# No Good Deed
## A FATHER'S JOURNEY

Mr. Frank L. Miller

Copyright © 2013 Mr. Frank L. Miller

All rights reserved.

ISBN: 0615767915

ISBN 13: 9780615767918

Library of Congress Control Number: 2013903381
Jockers & Stack Publishing
Denton, Maryland

# TABLE OF CONTENTS

| | | |
|---|---|---|
| Chapter One: | Where It All Began | 1 |
| Chapter Two: | 1990 and I Am the Establishment | 33 |
| Chapter Three: | Summer 1994/Therapy Decisive or Divisive? | 63 |
| Chapter Four: | The Fall of '94 | 71 |
| Chapter Five: | Zero Tolerance for Drugs? | 87 |
| Chapter Six: | The Board Hearing – December 6, 1994 | 107 |
| Chapter Seven: | Appeal to the State Board | 117 |
| Chapter Eight: | The Search for an Advocate | 121 |
| Chapter Nine: | Motivations of My Own – February 25, 1995 | 143 |
| Chapter Ten: | '95–'96 Involuntary Transfer to Secondary | 165 |
| Chapter Eleven: | November 1995 Circuit Court | 183 |
| Chapter Twelve: | Can You Compromise Your Kid's Future? | 189 |
| Chapter Thirteen: | The Plot Thickens – Complaints from Northern High | 197 |
| Chapter Fourteen: | Slip of the Tongue | 205 |
| Chapter Fifteen: | The Hearing | 223 |
| Chapter Sixteen: | You're Only as Safe as Your Next Evaluation | 265 |

| | |
|---|---|
| Chapter Seventeen: | The Classroom from Hell — April 1996, My Diary .......... 279 |
| Chapter Eighteen: | The Next Day ................. 305 |
| Chapter Nineteen: | July 16, 1996, Andrew Takes His Turn..................... 317 |
| Chapter Twenty: | Job Search ................... 335 |
| Chapter Twenty-One: | October 30, 1996, Marriage Quakes ...................... 353 |
| Chapter Twenty-Two: | The Case Before the Court of Special Appeals, November 7, 1996 ..... 369 |
| Chapter Twenty-Three: | November 25, 1996 — Psychological Warfare.......... 393 |
| Chapter Twenty-Four: | My Luck Has Got to Change .... 427 |
| Chapter Twenty-Five: | Nothing Left to Give ........... 443 |
| Chapter Twenty-Six: | Graduation Pictures............ 455 |
| Chapter Twenty-Seven: | Blood — Is It Thicker Than Water or Just Thick? ................. 469 |
| Chapter Twenty-Eight: | June 17, 1997, Closure? ......... 477 |
| Chapter Twenty-Nine: | November 1999................ 491 |
| Chapter Thirty: | Summer 2000.................. 501 |
| Chapter Thirty-One: | Christmas Blues ............... 509 |
| Chapter Thirty-Two: | Department 410, Los Angeles County Family Court........... 535 |
| Chapter Thirty-Three: | Breaking Up Is Hard to Do — Fighting for Our Gal ........... 555 |
| Chapter Thirty-Four: | The Awakening................ 591 |

# SYNOPSIS

This is a nonfiction account outlining the personal and professional challenges the author faced working as a school psychologist and having to take on his own employer to seek help for his disabled daughter. For a variety of reasons, to protect the privacy of individuals he deeply cares about, as well as to protect himself from legal issues, he has changed the names of the principal characters and locations. All the rest is completely true, and based on the journals he kept when the events were taking place. The author kept journals to maintain his sanity, and as the story, stories developed, they became this book about no good deed going unpunished. The story begins as an autobiographical account of growing up in a suburban Long Island environment, his experiences going to college during the wonderfully turbulent sixties, and how these experiences forged his strong sense of advocacy for disabled children and created a conflict in roles between 1960s flower child and father.

This story chronicles his free-spirited days trying to pursue an undergraduate degree in the late Sixties and early seventies amid turmoil over the war in Vietnam and strikes on campus after Kent State. It highlights the difficult choices between a day in the country versus a prisoner held captive between the four walls of academia that somehow seemed irrelevant in the whole scheme of things. The story captures the completion of his undergraduate and graduate degrees, moving into a career, and his marriage to a young woman with two children whose natural father dies a violent death.

This story is about the special challenges that parenting a child with learning disabilities can present, challenges that peaked when she became involved with drugs at fifteen. He devotes much of the book to the protracted battle he waged against the school board that employed him, his attempts to secure help from a network of allies who turned him down, and what he came to see as the failure of the system to protect parents of disabled children. The accounting is a no-holds-barred portrayal, with all his strengths and weaknesses, successes and failures, and the conflicts he was forced to resolve within himself, his profession, his marriage, and his family.

# A MODERN TALE OF ADVENTURE

*Long ago and far away there was a place where powerful Administrators roamed the land, making summary judgments about what to do with the less fortunate members of the kingdom. They imposed their will on the weak because the weak had no voice of their own, and Administrators thought they knew what was "best" for them. The Administrators were kind-hearted for the most part, but they really didn't know any better. Then one day a hugely powerful knight, forever known as the KNIGHT OF THE IDEA, charged forth, proclaiming:*

*"From this day forward no decision shall be made without the benefit of the order of due process. And all the knights in the land shall gather together to protect the rights of the disabled."*

*From the west rode the Knights of the Mind, the Psychologists; and the Knights of the Hearth; the Parents. From the south rode the Knights of the Book, the teachers. From the east rode the Knights of the Word, the Speech Therapists, and from the north rode the Knights of the Gifts, the Special Teachers; and the Knights of the Programs, the Administrators.*

*And the KNIGHT OF THE IDEA rose up to lead them in their quest for free, appropriate public education for all disabled children across the land. And he promised to smite any among them who chose to force his ways on the others, to usurp the rights of the many for the selfish needs of one. And from that day forward justice prevailed in the land. All of the knights gathered together to decide the most appropriate course of action for the weak and less fortunate, and until they all could agree, no decision was made. This came to be known as consensus. And ideas from all over the kingdom came together to form a single IDEA known as the INSPIRATION ENLIGHTENED PROPHESY, the IEP. And the kingdom prospered and grew strong.*

## CHAPTER ONE

# WHERE IT ALL BEGAN

People are always asking me exactly how all of this trouble got started in the first place. "How should I know?" I tell them. "I'm too emotionally involved to be objective. Go ask somebody else." But who else is there? Who else but my wife Caroline and I know what happened? Did it strain our marriage? Without a doubt. Did it make our marriage stronger? Certainly. And it's still not over, though the events of the last eighteen years have faded from daily view. Is my family stronger now than it was ten years ago? Depends on how you define "family." Our son was an integral part of our nuclear family for a time. He finished school, got married, and had two sons. Then the woman he married, whom we had serious misgivings about from day one, revealed her true colors and refuses to allow our son or two grandsons to have any contact with us. So they are lost to us. Our rebellious adolescent teenager Sarah got herself straightened out and got married to a great guy and had two sons and is closer than ever to us, but not until she put us all through the ring of fire that continues to reverberate to this very day.

We grew closer to Caroline's father, until he passed away. He always was a good listener, in contrast to my own father. Throughout our ordeal, every time my father answered the phone, it was with, "I hope you have good news for us." After three years he got tired and depressed when it was nothing but bad news. Then my sister went through a divorce and they shifted their attention away from me and to my sister. My parents would have preferred for me to have had my own family rather than adopt my wife's from a previous marriage. That's not what happened. My family never really accepted my children (from my wife's previous marriage) as grandchildren. Without the blood they didn't count. The fact that they were not my biological children didn't matter much to me then…still doesn't. I love my children for who they are and the quality of our relationship, not our bloodline. When my father passed away, my mother and I drew closer for a time, then my two sisters reared their ugly heads and now I don't have contact with the three remaining blood relatives I have left in this world (and am better for it as you will see). Most importantly, a new member of the family has brought all of us to a place we never thought we'd be. Families can be linked by blood and by history; they can also be bonded by the simple act of commitment. When I adopted children, I made that commitment. For life.

What happened to this family has cut wounds that may never completely heal, for more than anything, it demonstrated to me that your children never really belong to you, they just live with you until they a) leave on their own or b) you throw them out; and that no matter what you do or say, when adolescence hits, all bets are off and it's hurricane season. You can choose to evacuate, like a lot of parents do when the storm warnings are posted, or, like us, you can hold a hurricane party. You can just ignore the wind outside and bury your heads under a pillow, hiding in a closet, or, like us, you can stand out in the storm and weather it the best you can, dodging the flying shingles and tree limbs, and believe me, you'll be completely changed, all of you, when you weather a storm like this. We are still surveying the damage and will be for years to come. And the most frustrating part is that the storm just moves on, unhurt by the land it has destroyed. Storms, like wars and other catastrophes, have a way of bringing out the best and the worst in people, and the bonds that are formed can be as powerful as the divisions that arise when people are put to the test. Herein lie the stories of a family in a small community, and the storm that changed them forever. These life-altering events stressed our roles as parents, educators, employees, and child advocates. But it cleared the fog from our eyes and strengthened our commitment to our children, our professions, and, most importantly, to each other.

I had been an educator and child advocate for over twenty years when this all happened. I had fought long, hard, and alone for kids in my job as school psychologist. Did anyone think I would fight any less hard for my own daughter? Why would a school system work against a loyal employee who fought hard for kids? Isn't that what education is all about? You would figure a school board would be glad to work with a group of parents who were concerned, well-educated, and supportive. There were hidden agendas in our case, and personalities and power struggles. Where small men rule, petty acts are merely a reflection of their cold hearts and deeper insecurities.

We lived in the country, where being twenty years behind times extended not only to the low crime rate and affordable real estate, but to the staunchly conservative and sometimes uninformed ways of thinking. Open spaces and closed minds seemed to go hand in hand. Low crime and local corruption did as well. A population of well-meaning and kindhearted souls who were uninvolved for the most part. Oh, they'll be out there on the baseball diamond, count on that, but a budget hearing or a board of education meeting? Not likely. And when the chips were down for us, when the wolves were at our doors, though many secretly, privately cheered us on... no one spoke up. Only a few had the courage to stand up for their beliefs, and to them we dedicate this book.

It's certainly true that the stress and pressure our family has been experiencing increased significantly in the fall of 1994, but the events that began to spiral out of control had roots that extended many years earlier. In order to do this, I'll have to take you back, back into the past. Back even before my first few months here as a provisional employee in 1988, back before professional positions in West Virginia and Virginia. It started back in the sixties; for more than anything, I am and will always be a *child of the sixties*.

In order for anyone to understand what's happening here, you have to go back, way back. I was born in New York. Even when I was three and four I never took no for an answer. I wanted to know why. Give me a satisfactory explanation and I was okay; anything less than that was a challenge for discussion. In high school I took classes in political theory and studied Plato and Socrates. When I graduated from high school in 1967, I was a well-trained independent thinker, and I spent my last summer as a "square." That's when I moved into a state of mind that refused to take no for an answer, and when my ability to question authority became refined at the same time, my *bullshit detector* was tuned into the "extremely sensitive" mode of operation. That's when I, along with the majority of my generation, moved into the realm of the *experienced*. Experienced as in, "Have you ever been experienced, well...I have." And as Jimi (Hendrix) well knew, and Aldous (Huxley) before him, once you've walked through those *Doors of Perception*, you can't turn back...even if you care to. It was a state of mind that allowed, even insisted, that you take nothing for face value, but question everything, from the type of soap you use to the people you support in politics; from the kind of car you drive to the type of job you have; from the decisions you make about the movies you watch, to the laws you chose to obey or not. *Question Authority* bumper stickers are popular with today's teenagers, and they think they invented the concept. Anyone who was around in the sixties knows we had mastered the art of teenage rebellion in numbers so vast that it had a major impact on society at large.

Where It All Began

Make way for the baby boomers, and "BOOM!" it was. So it's time for a flashback, baby-boomers, the year is 1960, and we were all listening to Roy Orbison, Elvis Presley, Fats Domino, and Chubby Checker. Robert Young and Ozzie Nelson were our father figures, and life was good. It was the end of the fifties and we were still on a roll.

## Born Under A "Bad" Sign

John F. Kennedy was alive and well, and we had our first president elected who led with charisma. I really don't think I could have been born at a better time. I popped into the world on a cold morning in November 1949. I grew up in suburbia on a tree-lined street with sidewalks and lamp posts, where kids played kickball in the streets, "Car Car C-A-R stick your head in T-A-R." Stepping out of the way and rushing back into the street once the trespassing car was gone, much like water pouring into the levee once the sluice is opened. Our street dead-ended at a large wooded area. Walk around the fence and into the woods a short way, and a path opened up. It was well worn and the tree branches were set way back so the walk was easy. First pond was on your right bordering the golf course. We'd lie on the bank by the green on a warm summer day and watch the golfers shoot down toward us, staying low so as not to spook them or get a golf ball in the face. In all the years I lived on the street next to the golf course, I can only remember one person getting hit with a golf ball, and that was Kathy Ritter, one of my sister's friends. Funny thing was that she wasn't even on the course, but standing in her backyard. Someone hooked a good one, for it cleared the chainlink fence and the stand of cherry trees and landed square on her right ankle. Just goes to show, stuff happens when you least expect it.

I also remember Kathy's big brother Scott. He was one of the neighborhood bullies. I had the misfortune of being one of the smallest kids on the block. I didn't take any stuff from anyone, even back then. Trouble is I didn't have the physical skills to back it up. I wouldn't run, I'd just stay there and hold my ground. More often than not, I ended up *on* the ground with a healthy share *in* my mouth. Scott got me down one time and had me in a scissors lock. He wanted me to cry uncle and he'd let me up. It was hard to breathe much less utter anything that made sense, but I wasn't gonna cry for this bully. Luckily, my mom came outside. Though I thought she would rescue me, the best she could come out with was, "If you don't know how to play nice, then go in the house." Scott let loose of me then, but I had to go in, so the whole thing was a disaster. I never came crying to her after that. Thanks, Mom! Maybe in her own way she was trying to toughen me up. "If you're going to get yourself in trouble, don't look to someone else to pull you out."

## Billy Goat Mountain

Growing up on Long Island in a suburban neighborhood with a large sandpit and woods at the end of my street turned out to be a kid's paradise. The sandpit (Colonial Sand and Gravel) was the sand used to build New York City. Hundreds of acres of trees and ponds and, well, …sand. *Billy Goat Mountain* was a special trip. You'd have to pack a lunch and a canteen of water. Imagine an island covered with dense vegetation and tall trees in the middle of the ocean. Now drain all that water away so what is left is a mountain with steep sides surrounded by a sea of sand. This edifice was located in the middle of a sandpit hundreds of acres in size. They dug away everything but this piece, leaving it and its trees to stand as a monument to the kids in the surrounding neighborhood. A narrow road led up to the mountain, but from there you were on your own. The path up the mountain itself was steep and made of hard-packed sand. If you could make your way up the ten or fifteen yards, there was a huge steel cable you could grab on to. You could then pull your own weight up the cable to the top and victory! I don't think a single girl ever made that climb, so it was our own exclusive club with one rule: make it up, you're a member. *Billy Goat Mountain* was so named because they say a billy goat's skull was found up there. When you're a "city kid" or even a "suburban kid," the idea of a dead animal skull, especially of one rarely seen on the tree-lined streets of town, is exotic, even mysterious. *Billy Goat Mountain* was also a rite of passage, as well as a cherished memory. Adventure, mystery, independence, risk, self-worth, working to get where you want to go. These and other values were forged in the pits. Facets of my personality that would get me far, but would also get me buried up to my neck in the sand, metaphorically speaking, struggling to get out and back on top.

My folks were pretty glad to get me out of the house on weekends so they never worried about my heading off with Michael Deegan, my best friend, to the woods or sandpits. That is, until some fool kid over in the next town would get trapped under a mountain of sand and suffocate, or fall off the edge of something. That's when Mom and Dad would panic and issue the edict: STAY OUT OF THE SANDPITS! Now, I knew they were safe. We were smart about where we went and where we didn't go. It was our home. So to have to explain to them that this dummy tried to walk off a soft wall didn't get us very far. There were overhangs that would fall on you, smothering you before they could dig you out. We knew to avoid these spots. Others were sheer cliffs that would break off if you ventured too close. We knew just how to sneak up on an edge, crawling on our bellies, pulling ourselves along with our elbows, until we carefully and quietly reached the edge for a look that rivaled the Grand Canyon.

I was the kind of kid who was honest, so when I was told not to do something, I wouldn't. I can remember one day when there was a bunch of us playin' in the woods and they decided to head to the pits. "I'm not allowed." What! Who's gonna know? There was like this line in the sand, and I wouldn't cross it. They went on without me. I'd suffer for a few weeks until things cooled down, and then, with a deep breath, I would cross the line. If no one asked me anything, and I was sure to really shake the sand out of my socks, everything would be cool. Kinda like the old policy on gays in the military: *don't ask/don't tell*. I didn't bug my parents and I never challenged them, I did what they asked me until it was no longer a "hot item" and then I would go back to doing what I always did. They never knew and I somehow survived.

This was the first time I ever did something other than what my parents allowed, and I did it not to intentionally disobey, but because I felt I was operating on a different level of knowledge and understanding than they were. Here was a quite literal "line in the sand" and it seemed too artificial, so meaningless. They didn't know the pits were safe, and there was no way I could explain that to them, and because I respected their desire and need to keep me safe (I was safe in the pits), I didn't really look at my going down to the pits as a violation of their desires and instructions. I knew better than them. The same pattern of thinking and behavior carried got me through adolescence. Today it seems kids aren't as smart as we were. They challenge and argue and lack the respect for parents that we held. They may do the same stupid stuff we did when we were young, but they do it out in the open, it's more "in your face," and that promotes conflict. As well, I think many lack the good judgment of knowing what is safe and what is just plain stupid.

## Walden Pond Is No More

We moved when I completed the ninth grade, and it was just as well, because the pit began to gobble up more and more of the woods. It started moving in the direction of our street when I hit my teens. By '63 they were up to the ponds, and by '64 the ponds drained down into the pits, and the woods with them. We used to climb down into the pits on the trees they shoved down there with bulldozers. By the time we moved in the summer of 1964, instead of a mile from the avenue to the edge of the pits, it was just twenty feet. They put up a huge chain-link fence to keep people out. As though they'd want to see what was left of our woods and ponds. It was like we'd been "in charge" of the woods and ponds for so many years, we'd cared for them and kept them litter free and damage proof, and now some unseen power was swooping in and destroying what we had so long sought to preserve. All for a few shovelfuls of sand, a sidewalk or high rise somewhere in the big city.

## Salem School Revisited

They say you can never go home. That once you have left a place and it exists only in your deepest memories, coming back to rekindle those feelings can only lead to disappointment. I left the island when I was seventeen, and when I completed graduate school at age twenty-four, I had the urge to visit the town where I grew up. One spring I drove north to New York and stopped by my elementary school, Salem School. I was pleased and surprised to see that my first-/second-grade teacher, third-/fourth-grade teacher, and even my fifth-grade teacher were still there. I got a chance to talk with them after school. Their recollections of me were insightful. My first-/second-grade teacher remembered me by my eyes. Interesting. Probably because she was always trying to engage them. "Look at me, young man!" She remembered putting things on the board and hearing me sobbing. "What's the matter, Frank?" "I can't do it," I sobbed. "But I haven't even written the work down yet," she cried. "I know, but I already know I won't be able to do it." Talk about anticipatory anxiety. And I remember that feeling. My early years, the struggles I experienced when I was in school not only gave me great insights into my own children's struggles, but very likely set me up for the career I would pursue as an adult.

I started school at four years, ten months old, and was always the smallest and least mature. My third-grade teacher remembered me as a difficult child. She acknowledged that I needed a lot of attention. When I told her I was a school psychologist, she seemed to understand. She also told me that the first-/second-grade class I was in was something special. She remarked that one student was a lawyer; two became doctors. One of my classmates went on to be the president of a woman's college and the curator of a major museum in New York City. I actually felt like a failure because I'd only earned my graduate degree. Still, this was whence I came, and the standards and the will to achieve were there, and I fed off them. My ability to think and write was formulated there. Middle school shaped it further, and then it was off to Cold Harbor High School and the last shot of inspiration.

I used to wonder if I had done my own children a disservice by living in a rural setting, where some of the opportunities and challenges are missing. Instead of them sitting in class with future lawyers, governors, and presidents, they sat next to farmers, chicken pluckers, and railroad men. Funny thing is, many of the kids of the chicken pluckers have done better than my own two. It just goes to show that every area provides unique challenges, different sets of intellectual and academic opportunities, and that some kids choose to seize them and others don't.

## Cold Spring

When we outgrew our little house in Port Washington where the sandpits lie, we moved further out on the island to a nice neighborhood with an even more prestigious school system. Cold Harbor High School was a very special place. My parents had moved to Cold Harbor to provide us with some of those unique academic and intellectual opportunities. Neither of my parents had a college degree. My mom had two sisters, one who married early and one, my favorite aunt, Meam, who never married but stayed home. In those days college was not a top priority, and after the war (World War II) the returning serviceman had other things on their minds, like getting a civilian job, a wife, and a family. My mom worked for American Airlines when she met my dad. He would take technical courses at night while he worked during the day as my older sister came along in 1948 and me a year later. My dad worked for a defense plant for many years until he got laid off in his forties. My folks went through some tight times until he got the job that held him over until retirement. My mom was a full-time mom, although she always found a little something here and there. Once she worked for a well-known opera singer, and then for one of Franklin Roosevelt's sons (James) as an office manager. My mother and father both instilled in me the need to study and apply myself, and they provided the opportunities.

Cold Harbor was a small town on Long Island Sound with a small harbor filled with sailboats and surrounded by restaurants. The town was on one side of the harbor and the Biological Lab on the other. The lab was run by Dr. Watson, of Watson and Crick fame. They received the Nobel Prize for discovering the old double helix, Mr. Deoxyribonucleic Acid, or DNA for short. The building block for all life. The lab was dedicated to others like him whose minds were geared to pure research. The genius of studying life forms through microscopes and creating unique ways of interacting with creatures and life forms too small to be seen with the naked eye.

Cold Harbor had been a whaling community at one time. I lived there for four years until I went away to college in 1967. I never set foot in the Whaling Museum at the foot of my street. The shoppes in town were just that: shoppes. The Gourmet Shoppe where you could pay up to $5 for a loaf of bread, and this was 1960s. They had the riding shop, and antiques, and a restaurant, and pharmacy, and post office, but mostly it was for the tourists. For New Yorkers from the five boroughs who took Sundays to drive out to the country, Cold Harbor was country, with two- lane roads winding through farms and wooded acres. It had the shoppes and the restaurants where people could sit on the wooden stools and eat freshly opened clams. We lived up the street from the town proper and at the bottom of the hill from the high school. Some of the more affluent residents of the area, some at the lab, others at two exclusive enclaves, one Rhododendrum Hollow and the other Floyd's Neck, didn't want to send their children to the consolidated high school with working-class stiffs, not to mention people of color, so they set up their own district. And what a district it turned out to be. Cold Harbor celebrated its fiftieth birthday in 2012. Alumnae from Cold Harbor were CEO's of Fortune 500 Companies, world renowned physicians, and even a Judge on the short list for Supreme Court.

The building was beautiful, all one floor and all glass. The high school was grades seven to twelve and only 1,100 kids. Different departments of study were in separate wings—they had a humanities wing, science wing, math wing, art and music wing—all connected by glass walkways, and the classrooms opened up to central courtyards with trees and flowering plants. On hot spring days we'd literally open sliding doors onto the courtyard and attend class in the courtyard. Some of the more restrictive teachers forced you to remain indoors, but we always managed to slide our chairs onto the sidewalk, bodies out, eyes and minds in the room. We had a large cafeteria, an auditorium, plus a commons area, a sunken living room with couches, fireplace, and study tables. This area was reserved for seniors and juniors who were in the National Honor Society. This made being seniors and brighter, more academic kids special. They placed a high value on academic excellence. There was a lab area with lecture halls, a central teacher desk and seats on risers just like you see in universities. Those who were involved in science experiments (I was) could sign up for a private room for the semester. I distilled raisins into 130 proof alcohol. I knew that, because part of the project was measuring the specific gravity to determine proof. I even snuck some out and tried to drink it, but the stuff was so strong it would peel paint, and no amount of grape juice was enough to mask its potency. It was there that I developed my love for the sciences. Mr. Weaver for biology and Mr. Port for chemistry, Mr. Paul for physics. I studied planaria, little aquatic creatures no bigger than this (<--), for two months, watching them, cutting them in half, and watching them regenerate. Even had one with two heads. Wrote it all down in a little notebook and had another friend take their pictures for my paper. I was *into it* and completed labs with A's and was determined I would be a doctor or dentist when I went to college.

I may not have been the top student, but I liked to read and we had the courses in political theory and philosophy alongside physics and chemistry and Boolean Algebra. Our history teacher Mr. H used to bring history alive with voices and characterizations of various personalities. As I look back I realize that this time, this place, was fertile ground for my lifelong philosophy. Central to it all was one idea: that every man was responsible for his own actions. Attending elementary and middle school with a predominantly Jewish population, and being well-acquainted with the Holocaust, then getting filled up with Plato and Socrates and Galileo, I was well versed in making up my own mind. "I was just following orders" was for Nazis, not me, and I began to question authority like never before. The irony is that I never questioned my teachers; they had earned my respect. It was authority that did not deserve respect that was vulnerable. I reasoned, and I questioned, and I did what I felt was right, and let the consequences be damned. The interesting thing is that we all went on to college. Eight-five percent of my graduating class, and many of our teachers as well moved on to prestigious colleges and universities. It was like we all grew up together and our teachers moved on with us.

# 1960s

For those of us who were there, the sixties started in November 1963, the year our president was assassinated.

# No Good Deed

It shattered our innocence as well as our dreams. I was in the ninth grade at CPW Junior High School on November 22, 1963. That's where I was. I was sitting in Mr. Meyer's math class when the announcement came over the PA. First it was a quick blurb, "Senator Dirkson...," and silence. And then it came back on. "CBS now interrupts this broadcast for a special announcement." Static and an unearthly silence, then: "President John Fitzgerald Kennedy died at approximately 1:30 after being shot by an unknown assailant while riding in a presidential motorcade in Dallas today." I don't remember anything else that was said after that, and I remember feeling pretty much the same way then as I do now as I sit here writing this on my laptop. Tears and a faraway sadness that lurks in your chest and swells up into your face and eyes like a wave that warms and chills you at the same time. We wandered down the halls to our next class, encountering our friends as though in a dream. It was a realization that things would somehow never be the same. And they weren't. After the Kennedy assassination came Martin Luther King's, then Bobby Kennedy's, and that god-awful Nixon (and Rumsfeld and Cheney, though we didn't know it at the time), Vietnam, Watergate, and then, like a ray of sunshine, *Meet The Beatles*, *Sergeant Pepper*, *Magical Mystery Tour*, Jimi Hendrix, the Allman Brothers Band, Jefferson Airplane, Janis Joplin, Eric Clapton, the Who, the Rolling Stones, and *Woodstock*.

I remember when the *Beatles* made the cover of *LIFE* magazine with those crazy haircuts. Then in February 1964, they arrived at Idlewilde Airport. They had firmly established themselves in our hearts as well as our minds, and we could all mark rites of passage with their albums. *Rubber Soul*, my first kiss, *Help*, second and third base, *Revolver*, my first taste of gin. By the time they released *Sergeant Pepper* three years later, in June 1967, I was graduating from high school and ready to head into my last summer after high school and before college. We all listened to *Sergeant Pepper* with acute and impressionable ears. These four guys were gods to us, spiritual leaders, and they spoke more directly to us, more personally to our thoughts and feelings, far more than our ministers and pastors and parents ever did. They touched our hearts, our minds, and, yes, even our souls. The generation gap was there and widening. When John said the *Beatles* were more popular than Jesus, he wasn't bragging, he was making a statement of fact. The *Beatles* were more relevant to us, they were of us, with us, for us, and they spoke to us; advice that made sense and carried weight. And in those days they weren't telling us to kill and maim, they were telling us "All you need is love," and the joys of life, and living every day to the fullest. And we listened, and we heard them.

I can remember all the talk about the first drug reference in a song. From "Day in the Life," "Woke up, got out of bed, dragged the comb across my head, went upstairs and had a smoke, somebody spoke and I went into a dream, ah a ah aaaaaaah...." Talk was, it wasn't tobacco he was smoking, and he must have inhaled. We later found out later that John's first drug reference in a song was from *Revolver;* "Tomorrow Never Knows." That whole song was an ode to a radical change in consciousness. "Turn off your mind, relax, and float downstream, this is not dying...." With all the background sounds and flowing rhythm, it told us he was into it years before anyone thought. So, by the time "Lucy In the Sky with Diamonds" entered the plausible deniability phase, many of us—most of us—had been there and done that. It was no mere coincidence that Lucy Sky Diamonds spelled out the acronym for LSD, newspaper taxis and girls with kaleidoscope eyes notwithstanding. It was a great time to be alive, a great time to be young. We were all members of the secret society, the subculture. We were all connected by the times and by our common experiences. It was one of those rare moments in time when the culture, *the youth culture,* connected many of us across time and space. We were the youth culture, the counterculture, and there were a lot of us...boomers all.

## The Lake

My family had a summer cottage on a lake in the Berkshires. I spent every summer there swimming, boating, hiking in the woods, and just having fun. Some of the kids were rich kids whose parents owned two homes, one on the lake and another in one of the hotter regions of Connecticut. Bill lived on the lake for the summers with his parents and his sister Dee (my first girlfriend). Their dad owned a construction company. Tad was another part of our group. His dad was an eye doctor. Some were locals who came up to use the beaches and launch a boat. I had friends in both groups. One of them was Kenny. His dad was custodian at one of the local elementary schools. Kenny and I were drinking buddies and he knew the local gals, so we made quite a team. He also knew the hot spots to go and offered some kind of protection for an out of towner, especially a New Yorker. I became fast friends with his friends and family alike. They were good, honest, hardworking people. They accepted me and I enjoyed being around them. They invited me to parties and weddings, and I helped to merge the two groups. Girls were the most frequent common denominator. By 1967, our senior year in high school, plans were already laid out for us. I had applied and been accepted to college; Kenny missed graduating by a half credit. He went to Vietnam; I went to Virginia Polytechnic Institute.


## I Met Mary Jane And I'll Never Be The Same

Though I didn't try smoking grass that summer, Kenny met this wild chick from California who had. She turned him on to it, and though my interest was piqued, I believed all that stuff they said about drugs and how bad they were. I was happy with my beer and an occasional drink of Gordon's Gin or Schmirnoff's 100 Proof Vodka. After I got to college, though, there were more than a few of my friends who had smoked the weed. And these were regular guys, not drug addicts, but engineers and architects and business majors and psychology majors. Smart kids with good heads on their shoulders, and the information they gave me along with the stories about how nice it was proved once again that maybe Mom and Dad didn't have the full story on this. I was seventeen going on eighteen, away from home for the first time in my life, and I had to begin to make some of my own decisions. And the arguments against alcohol were strong. "Hey, man, do you really like getting all stupid and falling all over the place? And do you like barfing all over yourself and your date? And how about those humongous headaches the next day? With marijuana, you have a nice buzz, you are more aware of your environment, food tastes great, music sounds unbelievable, and things are just …funnier. And you don't get sick and you're ready to go the next day. You never get mad or crazy, or into fights, and you just feel good all over. Folks have been lying to you about this stuff, give it a try." Maybe, just maybe, the folks were wrong about marijuana. Here was another line drawn in the sand, and it too looked artificial. How can smoking a plant make you crazy? So when a close friend asked me if I ever smoked dope before, I said, "No, but you know I was really thinking about giving it a try." I did that afternoon. "I'LL NEVER DO IT AGAIN!" I cried as my brain ran in more directions than it ever had before in seventeen years. But the door was open a crack, and I just wanted another peek. It changed the way I thought about myself in a very positive way. It cleared out cobwebs that had been there for years. I finally started feeling really good about me, who I was, and who I wanted to be. It was my drug of choice for quite some time. What started out with just a few kids on my dorm floor turned into the entire floor with a few exceptions, and then almost the entire dorm went green. Good news travels fast. This was a conservative, Southern, agricultural, cow college, too. By the time the 1970s hit and "everybody" was cool, I had a head start, quite literally. Not only was my head further along, but so was my hair. It tumbled down my back in long blond waves. I had also wandered down some other psychedelic pathways and made friends with things I could smoke as well as pills that took me on faraway journeys.

# Rhode Island

This story would never be complete without a chapter about my arrest in Rhode Island. That's right, I've been arrested not once, but twice. Rhode Island was a total charade. In brief, it was quite literally the summer of '69 and our summer cottage had been sold. I was living in New York but hankering on getting back to Connecticut. The boys, Tad and Bill, and Kenny and Fran had a weekend planned for the beach in Rhode Island, so I planned to leave work on Friday and meet them there. They would go up early and secure a campsite, get a bite to eat, and then head down to the strip where music and the ladies met at a little club called *the George*. Everything was working like clockwork. I drove the five hours up to Rhode Island and went straight to the club, where we all met up. There was Bill and Fran and Tad. As it worked out, Bill and I struck paydirt first, two cute gals. They danced and talked with us, and we asked them if they wanted to go back to our campsite. Things were different then; you could trust people. There was a good vibe in the air and things were free and easy.

    The four of us headed backed to the campground. I was driving my car with my gal next to me and Bill was driving with the other girl in her car. When we pulled in (Bill first), there were people in our campsite. They approached Bill's car first, and then this dude in a gray sweatshirt approaches me. "Can I see some identification?" he demanded. "Let me see yours—what're you, a cop or something?" I replied. Turns out he was. Forest ranger. He whips out his badge and asks me to get out of the car. By this time I was getting a little nervous. Especially with the illegal substance I was carrying on my person in my left-hand pocket. He inspects my license and registration and then asks for my camp permit. I explain that I was in a party of five and Tad's and my names were on the permit. Ranger Rick then walks around to the back of my car and asks me to open my trunk. By this time I had torn out the bottom of my pocket and allowed the contraband, a wooden pipe and chunk of Turkish hashish, to slip down my pant leg into the brush. I came around behind, renewed in my efforts to stand up to this invasion of my civil liberties. "Open the trunk," he demanded. "Where's your warrant" I retorted. "This is my mother's car and I can't give you permission to search it without *her* permission." "Have this man arrested for trespassing in a state park and get a warrant to search his trunk." "Okay, I have a six pack of beer, still warm, that my mother bought for my father, in the trunk." And with this remark I opened the trunk, reached in and grabbed the still warm six pack of Miller beer and showed it to the ranger. "Arrest him for possession of alcoholic beverages in a state park." So even though I did not buy the beer, and even though I was old enough to purchase beer in New York at eighteen, I was going down for having it in my trunk, in a state park. No search warrant and definitely an illegal search and seizure, not to mention arrest.

They took Bill and me and the two girls, who we came to find out were underage (as though it made any difference that they were seventeen when we were eighteen) and they brought us to the local lockup, where we waited for the rest of the gang to be brought in. Seems this ranger had illegally searched Tad's tent and, finding several cases of beer, laid in wait for the perpetrators to show up. And believe me, beer was the last thing on our minds. When Tad, Francis, and company showed up at the jail several hours later, with cases of beer and smiles on their faces, I was glad that they were taking it in good humor and went along for the ride. The girls had to stay in the lobby of the local lockup and wait for their dad. When he arrived he was more upset with the Rhode Island constabulary than his kids or us.

Rhode Island's finest then put us in the back of a paddy wagon and drove us to the county lockup in town. There we were held without bail, no food or water, until court the next morning. The cell was a duplex and was made of iron slats two inches wide that crisscrossed to keep perps in, and out of trouble. Tad, Bill, and I were in one side and Fran and another buddy were sequestered in a coat closet. This was because our cellmate (on the other side of the slats), a quite-drunk Georgian, let fly a rebel yell every so often, punctuated by a rather interesting sound effect. The cells were empty except for two bunks, each hinged to fold up against the wall, and suspended by two chains attached to the center wall. After a rousing "EEEEEE-HAAAA!!" the gentleman from Georgia would lift his upper bunk and then slam it down until the chain stopped its downward movement, rendering a rather resounding crash that reverberated throughout the holding pen. We curled up two on a bunk and tried to sleep, but there was no sleeping.

Come morning they let the Georgian go. I think they released him to spare him the cruel and unusual punishment of having us bang the bunks a bit in tune with his hangover. We got hauled back outside and placed back in the paddy wagon for a ride to court. The judge presiding that day must have been a preacher on Sundays and judge the rest of the week, because he starting admonishing us and lecturing us, and at one point I really thought he was asking for my opinion. We were held without bread and water, but we were allowed a phone call. Each of us was required to call our parents and have them in court the next day. Tad's mother and father, Bill's dad, Fran's dad, were all there from Connecticut, the bordering state. I was eighteen. I refused to call my parents in New York, five hours away, in the middle of the night to get me out of something I had no business being in in the first place. I took care of myself, and I was damned if I was going to hassle my parents for this bum rap. They could keep me in jail, I didn't care. I was not going to call my parents!

So here we five are lined up in front of the bench. "I want you parents to stand behind your boys." They complied. Here I was standing proud, on my own. And then this judge, this representative of the court, starts lecturing about the country and its great standing, and asks, "What gives *you* the right to violate the laws of this nation?" He paused just long enough in his oration for me to speak up. At the time I was not familiar with the meaning of a *rhetorical question*. I was merely showing respect for the court by providing an answer, and I said, "Well, if you really want to know—" That's all I got out before he interrupted me loudly, glaring at me sternly, "Young man, you wait until I've finished!" So I did.

Then after he had drooled and slobbered his fundamentalist tirade all over the courtroom and us, he looked back at me and said, "And what do you have to say for yourself, young man!?" And I will remember this speech as long as I live. What I said was this: "Well, you asked me what gave me the right to violate the laws of this country. I'm eighteen years old. I'm old enough to get drafted and fight, and even give my life for my country, and yet I'm not old enough to vote to change the laws, and I'm not old enough to drink, which is why I'm in this mess in the first place." He seemed stunned for a moment, then his gaze froze and he said, "One more word out of you and I'll hold you in contempt of court." I knew to zip it at that point. The clerk leaned over and told me he'd done just that a week ago and that I could consider myself lucky. I later heard they hit another kid up for a $2,000 fine for possession of marijuana. Did I feel lucky? You bet! Me and my big mouth. But more about that later.

Well, we were all assessed $50 fines and were released. Bill's dad paid the fine for me because I didn't have that kind of money back then. I paid him back. Tad's mother came up to me and said, "Of course you realize you are no longer welcome in our home." I don't know if that was because I spoke up or because I got the blame for buying the beer and getting her little boy in trouble. I only found out years later who actually bought the beer—Tad's twenty-one-year-old next-door neighbor Jeff. That's another thing about me: I make a good scapegoat. The next time I would see any of these guys was at a bachelor party for Tad a few years later, I went on with life and lost touch with the Connecticut crew. It would be eighteen more years before I would be back on the lake with my own family. The next time I would pay a visit to Rhode Island would be forty years later as president of my State Association of School Psychologists, representing my colleagues at a Northwestern Regional Conference. But forty years earlier, in 1967, I headed back to college and my life down South. My friends were into the beer. I was responding to a higher calling. It was the sixties, after all.

## Listen To The Music

The music was also reflecting similar experiences, and the two seemed to go hand in hand. And although it's true that music had a profound influence on us all, it's difficult to "blame" the music for the times it reflected, any more than one can "blame" the newspaper for leading to an increase in crime. Any medium both reports and projects an influence on those to whom it reports. I can recall my first impression when a new Beatles album would come out and John Lennon's appearance went through all of the changes emerging personalities reflect. Smiling face on *Rubber Soul* to the line drawing on *Revolver* surrounded by surrealistic swirls. Then *Sergeant Pepper* with his "Fu Manchu" mustache, hair parted down the middle, all dressed in bright "I say Hello!" clothes. And then *Magical Mystery Tour* with its garish Busby Berkley cover, John shoveling spaghetti onto the fat woman's plate in an act from theater of the absurd. And then...*Abbey Road*, showing John with long hair flowing down his back, dressed all in white. I can remember thinking to myself at the time, "This time he's gone too far..." and then I'd look in a mirror at my own hair, now parted down the middle, and my mustache reaching for the bottom of my chin. So? And then my hair began its slow and graceful march down my shoulder blades. "Hair. Gimme it down to there! Gleaming, streaming, screaming flaxen waxen...." A statement of being young and being free and being different. And later: "Almost Cut My Hair." "Think

I'll let my freak-flag fly," David Crosby's song about hair as a political statement, and a willingness to stand behind your beliefs, despite the problems straight society presented. Long hair helped me to realize in a small way what it was like to be black in America. "It increases my paranoia, like lookin' in your rearview mirror and seein' a police car...." What it was like to get stopped by police and frisked, even arrested just because you "looked" a certain way. The music was there to support us and comfort us, justify us in our glory. And encourage and empower us: "And I'm not...givin' in an inch to fear. I... promised myself this year." Which leads me to the second time I was arrested. Unlike James Frey, who fabricated wild stories about vicious felonies and incarceration, I'm almost embarrassed to admit that my crime was...hitchhiking.

## Walking Like Jesus

It was Christmastime and I was in Florida for the holidays, Christmas 1971. I had my red Volkswagen Minibus and my long blond hair and I was down at the strip off Highway A1A, making my presence known, strutting my stuff, as it were. Cops back then hated the look and the freedoms we expressed that they couldn't even begin to understand. This was the time of the great divide between straights and freaks, and the cops were on the other side. They hated us and we hated them. They would bust you for anything, even walking or standing too long in one place. Here we were a stone's throw from the beach, a pedestrian strip with shops and restaurants and hundreds of college kids. One of my buddies was getting rousted by one of these officers sworn to protect and serve, so, true to my nature, I stepped up and asked him ever so politely what he was arresting my friend for. "Same thing I'll arrest you for...loitering." Now the absurdity of being arrested for loitering at a beach was beyond the pale. I laughed. Out loud. And commented, "Loitering at a beach, you've got to be kidding!" He turned my now cuffed friend over to his partner in crime prevention and turned his attention to me. Look, you either move your ass or I'll make room for two in the back of my car." As I started moving away, he called after me, "I'm going to be watching you, pal. I could follow Jesus around and find something to bust him for, so you better walk better than Jesus."

The next night I was back at the strip, parked my van facing the ocean, and walked across the street to the main thoroughfare. On one of my trips down the sidewalk, a friend pulled up to the curb in the RIGHT TURN ONLY lane and stopped at the light. He rolled down his window and called out to me, "Hey, dude, what are you up to?" I leaned down to acknowledge his greeting and we agreed to meet across town at a local club called the Propeller. The light turned to green and I stepped back onto the curb and into the loving arms of my favorite police officer. I turned and walked in the other direction. "Hey you! With the pants!" He was no doubt making a fashion statement about my purple velour bell-bottoms, but I don't respond to "Hey you with the pants." I have a name, or even an "Excuse me, sir, can I speak with you for a moment?" Next thing I know I am being grabbed from behind by this policeman. I jerked my arm free, and now he and his partner have both arms and I am being shoved up against their cruiser. "You want me to add resisting arrest"!? he asks me. "Arrest!? For what!" I exclaim. "Hitchhiking." "Are you crazy, that's my car right over there," I reply, pointing to my red van parked right across the street. "I saw you get out of that car with that blonde girl. That's hitchhiking." "Uh, for one thing, don't you have to be *in* the car in order to get *out* of it? I was merely talking with the driver when he stopped for the light, and no, that wasn't a blonde girl, but a dude... man." Next thing I know I have handcuffs on me and I am being shoved into the back of his squad car. I got booked for hitchhiking, released on my own recognizance, and ordered to appear for trial in three weeks. Though most students had already returned to classes by then and paid their fine via the US mail, I stuck around just to make my appearance and enter my plea of NOT GUILTY! I was found not guilty but still had to pay $10 in court costs. So, yes, I have been arrested two times, but if you try to dig up the court records to verify my claim, good luck. Their jurisdictions most likely pocketed the money and more than likely never recorded the infractions. So much for my criminal past, and to think about all the things I could have gotten arrested for! I consider myself a very lucky man. Me and Arlo Guthrie, famous for the Thanksgiving Day Massacre. His crime? Littering. Pick up a copy of *Alice's Restaurant* for a good laugh and view from a similar perspective.

## To Inhale Or Not To Inhale

We've had plenty of revisionists around these days, but I'm here to tell you, the music, the culture, the times were all driven by the drugs. The antiwar movement, the artwork, the woman's movement, the environmental movement, and the wholesale acceptance of Alternative lifestyles sprang right out of the introduction to the new ways of thinking only drugs could provide. Creativity blossomed as people copped a buzz and painted or sculpted or just thought about time and space. Open-minded, freethinking, intelligent, creative, tolerant individuals who had a clear vision of what this country was all about stepped forward and expressed these views. Some did it through their music or their art, movies, paintings, theater; the rest through public stands on the major issues of the day. Things we grew up to believe and accept: a woman's place is in the home, it's your duty to defend your country, homosexuality is wrong, black people are inferior, national leaders wouldn't lie to the nation, etc., were shattered with new insights and experiences.

Grass was nature's way of showing you the truth, rather than a distorted reality; it was a clearer vision. Paranoia has a way of making you take a long, hard look at life, especially your own life. Oh, it could be scary having to look at yourself with clear glasses, but it moved us all to a higher plane of consciousness, one on which we had to be kinder and more considerate of others, especially those less fortunate than ourselves. I became more understanding, more giving, more forgiving, though it also made me less tolerant of those with closed minds who hadn't made the move up. I might understand why the real estate developer was more interested in money than preserving the forest, but it was more difficult for me to excuse him. Pete Townsend said it best: "No one knows what it's like to be the sad man, the bad man, behind blue eyes." I still have to have logical explanations, a solid rationale for doing something, and when my "superiors" lie to support their views, it's more than I can take. My weakness was, and probably still is, that I have always thought I could use words to express this level of consciousness, that reason would prevail. Some people just don't "get it," though. And there's that Buddhist saying that "those who know, don't speak, and those who speak…don't know." "Though there may be many points of view, there is only one truth." "You have a right to your own opinion, but not to your own facts."

## Balancing School And The Cosmos

How I managed to stay in school without flunking out is not only a miracle, but a testimony to my solid educational background, or maybe my intellectual inheritance, and an uncanny knack of knowing just how much I could get away with. I managed to graduate with a degree in psychology in spite of the numerous extracurricular studies I conducted with a wide-range of pharmacological substances. I used them to experience a different state of consciousness, to explore my inner self, to learn about the town I lived in, the county, state, country, world, universe. We figured out Einstein's theory of relativity. And I still understand it today, not in his language of math (which only proves it, not explains it), but at the gut feeling level. Here 'tis: Nothing exists by itself, but only as it relates to something else. It's *all* relative, hence the theory of relativity. We even had a *frame of reference* hanging in our room. What's really peachy keen about this concept is that it proves that nothing exists, only the relationships between them. How's that for a dose of reality? Majoring in psychology with all of its neurophysiology and sensation, perception, and motivation courses brought a technical reality to everything I was experiencing, and an ever-growing *we* were experiencing. It was the creation of group thought, the communal oneness that we all experienced in the sixties, and it was everywhere you went. Trust, hope, love. It may have only lasted a short time, but, like a shooting star, it was brilliant and everlasting in our memories and our souls.

## The War

Back in the sixties we tried to go along with it. *Go with the flow* was one expression we used. The war was hard to ignore, though. If you had a student deferment you were cool, but we all knew kids, young men, friends, relatives, who were drafted and forced to participate. The Vietnam War soon became the most central focus, and the student protest caught on like wildfire. We had no business in this small country ten thousand miles away that was fighting a battle for unification. Why were American boys being sent over to a wholesale slaughter? For what purpose? And when many of our friends, including my friend Kenny, came home, they shared something with a lot of us: their love for marijuana and their hatred of the war. They joined us in protest of the war. When the *Vietnam Vets Against the War in Vietnam* threw their medals over the fence and onto the lawn of the White House, it was the beginning of the end. It's just sad that we had to topple a president to do it. But then again, Nixon had declared war on the kids back home even if he never declared one in Vietnam. He went after us with a vengeance, and his administration was as mean spirited as he was. He simply didn't get it.

Nixon kept the war raging despite getting elected with a secret plan to end the war. Our peers were getting shot to pieces and the war wasn't ending; it fact it was escalating when he moved into neighboring Cambodia. We experienced a collective guilt, not only for our family and friends, for our brothers who were over in Vietnam while we stayed home safe on campus, but for our yellow brothers who just wanted us out of there. We protested the war, and we spoke out against authority figures like Nixon and Agnew and Mitchell whose minds were as closed as ours were opened. We couldn't believe their big lie and were bent on convincing others not to buy into it. When they started shooting us at Kent State, we figured that there were things more important than going to English literature. We tried to organize a strike, and when the rest of our university protested, we began to realize that not everybody was as involved or committed or well-informed as we were. Divisions were widening and emotions escalating. The "rednecks" hated the "freaks" and the "brown-nosers" hated us and we tried to understand them, and the administration was on us, too. Peaceful protest turned to nonviolence in the form of rallies and then disruption. I ran from the police and got my share of tear gas. And I saw the force of the federal government with riot police at UVA, and Washington, DC. These were some wild times.

I had an opportunity for my third arrest, but decided that getting kicked out of school would end my college career. I was already on the edge with my lackluster grades and academic probation followed by a short stint of conduct probation for a physical altercation I got involved in when I punched my roommate in the face. He made the mistake of shoving me in the chest after I had pulled an all-nighter with mega doses of "NoDoz" caffeine pills. After the killings at Kent State a group of students on my campus decided to take over the English building. The doors were chained shut and a list of demands was drawn up, primarily asking the university to shut down in protest of the National Guard killing innocent college students. We were all there for peaceful protest, and given the choice to remain until morning, when we would be arrested for trespassing, or to leave before the police arrived, I decided to leave the building before the police got there to arrest the 107 students who were brave enough to get arrested to make a point. I was with them in spirit and in person for most of the night, sneaking out the back window before the police hooked up a pickup truck and tore the front door right off its hinges and forced their way in. My girlfriend at the time decided to stay and I respected that, although I couldn't figure out how she would get this one past her parents. Her father worked for a powder plant, a corporation that did not provide fluff for baby bums, but gunpowder for the war. I can remember one dinner he attended with Spiro Agnew as the keynote speaker. So much for the "nattering nabobs of negativism." What is really scary is the way that history repeated itself with the Bush administration (hello, Dick Cheney and Donald Rumsfeld) and lies supporting another illegal undeclared war perpetrated on the sovereign nation of Iraq. Trouble is the college students these days are lining up to be cannon fodder rather than lining up in protest. There are just so many disparate groups with so many divergent viewpoints that there's no one common thread to unite them. Some are so concerned about the "ethical treatment of animals" that they seem to ignore the ethical treatment of the human animal. There is also a fringe group of Earth Firsters and ecoterrorists who quite deservedly get a lot of bad press and make the rest of the nonviolent fringe pale in comparison. Nobody seems to do anything in moderation these days; they all go over the top, and that includes drug use. What used to be experimentation or recreational use seems to quickly slide into full-blown addictions, which takes all the fun out of the recreational use we enjoyed for those few years at school. It also has a lot to do with the context, the times in which drugs are taken. Today is very different than it was "back in the day" when we were growing up. Back then it was us versus them, the freaks versus the straights, the culture versus the counter culture. As challenging as it was for us, it was easy to pick sides, to figure out whose side you were on. Not so today. Back then, the vast majority of us did drugs and for the most part the drugs were clean and recreational in nature. Not so much like today with dangerous drugs and dangerous people dispensing them. This was the world my children, my grandchildren would be facing, but for me, it was easy. Life was good.

## The Check's In The Mail

For all the talk there is today of how evil drugs are, it's sad to admit that everyone is afraid to admit their participation, and the acknowledgment that we would not be where we are today as a country in the arts, theater, culture, even technology were it not for the drug movement of the sixties. I personally applaud anyone who has the courage to admit his or her part today.

Hard drugs are a nightmare: cocaine, heroin, crack. They can seep into your soul and poison it and everything you touch. Grass and hash were uppers, happy trips, and LSD, also known as "acid," was a roller coaster ride with peaks as high as Mount Everest and a few totally terrifying journeys into hell known as "bad trips." They basically put you in touch with nature and good feelings, good thinking. Some people use drugs, other abuse them, still others are used by the drugs. Problem is, it's hard to tell who is who. Some people, most people, can smoke a little weed and walk away a better person. But just like alcohol, there are some whose genetic wiring is geared toward addiction. One puff or one drink and some people are hooked.

## Hindsight One

Sometimes I look back and wonder if I should have ever walked through the door in the first place. Hindsight is usually

20/20, but when you consider the profound changes mind-altering drugs bring to you, it's nearly impossible to make a simple judgment; was the overall effect good or bad? I'd have missed out on a great deal, I know that. And most of the naysayers who are so profoundly dead set against drugs have never been there. How can they judge? Anyone looking at a junkie or a crack addict or some spaced-out drug burnout has to stop for a minute. And that applies to all those who never inhaled as well as those who dabbled in the subculture. My thought patterns are richer, fuller, more colorful. It's almost like comparing a black and white photo to a color photo.

There's a certain sadness that goes along with it, too. A kind of "knowing too much." Drugs change you in ways you can't imagine. You appreciate the highs in life so much more, but the lows can be pretty dark. That can be bad. Then there's this sense of altered reality that we really don't control our own destinies. That can be scary and force people back to the "I'd rather not know." It's what I sometimes refer to as the *illusion of free will*. If everything that happens is set to happen in one prescribed way, then we are all just going through the motions. If the script is already written, then why even try? Are we actually in the driver's seat guiding the vehicle of life along, or are we strapped to a sled careening down the hill, thankful it just made that last turn? And if nothing exists, than what is real, what is reality? I can understand it when drug users suggest that their drug experiences are the only "true" picture of reality and that "straight" (non-drug-user) people are the ones living in a fantasy world. But for sure, once you walk through the *Doors of Perception*, you can never go back, though you can push it into the back of your mind and restore the sense of self-control.

Although part of me is glad my children joined me in this special world, there is another part of me that is saddened that they did. And my own kids don't have my genetic wiring. They have their natural father's. He was a drug abuser. He was an alcoholic. He was an angry and violent man. He said he'd never live to make thirty. He died at twenty-nine. And even more frightening, he died a violent death. His daughter, my daughter, almost followed him to the grave.

## If You Can Beat 'Em, Join 'Em

And I heard them say, you can't change the country this way! You need to become part of the establishment and change it from within. After I got tear-gassed in Charlottesville and saw the force the government was willing to turn against its own children to restore order, I knew any civil revolution had to be peaceful, and that I had to effect change in a nonviolent manner. And so I made a conscious decision to complete my education and become part of the establishment, and to dedicate myself to social change constructively. I loved psychology, but there were no jobs in it, so I picked up education courses so I could teach. Teach what? They didn't even teach psychology in the high schools back then, so I had lots of hours in English, so I decided to pursue my degree in English education. I minored in sociology because it was the study of human behavior in groups. When I couldn't get a job as an English teacher in 1972, I went out for any job. I worked construction and I worked in a factory. Then one night I was at a party and got to talking with a friend who'd gone back to graduate school. She was telling me about a new field that was opening up. It seemed suited for my educational background and interests, a blend of my love for psychology and my love of children and education: SCHOOL PSYCHOLOGY. Since graduating in 1974 with my master's plus in this field, it's the only thing I've done professionally, and it's the only thing I truly love doing. And not only am I good at it (I should be after almost forty years), but I remained truly committed; I never sold out. I am and will always be a child advocate, spelled "I-will-fight-for-kids." And this, my friends is how I got myself into the situation I soon found myself in.

# CHAPTER TWO

# 1990 AND I AM THE ESTABLISHMENT

Three decades later, and I've straightened out my act, primarily for my kids. For starters, I gave up drugs. Partial credit goes to Elton John and Bernie Taupin's lyrics to the song "Rocket Man", "Rocket man...burning up his fuel up here alone...Mars ain't the kind of place to raise your kids...In fact it's cold as hell. And there's no one there to raise them...if you did." I always took that to mean you can't be a parent with a head all screwed up on drugs, and he's right. And alcohol is part of that, too, so I gave that up substantially. I didn't travel, I was home every night, and I didn't drink in excess, do drugs, or gamble. I read stories to my kids and took them to the bathroom at night so they wouldn't wet the bed; I built snow forts and sand castles, bought them bicycles and toys. We never left them with others, but took them with us, to the movies, and out to dinner, and on trips to towns along the East Coast. We talked to them, and listened to them, and had family chats about sex and drugs and friends and relatives. We ate dinner every night around the table. We were there for them. We made all the essential sacrifices a parent makes for his or her kids. But you always have to remember there's one thing you can't be for your children: their friend. At least not when they're under your roof and you're responsible for them.

*Friends love and accept you for who you are. Parents love you for who you can be.*

Somewhere along the line, when parents realize they have done the best they could, they release the little birds to the wind or the hurricane and sit back and get on with the rest of their life. It's only then that you wait for that gentle rapping on your window as they come back adults. If you're lucky that's all it is, a light rapping, not a steady pounding that shakes the very walls of your formerly peaceful homestead. If you have done right, the theory goes, your grown children will be an asset to you in your sunset years. It is only then that you can be on more equal ground and maybe even enjoy each other's company as friends do.

## He Doth Protest Too Much — Hypocrites Be Damned

But as long as they are under your roof and you have parental responsibility for them, you have an obligation to implement the parental role of caretaker, role model, provider, and chief authority figure. This role often contains inherent conflicts, especially for those among us who sowed more than our share of wild oats. Next question. Do you tell your kids about your drug use? Or, more specifically, did I tell my children about my own adventures into altered states of consciousness?

Well, when they were little, there was no need. They didn't understand the drug subculture, and they were into the "Just Say No" program first lady Nancy Reagan was pushing. Even her own daughter didn't buy it, and you wonder why *their* relationship was strained. But then the generation before us didn't understand drugs; they never tried them, were scared to death of them, and were even more scared to think their kids were into them. My parents missed out on the sixties. They did okay by us, but it wasn't the talk-to-your-kids generation. I didn't know people had sex for pleasure until I was fourteen. I thought I was going crazy wanting to see women naked, and...wanting to...touch their bodies. When I tried to talk to my father about it, his angry response was, "You shouldn't even be thinking about that stuff!" Slammed that door, he did. My mother hooked me up with a minister who, realizing I might not be the only kid in this situation, formed a bull session with kids from church, some my age and some of the older, more experienced boys. Boy, was I relieved to hear that not only were my secret thoughts okay, lots of people liked to look at and touch naked bodies. I breathed a sigh of relief, and a bigger sigh of longing thinking about what I had to look forward to!

This repressed generation who couldn't talk about sex surely couldn't talk about drugs. That subject was something they knew nothing about. I figured since I was here on the planet, at least they must have known something about sex. As with every generation, I wasn't going to be a hypocrite and lie to my kids, and I wasn't going to wait for them to come to me. We started family talks when they were young, and whenever a topic came up, we would sit down and talk about it, logically, calmly, reasonably. I hoped to do better than my own parents, who kept me in the dark. I talked with my kids about sex, about drugs, about life. They'd giggle sometimes, but it opened doors. Drugs were part of those discussions, with me, Dad, being more experienced and having a bit more to tell. "Did you ever do drugs, Dad?" deserved an honest answer. I didn't tell them everything, of course, just an overview, with an emphasis that I no longer indulged and why. That it wasn't fair to them to keep using. They were both anti-drug and I supported that. I helped write *Just Say No* skits about peer pressure, and supported them in their disdain for drugs—disdain, in part, because of their natural father. Kevin never gave up the drugs, hard or soft. He was a hard drinkin', hard ridin' biker dude who did whatever he got his hands onto or his nose into. His violent behavior near the end of his short life was enough to scare anyone away from drugs, and his natural children were no exception. I think their initial anti-drug stance was in reaction to Kevin. When he finally died at the hands of the police, we all breathed a sigh of relief. Kevin still haunts us years after his death.

Did I send mixed messages? Admittedly, yes. If I was at a concert with them and smelled the pleasant aroma of herb, how could I not allow a smile to come across my face? If I saw a lovely lass dancing at the Grateful Dead concert, could I deny that her glow was drug induced? DC on the Fourth of July was patriotic, but were most of the good vibes, good music, and laid-back people at the country-western sound stage or the Lawrence Welk Polka Fest, or the NORML smoke in? So that's where we (the kids and I) spent some time. It was a good vibe, the sixties all over again, and it felt good to be part of it. Tolerance for other people's beliefs and lifestyles. Acceptance, forgiveness. All of the values and attitudes that made *Woodstock* survive for three days with no violence. In 1969, and again in our violence-driven society with *Woodstock 1994*. And though drugs were not a major part of Woodstock '94, their spirit was there—the same spirit of tolerance for other people's ways of living. There truly is enough violence in our society to keep authority figures busy. Time is poorly spent hunting down the perpetrators of victimless crimes. And for those who say everyone who takes drugs or who lives with someone who takes drugs is a victim, I say there are no absolutes when it comes to drugs. And as for that message from my own childhood, ALL DRUGS ARE BAD, I ask about Prozac and Lithium and other drugs that help people to survive from day to day. If you come to accept the truism, and then come to find out that, well, a little grass didn't make my head fall off, then you can "safely" assume that there's nothing wrong with any drug. ALL DRUGS ARE GOOD, which is equally false. So you venture into dark territory not knowing what you'll run into or how it will affect you.

Over the years as I have talked with former drug users, they seem to break into two distinct groups: those who did not like themselves and used drugs for escape and went too far and really messed themselves up bad (burnouts we called them), and those who liked ourselves and really only used drugs for recreation and even for education to learn about ourselves and our world. I count myself as in the second group. We may have teetered near the edge, but had a FOUNDATION of strength that pulled us back from the precipice. The difference between the two groups is that one learned to STAY AWAY FROM THAT SHIT! and the other, I don't need it anymore, I've learned all I can from it. That foundation I refer to is your self-esteem, your history. Most of the individuals in the first group came from bad situations, victims of abuse or neglect, and did not feel good about themselves. The rest of us came from good homes with loving, supportive parents who gave us that foundation, that solid psyche from which we ventured out and to which we came back. We didn't get lost. A little paranoid, a little scared, but not lost; when we knew we were too far out there, we turned around and headed back to shore. Many were less fortunate. They went on what they thought was a day cruise only to find out they were on the *Titanic* or a small ship heading into a hurricane. Many of them did not survive the experience.

The big question is, how do you 1) explain this to your children, and 2) how can you separate one group from the other? Don't forget, my daughter came from one of those loving, supportive families, with a host of fine memories, but she dropped right off the edge. Why was her self-esteem so low that she could lose her way? What could we have told her differently to keep her from drifting out to sea? What would cause a wonderful child who was so anti-drug, who lost a father to the curse, to turn to drugs the same way he did, and get seriously lost in the process? Did we somehow fail her? Did we tell her too much or not enough? Or...was she somehow genetically predisposed to follow in her father's footsteps? An addictive personality?

I have gone over my role in her downfall over and over again. I have thought about the many talks we had about drugs and decision making. I have always believed that for education to have an effect, it has to be honest, with the good *and* the bad, with the learner making his or her own decision. In order to maintain credibility, especially with adolescents, you can't try and sell them a bill of goods. Their bullshit detectors are too finely tuned. In order to keep the channels open, you have to be honest. When they were teenagers, I told my children that there were two sides to drugs. If you used them sparingly and didn't let them get hold of you, it could be okay. Not unlike alcohol, the legal drug; use it sparingly, and a drink now and then won't lead you directly to the gutter. Take notice of your heritage and your father's problems with drugs, and know that you too may have addictive personalities. I told them to be aware that recreational drugs are still illegal, and that there are serious consequences for getting "caught" with them that society doesn't understand or forgive. And the ultimate height of hypocrisy: those that speak the strongest against it are most likely the same people who indulged the most in it. Like any drug, alcohol, marijuana, tobacco: be aware of your family history and the warning signs of abuse, and please, please, leave it alone until you're old enough to handle it. Fifteen-, sixteen-, seventeen-year-old kids have no business taking any drug into their systems. They haven't formed their own central core yet to start rearranging it. And be aware of your strengths and weaknesses. Know when you're in over your head. Kids can't do this. Hell, adult abusers can't; how can you expect kids to?

I was lucky, I guess. I didn't have the family history of abuse, alcohol, or drugs, and I had a strong central core. I recognized my limitations and pulled myself out. I quit tobacco cold turkey, never going back, and walked away from the pills quickly, merely dabbling in the softer glow of grass. Did it change me? Profoundly. For the better? I'd have to say yes. Before drugs I was afraid, and I didn't like myself. Heck, I didn't even *know* myself. Now, I fear nothing, and I have the strength of my own convictions. This came from self-analysis from my drug-related experiences. Drugs opened my mind and my life to the beauty I behold today.

Do I recommend, would I recommend, taking drugs to anyone? Back then we wanted everyone we knew to turn on. We wanted to share it all. Now that I realize the death sentence it holds for some, I wouldn't want the responsibility for anyone else. Most important, I wouldn't want it for my kids. But somehow, they didn't need Dad to sell them on the wonders of modern chemistry. Despite the fact that their biological father died a violent death as a result of drugs (or maybe even because he died that way), they were drawn to drugs like moths to a flame. The biological imperative, their powerful genetic link to their father, kicked into gear. Some of the same reasons that kept them anti-drug as children drew them to it as adolescents.

I no longer used drugs, and I made this clear to them. I talked about the psychological effects, the permanent changes in personality, and the legal implications for someone in the business I was in (education) and the many careers they planned to pursue. But there was nothing I could say to turn them away from their own experimentation. They know it all and have to find out for themselves what it's all about. My job, our job, as parents is to not to enable them, to allow them to use our money for a drug-centered lifestyle. Like any and all substance abusers, if you are there to pick them up every time they fall, they will count on it. You cannot help them; only they can help themselves. And the answer to the question, "How far do they have to sink before a parent reaches out to help them?" It varies for every person. But the answer is simply this: YOU DON'T REACH OUT. It is their journey, and the paths they choose are ones they walk alone. When they get in trouble and are hanging by the tips of their fingers from a ledge, you can't help them; they have to help themselves. They have to hit the bottom so hard that they don't bounce back up. Only then are they able to realize they have to stop, have to quit, to recover what they had before. A parent has to stand by and watch, as difficult as that may be. Be there when they are doing right and need that love to light the way. But turn your back when they continue down this awful path of destruction. Helping them, even at the very last minute, only sends a message to the most primal centers of their brains that Mom and Dad will always be there to snatch them out of the jaws of death, so the next time they choose to "walk on the wild side" they will be thinking you or some other loved one will be right there. Think Hendrix and Joplin and Morrison and Belushi and Presley and Phoenix and Ledger and Jackson and Houston and...well, you get the idea.

By now you may be wondering who their father was, and how did we come to this place. How did such a nice family who did all the right things end up with a daughter hooked on heroin? Where did it all start? With their biological father, Kevin.

## Kevin

From the time I was young, I have always imagined that one day I'd have children of my own. For a variety of reasons it didn't work out that way. I have made my wife's children my own. I was living and working in Virginia when they were born to Caroline and her first husband, Kevin. Kevin was a good guy who went bad. Drugs helped get him there. He fancied himself the bad-ass biker, a "born to raise hell" kinda guy who fit in just fine during the sixties. Even bikers were mellow back then, and since everybody hated authority and distrusted the police who invaded our campuses and our private lives, biker types fit in just fine. We shared their disdain for police brutality, and the "pigs' " tendency to single out individuals who were a little different. If you were poor or shabbily dressed, if you were the wrong color, you were a target. And now those with long hair and bell-bottoms, war protesters, and assorted draft dodgers became instant targets as well.

## 1990 And I Am The Establishment

I can remember the first picture I ever saw of Kevin in 1980 when I first moved to town. It was in *Easy Rider* magazine; that's the one with the biker chicks naked from the waist up, tattoos and all. He was riding his Harley, long hair flowing behind him at some at bike week in Daytona. The circumstances under which I was shown this picture were rather interesting. I'd just moved to a new state for a new job and had my eye on this pretty, long-haired brunette. I found out she had two young kids and was divorced from this bad-ass biker. He'd been in state prison, according to the dude with the magazine, and this wild-looking dude didn't take kindly to assholes trying to put the moves on his old lady, ex or not. I decided for my health and well-being to find someone else to date. My feelings got the better of me, and I finally got the courage to ask her to lunch despite the imminent threat of her ex-old man.

The kids were three and four when I first met Caroline, and Kevin had made good on his promise to divorce them if Caroline divorced him. He never contributed any money or anything else. Caroline was essentially a single mother raising two small children when I came on the scene. She'd been divorced a little over a year.

To be truthful, there is an inherent unbalance when a man marries into a ready-made family. Unless you're some kind of weirdo, your primary love interest is in the mom. You notice her, you like her, you love her. The kids, unless they are genuine pains in the ass, kind of go along with the deal like bald tires on a custom sports car. You might love them, you might hate them, but they're an integral part of the deal, and you can't do without them, though you know they aren't a permanent part of the vehicle like the engine or the seats. And you know that in a few years they'll be gone, rolling off to some distant future of their own. The only difference between tires and kids is old tires don't come rolling back all the time, and you don't usually haul them around in the back of the car after they've run their course. No, kids are different. They're yours (or someone's) for life.

When you marry a woman with kids there's usually another father lurking around somewhere. He may or may not be attached to the kids, but you can bet on one thing, more often than not, she has done little to strengthen the father-child relationship. A divorced woman doesn't typically *like* her ex-husband. If he was a drunk, gambled all their money away, used drugs, fooled around with other women, or was violent...she probably threw his ass out. She did it to protect her kids, to protect her vision of family, and most importantly to protect herself. Remember, at one time she loved this guy. Enough to marry him and bear his children. Now she was throwing him out with more than a few conflicting emotions about giving up her better years, and her financial security, and sometimes even her virginity. Now she was establishing the proper mental set to chuck the guy, so this is where the love/hate thing comes in. Never forget...hell *hath no fury like a woman scorned*. And, if the lousy bastard beat her to the punch, i.e., he ran out on her first with another woman (younger and prettier being the hardest to deal with), then you can imagine the depth of feelings she has for this man, and how this might tend to generalize to all men.

Women in this setting, single women, form a boundary of protective armor around themselves that is so thick, it can stave off an atomic weapon. Inside are their ego and their children, little ducks comforted by the warm wings of the mother duck with fangs like a werewolf. It takes a very accepting man and woman to break down this boundary and let another man in. To trust again. To love again. To share their children again. To be whole. When a man comes into this ready-made setting, it's three against one from the start, and though you will always put her *first* on your list, you will never be first on hers. You will always, always come after her children.

I loved the woman, and despite my mother's insightful warning when I first told her of my new girlfriend with two children, "Oh, don't get involved," I got involved, full tilt. My darling Sarah was three years old, and her brother, Andrew, was four. Sarah was a doll baby, the kind of kid who would crawl up in your lap and lay her head on your chest. Andrew was a little more difficult. He had seen more of the violence his father had inflicted on the family and on his mother. He was the one who had to be protected from his father's wrath. He was a little bit older when his father took a gun out and started shooting at the family. Caroline's dad had to grab both of the babies, one under each arm, and run for safety. Andrew was a bit overprotected by Caroline and was a momma's boy when I entered the picture. Andrew whined and cried and never really made up to me. I tried, I mean I really tried. He wet the bed almost every night. Mom would say nothing (and I certainly wouldn't have at those early stages of our relationship), but I was a psychologist, after all, so I devised a plan. He went to bed at nine. He would get nothing to drink after seven. I would wake him up at eleven when I went to bed, and at two when I got up to pee, and then again at six when we rose. I would wake him up (not an easy task), walk him into the bathroom, steering him like a little car with gentle hands on his tiny shoulders, slipping around in his pajamas with little feet in them, and I would unzip his little suit and sometimes even hike his tighty-whities or his Superman Underoos down to his ankles, but that's where I drew the line. He'd pee and shake that little winkie all by himself, and then I would walk him back to bed. I did this for weeks, praising him for the dry bed until we eventually got him to perform this nightly ritual on his own. Sarah never wet the bed or whined a day in her life. Her challenges would come later.

Enter the good Samaritan, or, as Caroline has been known to describe me in fits of anger, *the knight on the white horse*. I had purely selfish motivations. I needed a woman. And after years of playing the field and then settling down with the wrong woman (a cheating little vixen named Teresa who gave me the crabs), I was ready for a stable, steady relationship that a woman with a home and two kids would bring. I was ready to commit. And I did. I also figured that rather than having a tough act to follow, this would be a breeze. After Caroline's first husband I'd look like a prince. I didn't drink or use drugs or gamble, and I was committed to being faithful. It seemed ideal, too, because where most biological fathers are very much in the picture, Kevin was not. In most divorce cases, with a new boyfriend, not only are you sleeping with their wife, but you're playing father to their children. Kevin was different. His new girlfriend didn't like kids, and the two of them were so into the drugs they consumed, they couldn't care less about anything else. Besides, he told Caroline when he divorced her, "You divorce me, I divorce you and the kids!" And lowlife that he was, he was a man of his word on this. He never even bought her a gallon of milk or a loaf of bread. To be truthful, Caroline never asked for a thing, preferring not to be indebted to the man, assuming it would be much easier to do it on her own than to be dependent on him for anything. If he never contributed to her or his children's welfare, then he had no claim to them either. And that was just fine with her. Herein was the origin of her complete independence from him...and all men. She was a single parent, a single MOTHER, and proud of it. And she worked hard for her kids and for herself. Oh, she had her male friends and her fun, too, but it was on her terms...not theirs. Caroline kept me at arm's length for quite a while. Even after she agreed to marry me, she had doubts, and even years later when she got really steamed, she'd tell me she should have turned around that day she was headed down to the church to marry me; she should never have gone through with it. But she did.

Originally, my first reservations were about Kevin. I loved Caroline, was close to Sarah, and Andrew was coming along okay. It was the man on the motorcycle that had me worried. His girlfriend would leave threatening notes on our doorway, and he cut the tires on my van one night. Not just one but all four. He even assaulted his mother for money one time, and there was no telling what he might do to me and Caroline if he took a notion. For the first and only time in my life, I considered carrying a gun. Although it was good that he was not a regular part of their lives, Caroline lived in his grandmother's house and maintained a close relationship with Kevin's mother, the kids' grandmother. It all came to a resounding conclusion when he was shot and killed. That ended it all. Or so we thought.

## Huttonsville State Prison

Kevin's original crime was nonviolent; he tried to rob a post office. He thought he could get the money order machine and just print himself out thousands of dollars and hit the road. He got $1.50 in pennies. And ten years. It turned violent when he tried to shoot it out with the police after they caught up with him. All three went to jail, he and his two buddies. All three are dead now. Two in a car crash. Kevin would have spent every bit of those ten years in prison — he didn't believe in time off for good behavior — but he was married to Caroline. She went to bat for him and appealed to the governor, Arch Moore. In a rather ironic twist, he ended up going to jail for embezzling state funds. Caroline was a good woman and convinced the governor to let her husband out for a Christmas pardon. She then worked hard to get pregnant, hoping this would settle him down. She made a nice home for him and found him a job in the mines and gave him his son, but it wasn't enough. He took to picking up fifteen-year-old groupies and taking drugs. Despite kid number two, Sarah, he was still the bad-ass biker. In what may prove to be an even more lethal twist of fate, he came to the hospital after Sarah was born. He never wanted her and tried to convince Caroline to terminate her pregnancy, but once she felt life inside her, Caroline knew she'd carry her all the way. Sarah was born six weeks early and weighed less than five pounds. They didn't know if she'd even live. Kevin wasn't the type to hang around hospitals (bad vibes, man) even if his wife was in there giving birth to his premature daughter, but Sarah was weak and needed a blood transfusion. Caroline had lost too much blood already, so they called on Kevin. He came in and donated blood to his tiny little daughter and got high with her at the same time. He was stoned out of his mind on marijuana when he came to the hospital that night, and no, he didn't have the sense to refuse the taking of his tainted blood.

# Desperado's Last Campaign

Kevin said he'd never live to be thirty, and he never did. He'd gotten into trouble with his mother over money she wouldn't give him for a concert. He dragged her around the house by her hair until he found her purse, took her money, and then, just to show her, took her car, a 1974 Lincoln Continental Mark IV. He got arrested, of course, and went to jail, but Momma bailed him out and sent him to Texas to cool off with his sister. He came back to get his stuff and his girlfriend, whom he found in bed with another guy. The other guy had the good sense to get the hell out of there; Diane didn't. She was taking one hell of a beating.

The beating worked its way out of the house onto the front lawn, where the neighbors took notice. Police were called in for a domestic disturbance, and they sent two officers, a male officer with some experience and a younger female rookie. When they drove up, Kevin was working Diane over on the front lawn. The officers ran up, calling for him to freeze. He ran into the house. While they were seeing to Diane, Kevin emerged from the house, butcher knife in hand. He first attacked the male officer, plunging the knife into his side. The officer dropped to the ground. The female rookie jumped on Kevin's back. He threw her off onto the ground and went after her. He tried to stab her in the chest, but her bulletproof vest prevented his knife from penetrating her flesh. Thinking kill or be killed, Kevin went for the two places the vest didn't cover, her armpit and her neck. He was in the middle of plunging the knife into her neck when the male officer recovered enough to draw his weapon, issue a final warning, and then shoot him twice, once in the arm and once in the upper leg. The bullet bounced off his thigh bone and entered his stomach and chest cavity. Both police officers survived. Kevin

## 1990 And I Am The Establishment

died at five in the morning April 1, 1982. He always said he'd never see thirty. He was twenty-nine years old.

His children, Andrew and Sarah, were four and five years old. I had been dating Caroline for about a year by this time, and we both worried that having their father die this way would haunt them. When we thought about it, though, maybe it was better this way than to have a father alive wreaking havoc on the world. His death brought a sense of relief to the family. We would give the kids bits and pieces of the story as they grew older. We visited his grave and put flowers on it. We showed respect for him in death that he would never have had in life. Andrew has never discussed it, or even asked to see any of the newspaper clippings I saved on the event. Sarah asked one day to see them and, against my better judgment, Caroline let her go into her room by herself, close the door, and submerse herself in the tragedy from ten years earlier. Sarah was fourteen years old. Though he has been dead for over thirty years now, he still haunts this whole family: his ex-wife, his children, and me. In a recent letter to her counselor, Sarah wrote, "I look like my mother, but I'm a lot more like my real father." It bothered me to read that, but not for the reasons you think. I wasn't jealous; I was scared that she just might be right.

Fifteen years would pass and the strains on our marriage were starting to bend it to the breaking point. Sarah and Andrew were both young adults, and yet they were still creating problems for our family. Neither had gone on to school, and Sarah barely earned her high school diploma. They were on their own, yet they were still part of our lives, a lot more than I wanted them to be. I had raised both of them, they were now over eighteen, and still mom was more focused on *their* needs, *their* lives, more than our marriage. I was even considering asking Caroline for a divorce. I was sad, lonely, depressed. I woke up one morning and called my mom. She advised me to "Hang in there, Caroline's a great gal," etc., which I needed to hear. She told me that when your kids grow up, you have to refocus on your marriage. "You can't marry your kids," she said, and it's true. Your kids grow up and leave you, and they find love interests of their own who provide the direct nurturing mother used to, and then they start families (accidentally or intentionally) of their own, and provide their own nurturing.

I finally worked up the courage to confront Caroline. "You spend so much time doing for these two kids at my expense that I really wonder what we'll have in common once they're gone." I said this not so much as a threat or an imminent warning as a plea for her to begin to focus on me, on us, and balance her love between her kids and her husband. Little did I know how this fear would spin out of control in ways even I could not imagine.

## Do You Believe In Ghosts?

Caroline had a neighbor who was what some call a "sensitive." He could see things that most people couldn't. Caroline had been consulting him for card readings for years and convinced me to go see him one night. Naturally I was a bit skeptical. I was even more skeptical when he told me I would have serious trouble with a blonde woman in my life. He was nice, and he didn't charge me anything (he never took money), and he didn't profess to being able to tell the future, but the truth was, I didn't know any blonde women, much less any that were troublemakers. Two weeks later I was called down to Virginia to settle a dispute between my parents and my sister and her husband. Guns were fired into the night as we all ran for safety—my sixty-year-old parents, a baby, a five-year-old, and…my blonde older sister.

That's why I believed him when Mr. Shanks told Caroline that he saw Kevin several months after he died, standing in her backyard, looking at the house. He said he had the sense that he was there looking over the kids. Years later we would feel his presence again, looking over his children's shoulders as they ventured into the world of serious drugs.

## 1990 And I Am The Establishment

Any man who comes into a situation with a single woman and child should consider himself lucky if there is a living, natural father in the picture looking out for the welfare of his children. For all the inconvenience, it would be a helluva lot easier to deal with than the legacy this dead man left us. Many of the problems we've experienced as husband and wife, and many of the problems we've had with the kids and over the kids, have their roots in this man. His genes and the tendency for addictive behavior, his anger, and the scars he left on his wife often kept us from the intimacy we so deserved.

Throughout this series of life-changing experiences, I made a point of reaching deep to the bottom of my soul to understand my motivations, my needs, my sacrifices, and my gains. I accepted the ready-made family. It was a package deal, but with the headaches and the grief come a measure of control. It's the old accountability/authority model. If you're to be held accountable (as a parent or employee), then you deserve the authority to make the decisions as well, even if it's shared authority. The frustration comes in when somebody else is calling all the shots, and then you get the blame for the failures. With Caroline, it's been a mixed bag. At times she deferred to me, at others she consulted with me, and yet at others it boiled down to blood; they were her kids and the final decision was hers. That led to the three-against-one scenario, Caroline and the kids against "bad dad," and a few what-ifs. What if Caroline and I had our own child? How would that have affected our relationship and her relationship with her kids? How would they have related to a half sibling, someone who shared genes (blood) in common with their mom and me? And what if...what if, rather than Caroline being the only one to bring children into our marriage and allowing them to come between us as husband and wife, what if I had children of my own? How would that have affected the dynamic? Just for the sake of argument, I decided to write a story about it. I had no "baggage" when Caroline married me. I had no ex-wives or children, and it was just me. I had no debts or legal problems, no addictions to alcohol, tobacco, drugs, or gambling, no prison record. But what if I did bring a small suitcase into the marriage? I mean, after feeling part of a dynamic where I was always the odd man out, with Caroline aligned with the two children against me, how would she feel, how would they feel, if there was a knock on the door one day and a young man presented himself to me as my long...lost...son? How would they accept him? As readily as I accepted them?

## The Sixties Come Back (To Haunt Us)

It's the early nineties and the kids are entering their teenage years. "Retro" wasn't even a word back then, but believe me, the sixties were coming back, and it felt like a new age of Aquarius. I was kind of excited when my kids started to pick up on the new wave of energy; the clothes and lifestyles of the hippies were coming round again, tie dyed shirts, sandals, beads, flowing dresses, patchouli oil, "head shops," and...the music. When I was young I often wondered what my kids could do to freak me out. At the time the only thing I could think of was turn into narcs. Straight, short-haired nerds who busted those free-spirited amongst us. And for someone like me, a left-leaning, liberal Democrat, having a conservative Republican for a child would have freaked me out. But no, my kids were a lot like me, and I thought it was neat that they were leaning toward the spiritual side. Not only were kids starting to listen to Led Zeppelin and Jimi Hendrix and the Doors again, but new musicians; Alternative rock was coming to the forefront, capturing another generation's angst—Nirvana, Counting Crows, Pearl Jam, Cracker, Alice in Chains...the X generation. Our children may not have had the Vietnam War, and Iraq was years away, but they had something even worse: a deadly sexually transmitted disease known as AIDS. Jobs were just as scarce as ever, and the promise of a college education and good jobs was lost in the downsizing and lack of job security for our generation. Pollution and environmental decay are not just a theory or threat. The ozone hole is open, and droughts and streaks of ninety-degree days and snow storms, floods, tornadoes, and hurricanes have brought the harsh realities of global warming to bay. And terrorism, something that happened to other countries, is right here in our homeland, not to mention the terror of rapists and serial murders stalking the highways. And for those who felt safe in their own homes at least, there's Polly Klaas being ripped from her own bedroom slumber party, and home invasions as burglars get more desperate and more brazen. And then there are carjackings, children murdering their parents, and people going nuts and shooting up fast-food restaurants and kindergarten classrooms and government buildings. Who wants to work for the post office these days? Instead of an occasion nip in the butt by some errant mongrel, it's Uzis in the lunchroom. No more lead-free lunch. And Mac 10s instead of Big Macs at the local fast-food emporium. Point is, our kids did have a lot to worry about, and the music has once again captured the spirit and mood of a generation, their angst, their frustrations and fears and longings; longings for the good old days of the sixties, when flower power was the rage. And right along with the music and the clothes and the antiauthoritarian attitudes were the drugs that opened all those channels of communication.

## Just Say Not Right Now

All of the kids who "just said no" turned into teenagers, and the only "No" they were saying was to US, their parents, the square generation. For all of the grand notions we might have had that our kids would see us as COOL and open to talk to...well, just like in our day...that's the *other* kid's parents. Not yours. You can't be your own kid's friend, you're their parent. Oh, it's easy being COOL to your kid's friends, talking about the music then and now, and the good old days, but then you're not having to tell *them* when to come in, and when to go out, or not to color their hair pink or not to pierce or tattoo body parts. So the doors you thought were left open with your kids suddenly slam shut. And you wonder, if I hadn't shared with them my tales of sixties debauchery, would my kids be experimenting like they are, or not? Did my actions legitimize their current behavior? Some say that the best course is to LIE; it puts you in a better position of "maintaining the high ground"; DRUGS ARE BAD. Even though that *high ground* is a cloud of marijuana smoke that the kids can smell a mile away. A friend once told me that research has it (good old research) that kids of the sixties' drug users have a significantly greater chance of using drugs themselves *whether their parents shared with them their stories or not*. Seems that a subtle, unspoken message is communicated, even with those who were silent or outright deceitful about their former drug use.

In the early predrug sixties, parents and teachers and other authority types told us ALL DRUGS WERE BAD. They lumped marijuana with heroin, and so once you found out marijuana didn't make you crazy or "hook you," you figured, "If they'd lie to me about grass, then they probably lied to us about the other drugs, too." This was dangerous, because though some did lie, most told stories out of ignorance. They'd never done any kind of drug; they simply didn't know. But then those were the days when we all trusted our leaders not to lie to us. That was before Richard Nixon told the big lie, shattering trust in all our leaders and national institutions. It was a new freedom, thinking for ourselves. We were venturing out into unknown territory, new frontiers, and though it was fun at first, it became a living hell for many of us. And even those who pulled back and moved on with life without permanent scars had the mark of drugs upon us. So our use, like a yoke, or a medal around our necks, comes down to be bestowed upon our children, like it or not. But there was a cruel irony that involved our kids (typical teenagers knowing more than their parents) who then applied that to drugs, something we *did* know more than a little bit about. That they rejected the bad news we gave about drugs, thinking "it will be different" is the scariest part. For the drug scene is *very* different than it was in our day, even though the drugs are pretty much the same.

And so our drug-free kids jumped in full force and joined the secret society that drugs demand, and Mom and Dad were locked out. Sarah first, and then Andrew much later. I can't tell you how many times I think of the term "sins of the father." It's like, I thought I got away with my use in the sixties. I experimented, had fun, got burned, backed away, and came away a whole person with most of the brain intact... whew! Here I am many years down the road and my use has come back to haunt me again in the form of my kids. Sarah was first. And she jumped in the deep end.

## Sarah's First Rebellion

Sarah started with her first surprise back in 1992. That's when she slipped a lipstick in her pocket at Value City. We found this out when the store detective stopped us in the vestibule on our way out, flashed her badge, and explained that the girls (we were with a friend of Sarah's) had things on their person they hadn't paid for. No, not our girls, but when Laura, the friend, pulled out the lipstick with this "look" on her face, I was quick to think, "I knew she was trouble!" That is, until Sarah also pulled out a stick. You could have knocked me over with a baby's breath. We talked her way out of this one, but redoubled our efforts. We got involved in family counseling, put her on a behavior management plan complete with levels, and tried to pull the family together again.

## Teaching Tolerance

Sarah's next little adventure was to get a huge crush on an African American boy. I don't think I would have minded it as much if he had been from a good family, but he was a hyperactive kid I had seen professionally who needed desperately to have some attention, and Sarah provided it. A father is naturally jealous when his daughter takes on her first boyfriend, but I can't begin to describe my feelings when I saw her following this little troublemaker around. It bothered me more that she had crossed class lines, though no white person can honestly say that race doesn't enter into your mind a little, as much as you'd like to keep it out. You can't encourage your kids to make friends with all kids, black, yellow, brown, white, and then get all puffed up when they fall in like with a friend who is a different shade. When we saw them at the dance, we were taken aback, but what could you do? We quietly discussed it at home, talking about how other people in a small rural country-and-western town would treat her if she crossed the color line. We talked about burning bridges and how it would be very different to meet someone of a different race when she was older and at college, but small-town high schools didn't always understand and accept that behavior. Caroline and I were aware of the need to stay cool and not drive her to him, but wanted her to understand the consequences of her relationship. She denied having any romantic connection with Shontay (she lied), but when Shontay and his friends began calling the house at all hours, we know something wuzzup. I wanted to face it head on and invite him to the house, bring him into our world, but Caroline was not into encouraging that, and Sarah certainly wasn't into it. This turned out to be a crush that didn't amount to anything. He later impregnated one of Sarah's pals, and they got married and have several kids. Oh well.

## Sneaking Out

Sarah's behavior grew progressively worse as she careened from one troublesome incident to the next. Her next major upset after the shoplifting was sneaking out of the house at night to meet some boys. Sarah was about fifteen at the time and had a friend, Mary, stay overnight. Caroline had already gone to bed, and I was in my room listening to music when the phone rang. Sarah answered it on the first ring. Several minutes later she poked her head in my room and asked if it was okay to go out for a walk. Sure, I said. And after they were gone for a while, I followed them out. I mean, I'm not stupid. I decided against a confrontation, but listened to the conversation out in the street for a while and then came back to the house to wait for them. I was waiting for them when they returned from their walk. "Hey, girls. Have a nice walk? Bump into anyone?" They denied it, and so I told them I had walked out to see what they were up to. No big thing. Sarah was defensive and angry with me for not trusting her. Well...I didn't make a major thing about it, since they didn't go off in a car, just stayed outside chatting. I even agreed not to tell Mom. I remembered what it was like to be a kid, so I let this one go. I told her if she wanted to meet boys, it would be preferred that they come here to the house rather than her sneaking out to meet them.

The next night she asked if two young (male) friends could come over to watch movies with Mary and her. Sure. They went up to the loft and watched a movie, and then asked if they could go out for a walk. It was late, after eleven, and it was raining, so I didn't think they would go far. As well, they took Maggie with them (our short-legged bulldog). When eleven turned to twelve, and twelve turned to one, I woke Caroline and filled her in. We were close to calling Mary's parents when they walked in at one thirty. Actually, they didn't walk in, they stood outside. Mary got into the backseat and Sarah stood outside. I walked to the door and said, "I think it's time you boys headed home." We talked with the girls some that night and arranged a meeting with Mary's parents the next day. Topic of conversation, *responsibility*. Turns out they walked down to the river to sit on the dock. Real safe place on a rainy night. Mary has asthma, which could have caused additional problems. Two girls with two boys we don't know that much about, Mary's parents trusting us to care for their daughter, and Sarah putting us all in jeopardy. It was another step in her path of ignorance, tempered with defiance. Her failure to understand and accept convention (social rules) and her reaction when "caught" was a defiant attitude and defensive posture, blaming me for not trusting her when it was her betrayal of trust that was the cause. This was compounded by a complete unwillingness to accept any consequences for her actions or show any remorse. This made bad behaviors even more difficult to deal with. Most kids act contrite when they are caught red-handed; they apologize, they say they're sorry. They play the game, and when the heat dies down enjoy their new freedom. Sarah never let it cool down. We were the jerks for imposing all these stupid rules. We were wrong for not trusting her. So what if she screwed up Monday? This was TUESDAY! You can understand why we were beginning to get a little crazy. What is a parent expected to do? Give up and let them do what they will, or continue to set limits, enforce rules, and establish consequences? We redoubled our efforts to communicate clearly and concisely what we expected of her, and what the consequences would be if she followed the rules and what would happen if she chose to not follow the rules. We wrote them down. We talked about them. We had her sign behavioral contracts.

We supervised her and we followed up on everything the best we could. When we got into cross purposes with her misbehavior and her lying, we finally sought professional help. We contacted a clinical psychologist someone had recommended. He was okay, but he was a strict fifty-minute person, and you'd be right at a crucial point and he'd say, "We'll have to stop now, hold that thought." For two weeks? I'd start listing all the stuff Sarah had done to us over the two-week interim, and she'd start her tirade about how we didn't let her do anything, go anywhere, or have anything. It would dissolve into attack and blame. We stopped going to him. We'd have to try and work things out for ourselves.

## Sarah Takes The Plunge

In the summer of '93 we were all on vacation in Connecticut. Sarah turned fifteen and it was the Fourth of July. The whole gang was there; the Carnellis, the Bartles, and my friend Kenny from long ago. He'd been married with a son, and was now divorced and remarried with a second son. Kenny never finished that high school diploma, but had a decent job at a local assembly plant. His second wife, Tina, was a real steadying influence on him and pulled him out of the bottle some twelve years before. He was clean and sober when we started going back to visit Connecticut in 1986. Jamie Peace Hall, Kenny and his first wife's son, was a senior and had just graduated from high school. He was small like his dad, and cute, at least from Sarah's perspective. Andrew was sixteen at the time and it was kind of nice that the kids, *our* kids, were hanging out and getting along. So when they asked to go out to a carnival in town, who was to say no? I mean, it was the first time Sarah went out in a car with a boy, but her brother was with her and this was Kenny's son, one of my old friends, why not? So off they went. What I didn't know was that Jamie's friend, the one with the car, picked up his girlfriend, and when she whipped out a joint, my drug-free kids weren't into saying no, so they indulged. So in one of the classic ironies of life, a longtime friend's son, the same friend who got me thinking about drugs some twenty years earlier, his son ends up turning my own daughter on at fifteen, the first time she was even allowed out in a car. I didn't find this out until months later, many months later. By that time Sarah was into the drug scene full bore. Here was yet another example of a simple decision, trusting my son and daughter to make good decisions, and for their friends to do the same, resulting in bad decisions that would have monumental repercussions down the road.

# The Car Accident That Changed Everything

Each event in life has its own power, and like the drugs or alcohol that fuel them, they rapidly begin to add up, multiply, and accumulate into a quickening mass. The summer of 1993 turned into fall and Sarah moved into high school. On a bright sunny day in October, Caroline dropped Andrew and Sarah off at the garage to pick up my truck, which they would then drive to school. It's 7:40 in the morning, and teachers, students in cars and big yellow buses, parents, and others are on the way to work. Caroline pulls up behind Mrs. Bilbrough as she waits at a red light at the intersection between State Route 404, a four-lane divided highway, and River Road, a two-lane country road that leads from town across 404 and on to the high school a mile up the road. The kids pull in behind their mother, who is also waiting for the light to change. The light turns from red to green, and Mrs. Bilbrough pulls across the highway, one lane, two lanes, median strip, three lanes, four lanes, and off the travel section of the road. Caroline is behind her, one lane, two lanes, median strip, and as she enters the third lane of the highway, she is struck with such brutal force that the hood of her car is ripped off and lands a hundred feet down the road. She'd just been hit by a 30-ton Mack Truck loaded with sixty-seven thousand pounds of sand as the driver barreled through a light that had now been red on his side for eight to ten seconds. The initial impact occurred at the right front fender. Glass shatters and the force spins the van around, shooting it away at a ninety-degree angle. The truck, unimpeded in its movement, catches up to the van and strikes it again from behind, caving in the rear quarter section, shattering glass, and further collapsing the vehicle. It spins another half circle and ends up facing the wrong way on the highway, steam pouring from the radiator as vital fluids leak onto the road. Andrew and Sarah witness the entire spectacle. They pull their truck off to the side of the road and get out frozen in space, too afraid to approach the shattered vehicle that still contains their mother. Is she dead? Is she alive? It took the rescue team thirty minutes to safely remove her from the vehicle and transport her to the hospital. It would take years off her life, and years to recover.

## Sarah Sinks Deeper

Sarah's behaviors continued to worsen as she sunk deeper into the drug culture, unbeknownst to any of us. Although we suspected that she was using drugs, we weren't sure, and thought her behaviors were more a function of adolescent rebellion compounded by mild depression. She grew more distant and withdrawn. Her clothes and hairstyle changed from sunny and cheerful to dark and gloomy. Torn stockings and black fingernail polish and darker eyes became the order of the day. Her skin began to turn a ghostly white, and her mood grew ever darker. She would avoid us like the plague, getting home and retreating to the cavern of her room, venturing out to raid the refrigerator or use the bathroom. She rarely joined us around the dinner table and barely spoke two words to us for days at a time. At one point we developed a behavior contract which required her to say three things to us per day: "good morning," "hi, I'm home," and "good night." Having been there, and being fairly knowledgeable about the symptoms of drug abuse, we weren't exactly novitiates. We saw the signs and we addressed them. We talked to both Sarah and Andrew, though we were more concerned about her.

We also took an additional step. A family lived a few houses down from us. We didn't interact much with them when we first moved in because he came across as a know-it-all. For example, he quickly told us we paid too much to have our house built, and then showed us his glorified doublewide he paid "almost nuthin' " for. His kids refused to wait at the bus stop with the others and had an extra stop added for them. They didn't want their kids mixing with the country club kids. To further avoid the pressures to join the country club, which just happens to be less than a half mile up the road, with an eighteen-hole golf course, tennis courts, swimming pool, and clubhouse, he put in his own swimming pool. He started by inviting the kids over, and then we reluctantly went over. We don't like being beholden to people. He used to try and make us feel guilty if we exercised our membership rights at the club pool, though I wanted to get my money's worth. I don't golf, and we don't eat out in that style very often. So my annual dues were for the country club pool, and I intended to use it. But we ended up being neighborly as well and spent time at their pool as well. By the summer of 1994, the two families were pretty close, walking into each other's homes without knocking, taking care of each other's pets when one went on vacation, and generally helping out with chores, chopping wood, or building decks.

## On The Outside Looking In

We had reason to suspect Sarah was involved in drugs. In addition to the drastic change in lifestyle and dress, we'd intercepted some cryptic notes, and though we had no smoking gun, or joint, as it were, we needed to find out. Who better to ask to keep an eye on Sarah than our pool-owning neighbor, friend, surrogate father, and...newly hired teacher/coach at the high school? He assured us on more than one occasion that he would keep an eye on her, and that his ears were open, and we basically had nothing to worry about. In his words, she was "on the outside looking in." We followed his advice until one of Sarah's notes was quite obvious in its drug references, and some of her art projects had taken on a rather ominous tone. Mom searched her room and found what we had suspected, but not known for sure—that she was using drugs. A plastic pack with a marijuana bud was all we needed. We confronted Sarah and also called Coach over to let him know. I remember him sitting in my chair as I dangled the packet in front of his face, "Outside looking in? What do you call this shit?" I was upset, he knew it, and he had little to say. He had misjudged the situation. Mr. Know-It-All didn't know so much after all.

## We Take A Stand And Just...Say...No!

We got motivated. Without a great deal of discussion we decided that a sixteen-year-old on drugs was not something we could support, and that we would take strong measures to stop it. For all the recriminations of why she started and who was to blame—Kenny's son, Dad, Mom, Real Dad, Coach—it was our job to stop it, and we did everything we could. We signed her up for an evaluation at the local substance abuse counseling center. They evaluated her, decided that, yes, she did need treatment, and designed a program for her. We also put together a level system, behavioral management that targeted a number of problems behaviors, including her sullen attitude and come-home-hide-in-your-bedroom-for-hours routine. Her hair dyes and black fingernail polish and overabundance of jewelry and other badges of the drug culture had to be cut back. Her failure to speak to us for days at a time had to stop. If it were "just" the drug use, we could have dealt with it, but it was all the negative behavior that went along with it. Remember, I used drugs for years, and they made me happy. I was fun to be around when I got high. Yes, I grew my hair long, wore different clothes than I had before, and found new friends, but most of my friends were college students who had plans and goals to meet. We all had to find that balance between copping a buzz on the weekends and passing a chemistry exam. And, most importantly, we did our bests NOT to alienate our parents or other adults. They were our sole means of support, you know. So in a real sense it wasn't the drug use that bothered us about Sarah as much as the extremely antisocial behaviors she was exhibiting. We meant to reinforce her for having appropriate behavior and withdraw privileges when she did not. The discovery of her substance abuse was reason enough to "reel her in," as I used to say, to let her know that we were her parents and had limits to what we would tolerate. About the same time, stresses built up in the family with Andrew, not to mention Mom and Pop, such that we felt we needed help from an outside source, and we could no longer rely on our neighbor, the coach. The previous therapist, Mr. Nifty Fifty, was no longer an option. His advice and a lack of change in anything lead us to Dr. Mom, a family therapist in the next town. She worked with us as a couple, the kids individually, and the family as a unit. She would save our marriage and what was left of our family.

## CHAPTER THREE

# SUMMER 1994/THERAPY DECISIVE OR DIVISIVE?

By midsummer 1994, things had settled down considerably. Sarah was behaving much better, and everything was cooling down—so much so that when I decided I was going to *Woodstock 94*, Sarah was on line to go with me. By the end of August when the date approached, we were both ready. Maybe it was time for some father-daughter bonding. By this time we were attending counseling sessions with Dr. Mom, just as the counseling center services were fading into the background. Here's why. Even though we referred Sarah to the center and gave them personal interviews and lots of private and confidential information about ourselves, and even though Sarah was a sixteen-year-old minor child still under our care and protection, the center treated us like the enemy. Now I can appreciate the need for confidentiality. Who is going to want to be open and honest if they know the information is going to be blabbed everywhere, especially to your parents? But we knew about her drug use;

we brought her in, after all. And we were trying to be open and honest about her problem. It came to a head over two issues. One involved the lack of an effective group to put her in. Most groups had more "sophisticated" users, who also happened to be older, and male. History has demonstrated that these men often hit on the younger girls. This was *all* we needed. The group Sarah was put in was for young, female alcoholics. She was in a group of two. She didn't see what she was gaining from it. Most of this information came directly from the counselor, who did not appear to be too "involved" with the therapy to be honest.

One day we dropped Sarah off for a session and arranged for her to meet us at the corner restaurant, where we were meeting some people. Our meeting ended sooner, so we drove up the block to meet Sarah at the center. I pulled up and asked this woman out front if she'd seen Sarah. I was well dressed in a suit and tie, with Caroline also nicely dressed, seated in our shiny new car. "Who wants to know?" "We're Sarah's parents and we were supposed to meet her in town after a conference, and since it ended early we came here to get her. We didn't want to miss her." "Well, I can't give out that information." "Why can't you?" "Confidential." "Well, I would say that since we dropped her off here an hour ago, I'd think it's safe to say we already know she was here." I mean, this person was taking the confidentiality limits to the limit. We eventually met up with Sarah, but this left a bad taste in our mouths. In the midst of this, her counselor was involved in a car accident. Nobody had the courtesy to call Sarah to cancel, so she showed up for her appointment, and no one was there. She came home upset. I called to see about rescheduling, but don't remember if this was ever done. They insisted that she had an appointment for August 14 and she never showed, but I don't remember making any appointment and neither did Sarah. Besides, Sarah and her two friends from Pennsylvania and I were at *Woodstock 94*. This was our first disillusionment, that a drug counseling center would exclude parents who wanted to help, that they would fail to provide adequate services, and that they would fail to follow up after the therapist's car accident. It just seemed like they didn't care, or that they cared more about their rules and maintaining confidentiality than they did truly reaching out to people in need.

When we returned from *Woodstock* we simply supplanted Sarah's family counseling with individual sessions with Dr. Mom, and this seemed to meet our needs. These sessions continued for several years.

## Selecting A Counseling Center

For future reference, make sure you turn your children over to a counseling center that gets the child to sign a release so that the counselor can talk to the parents about important matters. Make sure they keep in touch about scheduling appointments. Some adolescents are notorious about being disorganized and forgetting to keep appointments, so it helps to keep the communication channels open. And without communication between family members, the substance abuser is pulled from the family rather than being encouraged to rejoin it. Centers that assume it's the parents' fault will not gain the trust of the parents and will soon inflame the already tenuous parent/child bond. For therapy to work, it has to include the parents and child. Confidentiality is essential; the parents don't need to know the "gory details," and they don't want to...they need to know how deep their child is in, what is causing him or her to sink into the morass of substance abuse, and, most importantly, how they can pull him or her out. A strong family bond and open communication is central to any working relationship.

Also make sure the center provides group as well as individual counseling and that the group is appropriate. We later came to find out that one of Sarah's friends who stayed with the program was stalked by one of the other older male group members. Who needs more problems?

# Woodstock '94

By the time I got to Woodstock, twenty-five years had come and gone. I missed it the first time because I was committed to my summer job delivering car radios, and by four o'clock Friday, "The New York Thruway was *closed*, man," and I knew I'd never get around the twenty-mile backup since my helicopter was in the shop for repairs. I was resolved that I wouldn't miss it this time. I lived in New York in 1969, I was nineteen and home from college for the summer, and I was definitely into the music and all that went along with it. We (meaning my crew from Virginia Tech) were of the mind that the *Atlantic City Pop Festival* was going to be IT. I mean, can you blame us? Jefferson Airplane, Canned Heat, Johnny Winter, B. B. King, Creedence Clearwater Revival, Janis Joplin, and more. We had tickets and we went, and it was great, though it wasn't *Woodstock*. By August I was ready for a really big event. My boss at *Precision Electronics* had a different idea. No! I couldn't have Friday off, and No! I couldn't leave early to beat the traffic heading to upstate New York. So I spent Friday sitting on my ass. By the time I got off work at four thirty, the backups were several miles, and I knew I'd never make it back in time for work on Monday. Had I known that my boss had planned to fire me that following Friday, things would have been different. That's why hindsight is always 20/20 and future vision leaves you blind as a bat. It does keep the surprise in life though. Maybe now you'll understand why I was committed to going to *Woodstock '94*. I had the time and the money, and the overwhelming desire to go. And no Schmuckuvaboss to tell me NO. I'd read up on it, had reservations at a campsite on the other side of the Hudson River, and figured I could use this as a base camp. I had camp gear and food and everything. Everything, that is, except tickets. Details, details…I had pliers, and wire cutters, and a shovel. I figured if I couldn't get over the fence, I could go under it or through it. I just knew we'd get in. Just in case I brought some cash in case I had to…buy our way in.

Well, Sarah was committed from the word go. We were pretty close that summer, and she wanted to do this great festival with her dad. Andrew, on the other hand, Mr. Cautious, did not want to take a chance without tickets. Now he would gladly go if Dad forked out the $120, but no way was he going with a pair of pliers and a shovel. So Sarah and I left without him, with plans to meet up with two of her friends from Pennsylvania at the campsite in New York. They were returning from a family vacation at Lake George and we'd meet halfway.

I looked forward to *Woodstock '94* not only for myself and the music and festival atmosphere, but for Sarah. I knew she would enjoy it and that we could enjoy it together. In the same way that Mom and Andrew are bonded over shared interests, Sarah and I are as well. We share a love of music, travel, and adventure. Mom and Andrew aren't really into this scene, so in a way I was glad Andrew wasn't coming. All he'd do was complain anyway. "This food sucks, those bathrooms smell, and where did all these stupid people come from anyway?" When I knew there was a chance of two of Sarah's friends coming, I was even more relieved Andrew wasn't coming... Andrew and Sarah do not get along, so I was glad with the prospect of Dad and the "girls" going. I was truly excited. Face it, what normal male wouldn't want to go somewhere with three cute young ladies. I was proud of my daughter then, and her friends were full of life as well. Just good clean fun with Dad watching over the girls. It was funny, sometimes they'd lead and I'd follow, other times I would lead. There were times when they were in front and some dudes would spot them. I loved to see the expressions drain out of their faces when they saw Dad bringing up the rear. I rented a van as a convenient home away from home, plenty of storage and sleeping room if other settings didn't work out.

*"Woodstock" wasn't a place or an event so much as a feeling shared by participants.*

## No Good Deed

I was put off a little with the media hype about the "commercialization" and "yuppification" of the Woodstock spirit, and was even resolved to indulge in the rebel spirit I have nurtured since the sixties and sneak in without benefit of tickets. In the end I ended up purchasing tickets for myself and my three companions: sixteen-year-old Sarah and Amber, and Amber's thirteen-year-old sister Ariel. We only paid face value for one ticket; the rest we got at discount in the gold parking lot waiting for the shuttle to bring us to the Garden of Eden. The gold parking pass was a gift from a fellow camper at a state park across the river from Saugerties.

Once we got inside, we were quickly caught up in the Woodstock spirit, an intense feeling shared by three-hundred-thousand-plus people that quickly rose above the logos on the soda cans. Woodstock, not so much a place as a shared cultural experience, like Christmas, where for three days everybody is nice to everybody. Or as I describe it to others who weren't there, "The only place on the planet where if one person sneezes, 350,000 people chant 'God bless!' "

To truly appreciate the Woodstock experience, you had to be there, and I don't mean watching it on pay-per-view or MTV, or in the press platforms high above the crowd; not even backstage, insulated from the mud and the mass of humanity from which this unique form of energy emanated. You didn't have to be in the mosh pit or one of the many mud zones to get the feeling, but it helped. Just being close, having the "mud people" brush elbows, leaving dark smudges on your sleeve, or offering a friendly hug got you there (No, thanks...Cool, man, see yuh). Trying to get from point A to B when all the normal pathways were gridlocked with happy people helped, just as devising unique methods to detour the normal causeways did. Tent weaving was the most popular, a sport of cutting in and out of the thousands of tents covering every inch of ground like a huge maze, all the time trying to keep going in the general direction you desired without stepping on A) sleeping people, B) clean blankets, or (C) someone's cold pizza. Thank goodness tents are shaped like teepees so that, close as they were, the complementary angles offered a friendly "V" to step through. I heard "excuse me" offered and accepted more in two days then I had in the forty-four years I'd spent on the planet. I had a complete stranger rub a cherished ice cube on my back just because I looked hot. Cindy became my friend for life at that moment. She was an airline stewardess.

We felt chills when Joe Cocker sang "With a little help..." and goose bumps when Crosby, Stills, and Nash sang "Woodstock." We shivered when Melissa paid her tribute to Janis. I was even impressed when my kids' favorite band, Nine Inch Nails, appeared on stage fresh from the mosh pit covered from head to toe in mud. That said more to me than anything I have heard, on or off stage, in the last twenty years. The band was *one* with us, *and* they were going to entertain as well. No prima donnas, no divas here, man!

In the end the mud was gruesome; it was tough to walk even five feet without the glue-like substance trying to suck the shoes right off your feet. And sleeping with four people in a tent is hard enough without an inch of muddy water running off the nearby hillside. But throughout it all we smiled, and felt a warmth and kinship that we didn't feel before, and won't feel again for a long time. It resides within all of those who were a part of it. And though I am a sixties child and proud of my generation, I recognize the even greater challenge Woodstock '94 presented; so many people, from so many subcultures (we were only one back then); the punks and the grungers, the yo-boys and the fraternity kids, the bikers and the yuppies and the hippies, all united for the music, the party, and the shared desire to get along no matter what. And they did...again. And we were there. What a great jump start on life. Sorry you missed it.

We came back from Woodstock invigorated. The music, the people, the party were all great, and with my planning and direction it went well. Everybody got along fine, there were no arguments or problems, and we breezed in and out. No traffic either way. Sarah and Ariel and Amber would be among the few if not the only kids in their school that went to Woodstock. They had fun with no drugs or alcohol, and actually went with a dad, and everything was cool. We were excited and I wanted to let folks know that a local family had participated in this grand event, so we gave the local editor a call and he interviewed us. I never thought for an instant that anyone would look at this father/daughter venture in any negative light. But then, hindsight is not always 20/20. One of Sarah's teachers, one who didn't much like me anyway, commented on the wisdom of taking a kid with a drug problem to Woodstock. I think the quote was, "Taking his daughter, a drug addict, to Woodstock, is like me taking my son, an alcoholic, to a bar." As I've said before…Woodstock wasn't about drugs or alternative lifestyles, it was about music, and 350,000 people getting together for three days without an act of violence. Oh, sure, there were drugs present, with alcohol being the most pervasive, and there were plenty of alternative lifestyles on display, but like any major city—New York, Washington, DC, Baltimore—you'd expect that drugs would be used and alternative lifestyles would be present, but, like New York and DC and Baltimore, Woodstock was more than that, much more. And it was peaceful, without a single act of violence. Which is a hell of a lot more than you can say about New York, Washington, or Baltimore.

## CHAPTER FOUR

# THE FALL OF '94

School started back in September and fall arrived in October. Everything was cool, or at least that's what we thought. October 13 was a Thursday. Similar to the main character in the movie "Rainman", I'll forever remember that combination. I know because I had replayed the events over and over so many times in my head. In truth, it was a rather quiet day. I went to work with only one more day until the weekend. Came home and got ready for dinner. We were still one of those families that made a serious attempt to sit around the table for our dinner meal. We would talk and relax until everybody headed off in different directions. The only thing that was a little different was the phone call. The coach and pushy neighbor from across the street called, and Sarah went off to talk to him. What was that about? "Oh nothing, just something that happened in school." I know that Sarah went to school Thursday morning, and finished the day at volleyball practice. She rode home with a neighbor, and then sat around the dinner table with us. Nothing seemed out of the ordinary.

## Torpedo Juice

The next day was Friday, and I remember Andrew talking to me about the major stories that were circulating around his school. Seems that the JV football squad had gotten soundly trounced, 54–0 or something like that. Word had it that many, if not most, of the players were under the influence of drugs; LSD, in fact. Saturday morning, our friend, neighbor, and coach of the JV football squad stopped by with his pickup truck (the same one he bought on my recommendation) for our Saturday ritual, the ride to the dump. On the way I made idle conversation along the lines, "I hear your boys got the shit knocked out of them last Thursday. I also heard they may have had some help from some hallucinogenic substances...." Coach's only response? "Oh, yeah? Well maybe I'll have to look at the game films again." We moved on to other subjects.

Unknown to me at the time; the secret he was harboring concerned my daughter. I would have to wait until late Sunday night before I would be let in on this little secret. Sunday evening I found a note on my pillow. I read it and my stomach sank. It was from Sarah and it turned out to be a confession. Despite all the counseling and family talks and behavior contracts and substance abuse classes, she had taken LSD, but "it was some time ago," and she didn't like it, and she would never do it again, and PLEASE don't tell mom. I'd have to sleep on this one.

It seems that Thursday afternoon had been a busy one for the football squad. A new shipment of LSD had come into town, and some of the older boys were trying to convince the younger boys to give it a try. "Try some of this! They call it torpedo juice, and you'll play one hell of a game." So this little fellow from a farm on the outskirts of the county, who'd never done any drugs until that day, took a little tiny pill and swallowed it down. Why anybody would want to go out on a football field with the love drug LSD coursing through their veins is beyond me. But this fellow was not what you'd call experienced. The specter of a 230-pound fullback running at you with "Kill!" in his eyes is a little different from sitting on a grass-covered piece of ground looking up at the clouds while butterflies melt into the sun. Arthur, the little farm boy from the country, started to have some really bad visions, including being in the middle of a combat zone, a war. Soldiers, big ones with broad shoulders and gigantic heads, were running at him from every direction with mean looks on their faces and guns in their huge hands. They wanted to kill him. When the coach wanted to send him back to the front lines, poor Art broke down. "Coach! I can't take it anymore. They've got guns, they're trying to kill me out there, please don't make me go back."

Coach may not have been a rocket scientist, and he played his boys hard, but when Art started babbling about guns and soldiers and getting killed, coach feared the worst. Maybe this kid had sustained a head injury and needed medical attention... NOW! Time out was called, and arrangements were made to call in the life flight medivac helicopter. Somewhere in the confusion, good old Art came around enough to admit, "Ummm, wait a minute, coach, I'm not hurt and I don't think I'm crazy, but I sort of took something before the game..." and the whole "torpedo juice" story came tumbling out. The helicopter was canceled, but they still had Art's mom transport him to the local hospital for blood work and crisis control (more like trip management). LSD was reportedly confirmed in lab tests.

## The Investigation

What Coach did next was understandable, but it explains his motivations and his weakness of character. As he would later testify at Sarah's expulsion hearing, he was in a jam, and he had to figure his way out. How did his players get the stuff? And who did he turn to but his friend, neighbor, and known substance abuser, his little snitch-to-be, Sarah. That's why he called her Thursday night at our home, to pump her for information. The gist of the conversation, as Sarah later recounted, started out easy. "Come on, ol' girl, you can tell me, this is Coach you're talking to...no one will ever know where I got the names, I just need to know who was involved and who was selling the stuff." When that approach didn't produce anything, he switched to another tact: "Hey, look! I just came back from the emergency room with one of my boys who was out of his head on drugs. I need to know who sold him the shit, and don't you lie to me!" This must have gotten her attention, for she spilled the beans. As an aside, he asked her if she also took it, and somewhere along the line she admitted to him that she did.

In what appears to be a string of sad coincidence, Sarah had a panic attack on that same Thursday and ended up crying in the girl's room at the high school. Coach's teaching assistant had come and gotten him, and he talked Sarah down. Trouble is, no one ever called us. Was he protecting her, trying to cover for her, or himself? At this point, my sixteen-year-old daughter with a history of drug abuse, including treatment programs and counseling, is confiding in a neighbor, and Mom and Dad know nothing about it. Coach sort of blurred his roles and responsibilities. Was he acting as a 1) coach, 2) teacher, 3) neighbor and friend of the family, 4) counselor, 5) school official? This guy was supposed to be keeping an eye out for her. And keeping us informed. Instead he was leaving us, her parents, very much in the dark.

Now it may be all right for police officers to question suspects in this fashion, but if the suspect is only sixteen, then his or her parents are usually involved. And if the suspects are over sixteen, and have any sense at all, they know that they have a right to have an attorney present. Now this was not a police matter, and this wasn't even an officially sanctioned investigation. The principal and other administrators were not aware of Coach's phone call to his friend and neighbor's daughter, and if they were, I don't know how comfortable they'd be with Coach conducting an investigation of a case in which he was personally involved. This thing reeked of conflict of interest. He had no business as a coach investigating drug use by his football team; this was an administrative function. And when he called my daughter, he did not represent himself as a school official or investigator, just Sarah's neighbor and friend. Our friend and neighbor. And he promised her protection if she gave him the information he requested. If he had never asked about her own involvement, none of this would have happened. If she had refused to talk to him. If he had brought it to me first. This man, trying to be all things to all people, opened the can of worms that turned out to be a barrel of rattlesnakes. And no one could put them all back into the can again. But here it is Sunday night, and I've got this note, my first introduction into this thickening quagmire.

## The Coach Tells All...Or Does He?

Since it was Sunday night and Sarah was sleeping, I decided to let all of this sink in first. Then the phone rang. It was Coach. Did Sarah talk to me? "Not exactly, but she left me a note." "What did it say?" he asked me. Well, with my wife Caroline standing right there, I wasn't about to use any buzz words like "hallucinogens" or "LSD," so I said she mentioned "some letters (L, S, D)." "That's all?" " Yes." "We need to talk," he said. And with that I walked over to Coach's house. His kids were in bed and wife out of the room, and we talked, or sort of talked, that is. I revealed the contents of the note, and he neither confirmed nor denied any of it. He indicated that Sarah had been quite upset at school on Thursday; in fact, she was curled up in the girl's bathroom refusing to come out, and his aide had come to get him. Sarah was apparently upset about a remark Caroline had made four days earlier in anger, that she wished it was Sarah that was going off to school next year instead of her brother Andrew. Sarah interpreted this to mean Mom wanted Sarah to leave. I knew very little about this conversation other than the remark, and didn't understand why she would wait four days to get upset about it. I asked Coach point blank if he thought she had, in fact, taken anything, and he refused to give me an answer. After ten to fifteen minutes of beating around the bush—he maintained that she had come to him in confidence, and he couldn't betray it now—he said that he had given her until Sunday night to tell me, and if she didn't, he would. And yet here we were, Sunday night, and I only had part of the story and he was refusing to give me the rest. He was refusing to tell me about my own daughter, using confidentiality as a shield to protect her, but in reality the protection was for him. From the start he could not get his story straight. She did not go to him, he went to her, on the phone Thursday night. This was in the capacity of friend and neighbor, not teacher. On Friday he called her to his office again on a more "official" basis, and then essentially turned her over to the assistant principal with a cover story, a lie to "protect" her. And now here he was standing before me telling me of his involvement, but only the parts he wanted me to know. Like, for instance, he talked to Sarah on Thursday, after she came out of the bathroom, and he settled her down. When I pressed him for his opinion, he refused a number of times to give it, but finally suggested that, yes, in his opinion, her behavior, crying uncontrollably in the bathroom, suggested something abnormal. Was it drugs, was it LSD? He didn't answer, but his look and body language suggested that it was.

## The Most Difficult Decision For A Parent

Here is the sequence of events: Thursday, Sarah is upset in the bathroom and Coach's aide calls him in. He talks to her but does not talk to either Caroline or me that day. Later that evening he attends the hallucinogenic ball game, LSD, 54; NHS, 0. His player is hauled to the emergency room in a panic. Coach calls Sarah at home to find out what she knows. Friday he calls her in to work out a cover story. She is to tell the assistant principal (AP), if he calls her in, that she had it (the LSD), but she flushed it. If anymore is made of her having it, she is to be sure and tell them she has a history of drug problems and is currently in counseling. When the AP *coincidentally* calls her in, this is what she tells him, and by Monday night, October 17, a full four days after the alleged incident, Mom and Dad hear nothing from the school on an official basis, and know nothing for sure from anyone, including Coach or Sarah or anyone in an official school capacity. Sunday I get the note and get a half-baked explanation from Coach. I sweat what to do for the next twenty-four hours. Monday passes with no call from anyone in an official capacity at school, and I am wondering if once again Sarah is going to dodge the consequences of her substance abuse. I am wondering to myself just what Coach's involvement is in this whole endeavor and wondering why we were not called on Thursday if she were in fact crying uncontrollably. If Coach suspected she was on something, he had an obligation to tell someone, her parents or school authorities. He did neither; he apparently tried to handle it himself.

## Dad's Inquiry

So here I am Monday night, nothing from the school, and knowing my daughter may have done something she shouldn't at school. Mom had to teach a parenting class Monday night, so I figured that would give me time with Sarah alone to figure out what exactly was going on. No need in upsetting Caroline when she has to go deal with a group of parents. So with note in hand, I ask permission to enter Sarah's room. So what's the scoop? She is curled up on her bed. Her responses were vague about when she did…whatever she did. "Some time ago," a relative term; since school started, but not recently. I try to tie her down, and she withdraws. "What d'ya mean. 'some time ago'? That could mean a few weeks or a few months or a few years. You know what we have been through. I need to know if you still have a drug problem…if you are still using." She was not very forthcoming, so I had to reveal my source and

## No Good Deed

tell her I'd talked to Coach. I told her that what he told me led me to believe that there was more to the story, that it was more recent, for one thing. I avoided putting words in her mouth; I wanted her to come clean on her own. She was into total denial. I even threatened to bring Coach in, and had to live up to the threat. I was still calm at this point, but finding myself increasingly agitated. I called Coach and he walked over to our house. He tried to convince Sarah to tell me what I wanted to know. She withdrew further. At this point she was curled up in a fetal position. It was clear we were getting nowhere. Coach and I went out in the kitchen, but he still wouldn't tell me what he knew, hiding behind his so-called confidential relationship with her, and I was left there not knowing what the hell was going on. He left. Caroline came home at 9:30, tired, but there was one more mission for her. Caroline and I both went into Sarah's room, and for forty-five minutes we pumped and cajoled and begged and threatened, and finally, finally, she broke and the story poured out.

Sarah told us that a friend called her over to this kid's car Thursday morning in the school parking lot. "Hey, wanna trip today?" she asked. Her friend Barbara stood there with a piece of paper on her tongue which she showed to Sarah. "No thanks. I don't have any money anyway." "You can pay me later, here," the other kid said. With that she took the paper and shoved it in her pocket. As the day proceeded, she had her little breakdown in the bathroom, an incident completely unrelated to what was still in her pocket. She then talked to the aide, and then the Coach, and though he insisted he "calmed her down," she later went back into the bathroom, ripped the paper in half, flushed one half, and ate the other. Remember, this is a girl with problems, foremost impulsivity. She then went through the rest of her school day, spending the last part in the library, going to a full practice for volleyball, riding home with a friend, and sitting around the dinner table with Mom and Dad. Wouldn't you figure someone would have noticed something about her behavior? If not her teachers or volleyball coach, then maybe the two individuals who knew her the best, her parents? Parents that had more than a rudimentary knowledge of the effects of a powerful halllucinogenic drug. Sarah told us about Coach calling her that night, and the assistant principal calling her in the next day and how, using Coach's cover story, she lied her way right out of trouble. Did she really take LSD? To this day we don't know. She thinks she did, but what does she know? Maybe when she tore that blotter acid in half, a piece of paper with a drop of liquid LSD dried into it, maybe she flushed the drop and ate a bit of paper and nothing more. And maybe, just maybe there was nothing on that piece of paper at all. She got kicked out of school for eating a piece of paper. Will we ever know?

More than fifteen years later I bumped into Barbara's mother in my health club. It was one of those moments that I have learned to take advantage of. I was on the leg machine, she was standing a few feet away. "I think our daughters went to high school together," I remarked. "Who's your daughter?" she asked. "Sarah Matthews." I replied. "Yeah, I remember her." I paused a few seconds, finished my routine then casually remarked, "I think they were partners in crime." That opened the door to a half hour conversation about the events that had taken place so many years ago. It all came together when she said, "You know Barbara said she doesn't think there was anything on that paper she took, she didn't feel a thing." After sixteen years, she essentially confirmed what I had always thought: these two girls' lives were changed when they were expelled from high school for chewing on a piece of paper.

## Decision — Enable Or Face Up To It?

We wait for the dust to settle. Here is a girl with a history of drug use (marijuana). We have had her in drug counseling, family therapy, individual therapy, regular urine screenings, and here we are five months later, back where we started.

What do we do? Do we cover for her and perpetuate the lie? Do we enable her drug use? I pull out the policy, and reading the section on Class III offenses:

> Assault and battery against a teacher, weapons, bombs, rape, felonious acts, arson, guns, robbery, alcohol (second offense) and drugs—automatic suspension for five (5) days and referral to the expulsion panel.

Now I was only vaguely familiar with this policy, but I recalled a student who had brought a handgun to school the previous year. He got his five days and was back in time for homecoming. My thought, our thought, was to turn her in. Let her face certain consequences: suspension, and having to appear before the expulsion panel with a plan for getting herself straight and expulsion hanging over her head to keep her that way. That night I called the principal, using the words, "I am not going to cover for her or lie for her; she needs to face up to her consequences...." The principal seemed surprised and, without saying anything else, thanked me and told me she would call Sarah in to her office the next morning and asked if I would like to be present. I would, and I was. It was October 18...it was a Tuesday.

## The Confession

Sarah was asked to tell what happened in her own words, and then was taken next door to write it all down. She didn't want to "rat" on her friends or the dude who gave her the stuff, but Dad insisted that she cooperate, that she be open and honest, and she was. Before I left, I had this thought in mind: WHY? Was the transition from middle school to high school too tough, were her learning disabilities coming back to haunt her again? Before I left, I told the principal, "I'm not trying to get her out of anything, but she does have a history of being learning disabled, and I wonder if this might have anything to do with her current behaviors. Could you, as a professional courtesy to me, see that Sarah be evaluated to rule out any learning problems?" The principal said it would have to go through a screening committee first, and I reiterated that with her history of learning disabilities, I didn't think they would have any problem recommending her for an evaluation. Don't forget, I was a school psychologist with this system and knew their procedures. With that I left her office and returned to my school. Little did I know what this short meeting would set in motion — repercussions that would spin off for years to come. Had I known then what I know now, I would have never set foot in that office.

## Suspension And Using Her Time Wisely

With the next scheduled event being suspension, we geared up. For starters Sarah would not spend her five days on vacation. I made arrangements for her to help out at the local nursing home. They were glad to have her, and Mom and I wouldn't have to worry about her. As well, it was an important lesson about consequences in a location where people lived who really had problems. We also put our behavior management system into play. I am a school psychologist, after all, and have a little experience with structured programs, so I designed one for our needs. Desired behaviors were spelled out and expectations and a level system were designed with her starting at the bottom (Level I) and working her way back to full privileges (Level V). I put lots of things in there, from television and music time to social events and friends. We also included a "Daily Log" to communicate our expectations for school behavior as well.

You may wonder why we put this plan into effect. Why couldn't we just sit down in a family group and talk about it, reach understandings, make agreements? That assumes that you're dealing with adults, honest adults who live up to their word. Sarah's long history of deceit and continued violation of our family rules prevented us from sitting down like this anymore. Sarah wasn't always great at listening, especially when she had screwed up. You all know the expression "the best defense is a good offense," well, Sarah was a master at getting emotional and getting loud and stomping about every time we attempted to sit down and quietly discuss what her consequences should be. We quickly got emotional, reacting to her tantrum, and things would deteriorate. One of the first rules in parental discipline is to keep the emotions out. No matter how angry or upset you might be, you are to maintain a calm, rational demeanor. I was taught in graduate school that sometimes it was better to let an external force set the rules. We turned to Dr. Mom.

Dr. Mom proposed the team concept. If Sarah screwed up and waited to see what Mom and Dad were going to do, ready to explode and scream and cry, "I never get to go out and do anything! I'm *always* getting grounded. *You* don't understand!" etc., we were to quietly tell her that it was out of our hands. From there on in, a *team* would make the decisions. The team would consist of Dr. Mom, Mom, and Dad. Since we felt we needed help to control her behaviors, the family counselor, in consultation with us, would determine the consequences. In this fashion, we would get the emotionality out and let the team run the show. The thinking was simple. Sarah could yell and scream at Mom and Dad when they "punished" her, but she couldn't get mad at the team or Dr. Mom. If she wanted to spend the night out with someone we didn't approve of, instead of us telling her no, we'd tell her we had to consult with the team. That meant calling Dr. Mom on the phone. After consulting Dr. Mom we decided to set firm limits for Sarah. With her drug problems, her learning disabilities, her short attention span, and her oppositional behaviors, she didn't always know what to do. That is why she was constantly breaking the rules. She was testing us. Like the two-year-old who grabs the power cord on the lamp and looks at Mom—"No!" Some stop at that, but others give a little tug and look back at you to see if you really mean it. If you don't increase the "No" or moved to stop them, the lamp will end up on the floor. With Sarah, it was "tug and look" all the time. Curfew at eleven? Let's try eleven fifteen. If I get caught, I'll pretend I didn't know. "YOU SAID ELEVEN THIRTY. YOU SHOULD BE HAPPY I'M HOME EARLY!"

Dr. Mom provided the general approach and I developed the behavior management plan, a structured plan to set firm limits. Establish consistent rules and standard consequences (response costs) that would lay everything out for everybody ahead of time before the events and the emotions that accompany them increase the heat. These plans are put into use in classrooms and in special schools, anywhere a population of children (and even adults) are that need a little more than a kind word or simple explanation. We tried that. It didn't work.

The plan was based on sound practices of behavior modification developed by behavioral psychologists I knew well. It was designed to target behaviors that were problematic for our family and to tie privileges and consequences to her behaviors. For example, Sarah would go days without talking to us. She'd come from school and go in her room and close and lock the door. Though we used to sit around the table for dinner, she often would say she wasn't hungry and fail to join us for dinner, only to venture out when Mom and Dad had finished eating and were in the living room watching the news. "I thought you weren't hungry" or other similar inquiries would only precipitate yet another confrontation. When she did talk to us, she'd look at the floor. We began to just avoid her, just to minimize conflict. We didn't know at the time that these were the signs of depression. The contract was designed to encourage eye contact and, at the very least, small tidbits of conversation. One of the requirements was that she say at least three nice things to us per day: " Good morning," "How was your day?" and "Good night." The rest of the time we would respect her privacy and leave her alone. Every rule in the contract was there to address a long history of problems in that area. Music too loud, too much time on the telephone, not carrying her weight in chores, inappropriate dress, curfew violations, etc. The plan was simple. You meet our expectations and you get more freedom. Fight us, and you lose freedom. Respect curfew and you get to go out the next time. Come in late, and you miss the next time; simple. Most important, the plan worked. It restored peace and quiet to the household. It eliminated the disagreements. "Trip tickets" were used to put down in writing the curfew time. We would discuss it, agree on it, and write it down on the ticket. We'd all sign it. It would go on the refrigerator until she came home. That way we all knew where she was going, who she was going with, and what time she would be back. After the contract was written, we sat down with Dr. Mom and reviewed it with Sarah. She grumbled but agreed, with a few revisions, and signed it. As with any contract, Sarah had a lot to gain as well as us. For starters, we promised not to yell or raise our voices. We also agreed to give her more freedom and privacy as she earned it.

Here is the preamble to the contract, the rationale for it, basically:

## Expectations for Miller Family Members

All members of the family are expected to follow basic rules. Parents are expected to be home and to set examples by word and deed of what is expected of other family members. Parents are also responsible for setting realistic expectations that promote the development of happy and successful children as they progress from childhood through adolescence and adulthood. Privileges that result from being in this family are not automatic. They must be earned by appropriate behavior. Appropriate behavior means it meets the expectations parents establish. Because this has not been effective in the recent past, the team approach will be used. The team will set the expectations and judge privileges based on meeting of expectations. They will determine the privilege level for a two-week period each Friday/payday. Privileges will be in effect for the next two weeks. Grounds for immediate loss of one level: 1) Knowledge that team member was given inaccurate information with the knowledge of the informant. 2) Drug use. 3) Violence. Team consists of both parents and attending counselor. Requests for privileges not covered in this contract must be submitted in writing to team for approval. Team will avoid long lectures or withholding emotional support.

# CHAPTER FIVE

# ZERO TOLERANCE FOR DRUGS

Sarah's appointment with the expulsion panel was scheduled, and I prepared to make a short but thorough presentation. I started off by indicating that if Sarah were before this panel for an act of violence or for dealing drugs, I would not be here speaking up on her behalf. I did not condone her actions on the day in question, but I acknowledged her long history of learning and behavior problems, and a willingness to work with them to get her the help she needed. I told them about the behavior plan and the counseling, and how we supported her and expected her to face consequences for her actions as well. They responded briefly and we thanked the panel and left. I fully expected her to be put on "probation" and monitored for any further problems, then she would be O-U-T. Imagine my surprise when we received the letter from the superintendent dated November 9, 1994, indicating that he was supporting the recommendations of the principal and expulsion panel that "Sarah be expelled from school for the rest of the 1994-95 school year effective immediately." Now, this caught us all by surprise. We both had to go to work the next day and had no plans for Sarah; could she at least come to school for this last day and give us a time to regroup? I called the principal, who called the superintendent and chairman of the expulsion panel. The answer was an emphatic "No." So here was an extremely depressed, extremely upset teenager on her own. I arranged for her to spend the day at the nursing home and dropped her off.

As luck would have it, the *challenge grant* team was meeting with the facilitator at a local hotel that day. I was a member of the steering committee, so you'll appreciate the irony of my participation at this grand meeting as a member of this team who was charged with spending $1.5 million in state funds on innovative programming for kids. I was there with the assistant superintendent and director of personnel (both members of the expulsion panel) and all of the other board office administrators, while my daughter, my little girl, was undergoing agony at these guys' behest. I recall standing outside with the assistant superintendent, trying to understand. "How is it that with nine separate Class III (expellable) offenses, my daughter is expelled for admitting to drug use, while others who bring in weapons, including handguns, remain in school?" When he shuffled this off, I gave him a specific example of the student by name who brought a handgun to school in a book bag after his girlfriend broke up with him. I had been involved with that situation, so I knew. It was there that I learned for the first time that gun-wielding students, along with those who bring in knives or bombs or burn a building or rape a student or assault a teacher, are permitted **discretion** under this policy, the *Student Code of Conduct*. They'll work with *them*. The only *exceptions* are drugs and alcohol. Alcohol for a second offense and drugs for even the first-time offender, even with a discipline record clear as the newly driven snow, result in automatic expulsion, no mitigating circumstances, no excuses, no consideration, no discretion…only expulsion. That's what is meant by "zero tolerance." She was out, no questions asked, until next school year. When I got home I pulled out the policy and read it through again, this time all the way to the end. And sure enough, at the extreme end of the policy, separated by several pages and several sections unrelated to the drug/alcohol procedures, was a special section on drugs and alcohol labeled, you guessed it *Special Section on Drugs and Alcohol*. It was there that the "zero tolerance" rule was explained. If only I had read a little further...

## Sarah Disappears

But this day wasn't over; in fact it was only starting to get interesting. A few minutes into the next session of the *challenge grant steering committee*, I got called away to the phone. It was Caroline. Seemed as if Sarah walked away from the nursing home and was missing. Could I go find her? Where was she? Where might she go? It was the beginning of our little hell. I remember thinking to myself, if anything happens to her, Mr. Assistant Superintendent, you'll live to regret it. I decided to try a few places and ended up at a friend's apartment. She was there. We talked and she agreed to call her mom and come home with me.

What bothered me the most was that had I not brought her forward, none of this would be happening. Her attempt at honesty, her openness, was the cause of this action, nothing more. What also bothered me was my understanding of state laws that protected students with drug problems who came forward seeking help. Reading over the policy, it carefully laid out the procedures when a student was found in possession of a CDS (controlled dangerous substance), how the substance was to be handled, and how the police labs were to confirm it. No one ever saw the "substance" Sarah allegedly took; there were no witnesses, no physical evidence, no powder, pill, or blood work, no judgment, only her word. It made me wonder how this was legally, morally, and ethically correct. And in light of the fact that the little creep that approached her in the parking lot that day was known for dispensing "look-alikes," who knows (even Sarah) what, if anything, she took that day? Was it possible for her and her friend to be expelled from school for the rest of the school year for simply eating a piece of paper?

## The Rights Of The Accused

Having been closely involved with my home county's expulsion and suspension policy for disabled youth, I knew that the school districts were required to conduct a special meeting, called a manifestation hearing, on her case before she was expelled. None of this was done. Sarah had a history and identification as a child with a learning disability (she was identified in West Virginia and received special education and related services there and briefly here before asking to try and go it alone). The thrust of a manifestation determination hearing is to determine if there is a relationship between the child's disability and the behavior that he or she is being disciplined for. Many individuals "self-medicate" if they are not properly treated, and often the very behaviors they are called out for (impulsivity, poor decision making, failure to link consequences to their acts) are a function of their disabilities. In my heart I knew then that I would appeal to the local board of education. Just wait until they hear the facts of this case! Wait until they find out how she was expelled *after* I turned her in. And wait until they hear about the ramifications of their own policy, one that allows the violent offender to return to class, while the quiet student with the disease of drug abuse is excluded from the school community. The policy was outdated, it was cruel, and it was wrong. And boy, would they be nervous when I told them they had violated federal law when they expelled her without a manifestation hearing to see if her learning disabilities were in some way related to her current substance abuse problems.

And we turned to a trusted friend and attorney to help up out. He indicated that he had a new partner and arranged for us to sit down with him. The decision was to appeal to the local board based on the lack of supporting evidence, the fact that she turned herself in, and that she was disabled. Sarah's hearing before the board came up December 6, 1994.

**LEA** (Local Educational Agency) — This is a term the federal government uses to describe the local school system, whether it's a district, county, or city system. SEA refers to a state educational agency.

**Manifestation hearing** — As a result of US Supreme Court decisions and, more recently, the reauthorization of the federal law guaranteeing education for disabled children, any disabled child who is considered for suspension or expulsion requires a formal hearing to determine if there is a causal link between his or her disability and the act for which he or she is to be disciplined.

ADHD (attention deficit hyperactivity disorder) — A physical abnormality occurring in the brains of children and adults that interferes with the ability to inhibit or stop nerve impulses. The result on behavior is varied, though it often causes the individual to be impulsive, distractible, and sometimes active or restless.

One of the rights of the accused is to have a hearing before the board. Instructions are all laid out about who to appeal to, how long you have, and how any subsequent hearing will be conducted. They also speak to the right to present testimony and call witnesses. My thought was that Sarah has never been a discipline problem at school, not so much as a referral or even having to stay after school, much less a suspension. She was "squeaky clean" at school. She clearly did not want to "get in trouble," as her testimony would clearly reveal. It doesn't take a Supreme Court justice to know that my next step would be to gather a few character witnesses to speak on her behalf. Who better than teachers who knew her? I called a few at the school before I went to work, leaving messages for the most part. I also asked my "friend" and colleague, the other school psychologist in the district. I asked her if she would testify. She understood kids with learning disabilities, especially adolescents and their impulsive acts. She was assigned to the high school, after all. She was on the BEST Team (for helping kids with drug problems). Imagine my complete surprise when she took personal offense to my request. Rather than tell me her concerns or her reluctance to speak up on my daughter's behalf, she called my boss—the same boss who also happened to be a member of the expulsion panel, and director of personnel. "Frank called you!" he exclaimed. He also took personal offense to this action to find advocates for my daughter. The idea that I would want teachers, board employees, to testify against the board was too much for him. So he came after…me. Loyal to the superintendent, with an office right next door to the superintendent and his assistant, all members of the expulsion committee as well as the "good old boys' club," he would defend and support their decision and any attempts to question it, especially by an UNDERLING, would NOT BE TOLERATED! This would be the start of pattern of harassment and intimidation that would last more than two years. Through it all I remained faithful to the mission, the case, and our right to appeal unfavorable and unreasonable decisions. I would do it for my daughter, for other students affected by an unfair policy, other parents, but most of all, I would do it for me. I would be true to myself and my daughter.

## The Conspiracy Unfolds

The personnel director was a man with whom I had worked for six years. He was a conservative, old-school style, authoritarian administrator who (as rumor would have it) was kicked upstairs after he tried to fire a coach the year after she was awarded "Coach of the Year." The fact that she was also female and African American made his move all that more unbelievable, and the personnel director was slid out of the high school and into a central office position. Already crouching in the board office was another cur, a man who (as rumor would have it) left *his* previous position under a cloud), the superintendent. He was not only short in stature, but short on personality. He also had these tiny little hands, like a doll's hands. And a nervous twitch in his face. This man was simply despicable in every way. This man also hated me with a passion.

The personnel director lied to me when he hired me. He looked at my credentials, and he told me I would have no problem getting certified in the state. When this turned out not to be the case, I was disappointed. I was shocked when they informed me that they now planned to dock my pay. I protested understandably. To keep my job in the district, I had to take six credit hours of college classes despite holding a master's degree and thirty-six credit hours representing twelve courses I had passed, certification as a school psychologist in two neighboring states, and being a nationally certified school psychologist. I also had fourteen years' experience as a school psychologist. I filed an appeal with the various State agencies, lost, and took the classes. I met the requirements by the next school year. I also received my full pay after pointing out contract wording that read that I was to be paid for my *current or anticipated certification*. The finance director who opposed my receiving a full salary was forced to pay it, and it did not make him very happy. The finance director moved up to superintendent when the previous superintendent retired, and this small-minded (and short) man was the same one who signed off on the decision of the expulsion committee, which included the assistant superintendent and the personnel director, my immediate supervisor. The whole thing was a closed set with no opportunities for a legitimate appeal. It was circuitous, almost incestuous, and reeking of conflict of interest.

## FLOW CHART

The Superintendent

Assistant Superintendent

Director of Personnel     Director of Instruction

Special Education Supervisor     Principals & Supervisors

Psychologists Teachers Specialists (Music Art) Coordinators

Just to help put all of this in context, let me explain a little bit about how LEAs (local educational agencies) work. For the most part, school systems are run by boards of education. Some are elected, others are appointed. In my home state they are appointed by the governor (more recently the law was amended to allow half to be elected). In making the appointments, the governor typically goes by the recommendation of his local party, in this case the County Democratic Central Committee. School board members meet once a month and vote on policy and procedures, personnel, expenditures, etc. They meet in public, but before and after every meeting they go into "executive session." Now, "executive session" is supposed to be reserved for personnel matters; that's so no one gets embarrassed if he or she is being fired or suspended or otherwise disciplined. But this board must have a mountain of personnel matters, because they meet behind closed doors before every meeting. Then when they come out into the public session, they simply walk through every step of the agenda, muttering, "All agreed...Yes or nay" when asked to vote on something. I refer to it as the "dog and pony show." Without exception they agree with everything the superintendent proposes...er, recommends...every time. This may be a public meeting, but they do not encourage public discussion. Oh, it's the public's children they're educating, and it's the public's money they're using to pay their salaries and everything else, but they don't want unfettered public input. They have their little citizen advisory committees and councils with parents on board, but you better keep quiet at the board meetings. They do have a "sounding board" that allows the public to sign up and speak to the board (that's required), but it's after most of the parents leave, after the recognition ceremony where their kids receive certificates for being the spelling bee champ or the winning volleyball team, etc. And speakers only have five minutes, no more, and when you're finished you're lucky if you get a "thank you." Neither the board, the superintendent, his staff, or administrators speak. Not a whisper, not a soul will respond to your questions or concerns. Your objections are "duly noted" and then forgotten. They don't even appear in the minutes of the meeting. So much for public input. And this is a public meeting? Where the men and women who control our $23 million budget and our children's lives are not answerable to anyone? It just doesn't feel right, and these "sunshine laws" are in full eclipse. Like a lot of things about this group of individuals, their monthly meetings were a sham.

Now then. The board and superintendent answer to the county commissioners, who dole out more than 75 percent of their local dollars to the board of education. They submit a budget to the commissioners, and they toss it back and forth until they agree on a funding level. In hard times the board tells teachers, "The commission cut our budget $1 million, so we can't give you a raise this year." When times are good and they only get cut $250,000, they still complain they have no money. The kicker is this: In West Virginia times were hard. Every year we lost money. If we spent $20 million one year, we only had $19.5 million the next. We had to cut positions and ran a deficit for years. In this state we always got our $20 million, let's say; what they'd argue over was the *increase*. So every year the superintendent would add positions, usually administrators, or coordinators so his administrators didn't have to work so hard, and every year class size got bigger and teacher salaries stagnated. This would become a bone of contention between the superintendent and me down the road, but we'll leave this be for a while. Even in lean years there's a law on the books called "Maintenance of Effort" which guarantees that the county commission can't give the board less than they gave the year before (adjusted for inflation).

The other entity the local board had to answer to was the big guys, the feds. Now we don't get a big chunk of money from the federal government, but there are a lot of federal programs, from food subsidies to reading programs and building programs, that are essential to the operation of schools. One program is the one that guarantees that education for disabled kids. The rule is simple. If you don't meet precise guidelines for guaranteeing a free appropriate public education (FAPE) for all children, including the disabled, then you will not only lose money for the special education programs, but ALL YOUR FEDERAL MONEY. This isn't like highway funds where you can say stick it, we'll build our own roads and put up a toll booth; this is major bucks, and public education is free. No parent pays tuition; he or she just sends his or her kids to school and pays his or her taxes once a year. Now, to guarantee this happens, the federal government passes public laws and regulations that the state governments (SEAs, or state educational agencies) must implement. The states then monitor the LEAs, the local systems, to make sure they are doing their job. This is known as compliance monitoring. LEAs have to develop and implement local policies and procedures of which the boards of education approve. They have to make copies of these LOPs (local operating procedures) available to the public and to the teachers, administrators, and others who are responsible for implementing them. They also have to conduct training to make sure everyone knows what he or she is doing.

# The Tightrope Walk Of The School Psychologist

School psychologists are one of the "lower echelon" school system employees who implement many of these procedures.

Just what is a school psychologist? Simply stated, we deal with any learning or behavior problems a child in school may have. Despite our sometimes lowly status in many school systems, our responsibilities are many. We are on the front line, meeting with parents and teachers and students on a daily basis. We observe them in the classroom, we conduct evaluations (give them tests) to determine their intelligence, their aptitude to learn, their learning style (how they learn), their actual achievement (what they've learned in reading, math, spelling, history, science, etc.), their behavioral and emotional status, and we judge their motivation and attention and frustration level and their commitment to task. We also gather information from previous tests or records. We talk with those who deal directly with them, their teachers and parents and principals and doctors, and we make recommendations for positive change for the child. We are, by role and definition, change agents. We are also, by design, training, and philosophy, child advocates; the child comes first above all else.

In order to call yourself a school psychologist, you need an advanced degree. I have a graduate degree. Most of us have undergraduate (four-year) degrees in psychology. Mine was a double major with a degree in psychology and English education (teaching on the secondary level). I also had a minor in sociology. My graduate degree (master's) is in psychology, plus another year in my specialty (school psychology), which included courses in special education, school law, psychological testing, school administration, and more. I was awarded an *educational specialist degree* recognizing the two years of study beyond my bachelor's degree. After that I was required to perform a supervised internship. In order to maintain my state certification, I have to take professional development and other college courses. I also opted to be recognized for national certification and submitted credentials and took the national examination. Every three years I have to reapply for national certification and provide documentation of continued in-service/professional development and other activities.

Over the last thirty plus years, I have been employed by five public school systems across four states, which has given me a wealth of experience on how different states and different LEAs (local boards) interpret, implement, and enforce the federal laws that protect the disabled in their districts.

And if that's not enough, I am bound by a code of ethics designed by the best minds in the profession of school psychology, one that encourages its members to hold to the highest standards of excellence in providing services to disabled children and their parents. Procedures are in place to censure any psychologist who violates these standards and puts anyone, be it teacher, parent, or even employer, ahead of what is in the best interest of the child. The system is designed to assure consensus, to assure that decisions that are made are in the child's best interest, and although it is clear that no one expects a disabled child to receive the BEST education, it must meet criteria for the MOST APPROPRIATE one. And here is the rub. What do you do if your employer tells you to recommend or not recommend something for a child when you know it is not in the child's best interest? It is a tightrope all of us walk, and I made a decision long ago that if there were ever a choice to have a parent or a teacher or an administrator mad at me, I'd sleep better at night knowing the parent and teacher were happy. Needless to say, this has made for some interesting moments with administrators. Read THE KNIGHTS OF THE IEP again at the beginning of this book to understand how I see all of these players working together.

My job in all systems I have worked in boils down to taking referrals from teachers in the schools to which I am assigned. This has varied from as little as two schools all the way up to ten schools during the hard times. I examine the referral, determine a course of action, and gather as much information on the child as I can through interviews and reviews of records and work samples. I will handle a referral for a behavior problem a little differently than one for a strictly learning problem, though I need to know the two are not related causally. I screen kids for ADHD (attention deficit hyperactivity disorder), I set up behavior modification programs, I observe in class and make direct recommendations, I conduct individual assessments, I integrate all the findings on children into formal reports, and I attend meetings to discuss findings, student needs, and possible solutions. I follow up with referrals to outside agencies as well; doctors, clinical psychologists, psychiatrists, etc. The job of a school psychologist is a difficult one with a great deal of responsibility, and it is never boring. All you deal with are problems, and you are often between competing forces, many angry with each other, and your job as peacemaker is often at great emotional expense. I have not been without controversy, but I have always fought hard for the children I serve, and for this reason I sleep well at night. I am first and foremost a child advocate. When an administrator has asked me to compromise myself, I always point out how this will violate federal and state law and how doing so will place the local board in jeopardy. If he or she is not dissuaded, I allow his or her decision to prevail, but I do not do so silently. In four states, five districts, I never had more problem than I did in this school district.

## Public School Supervision By The Director Of Personnel

In the eight years I worked in the district, the only contacts I had with my supervisor, the personnel director, were negative. He never once set foot in my office the entire eight years I was employed by the system, that is, until the very last day when I was moving out of my office after turning in my resignation. That's right, out of almost sixteen hundred days I worked for the county public school system, he never came by to say hi or ask how things were going or if I needed anything. The only time I saw this man was in his office and when I was in trouble. The only other exception was evaluation conferences, and those were in other people's offices, never mine. If I needed help my first year because principals were asking me to bend or break county rules or federal law, he was never there. "I don't return phone calls" was his excuse. When I got in "trouble," my building principal, Mr. Dave, was there for me, and he often ran interference between other principals and the personnel director.

At the end of the first year, Mr. Dave, my protector, left the county. He not only left the county employ, but he left his house and his wife for a job in another state (he maintained contact with his two daughters, I am proud to say). He was my advocate. He ran interference for me because he knew where I was coming from. When he left, I was alone. Left alone, the next year was brutal. The principal I'd had some problems with moved into my home school (where my office was). By the end of the second year, as a decision to offer me tenure approached, I got nervous. Most school systems have a probationary period, usually two years, before you are offered a "continuing contract." Anytime during these two years you can be notified that you will not be rehired. No reason has to be given. You cannot protest or grieve it. You just find another job at the end of the school year. (And good luck finding one if you haven't been renewed.) In this district they had to give you notice before April 1 that you would not be renewed for the following school year. I had mostly good observations and answered negative evaluations with solid arguments. I had worked hard and felt my status was secure. Little did I know that the personnel director was not in my corner. I'd hardly seen the man, and every "problem" had been resolved. Still, I would hold my breath until April 2. Then, on March 30, my grandfather died.

I knew I would not be present for an April 1 conference since his funeral was four hours away. On the thirtieth I approached my immediate supervisor, my building principal. I told him my grandfather had died and that I would be applying for family leave for Friday the first of April. I also told him that I would be available for any conferences the next day, March 31. He assured me that anything could be taken care of on Monday, April 4, when I returned. I asked him if he was sure. "Go take care of your grandmother," was his answer. I was on the job the entire next day, the thirty-first, and when four o'clock came, I left knowing I had a job with security. I later found out that while they thought I would cooperate with a "late notice," and when they called me in for an April 4 meeting, I made it clear before the meeting that I was glad I had passed the deadline for nonrenewal. They misjudged me. I gave them ample time before I left for the funeral, they missed the deadline, and they were now "forced" to keep me. Without coming right out and saying it, they alluded to the fact that were it not for this technicality, I might not still be with them. I don't think the personnel director had ever forgiven me for that. They tried some half-baked attempts to get me to resign, but I liked it there despite them, and after three jobs in two other states, I was ready to stay put. That was 1991. I was forty-one years old. I continued to do my job, to work hard, and to earn the respect of the teachers and parents I worked with. Things were settling into a nice groove. My wife was also employed by the system, and both my kids were attending the system's high school.

The problem was, these folks hired someone to do a job, they did everything in their power to prevent them from doing it. I wasn't there to advocate for kids or to share my decisions with team members; I was there to do the principal's bidding or one of his cronies. If a teacher didn't want a particular child in his or her room, he or she would lobby against the child with full support of the principal. And hey, they were in the building five days a week; I only showed up once a week, what did I matter? Politics and personalities played more a role in what decisions were made then test results and what was in the child's best interest. I also came in after a psychologist who was a bit lazy. He did as little as possible, and so he was only too happy to go along with the school's decision, to sign off on what they wanted. When I wouldn't rubber stamp their decisions or sign off on their recommendations, when I actually did the evaluation and wrote a five-page report considering all the factors, they singled me out as an instigator. I wasn't a "team player," I wanted my agenda to prevail. I kept saying it wasn't "my" way, it was the right way. I would go to my supervisor and he would tell me I was doing the right thing, go in there, and follow the guidelines, and yet every time when I would run into an obstacle, usually a principal trying to force his way on the committee, I would be left out there alone, swinging in the wind. I fought this for four years until finally I was moved into another school building and into a successful and rewarding job experience. It was at this time that I heard very little from the personnel director. I rarely went to him; he was as useless as a strand of spaghetti in a bar fight, I relied on my own wits.

## The Good Years

I spent the next three years in a very successful setting, working hard and building a reputation. With the exception of a few minor glitches, it was smooth sailing. I became active in my school and community. I was elected president of the local Teacher's Association and also president of the County Council of PTAs. I was on playground committees and reading incentive programs and raised money for scholarships, organized banquets, and negotiated contracts for teachers with the board. I got along well with my building principals, especially my home-based one, and not only special education and general education teachers, but parents trusted me and respected not only my work, but my willingness to stand up for their kids. What I didn't realize at the time was that while I was making friends and earning respect from some, I was making enemies of others, and rather than earning their respect, I was beginning to scare them. I was a "lower echelon employee" a teacher, but I was building a reputation, even a power base, and the superintendent didn't like that. And, too, I misjudged him. When I went to "war" with him over the teachers' contract, I felt we were on equal ground; that he respected the level of professionalism I brought to my role. He couldn't have cared less. When I brought facts to bear that made him look bad at the bargaining table, I may have sealed my fate…and my daughter's. When I organized the parents group and began to see changes in the amount of input and impact parents were having in decisions that affected their children, I thought it was a good thing. When I organized parent and teacher groups to examine the superintendent's budget for the very first time, I was excited. But once again the superintendent was steaming, and waiting for the opportunity to set things right. And when my daughter "stepped in it," so to speak, he was waiting right there to make sure it was my face that got rubbed in it. And his henchman, his two directors, the assistant superintendent and the personnel director, were waiting in the wings. The assistant superintendent, the same guy who sat across the bargaining table from me as the board's chief negotiator, and me as representative of the teachers, would later sit in judgment of my daughter as chairman of the expulsion panel. And the personnel director, my supervisor, who missed his opportunity to have a progressive and beneficial school psychology program, who instead tried to terminate his hardest-working psychologist (and failed), would sit as the co-chair of the expulsion panel and my chief antagonist as director of pupil personnel. He was there ready to pounce at every perceived slight, every chink in my armor.

## Two Trains Collide

So here I stood, in the position of having to defend my own kid, this time against these same administrators. The other school psychologist, my colleague, called the personnel director incensed that I would ask *her* to testify on my daughter's behalf. He shared her indignation. How dare I call a fellow employee of the district and put her in such an untenable position!? This was tantamount to treason. I was not only questioning the expulsion panel's decision, but asking fellow employees to do the same. Forgotten in all this was the child who was at the center of all this discussion.

I was at one of my schools at the time and it was near the end of the day. The personnel director waited for me to finish a meeting I was in and then asked if he could have a word with me. Sure. He came in and sat down. His face was flushed red, highlighting his shock of neatly cropped gray hair. In an accusatory tone he demanded to know if I had "used the county telephones to contact teachers to testify against the board at your daughter's hearing." I was shocked. What the hell was he talking about? Had I made phone calls to colleagues about my daughter, who also happened to attend the schools I worked in? Yes. To obtain people to talk "against the board"? No. How about FOR my daughter? I had a perfect right to contact teachers to speak on her behalf, and I said as much. The policy outlined the parents' rights to appeal, and you could call witnesses from the board. "With the board phones?" he asked. Again I insisted I had the right to use the phones for *professional use*, to call parents. Past practice, however, is that teachers, being captive during the bulk of the business day, use their free time and these phones to make doctor's appointments, check on their sick children, order pizzas, check on car repairs, make reservations for dinner, order theater tickets, talk to their older kids, husbands, mothers, or relatives, or call the bank or mortgage company. And yet here I am being singled out for using the phone for a legitimate purpose, not to have people testify against the board, but to provide testimony behalf of a disabled child in the district, my daughter.

His point was made: past practice or not, any further use of the phone or computers or any office equipment belonging to the board of education to further my case against the board would be dealt with harshly. (And remember, this was in the days long before cell phones.) In his unforgettable words, "The focus will quickly shift from your daughter's case to you." Ask me if I felt intimidated. From that day forward I became an angel, but it was clear from that conversation that things would never be the same for me in the district. Once again I would have to walk better than Jesus Christ himself. War had been declared when I had the audacity to question an administrator's decision to the local board. Even if that decision wasn't just another "screw job" for a kid I had tested, but one that involved my family, my own daughter. And though I expected them to play hard, I also expected them to play fair. I would do my job, I would keep my nose clean, and I expected them to let the boards and other deliberative bodies deal with the facts. Boy, was I naive!

This was the first salvo in what would become a long series of actions against me. The next one arrived a few weeks later, on December 1, 1994. For years I had enjoyed one small "perk" of being an itinerant employee. Itinerants enjoy the luxury of traveling between schools. Though it gives you thirty minutes of freedom on company time, the itinerant misses the "family atmosphere" of being assigned exclusively to one school. You are often forgotten for half-day lunches. You can't do "Secret Santa" because you aren't there every day. You're sometimes spread between four schools and they all forget you when you aren't at theirs. It's human nature. At least you're accepted at your home school, but even then it's only a few days if you're lucky. You have to make a genuine effort to fit in and be included. The life of an itinerant is often a lonely one.

In this district the "freedom" is taken away because, rather than allow you to set your own schedule, you're forced to assign one school one day. And they usually pick the day. So you report to your "assigned" school and you shouldn't leave until the end of that day. But if you have nothing to do at your assigned school, and plenty at another, fine, travel to the other school. Occasionally a principal will give you permission to leave his school for another, or your home school to write reports, but they usually are territorial enough to want "their" psychologist all day. If you are at a school and you test kids and have meetings, you carry files with you. Carrying three to four files for three to four schools can get confusing, so you typically stop off at your home school to unload from the previous day(s) and pick up your files and test materials for the next school(s). This is usually done at the end of your work day, on your way home or on your way in before the work day starts. On your time. The perk? Charging travel between the home school and your assigned school, or between your assigned school and your home school, usually twice a week for a total of less than five bucks. Save it up for several weeks and you get a check for forty or fifty bucks; gas money. In December 1994, the personnel director cut off this travel for me. *Unless I left during the work day with permission from the principal,* I could not receive reimbursement. Principals seemed reluctant to let me leave, so I was stuck working on my own time for free, without the two- to three-dollar travel reimbursement to make it a little more palatable. So here we are in a county that sends administrators to national conferences annually, and they cheat us out of a few measly dollars that are placed in our travel budget for this purpose. I was not the only one affected, but it was the first example of how far they'd go to hurt me, and the rest of the folks be damned. You can imagine how this ingratiated me with my colleagues.

## CHAPTER SIX

# THE BOARD HEARING, DECEMBER 6, 1994

Board hearings are part of the due process procedure. They are designed in theory to afford your rights to be heard before action is taken against you. If an administrator and expulsion panel, made up of more administrators, hear evidence and make a mandatory recommendation to yet another administrator (the superintendent), who is also bound to follow the lock step—*if you did it, you're out*—then there has to be one deliberative body who can stop the process for a minute and make an independent decision. That's zero tolerance with a measure of due process to allow for mitigating circumstances. The board of education is that body, legally, ethically, and traditionally. The hearing occurs with the five board members at the dais, a raised platform with chairs behind this curved monolith much like a judge's bench. The superintendent is seated in a chair on the floor of the room at a table facing the board with his attorney. The student sits at another table with her parents and their attorney. Just like a courtroom. Well, almost. Let's just say it has the *appearance* of a courtroom. But like the "public" board meetings, there's a lot missing. What is especially interesting is that the administrators have their attorney, who sits at the table on the floor with them, and the board has their own attorney who also serves as the "moderator." He runs the hearing. And although he supposedly is "neutral," how interesting that he sits as an "impartial" moderator as well as their adviser. When he goes behind closed doors with them, does he advise what is in the student's best interest or the board's best interest? When he interrupts a parent or the parent's attorney to make a point, is this to further the cause of due process or to protect his client, the board? The answers are all too obvious. In reviewing the transcript of this hearing, it was almost criminal—when our attorney was getting one witness (Coach) ready to admit that he withheld information from us, the administrator's attorney didn't object to this cross examination, so the board's attorney did. "In the absence of an objection not made, I'm going to disallow that question." They had this thing covered from both ends, it seemed—rules of evidence being more what's left out than what's left in.

The board (i.e., the superintendent) had it all planned out. Three kids up for expulsion for drugs, one at four o'clock, one at five, one at six, time for a seven o'clock executive session, and move on to their regular board meeting at seven thirty. We were on first at four. By six thirty they canceled the other hearings and were worried about finishing us up to hold the regularly scheduled public board meeting at seven thirty. Ours ran until ten after seven, over three hours of witnesses and testimony. Less, a hired gun from the city across the bridge, was the attorney who represented the administrators. The board's local small-town attorney stood to represent the board of education and to "moderate" the proceedings. The board put on their case first. The assistant superintendent and chairman of the expulsion panel spoke first. It was basically "just the facts, ma'am"; however, he made one statement that stands out in light of all their talk later about the

## The Board Hearing, December 6, 1994

investigation they supposedly conducted. The primary question was this: *did they discover Sarah's alleged drug use through an investigation, or by her own admission four days later?* How does the personnel director's sworn statement ring: "It is my understanding from the expulsion hearing that I had that it was actually Sarah's parents who finally found out that Sarah had not been telling the truth, that she had been lying to avoid punishment, and when they found out that Sarah had indeed taken LSD on school property, it was Sarah's father, Mr. Matthews, who actually called and notified (the principal) that, yes, indeed Sarah did possess and use LSD on the school campus, so *that's how they (the school) found out with Sarah of her involvement.*"

So much for their investigation. The assistant superintendent, head of the expulsion panel, and lead investigator essentially admitted under oath that they didn't know until she came forward. Sarah went on to testify at the hearing, and was both open and honest. She did well. Even to the point when Less tried to confuse her, "Oh, so, okay, so you were *wrong* when you said earlier you made a mistake when you just told us that you told him that last year you had a drug problem?" Sarah never said that; he misheard it or was trying to confuse her with all the "you said…you made…you told us…you told him…," and she broke down in tears. Even the superintendent and members of the audience who heard it correctly spoke out. "That's not what she said!" Less lost points on this one. The truth was coming out as we hoped it would.

I was the next witness, and I addressed the facts as I knew them. I openly and honestly discussed Sarah's previous history of drug involvement, our contacts with the counseling center in town and our private family therapist. I spoke of her early history: premature birth, violent death of her father, delayed milestones, identification as learning disabled, special-education services in West Virginia, and here locally. I talked about Coach and his dual role as personal friend of the family and teacher/coach who revealed to me his suspicions and my need to question Sarah directly to protect his confidential relationship with her. I spoke about the reasons I turned her in, and my ignorance of the "zero-tolerance" aspect of the policy.

I also gave unrefuted testimony about my meeting with the principal when I brought Sarah to school to turn herself in, how I was clear about Sarah's history of learning disabilities, and how I wanted to have her evaluated to determine if her current behavior problems were somehow related. I was teased by our attorney for covering a bit of his closing argument when I said, "I convinced my daughter to be open, to be honest, and the irony is that she would never have gotten caught if I hadn't convinced her to come forward. There was never any witness, there's no physical evidence. The only reason that she got caught is that her father said, 'Sarah, turn yourself in. Be open and be honest, and get help.' And I appealed to the school for that help and yet I don't feel we received it. And I wonder what kind of message that gives Sarah, and, more importantly, what message does it give the other kids who are still in school because they lied about their involvement?"

Our family therapist, Martha, also testified. Her area of expertise was on ADHD (attention deficit hyperactivity disorder) and its primary features. She talked about Sarah's impulsivity, and her depression resulting from her father's violent death. The connection between her drug use and her ADHD was all unrefuted. Many individuals with ADHD who were untreated (i.e., not on medication) often turned to drugs; they "self-medicated." Less tried to undermine Martha, but she stood strong.

Maria, a highly respected teacher and coach, testified about Sarah's character. Less tried to put words into her mouth: "So you say that Sarah is a nice kid...Do nice kids get hooked on and use marijuana and lie to their parents about it?" Maria: "I'm sure they do." Less: "Nice kids do?" Maria: "I think you're putting me in a very difficult position. So you're saying that any child that's used drugs..." This is when the

## The Board Hearing, December 6, 1994

so-called unbiased moderator saw where this was going and, to protect the board's case, interrupted Maria before she finished: "In the absence of an objection not made, I'm going to disallow that question." So if the moderator, who is also representing the board and its administrators, doesn't like the answer to a question, he simply interrupts and erases the question. This allowed the board's attorney Less to continue his character assassination of a sixteen-year-old. The moderator's final words: "We can't go back and forth here." No, they just wanted to "go forth" with a predetermined decision.

We had called Coach as a witness originally, but, after seeing where his loyalties were placed, were afraid of putting him on. It was clear the administration (the superintendent) had gotten to him. He was there and squirming in his seat. At a break he approached the superintendent and Less, and he was called to "testify." Or more accurately, tell his story (lie) to make himself and the school system look good. He made it sound like he conducted his "investigation" with the full authority of the school administration. I'm sure the principal told him to call Sarah at home and use his friendship with the family and his personal relationship with her to get information from her. He lied on the stand when he quoted (paraphrased) what Sarah supposedly told him the next day, Friday, October 14. "She said three things." Trouble is, when he repeated the quote later on, they were three *different* things. "I said, 'We have names, I just want to compare to see if it flows or what. Nobody will know who said what, and you can go back to class. Okay?' So she tells me who this person was. I said, 'Sarah, did you have drugs yourself?' First answer was no, second answer was, 'I flushed it.' Third answer was, 'I had it.' " Later on he quotes this same conversation but a little differently; "No, she gave me three options. She gave me options. She said, 'I had it. I flushed it. I only took half of it.' "

Funny how the truth stays the same over time, and the lie is harder to remember because it is a story rather than a recollection. And most individuals can't remember what story they told the first time. And it was to cover his rear. He actually gave Sarah this very "cover story" when he had her in his office that Friday. "If (the assistant principal) calls you in, just tell him you had it and flushed it…Also tell him you were in counseling. They'll go easier on you." And when he was questioned about his previous knowledge of her drug use back in the spring (when he was also an employee of the school system with certain responsibilities), the moderator cut him off, thereby protecting the school system again when he admitted to having knowledge about a student with a drug problem that he failed to act on. Our attorney was going to ask Coach why he didn't refer Sarah to the drug team at the school. Coach: "I didn't know about Sarah's marijuana use until the Mathews called me up and told me that they had found items in her room." Our attorney, Ellis, asked him, "Okay, did you…" only to be interrupted yet again by the supposedly neutral moderator: "I'm going to stop this area of the cross examination based on an unheard objection that it's beyond the scope of the original testimony."

Despite all of this apparent subterfuge and legal wrangling, we left there feeling great! We had gotten a lot of good information on the record. The truth had been revealed. We'd had our "day in court." I was optimistic that the board would overturn the superintendent's decision. They had to. The sad truth was…they didn't. They upheld the decision. Sarah was suspended for the rest of the school year.

## To Tell The Truth The Whole Truth And Nothing But The Truth

Lies were concocted to protect her and the Coach when the football player got caught using drugs. The trouble started when I couldn't allow the lie to stand. I couldn't allow my daughter to get away with the lie. It had everything to do

## The Board Hearing, December 6, 1994

with the truth and facing up to your choices, something I still believe in. Later, "honorable" judges will suggest that maybe we would have been better off lying, "retracting her statement," or "mitigating" it. I will tell you, when you look at some of the consequences out there for such innocent acts, it becomes clear why people avoid detection by any means. Trouble is, it causes a lack of respect for all the laws, and those who are charged with enforcing them and judging them. When a judge tells you, "Hey, you confessed, you had a chance to lie, what do you want me to do about it?" there's something wrong with the system. When the truth doesn't work and the lie does, something is seriously wrong. When judges expect, even demand, that you offer "mitigating" circumstances, aren't they telling you to make up excuses for your behaviors? After all, what does mitigate mean: "to relieve, to temper, to make less severe." "Well, judge, I took the piece of paper I thought was a dangerous drug, but I didn't really get off that good. Oh, and I'm sorry." How do you help a person with a drug problem who lies and makes excuses for her behavior other than to hold her accountable while at the same time providing a safe alternative? Punishment or treatment? Her choice. When telling the truth leads to severe consequences that can be easily avoided with a simple lie, you know how most will choose. *You told the truth, so we're going to punish you. If you had lied, we'd have let you off.*

You'd have thought this country would have "gotten it" after Prohibition. I guess not. People will drink or take drugs regardless of the laws designed to deter this behavior. The attraction is too strong. We did away with punishment for alcohol use and abuse. There are a multitude of treatment programs for alcoholics. Treatment first, second, and third, and then the punishment—the consequences. Why is it so different for drugs? Shouldn't drug abusers be treated with some compassion, too? Give them a chance, and give kids, school kids, sixteen-year-old kids, more than one chance... after all, they are supposed to be learning, and what is it that we are supposed to be teaching them? Punish the lie, reward the truth? Make consequences realistic and appropriate. These are victimless crimes where the only one truly hurt is the substance abuser herself, and her family. When drug laws make victims suffer even more than the real criminals, then something is wrong with the system.

Three kids came before the board that night: Arthur, who got into the mock battle on the football field, Barbara, and Sarah. It was Barbara who called Sarah over to show her what she had on her tongue and convinced Sarah to join her in the adventure. I respect Barbara for coming forward as much as I do Sarah. Arthur got caught hands down. He had no opportunity to turn himself in or to come forward; he was the only one they had corroborating evidence on—blood work. Did he deserve what they all got? Certainly not, but he was the only one who was treated fairly, according to the policy. The board affirmed the superintendent's recommendation and the three kids were suspended for the rest of the school year, seven months of schooling. The only deliberative body that had discretion didn't exercise it. Though they had the statutory authority to override the superintendent's decision, they were told they could not, they were told (improperly, in my opinion) that with the board policy of "zero tolerance," they were required to vote for expulsion if the "findings of fact" proved the student in question had in fact violated the policy. They voted three to one to expel the students. So much for due process. So much for discretion. So much for justice. So much for helping kids who need help and seek it out at school.

## Local Board's Decision

The local board of education rejected the argument that they couldn't use her statements against her. Their position was that she was not "seeking help to overcome a drug problem" but was addressing questions in relation to the investigation. What investigation? Furthermore, they felt that she did not

## The Board Hearing, December 6, 1994

deserve protection under Section [504]* or special education provisions because "the student has not factually established such a status. On October 13, 1994, Sarah was not a special education student, nor had there been any request for an evaluation." They upheld the superintendent's decision.

Although there's no argument that Sarah was not a "special education student," she was not receiving special education services, and she did not have a current IEP (Individual Education Program) in place, she was still disabled, and I had requested an evaluation. There was unrefuted, sworn testimony to this effect. She was identified (learning disabled) and received special education services in two states. It was ignored. I had requested an evaluation. It was also ignored. It was incredible the way things were turning out.

---

*504: Section 504 of the Civil Rights Act of 1974, prohibiting discrimination based on race, class, sex, and handicapping condition. It opened the door for kids with disabilities to file for action under the civil rights laws. OCR, the Office of Civil Rights investigates these complaints directly.

# CHAPTER SEVEN

# APPEAL TO THE STATE BOARD

After the three-hour fiasco referred to as the board of education expulsion hearing, and their decision to uphold the superintendent's decision, we were shocked and deeply disappointed. I felt sure that once the board heard the facts, they would be unable to support the superintendent. How could they? I mean, Sarah may have done something wrong, but she came forward to do the right thing. She was open and honest, whereas the others who lied or failed to come forward remained in school. The policy itself was flawed as well. Making special support programs available to students who committed violent crimes against the school—rape, robbery, assault against staff, arson, weapons, bombs, etc.—and then treating nonviolent students differently just didn't make sense. The violent students were allowed discretion. Zero tolerance or the "automatic expulsion" only applied to two groups: kids who were caught abusing alcohol the *second* time, and *first*-time drug offenders. The kids who need the help, treatment, are expelled from school with no services or alternative programs, exiled from their peers and social environment, while the violent offenders with real victims are welcomed back. It just didn't make sense.

We addressed the board of education at the December 6 hearing in an honest and forthright manner. We attacked the policy, a policy that allowed discretion for knife-toting felons while taking a punitive approach to drug-addicted kids who needed treatment for substance abuse. It seemed so backward: punish the drug and alcohol abusers and provide "treatment" for the felons. Children who use drugs and alcohol have a problem, and it more often than not is not the drug or alcohol itself. There are underlying problems that lead to the abuse. The alcohol and drugs only become problems later on as use turns to misuse and then abuse and addiction. Teenagers and other adolescents abuse drugs and alcohol for a variety of reasons. They are depressed, they have low self-images, they have academic problems, and they have social problems. They come from dysfunctional families and they come from well-adjusted families. They come from families who use drugs and alcohol, and those who never did. And they turn to drugs for any number of reasons: to escape, to enjoy, to rebel, to mask feelings, to be accepted, to be different, just to do them. And they come from families who hurt their kids and neglect their kids, and they come from families like mine, who cherish and protect our kids. And even "good" families are far from perfect. Yes, we used to do drugs, but we gave them up for parenthood, and we most certainly don't condone them for our kids or your kids. But face it, we are children of the sixties; we did what we did, and then we brought children into the world. We grew up and gave up our childish ways. We teach our children the values of tolerance and forgiveness, of caring for the less fortunate. We teach our children honesty and integrity and the significance of standing behind your positions and your decisions. And we expect our educational system to teach a similar compassionate message. And we expect it to teach our children about the virtue of being honest and taking a position and standing behind it and others who share your views. This is what I thought was the American way.

Instead we find attitudes about drugs that predate the sixties and which allow people to view substance abusers as evil and deserving what they get. They forget that drugs, especially alcohol, are addictive to certain personality types, and that the abuser loses control and needs help to regain it. And when children and teenagers experiment with drugs, it's a sign that something is wrong or missing in their lives. The response should be compassion, not hatred. Like gays and others who live Alternative lifestyles, people who are different are treated as outcasts. And they make no allowances for the fact that these are children, our children. The board seemed to be saying, "These students purposely and intentionally with will and aforethought determined to ingest this foreign substance, and they deserve any punishment the board is willing to mete out." Forget the value of honesty, for the students who lied to protect themselves avoided any consequences. Forget the value of integrity, "I did it and am willing to straighten myself out with help, and I reach out to you for it" — for no help will be forthcoming, only punishment. And forget the value of compassion for those less fortunate, for despite the fact that these are children, some with serious problems, there is no concern or consideration for drug users, only disdain as they are removed, shunned, and sent into a yearlong exile. And for many, the punishment far exceeds the crime. And the sad thing is that years later, with many of these policies still in place, the drug problem has not gone away; if anything it has gotten worse. The zero tolerance policies and their sacrificial lambs proved nothing, only the need to soften the policies and reach out to kids. And they are not administered in an equitable fashion; they are often used as weapons against certain individuals: the poor, the disenfranchised, the politically incorrect.

We appealed to the board on these issues, and we appealed on the fact that county policies and even state and federal laws were not followed. No one told us about her problems until we found out about them on our own and brought her forward. County policy requires the school to notify parents when a kid's in trouble. No one ever called us. And state rules require a thorough investigation, although one was never done. It was only her word. And protections for kids seeking help with a drug problem were ignored. Coach knew about her drug problem from six months before, and yet he never referred her to the proper school teams. Her English teacher read and graded her journals the previous spring—writings laced with drug references and even drawings—and yet no one ever alerted us or referred her to the school's Substance Abuse Team, the "BEST Team" that provided help and confidentiality for troubled kids. And finally, no one ever looked at her confidential file revealing her status as a learning disabled student. No one set up a manifestation hearing to determine if her behaviors were related in any way to school failure or frustration. No one asked if her impulsivity or her oppositional behaviors forced her right down this path of destruction. Neither did they look at her learning disabilities to see if her thinking skills or her failure to fit in contributed to her actions that day. And no one ever asked if her impulsivity might indicate an attention deficit with its incipient need to fill in with drugs what has for ever been missing in her brain. The board didn't deliberate, they mandated, and the expulsion for Sarah was upheld.

# CHAPTER EIGHT

# THE SEARCH FOR AN ADVOCATE

We knew immediately that we had to appeal and went to meet with our attorney. He was willing to file one for us, but he estimated it would cost $4,000 or more. We'd already pulled together a month's salary (over $2,000) and couldn't afford twice that at the time. We talked it over amongst ourselves, and it is here that I began my search for an advocate. Someone who would take the case pro-bono or at a reduced cost. I felt the case was strong and had merit. Someone would take the case to establish the rights of school students whose rights were violated. We couldn't prevail on the discriminatory nature of the policy, how it punished students with problems (drug and alcohol abuse) instead of treating them. If this argument wasn't strong enough, then the issue of her coming forward on her own could be a focus. Constitutional law should provide protections against self-incrimination, and the only evidence they had was her word, backed up by us (hearsay), and we were taking her at her word. There was no physical evidence or witness, remember. If that didn't fly, then there were the protections that were put into place to protect students who came forward seeking help in the form of counseling for drug problems. Remember, she didn't come forward to get expelled, to get punished. She came forward for help. I testified to this at the hearing. And last, but certainly not least, federal protections were afforded students who were disabled, and she certainly was that, having been previously identified as learning disabled and served in both West Virginia and here in the Maryland. Every argument was strong enough to stand alone; together it should form an airtight case. The challenge was to find an agency, an advocate who would take up our daughter's banner.

With this knowledge and strong belief in this case, I began my search. I started with a tip about the state university's law clinic. I called, several times, and its director never returned my calls. I read an article by a professor in a neighboring state university promoting advocacy for disabled students who have been expelled. He is currently a well-recognized name in the field of law for children with disabilities. Over the twenty-five years I had been out or college, I seemed to have forgotten about the inflated egos some college professors have. He was a reputed expert in the field. He returned my calls but was rude and more than a bit arrogant. He was more concerned about how I got his phone number, indignant that I expected his help. Here was a man who dedicated his life to research and writing about the rights of the disabled; but when he was asked to help with just one, he acted like I was asking to sleep with his wife. A sad example of someone who fails to practice what he preaches in class every day. And all I was asking for was some advice and some direction to go. All I got was the cold shoulder.

If you count our family attorney, George, and his partner, Ellis, who represented us at the local board, and the two professors, I was now up to four attempts to obtain affordable representation with no success. The next person I was referred to was an expert on educational law. Trouble was, she was the state board's attorney and, though she was professional enough to return my call, was quite obviously not

## The Search For An Advocate

in a position to render me any legal advice. Attorney number six was employed by a state-funded disability law center, but we were over income. Like they say, in America only the rich and the poor can afford an attorney. Number seven was the ACLU. I figured the American Civil Liberties Union would be very interested in the fact that the Constitution and its protection from self-incrimination had been abandoned at the schoolhouse door. Students had no rights once they walked in the classroom. Their response was also disappointing; they were restricted to cases that focus on the rights of homeless persons. I thought that was a bit odd. People, mostly adults who, through choice, lack of effort, or, in some cases, sad misfortune, are out of work and out of a home take precedence over a young adult, a minor child with her entire life in front of her.

Since Sarah was learning disabled and her civil rights had been violated (she testified against herself and was then deprived of an education) I contacted the Office of Civil Rights. Some grouchy old curmudgeon cut me off quick; they "couldn't take drug-involved cases." Next I tried *Advocates for Children and Youth*. They sounded like an agency that would fight for kids. They sent me on a wild goose chase, from one person to another within the agency. Some were "not at their desks," others wouldn't return my call, and one was on pregnancy leave. They finally suggested a man who might take the case at a reduced fee; half of the usual $200 an hour. I called and spoke with him at length over the phone and eventually drove across the bridge to Baltimore to meet with him. He spent most of the hour trying to convince me not to pursue the case. But he agreed to take it. We met with him on one more occasion, and he wrote a decent brief that was submitted to the state board of education. Without even taking the time to hear the case, they decided against us. If that wasn't bad enough, they sent us a form letter with three sentences in it. That little misadventure only cost us $1,500. We paid the attorney and discharged him. We now had to decide the next step, court. The next attorney I contacted didn't do expulsions; the next three I called either failed to respond or said *they* didn't do expulsions. The next one (if you're counting, that's number fifteen) took my information and set me up with a conference call with three associates, who asked questions and would get back to me. When they did, it was, "No, thank you." The next one was also a "no response." Number seventeen was interested but had someone else in her office that was more up on special education and expulsion. She charged $175 per hour, and though she was great, I couldn't afford her or her partner. Looking back, after it was all said and done, $175 an hour would have been cheap. Not only would we have saved a lot of money, but we might have had a better chance of prevailing. You noticed I didn't say *winning*, I said *prevailing*. But more about that later.

I was getting discouraged. I took a referral from Dr. Mom and called a local attorney she was familiar with. She seemed interested, but was overwhelmed; however…her husband also practiced law. This husband-and-wife team would pretty much see us through to the end. The only other attorneys we used were as follows: one I had worked with in West Virginia who was a nationally known education lawyer, an associate of his who advised me on a number of related issues, and the teachers' association attorney. By the time the cash register was finished ringing from Sarah's defense at the local board all the way up to the end, we forked over a total of $25,000. And I was worried about $4,000. Justice comes at a price and lawyers sell the tickets. And these aren't like plane tickets or tickets to a movie or a show. There you're guaranteed a bit of entertainment or a service. With a legal case and lawyers, those tickets are more like lottery tickets. You might win big, and then again you might just be pouring more money down a rat hole. But just so you know we didn't throw all this money in the toilet, what follows is an explanation of how the case weaved it ways from the local board upward.

## The Case Goes To The State

Our attorney's arguments to the state board were numbered one through five: 1) The School District failed to conduct a prompt and thorough investigation, thereby depriving Sarah of due process. 2) The District failed to take into account state law ß 7-410 protecting kids who come forward seeking help for a drug problem. 3) The board's argument that ß 7-410 doesn't apply because "even though she had a previous drug problem it was for *marijuana*, not LSD, a different drug" is hollow, as was 4) that since she was drug free for a time, drug abuse protections don't apply, and, finally, 5) zero tolerance is the strict standard of expectations the District holds students to, and yet they fail to follow their own policies and procedures with respect to parental notification, prompt and thorough investigations, and protections for students who come forward seeking help.

Our attorney gave convincing arguments that blew holes in all of the district's specious arguments. He emphasized the admissions of both Coach and the assistant superintendent that without Sarah's cooperation, their investigation would have ground to a halt, and that they were obligated to inform parents that their daughter had allegedly ingested a controlled dangerous substance (LSD). About the only thing our attorney failed to note was the fact of Sarah's disability. And though I emphasized this, he chose to ignore it in his presentation to the State. It was a moot point. The State board met and, without argument, read the brief and ruled three weeks later. They failed to say why they upheld the local board's decision, only that they did. They did it with three sentences that took up less than half a page. For this we waited four months: <u>ORDER:</u> *Upon consideration of the letter of appeal, the Motion to Dismiss and/or for Summary Affirmance, and other documentation in the record, and finding that the local board did not violate the due process rights of the student or act in an otherwise illegal or unconstitutional manner, it is this 26th day of April, 1995, by the Maryland State Board of Education, ORDERED, that the*

*Motion to Dismiss and/or for Summary Affirmance be and the same is hereby granted. The decision of the System is therefore affirmed. See Md. Educ. Code Ann. 7-304 and COMA 13A. 01.01.03E(4); Adam McDonald v. Harford County Board of Education, 5 Op. MSBE 578 (1990) upholding an expulsion for the balance of the academic year for drinking and sharing of alcoholic beverages on school premises."*

So there we had it. No logical reason or explanation other than a reference to an *alcohol* case.

Don't tell me NO! Tell me why. This was no answer. It was a rubber stamp of the board's cursory decision. I still wanted my day in court.

## On To The Circuit Court For Judicial Review

We decided to take the case to the circuit court of his Honorable Judge. I went this route because I was advised to, and I assumed (wrongly I was to find out later) that you had to exhaust all your local administrative and state remedies before you could get into federal court. To be sure, I really believed that state courts would be open-minded, fair, and interested in the truth, a full review of the facts, and an impartial hearing of existing law applied against the facts we had presented in our case. That is what I thought a judicial review was. I filed this petition myself. I was fully intending to argue it myself as well, but judges and lawyers have this thing. Even after filing all my required papers, I heard nothing from the court (the judge), and yet I received this legal document from the other side's attorney telling me I was expected to file a formal "memorandum." To me it was asking me to give away my argument before the case was presented. "See you in court" was my response. I even called the court clerk to ask if I was required to file extra documents beyond my appeal, and request for the judge to review the state board decision. She didn't think so, and so I didn't respond to the board of education attorney's request. That's right, the

## The Search For An Advocate

board's attorney, the same man who moderated at the local board hearing, was now up front in defending the appeal to the circuit court. Next he hits me with SANCTIONS and a *motion to dismiss*. Seems that one of the ways lawyers make money is to spend their client's money writing memorandums back and forth. This way they have all of their arguments on paper before they even get into court. And despite the fact that the paper trail was already deepening like a new winter snow, I was told to respond or else. The court had a pile of documents already: they had the documents we presented at the local board hearing, and a full transcript of the three-hour hearing before the local board, not to mention the "briefs" that lawyer number two filed, and that number seven filed for the state board. They had it all, and we were ready to present oral arguments, and yet here we were being asked to send the circuit court judge yet another set of written legal arguments to prepare him for our oral arguments on court day. And the sanction...sanctions are like punishments or admonishments to lawyers who don't spend their client's money fast enough. I was being chastised for not following the rules, not playing their macabre game their way. "More paper, more paper, send us more paper!" I knew I was in over my head already. Going into a courtroom and arguing simple facts, common sense stuff is not how it's supposed to work. They have their own rules. Part of it is "We need a year to prepare for your case," but that's so we can read over all the documents that have been gathered during previous proceedings. In addition to all these transcripts of testimony, and psychological reports, and educational plans, and letters, and written decisions, we also need a memorandum, a summary from each side, so we can read one document and are refreshed on court day for the arguments. Remember this well, for these all-important memorandums will come into play later down the road.

Frustrated with the legal system and its cumbersome rules, I broke down and got back into the phone-calling business. Last but not least I spoke with attorney Liz. She had a nice voice and though she said she wasn't sure, she would at least meet with me to go over the case. I met her in her office. We talked and she took some of my documentation and indicated she would get back with me. In several days she did call. She said she was basically a researcher; however, her husband was also an attorney and he was a litigator. He might be interested in the case. She would share my file with him and have him call me. Several days later he called, and Caroline, Sarah, and I arranged to meet with him. He was what I describe as a "quick" learner. He pored through the briefs and had a very good sense of the arguments. More importantly he was the first attorney that was the least bit positive about our prospects, the first one that not only shared our enthusiasm, but our sense of "This ain't right." He laid out his terms, which were a flat fee for preparing the memorandums and appearing in circuit court on our behalf, $5,000. He would follow up our meeting with a written letter and payment schedule. We were back in business.

# What Do Learning Disabilities Have To Do With Anything?
## The Special Education Case

You may remember that I asked the principal to have Sarah evaluated when I turned her in for suspected drug use on that Thursday in October. In testimony later on, the principal says she "doesn't recall that," which is honest, but it goes to credibility...mine. In West Virginia I was director of special services. In this role I contracted with a highly respected attorney to help my district's administrators develop a policy for suspension/expulsion of handicapped kids. We did it in a one-day workshop and it was a policy with procedures that all my building principals could all live with, and that would meet the federal requirements of the recent "stay-put" provisions of the *Honig v. Doe* case that came before the Supreme Court. When I turned my daughter in for a possible expulsion, I was well aware of her disabilities and the law regarding suspension/expulsion of disabled children. It's my career, after all. Would I neglect to reveal the fact that she had a history of disabilities? As well, I wondered if there might be a causal link between those disabilities and her recent behaviors and, in that interest, was requesting a reevaluation. I distinctly remembered telling the principal that I "wasn't trying to get her out of anything, I just wanted to see if her previous history of learning disabilities was related to her current behavior problems." The principal responded that she would have to go through a screening committee first, and I didn't argue, though I knew a student with a history of being disabled didn't need to be "screened" first. Even when a student is "suspected" of having a disability, the district is required to evaluate. In the most recent reauthorization of IDEA, signed on June 4, 1997, by President Clinton, a district is required to afford a student all the rights and privileges of a disabled child as soon as a parent *requests an evaluation* for such a disability, even if the child has never been identified before, much less placed in a special education program for several years. A history of being previously identified as being disabled and served under an IEP is a far stronger burden of proof than a mere suspicion.

To reinforce my request, I approached my colleague, a fellow school psychologist (the same one who was incensed that I would call her to testify "against the board" on my daughter's behalf), and explained that my daughter was being referred for possible expulsion, and could she please prioritize her case and move her to the top of her list as a professional courtesy. I don't hold grudges and, above all, I am a professional and expect others bearing the title of school psychologist to be professional as well. Virginia mumbled something about being very busy, but agreed to get me a set of screening forms to fill out. I received them a short time later. What happened next was Sarah got expelled. She was prevented from returning to school for even one day while her mother and I prepared for her future. Having her evaluated somehow slipped off the front burner for a while. We raised this issue when her appeal was brought before the local board, but they rejected it along with our request to get her back in school. I think their attorney's words were along the lines of "(Special Education Team) decisions were out of their jurisdiction and should be pursued through other channels." The superintendent put it more succinctly: "what do learning disabilities have to do with anything?"

ARD (Admission Review and Dismissal) — A team of individuals from a variety of disciplines — classroom teachers, special education teachers, psychologists, principals, and parents — who meet to decide 1) what tests to give to children with learning problems; 2) what the results of the tests and other information mean; 3) whether the child is disabled; 4) what the child's needs are; and 5) what kind of plan is needed to enable the child to learn up to his or her capability.

## Formal Request For A Reevaluation

Two months after Sarah was suspended from school and five days before Christmas, the local board had upheld the superintendent's decision. I knew we would appeal the decision to the state board, and I also knew I had a right to another evaluation at county expense. I wrote the superintendent asking for him to conduct this evaluation, or to schedule a local due process hearing to explain to us why this should not be done. On January 13 we received his response. Three pages of blame and attack that ended with *"No, we will not evaluate her"* and *"No, we will not schedule a local due process hearing,"* as my daughter was in no way entitled to special education services or otherwise covered by the provisions of federal special education law.

I knew enough about the laws protecting special education students and the rights parents had to evaluations. I knew they were wrong, so I wrote the first of many letters, this one to the assistant state superintendent, Division of Special Education, for the State Department of Education. If anyone knew the law it was this department, which was responsible for enforcing it. The assistant state superintendent wrote the local superintendent back, "Unless there is additional information available, the school system must take immediate steps to conduct evaluations needed to determine if the student has a disability, or arrange for a due process hearing in accordance with applicable state and federal regulations." We were quite pleased, needless to say, and still willing to trust the professionals employed by the school system to do the job. I had full confidence in my colleagues to complete a thorough and comprehensive evaluation. I did not ask that an independent assessment be conducted by professionals outside the school district, I was comfortable with local colleagues. Sarah's evaluation was conducted several weeks later, and on February 28 a meeting was scheduled to review the results. We were relaxed and openly optimistic about the outcome. I *worked* with these folks; I never questioned their ability, their competence, or their professionalism. I also knew my daughter and the findings of her previous assessment. Learning disabilities may change, but they don't disappear. Three people would be involved in the meeting: the special education teacher from the high school performing the educational assessment, Miss Lori; the county school psychologist performing the intellectual and perceptual motor components, Miss Virginia; and the consortium school psychologist conducting the social-emotional (projective) testing, Miss Ann. I had full faith they would do a competent and professional job. Boy, was I in for a surprise!!

# And The Results Are In! Measuring Intelligence — The IQ

So what's an IQ anyway? The letters stand for "intelligence quotient," or a number assigned to just how smart you are. It's a way of comparing one person to another across a number of areas. The most commonly used IQ test at the time was the WISC-III, the Wechsler Intelligence Scale for Children, Third Edition, named for its developer, David Wechsler. The first WISC was developed in 1949 as an answer to the then-most-popular IQ test, the Stanford-Binet Form L-M. Here is a brief explanation of the WISC-III Cognitive Assessment (IQ test).

The test has two sections, a verbal section that measures language skills, Verbal IQ (VIQ), and a nonverbal section, performance IQ (PIQ), that measures hands-on tasks. A total or Full Scale IQ (FSIQ) is obtained as well. The test consists of twelve short tests or subtests, six in each section, that measure things like solving math problems in your head, defining words, explaining what you might do in a particular social situation, or answering factual questions, as in Trivial Pursuit. These theoretically test distinct areas of knowledge. The six performance tasks include puzzles and geometric designs the subject copies with blocks, and paper and pencil tasks. The tests are all standardized, that is, the examiner (who gives the test) asks the subject (the person taking the test) the same questions in the same way. If the subject asks questions of the examiner like, "What's a doormat?" the examiner can 1) repeat the question or 2) say: "Can you tell me more about that?" or 3) "Can you explain what you mean?" The idea is that the test is the wall and the subjects are the balls. Examiners judge how fast the balls hit, how far they bounce, and in what directions. Right and wrong answers are awarded points that are called raw scores. Raw scores are then converted to scaled scores that depend on the person's age. It wouldn't be fair to expect a ten-year-old to know as much as a twenty-year-old, so you're compared with people your own age. Each subtest score earns a scaled score from 0 to 19, with 10 the average. Each section (VIQ/PIQ) also earns a composite scale score from 0 to 180, with 100 being the average. Average scores mean that the majority of people who took the test earned this score or close to it (plus or minus ten [10] points [90-110]). How do they determine the average score? They give the IQ test to hundreds, even thousands of people, of all ages, sexes, geographic locations, socioeconomic levels, races, and occupations (or parents' occupations) in the United States. They plot the scores and, using statistical analysis, set the ranges for average, and just how much is way above or way below. On the WISC-III, if a score is fifteen points above or below (85 or 115) it is said to be significantly above or significantly below the mean (average). Fifteen points is considered to be a number to pay attention to, more than just eight or ten points, and fifteen is called a standard deviation and is a measure of how far scores may differ before it begins to mean something.

IQ tests are given to help determine if children have disabilities. If a student's IQ score is 70 or lower (100 points minus two standard deviations—$2 \times 15 = 30$) they might be considered "intellectually deficient." We used to call kids with these low IQs "mentally retarded," but the social stigma was so bad the test creators gave it more considerate (politically correct) names like "mentally challenged," "mentally deficient," "mentally handicapped," or "intellectually deficient." The newest IQ tests have backed off from names to descriptions. An individual who scores 70 or below on the WISC-IV, is said to have a score that is "extremely low." When you consider the names that were used to describe more extreme cognitive limitations fifty and sixty years ago, you'll appreciate how far we've come. Individuals with IQ scores below 70, below 55, and below 40 were, respectively, morons, imbeciles, and idiots. Can you imagine sitting down with a parent at a formal meeting and telling him or her that his or her child was an idiot? Talk about jaw-dropping revelations.

It all boils down to the same thing: if you answer most of the questions on the twelve subtests wrong, you get a low raw score, and when that score is compared with all of the other twelve-year-olds who took the test and yours is 30 points below theirs, and you also have similar problems with real life skills (dressing, finding your way around the community, writing checks, making and keeping friends, etc.) then you may qualify for special education with a mental or intellectual disability.

The most popular disability, and the most plentiful, isn't "intellectual deficiency," though. Lots of people have this disability, or think they do anyway. They aren't even embarrassed about it. It's called a learning disability. Lots of famous people, like Nelson Rockefeller and Albert Einstein, had learning disabilities. It's a real popular disability because you have to be smart to be considered learning disabled, and it is a very reasonable explanation for smart people who can't quite get it together. Lots of underachievers are mislabeled learning disabled, or LD for short. A few who are just plain lazy can be misdiagnosed as LD. One very real type of learning disability is dyslexia. That's where people reverse the order of letters in words. But there are a lot of other types of learning disabilities; dyslexia is only one rare example. Other examples involve the way people see things or hear things or express themselves in words or on paper, or how they organize information, including numbers.

How do you tell if a person has a learning disability? Well, the answer is a lot more complicated than this, but, simply stated, you give him or her an IQ test to find out how smart he or she is, and you look to see if he or she can perform verbal tasks better or worse than nonverbal tasks (that's one kind of learning disability), then you look at those twelve subtests to see if he or she has high and low scores (cognitive strengths and weaknesses) that indicate he or she can do some things really well and other things not so well. Next you look at the person's potential to learn from those IQ scores, and then you give him or her achievement tests in reading and spelling and math, and you compare. Achievement tests also have right and wrong answers (raw scores) and scaled scored based on an individual's grade level or age. They also use a similar scale, with 100 being "average." That way you can compare scores. Someone with a 100 IQ should be able to score close to 100 on his or her achievement tests. If he or she doesn't, and there's a "significant" difference (15 points again) then you can say there is a significant discrepancy between ability and performance and then check out a few other things (make sure the person has been in school and had the opportunities to learn and doesn't have sensory problems like visual deficits or hearing problems that might look like a learning disability but are really happening because they can't see or hear), and you can reasonably assume that the person's learning disability is preventing him or her from using his or her intelligence to solve math problems or read words or write stuff down. Now you're a psychological diagnostician!

Sarah's results on the tests my colleagues, the school district's employees, gave her were amazingly similar to those from eight years before when she was in West Virginia. Not only was her Full Scale score within three points, but her performance score was in the same range and her Verbal score increased from her previous assessment:

|                  | 1986 | 1995 |
|------------------|------|------|
| Verbal IQ:       | 88   | 104  |
| Performance IQ:  | 100  | 92   |
| Full Scale IQ:   | 92   | 95   |

More importantly her pattern of strengths and weakness was the same. Remember, the IQ scores are made up of ten subtest scores, five each for Verbal (language tests) and Performance (hand-eye coordination tests). These test scores range from 0-19, with 10 the average, and 3 points considered significant (standard deviation). So any score that is 8, 9, or 10, is average, and 11, 12, and 13 are better than average (high average) and scores that fall below, 5, 6, and 7, are below average. In her January 1986 WISC-R, all of her subtests were within normal limits except three:

|  | 1986 | 1995 |
|---|---|---|
| Arithmetic | 4 | 5 |
| Object Assembly | 6 | 7 |
| Vocabulary | 7 | 9 |
| Picture Arrangement | 12 | 14 |

Two evaluations separated by nine years with the same Full Scale IQ, similar Verbal and Performance IQs, and, even more importantly, cognitive strengths and weaknesses in the same areas! Her learning disabilities, as demonstrated by her individual subtest scores on the WISC-R and WAIS-R (Wechsler Adult Intelligence Scale-Revised) were consistent nine years later! Academic achievement also revealed huge gaps between areas, gaps known as "significant discrepancies" between ability and achievement. With average IQ scores one would expect academic achievement in the average range (90-110). On one test, the Peabody Individual Achievement Test-Revised (PIAT-R), her score ranged from 102 in reading (recognition) down to only 80 in mathematics. That's a 22-point difference, and remember, you only need 15 points to be significant.

On the only test designed to go with the Wechsler Intelligence Scales, the WIAT (Wechsler Individual Achievement Test), her standard scores ranged from highs of 132 in oral expression and 123 in written expression down to 85 in math...a 47-point difference! On another section of the same test, scores ranged from 121 for reading comprehension down to 89 and 84 for math reasoning and numerical operations respectively. These discrepancies were not only significant, they were *highly* significant. Though her reading and language skills had improved, her math skills were significant weaknesses. Her continued eligibility for special education and related services was clear. All you need for the state-suggested guideline is 15 points. Her discrepancy, her difference, was *three times that*, or 47 points! Emotional problems had been ruled out by Miss Ann, their examiner, but Sarah was still learning disabled. In a way I was relieved to find out. Not that I was happy she was still suffering from a disability, only that it explained a lot to me about her failures in school, her frustrations with learning, and maybe why she was turning to drugs.

When we sat down with the school district's assessment team to discuss Sarah's test results, the discussion went along fine until we started to talk about her needs. Sarah was not in school, you'll remember. Her expulsion was still in effect. But I wanted to confirm her status as a learning disabled child. I had no ulterior motive other than to confirm what I had maintained all along, that she was in fact still disabled. If her expulsion was illegal based on a disability and lack of a manifestation hearing, then her previous identification from 1986 was sufficient. Confirmation was only gravy. I wanted this as a logical step. I asked for an evaluation, she was tested, she was clearly eligible (at least from everything I ever knew about learning disabilities over a twenty-year career), and the results were done in house by their psychologists, resource teachers, and consultants. That's why I nearly died when they refused to discuss her eligibility, but only how great her grades were. The school psychologist, Miss Virginia, and the resource teacher, Miss Lori, and the special education supervisor refused to acknowledge what was right in front of their faces. Hundreds of kids were identified and placed in LD programs with scores far less revealing. That's when I realized what was happening. They were never going to admit she had a learning disability, or any disability, for that matter. In doing this they would admit to having made a grievous error.

A month later at a subsequent hearing, the school board's hired gun from Baltimore made a statement to the court of special appeals that Sarah had been evaluated and found "ineligible" for services. This was the "fact" he was afraid of having on the record: their own team conducting an evaluation and confirming that she was, in fact, disabled. But sitting there in April of 1995, there was no way of knowing what was to come. I was willing to rely on my unrefuted testimony that my daughter was previously identified as LD, and that the school system should have considered this before they expelled her. My primary focus for this evaluation was to determine her *current* educational needs. If she was still suffering from her learning disabilities, I wanted that to be known and, more importantly, to then examine her educational needs (did she need extra help in math, for example) and then use the test results to design a program for her when she returned to school. My intentions were true; I had no hidden agenda to use these current results to support or defeat the expulsion case, I simply wanted to help my daughter. *They* considered the possible linkage between her current status as learning disabled and the legality of their expelling her. They could not acknowledge her disability without admitting that they had erred in expelling her without a manifestation hearing. They would do anything to hide that fact. My motives were pure, and I couldn't understand why my peers, my colleagues, teachers, counselors, even fellow psychologists were lining up to interpret facts that were clearly indicating Sarah was disabled, as ineligible. Someone had gotten to them, and in their loyalty to the board, their job, their superintendent, they forgot their loyalty to their profession, to this child, to their own souls. They sold out. With all the talk about jury tampering, committing perjury, and coercion of witnesses, it's amazing how much went on in this young girl's case.

## What Is It You Want?

I've reviewed the transcript of that meeting to discuss her test results a number of times, and on it I'm quoted talking

## The Search For An Advocate

about her needs and what services would be provided based on those needs. Was I looking for private school, or home schooling, or a quick return to school? No, all I wanted was basic consultation services once she returned to a public school setting. That's it! Somebody to "keep track of her," in my own words. We talked about getting her ready for SATs, the accommodations she would need, and getting her ready for college. Making sure she had the appropriate courses (Algebra II and others). I kept trying to clarify the issues, and I'll quote directly from the transcript of the April 5, 1995, ARD: "Well, I always look at it in two steps. One is eligibility and the other step is needs, and from there we go to IEP, and then from there we go to program. So we've got a little distance between those two things. I would only say that I would like to see the eligibility determined now, because I think that the scores support that, and there is a history of her doing well with direct services that move into a consultation model with indirect services. And rather than have to do this all over again in a year (when she returned to school in the fall), if she does hit a lull, it would seem to make sense to me to determine her eligibility, to say that she doesn't have needs at this time...but we could monitor her for a year."

Due process is provided for disabled children and their parents in any number of documents, and it essentially boils down to this: Parents have certain rights, and the steps from testing to placement in special education programs take place in a very organized sequence. Parents give permission for assessment. Examiners administer the tests. A meeting is held to go over the test results and what they reveal. The team of parents and educators compare test results with state and federal eligibility criteria and decide if the child meets the criteria. Once he or she is determined eligible, his or her needs are discussed, then a plan is developed to address the needs (IEP) and then the team decides where (in what class and what special education teacher) the plan can be implemented.

## Conspiracy: The Hidden Agenda

That's where the hidden agenda came in. My colleague—the other school psychologist employed by the county, I believe, for she is not identified in the transcript—speaks up, "The way I understand it, if they only need accommodation, then actually they would be more likely to fit under a 504 plan rather than special education." I shot back, "That's if she's not eligible under IDEA," and the fireworks began. They started blabbering about having to have an *educational impact* and having a *condition,* a term reserved for seriously emotionally disturbed children. I was now upset. They were not working with a parent for the benefit of a child, but against the parent in every way they could, arguing semantics and every reason why she was not "eligible for special education." They ended with the circular argument that "So, she does not need specialized instruction. And if she doesn't need the specialized instruction, we are not going to call her learning disabled." This prompted my now infamous response: "So if you're blind and you do very well in a classroom because you can read Braille, does that mean you're not blind anymore?"

After an hour and a half, we finally got the team to agree that she had a learning disability in math. To be honest, many LD students do not deserve, do not need, special education if they are compensating for their disability. Earning passing grades is enough. And though her grades were passing, she still flunked the functional math test needed for graduation and had earned a 3 percent on the PSAT for math (Preliminary Scholastic Aptitude Test). That means 97 percent of the people who took the test did better than she did. The team report was filled out and signed by all present that she was learning disabled, and that they agreed that the "documentation support(s) the conclusion of a specific learning disability," but it was a monumental struggle. We did not discuss needs any further, or develop an IEP. We just stopped there. Why? There were two reasons: one, because it was all we could do to get this far, and two, because she was not in school. Why develop individual education goals for a student who won't be back to school for five months? We would wait until she was back in school, and then we would reconvene the school's special education team to discuss her needs and possible placement. Then and now I never wanted private school (meaning thousands of dollars for the board) or even direct services, meaning a special education teacher would have to spend time with her each day. All I wanted was someone to monitor, to oversee her educational program, Level I or Intensity I, even Consultation; someone with expertise in specific learning disabilities to watch over her where I couldn't. I had asked Coach to watch her because I was worried about drugs. That failed. Now I was asking someone to watch her because I was worried about her finishing high school. That's all. This was April 1995. I had no ulterior motive other than assuring my daughter's success once she returned to the public school setting in September of 1995.

That same week the state board of education met to read arguments about her expulsion. In May they rendered their decision upholding the local board's decision to expel Sarah. Five months and several thousand more dollars for nothing? Maybe the superintendent's threats to Caroline that we were wasting our time were valid. This was the "good ol' boy network," as he'd described it. At the time our attorney had advised us to appeal to the local circuit court. If I knew then what I know now, I wouldn't have wasted a minute of my time or a nickel of my money on this sham of a process. I would have gone directly to federal court. But what did I know? I thought you had to start with local and work your way up to federal. But here we were trying to get our day in court, so we appealed to the courts and filed a request for a judicial review at the circuit court of our home county. I'd filed the appeal on May 24.

On May 25 I would come to understand just how far my employers would go to stifle dissent. On this day, one day after I filed my appeal of the circuit court ruling, I received the first in a series of formal reprimands from my superiors. The next day I received my second reprimand. They were obvious messages for me to back off. A line had been crossed between my role as parent and my role as employee. They crossed it by formally reprimanding me for matters that had nothing to do with my job performance. I knew things would get rough, but I didn't know how rough.

# CHAPTER NINE

# MOTIVATIONS OF MY OWN— FEBRUARY 25, 1995

Conventional wisdom has it that psychologists go into the field so that they can work out their own problems. In other words, you go to school to be trained to analyze yourself. You become a psychologist to learn how to observe, how to be perceptive. I maintain that just the opposite is true. I did not become a psychologist to be perceptive. I *was* perceptive; that's why I became a psychologist. I was able to read people like books. I knew things about them they didn't even know, and when I turned the spotlight on myself, I gained insights into my own motivations. Over the years I have become quite comfortable being me. If it's *Physician, Cure Thyself,* then for shrinks it's *Psychologist, Know Thyself.* I can be hard on myself, too. I take to heart not only what others say about me, but what I discover about myself. Maslow, in his hierarchy of needs, talks about stages of development people go through. The highest state is "self-actualization."

This is a stage in which you are fully aware of your strengths and weaknesses and have gained maximum control over the latter. All of us strive for this level of consciousness in this field. To help others get right with themselves, you have to set a good example and be in the position of improving yourself. I mean, who's going to pay a therapist $90 an hour who sits there and cries, or gets angry with you? How about $50 an hour for one who sits there and picks his nose, or passes gas every time you tell him some deep dark secret about yourself? That's not what I'd call "aroma therapy."

From time to time I've done "reality checks" on my actions with respect to this case of Sarah's. Do I have any hidden agendas or cross motivations? Both Caroline and I were employees in the same school district Sarah was enrolled in. Both of us had been asked to make ethical compromises, as many others had, as a condition to employment. This latest series of incidents taxed our ethical compasses. Caroline and I go to work every day and are front men for the district; we sell their line that we all work for the *best interests of children* in the district, something that has been most difficult to do knowing what we do about the manner in which these children, our daughter and her friends, were dealt with in this case. It's almost as though we needed to persist to force this system to "clean up its act" for the benefit of other children and families, as well as to enable us to be a part of this system and remain true to our calling: child advocacy. We've been accused of forgetting who pays our salaries, who we work for; of lacking loyalty to our employer, even "biting the hand that feeds you."

Sarah's situation was very similar. The corruption is the longstanding problem with drugs at the district's largest high school. We were aware of it, especially when my daughter was caught at home with the marijuana and she filled us in on how widespread it was at school. At the time we wanted to ask school officials about how often they brought in dogs to search for drugs, or whether they could do urine screening

## Motivations Of My Own—February 25, 1995

of athletes. We took care of our daughter's situation in the spring when we found her involved in drugs, but we didn't take that next step, going to the school or going public. Why? Because we didn't want to put our children in the position of having parents who "narced" on the school. It wasn't any of "our business."

When they expelled Sarah they *made* it our business. We urged her to turn herself in and we looked to the board and the administrators to do the right thing. But they didn't. They used her and the other students as scapegoats to give the appearance that they were "tough on drugs," all while they were allowing it to go on unchecked. The very act of expelling these kids for being honest effectively sent out a very strong message to other students, DON'T TELL. It merely forced the problem underground.

And so we are now forced to pursue this to its ultimate end. Not only for the sake of our daughter and the other kids this time, and the next kid who gets caught, but for the sake of our district's integrity, so they can look at the drug problem in a more honest, more realistic manner and take actions to make the school system safer, drug free, and more open. Child advocates don't punish and isolate children, especially those who are nonviolent and in need of help and guidance; they reach out to them. *Treatment* is what they need, firm but fair limits clearly spelled out, and logical consequences for their actions. And though violence is abhorrent, even violent children deserve consideration—crisis intervention, conflict resolution skills, as well as counseling to help them deal with the rage and anger they are venting—for expelling them only turns them over to a community ill-equipped to handle them.

In this interest I wrote a letter to the one group I felt could have an impact on county policy, the Citizens Advisory Council. Trouble is, the chairman is also assistant superintendent, and chairman of the expulsion panel. I wrote him the following letter anyway:

Mr. Chairman
Citizens Advisory Council
Main Street
USA

Dear Mr. Chairman, March 22, 1995

As you are well aware, I am in the process of appealing a decision rendered by the board of education with respect to a violation of the current *Student Code of Conduct*. Whatever the outcome of my daughter's case, I continue to have a range of serious concerns relative to this policy and its impact on the safety and health of all students attending district schools. I refer of course to the fact that students with drug and serious alcohol problems are too often excluded from their public school experience, with no provisions for alternative education, much less treatment. At the same time, students who commit violent acts against students and staff are offered opportunities both within and outside the regular school day. I have a serious problem with a "zero tolerance" policy that isolates children with substance abuse problems and allows "discretion" for students who bring weapons, including knives and handguns, into our public schools.

In this interest, I am requesting that the Citizens Advisory Council conduct a thorough review of this policy and its impact on the health and safety of our schoolchildren. A policy that forces students and their parents to lie to avoid the mandatory provisions of this policy also prevents these same individuals from receiving the help they so badly need. Public input from parents, teachers, administrators, students, and other members of our community is strongly advised. Recommendations should be forwarded to the board of education for immediate action.

In light of your position as assistant superintendent of schools for the district, not to mention your role as chairman of the expulsion panel, I respectfully request that you step down from your role as chairman of the advisory council during these proceedings and deliberations. This would avoid any appearance of conflict of interest.

Sincerely yours,
Frank L. Matthews

Of course, you can guess what his response was. I mean, here was the man who expelled a twelve-year-old in 1986 for bringing in three marijuana seeds. This one went before the state board and they upheld this decision. He believed in the get-tough policy. "It worked. Why should we change it?" And as long as he was assistant superintendent, chairman of the expulsion panel, and chairman of the advisory council, which consisted of parents, some whom might not approve of his policy, then he better stay right there to make sure they didn't change it on him.

He wrote back explaining the only issues the advisory council bring up are those the board or the superintendent suggests. How is that for a closed loop? Or more like circling the wagons. So the Citizens Advisory Council only discusses issues the superintendent wishes and *allows* them to discuss. Sounds like another dog and pony show, doesn't it?

I was not to be deterred, so I decided to work around them, and when I was contacted by a member of the Advisory Council I had my opportunity. I received drafts of their Revisions of the *Student Code of Conduct* and gave the member my input, which she shared with the committee along with her own. I kept my suggestions fair and professional. For example, I pointed out that it would be helpful if parents were apprised of their rights, especially if their children were coming under questioning by the board for possible expulsion. The new policy that finally came out wasn't perfect, but it made sure that parents reading about procedures for Class III offenses would know to look at the end of the document for *Special Considerations for Drug and Alcohol*, the section I missed. After each section of the policy appeared the following statement: "See *Special Considerations for Drug and Alcohol*." They also made it quite clear that special education students would be handled in accordance with federal guidelines. And, most significantly, they opened the door for an alternative school program for drug and alcohol cases. My daughter would not have been expelled had this new policy been in effect. I had some sense of satisfaction in this, since my fight was to make sure what happened to her did not happen to another student.

Anyone expelled today for drugs should know going in what he or she is up against. The Code of Conduct is explained to every student in every classroom the first day of school, and teachers sign a roster that they have received a copy, handed it out to students, and explained the zero tolerance section. If there is any vindication for me, this is where it lies.

If I could write my own policy, my student code of conduct would look like this:

I. Zero Tolerance/Mandatory Expulsion vs. Discretion in All Cases

A. Acts of violence against school
1. Vandalism/arson
2. Crimes against students/staff
3. Weapons
4. Distribution of CDS

B. Separation from day school for remainder of year — first offense
1. Alternative School for Education–day program
2. No contact with general population (no social events)
3. Remedial programs
a. School beautification projects
b. Community service projects
c. Conflict resolution workshop required
d. "Scared Straight" prison visits

II. Substance Abuse—First Offense, Clean Discipline Record (Maintained Four Years)

A. Suspension-ten days—required to make up work at day school—research on drugs.
B. Immunity from prosecution—Parents/student who turns self in
C. Remedial programs
1. In-house therapy
2. Regular urine checks
3. Community service
4. School service
5. "Scared Straight" ER visit

D. Second offense/CDS in specimen—removal from day program to evening program
No contact with general population—referral to drug rehabilitation program

III. Student Review Committee

A. Peer review for problems/counseling
B. Peer mediation/conflict resolution/crisis intervention
C. Substance abuse education—required course for graduation—recovering peers

IV. Gathering Information on Substance Abuse

A. Parent/guardian must be present when minor child is interviewed for Type II and III
B. Witnesses who provided report must be produced—anonymous sources not used
C. Regular searches of school with dogs unannounced
1. Lockers
2. Cars
3. Grounds

D. Urinalysis for all those who wish to participate in team sports; student's right to privacy vs. protection from dangerous practice

E. Parent pledge—voluntary agreement between parent/student for routine screening
"Urine the Clear" program (You're in the clear)

## A Simple Recommendation: Retention

In my mind I had two distinct roles: as father, and as a loyal employee. I planned to balance both roles in a professional manner. I would keep my personal case and my personal life out of my daily job. When my daughter's case came up, I would be a worthy adversary against the board. I would be an adversary only because they were forcing me to be one by their refusal to return her to school and provide the services she was entitled to. In all other cases I would be a loyal employee, fighting for the reputation of the board, selling their product to the public. I had every intention to continue my advocacy for children and to put the board in the best light possible. But they made this next to impossible for me. They set me up.

The first reprimand was from the principal in one of the schools I served in the district. I had been assigned to this school since first arriving in the district. It was my first home base, and the staff and I worked well together. I started out with Mr. Dave, the best principal I've ever worked under, and then a brief sojourn with another who made me give up my office and home base though I remained in his school as his psychologist. We got along better after I left. The third principal at this school came in from a small school in the southern part of the county. I got along fine with him, though he was headstrong, arrogant, and not open to discussion. Anyone that knew Mr. B knew it was his way or the highway. He was hands-off special education at his previous school, allowing us (the two resource teachers and me) to handle meetings.

## Motivations Of My Own — February 25, 1995

When the going got tough, he knew he could count on me to help out, like the day we had to carry an unruly student out to a waiting patrol car. We all got along fine. We did here at this school as well. He knew my work, that I did my job well, and he trusted me. He rarely attended meetings or second-guessed me. That is until the heat got turned up on me, and him. He might have counted on me, but when the going got tough I could not expect the same support.

The case was a simple one. Part of my job was to help determine which kids were in need of evaluation and which needed other interventions I was trained in and willing to provide. My background and training, not to mention two decades of experience testing close to two thousand kids, gave me a clear insight as to what to look for in a student. Even before I gave the test, I could give pretty good odds on who would qualify and who would not.

Mr. B was insistent that I test this little girl who was developmentally delayed. She was born prematurely in December. Had she been full term, she would not have even been born until February, well past the December 31 cutoff for starting kindergarten. She struggled at four years old through kindergarten, was recommended for retention by her kindergarten teacher, and would have been retained except for one thing. Her parents were planning to move to Florida, a state that only provided a half-time kindergarten program. If she truly needed help, they argued, then why take her from a full-day kindergarten program here and place her into a half day program there? Why not promote her to a first-grade setting? If she still had troubles then they could always retain her at the end of first grade. This is where I came in...at the end of a very difficult first grade. Turns out they didn't move and were still here in the district. This little gal, not yet six, was placed in first grade and struggled the whole year. When I examined her history and her grades and her work, and the precise nature of her problems, I recommended retention in first grade. "Test her for special education," Mr. B said. "She is developmentally delayed, not disabled," I responded. "Test her," Mr. B repeated. So I did. My evaluation confirmed everything I said previously: she needed to start first grade again. She was not disabled, she was just a five-year-old ready for first grade, not second.

The special education meeting to share my findings with the parents was scheduled, and as a courtesy I stopped in before the meeting to talk with Mr. B about my recommendations to the team (classroom teacher, special education teacher, administrator, parents). I was being careful, even cautious in those days. I knew he was "quota conscious" as a result of the state "report card" for the school system that rated how many kids were promoted, how many came to school each day, how they scored on group tests, how many dropped out, etc. The funny thing was that most educators had little control over how kids scored on the tests or if they came to school. But there was one factor they could control: retention rates. Pass all the little children on and you get a 100 percent promotion rate, and the state smiles down on you. Mr. B loved this rule because he didn't believe in retaining kids anyway. And the superintendent didn't either. So here we are in Mr. B's office talking about this little girl he had wanted me to test because he didn't want to retain her, hoping instead she'd qualify for special education. In the office with us was the assistant principal. Mr. B had read my report, which suggested that the little girl was not disabled and therefore not eligible for special education. He also saw where I presented my case about her being delayed and needing to repeat the first grade. He then proceeded to tell me I was not to recommend retention at the meeting. I had done what he had asked me to do, evaluate her, despite my sense of what needed to be done. My test results supported my suspicions and my recommendations. I will always remember the expression on the assistant principal's face when I dared to say, "Mr. B, I have to recommend retention to the parent. It's my professional responsibility to give parents all of the options I believe are viable." Randy, the assistant principal, looked like someone right before a balloon that is overinflated gets ready to explode. That balloon was Mr. B.

## Motivations Of My Own — February 25, 1995

No one ever questioned Mr. B, much less disagreed with him. She thought he'd blow for sure. I also remember the expression on her face when he said, "Okay, but you make it clear at the meeting that the final decision to retain her is mine, not the team's." I agreed to do that, and you could see the relief spread across her face. I would make my recommendation, the team could support it or not, and the decision, the responsibility for changing that recommendation, the "veto," was his. By the way...federal law allows no veto, only a team consensus.

And that is precisely what I did. Both parents attended the meeting, along with the special education teacher, the regular class teacher, the speech therapist, a number of others, and me in my role as school psychologist. Who was missing? An administrator. The assistant principal was busy, according to the building secretary, and would be there as soon as she could. This was the same assistant principal who held her breath when I made the statement regarding my responsibility to the team, to the parent, and, most importantly, to the child. Mr. B, the building principal, the same one who reserved the right to veto any decision this team made, was not present.

We all presented our individual pieces, and I went over the results of the psychological assessment I had recently completed. The little girl was not learning disabled; that was good news. Her IQ was within normal limits with no particular strengths or weaknesses, and her achievement testing confirmed that she was developmentally on track...for a *beginning* first grader. Trouble was, this was May, the *end* of her first-grade experience. In addition, her delays were a carryover from the previous school year when her kindergarten teacher recommended that she repeat the grade. Her parents insisted that she be promoted to first grade and she was, and now she was a year behind her grade level peers. We looked at a number of options. *Reading recovery program* — fine, but it ended for second graders in December. *Family class* — mom did not want her in the same room with the same teacher for three years. *Learning disability program* — But she wasn't eligible; she was not disabled. We kept coming back to...retention. Not wanting to be the driving force behind this recommendation, I took a poll. In the past I've been accused of unduly influencing others, primarily because I do my homework and make persuasive arguments. Let everyone vote independently, I thought. Every member of the ARD, including the parents, was in favor of retention. But remember, we couldn't make this recommendation without an administrator present. I got up and flicked the call button on the intercom. Maybe I am paranoid, but it seemed too pat that the assistant principal was sitting right there by the intercom, answering my question before I even asked it. "Yes, Mr. Matthews, I'm on my way." So she joins us. I give her an overview of all that has been discussed, and then turn it over to her. "Well, we can't make the recommendation for retention as an ARD," she says, and Mom starts to cry. ARD stood for admission review and dismissal and was a function of the federal guidelines for developing and reviewing programs for disabled children. "Do you mean I have no say in this!?" the mom sighed. "Oh, yes, you do, you have a very important part, but you need to discuss this with Mr. B," the assistant principal intoned. I added to the discussion, telling the parents that this would be difficult because "the principal is not a big advocate of retention, and you will have your work cut out for you." The meeting ended. I go about my duties and return to my home school.

## The Next Day — Worrying About The Parents

The next day I am worrying about these two parents. I can see them trying to explain why they want their daughter retained. The principal needs to know what's up, so I write him a short letter stating my position and why I feel she should be retained. I felt it would help the parents out as well. I hand deliver it to the principal at the end of the school day. He grabs the letter out of my hand and calls for me to come into his office, where he proceeds to explode, literally screaming at me with his office door wide open.

"HOW DARE YOU INTENTIONALLY COUNTERMAND AN INSTRUCTION I GAVE YOU? I TOLD YOU *NOT* TO RECOMMEND RETENTION FOR THIS GIRL, AND NOT ONLY DID YOU DO THIS, BUT YOU TOOK A VOTE OF ALL OF THE COMMITTEE MEMBERS IN FRONT OF THE PARENT!" He banged on a pile of books on the corner of his desk so hard they crashed to the floor. He approached me, coming around from behind his desk and waving his finger in my face, and continued, "YOU'LL NEVER WORK IN THIS DISTRICT AGAIN IF I HAVE ANYTHING TO SAY ABOUT IT. THIS IS INSUBORDINATION, AND I INTEND TO REPRIMAND YOU FOR IT!"

I recovered and attempted to clarify my position and, more importantly, my understanding of what we had discussed just prior to the meeting: I was authorized to make the recommendation, just as long as I made it clear he had the final say. He insisted he had told me otherwise. "Well," I said, "let's get the assistant principal in here. She was present during that discussion." The assistant principal was called in and, when asked for her recollection, to my utter amazement she agreed with him. "He told you *not* to recommend it." I started to explain to her my thinking and how I would never have agreed to this arrangement, but I realized it would be a waste of good air...I'd been set up, and the trap was sprung. They would even lie for each other. I walked out, tail between my legs, secretaries and teachers doing their best to look at the papers in their hands and avoid eye contact with me. I slinked out of the building and headed straight for the office of my supervisor, a former school psychologist. He was standing in the parking lot having a smoke, and I spilled out the story. He was sympathetic, but could offer no solution. So what else is new. I was starting to wonder if anyone had a backbone in this district.

As I look back at this situation, and similar situations in my fifth position in my fourth state, I realize that it's the same no matter where you are. The classic battle between the administrators and the nonadministrators, and when the going gets tough, they circle the wagons and lie for each other rather than admit that an underling was correct. It's a battle I fought in the first job I had in state number one, state number three, and at the end of my career in state number four, right up to the last months of my employ. And why did I not have problems in state number two, you ask? Because I was an administrator as well as a school psychologist. And if you are wondering why I "didn't get it" after over thirty-eight years, let me tell you, just because I "got it," and believe me, I got it good, didn't mean I could behave any differently. I was, and am, a child advocate with a distinct role, one that became more clearly defined to me over the years, such that even though the ambushes and ordinance they hurled at me was intense and frightening, I had only one mode of behavior: to continue to charge into the furor with my little children at my side. Had I not continued to protect them, even at great expense to myself, I would not have been able to function or sleep at night. My programming was sound, it was solid, and even when I tried to compromise, to meet them halfway, I knew where the lines were and I respected them. Such was the role I chose as an advocate for disabled children.

## Making Peace?

I called the principal's office Monday to ask if I could stop over to talk with him. We sat down in his office and he closed the door. He was calmer. We talked nice. I apologized for any misunderstanding and asked for him to give me another chance. Remember, I'm pursuing an appeal of the board of education's decision to the circuit court. I need to keep my battles on one front, and I don't need additional trouble with supervisors, even though I had tenure. He apologized for yelling at me (a rare occurrence, I'm told) and agreed that although his first inclination was to ask to have me transferred out of his building, he would be willing to work with me again. I reminded him of the times I'd helped him out of jams, including the time I'd helped him carry that angry, kicking, and screaming boy out of the school to place him in a police cruiser. That's why I was so surprised the next day when I received a letter of reprimand. It didn't fit. Why, if we both "made up," did he still file a formal letter against me? When I got the second one from another principal the very next day, I understood why.

## Strike Two!

Mountain View was not only my favorite school, but it was where my wife, Caroline, worked as the elementary guidance counselor. She got along fine with the staff and the new principal. I had worked there for six years and established a tremendous rapport with the teachers. The case involved a youngster whose parents were extremely upset. They believed that not enough was being done for their son. I compiled a three-year chronology from my records for the principal so she could adequately defend our extensive efforts. We were finally getting the psychologist from the consortium to evaluate him for SED (serious emotional disturbance), and it looked like he would be one of the rare kids who qualified. In this district, they did not allow their own psychologists to identify disabled children who might be emotionally disturbed; they relied on a clinical psychologist and extremely conservative criteria to label children with this classification. The student was a very bright youngster who did absolutely nothing in class except disrupt, get kicked out, and spend the day in the office, day after day after day. I would say that he was in the office on more Wednesdays than not, and I couldn't account for the rest of the week. I had set up behavioral programs for teachers and parents, I encouraged staff members to consider a small self-contained classroom where he would not be overstimulated and a more structured behavioral program could be implemented. This was a classroom designed for children like this with behavioral and emotional problems, children who, by the federal definition, were emotionally disturbed.

## The Gatekeeper

The clinical psychologist contracted by the district was conducting the evaluation. Initially, at the first IEP Team meeting, he hinted that he was going to recommend placement, but didn't have enough information. It seems the social worker hadn't completed her home assessment. This would buy them more time (and lose the kid more time). Several weeks went by and the social worker did her home study and another meeting was scheduled. Just before the second meeting, the building principal looked frustrated. It seemed that the clinical psychologist had changed his mind and was not going to recommend the student as eligible for the program after all. I was shocked. I thought it was in the bag. I then took a bold step. For fourteen years I evaluated students who were placed in programs for emotionally disturbed children in both Virginia and West Virginia. In this state, number three, it was highly politicized for some reason, and only the clinical psychologists were allowed to render this diagnosis. I recalled a time when I attended graduate school with other psychology students working on their master's degrees. Some were in a one-year program designed to allow them to work in a clinic. Others, including me, were in a two-year program designed to allow us to work in the public schools as school psychologists. As it turned out, the one-year clinicals were allowed to diagnose emotional disturbance in the clinics, but the two-year school psychologists were not allowed to do the same with students in our own school buildings. Together with a whole host of school psychologists, we lobbied and had this turned around such that we were also allowed to evaluate, classify, write behavior plans, and even counsel students with emotional disturbances.

## Motivations Of My Own—February 25, 1995

You can imagine my surprise when I moved from West Virginia to state number three, a so-called progressive state, only to find out that once again the clinical psychologists were in charge, in this case only those with doctorates, or PhDs. The clinical psychologist from the consortium that served my district told me in an in-service on the subject that he was in fact the "gatekeeper," a clear violation of federal guidelines which allow school psychologists to participate in this decision-making process. His assuming the gatekeeper role also excluded important and essential input from all of the other members of the team: the teachers who saw the child every day, school administrators who were involved in discipline, and special education teachers with knowledge and expertise in all of the various disabilities, including emotional disturbance. Were these specialized teachers somehow able to teach these children but unable to recognize and help to identify them? And what about the school psychologists and parents of these children? I'd attended school meetings where twelve members of the school staff, school psychologist included, sat around and agreed on the diagnosis of emotional disturbance only to be overruled by a single team member, the clinical psychologist. I had attended meetings that included principals, classroom teachers who were with the child all day, and specialists in music, art, gym, special educators, guidance counselors, professionals all. All twelve agreed in classifying him emotionally disturbed, and one man exercised a veto he had no legal right to. I had nothing but contempt for this process or the man who wielded his authority so indiscriminately. To be honest I believe he held a similar impression of me. But he had the power. For now...

Here I was, knowing full well that this youngster could benefit from the services, and yet we were stymied by the system. I suggested something quite ordinary, and yet something quite radical just the same. I offered to do my own assessment, to make my own recommendations to the team, and the building principal agreed. My results confirmed his eligibility. I followed all the right procedures, gave him all the right tests, and had teachers rate him on behavior scales, and I used the federal and state guidelines to conclude he met the criteria. I shared this with the building principal and gave her a copy of my report. The principal spent the next week telling all the teachers that if the issue was raised at the meeting, they were to support it. The day approached. May 1995. The clinical psychologist and the principal were sitting in her office. I was invited in. The psychologist and I argued for some time about who was able to make this recommendation and how, according to him, it was his call. I looked at the principal, who avoided any eye contact; all I saw the top of her head. She said nothing, so I held my ground. The clinical psychologist suggested a compromise. "Label him as eligible under Section 504 and not special education laws, and I'll support his placement in the program without having to classify him as emotionally disturbed." "Fine," I said, "If he gets the help, I'm not hung up on what we call him." With that assurance we entered the meeting.

## The Ard—The Real Meeting

After some discussion, we got to the part of the meeting where the clinical psychologist assured me he would recommend we make a placement in a special class under 504 rules which allow "reasonable accommodations for individuals with disabilities." I began to talk about the specialized classroom in the neighboring school that was designed for children with behavioral and emotional problems and how I felt this was a good place for him. The clinical psychologist interrupted me, "I think you're getting a little ahead of yourself, we need to determine eligibility first." He wanted to clear the table; according to him, the child was not emotionally disturbed. He was not learning disabled. I was okay with that. I was not happy with the next words out of his mouth. "Now we can reschedule a meeting with the chairman of 504 Committee (who was not present) to discuss his eligibility for that service." Now wait just a minute. What happened to all the assurances of placement based on 504? We were going to take away all his protections of disability LD, SED (for seriously emotionally disturbed) for a possible 504 eligibility at yet another meeting down the road? That was *not* my expectation or my understanding (not to mention the agreement we'd come to earlier that day), and I moved the recommendation for services based on my finding of emotional disturbance back on the table. We argued heatedly for fifteen to twenty minutes. At the end I called for a consensus.

The student's third-grade teacher number one: "SED." Third-grade teacher number two: "SED." Guidance counselor: "SED." Gym teacher: " SED." Resource special education teacher: "SED." Mental health counselor: "SED." School psychologist: "SED." Clinical psychologist: "Not eligible." The principal—now remember, she was the one who encouraged me to conduct my own evaluation, who walked all around the school with my report in hand encouraging all the teachers at the meeting to support my findings—incredulously, she voted "not eligible" and every member of her staff looked at her in complete surprise. After spending weeks telling them to support the SED diagnosis I formulated, she was voting against me *and* her staff. And, more importantly, she was voting against this student. Then it came to the parents, the most important part of the team. Dad spoke up first when he said he agreed with the rest of us, his son needed the class: "SED." The meeting closed down with clinical psychologist remarking, "Well, I guess you win some, and you lose some." This was the first time he was ever overruled, but it wasn't over yet.

## The Secret Meeting

A week later the special education supervisor, the same administrator who sat in my daughter's meeting the previous month and made sure *she* didn't qualify for services, reconvened the ARD *without* the two classroom teachers, or the mental health counselor, or the guidance counselor, or the school psychologist. They undiagnosed him. He was no longer found eligible for the SED program. The handwriting was on the wall. Administrators proved that decisions could be made top down, even when all the members of the legitimate multidisciplinary team felt differently. And we're not talking about one psychologist "forcing his way on others," we're talking about an administrator (in this case a special education supervisor and out-of-district psychologist) forcing her way on a team by meeting without the major players present. No school psychologist or classroom teacher or mental health counselor. Politics at its worst, playing games with children's lives. Violating the spirit and the letter of the law that was designed to protect the disabled. It was beyond disgusting, it was contemptible.

I didn't protest, I was just confused, sickened. I didn't understand what had happened in that first meeting with the teachers and everybody. Why had the principal voted against us? I really wanted to figure out what happened. I went in to talk with her. The best she could come up with is that we (the clinical psychologist, the principal, and I) had agreed behind closed doors to go with a 504. Then I went into the meeting and switched to push the emotional condition. I explained to her that I did this only after the clinical psychologist failed to live up to his commitment to support the 504 placement. I was not going to be party to taking this kid out of all services unless something else was in place (he was receiving some support in a special education program designed for children with learning disabilities). The principal felt I should have trusted the clinical psychologist to support the 504 at the subsequent meeting. I had already seen this man in action. I did not trust him. Even more importantly, he does not call the shots for 504 placements, only special education, and I wasn't taking the chance on another meeting with different players. All the members of this team agreed about his needs for help. What was I missing?

I think I walked into her office on at least two other occasions, I was so bothered by this decision. I was there to chat and figure it out. I needed to understand. She never seemed angry and she never suggested that I had done wrong, only that she felt I had broken an agreement with her to support the 504 finding. This is why I was so surprised when, the day after I got the principal Mr. B's reprimand, and almost three weeks after the meeting to place the student at this school, I received reprimand number two from this building principal. She accused me of failing to be a team player. Excuse me? I mean seven out of nine were in favor of my recommendation, so who's let the team down? I was not going to let either of these reprimands stand if I had anything to do with it.

I contacted my union representative and the teacher's association attorney. All it took was a quick phone call between attorneys to fix this one. Seems it is highly unethical for an administrator to pressure a professional about an opinion. Mr. B's letter stating, "I made it very clear that I did not want you to recommend or discuss retention in a formal meeting with any parent. Retention is an administrative decision and is not a decision which is made by a special education committee" was highly inappropriate. There have been court cases about what special education team members can and cannot discuss, and retention is clearly in their domain, even if the final *decision* is administrative. Their attorney (the same fellow from Baltimore I would meet later on) felt that this letter could open the county for any number of lawsuits, and would withdraw it. The other principal's written statement, "When a decision is made to which you are a part and to which you agree, I expect you to stand by that decision regardless of any possible decisions that may be made by another committee or group of individuals at some future time," was also problematic. This was a legally constituted special education team, and regardless of "the fact that we entered a public meeting with the understanding and agreement that certain things would happen and then during the meeting you changed your position without letting me know is unprofessional and not in the 'team' spirit in which we make decisions and operate." But that's just the point. Meetings with parents and professionals can turn in any number of directions. They aren't supposed to proceed according to some preplanned agenda. I had a right, a duty, to make my professional recommendation to the special education team as the situation developed. The interesting thing is that it was she who changed her position, from supporting the placement to not supporting it, and it was she who stood against the "team spirit" by supporting an outsider (clinical psychologist) rather than her own staff and the school psychologist she'd asked to conduct the evaluation. Both of these should have been tossed out on the lack of merit as well as the technicalities involved. But then again, in public education administrators can't screw up, so even if they are wrong, someone else catches the blame. And in this case it was me. I "win" both grievances, and in August the superintendent calls me into his office. And it wasn't for an apology either.

# CHAPTER TEN

# '95–'96 INVOLUNTARY TRANSFER TO SECONDARY

In the spring, my so-called colleague, the other school psychologist, informed the administration that she was leaving. With one of our three school psychologists leaving, I knew the middle and high schools would be opening up and felt I would like a chance at a different caseload, not to mention different work day, seven forty-five to three. For eight years I had been going in early, seven forty-five, and staying until four, the elementary dismissal time. The other two psychologists came in the same time I did, at seven forty-five, but were free to leave at three. This was due to the fact that they both worked in secondary schools, grades seven through twelve, while I was at the elementary level, kindergarten through sixth. I just wanted *one* secondary school with earlier hours. The other reason I wanted a change was to give me a break from the torrent of new referrals and screenings for children suspected to have attention deficit disorders and other conditions that pour out of the elementary settings. By middle school most of the original diagnoses have been worked out, so it's more reevaluation and behavior management for adolescent energies.

I asked to be taken out of one of my elementary schools and placed in a middle school instead. Here's what the superintendent said: "Because we only have two psychologists, I am dividing the schools in half." So far, so good. "I am grouping the five elementary schools together (what?!) and the two middle and high schools together, and will be reassigning you to the *secondary schools* since you have more experience on that level than Lucy (the remaining psychologist)." What is it they say, be careful what you ask for because you might get it? But this was a crazy idea. He could have pulled a former school psychologist who moved into central office back into service, or divided them by size or caseload, but this didn't make sense. Wanting out of *one* of three elementary schools was my wish, picking up two more would have been a crusher, but giving them *all* up? And being exclusively in the secondary level was something else. Over a twenty-two year career I had always had an elementary school in my caseload. This would be the first time I didn't. My emotions were mixed. I loved the elementary setting, I just wanted a balance: older kids and a more realistic caseload, fewer referrals and a shorter work day. And, in his words, I "had the most experience." This was a promotion, wasn't it? So I took it like a trooper. I acknowledged that it would be difficult after always having only elementary schools for many years, but I would look at it as a challenge. I would accept the new position, the transfer. Why did I have this sinking feeling that I was being punished?

## What About Later?

I asked the superintendent what would happen once we hired a third psychologist. "We'll divide the elementary schools between the two of them," he said. "Oh. I have four schools, one has three, and the other has only two!?" I thought to myself. Maybe this isn't a promotion. I have four schools, and the less-senior people have three and two!? So after putting in eight years, senior psychologist, I get more work, and Lucy gets what I would have died for; only two schools. Still cool, I asked if him this would change down the road and his pat answer revealed his attitude. "You can always put in for a transfer at the end of the year." This meant no special consideration, only that I could request a change and they might...consider it. My seniority meant nothing, I was not being given the professional courtesy to choose, or to even have input regarding my caseload, and I was being given the most schools. True, the referrals and testing load would be lighter, but four schools meant four principals, and many assistant principals and even more guidance counselors to deal with, not to mention special education teachers. And most importantly, I had little experience in the high schools; I was most comfortable and more familiar with the elementary grades. I felt I was being given the worst assignment of many.

I certainly felt like I was being punished, not only for my court actions, but for my fighting and winning the grievances. What else could it be? Was I paranoid or was I suddenly being treated differently (i.e., discriminated against) because I had dared to disagree with the superintendent's decision to expel my daughter? And he wasn't finished either. He told me he would have preferred to have left me in the elementary schools, but I had created so many problems there, he had had to transfer me from every elementary school I was in. "Right or wrong, you're alienating principals, and I'm running out of places to put you. No elementary principal wants to work with you." I pointed out that I'd not had a single complaint from a parent, a student, or teacher, just "a few administrators," and he responded, "That's all we *have* is a few administrators." I told him that despite what he might have heard or thought about me, I was a loyal employee. I was not only doing my best to protect the rights of the students and parents I worked with, but the school system as well. Principals, the schools' chief administrators, should be expected to respect the law.

When they failed to do so, it was the duty, the responsibility, of others (school psychologists in particular) to bring this to their attention. They might enjoy the benefits of "ignorance is bliss" but they could ill afford the pleasure. It was the start of being punished for being an advocate, and an approach that went after you personally rather than try to argue the facts.

Maybe some principals did get upset with me, but it certainly wasn't because I skirted the law; to the contrary, I respected it and held them to the standard of respecting it as well. Did some consider me a pain in the ass? I'm sure, but I had the respect of parents, teachers, and other professionals. I was one of the few who protected the rights of kids in the face of headstrong and sometimes power-hungry administrators. When I asked the superintendent what he would have me do when I became aware of violations of federal law, the superintendent indicated it was my place to ask principals on what "legal basis they based their decisions." If none could be provided I needed to bring them to his attention. With the exception of some philosophical differences with one principal a few years ago (he thought I was getting too chummy with the parents, fighting too hard for them rather than supporting his teachers) and my recent problem with Mr. B. (the desk clearer), I got along fine with the rest of my principals. He was really blowing things out of proportion. I asked him specifically about one principal, the one for whom my wife worked. "How about the principal at my wife's school? We really didn't have a problem there, just a misunderstanding."

You'll recall the recent meeting with the clinical psychologist and her, and how she changed her mind at the meeting, supporting his view rather than my own. You have to realize that there were three weeks between the meeting and the reprimand she wrote up on me. I was wondering why, after three weeks of silence, she suddenly decided to write me up. I was about to find out.

"Have you talked with her lately?" the superintendent asked me. It soon became apparent that he had, and may have convinced her that she *did* have a problem with me after all. It's not hard to imagine the nature of the conversation; "I think you understand the problems we have had with Frank lately, not only his interfering with this team decision of yours, but all of the trouble he's been causing with these appeals on behalf of his daughter. You know that Mr. B had to write him up for the same problem. Frank's simply not a team player. He's a troublemaker; too concerned about those kids and their parents. He doesn't understand we have schools to run. We can't get these parents all fired up over these issues. They trust us, and don't need someone like Frank putting ideas into their heads. He needs to be taught a lesson when he takes these positions siding against us, and with the parents and these kids. I know you support your peers and me and will do the right thing. We need to stick together on these things. I'm not telling you what to do, but if he didn't support your decision, I think you'd be foolish not to write him up. Especially if there's any more trouble out of him. Then I would have to hold you…responsible."

I'm convinced that is why she wrote me a reprimand some three weeks after the meeting and after numerous collegial discussions between us about what exactly went wrong at that meeting. She told my wife, Caroline, who taught in her building, that administrators are owned body and soul. I am convinced she had no intention of writing me up; the superintendent put her up to it in the same fashion he put Mr. B onto writing me up after we had talked and settled our differences. He doesn't order them to do it; he just made them an offer they couldn't refuse. The superintendent would use the same tactics throughout this endeavor with every other administrator who had dealings with me. He would have completely gotten away with it except for one man, the only man (or woman) with integrity. He said "No," and he suffered the consequences, as you will come to see.

## 1995–'96, A Year Of Infamy

So here I was, assigned to two middle and two high schools. What a total bore. Reevaluations and meetings with teachers who hold every kid accountable and don't always care about their disabilities. My schedule was set and I was stuck at the high school two days a week, even though they didn't have the caseload to support it. I like to be busy as long as I am not overwhelmed, and with this rigid schedule I was twiddling my thumbs on some days and running myself ragged on others. When I asked for flexibility to move between schools, it was denied. In October they hired the new boy in town, the third psychologist. He had worked in clinical settings, but never as a school psychologist. They hired him anyway. And they awarded the paid mentorship to…Lucy, my less senior colleague. I was the senior psychologist, but the mentorship and extra pay went to the less-senior psychologist. Things were getting nasty. I applied and won a position on the Governor's Council on Disruptive Youth, and was denied leave during the day to attend the meetings. Though it was my turn to represent the county at the state department meetings, I was turned down. Someone out of the central office would go, the same gentleman who was notorious for not sharing anything with his fellow psychologists, even the state department memos meant for all school psychologists. I was being shunned. The only positive response I got was when I documented 130 reevaluations on my caseload and they took away one of my schools…the only one I had wanted to keep.

## Sarah's August Iep Meeting

In August 1995, Sarah was getting ready to get back in school after her eight-month suspension. Her expulsion case was heading to the circuit court in town. There was some tension in the air, but we were all acting like professionals.

I was doing my job, keeping my mouth shut, and letting my attorneys fight the battles. Since we never developed an IEP (individualized education plan) for Sarah at the April meeting, we wanted to make sure we had one in August before the start of school. We wanted to make sure everything was in place for her junior year. The school folks gave us a date and we were anxious to meet with the new guidance counselor and new principal. The special education meeting included some other new faces we hadn't planned on, though. Since the one psychologist had resigned, Lucy sat in for her. No problem. In addition to the resource special education teacher who gave the educational assessment was the new LD teacher. She was from Alabama, but had lived in the county for a number of years. I had known here when we both worked as members of the PTA when our daughters attended the elementary school several years back. I really didn't know what to think of her, although I had heard comments that she was a prima donna of sorts.

With all of the new players present, I felt it was my role to summarize the deliberations from the previous IEP meeting. I shared Sarah's test results from the previous school year, and her needs, and suggested that we could open discussion to determine what if any services she would need this school year. I felt that the most important component was that her teachers recognize the fact that she was learning disabled, and to have some contact with the special education teachers if any problems arose. I was not looking for a lot of services, just someone with the training and expertise to monitor as she returned to school. The special education supervisor interrupted.

I was getting ahead of the game. "We still have not determined eligibility, in fact we are missing one of the federally required evaluation components: a classroom observation." I could feel my blood pressure rising. After going round and round at the previous meeting in April, we at least agreed about one thing, Sarah's eligibility as a learning disabled child. I wasn't about to step backward to gather additional assessment data seven months later. Eligibility had already been agreed on in the spring. The previous team had considered all the reports discussing Sarah's academic achievement, her cognitive deficits, her group test scores. What more information could a ten-minute classroom observation provide? "If the board wants to press this issue," I told them, I would file for a due process hearing and have an outside evaluation conducted at county expense. We had already agreed on the eligibility; we needed to move forward to discuss her needs and decide what kind of program she needed to meet her needs. My greatest fear was that her frustrations from her learning disabilities had contributed to her drug abuse, and I was adamant about avoiding this dynamic again.

The meeting cooled for a while and results were reviewed. That's when the other school psychologist and the new teacher chimed in about the discrepancy formula. This formula, concocted by a special commission ten years, earlier was a statistical chart to use as a *guideline* to help teams determine if a student met the eligibility requirement for a "significant discrepancy between ability and performance." The formula was not to be used as "sole criteria" for making this determination, largely because learning disabled kids IQs were depressed as a direct result of their disabilities. The federal government was clear that placement and eligibility decisions were not to be based on single factors. To look at a single score, a full scale IQ that was depressed not due to mental retardation, but specific areas of weakness, missed the whole point of an IQ test that included twelve subtests. More importantly, in the eight years I was in the district, the "discrepancy formula" was never used. At least not until now. And I said as much. "I guess I've been doing it all wrong for eight years as a school psychologist and member of the special education teams here, because I have never seen this formula ever used in any of the elementary schools." This is when the coordinator spoke up, this brand-new-to-the-district so-called expert told the IEP Team, "Whale, Ah kin tale yew, we use it all the tahm!" Maybe in her former district way down South, but not here, and where did she get off being in the district all of two days, telling me, with eight years experience, how "we" run things? Sounded to me like someone had gotten to this team, too.

Well, we were getting nowhere fast, so the new principal, gregarious and seemingly honest, broke in. He essentially stopped the meeting and made a suggestion. Since Sarah had been out of school for almost a year and was starting back in, why not give her a chance? Why not let her start school fresh and see how she settles in? If there are any problems, reconvene the team and do what has to be done. Caroline and I reluctantly agreed. On the way out he pulled me aside in the next room and told me, "Look. I'm new here, I don't know what has gone on before and I really don't care. Let's focus on Sarah. If she starts to stumble, we'll call another meeting and I'll make sure she gets the special education help she needs. I'll be the strongest supporter of getting her special education help." It was a promise he would not be able to keep, though I don't think he knew it at the time. After all, he too had only been on board a few weeks. He didn't know the forces he was up against.

We would monitor her progress carefully over the next few weeks and months. I would be drifting that fall between doing what was in the best interest of my daughter and being the loyal employee, i.e., not raising any more trouble. I would do my best to do my job and allow things to get back to normal. I did *not* want trouble. I wanted normality, and I wanted my daughter to do well, to graduate, and to go on to college. Sarah had paid her debt, she wanted to get back into school and on with her life, and we all wanted things to get back to normal. I did not want people to hold my problems with the system, my frustrations, my anger, against my daughter. I wanted to declare peace. Little did I know that a personal vendetta had already been launched against me, one that would take on an extremely personal and even vindictive tone. I would soon learn just how low the superintendent was willing to sink to "get Frank Matthews."

# Hank Matthews, The Death Of A Friend

For the past four years at my home school, I had befriended the music teacher, Hank, the "Other Mr. Matthews." We shared a love for the Beatles and football games. He even went with us to the Maryland/WVU game. We were all concerned when he was hospitalized for stomach problems and saddened when we found out it was cancer. I visited him in the hospital on a regular basis during the summer of 1995. I brought in some of his *Peanuts* characters to put up on his wall; his "children," so to speak. We talked and laughed and enjoyed each other's company. I talked with his social worker and discovered that he was terminal even before he knew. When he died, we were all very sad. He died on a Wednesday. I was at my high school in the district.

You'll remember that I was only recently transferred from the elementary where he taught. I had a lot of friends there and I was close to the kids and the staff. It was a time to grieve, a sad time for the school family to come together in mourning. I approached the principal of the high school I was working that day, Mr. S. He and I had worked together when he was the assistant principal at the elementary school where Hank and I had worked. I told him Hank had died and he told me he was sorry. I asked him if it would be all right if I finished up my work and headed over to the elementary school. "I'd like to be there with the staff, to help out if I could," were the words I used. Hank was the music teacher and every kid in the school knew and loved him. Without hesitating Mr. S. said sure, and I walked away. Before I got fifteen yards down the hall, he ran after me saying, "Just go, go now, we'll cover for you. You need to be there." And I left. I spent the day doing grief counseling with the kids. It was heart wrenching. Kids loved Hank, and it was tough thinking about him being gone. The staff was similarly affected. It was a sad time. Emotionally draining. As I came from one classroom and walked across the lobby, I spotted the personnel director. I approached him. The first words out of his mouth were unbelieveable: "What are you doing out of your assigned school?" he said in a demanding tone of voice. I was dumfounded. It was like somebody making a scene at a funeral. Was nothing sacred? I told him my immediate supervisor, Mr. S, gave me permission to come. But even that wasn't good enough for this bastard. "Who you invited you here?" It was so inappropriate that someone had to be "invited" to a school he had covered for four years where a tragic loss occurred. All of a sudden the contract is shoved in front of my face again: *where does it say you can leave your post for grief counseling unless you have been formally asked to do so?* I walked away from the man. I had nothing to say. I can't begin to describe my emotions; embarrassment, humiliation, grief, anger, all wrapped into one. But what was to happen a week later would even surpass this.

## Exploiting The Death Of A Child

During the 1994-95 school year I had devoted a great deal of my time to a youngster who had survived against all odds. At age two Jackie fell into a septic tank and almost drowned. He was pulled out after twenty minutes under this putrid water, revived, and recovered to a remarkable extent. But he was now in school and having a variety of learning problems. I was closely involved in the case. Mom was extremely protective and was unable to accept that he had any problems at all. The doctors told her he would be perfectly fine. Physically. But neurologically there had to be some damage. He'd been deprived of oxygen too long. But this little fellow with the big smile captivated anyone who knew him, me included. I sat in on numerous meetings with his mother and his teachers and convinced her to have him seen by the Diagnostic and Advisory Clinic for evaluation, and I pulled some strings to have him seen quickly. I sat in with her when she brought him in for testing at the clinic and was with her all the way through the explanations, and meetings. It was a case I followed as closely as any. Even more than usual, I took a personal interest in this family and this youngster.

On the evening of October 22, 1995, Jackie's mother was driving home after dark when she lost control of her car on a curve. Her Ford Tempo careened across the road and slammed into a telephone pole. It immediately burst into flames. Badly injured herself, she tried to reach into the back seat to rescue her son. It's fortunate that he was already gone, because she was unable to get to him for the heat and flames. He was consumed by the fire. In less than a week, the same elementary school had to deal with the loss of one of their beloved teachers and now a first grader, a popular and well-loved student. I went over Monday afternoon and sat with staff members, the teachers I had worked with on his case, the teacher who had him in her class, others who knew and loved him. It was another heart-wrenching experience. Since I wasn't "invited," I had to wait until my day ended at three to go over to the school to help out where I could. But this was my time, and I would do what I could.

## Jackie's Memorial

Wednesday the paper reported that a memorial service would be held for Jackie in a neighboring town. One o'clock. I wanted to be there, I knew I needed to be there, but my fear kept me back. I went into the other high school. Turns out, the special education teachers had no one for me to test. They had no meetings for me to attend. In fact they had little time to even talk with me, "busy, busy." So I went back to the library and pulled out work from a previous school and wrote a report. By noon I was completely done. Nothing more to do. So I approached the same principal who had so graciously granted me leave the previous Wednesday. I told him I literally had nothing to do, they had no one for me to evaluate, and no meetings. I told him I had written two reports from another school and was without a thing to do. I asked him if he had heard about the death of Jackie, and he indicated he had. I told him that I knew him and had worked with him and his family the previous school year. I also told him that they were holding a memorial service that afternoon at one, and would it be possible for me to attend? He indicated that it would be all right. I told him I would eat lunch and then call Jackie's elementary school to see what time staff members were leaving, so I could meet them outside the church and walk in with them. He said that sounded fine and told me he was sorry for my loss. I called the secretary at Jackie's school; staff members were leaving at noon. I left at twelve fifteen since I was closer to the church, and arrived at twelve forty. It was a small church that was more like a double-wide trailer. Though it was October, it was a warm, sunny day. There were people milling around outside where I stood. Several vehicles arrived with school staff and I recognized a number of other board employees. A total of twenty-five were there, including the superintendent himself. I stood in the back of the paneled room with folding chairs and a few pews. There must have been over two hundred people in there and it was hot. I can think of a lot of other places I would have rather been but there. The mother and family arrived late and came in and sat down. Her hands were bandaged from burns she received trying to rescue her son. There must have been twenty-five people in her entourage. This displaced twenty-five others who had already sat down, and they crowded into the little space remaining along the sides and back wall. The service started at one fifteen and ran for fifty-five minutes, ending at two ten. Jackie's last school picture was resting on a table in front. Grief was thick in the air that was as thick as a sauna. After the service everyone streamed out behind the family and stood in front of the church. It was cooler out there. No one wanted to leave until his mom left, and she stood alongside the big black limo, hugging friends and family and teachers as they paid their respects. I finally drifted off and got into my car and drove home. It was about two thirty when I left. I drove past the school at three, so I just kept on going home. It was the end of my work day. I needed a rest. I was emotionally drained.

## In Trouble Again!?

The next day I got called into the office of my principal, Jack Armstrong. Did I attend a memorial service yesterday? Did I have permission? "Yes" to both questions. Seems as though the superintendent saw me there, and wanted to make sure I had taken a personal day to attend, like all the other board employees. Well, as sure as I was sitting there, I knew that no one had claimed a personal day to attend the funeral of a student from their school. I verified this, of course. I got the names of all twenty-five teachers, instructional assistants, and administrators, and I discovered that only two had asked for personal leave. One was a relative who taught at the high school, and the other was a friend of Jackie's mother who also taught at the high school. An instructional assistant from Mr. S's school knew Jackie's mother. She reportedly took "comp" time. All the rest, including teachers that never had him, just knew him, as well as aides who knew him but never taught him, were there, and all were allowed to attend on school time without taking a personal day or a day charged against your sick leave bank. Since I was not a "current faculty member at that school" I did not have blanket permission and was told I would have to take a personal day. I was chastised for not getting permission from my immediate supervisor as well (Jack Armstrong at my home school). According to the rule makers, Mr. S at the high school was not authorized to give me release, only my immediate supervisor at the middle school to which I was assigned. I had always been told to check with my building principal before I left his building, and I did this religiously. I was not at my home school the middle school, but another assigned building, and I did check with my "immediate supervisor" in that building, Mr. S.

As far as personal leave, it's *not* your home-based principal, only the assistant superintendent, who can grant personal leave under specific conditions, and one was forty-eight-hour notice. Kinda hard to do when the announcement only made it in the paper that morning. And besides that, why would it be a personal day when I was not related to the boy and didn't know his mother on a personal basis or live near them. My contact with them was purely professional, a direct function of my professional responsibilities; identifying, evaluating, and following up on a child in one of my assigned schools. Due to the special nature of this family's circumstances; almost losing him earlier, and struggling to make sure he received the services they knew he needed, I also took a special interest, a "personal interest' in them, but it was all an extension of my professional duties, not because they lived in my neighborhood for example. I took the day as a personal leave day and filed a grievance. It simply wasn't fair. As well, with Sarah's court case coming up I needed every personal day I had available. Employees were only allowed three, and once they were gone, you would be docked a day's pay. I could not afford to lose any wages with my ever-growing court costs and attorney's fees. Even more importantly, I had to resist actions which were clearly discriminatory. Rules that weren't enforced for anyone else were being applied full force to me. It simply wasn't fair. Say, for example, ten people are speeding and you're the only one that's pulled...you can't complain because you were speeding. But this was a case where no one ever got stopped for speeding, and here I was getting pulled over for going two miles over the limit. As a member of the Teacher's Association, I also had the protection of precedent... known as "past practice" in educational jargon. If a school district routinely failed to enforce a rule, then they were essentially prohibited from enforcing it selectively on a discriminatory basis. Hey, I had done my homework, I had a list of twenty-five people, board employees, who were allowed to attend the funeral with less contact with the student or family than I had had. I could prove they were singling me out. I had to fight back to protect myself. But the network of lies was spinning out of control, and once again I would get caught up in it.

## How Conspirators Operate

The superintendent doesn't go to people and say, "I need you to lie for me." What he does instead is put the *squeeze* on them. For example, he very likely went to Mr. S and said something along these lines: "You should never have let Mr. Matthews go to that memorial service; you weren't authorized to do so. Permission for personal leave comes from *my* office. You would really have put yourself out there giving him permission like that. What would the taxpayers think if we're paying him his salary to attend funerals around the county? Now I know you wouldn't have given him permission like that. Did he ask you for personal leave?" So it's a forced choice: admit he gave me permission to go and put his own job on the line for not following policy, or lie and say he never did grant permission, he assumed I already had it. He took the coward's way out. Catholic or not, it was a bad thing for him to do and he will pay for it in his lifetime. Bad karma.

So now you get an inkling on how low the superintendent will sink. He will exploit the death of a six-year-old boy and his memorial service to castigate me. Rather than applaud me for my dedication and caring, appearing for a memorial service in a hot and crowded church, I am singled out from twenty-five others for dereliction of duty. It was but one of many cowardly acts this man demonstrated during the course of these proceedings.

Most of his other acts were petty. Like October 30, having the principal take me off the high school's problem-solving team until I was caught up. I wasn't behind. This was where I could make suggestions as to help students with substance abuse problems. What did they have to hide here? Two days later, on November 1, I was also removed from the drug team at the other high school, this time for "perseverating on personal situation." The team consisted of a several educators (special education teacher, school nurse, guidance counselor, and the county addiction counselor) who took referrals from teachers on kids they suspected of drug or alcohol use. They operated confidentially, with their focus on helping kids with addictions get help. I was well-suited for this team because I strongly advocated a treatment approach to kids with drug and alcohol problems, and this team did just that. My mistake? I had asked a few questions about a case they were discussing.

It seems that the previous school year a high school girl had walked into the nurse's office with abnormal vital signs. She was incoherent, agitated, and her blood pressure was soaring. I asked the nurse what she'd thought was going on, and she said she thought the kid had taken LSD. "What did you do?" I asked. Remember, I was new on the team and wanted to know what the procedures were. The nurse told me that she immediately contacted the girl's mother, who came and got her. Whoa! What was an innocent question opened up a whole train of thought in me. I'm drawing parallels to my daughter's case, wondering why we weren't called to school on that day to take Sarah home, but more importantly wondering what happened next. I asked the nurse what follow-up there was. "There wasn't any. The mother apparently had a drinking problem of her own. Why bother to call her when she wouldn't do anything about it?" the nurse responded.

What was most surprising to me is that no follow-up had been made to report it to the administration. My high school daughter also came to school in an agitated state, possibly under the influence of LSD. The school administrators failed to contact the parents. Instead they conduct some half-ass investigation and then sit and wait to see what will happen. And as for our reaction, our role as responsible parents? Unlike the alcoholic mother who ignored her daughter's altered state, once we knew what our daughter had done, we not only acknowledged it, but we acted on it. We brought her forward for a cooperative effort with the district, and were treated to expulsion/punishment instead of the treatment we had so desperately sought. I had a right to ask questions, I was a member of the team as well as a parent, and it was pretty obvious that two high schools in the same county were treating student drug use in very different ways. Did I have a personal interest? Certainly. For my daughter's case, sure, but what about other cases that came before this committee professionally? I had to know. For trying to reach clarity I get kicked off the team. Double standards were in effect and it was clear some cases were treated very differently than my daughter's case was. Beyond the personal, I was beginning to wonder if the school district's purpose was to help students with substance abuse problems, or to punish a few to make an example and shove the rest of them under the proverbial rug.

## CHAPTER ELEVEN

# NOVEMBER 1995 CIRCUIT COURT

We ended up going to court in November 1995, more than a year after the expulsion. The judge had all the documents in his possession, including memoranda from the attorneys. You'll remember that I wanted to do this myself, but with memoranda and sanctions and all the rules of engagement I failed to grasp, I was forced to engage Morris for an attorney. We knew we were off to a bad start when the judge first appeared on the bench. He expressed confusion. He didn't even know what type of hearing this was; who were the plaintiffs and what was the basis of our appearance? Our attorney explained how it was an administrative decision we were appealing for his review. Our attorney indicated he saw no reason to read the memorandum, since the judge already had them on hand (for thirty days prior to the hearing). These were the same all-important memoranda I received sanctions for not filing. I was forced to hire an attorney for thousands of dollars to draft the memoranda and make sure they were in the judge's hands well before the hearing. These were the documents that the judge needed to understand the case. And the judge doesn't know who the plaintiff is or what kind of case it even is!? That's when the judge admitted that he hadn't read the memoranda, could they fill him in.

I was astounded. We'd waited a year for our day in court and he'd had these memoranda (case summaries) for thirty days, not to mention the rest of the documentation he'd had for seven months. Had he even read those documents? I would say it's a safe bet that a judge who didn't take the time to read a three-page memorandum would not have taken the time to read through a three-hour transcript. The problem is, *that* is where all the facts lay, my testimony about Sarah's disability and her counseling and our turning her in, and the dishonesty and policy violations by the board. It was all there. Unread, apparently. So our attorney did his best to muddle through. He wasn't prepared to have to explain everything in detail, and he was not as familiar with the case as I was. I was passing him notes, some of which he responded to, others he ignored. I was not permitted to sit at the table with my attorney, though both of the board attorneys were at their table. It was my party, I had prepared the documents for it and was paying for it, and yet I had to sit on the outside looking in. So much for the justice system. Why is going to court so bad? It just is.

I got a little nervous when the judge jumped all over our attorney for his three-prong attack: "First you're saying she didn't do it, but if she did, then she has protections from this state law about drug users. And I don't know what learning disabilities have to do with anything." (Now doesn't this sound an awful lot like something the superintendent once said? Now you don't suppose these two "gentlemen" are part of the infamous "good old boys" network?) Well, my attorney couldn't respond. I could have, but I had to sit on my hands. It was a fiasco. The board's hired gun from across the bridge got up and denied a disability ever existed, and said that I never suggested she had one, she was never in counseling, and I only brought all this up after the fact. My only hope was that hearing these specious arguments, the judge would go back over the record to see who was telling the truth. If he had he would have seen that the record supported our side, not the false claims here from the board's attorney.

## What's Next?

The circuit court judge's ruling came a little over a month later. And to our profound disappointment, it was right out of the board attorney's playbook. It was as though the judge never heard any of our arguments based in fact, and heard and believed all of theirs based on outright lies. In the judge's ruling were statements that included "Well, if she had been identified as disabled earlier, instead of only after she took the LSD...." Fact is, she *was* identified with a learning disability in second grade. And she was served in special education in West Virginia, and here in the local school system. These facts...FACTS...were ignored. His opinion continued, "If she had been involved in drug counseling it would have been different." And once again, the facts, including her evaluation at the Drug Counseling Center and my recorded testimony in the documents about continued treatment, sat in dust-covered volumes on the judge's desk. And finally, though criminals have all sorts of rights when it comes to how evidence is obtained, according to this court, students don't. Her confession stood, even though it was first coerced (if she'd told Coach to go to hell, no one would have ever known) and then part of a tacit agreement to cooperate to get the help she needed. Why else would I have turned her in?

We were devastated. But since he so blatantly ignored the facts of the case, and they were clearly that, FACTS, not interpretations, I felt we needed to go beyond this judge to a higher court. We told our attorney we had to go on, how much would it cost us? Ten thousand dollars. Whew! We were looking to our line of credit and our cars, and then a miracle came forward, and Caroline's parents gave her $5,000. Her uncle had already given her $2,000, and my aunt $3,000. Our family provided the defense fund we needed to seek justice. Our attorney, Morris, sat down with us at J & T Restaurant and mapped things out. He followed up with a letter laying out the agreement and payment schedule: $2,000 now, $3,000 in July 1996, when preliminary arguments are heard, and $5,000 at the actual hearing.

We got some good news over the summer when Morris phoned to tell us that the Maryland Court of Special Appeals had agreed to hear the case and that they had waived the preliminary hearing (no, we didn't get any of our money back or a reduced rate). Our attorney felt it was a result of one of three reasons: 1) There was no need to clarify the issues, they were clear cut; 2) There was no chance of mediation, the two sides were too far apart; or 3) Here was a good opportunity to establish case law—students' rights/rules of evidence/state law for drug users coming forward/rights of disabled students who don't have active individualized education plans (IEPs). Either way it looked good for our side. They scheduled a date sometime in November 1996, and it was sit back and wait. This case wasn't one I had to work on or lose sleep over; heck, we were paying him ten grand to do that. When Morris filed his brief in July, I read it through carefully. To be heard by a court you have to provide them with a packet of documents along with written arguments for the court to consider, remember. I read them carefully and since Morris and I had met before, I have to admit he picked up all the points I wanted him to consider. I couldn't change a word. We submitted and waited for the board's attorney to respond. And respond he did. His usual blather, and as usual I got mad, and then I realized once again that they had no case and I started feeling good again. He had to build his case on lies because the truth was on our side. The second highest court in the state was going to hear Sarah's case, one I had helped put together, and it looked good. Not only for Sarah, but for all of the other students in Maryland who have been illegally questioned or searched. And those who have been caught up in these draconian zero tolerance policies and kicked out of school. Our pain and suffering might prevent similar tragedies for other students and their families. I was hopeful. I could wait until November. Another year. But maybe things would have settled down a bit by then.

# CHAPTER TWELVE

# CAN YOU COMPROMISE YOUR KID'S FUTURE?

Well, August 1995 quickly turned into September, and it turned into October, and then into November. Sarah was back in school, having served her one year in exile. She had been evaluated in April '95, and though eligible as learning disabled in math, no services were recommended. In August she was denied services again, but we were willing to wait and see how she settled in.

How was Sarah doing? She was not doing too well. We worked with her at home, we encouraged her, we tried to strike that balance between enjoying harmony at home and pressuring her to study, read, do your homework. By mid-November I had had several conversations with the principal at the high school, who had promised me he would act if she began to struggle. I had regular contact with him and two pairs of eyes on Sarah because I was in the building twice a week. My conversations with the new principal were pleasant talks, bull sessions. We made some fine-tuned adjustments to some things and I talked to him about my dilemma. Do I keep my mouth shut to make things easier on my job, or do I stand up as a parent for my daughter? Her expulsion case was coming before the court, but I was even more concerned about her passing her courses. Would he call a meeting? He made this face and he looked at me almost embarrassed. "Look, Frank, I can tell you, between you and me? There's no way they're going to label her LD." I knew then that they had gotten to him, and that he was telling me to do what I had to do, but that it was hopeless from his perspective. He knew what was going on behind the scenes and was honest with me about what he knew. He was also making it clear that he could no longer help me. I was on my own. I decided there and then that I would get him out of the middle and formally request an ARD, a meeting to decide what services, if any, Sarah needed. In this interest I wrote a letter to him on November 16, 1995. We essentially asked for a formal IEP meeting to be scheduled between Thanksgiving and Christmas. Plenty of time for them to make contacts and arrangements.

Almost a month went by with no response. My weekly talks with the principal stopped. I waited until December 11. Why the eleventh? If they hadn't contacted me by then, there wasn't enough time to provide us with the required ten-day notice for a meeting prior to December 21 when school was out for Christmas break. When the eleventh came and went, I planned to contact them, not for an ARD, but for a due process hearing. Maybe it was time to let an outside party come in to settle this thing once and for all. It was over a year since they expelled her, and in doing so they refused to honor my request to evaluate her. The state department directed them to test her; they did, and then they refused to acknowledge her eligibility earlier that year in April. We finally compromised by agreeing she was disabled, but not developing an IEP for her until school started in September. Sarah was still out of school in the spring of 1995, so we agreed to wait until school started, and they sandbagged us again, wanting to redetermine eligibility based on the lack of a ten-minute observation.

Once again, we agreed to wait, this time until November, and now they ignored us! I had Sarah's attorney draft the letter only because I figured that would get their attention, but I had every indication of running this show myself. After all, I know a few things about special education. Our attorney's letter was written on December 14. I got a call from the principal on the twentieth, the day before we were to pack up for our Florida vacation. He wanted to know if we wanted to meet the next day. I declined. We deserved more than one day's notice, especially the same day we're flying out to Florida. I was polite, but I turned the ARD down. He asked about a date after the start of the year, but to be honest we were so frustrated, we didn't want to deal with these people anymore. We didn't trust them. Even the people we did trust, like the special education supervisor, had been compromised. We needed a third party, an objective party. We wanted an impartial due process hearing officer to determine the outcome of the case, and our attorney's notice on December 14, 1995, was just that, a request for one.

The principal's December 21 letter in response confirmed our suspicions. He was backing off his commitment to push for an LD placement, even to support the decision from the April ARD that recognized her disability, for in his letter he wrote, "According to the ARD minutes from the meeting held on August 25, 1995, the ARD Committee determined that Sarah was *not eligible for special education services*." ARD minutes?! We had never received any, despite a four-month interim. We got his letter on our way to the airport, but I still had time to hand write a note declining for a number of reasons the January 8 meeting they wanted to hold.

I wasn't about to rehash the eligibility decision reached at the April meeting. In my own words, "Another ARD with the same players holding the same opinions is not productive in my mind." They scheduled the ARD during our work day, two o'clock, convenient for the Northern staff though not for either of us, who work until three and four. Our teacher contract specifies a seven hour, fifteen minute day with two exceptions: faculty meetings and parent meetings. The principal is completely within his or her authority to schedule an ARD after teachers' regular hours. For other kids, not your own. The school could have legally required the teachers to stay after to attend Sarah's meeting; we would have been prevented from doing so since it was our own child and within our work day. And with the scrutiny I had come under, I wasn't about to ask to leave a building early. The convenience of the parent is primary. I should know, I've sat in plenty of 7:30 meetings before school or 5:30 meetings after school at the elementary level. It was clear, they were circling the wagons, getting ready to do battle, and the saddest part was that they left the little girl, Sarah, standing outside, alone.

## The Hired Gun And Myron — Due Process

On January 17, 1996, a Wednesday, we got a letter from their attorney, hand delivered to me by the special education supervisor herself while I was at work. They delivered a copy to us, with the original to our attorney. The board's attorney, the one from across the bridge, had set the date, time, and location of the due process hearing, Friday, January 26, nine o'clock in the morning at the board of education. A fellow I will call Myron was the impartial hearing officer (HO). We'd been waiting over a month and heard nothing, and now here they were setting a hearing date a little over a week away, but, more importantly, with a five-day disclosure rule we were required to have all of our documentation in their hands (and theirs in ours) by Sunday, January 21. With only three days, including Saturday, we knew we'd have to hustle, and hustle we did. I knew we could assemble our documents and witness list in time, but then it was duplicating and making sure the hearing officer and opposing side (school system) each had copies, before the five-day disclosure deadline had passed.

On Friday, two days after the first letter, I received another one from the board's attorney, this one also hand delivered by

## Can You Compromise Your Kid's Future?

the special education supervisor. This one rambled on about how they had heard nothing from "our attorney" despite "numerous letters and phone calls" and they were hereby calling off the January 26 hearing. I called Myron, the hearing officer, to find out what he needed and noted it down. I told him we were ready to proceed and, more importantly, that I was *not* represented by counsel for this due process hearing, only the civil matter. I was presenting this case myself. In fact I would be glad to bring him a letter from Sarah's attorney indicating that he was *not* representing us in the special education case. I felt the board was blowing smoke, trying to rush us and then slamming the brakes on, hoping we'd rear end them. Myron was cordial and very understanding since I was a parent and not an attorney. He seemed to understand that I was doing my best to work my way through all the twists and turns of the legal system. We used every bit of Saturday to finish making copies of all the documents and made arrangements to hand deliver the packets on Sunday. I called our attorney to arrange to meet him on the way to pick up his letter indicating he was not representing us. We then drove seventy-five miles across the bay to the Western Shore to hand our packet to the hearing officer. His wife was very nice. She let us in and allowed us to meet with Myron before we headed back home. Then it was back in the car and across the bridge to hand a similar packet to the board's representative, the special education supervisor. She had hand-delivered stuff to us. I was following suit. Imagine her surprise when she responded to the rapping on her screen door and saw me standing there with a packet of information. I quickly handed it to her and walked away. We had beaten the deadline. They had not.

## Conference Calls At Northern

Monday the phone calls started coming in from the board's attorney. I was at school and I was inclined to refuse to accept them. For one reason, I wasn't allowed to use board of education phones during my work day to discuss "personal business," especially business that related to my daughter's case. The personnel director had made that abundantly clear. Secondly, I made the deadline, he didn't; what could I possibly have to say to him? I refused the call. This time the special education supervisor's secretary called back. I agreed to talk with her. Then she put the board's attorney and the hearing officer, Myron, on the line. Talk about bait and switch. I couldn't refuse to talk to Myron. He was the hearing officer, but they tricked me into getting on the line. Picture this, here I am in the teacher's lounge with someone at the computer and three people trying to get the Coke machine to take their money. Here I sit, on the telephone (the same one I could get fired for using on company time) with two attorneys and the special education supervisor, all yelling about how I was muddying the waters and they needed an extension.

The same individuals who waited thirty-four days to spring the hearing date on us last minute (a date that is supposed to be set at the parent's convenience) is crying *I'm not ready* when we spring to action. The board's attorney rambled on. They wanted, they needed, they deserved an extension until Tuesday, January 30. I refused. They knew about the twenty-sixth. They knew the time, the location, even the identity of the hearing officer for *weeks* without telling us. They spring it on us last minute, we meet their deadline, and they cry foul?! Because they haven't heard from our attorney, who wasn't even representing us? All our attorney did was write the December 14 letter to request a due process hearing on our behalf. From that point on they should have dealt directly with our attorney. They didn't. They had the principal call *us* at home. They had the principal write *us* a letter. They had the principal schedule an eligibility meeting with *us*, all without the involvement of "our attorney." It wasn't until it was convenient for them to use it that they did. Dirty tactics. Double standards. Duplicity. Hypocrisy.

## Can You Compromise Your Kid's Future?

Despite my refusal to give in, the hearing officer, afraid of an appeal, granted them the extension. "It was only four days and two were over the weekend," he explained. Truth be known, I could use the extra time to prepare our case, but it was the principle. They tried to ambush us, we were ready for them, and they wanted leniency. Their attorney got his extension, and I got four more days to prepare my case. I should have smelled a rat right there. Could I trust Myron to be truly impartial or not?

Thursday the twenty-fifth was the last day for submission of documents. We had all of our stuff ready to go. Caroline gets a call from the special education supervisor's secretary. "You'll never guess. We found all of Sarah's special education records! The same ones that were lost for ten months! In a closet at one of the elementary schools. Stop by TOMORROW," she says, "and we'll have them ready for you." Only problem about TOMORROW is that tomorrow is one day late for submitting documents. With other more pressing issues at hand we didn't make a whole lot of it. Like Hillary Clinton's files that suddenly appeared under a table in the White House, Sarah's files conveniently reappeared in her elementary school one day too late to use as evidence. The records would have provided documentary evidence of her learning disability, a special education service this school district was all too aware of.

That same day I received our packet of information from the board and pored through it. The only surprises were two names on the witness list: one was one of our close friends from back home in West Virginia, the same friend we brought here and recommended for a position. She and her husband and son moved here to the Eastern Shore to work with us in the same school building where my wife and my offices were located. They lived with us while they were moving to the area and we provided all the support they needed when they arrived. Yet somehow, without a word to us, Maureen, our friend and colleague, was being asked to testify for the board. The irony was that when we all lived in West Virginia,

Maureen was in charge of special education and knew all about Sarah's history of learning disabilities and special education status. What could she say that would hurt us? But at the hand of the board's attorney, anything was possible. It certainly strained that friendship.

# CHAPTER THIRTEEN

# THE PLOT THICKENS—COMPLAINTS FROM NORTHERN HIGH

To fully appreciate what happened next, we have to go back a little to the fall. Remember, I am now operating in a new setting, a secondary or high school setting, with new special education teachers, including the newest addition to the staff, the young lady from way down South. I had learned to do my best to separate my daughter's case from the job I was set to do, psychological reevaluations at the secondary level. As long as the folks I worked with were professional and performed their jobs well, we'd have no problem. I don't hold grudges. I am quick to forgive and forget. My wife says too quick. Treat me nice and I don't care what you did to me before, I'll return the gesture. But try as I might, there was something about how these people conducted themselves in Sarah's case and how they behaved in special education meetings for other disabled students. That link was an attitude that *they* decided who went into their classes, who *stayed* in their classes, and, most importantly, what level of service (how much direct help) these kids would receive. After over twenty years in public education and eight in the elementary schools, where *teams* made decisions, I was more than a little surprised to find that the results of my two-hour assessments were taken very lightly, and my interpretation of results and analysis of his/her current status in light of the student's background and history were treated with equal disdain. *They* knew what was best for their students. And despite the fact that there might be a perceived conflict of interest since they were having to develop individualized educational plans and implement lesson plans for all these kids and then teach them, they maintained a position of authority that superseded the rest of the team members, including parents and the school psychologist. This did not sit well with me, but since I was the "new boy" in town, I sat in silence to watch "how things were done."

A number of factors brought this to a head. One involved the simple fact that they stuck the new special education teacher in the meetings for the first half of the year, and often had the brand new assistant principal sitting in as administrator. So here I sit with eight years experience in policy and procedure in the district, listening to these folks new to the district tell me how "things were done." The second problem arose when I began to reevaluate students I had seen previously at the elementary level. These were kids I knew very well, and a lot better than they did.

## Another October Surprise

Picture this. A severely learning disabled student I saw in fourth grade is now in tenth grade, reading on a third-grade level, struggling, and becoming a "behavior problem." The guidance counselor tells me he has a "bad attitude." He is receiving *no direct services*. Only monitoring, which boils down to having the classroom aide have someone fill out a checklist every so often to note his progress in the regular

## The Plot Thickens—Complaints From Northern High

classroom. Uh, hello?! Might there be a relationship between his reading problems and his behavior problems? Anyone who knows anything about kids understands that they would much rather be considered "bad" than stupid. The meeting starts and this special education teacher new to the county whips out the now infamous "discrepancy formula." I inquired about this after seeing it for the first time at my daughter's meeting. I was assured it was "to be used as a guideline, not a requirement for eligibility." But then this special education teacher is telling the parent that he may not even qualify for the program, and asks me to provide her with his full scale IQ (FSIQ). She is asking me for the knife to sever this student from special education. She will then use (misuse) my data. For starters, full scale IQs for learning disabled kids are often invalid. They're depressed (lower than actual IQ) as a direct result of their specific cognitive deficits, even more so if there is a significant difference between verbal and nonverbal skills. Secondly, it is to be used as a guideline, not a requirement, and if a student has been identified and served for six or more years, why is his or her eligibility, his or her need for services, even being rehashed? The student was LD in high school and reading on a third-grade level. What are you going to do, dismiss him from services and throw him into mainstream classes with no help from the special education staff? This *brand new to the district* special education teacher is erroneously telling the parent this is a requirement, and I'm sitting there knowing this is not true, at least not in this school district. I've been here eight years, she's been here less than eight weeks. This special educator was from another school district that may have done things a bit differently. Thirdly, why is she asking me for a score that was written up in a three-page comprehensive psychological report she has had in her possession for over three weeks? My ethical alarm went off and I refused to give her a single digit out of a three-page report. I placed the report on the table in front of her saying, "Here's what I have to say about this young man." I also turned to the parent and explained to her that it was my understanding that the discrepancy formula was not a requirement but a *guideline*, and that in my opinion her son was qualified and deserved more services than he was currently receiving. I was clearly upset: with the process, with the teacher, but, most importantly, what was being allowed to happen to this kid. Maybe they *didn't* single out my daughter for special treatment, maybe they treated *all* kids this way. Did that make it right? Or excuse it? Hardly. The sad thing was that the services did not change for this student. He remained in the regular classroom without any help from the special education teachers. Why? Because my ability to advocate for students, my ability to "fight" for them, had been lost. I had been quite effectively neutered.

## Meeting With Mason

I truly did not want to make waves—my job, my career, was on the line—but I was upset enough at this point to talk with the new-this-year assistant principal Mason, who had attended the meeting. On my own I asked him if he had a few moments to talk. We closed the door to his office and I asked him what were his impressions of what had gone on in the meeting. He said he thought I was out of line by refusing to give a teacher the information she wanted (FSIQ), and that he was uncomfortable with my behavior. Administrators are like clerks, bureaucrats enforcing rules they don't understand and sometimes putting their own spin (interpretation) to them. Follow rules if it's convenient, break 'em if it's not...who'll catch you? Seemed to be my experience with a lot of administrators. So it fell on deaf ears when I explained to him why I took the position I did: because it was my responsibility as school psychologist to protect my results from being misused. Furthermore, I told him what the special education supervisor had told me about the discrepancy formula, and pointed out that though the special educator might have done things differently in her previous assignment, we did not use the formula like that here. I followed up this conversation with a formal page-and-a-half letter. It appears below. He never responded directly, instead sent me a letter in which he indicated that he forwarded my letter to his boss, the building principal, Mel. Mel passed it along to the special education supervisor, and though I never received a response to my expressed concerns and remedies for positive change, this letter would resurface some months later.

November 1, 1995
James Mason
Assistant Principal
Northern High

Dear Jim,
    I thought I'd drop you a few lines to provide you with a little more detail about my concerns with respect to the special educator's role as chairperson of the ARD. Although she appears to be acting in a thorough and professional manner, there are a number of problems with the way in which she conducts these meetings. With the number of students awaiting reevaluation and special education eligibility meetings to attend, I think the sooner we resolve some of these issues, the better.
    For some reason, she does not appear to have a working knowledge of the psychological report I provide well in advance of the meetings. Then, when she fills out the *LD Team Report*, for example, she asks me for information I have already addressed in my presentation to the team members. Even more disturbing is the fact that she feels that she can question my interpretations in front of colleagues and even parents. I sometimes feel that I am being forced to reexplain and even defend my findings, when she has all of this information already in front of her. Although I am always willing to clarify my results to parents who have *not* had the opportunity to read the report, I feel that having to do this for the

special education teacher's benefit is not only a waste of the committee's time, but essentially undermines my credibility.

It was fortunate that the parents were absent from our most recent meeting on October 31, for this special educator's comments were directed at my well-documented findings. For example, she minimized the significant discrepancies I identified, not only between individual cognitive areas on the IQ test, but between the student's ability to perform mathematical calculations and his application of this knowledge to actual practice. This is a young man who quickly solved difficult word problems in his head, and yet has failed the functional math test three times! Her position was that he did not qualify for special education services in math, because the only discrepancy she found was in written expression. In other words, only *her* test results count. The standards call for a multidisciplinary team to conduct assessments, and though her role in gathering detailed data in academic subjects is important, so too is the psychological which covers overall ability, discrepancies between individual cognitive areas, as well as differences between abilities and actual academic performance. The psychologist must also address the numerous behavioral and emotional factors that can affect these discrepancies. Committee members should be encouraged to make decisions using all of this available data.

Of equal concern is the manner in which this special educator uses the "discrepancy formula." Although the special education supervisor has made it clear that this is to be used as a guideline, not a requirement, this special educator insists on applying it to students who have already been identified as learning disabled, many for three to six years or more. I do not feel that this is an appropriate use of this tool, as it is confusing to parents and educators alike, and should only be applied to initial assessments, as a guide, along with all of the other data. As well, it is inappropriate to use a full scale IQ when learning disabilities are present because they tend to depress IQ scores. When she insists I give her the "IQ score" to plug into this formula, she is asking me to provide data to the team that is not valid for that purpose, a violation of my professional association's code of conduct. Psychologists are carefully trained to guard against misuse of their data.

The primary function of the eligibility team is to provide an opportunity for the individual examiners to report their test results, including scores and interpretations of these scores. It is unprofessional, in my opinion, for another team member to question the results or interpretations of another examiner in an open meeting. If there are any questions or concerns in these areas, they need to be discussed prior to the meeting. My reports are provided in complete written form well in advance of the meetings, and I welcome questions about test results, interpretations, or recommendations by colleagues, but not in an open meeting. The formal meeting is for results to be explained to other team members, including parents, who are free to ask any and all questions they may have. Team members should confine their questions to clarifications about results, not interpretations presented by qualified examiners. Team discussions should center around how these results will impact the student's educational program and what the least restrictive placement might be. It is these recommendations that are open for discussion, the give and take that hopefully results in a plan that best meets the unique needs of that individual student.

Curiously, when the meeting moved to this critical step at the meeting last Tuesday, she skipped over it in favor of maintaining the student's current level of services: *Intensity I* — i.e., no direct services. When I suggested that the committee discuss this essential requirement, she offered a variety of excuses including, "(He) doesn't want to come in here because his sister is mentally retarded, and he doesn't want to have anything to do with special education." When I suggested that he might be an excellent candidate for *Inclusion*, a model which allows special needs student to remain in the general education setting with help from two teachers, one general education and one special education certified, she indicated that this was not feasible due to scheduling problems. This, of course, is not a concern of the eligibility team, but is an administrative function, which I pointed out. The team is required to cover test results, eligibility, needs, and placement in the least restrictive environment. Administrators are present to work out the delivery of services.

If we can address these concerns now, we can prevent any further disruptions to meetings that are inevitable if these conflicts are allowed to continue. We are all trying to perform our tasks to the best of our ability, and I fully expect that we can establish working relationships that will benefit all of the students we see.

                Sincerely yours,
                Frank L. Matthews, Ed.S., NCSP
                School Psychologist

# CHAPTER FOURTEEN

# SLIP OF THE TONGUE

Not as though I didn't have enough to worry about. Roamy caught me on a bad day. I had just completed a round of psychological evaluations at the middle school. Some were quite complicated, including students with severe disabilities who were in all-day special education programs. Their files were inches thick and required careful and thorough review and comprehensive assessment (testing) and reporting by me. I was exhausted. I was ready to concentrate on my other schools. Roamy, who teaches special education at the middle school, comes up and addresses me with what might be described as an impatient tone: "When are you going to get around to testing Sammy?!" It was the kind tone that suggests the bearer thinks you haven't done squat for her, or anybody else for that matter, have nothing better to do than wander the halls and play the busy professional all day, and that if it weren't for her, squeaky wheel and protector of all needy children, "Nothing would get done around here!" Now, this is an attitude I am abundantly familiar with. Like the flu or rainy weather, you can count on it visiting on a regular basis, usually at the worst time, and even at the best time it is unwelcome. When you're an itinerant employee, you are assigned to more than one school. I had four schools in my caseload and I had to spend a full day in each every week. This means that four days out of five you aren't in the other schools. When you cover an entire building, you may have six or more special education programs and teachers to deal with, consent forms signed by parents, coordinating psychological and educational evaluations, writing three- to six-page reports, and special education placement meetings. This, in addition to dealing with guidance counselors, administrators, not to mention a few regular teachers who have asked you to help out with a kid or two. You get pulled in a hundred directions. Although some appreciate your efforts and what you have done for them, some are, "But what did you do for me today?" They also assume that when you are not working for them in their building, you're not working. And if, heaven forbid, two weeks goes by and their kid hasn't been tested, then you're in trouble. They will lie in wait for you like the dog for the mailman, and their bark is as bad as a bite. It startles and scolds, intimidates and corners you all at the same time.

I really don't know which of these dynamics was at work, but for my part I felt unappreciated, even put upon, and I responded curtly. I snapped back, something along the lines that I was not going to drop everything and test her kid just because she wanted me to. I had other priorities. Well, she went to the principal with it. "Frank said he wasn't going to test Sammy." Now in a profession that is 95 percent women (sex police and feminists, get ready), men who are not in power positions are at a distinct disadvantage. Why? Because of the few males in education, many of them are in the power positions. They rule over huge groups of women who aren't in power positions. The male administrators are outnumbered and they have to respond to their vast majority of women constituents; they have to keep their troops happy. So if there ever is a contest between a male and female teacher in the principal's office, who do you think the principal will side with? The man, and be accused of being a sexist, or the woman and be seen as the champion of the women against the unruly male? "You mean you raised your voice to her? We can't have this." And it's no better when faced with a female administrator who is defending her women staff members even more fiercely. Admittedly, I am from New York, and I tend to express my feelings openly, and my tone of voice is often, too often, misconstrued and taken personally. I kind of wish I had a little Dr. Phil to travel around behind me like a guardian angel, letting folks know, "It's not about YOU, that's just the way Frank is. Don't take it personally, he's just had a bad day."

Like it or not, I have dealt with this for over twenty years in education, and I'm constantly at the mercy of coworkers (mostly women, because they make up 95 percent of the public schools), not *all* women certainly, just that specific breed who are constantly running to "mommy or daddy" to tell on big brother. "And then he called me a stupidhead." Keep in mind that I was raised in a female-dominant setting with two sisters, one older (by eighteen months) and one younger (by eight years). When one of them (usually the older one) decided to pick on me, it was a) go to Mom and Dad and be chastised for not dealing with my own problems and running to them to solve them, or b) not going to Mom and Dad and dealing with it on my own and getting heck for picking on, hitting, or otherwise dealing with my sister. How many times had I heard, "What, can't you take care of yourself?" or "She's a girl, you shouldn't be picking on her." It was the classic damned if you did, damned if you didn't. And my older sister was downright mean. Over the years she threw a radio at me, slammed my knuckles with a plastic hairbrush, talked me into sticking my head between the rungs of a chair from which I was unable to extricate myself without the help of my mother and a saw, borrowed and destroyed my sled, snow skis, and who knows what else while I was away at college and she was not, and ratted me out at every opportunity. I have always longed for someone to mediate a dispute with some measure of justice, and believe in my heart of hearts that if you have trouble with someone, have the courtesy to bring it to them first before you go TELL on them.

What's missing is the striving to be professional, to approach the individual with your concern to say, "I don't like the way you spoke with me about Sammy." That would put them on equal footing with you. No, they have to run and tell, run and tell. Having grown up with two sisters and no brothers, and having been on the receiving end of this same dynamic for my formative years, let's just say I am sensitive to it, recognize it, and am continually disheartened by it. I got hauled in on a regular basis for doing absolutely nothing other than get on the wrong side of my sisters, and Dad always took their side against me. In my almost thirty years of this business, I have had disagreements with men coworkers. I cannot recall a single incident when one of them failed to deal with me directly, choosing instead to run to the boss and tattle on me. Men don't do this. They just don't. And most women don't either, just *some* women. But this woman was one of those run-to-Daddy types, and she was going to get him in big twouble for the way he talked to her.

And so I get called in. And it's that "here we go again" feeling. Here I am in the principal's office, not at five years old or seven, but forty-five and forty-seven, forty years later, and I haven't learned a damn thing, apparently. So here I am, under the most intense scrutiny of my professional life. Trying so hard to please everybody and not screw up, and here I got someone mad at me. Again. This time it was different, though. This principal (Jack Armstrong) was great about it. He was not going to get in the middle of it, he was only passing it along to me to work out. I explained why I wasn't able to get to the case as quickly as she wanted, that I hadn't refused to test Sammy, only not that day. He encouraged me to get with her and make nice, which I said I would. He was telling the kids to "work it out." Terrific! What a great dad he was. For my part, when you hear the same criticism from different people over the years, you have to take it to heart;

you have to take some ownership in it. And I have to admit to being somewhat impulsive, somewhat intense, and curt at times. I may not always take the diplomatic route, preferring or being predisposed to taking the direct path, the straight path, to the response. I have been accused of being too direct, and I try to consider this when my blood pressure and my Germanic temper go up. Being ADHD and impulsive and living in the moment doesn't help either, by the way.

I am in litigation with the board of education, my employer. I have been put ON NOTICE in any number of ways about my unprofessional behavior, using school phones for personal business, etc. I am under tons of pressure. My eyeballs are bulging, my brain ready to ooze out my ears. Every perceived misstep is documented and catalogued and made part of my permanent dossier. To say I was being held to a much higher standard is extreme understatement. So I really don't want anyone upset with me. I want them to be happy with my work, to be happy with me. Now Roamy is what I would term a "man's woman." And I mean this in the most positive manner. She is confident, gregarious, upbeat, even a bit brash or loud. Demure she is not. When she comes into a room she takes over; she commands attention. Her stories are colorful and amusing. Her husband is in law enforcement, and you can picture her belting down the brews with the gang at office parties. That's why I was rather surprised when she failed to come to me first instead going to tattle on me to the principal. But now I have a chance to make this right, to pull myself back from the brink. It is with the previous mental set — tough gal, need to impress her, be contrite — that I asked if she had a few minutes. She welcomed me in and I closed the door. I began by apologizing if I had cut her off the other day, I explained that I was under a great deal of pressure and sometimes reacted badly. I didn't always consider people's feelings. (So far, so good. Now shut the hell up, Frank, and go about your business — but no, the adrenaline is pumping.) I then took it a step further to convince her of my sincerity. I gave her what I would call a "free pass," a signal she could send me if I appeared a bit intense or overbearing. I told her to not take me too seriously or take it personally if I barked, because I was not myself these days. "If I ever appear to be overbearing again, just tell me to *fuck off*, and I will." She said no problem, and I got up and left.

## Me And My Big Mouth

If you know anything about kids with ADHD, remember... that attention deficit hyperactivity disorder? Well, they also have trouble controlling their behavior. It's called Impulsivity, and it basically means the behavior occurs before the brain has a chance to say STOP! It's one of the classic features. It's why they (we) are constantly in trouble, because we act first and then go, Oops. Too late. We don't have good brakes, so we constantly run into things. When you look at the other behaviors that go along with ADHD—talking too much, restless in confined spaces, distractible, difficulty focusing our attention, etc.—you can imagine our frustration. I know there is this "something" about me that drives people away, this intensity, this frenetic talking, and failure to listen (focus on what others are saying), and even a reluctance to accept the consequences for my mistakes, that fatal failure to see the connection between what I did and what somebody else is making me do as a result. "What do you mean I was speeding!" The thinking part of my brain knows these things and is constantly running over the other side and beating on the walls for me to be quiet, or coming over and tapping me on the shoulder and saying, "Shhhh" or even "Shut the fuck up!" But sometimes, as hard as I try, there's a force in me that's stronger than I am, and things happen before even I know its coming. This "free pass" was just one of those moments.

The other side of ADHD is ODD, oppositional and defiant disorder. This is the part that says, I'm mad as hell and NOT going to take it anymore. It's that part of the ADHD's brain that says, I have to organize this stimuli, this information, my own way, and if someone else tells me to do it his or her way, then…well…I can't. I have to do it THIS way, it's the only way I CAN do it. You can imagine how the ADHD/ODD kid (or adult) deals with AUTHORITY FIGURES. They don't like being told what to do, they don't take orders well, and they react defiantly, not because they want to, but sometimes it's the only way they can react. Corner a dog and he'll come out fighting. Ordering an ADHD person to do something is like cornering them psychologically. Ask them. Let them do it in their own time and their own way, and you will get 110 percent compliance. Otherwise you get argument and anger and discomfort. It's tough. I don't go out of my way to cause disturbance; in fact I work twice as hard as most people just to keep the bosses and the people I work with happy. Happy and off my back. So when, after moving two-hundred tons of gravel, I finally sit down and someone, anyone, comes over and says, "Get to work!" or "Would you please move your wheelbarrow?" or "Would you mind sweeping up that gravel in the driveway?" I boil over. Righteous indignation, I think it's called. Of course, the person asking the question typically doesn't know about the gravel you've moved or anything else. He or she just asked a simple question and got attacked. Live inside this brain for a day or so and then tell me you weren't asking a whole lot. The gravel I moved for my daughter was in the boxcar-load size, and I was still trying to keep a clean office, with the gravel police inspecting for gravel dust, or that one tiny little pebble I neglected to pick up. It was tough. I would be hearing from Jack Armstrong about this slip of the tongue, but that story will come a little later. Believe it or not, there are bigger fish to fry.

# The Worst Week Of My Life — December 11–15

We knew this week would be one to remember. Caroline and I were subpoenaed to court to testify in a child custody case.

## No Good Deed

As the fates would have it, they were before the same judge who heard our own daughter's case on November 9. We were waiting to hear a decision according to his schedule, or thirty days after the hearing. His decision was due within days. Then there was the ten-day deadline for the board setting up the special education meeting we'd requested for Sarah in the middle of November. We were bound and determined to request a formal due process hearing if they missed the deadline, to bring in an impartial hearing officer to rule on Sarah's special education status. Word was out that the board was dead against labeling her LD and would fight it out. As usual they were circling the wagons, but this time they had the Indians inside the circle with them. As if this weren't enough, I had my "informal meeting" with the superintendent to discuss my concerns about the personal day I was forced to take for Jackie's memorial service, the little boy who died in the car fire. Seems like the superintendent would have something more important to do than take attendance at funerals for six-year-olds, but when he gets on a roll to destroy someone, no one better get in his way.

Monday went by okay without incident. Tuesday, Caroline's custody hearing for one of her students ended with the kids going back to their abusive parents. The special education supervisor insisted on meeting with me to express her dismay that I had tried to "set her up" with the superintendent. I had asked her to give me flex time to leave the high school, where I had ten days with no one to test, to return to the middle school, where I had kids to test, observe, consultations, behavior contracts, ADHD screens, etc. I had ample documentation and thought this was a legitimate request. The only subterfuge was that I wanted her to rule on it before the personnel director got back from his heart bypass, because he went out of his way to ignore my requests just because I made them. Forget what makes sense or what is in the best interest of the school system. Frank wants it? Forget it. The special education supervisor's problem was the fact that I hadn't filled her in on everything else going on. In my mind

I saw no connection between events; in fact, I was trying to keep my mind clear and not get paranoid and see conspiracies hatched behind every tree. She suggested that the grapevine was rattling about me taking all of these illegal days off (for the funeral and my late friend Hank Matthew's mourning), and that this had to be another attempt on me to steal more days from the school district. When I asked her what days she was talking about, she mentioned Hank's funeral. I explained the situation to her. My supervisor and I were lied to, told that everyone had taken personal leave to attend the memorial service for the six-year-old. This wasn't the case. I filed a grievance (4-205-c). I would be meeting with the superintendent on Thursday to resolve that very issue. I was not trying to pull a fast one and had no ulterior motives. There was no connection between my request for flexibility—spelled spending time where I was needed most—rather than sit at the high school with nothing to do. The superintendent's allegations about me stealing time were untrue. The only grapevine rattling was the superintendent's. I saw no connection because there was none. Apparently someone did, or was trying to tie unrelated events together, as I later discovered. The supervisor understood my position and we parted amicably. I was almost feeling bad about filing for a due process hearing about Sarah's need for special education. Wednesday I taught my last class at the college for the semester, and Thursday I went to the custody hearing for the student I was working with.

The witnesses were sequestered, and when I got called in before the judge, I was sworn and handed the letter I wrote and asked if it was the report that I had written. Well, it wasn't a report, and I was under oath, so I stumbled and then clarified that, "I wouldn't characterize this as a report. It is a letter I wrote." Well, the other side objected, and the judge made a big thing about the purpose of the letter—was it written about the girl in question or for this proceeding, and what business did the board of education have getting involved in custody suits? I did get to squeeze in a word that I wrote this letter not as an expert opinion, but my sense of what was in this girl's best interest after having worked with her for eighteen months. And, that I had completed a comprehensive psychological report on the student in question. The judge's eyes narrowed and he mumbled something about "I hope this isn't a special education case." (Was he thinking about his last special education case? My daughter's?) I don't think he even knew who he had on the stand…the father of the girl he was to make a special education decision about.

I was under oath, mind you, and I needed to answer his question honestly, was this a special education case. Well, I said, "Yes, your honor," and that's when the volcano blew. He directed his wrath at the two attorneys, how they hadn't given him all the information, and how he was being asked to render an opinion without the facts, and it would be overturned on appeal. By this time the stepdad's attorney was too confused to ask me any questions, and the natural father's attorney asked me a question or two. I interjected that it was my opinion after having talked with both fathers, that her real dad seemed to have his motivations confused, between anger over his ex-wife and his feelings for his daughter. I was then dismissed without having said a whole lot more. I left feeling frustrated. How would this affect me on the job, or Sarah's case?

So I go back to the middle school feeling pretty down, and I get to school and Jack, the highly respected principal, my primary supervisor and sole supporter calls me to his office. I'm thinking he's picked up on my blue mood and wants to perk me up, and I start telling him about my court appearance, and he rather frankly says he's not interested in my court appearance, he wants to know what happened at my meeting with Roamy. Up to that moment my conscience was clear. He asked me if I met with Roamy to straighten out our misunderstanding, and I very proudly said I did. He leaned forward in his seat with what I would describe as a quizzical look and said, as serious as any man could, "In the course of this conversation, did you tell her, that she could…'tell you to fuck off'?" The blood drained out of my whole body. I felt embarrassed, humiliated, defeated, and about as stressed out and stupid as a man could feel. What could I say? "Well, I guess that's something I might have said...yeah, I said it." And I won't waste words repeating what I tried to do in the way of explaining my way out of this one. There weren't many, I can tell you. Just a context of what I was feeling and how I wanted to convince her of my sincerity. How I misjudged her. I was sorry. But hey, I didn't tell *her* to fuck off, I just gave her permission to tell *me* to fuck off. It would never happen again. What now?

He was clearly upset with me. I felt like a little boy who had let down a trusted mentor. I respected Jack, and his credibility was on the line here, too. I was so low already I really couldn't imagine how much lower I could sink. Jack didn't lecture me; he didn't say much. With a man like Jack, a few words and the look on his face said it all. His integrity and his expectations. He told me how the special education supervisor had come to him with the report. Apparently I had Roamy pegged correctly in regard to her affinity for going to the top to complain about someone; she loved to tattle on people, and in this case on me. Was she trying to solve a problem and make one for me? Jack was trying to work with me and he had insisted that the supervisor let him handle it. He felt that she would honor his request. He also believed that if she didn't, or the superintendent found out from some other source, he would use this to the fullest extent. He would make mincemeat out of me. I think Jack's words were along the lines of "If the superintendent were to ever get hold of this, you'd be history." I need you to get with Roamy and make this thing right, and then I'll need a letter from you telling me what you did. This way, if the superintendent wants to know what action I've taken, I can tell him I've dealt with it. He'll want you to be formally reprimanded, but I have had my go-rounds with him, and I know any man deserves one mistake. I've heard all of this stuff about Frank Matthews, but I've ignored it and tried to give you a chance, and this makes it hard."

On that note I slithered out of his office. I did exactly what he said. I made nice, and wrote down a little something for the files. I don't know what bothered me more — the fact that

I might have inadvertently given the superintendent just what he needed to bury me, the fear that it would always be there dangling like the veritable sword of Damocles, or the fact that I had let Jack down. Luckily Roamy was in her room alone and I asked her if I could come in. I was humble beyond description, and I think she understood. The pressure was gone between us and I wrote Jack a short letter about it never happening again. No excuses, just never again. I also asked him if I needed to get with the special education supervisor before my meeting with the superintendent that afternoon, and he said no, he had assured her he would handle it and he felt she would respect that. As Jackie Gleason used to say in his role of Ralph Kramden, "Me and my BIG MOUTH!"

## Appeal: Personal Day

I needed to talk to somebody, and Tony G. the guidance counselor was my sounding board. He was available. I also talked to my wife. How much stress could one man handle? Now it was try and get something done and get my head ready for my meeting in the afternoon with the superintendent. I had to talk about my having to take a personal day grievance for Jackie's memorial service. I have to tell you this was the most stressed and the lowest I felt throughout this whole venture.

We had the hearing before the superintendent. They even had their big city attorney there. The principal from the other high school was there in person. I was surprised since this was just an explanation of the facts. I was to find out why very soon. The superintendent put the principal up to testify. "Did you give Mr. Matthews permission to attend the memorial service on October 25?" Principal: "Mr. Matthews approached me on the day in question and told me (TOLD ME?) he was going to the service, so I reasonably assumed he had already secured permission." I was blown away. When I got to speak I tried to be as professional as possible to relate my recollection of events without calling him the damn liar he was. The assistant superintendent talked about types of leave, personal, sick, conference, and that the contract simply didn't have a clause for compassionate leave. [No, man, that comes from the heart, that is if you have one]. My union rep took me out in the hall to confer. "Did you hear what they were saying in there? They were only too glad to return your personal day as requested, but then you will be considered AWOL!"

A teacher who is AWOL is in bad trouble. That's like walking out of your classroom in the middle of the day to go to Sunny's Bar and Grill for a beer. It's also grounds for immediate termination! It was my word against the principal's, and you can guess who the superintendent was backing. Not only did he stand behind his principal, but he had the knife poking him in the back at the same time. The superintendent was all this talk about what time I got back to my building (the funeral was over at two ten, they hung in the parking lot until two thirty or later, I drove past my building at three, the end of my workday). He was trying to say they all got back at two thirty. Not unless they were direct-wired and faxed themselves there. They were fifteen or twenty minutes further down the road and couldn't have gotten back before three fifteen to three thirty. And though they did return to their buildings after the funeral, they work till four; my day was over at *three*. When I pointed out this not-too-subtle fact, he spouted administrivia: "The work day is seven hours and fifteen minutes." My response, "Well, if you want to play it that way, I arrived at the building at 7:30…I'll let you do your own math" (two forty-five). The bottom line was they didn't care about the facts. The lie was all they were willing to entertain, and they supported this by other unfounded accusations about my "pushing the limits" and taking time away from the taxpayers for other non-job-related activities, allusions to the grief counseling I did when my friend and colleague Hank died. We conferenced in the hall, and I told my union rep that I heard loud and clear what they were saying: take the funeral as a personal day or get fired. I was willing to concede this skirmish, and glad to get out of there. I withdrew my grievance. Friday was uneventful, but it's clear that they (meaning the super and the directors) were out to get me any way they could. There was a bounty on my head. The special education supervisor said it, Jack said it, and in certain ways Mel did, too. Was I intimidated? Sure, but they still got their due process letter the next day. I wasn't going to give up on Sarah's need for special education services. I was still ready to rock and roll, I just wanted to hear some decent music.

I thought long and hard how to deal with the other principal when next I saw him. I was beginning to get a fix on the superintendent's MO (*modus operandi* — method of doing things), and it was clear. Put pressure on your staff to do the "right thing" even if it meant lie, deceive, or betray someone. This was confirmed, at least in my mind, when I asked the other principal for an opportunity to sit down.

He went on about how he had really had the riot act read to him for letting me go, and that he hadn't understood the policy on personal days. I told him I understood why he did what he did, that he must have been under enormous pressure from the superintendent and had to do what he had to do. I was giving him an out, an "I understand and feel for you, it must be tough having your balls in this man's wringer." His response was this: "I'm a good Catholic and I know the meaning of sin, and my conscience is clear. I sleep well at night." He was essentially denying that he had lied. "I simply misunderstood what you were asking me." Sure, sure, not only does the guy lie, but he's afraid to own up to it. I lost what little respect I had for the man right then. He later reported to the superintendent that I had "called him a liar." Read my mind. Guilty conscience, man?

## The Spies Within

After the Mason letter and my due process for special education request, I noticed the attendance at my special education meetings was up. Now supervisors and assistants began to appear for no apparent reason. One was a smoking buddy of the special education supervisor and had no vested interest in any of my other schools, but here she was at North. I even asked Mel what she was doing there and he couldn't tell me. His response was along the lines of, "Of all the people who come into my building, she is the only one I have no idea about." I had the feeling she was there to spy on me. And one meeting I discovered that I was wrong. She was there to do more than spy on me, she was there to set me up.

It seemed innocent enough. I'd be in the midst of explaining a range of scores to a parent and she would interrupt me mid-sentence with a "thoughtful" question. "But Mr. Matthews, I thought you said she had visual motor strengths. Didn't you just say she had visual motor weaknesses just now?" So I would have to explain to her how the subtests were all visual motor, and how out of six you could have both strengths and weaknesses, a point of distinction I would make at the appropriate time in my explanation. After her third interruption, I held my hand up like a traffic officer and said, "Could I please finish?" I had behaved professionally in a difficult setting... or so I thought.

January 26 was the Friday before Sarah's special education due process hearing. I would be running this on my own. I was nervous but I had prepared for weeks and weeks. I was ready. I just had to relax and get ready for the day. What could screw it up? Then I received a phone call. It was from the personnel director's secretary. She was calling me to set up a meeting on Monday the twenty-ninth, the day *before* the hearing, now scheduled for January 30. The last thing in the world I wanted to do was engage in more back and forth with this man who hated my guts, the day before this major hearing. I told his secretary I was unable to give her a commitment because I didn't know my schedule of meetings until I arrived at the school Monday morning. She hesitated, indicating that the personnel director had already left for the day; he was feeling sick. She promised to get back to me.

Approximately twenty minutes later, that ol' personnel director crawled out from under his sick bed and showed up at the middle school where I was working that day. I was walking down the hall when I saw him, and when I did, I panicked. What was so important that he would come in "sick" to schedule a meeting with me, one day before I had to present at my daughter's due process hearing? It could only be one thing. He had found out about the F-word incident and he was going to haul me up on sexual harassment charges. I had to get to Roamy before he did. I ducked down a back hall and into her room. Luckily she was there and had no kids. I spilled it all out. She basically looked at me like I was nuts. "We don't have a problem. No big thing." Then the personnel director had me announced on the ALL CALL. I scurried out and met him in the media center. His demeanor could be described as upset, somewhat angry, and firm in his insistence that we meet on Monday. I set a time. I asked him what he wanted to discuss with me and he simply responded, "There's some things you need to see."

Well, I just wanted to make it through the day and go home. I knew there was no way in hell I was going to let this man, the director of personnel, get to me twenty-four hours before Sarah's hearing. I was presenting the case, I had worked for weeks preparing it, and I needed to be relaxed and on top of my game. Plant some seeds of doubt, show me the naked pictures of me with the cocker spaniel, gun to my head, held up for harassment charges, who knows? I couldn't afford to have my concentration ruined. They'd gotten to other people; they'd get to Roamy if they had to. No way I was going to school Monday. They could have been passing out a million dollars and I would have been sick. But Friday wasn't over yet, one small thing. Well, two, small things...two letters in my mailbox. This was what is known as the full court press. One letter was from the special education supervisor: "How dare you beat on my door!" She was upset about my having served her at her private home. She could serve me on the job, I couldn't, and when I did it on my own time, I was chastised for violating her privacy at home. There were just too many double binds to steer clear of. And the bottom line was they got their postponement anyway.

The other letter was a thick envelope from my attorney, Morris. The circuit court turned us down. To my surprise the judge at the civil court agreed with the board of education: Sarah was expelled for good reason. That was very bad news. After reading through his decision it was readily apparent that he never read any of the documentation we provided! He had the most basic facts wrong. But as disappointed as I was that he had ruled against us, his gross errors in judgment and his missing crucial facts would provide us ample opportunity for appeal. His strongest argument, and the only one we agreed with, was, "If she was special education, then they couldn't have expelled her like they did." Thanks, Judge, you gave us our best argument. I recall his comment about not having all the right information for my case earlier in the week ("This isn't a special ed case, is it?") Even he knew his decision could be appealed. And yet here it was in its full splendor. He was supporting the administrators and the board and the state board, all of whom erred by expelling a special education student without due process. It stunk. The whole thing stunk to high heaven.

# CHAPTER FIFTEEN

# THE HEARING

## The Personnel Director's Meeting

On Tuesday, January 30, the hearing was held, and I did an adequate job with the odds against me, but more about that later. Suffice it to say that we did not settle anything except to set a date for another hearing. And the meeting that the personnel director so desperately had to hold the day *before* my hearing? Well, it was almost forgotten, an afterthought now that the due process hearing had been held. This seemed to confirm my earlier suspicions that the intent was part of their psychological warfare, to make me anxious prior to the hearing I had requested and where I would present testimony against the board. The hearing is held without the personnel director's all important, have-to-see-you meeting, and when do I next hear about it? Three days later he had his secretary call my office and ask for a time on Tuesday, February 6, to meet. *Ten* days later. I agreed to meet at two o'clock.

He greeted me and invited me to his office. He then invited the special education supervisor into the meeting and sat down and closed the door. He shuffled some papers on his desk and said that when he got back from his surgery (he'd had a heart attack and surgery and was out for a number of weeks), there were these letters, six of them, written about me. He said the superintendent had asked him to investigate and that he wanted me to read them, or scan them, and react.

I took the letters (there were only five; one was a copy of a letter I had written—the Mason letter). I scanned them and asked him if these were my copies. He said no, and went out and returned with copies he handed me. He and the special education supervisor seemed to be waiting for me to say something, to react, and I sat in silence (for once). This prompted him to ask me if I was going to respond. I told him that I had learned a lot in these court proceedings, and that one thing in particular was this: that if you let any allegations stand unrefuted, they stood as fact, and that there was a great deal more to these stories then these versions. However, some of the issues that were being raised in these letters were the same issues that I intended to address at the second due process hearing, scheduled for February 20, and it wouldn't be appropriate for me to respond until then. He then asked what kind of timeline I was working on. If I waited too long, "the superintendent will be down here banging on my door." I asked him what kind of response he wanted, verbal or written. He indicated written, and I said, "Fine, how about the twenty-first?"

Here are the "serious" allegations contained in those five letters.

**Allegations:**
"...displayed some uncooperative and unprofessional behavior toward the special education teacher..."

"...not working with the team and his demeanor was offensive to the special education teacher..."

"...contradicted (the special education teacher) regarding the use of the discrepancy chart and told the parent it was being used incorrectly."

## The Hearing

"...refused to verbally give the results of the Full Scale IQ score to the special education teacher, commenting that she was going to apply it incorrectly against the discrepancy chart."

"...reluctantly threw the paperwork to her across the table."

"...refused to report the full scale (sic) IQ so that the discrepancy chart could be used according to county policy."

(When asked for the student's IQ in the meeting I refused to provide a single number, when I had prepared a three-page report that placed this number and all the rest into the appropriate context, thus preventing her from over-simplifying the case by using a formula long discredited in the field. In fact there was no "county policy" on use of the discrepancy chart, and test results are expected to be interpreted by the team member with training in that area, in this case the school psychologist, me)

"... refused to give the special education teacher his test scores..."

(I did, however eventually allow her to reach across the table and retrieve the report so she could continue to conduct the meeting.)

"...student clearly had a learning disability... (Mr. Matthews indicated that) he believed the student's bad attitude in high school was because he was a frustrated student."

"... had the audacity to hold out his arm and put his hand up when (one team member) was ready to speak, indicating that (she) should not speak. (She) found this action very offensive."

"...he questioned school/board policy...and advised the parent to call the principal. Then if the parent was not satisfied, to get a group of parents and to go to a board of education meeting because the squeaky wheel..."

"...he chewed gum..."

One of the "serious allegations" was about my culinary habit of chewing gum when I was nervous, and my sour stomach brought demon breath to my lips.

Now then, the allegations listed above are verbatim. I place them here in their exactitude for two reasons. One so you get the straight facts as they read, not my interpretations of them (you'll get plenty of them later), and two so you can see for yourself how each allegation describing the same incidents differ widely from one witness to the next.

The personnel director gave me copies of these alleged incidents, then indicated that he would conduct an investigation and make his report directly to the superintendent for action if necessary. I asked him if it turned out that others were at fault, could I expect action would be taken against them? He hesitated, and then said yes. The whole conference was over in ten minutes. Asking me to respond to these allegations was like asking me to show my hand before the big showdown. I wasn't about to do that. He got a response on the twenty-first, all right: "Dear John, Feel free to conduct your investigation and rest assured that the allegations against me are completely without substance." I figured he could find out what brand of gum I was chewing, and which hand, right or left, I used to tell the supervisor of special education's assistant to stop interrupting me. I thanked them and left the building. I returned to the middle school for the remaining forty-five minutes of my work day. This short meeting confirmed what I had always suspected, that the superintendent was running the show and that he was directing principals, supervisors, directors, coordinators, and now my fellow educators to get Frank Matthews, any way, any shape, any form. I was for all intents and purposes: Wanted, Dead or Alive.

Here are my responses to the "serious charges" in the letters from the meeting.

1) Most of these "incidents" are factual, but taken out of context. I was being asked to misrepresent data from my psychological, and when I refused to give one score instead of the entire profile, which presented a more complete and accurate picture, and the special education teacher insisted, I just give her the IQ. I

## The Hearing

closed my report and placed in on the table in front of her, saying, if you want the numbers, *you* find them; this (my report) is what I have to say about this young man. My point was that I wrote a four-page report and wasn't going to let my data (the full scale IQ) be misrepresented at a meeting. Even among the "eyewitnesses" there are at least three versions: *tossed, threw, allowed her to reach across*, and mine, *placed in front of her*.

2) There is no county policy on use of the "Discrepancy Formula."
3) These "incidents" occurred back in October and November and yet no formal conference was held to discuss them, no letter was handed to me about my actions, and the building principal has never discussed the matter with me at all. All of the preceding are requirements of our Teacher's Association contract; prompt notice, written notice with conference, and opportunity to respond. I went into the assistant principal's office on my own after the one meeting because I was upset and wanted to complain about the special education teacher's behavior. He told me he thought I was "out of line" but never used the words "offensive" or "unprofessional." I followed up this meeting with my letter to him on November 1, 1995, which he never responded to other than to indicate by letter that he passed it along to the building principal, who would deal with it. To date no action has been taken. This was after fourteen weeks had passed. The assistant principal thought I was "out of line" because he didn't fully understand what he was observing; he didn't understand county policy, the teacher's contract, or the tenets of my profession. All he saw was a new teacher trying to conduct a meeting. Sad to say, she didn't understand county policy or how psychological data must be presented either. That's the trouble when you have administrators who are uninformed and don't trust the

professional judgment of those who are. He essentially backed the wrong horse.

Later that week we received word that the circuit court had turned down our appeal. We received word of this on Friday, January 26. This just so happened to be the same day the personnel director demanded that I meet with him Monday, the day before Sarah's due process hearing. After the hearing and a week before the second round, he schedules his February 6 meeting, in which he suddenly presents the five allegation letters.

Of the four allegations, two were witnesses against us at the hearing, and two were assistants to witnesses. So here are four people, employees of the school district, involved in the evaluation of my daughter and the subsequent due process hearing alleging improprieties by them and others, and here they are filing "complaints" against me for unprofessional behavior. There have to be some questions about their motivations and their credibility, don't you think? Was it fair? Heck no. But I would start to learn the adage that LIFE IS NOT FAIR.

## The Hearing

I stayed home Monday to get right with my body and prepare for the case on Tuesday, January 30. By Sunday my whole body was a total mess, so I made "the call" to Jack that night. He understood and even said he'd call the high school in the morning to save me from having to make the "other call." I put the day to good use, revising questions and documentation, pulling together all the odds and ends so I'd be ready. Ready to enter the ring with no timeouts. In a way it is like an athletic event, a fight, or an Olympic contest where you do all your winning and losing outside the ring or rink or whatever. You train and practice and put it all into that one moment in the ring. Time it perfectly so you peak at

## The Hearing

the right moment, adrenaline pumping, body and mind alert and in synch. No way was I gonna let the personnel director screw that up for me. The phone did ring. Three times. The machine was primed. One ring, two rings, three rings...four rings...click... "Sorry, no one's home. You know the routine, name and number...beeeeeep..." "This is Toni from David Mercier's office. I tried to contact you at school but no one seemed to know where you were. Anyway...you're scheduled for four thirty this afternoon. See you then." Click whirrrrrr click click click. Forty three minutes later: ring ring ring ring click Sorry beeep ka-chunk click whirrr click. And once more, same as the last one, but each time silence, no message. Just checking... cowards. Just making me breathe harder, and pounding that old heart in my chest. "Hey, I heard the phone ring at 9:40. I was in the bathroom, and then I took a shower... what can I say?" Made my appointment with David, he's my acupuncturist, and it was amazing how this treatment and his calm voice drained the stress and anxiety right out of me.

I first got interested in acupuncture when I read how it was used to help addicts break the cycle of addiction. I figured that if this worked with heroin addicts, it had to be powerful. I suggested Caroline give it a try for her muscle spasms, and I followed for my blood pressure and tension headaches. It's fairly simple. You lay out on a table in a room with soft lights and soothing music. You strip to everything but your undershorts and lie back on the table with a sheet pulled over you for privacy. After you've relaxed for five to ten minutes the acupuncturist comes in and sits in a chair near you. He asks how you are and how your week has been. How have you been, physically, emotionally? It is every bit of a therapy session. Active listening, someone who cares about you and your well-being. He then puts down his clipboard and examines your pulses. There are any number of locations for different energy flows, and he reads them all. Then he places the needles into the nerve pathways to block or stimulate the flow of CHI, the energy source. He may insert and remove a needle in a "Breathe out...breathe in....breathe out" pattern, or he might leave them in for fifteen minutes. Sometimes he will end the treatment with a conversation where he gives advice and perspectives on your situation, how to handle things the next time, ways of looking at things differently. Sometimes he may leave you with ten to twelve needles in for you to relax into a deep sleep. Sometimes you can feel the energy rushing through your body or stress leaving it like a balloon that has just been stuck leaving the air to escape. Sometimes he'll ask you to lie back for a while to let things set in before you get up and dress. "See you next time." You never feel rushed, you just feel relaxed, respected, important, and cared for. After this last treatment, I felt 100 percent better and ready to go into battle.

## Opening Statement — January 30

"The first thing we need to address here today is the reason we are here today. There is only one reason, and that is the young woman who sits here with us, my daughter, Sarah Matthews. We will show that Sarah is a bright, capable, effervescent youngster, who is full of life and captivates everyone she meets. But we who love her the most, her mother and I, acknowledge that she has a dark side. A place she is only now coming out of. A place where things are confusing and frustrating, filled with depression and anxiety, even anger. I know because I've lived with her 365 days a year for almost fifteen years, when I became part of her family. Not only am I her adoptive father, but I am a practicing school psychologist, and as such I recognized her learning problems from the very start, and we have worked with her from the very start.

"When she turned to drugs to fill in what was missing in her mind, we were there to catch her and pull her out of the abyss before she sunk further. Let me tell you, it's not been easy, but she is worth every minute, every penny, every tear we've shed.

## The Hearing

"When I asked to have her evaluated, I had one thought in mind: Why is she continuing to slip back into the past? What is going on with her? Is it her learning problems from before, is it a new set of emotional problems spurred by adolescence? And so I asked to have her evaluated, and from that day on it has been an uphill struggle, a battle to realize the rights every other disabled child in this system takes for granted.

"As we present our case we will call witnesses, but where their memories or loyalties compromise their responses, we will provide a paper trail so clear it will show without a doubt that what we maintain is true. What I want you to keep in mind is that there has been a lot of confusion in a case that should be very straightforward. I mean, we didn't have to bring in independent evaluators; we were perfectly comfortable with the assessments this system's examiners conducted. We'll show how test results from two psychologicals nine years apart are strikingly similar. We'll show how the results on the psychologicals are consistent with the results of the educational tests, and that both are consistent with problems she is experiencing in the classroom. This is not a borderline case. On a one to ten scale, this is a ten in terms of eligibility.

"Sarah has all of the 'classic' indications of specific learning disabilities: a previous history of learning problems and identification as a learning disabled student, average ability, significant variations in cognitive areas and scaled scores on achievement tests, as well as a highly consistent relationship between these cognitive deficits and her academic deficiencies.

"If everything is so clear cut, you might ask, why is the board fighting so hard to keep her from receiving services? I'm as curious about this as you are. The hearing officer commented that he felt he was in the dark. Well, that's pretty accurate, because there's been a lot of smoke being blown around here, and it's our intention to reveal the source of that smoke and clear it away.

"According to the *Procedural Safeguards Parental Rights* booklet provided by the board of education (page 7), we have a 'right to have the hearing conducted at a time and place reasonably convenient to the parent and the student. Although the board apparently knew weeks in advance about the date of the hearing, they only notified us at the very last minute. And they didn't ask us, they told us. Then they complained that because they had made numerous attempts to contact our attorney and could not reach him, they wanted to postpone the hearing. What I can't understand is why no one ever called us in the thirty-four-day interim; I mean, the principal and special education supervisor knew where we were every day.

"Our attorney's January 24 letter clearly sets the record straight that 1) there *was* no communication from the board attorney between our attorney's December 14 letter and January 17, when they summarily set the date, time, and location of the hearing. Our attorney also writes that he was not representing us in this matter as I had indicated previously."

## The Opening Statement Has Been Delivered

The hearing went on as you can expect. Opening statements, my witnesses: Lucy, the school psychologist who tested Sarah at our request, The Special Education Supervisor who did everything she could to ignore the test findings (that Sarah was in fact learning disabled), and the building principal who assured me Sarah would be properly identified with a learning disability. They were primed. I wonder how much it cost in hours to coach them? They answered quickly so I wouldn't have time to object, and they gave vague answers... played stupid; "Me an expert? I don't know nothin' bout no 'screpancies." But I got my information on the record. Sarah's principal, was on and we were really making some progress... and I think Myron Stein, the Hearing Officer was ready to rule in our favor. He was ready to agree that Sarah was LD (learning disabled). He wasn't going to recommend she be pulled out of her classes for special services just

Intensity I (consultation model), but at least it would be an acknowledgment of her learning disabilities and provide our long-sought-after IEP. The board's high-powered city attorney smelled defeat in the air, which is precisely why he leapt up and proposed a settlement offer. He'd be right back. He left the principal on the stand to schmooze with the board's local attorney, and fifteen minutes later he was back with seven points. On the surface they sounded okay—no acknowledgment of her learning disabilities, no IEP, but all of the modifications and help we'd long sought. Accepting would be waiving our rights; rejecting would indicate we were after labels, not help. What to do? Conference. Dr. Mom, our family therapist, Caroline, Sarah and I went upstairs to talk. After weighing the pros and cons, Dr, Mom came up with an excellent solution. Ask for the seven in writing and forty-eight hours to consider them. We returned downstairs and that's how we left it that day. The Hearing Officer wasn't even going to hold me to the forty-eight, but he did want a response quickly.

Wednesday the thirty-first was an interesting day for a lot of reasons. I was at the same high school I got in trouble for attending the little boy's funeral. The special education director, the clinical psychologist, and a teacher were in my room again, so I made space in another office. Sat down with a kid for my evaluation. Heard the Assistant Superintendent outside the door for forty minutes before I finished my assessment, opened up to let the kid go back to class, and got my package from him at 9:40. Never opened it until I got home that afternoon. It was the board's high powered attorney's offer. He had outlined seven points.

The seven points were little in the way of offering, and asked us to give up much. But the board attorney managed to do something we couldn't. He formed linkage between the two cases. We thought about it, and for sure on the surface it appears to meet all our needs; that's the way it sounded when he read it off his notepad. But on close inspection, it left a lot to be desired. In the context of her expulsion and the myriad of games they played while we tried to get her tested and identified as LD, and then to receive the services she was entitled to, we were not about to let them off the hook on the errors they made with respect to IDEA or 504. At the very least there were technical violations, timelines being the most outrageous. If even one day is missed (and they missed by weeks, even months), the parent prevails and recovers attorney's fees. That is why special education people are so compulsive about dates of IEPs and psychologicals and ten-day notices (inviting parents to meetings, etc.). Dates are hard to miss, and with dated documents, violations are easy to prove. It's a paper trail. All it takes is one hearing and one missed date.

They agreed to give us what we had cried for almost a year, an IEP for Sarah. But was it? IEPs don't expire, and they don't contain only one goal, and they continue to make adjustments according to the disabled student's need(s). They wanted a closed contract (one year) with no obligation to reconvene the ARD for additional action. We were so badly burned before, we did not trust them enough to give them this power and authority, and I truly question whether it was legal. We were also concerned about the use of nonstudent tutors, meaning instructional assistants. Sarah was learning disabled and needed someone with expertise in this area, a special education teacher, not a teacher's aide.

We were also reluctant to have our hands tied and our lips sealed with respect to using this "program" in other actions, especially the expulsion hearings. Though we were still relying on her history of special education identification and services for that case, it would be icing on the cake to demonstrate that she was still disabled and in need of services, and that the district that had so long denied her services was now recognizing this fact. The mere fact that Less mentioned her expulsion case, the one before the circuit court, was revealing in itself; it suggested quite strongly that they were concerned about what happened in parent meetings affecting the eventual outcome of her court case. We could not allow anything to interfere with that. Less made the connection, the linkage, and it was a revelation we could not ignore. For so long they insisted that the actions they took in our parent meetings (refusing to test her, ignoring her test findings, etc.) were in no way related to the court action, but they could no longer make this claim.

We did not like the wording in which any disclosure would be a breach and render the services null and void. Even though we might be quiet about it, what would prevent them from leaking it and then turning around on us and stopping services for Sarah based on this alleged breach? We had gone beyond not trusting them to a much higher level of suspicion; they had lied to us and ignored us and mistreated us so badly, we were not going to give them any leverage over us we did not have to.

And last but not least, we had around $8,000 to $10,000 in the case, not including costs, and we were not about to waive any rights to attorney's fees. We were still convinced in the end we would recover something; we knew there were so many violations that even one technical violation would throw it our way. We decided we would make a counteroffer.

## Homey On The Range

Even while all this back and forth was going on between hearings, mine and Sarah's, other things were brewing at Northern. Sarah had called me from school. She was upset about something and wanted to go home. I gave permission. When I got home I found out why. The same teacher who complained that "Sarah's got a friggin' dirty mouth!" We talked with Sarah and she apologized. He (Homey, that is) runs a fast and loose classroom and then singles out students for doing things that everyone else does, like curse. This is the same gentleman who singled out my son at a dance two years ago when he spilled a soda. "Way to go, Andrew, a klutz like your old man," He hollered across the high school lobby. I went right to the principal on this one. He lied his way out, as you would expect. Well, seems with hunting season declared on the Matthewses, he figured we were safe targets, so he stepped forward again. This time it was, "When are those Matthewses going to give up on this case? I mean, they should talk. Got a drug addict for a daughter and then take her to Woodstock. That's like taking my alcoholic son to a bar." Word came to us from some of Sarah's friends who were upset that he would say these things in class, in front of other students. This had to stop!

Caroline and I met with Sarah's high school principal Thursday and laid it out. Tell Homey to close his mouth. The principal whom I'll call Mel assured us he would deal with the man and we went on to work. Later in the day, old Homey did it again. "I better not say anything to Sarah or her father might sue me. Why don't those West Virginia hicks get a life!?" In any other world this man would have been suspended or even fired for unprofessional conduct. Here in the district even harassment is allowed apparently. I fired off a letter to Mel, though it was really the superintendent it was aimed at. I described a hostile work environment and harassment against my children. This made the third time this teacher made unprofessional, disparaging remarks against my family, and it certainly seemed like it was a pattern of abuse, Systemic. I got a letter back from the superintendent, but as you can expect it was a counteroffensive rather than anything of substance. But back to the hearing…

The board's high-powered attorney I'll call Less played his usual game of BE THERE AT FOUR THIRTY and then didn't show up himself. I'd arranged a location (my office), a time for the conference call and day, and Myron, the hearing officer, said he'd talk with Less. Less calls my *home* at three and talks to Sarah: "I don't know where my dad is." "When will he be back?" "Oh, four thirty to five." So when the hearing officer calls from a pay phone at four thirty, Less reports that I can't be found. I sit by the phone in my office from three thirty on, and call his office at five. We get it together at five thirty.

# The Hearing

The STUPID dishonest games Less plays! I'm ready to go on February 7, but Less can't make it. "My witness will not be available until the nineteenth," he insists. "Okay, I respond, "...but the nineteenth is a day off. I don't care about Less's problems, I tell him, "That's your problem. These hearings are to be at our convenience, not yours. I can't afford to miss a day's pay Wednesday we are off work, Tuesday we are not If you'll work with us, and schedule the hearing on our day off we won't be penalized for appearing to the tune of $432 " I tell him. "That's up to the superintendent," Less proclaims. No shit, Shirley, he *is* your client after all. And with this in place we agree to the twentieth. Of course Less never gets back to us about the pay, and the superintendent kindly informs us of the wonderful policy he constructed around this need. Take the day off and *only* lose $432. They are not making this any easier.

    The next event on the agenda came on Thursday the eighth of February. I was in my office at the middle school, and I get a call from the secretary to meet The Special Education Supervisor in the media center. Strange, why didn't she come down to my office? So I march up and there she sits, all sugar and spice, ready to go over a formal *observation* she conducted on me on the twenty-fifth of January. I mean, really. First off, I had no idea whatsoever that I was even being observed. The fairness or lack thereof of The Special Education Supervisor evaluating me right after a due process hearing against her was incredible. I figured they'd bypass my evaluation or wait a few weeks until spring. But not these morons. They observe me without notice, two school days before the hearing on the thirtieth. They pick a difficult case where the parents are upset with the school system anyway, and I have to go over my test results. Then they review it less than ten days after I have the same special education supervisor on the stand as a hostile witness. Oh, there were a few positive comments, but she made a big thing of me bringing in "irrelevant information that upset the parent." I filed my usual protest and moved on. They just don't know when to quit.

## Teachers Association, Where Are You?

I've been dealing with the Teachers Association, but they are so busy, they really can't spend much time with little ol' me. I have been asking for months for them to go on the offensive, but my Teacher's Association attorney whom I'll call Geraldine, seems content to wait until they take action and then poke holes in it. Until the next time. I mean, I have enough on my plate financially, emotionally, professionally, and otherwise with this hearing and the circuit court case; I can't worry about my job. That's what they're there for. I paid my dues for the association to protect my job, so they needed to do their part.

## Closing Remarks, February 20 — Background

I reviewed Sarah's problems from birth—her delayed gross motor skills, delayed speech, delays in school, retention and identification as a learning disabled student in second grade. I documented how she had been provided special education services in four school years: 1985–'86, '86–'87, '87–'88, '88–'89. Her grades were good. I explained how her behaviors became a problem in middle school.

I discussed her involvement with illegal substances in '93–'94, and the repeated urine screenings, individual and group therapy at the counseling center, family and individual counseling with Dr. Mom, and my request in October 1994 for a reevaluation. After some delay, this evaluation was completed in February 1995. Her ARD on April 5 was complete with clear-cut evidence of eligibility, yet no one would address it. Qualified examiners are required to conduct assessments for eligibility determination, i.e., they have the necessary educational background and training not only in test administration in general, but in the *interpretation* of the individual tests they administer. Yet, the special education teacher at the high school and the school psychologist's behavior at the April 5 parent meeting with us, as well the January 30 hearing, suggested that they were unable to form a professional opinion. I wondered aloud why this might have been. The state certified special education teacher indicated she was not an "expert" in test administration and couldn't even answer basic questions relative to the *significance* of the scores on Sarah's tests. I asked the special education teacher and the school psychologist the same straightforward question about whether the discrepancies they revealed were "significant" or "highly significant." Their responses were vague at best. It was obvious they'd been coached.

In my role as presenter as well as expert witness, I interpreted the results for the hearing officer: I pointed out her *arithmetic* score was only 5 where 10 is "average." This low score occurs in less than 5 percent of the normative population.

I further demonstrated from the tests their staff administered that Sarah's were not all "average" across the board; she had both strengths *and* weaknesses. This is the typical profile for a learning disabled student. Remember, for kids with low IQs, all their scores are low; with kids with high IQs, all their scores are high; and with learning disabled kids, they have both highs and lows depending on what areas their learning disabilities affect.

With 10 points the average, anything within a point or 2 is still okay. When you get 3 points away, you start to take notice, e.g., a subtest score of 7 is too low, learning problems may be present; 13 is high, the student may be bored; etc. Three points is the "magic" number.

# Frustration Merry-Go-Round

We had a right to request an IEP, a plan to address and correct Sarah's disability, after the April 5 meeting. We elected to wait until August when she returned to school. At this meeting, despite the lack of a notice, the special education supervisor wanted to revisit the *eligibility* question: did Sarah meet the requirements for needing help. A team of professionals agreed she had a disability, and now six months later, instead of acting to fix the problem, they were arguing over whether she even *had* a disability. They were using a technicality to do it: "we didn't conduct an observation of her in the classroom." We never said they couldn't do an observation; they had permission for six months, it was their fault, their neglect that it wasn't done, yet they were using it to delay services. That's known as compounding an error. We even argued that both of their psychologists conducted observations of Sarah when they tested her, but closed minds are just that…closed to any ideas that make sense. They did not want to confirm Sarah's diagnosis, much less address her needs and provide special education and related services. They wanted to stonewall. What could we do? We started this process last December, had testing in February, met in April, postponed a decision until August, and here they were delaying yet again.

We agreed once again to wait; to allow Sarah to settle into school with assurances from the ARD chair, Mel, principal of Northern High, that we could reconvene the ARD if she began to struggle. September turned into October and then November. When we tried to hold Mel to his word to reschedule a meeting, he hesitated. We were now approaching a year after we originally asked for help. We were through waiting, and we requested the hearing we were now involved in.

At this point in the discussion I tried to bring in the issue of timelines. I was told by the hearing officer that I could introduce this as pertinent to the case. They didn't just miss deadlines by a day or two; they missed them by weeks/months and refused to do anything until they were forced to. But Less objected and Mr. Stein, in complete opposition to what he promised me over the phone ("He'll object but I'm gonna let you bring it in"), sustained his objection. For the second time I was not allowed to bring in a key element to the case. It really made me wonder who got to the hearing officer. Was he truly an "impartial hearing officer?"

# The Hearing

I decided to move to closing. I said this: "Sarah is a learning disabled student. And though her most obvious problems are in math, her learning disabilities are numerous. Learning disabilities affect not only academic subjects, but all areas: her ability to think, reason, make decisions, organize her activities, take tests, write reports, recall previously learned information, listen in class. Sarah has special needs. She is eligible for special education and related services. Sarah doesn't need a tutor, she needs *specialized* instruction. She needs a qualified instructor, not an instructional assistant, or a peer tutor, or a remedial math teacher, or a reading teacher, but a *fully certified special education teacher* with an IEP, and related coursework specifically geared to the specific learning disabilities identified in the reports completed by the examiners. There's been a great deal of discussion about 504 plans, and though I'm not going to tell you that 504 and IDEA are mutually exclusive; there is overlap in the populations they serve, and IDEA takes precedence over 504. If you can receive services under IDEA you'd be foolish to accept a 504 plan without the funding, without the enforcement, and without the protections that accompany IDEA. Protections like annual reviews and IEPs and no change in program without parental consent. IDEA is the automobile and 504 is the bicycle; they may both get you there, but in a very different fashion."

## After The Hearing

At the end of the hearing I felt I had done my best to present witnesses and documentary evidence that would support the contention that Sarah was learning disabled and in need of services. I broke it down and explained it thoroughly. The board's attorney, having to rely on the lie, did not want to present his closing remarks and give me an opportunity to rebut, so he had the opportunity to hear all of my arguments and then go home and write his closing remarks. I didn't find this to be fair, and they sprang this at the last minute, but the hearing officer ruled he could do it. They also gave me the option to write my closing, but I was prepared for an oral presentation and an opportunity to hear the board attorney's closing and a right to rebuttal. Many of my arguments were heartfelt and could be best expressed in person. I chose to speak mine, though I feel the board attorney's should have been oral as well. His thirty-page written closing was nothing but garbage, bringing in half truths and innuendos that would never have gotten admitted to evidence if he'd tried it in front of me, and it stands as his final word, with no opportunity for me to rebut. If both sides give oral closing, I would have had the chance to bring on rebuttal witnesses. With written closings it doesn't happen. So he can talk about the principal's testimony standing unrefuted, even though he never made it to the stand on the twentieth for me to refute his remarks. And he can bring in my "personal/professional dispute" with another special education teacher even though he never called her as a witness, and I never got the opportunity to cross her or Mel about the letter he refers to (Mason letter). He insults Dr. Mom, misquotes Caroline and me, and generally rambles on for thirty pages. This whole process reeks to high heaven. Briefs are briefs, and a hearing should be just that, with both sides presenting oral argument, not one ready to and the other bowing out at the last minute with seven days to respond. The system is stacked against the honest.

## Parents Don't Stand A Chance

I was completely shocked by the rules of this process. My views of the justice system were eroding and my view of the impartial hearing officer was that he was not impartial, did not listen enough to call him a "hearing" officer, and any claims to a professional title of "officer" was also sorely lacking. This whole thing, like the appearance before the circuit court, was nothing but a sham. The process is set against the parent from the word go, even who is called as witnesses. I mean, if the parent calls board employees, they are compelled to appear, but they are in fear of their jobs and their loyalty is to the board, and their lawyer gets to coach them and then they get paid to do the board's bidding. The parent doesn't have a chance. Even if they secure a teacher or other board employee as a witness, they are loyal to their jobs and in this county in fear of losing them. Even teachers loyal to the child/parent will have a tough time standing up in court with the superintendent looking over their shoulders. And if the parent brings in someone from the outside, the person is perceived as just that, an outsider, someone paid to testify. The entire process is corrupted, with *ex-parte* conversations and half truths and innuendoes ruling the day. How can the truth come out in a setting as contrived as this?

## The Decision

After wading through all this we finally get a decision from the hearing officer. What a waste of time and money and emotion. He never let me bring in all the facts like the issue of timelines, even though I was told I didn't have to bring up every issue I planned to address before the hearing (what are arguments for, anyway?), and even though I provided it as a central issue at the five-day disclosure prior to the February 20 hearing. So with the facts muddied and timelines the only clear-cut issue out, we lost any advantage we might have had to prevail.

What we got from Mr. Myron Stein, the Formal Hearing Officer, after countless hours and money for consultation fees from attorneys and phone bills and copying charges was... nothing. His decision contained no less than thirty-three spelling and typographical errors. It was typed, not word-processed, but typed...on an ancient manual typewriter whose margin controls were off. Sentences disappeared off the page never to be seen again. It was beyond unprofessional and deep into the incompetent range. And his ideas and conclussions (sic) were every bit as bad as his typing skills. I was aghast.

According to Stein's Conclussions *(sic)*, the term *specific learning disabled* is a "diagnosis." The term as I understand it is a medical term reserved for physicians and clinical psychologists in the business of *diagnosing* conditions such as emotional disturbance or psychoses. In the public schools under IDEA, specific learning disabilities are determined by a team rather than an individual. The team carefully compares the student's functioning with a set of eligibility criteria. The criteria requires that certain kinds of individuals be involved (qualified examiners). They require assessments, written reports, and presentations to the group, who, familiar with the criteria, entertain the examiners' interpretations and recommendations and decide independently and as a team if the student qualifies.

The IEP team that met on April 5, 1995, agreed that Sarah met the criteria for eligibility. By law they were required to discuss her needs as outlined by these same assessments and develop an IEP to address her needs. Placement in the least restrictive environment would flow from this IEP. Although we were willing to wait until she reenrolled in school in August, we were not willing to wait while they conducted "observations" and other assessments to *redetermine* her eligibility. We reluctantly waived our right to an IEP at the August meeting. We refused to waive these rights in November and December, and requested a hearing. The hearing was to review the system's actions in light of current law. Stein was ignorant of the law as well as the rules of spelling, and his "decision" reflected this. And here we were almost a year later with nothing more to show for it than a lot of binders full of documents and hurt feelings all around us.

## Response To The Decision

The system seemed to want to have it both ways. In the August 28 ARD they used "statistical score discrepancies" to decide that Sarah was "not eligible for special education services," in complete opposition to the decision the April 5 ARD arrived at. When, at the January 30, 1996, hearing, we carefully demonstrated that Sarah met the eligibility criteria for specific learning disabilities based on a commonly accepted analysis of the test scores ("significant discrepancy between ability and achievement"), the system turned their argument to "Well, she may be *eligible*, but she doesn't have any *need* for special education services." What makes these arguments even more specious is their circular nature. If she doesn't deserve an IEP because she doesn't have any *need* for one, how is that she has so many *needs* for a 504 plan?

We maintained all along that she clearly met the eligibility criteria for specific learning disabilities and that her needs for special education were spelled out in specific cognitive deficits on the WAIS-R (intelligence) and the WIAT (achievement test), and that her failing the functional math test and earning a percentile of only 3 on the PSAT suggests that group tests are consistent with individual tests, i.e., deficits in math reasoning/computation. More significantly, we provided ample documentation in the way of low test scores in geometry as well as anecdotal records that were uncontroverted regarding her frustrations at home with math and her needs for help from parents and a long list of friends and acquaintances. She was identified as learning disabled in 1986 and required specialized instruction to overcome her deficits. Her disabilities didn't go away; they just went into hiding in middle school, only to reemerge at the high school level. I'm convinced that her difficulties in school and her frustrations in learning directly contributed to her declining self-image and resulting behavior problems. She was disabled, she had learning problems, she had needs, she deserved the services...period. She was punished for her suspected drug use, she took her expulsion with courage, earning six credits at night school, and now she was back in public school and she needed help. And they weren't providing it.

## Complaints To Ocr/Msde-Dse/Osers-Osep

To be honest the idea to file complaints against the board of education had a variety of reasons for coming into being. Top on the list was my credibility. After serving in a role as school psychologist for over twenty years, including eight years with administrative responsibilities, I felt I had a pretty good handle on special education policy and procedure. When I was in Virginia I had to be well versed in it. I was there when 93-180, the first law, was implemented to provide services to handicapped children in 1973. It was whipped together just before 94-142 came into place. This law guaranteed a free appropriate public education for all children with handicapping conditions. It required schools to open their doors to the disabled, and it closed the doors of the private schools and public institutions as parents brought their children home to live with them and attend their neighborhood schools. We were at the forefront of developing policies and procedures that would meet both the spirit as well as the letter of the law for the education of the handicapped. That was in 1974. Having been both a practitioner as well as an administrator, I appreciated the view from both sides of the fence. And when Less tried to tell me I didn't know much about special education, well.... And when he criticized me for demanding "sweeping changes in special education" when we offered our settlement agreement, I was aghast. I was merely asking for what my daughter deserved and no more. Did I question my own knowledge and expertise? No. But others might, and I had a lifelong reputation to protect as well as my daughter and my job. I had a career.

My intent was to regain my own credibility as well as to demonstrate to them (the board attorney and the local administrators) that this is the way the rest of the world operated

## The Hearing

when it came to special education. In this way I could drag the system, kicking and screaming, into the twentieth century. The kids I had devoted my life to these past six years would benefit from the state or the federal government coming in and cleaning house. As the case developed, I realized too that establishing my credibility would not only preserve me in the long run, but it would protect me by giving me a stick at least as big as theirs. Little old me the teacher had little clout, but bring in the various branches of the government, and watch out! Boy, would I be surprised and bitterly disappointed again. Why? Because Polly would rear her ugly head again. Polly who? Polly Ticks, that's who.

The first salvo I fired was yet another round of defensive fire against the board attorney. Funny thing, but in gathering up documents he planned to use against me, he inadvertently sent me documents I had never seen that ended up helping me build my case. Less was trying to bolster the superintendent's position that I dominated IEP Team meetings. "Ran roughshod over them," in his words. Funny thing is that he never sat in on even a single ARD. Neither did his assistant. And in the six-plus years I was in the system, I can only remember the personnel director, my primary supervisor, sitting in on one. So this makes them experts on how I conducted myself in the other five-hundred-plus meetings. Of course, there were administrators, though for the most part most of them left the parent meetings for us to run. By "us" I mean the special education teachers and me. The special education supervisor began to attend more and more of the sensitive ones, and administrators were encouraged more recently to sit in as well, but we ran literally hundreds of IEP Team meetings with no problem. Either the special education teacher would run (chair) the meetings, or if there was a sticky one they would ask me to. I can't count the number of times I heard, "We need you in on this one, Frank." Only in instances where team members had hidden agendas, usually "I don't want: a) any more kids or b) this kid in my program," did I have to assert my advocacy role. I performed the background check and the comprehensive psychological, I reviewed all of their work and all of the regular teacher's work, and I wrote my two- to three-hour, three- to five-page psychological, and I was there for the benefit of the kid first and the teacher second. This only happened at two locations (other than the one-time incidents mentioned previously). They were both interested in maintaining the status quo, and they only looked to the school psychologist to rubber stamp the decisions they made before they even sat down with the parent.

## Let's See What The State Department Thinks

The board's attorney included in one of his five-day disclosures a document I should have seen but never did. Bill was a former school psychologist who now works for the Maryland State Department of Education–Division of Special Education (MSDE-DSE). His role is to make sure that school psychologists are used in the proper manner, and that procedures are followed with respect to special education law. He meets with a representative from each county school system. The idea is that he can bring them up to standards and use them to disseminate information to the other school psychologists in their districts. Trouble is, in eight years, the only document or notice about any of the meetings was the one Less sent me. Bud, our county representative, never was much good about bringing anything back to us. He was more intent on getting to travel at county expense and have a day to play the big shot. He never debriefed us and he never gave us a scrap of paper from his meetings or any of the mailings from Bill.

## To BE S.E.D., Sed, Or Not To Be, That Is The Question

This particular document talked about how the IEP Team process was where the power flowed, that any one individual could not override the decision of the team. (He apparently never sat in on some of the meetings in this county.) This particular memo spoke directly to seriously emotionally disturbed (S.E.D.) students. We aren't even allowed to see these kids. They haul in the "experts" from the regionally based consortium. The irony was that I had been involved in diagnosing and developing programs for S.E.D. kids for fourteen years when I arrived here. I quickly learned that I would not be doing them here. Instead, this one gal fresh out of school with no experience would do them along with the clinical psychologist, who told me in a meeting in response to a question I posed, "Yes, I guess you could consider that I am the *gatekeeper* for emotionally disturbed children's programs." I was concerned back then in 1988, my first few months in the county, that with all the programs at the middle and high school level, it certainly appeared to me that we were either failing to diagnose the kids early enough, or kids just didn't get "disturbed" until they turned twelve. I spoke to the need for early identification and prevention and all, but I just didn't know (and never did find out) that there was a political agenda when it came to S.E.D. at the elementary level. The new gal and I got at cross purposes a number of times, because I referred the kids to her, sat in on the meetings, and tried the best I could to learn the rules by which these kids were evaluated. I never did. They changed all the time. But Toni, the clinical school psychologist from the consortium had great advice. I had this young man who was quite disturbed, or at least *I* thought he was. He would fly into rages and throw things, like desks across the room. At home in his foster placement, he would sit and watch TV. Okay, I know that's normal, but with his penis in his hand? Toni had no advice for his penis play, but she did have some grand advice for his violent outbursts. "If he behaves inappropriately, just make him stand on a carpet square until he settles down." I can recall my response to this pearl of wisdom: "If you expect us to control his behavior with a carpet remnant, then it better be large enough to roll him up in." She didn't appreciate this bit of sarcastic humor. I did get a few laughs from the peanut gallery, though.

He wasn't much better. No matter what a kid had been through, if he or she wasn't "crazy" in his estimation, he or she wasn't SED. I can remember this poor little fellow Joey. He was living under the care of his mother, who was no help at all. His uncle and his girlfriend were only too happy to help out. This uncle only had one arm. He used to handcuff Joey to the bed to keep him from running away while he and his girlfriend had their way with him. I can't imagine the nightmares this kid had. He tried the best he could, but he was angry. He needed a program to meet his psychological needs as well as his educational needs. But because "he was learning," Dr. Dick didn't qualify him. Apparently it didn't matter how disturbed you were, as long as you could read or write you weren't eligible for the emotional support services. But I'm, digressing again.

When this memo from Bill, the man from the state office, finally made it into my little hands, I realized that he felt the same way that I did. Committees made decisions, not individuals. Although I was being accused of this, it was really something I respected, and if they were going to investigate using this as a criteria, then let them come on. I sent this letter with a letter of my own explaining how S.E.D. diagnoses were made in this system. I cited the case of the kid at Ridgemont. I could have cited a dozen more. I can recall a meeting where twelve people at the school "voted" for S.E.D. where Toni voted no and the kid stayed in the regular program. It wasn't until she burned her house down while she was inside that people woke up. She was rescued, placed in a hospital, and does fine on her medication. I wanted the spotlight to shine on the clinical psychologist, so my first complaint was on him and the procedure that allowed people outside the school system to diagnose kids inside. It went nowhere. Oh, they questioned the clinical psychologist and he said he never did that. I imagine they are more careful now. But who knows?

Having been turned down by the board attorney and his cohorts about cleaning up other areas of special education in the county, I felt that maybe it was time I contacted OCR, the United States Office of Civil Rights. I had already laid out the areas of concern in my "consent agreement" between the first and second due process hearings in February 1996. My complaint to OCR maintained that parents' meetings were not always run by the team, but by administrative restraint. I provided documentation of meetings in which principals "overruled" or vetoed committee decisions. I pointed out that screening meetings where decisions were to be reached about who was conducting assessment and in what areas (vision, perception, math achievement, reading, etc.) and which tests were going to be used never happened. I was lucky if I got a name and a consent form much less any background information on kids I was supposed to reevaluate. And at the high school, they didn't seem to care much about the results I obtained after the assessment. I was to show up, sign the paper, and let them place the student as they saw fit. In some instances they didn't even schedule a meeting to review my results. I could do that "on my own." "The kid had been in special ed for years, what changes did they expect from your two-hour assessment?" So if I did happen to feel the youngster needed additional time or additional help, forgeddaboudit. As long as a kid wasn't failing, he or she could stay in the regular program full time and get "consultation services." This amounted to an instructional assistant checking monitoring sheets on kids in the regular classes. Too bad if a kid I tested in third grade who was severely learning disabled needed more help in the ninth. He was "a behavior problem." I would be too if I was in the tenth grade and could only read on a third-grade level in world history. There were too many occasions in both the high schools where they were interested in only one number, and it wasn't even the IQ! It was the date of the assessment, so they could show auditors they had one done every three years. They seemed to care little for cognitive strengths and weaknesses or learning styles, much less academic achievement scores. I would submit my report well within timelines, usually a week after I completed the assessment. But they would have an IEP meeting or an annual review scheduled months away, or when they updated the educational testing. It was all done piecemeal, and it was not according to the letter much less the spirit of the law. So I filed my complaint along these very lines. OCR passed me over to Office of Special Education and Rehabilitative Services/Office of Special Education Programs (OSERS/OSEP). When I was director of special services in West Virginia, OCR came in to investigate my program based on a parental complaint. It was unfounded; we had followed not only our own procedures but state and federal guidelines as well. They went away happy. Where were they now?

I wrote the governor and lieutenant governor's office. Though I never got a response to my letter, they sent it right to the superintendent's office. Just to let him know what I was up to. Thanks. I contacted my congressman's office, and though he seemed interested and made some inquiries, he was rebuffed by OCR and OSERS, who basically said they could not get involved until the state did their investigation. The state did a cursory job; they essentially went around and asked all the people I complained about if they did it. They denied it. And by the time they got around to talking to other individuals in the county, the word was out. Open your mouth and you'll get the same thing Frank got. It was like, if the superintendent can get away with stifling Frank and stripping him of all his seniority, and Frank is...well...outspoken, well-respected, credible, and a former president of the teachers association and the parent/teacher association, well, if he can do this to Frank, what chance do any of us stand fighting him? And they all slinked back into their holes, afraid to say anything that would get back to the superintendent. "You

## The Hearing

know how vindictive the superintendent is, and he never forgets." So as the heat turned up on me, few folks came forward, just at a time when they needed to. If not for me, then for the kids we all served, for their own job satisfaction, for justice.

I also contacted my United States senator. Her office was even more helpful. Not only did her aide take a special interest in my case, but the senator herself made inquiries. Of course, she went right to the top, a Cabinet-level secretary. Pretty much the same response came back: we cannot get involved as long as this is a case under litigation (Sarah's), and we need to await the outcome of the state's investigation before we step in. To be fair, just about the time I was about to launch another salvo, this time a few smoking guns demonstrating one of their principals lied to the state investigators, my attorneys came up with the settlement agreement. Although it has worked out well for me, they don't know how lucky they are. Among other items, I had a principal, the same tyrant who knocked things off his desk telling me I was insubordinate for making a recommendation at a team meeting, *on the record* saying he "categorically denied overruling IEP Team decisions." Fine... his word against mine, except for one thing. I had a copy of the reprimand letter he wrote me speaking to this very issue, that I was not to make "retention recommendations at IEP Team meetings." He doesn't know how lucky he is. Saddest thing is, one "disgruntled employee" goes away and the rest of the investigative team breathes a sigh of relief and goes "ho hum" about their jobs. Shame on all of them. But I'm getting a little ahead of myself. Living through this sometimes has the feeling of a hurricane-wild river, out of control. In it are swirls and eddies that double back, and remember we had two cases rolling, Sarah's expulsion case and her special education case. Additional were the complaints I filed with OCR (Office of Civil Rights) and OSER (Federal Office of Special Education Resources). I was about to find out about a third and even more chilling case. My employment case...

## February 28 – The Complaints Go To My Union

Well, I gave my teacher's association representative a copy of the superintendent's response to my letter with a DRAFT of one I wanted to send to amend his record. I also enclosed a letter to my rep about my need to have one less thing to worry about…in this case, my job. With the due process hearings and the court of appeals hearing coming up, I shouldn't have to be looking over my shoulder at the job every minute. I wrote to my union rep that, "… those "six (five) letters are still hanging out there with all of these unfounded charges against me, and here's the superintendent directing me not to make any further unsubstantiated accusations about the competence of employees." He didn't like things I said about Homey. Talk about a double standard, Homey can make all of his remarks, and the special education teachers and company can make unsubstantiated remarks about my reputation, but if I try to return the volley I am insubordinate? That is why I wanted to respond and try to level the playing field a bit. Caroline and my local teachers' association rep both counseled me on waiting for Geraldine to review the letter. So a week goes by without a response from her or anyone in the state teacher's association office. And in the meantime the board sure as hell isn't waiting.

I go in Monday and Wendy, a teacher at the high school, tells me, "They're out to get you." Tell me something I don't already know. But bless her heart, they dragged her in on this one. They wanted her to sign a paper that she too had seen Frank Matthews violate confidentiality laws. "Here's another nail for his coffin," the special education teacher remarked. What were they up to now? Remember when Mel helped me out by moving me downstairs to the conference room, and then gave me "my own" computer to use? Well, I thought I had exclusive use. Come to find out others are not only using my room, but my computer, and not only that, they are snooping through my files. One staff member *discovered* my

The Hearing

confidential psychological reports on my computer drive. No shit, Shirley, I mean I only write 75 percent of my reports on that computer and leave a copy on the hard drive in the event my floppy breaks up, which they do at times. Good strategy to save three to six hours of work a week. Any rate, these bozos think they have the smoking gun on me now: leaving confidential files in an unlocked room for all to see. I lock my door every time, and never thought anyone would access my files clearly marked *Psychologicals*. If they do, *they* are the ones violating confidentiality laws, not me. It's like coming into my home at six thirty in the morning, walking into my bathroom while I'm showering, and then accusing me of exposing myself. No shit, Sherlock, I mean you won't find dirt unless you look for it. So now it seems they are siccing teachers on me. I headed this off at the pass the best I could, by going straight to Mel and complaining that my office has been used, personal effects are missing, and now they are violating my confidential files. Mel indicated he's get me a locking file and had Wade put a personal code on my computer. He said the "feud" between the superintendent and me was heating up. Sure, the special education hearing was ready to wrap, and we'd filed the appeal to the state court of special appeals.

## Meeting With The Superintendent, March 28, 1996

At two forty-five on Wednesday, March 27, approximately ninety minutes before a scheduled conference call between Less and Judge Lynch from the Office of Administrative Hearings regarding the scheduling of our state level due process hearing, I received a phone call at Northen High School from the superintendent. He indicated the need to meet with me and wondered whether I was "tied into something at the moment" or could I stop by on my way through town. I agreed to stop by; however, he quickly corrected himself, indicating another commitment he had, changing the meeting to the first thing in the morning on my way in to work. Again I agreed to meet with him. My impression was that his intention was to plant a seed of doubt just prior to this phone conference. The board attorney's sudden offer during this subsequent call to mediate this dispute after rejecting other offers was interesting in light of the superintendent's phone call less than two hours before. Did this sound like they wanted to settle instead of fighting in court?

I arrived at the board office at seven thirty-five on Thursday morning and the inner offices were locked. I went upstairs and collected test protocols from the coordinator's office. On my way downstairs the superintendent was entering the building at seven forty. He acknowledged my presence, directing me to have a seat and he would be with me shortly. After twenty minutes he invited me back to his office. The assistant superintendent joined us, memo pad in hand.

The superintendent introduced the conference as a follow-up to a series of letters written about my professional conduct and turned into the director of pupil personnel. He characterized these letters as a continuation of a long history of "concerns and personal conflicts" involving me and my "inability to work with other people in the county system." He indicated that there were "several principals who had asked that I be removed from their buildings so that they would not have to work with me."

In contradiction to an August meeting in which he indicated that he was transferring me to the middle and high schools as a result of personnel changes (resignation of the third psychologist) and my "experience" working at this level in previous positions, he indicated that this involuntary transfer had actually been an "opportunity for a fresh start." Sure, move me out of settings where I've been successful (elementary) and move me to where I am unsuccessful (high school). He complained that despite this move, he felt that I, "Continued to conduct myself in an unprofessional manner. He added that he felt I was arrogant, abusive, and abrasive."

## The Hearing

He further indicated that the "investigation" that the personnel director had conducted had borne out the "facts" reported in the letters he received. He held the letters, stapled together with my response attached to the front, commenting that it was "nice that you gave our head of personnel permission to conduct his investigation" and that despite my indication that there "was no substance to the allegations," he felt that there was. He further indicated, "Your relationship with the school system is in jeopardy," and that my good work was "no excuse, that there is no justification for your behavior as outlined in the written complaints." Sure, reporting psychological results completely and accurately, advocating for my students, informing parents, and asserting my rights as a professional. And, oh, yes, there's that hand-holding and gum-chewing stuff, too, don't forget. The superintendent further indicated that many of my professional colleagues "were frightened being around me" and "afraid of what I might do."

Up to this point I sat and listened without reacting. At this one, I let one slip. I "frightened people"? "That's a good one," I said. He reacted by pointing out that this was *just* what he was talking about. I asked him if I frightened him. He did not respond. Hmmmmm. It's been said that people are often frightened of things out of the ordinary, and me speaking up in my own defense was certainly that. The superintendent was not used to anyone speaking up. And when that person who is speaking his mind actually makes sense, well, that's even scarier. Maybe I really had frightened him. As for other people, I told him that I never raised my voice at meetings, or used profanity, and that I certainly never physically threatened anyone at any meeting I ever attended, so I strongly disagreed with this characterization.

The superintendent then proceeded to explain the actions he planned to take in response to the letters.

1. He would ask his assistant superintendent to sit down with the personnel director and write a summary letter

of the concerns, including my "long history of unprofessional behavior."
2. They would then develop a professional performance improvement plan for me, and that I would be held accountable for implementing it. He further indicated that I would have to conduct myself in a completely different manner, and that he expected significant changes in my behavior.
3. As superintendent he would evaluate my progress at the end of the school year. He would then make a decision about my continued service to the county. He closed by exclaiming, "No one runs roughshod around here, and your behavior, your wanting everything to go your way, is not acceptable behavior." (Sounded like the pot calling the kettle black to me.)

He then paused to allow me an opportunity to respond. I basically told him that I continued to believe that the letters contained nothing of substance. "I wasn't worried when the personnel director gave them to me, and after a more careful reading I'm still not worried, and if you think you're going to initiate termination proceedings against me based on these letters, I wish you luck. You'd better find something better than this if you think you're going to get rid of me."

He responded that he didn't say he was going to "terminate" me. I looked at the notepad where I was taking notes and read him back two quotes: "(My) relationship with the school system is in jeopardy" and "(He would) make a decision regarding my continued services to the county." "What exactly did you mean by those remarks?"

He responded that he had "changed my assignment twice, and he could change it again." He could also change the status of my certification to a second-class certificate, he could apply sanctions, or take disciplinary action.

I indicated that actions could and should be taken against some of same individuals who were making these accusations against me. He asked me if I was making a threat. I indicated

## The Hearing

that anyone who violated the law should be held accountable. He said that was part of my problem, that I wasn't aware that I had a problem.

I calmly explained to him, that if he was asking me to change in respect to my role as advocate for children, I did not plan to change. If teachers or administrators violated the law or the rights of disabled students, then I would stand with the students and their parents, even if it meant standing with them against the school system. If school officials lied to parents or gave them the wrong information, I would stand to correct them. He asked me if I thought that was my role. I explained to him that as a school psychologist, bound to follow my association's code of ethics, the child was my client, and that I would advocate for that child. I could not be party to violations of law or ethics with respect to disabled students and their parents.

He responded that if that was my position, he would see to it that I was given another assignment, that I would not function as a school psychologist for the county system. He announced that the meeting was over. As I got up to leave, my final statement was, "All I can say is it ain't over until the fat lady sings." His parting remark was a request for me to leave his office, that he'd heard enough of my arrogant remarks. I was already halfway out the door, still calm, still smiling. I reported the meeting to my immediate supervisor, Jack Armstrong, and to Pat, my teacher's association representative. I knew that I had been tenured for over five years, and that my observations and year-end evaluations were predominantly positive. I had scores of exemplary marks. I also knew the union's agreement with the board, and it did not allow top-down evaluations. Any violations, real or perceived, on their part had to go through my principals. To date I had no written complaints other than the bogus reprimands that were thrown out. I knew the superintendent could not evaluate me. How wrong can a person be? As I was to find out, the rules are written for the administrators, and they can follow, bend, or break them at will. And, sadder still, they have the full backing of the board and the courts.

Here's the letter he wrote me in follow-up:

County Public Schools
Superintendent of Schools
March 29, 1996
Mr. Frank L. Matthews

Dear Mr. Matthews,

I wish to summarize our conference held in my office on Thursday, March 28, 1996. Besides the two of us, my assistant superintendent was present.

The purpose of the conference was to indicate my concerns regarding your continued inappropriate behavior toward other professionals, including teachers and supervisors. You were given copies of letters of complaint received by the school system administration from several of your colleagues. Most of these letters were provided to you in an earlier conference with the director of pupil services.

I indicated that based on his investigation of these letters and a review of your past performance in the area of professional relationships, I was directing him to summarize his concerns as of this date. That summary would be presented to you and would be placed in your personnel file. I further indicated that my assistant and the director of personnel would develop a written performance improvement plan which is to be implemented by you, and I expected to see improvement in your performance. I also indicated that at the end of this school year it is my intent to review your performance, and to reconsider your employment relationship with the school system.

You were then asked if you wished to respond. Your response was both surprising and totally unacceptable. You made it very clear that you see no need for improvement, and that despite the complaints made against you, it is your intention to continue to behave as you have in the past. You

## The Hearing

also made several veiled threats about actions you may take against me and others in the school system. **You declared that you would advocate for children regardless of the requirements and expectations placed upon you by the school system. You made it clear that you consider yourself to be responsible for seeing that the school system and other school personnel put children first.**

It is exactly this self-righteous, arrogant attitude and behavior which has resulted in your colleagues' discomfort in working with you. During our conference, and in previous written communication to supervisors and others, you have presumed to define a special role for yourself in this school system that only you consider to be appropriate.

Toward the end of our conference you made it clear, again with obvious threat, that if I was going to try to terminate you based on these allegations that I could go ahead and try, but "it's not over until the fat lady sings."

Because of this remark and your continued display of insubordinate and arrogant behavior, I asked you to leave my office.

We will proceed to take the actions outlined above. You are to implement the requirements placed upon you as outlines in the performance improvement plan when it is provided. Should you decide to disregard these expectations, you will subject yourself to further disciplinary action.

                                  Sincerely,
                                The Superintendent,

Just as there is *truth in jest*, so too there is truth in the darkest of lies. If someone read this letter about an employee and his superintendent, it would certainly sound like a stubborn and resistant employee who was spitting in his boss's face after having been caught *in flagrante delicto*. Trouble is, I had done nothing wrong, and all his allegations and accusations had no basis in fact, it was all a setup. I was being framed, and I wasn't about to put my tail between my legs and cower. I knew my rights and I knew he couldn't get away with this sham. If you know you're going to get shot in the morning, why give them the satisfaction of cowering first? Though I got a lot of flak from my union rep, I will never regret speaking up in that meeting and letting him know what I thought. It was back in Rhode Island with the hanging judge, and I had to speak my mind. I knew in my heart this had nothing to do with me or my role as school psychologist and everything to do with my daughter's cases, the due process hearing and the civil proceedings.

Sure, I told him I would continue my behavior and saw no need for major changes. I was following the rules of ethics for my professional association, which required me to focus on the child. My only obligation when a conflict existed between the interests of the child and the school system was to inform them, not blindside them in a meeting with parents. I did this, including both incidents for which I was reprimanded in the previous year. I told the one principal that I was required to inform the parents of my recommendation for retention. I told the second one that I was primarily interested in placement for this youngster in a small, self-contained classroom, and it didn't matter how he got in, under IDEA or Section 504. When *they* changed the agenda in the meeting with the parents and wanted to take his protective label off and cast his fates to another meeting for 504, I spoke up as I promised I would. I did my job, I did my homework, I focused on children, and I kept administrators and parents informed, and if others had hidden agendas that did not meet the child's needs, then it would be over my strong objections. That was clearly my role. And I would pay dearly for it. But could I do anything less? I'm just not made any other way. And if I stand up for a child's rights, if I assert myself in his or her interest, if I defend him or her, then I am condemned? What are we all about in education after all? The superintendent's statement read, "Your response was both surprising and totally unacceptable when you *declared that you would advocate for children regardless of the requirements and expectations placed upon you by the school system.*" It was unbelievable. I mean, "HELLO!"

Aren't we all supposed to advocate for kids? And just what requirements and expectations were set up to counter this order? And why? And shouldn't they be resisted?

The superintendent stepped in it with one foot and then swung his other little foot around, and, yes sir, he stepped in it again with, *"You made it clear that you consider yourself to be responsible for seeing that the school system and other school personnel put children first."* Aren't we all responsible for this? I've always said I'll take a backseat at meetings as long as someone is guiding the process in the child's interest. If no one is, then I will step in to fill this vacuum. That is my job, my responsibility; it is my life's work. It's why I am in this business in the first place. I care about kids. I am, after all, a child of the sixties, and I am here to "use psychology," my knowledge, to benefit, not hurt others, and my focus, my priority, is the child. I am now a member of the establishment, the system, and it is here where the rubber meets the road that we each decide whose side we are on, and mine clearly is with the child.

## Biting The Hand That Feeds Who

Throughout this quest I was accused of being disloyal to my employer, the "man who signs my paycheck." Since it was brought up, I'll address it right here. Did I work for the superintendent? Not really; I always felt that I worked for the citizens and taxpayers. I served their interests, but most importantly their children's interests. Giving an order that contradicts my duty to them is wrong and it should be ignored. Oh, there are a bunch out there who insist that my option would be to follow the order or quit. But what happens to a system in which all of the child advocates, all the honest, hardworking, fearless people quit? It leaves those who don't care about kids; their paychecks are more important. It leaves the quiet ones who don't complain or "cause trouble," but don't do much good either. It leaves the liars and thieves who feel right at home with corrupt administrations. And it leaves the cowards, decent people who care about kids and honesty but are afraid to speak up. And not to leave everybody out, it leaves a small and sometimes dwindling core of people who get the job done, who are untouchable somehow by the strength of their personalities and their devotion to the job and the loyalty of their parents. They manage to advocate for children in a quiet way that gets the job done and keeps them out of the fire. They secretly and quietly respect and applaud the rabble-rousers like me, but they know it's not their way. They sometimes look to us when a tough meeting is coming up because they know we will stand up to the forces that work against kids. There is a mutual respect for these two groups. Every system needs them, but especially the corrupt ones.

A public school is not a private corporation. The superintendent was not chief executive officer of a company he founded. He did not start this $28 million business from a table top, working long hours. He didn't invent or engineer or design a unique product that he is marketing. He is a public official. He works for a public institution. He works for the citizens and taxpayers of this county. He is there to administer for them, for the children, their parents, and other citizens. It's their money he is spending, not his money or his family's money. It's *their* money.

So, yes, if I am self-righteous and arrogant, it's because I know the law and I know what other school systems do, and I am swayed not by threat or fear but only persuasive argument. Short of this, I will stand my ground. And this is not a "special role" I've carved out for myself, it is one that has been instilled in me through training, education, experience, and a familiarity with the law and the ethics of my profession. I do nothing outside of the expectations of my own profession, little bits of information imparted at conferences and training workshops, tidbits that many people leave behind at the conference door that I believe in and maintain in my daily practice. Do your best to identify student needs and formulate recommendations that will serve them. My only failure is my passion, my intensity, and without that what am I? Apathetic and listless.

## CHAPTER SIXTEEN

# YOU'RE ONLY AS SAFE AS YOUR NEXT EVALUATION

I read my union's negotiated agreement, and I knew the superintendent could not terminate me without going through the evaluation process. Over eight years my evaluations were good to excellent. More recent ones were exemplary. And the few reprimands and assorted issues from years ago were dealt with and put to rest. Little did I know that they would be resurrected like corpses from the grave, along with all the hearsay and innuendo the superintendent could muster. He wasn't playing fair; he was out for blood — mine — and he wouldn't quit until he had drained as much of it from me as he could. He started out by not even giving me a chance to implement my developmental improvement plan. These plans are put in place for both the teacher and the school system. It is developed with mutual agreement and action steps are designed to help the teacher to correct shortcomings. If the plan is followed, the teacher becomes a stronger educator and the school system gets a better employee. Of course, those teachers who fail to meet expectations or refuse to effect the needed changes are in line for termination. High stakes. I was motivated to meet every detail of my plan 110 percent. And I deserved the time agreed on to meet it. But the superintendent didn't want me to succeed, you will remember, so he decided to up the stakes. He was taking immediate action. He was threatening to dismiss me based on baseless allegations. Gum chewing, holding my hand up. I was not going to be intimidated by this man. I told him, "If you think you can initiate termination proceedings against me based on these complaints, well, I wish you luck. I wasn't worried about them when the personnel director showed them to me, and I'm certainly not worried about them now. If your intention is to get rid of me with these flimsy charges, then you'd better find something better." His response: "Who said anything about termination? I never said I would terminate you." I paused and then responded, "Well (and I read directly from the notes I was taking during the meeting), what does 'reevaluate the status of your employment situation' mean?" He replied, "I can discipline you, I can reassign you, and I can place you on second class." Second class, just like it sounds, is where they place those teachers who have failed to meet the terms of their improvement plan. Your salary drops to minimal level and you can be dismissed without any further grounds. The following Monday morning I got called in again for a meeting with the superintendent and his second in command.

## Monday, April 1, 1996, April Fools Day — Reassigned

Because I was put on report, and knew I had to be on my better than best behavior, I tried to walk "better than Jesus," as I was once advised. You'll remember that bit of critical advice came from a law enforcement officer back in the sixties who was hassling one of my friends. I politely inquired as to why he was bothering my friend, who wasn't doing anything wrong. "I'll arrest you for the same thing...loitering." Which prompted my witty rejoinder: "How can you loiter on a public beach? Hence his not-so-witty rejoinder, "You better walk better than Jesus, 'cause I could follow him around long enough and I could find something to bust him for." Needless to say it wasn't too long before I was pulling thorns out of my backside, but that's another story...

So here I am some twenty-five years later and I still haven't learned to keep my big mouth shut. I am not aggressive (taking over another's territory through violent action), but I am very, very assertive (preventing others from taking over my territory). The superintendent, being who he is, thinks the entire school system is his territory, and he probably never learned to share when he was a little kid. So he resented me telling him I was hired to do a job for the citizens and taxpayers, and that I intended to do that job. He failed to appreciate that by doing my job, I kept teachers and parents happy and lawsuits away. I'd evaluated over five hundred kids in the county over seven years and sat in on more than twice as many meetings. Out of those thousand-plus meetings I'd experienced problems in only a handful. I had not so much as a single complaint from a parent, much less a due process hearing from any of my cases. My only problem was the few administrators who got upset when they didn't get their way. They wanted to take their balls and go home. I couldn't play anymore 'cause I always won. I had the law on my side and darn it, I was right most of the time. And they didn't like egg on their faces when they discovered that though it was the federal law that provided the handcuffs, it was I who snapped them shut. Those were the cases the superintendent focused in on, and though I deserved his support on each and every one, instead I received his condemnation. But this wasn't about my job performance or my competency, or even my professionalism. He was out for blood, remember? My blood.

His response was that due to his concerns and my behavior at the Thursday meeting on March 28, he no longer wanted me to "continue in my capacity as a school psychologist." He believed there to be "irreconcilable differences" between the board and me. He was therefore *reassigning* me to…the *Alternative School* as of April 9, 1996. I was to report to the building principal as of that date for instructions relative to my new assignment. "In the meantime you are to use the remaining days to close down all your cases and return all of your files, memos, etc., to the appropriate building principals. This decision is in keeping with the superintendent's right to make placements in the best interest of the school system." He referred to the negotiated agreement that required the superintendent to sit down with teachers to discuss their new assignment. I was watching eight years of dedicated work slowly swirl down the drain.

On advice of counsel, the teacher's association attorney suggested that I not dare him to fire me anymore and make every attempt to make nice. I cowered…a little. I told the superintendent that he must have misunderstood my position on the Thursday meeting, that while I would continue to advocate for children, I would not have ever taken positions against the school system's administrators or supervisors… only other teachers. I also pointed out that the complaints included in the personnel director's stack of letters included only fellow teachers, and that the lone administrator was not complaining about my relationship with him, but only my relationship with another teacher. How was it I was being reassigned for problems with administrators, when I had none on record, none formally documented? It didn't make sense. Ahh, but it wasn't s'posed to.

I also asked him about how to finish up cases that obligated me to go over the results of my psychologicals, and he indicated that I was free to do this within the period between that time and April 9, and that after that date someone else qualified to interpret my results would do it.

When I pointed out that this new assignment; teaching in a special classroom for disruptive youth, was out of my area of certification, he indicated that he would be willing to work with me to obtain certification in this area. I explained that I had been certified and practiced as a school psychologist for over twenty years, and that my only experience in a classroom setting was student teaching some twenty-five years ago. I had no interest in a teaching certificate because I didn't plan on teaching. I indicated I had no interest in this. I was a school psychologist. I also asked him why I was not allowed to have my representative present during this meeting, and he indicated he had the freedom to sit down with any employee for a conversation. I pointed out that this did not apply to meetings where punitive actions were discussed, much less implemented, and he maintained his right to meet with employees without their representative present. So much for that section of the teacher's contract. Might as well use the document I helped create for…toilet tissue.

It is still a requirement for the principal to sit down with the teacher in a timely fashion and discuss the incident and the concerns. None of my principals ever sat down with me, and all of my formal evaluations were positive. This was a "top-down" evaluation from the superintendent, and it was not according to any established procedure. As well, it was clearly in retaliation for my actions as a parent, my appeals of his decisions, and my request for services for my daughter. It was not only unfair, it was so outside the law as to be unbelievable, but trust me, it happened, and it happened without so much as a whimper from my paid representative, the attorney for the educational association.

The superintendent reminded me to clean out my office and to return all files, memos, etc., to the principals before April 9. He then indicated that the meeting was over. He gave me a letter outlining his remarks and I left his office. My position in my March 28 meeting with the superintendent was that my responsibility was to advocate for the child. I maintained that I was a loyal employee, but that in protecting the board I was making sure others did not violate federal law state regulations or local procedures. If they did, it was my responsibility to speak up. I would not allow others, be they teachers or principals, to lie to a parent. Was that so wrong? I returned to

North High after stopping off at Lakeview to drop some things off. Below is the letter he wrote me in follow-up to our meeting:

Dear Mr. Matthews,   April 1, 1996

As you know, I have recently reviewed with you a number of serious concerns raised by your colleagues and supervisors as to how you perform your role as school psychologist.

(Yeah, chewing gum, holding up my hand, and speaking up on behalf of kids.)

When presented with these concerns in conference on Thursday, March 28, 1996, you made it very clear that you have no intention of changing your behavior toward other professionals with whom you work. Given this response and the other unacceptable statements you made during that conference, I have determined that I no long (*sic*) want you to serve this school system in the capacity of a school psychologist.

Effective Tuesday, April 9, 1996, you are hereby assigned as a teacher in the Alternative School, under the supervision of the building principal in charge of the "A Different Day Program." This reassignment and transfer is in the best interest of this school system.

You are to report to the principal's office at the Technology Center at 8:00 a.m. on Tuesday April 9, 1996, to receive further instructions regarding your new assignment. Please return all files, reports, notes, etc. regarding students with whom you have been working, to the appropriate principal no later than Thursday, April 4, 1996.

Sincerely, The Superintendent

Oh, great! After having suffered through the indignities of losing my elementary schools, and then finding myself bored to death at the middle and high school level, add to that the loss of all my seniority and status, throw in a few reprimands and humiliations, and then…then, just to top it off, take away my last shred of dignity by removing me from the career I've pursued for twenty-plus years. I'd worked in three states and four districts, but I'd always been a school psychologist.

I've worked hard and I've been dedicated and efficient...and respected. Now I am relegated to trying to teach a group of students who have been kicked out of every other program. The last time I was in a classroom as a teacher was twenty-five years ago when I student taught. I haven't even seen a lesson plan in a quarter century, and now I am to teach a full range of subjects with no experience or training. And these kids are often the most challenging. They are the ones with the most severe learning and behavior problems, who hate school and, even more, hate authority figures. That's why they're there. They have all been suspended and or expelled from the public schools for fighting, bringing weapons to school, drugs, or for chronic attendance problems. Many have been involved with the juvenile courts. Some are on medication for attention deficit disorders (others should be), and others are given that label we currently assign to juveniles who exhibit disruptive and oppositional behaviors: ODD — oppositional and defiant. Those who have crossed the line into actual criminal behavior (assault, shoplifting, arson, etc.) are given the additional title of "conduct disorder." Years ago they were "juvenile delinquents"; now we describe their behaviors. And a few have real criminal records, including assault with a deadly weapon.

These kids deserved an education, but was I allowed to help them in the ways I was trained, as a psychologist? No. What I was expected to do was teach. It was made clear from the very start I was not to play the role of psychologist, I had to forget my graduate training and twenty-three years of experience, I was to be a TEACHER. I was to control these students' behaviors from eight in the morning until three in the afternoon, keep them busy, keep them out of trouble, and teach them something. And now for the good news/bad news. It was my duty, and I didn't have to go it alone. I would be placed in there with another teacher and a classroom aide who had been in the classroom for eight months (good news), and yet I would have little to no control on how things worked; it was clearly her classroom, and I was the new kid (bad news). And as you will soon see I was placed in a no-win situation, sent out to sea on a rudderless ship with a mutinous crew and a captain and first mate who couldn't care less whether I sank or swam. But that is a story to be told a bit later. Right now I have a few days to close down my career of twenty-three years, eight here in the county system, and I need to get ready to move on to another challenge.

## Cleaning Up

I have two days to finish up my cases, move all my stuff out of my office, and report to work at my new assignment after Easter break. Teacher at the Alternative School. My career, my profession, was disappearing before my very eyes. And did I have the support of my association? My teacher's union representative, long silent, tells me to do what I'm told, to behave myself. "Go in there and do your job! I'll meet with you when you get back from Florida. In the meantime… keep your big mouth shut!" These words of comfort from my teacher association attorney finally springing to life after months of inaction on her part. And, oh, what great advice it was. Lawyers are called "mouthpieces" because they talk for you. They protect you in this fashion. Left on your own, you can get into trouble. I had appealed to the teacher's association time and time again for help. For months. And the best she could tell me was, "Wait until they take action and then we'll respond." And so now they have acted and the best she can tell me is sit tight and shut up? Was I missing something?

## And If You Want To Make Him Really Mad…

Though I thought I shared a professional relationship with the superintendent during my tenure as *president of the Teachers Association* and *president of the County Council of PTAs*, both roles put me on the opposite sides of several issues with the superintendent. He was used to presidents who went along with the status quo, figureheads who wouldn't think of rocking the boat or asking the indelicate question. I took my jobs seriously and I did my homework. As *president of the Teacher's Association* I was responsible for speaking out on behalf of teachers, to be their advocate. When the superintendent refused to support the third year of a pay increase the association and the board had agreed to, teachers were upset. We were in a catch-up mode and promised 9 percent. We got zip, increments only, which are for experience on the scale, not an increase. They went to impasse and the arbitrator (for which we, the association, paid $1,000 for our share) recommended 4 percent. We got...nothing. There was arbitration, but it was not binding. The superintendent claimed budget cuts and no money. Then he hired twelve new employees who were non-instructional. They weren't teachers to reduce the class size. They played musical chairs and moved people around, but with a little research I came up with the figure and the names of the new employees and the positions. This, along with several other moves, allowed teachers to bargain from a position of strength the following school year, and under my leadership we settled across the table for 4 percent for the first time in ten years. This must not have gone well with the superintendent, though he was smooth enough to keep it under his hat.

I played a similar active and proactive role as leader of the parents group, and, being an insider, had direct knowledge of what kinds of things needed fixing. The *County Council of PTAs* is an organization that consists of all the presidents of the local PTAs in the school district. The county *council president* is automatically a member of the *State Board of PTAs* (220,000 members in Maryland) and is the link, the liaison, between the state office and the locals. Activities and concerns at the state level are encouraged at the local level. I was required to hold four to five meetings a year, pass along copies of bulletins and notices from the state office and make sure local PTAs were run in a manner consistent with state and national goals. I was to make sure they kept their local bylaws updated, that they kept their financial records intact, that they had appropriate bonding and insurance (some PTAs raised $10,000–$12,000 in fundraisers). I even initiated liability insurance in the event someone was injured during a PTA-sponsored activity. I turned around the scholarship dinner so that more dollars went to the fund rather than the Country Club who catered the dinners, increased the awards from $500 to $600, and even added a third scholarship for the vocational students. When the issue of statewide issues came up for discussion, I voiced my concerns and participated on committees. The state testing program was one, and my actions locally and at the state level were recognized by parents outside the county. I think that the superintendent was seriously threatened by a teacher, a low-level employee (e.g., not an administrator), with so much power and influence. I mean, here's a man who keeps his administrators under a tight rein, and then this uppity teacher with a brain and energy comes on and starts pushing his weight around. He couldn't touch me. That is as long as I was in office. I finished my terms in June 1994. Sarah was suspended in October 1994. Is it possible that he used my daughter to get back at me? A way to punish and humiliate me? Just think about the funeral of the six-year-old for a minute and ask yourself that question again.

Sometimes it helped me to maintain my sanity by writing. Most of the time it just poured out to keep it from busting out at my cerebral seams. Sometimes I wrote fiction...took a little poetic license. Embellished. Like sticking pins in a voodoo doll. It made me feel better. It made me laugh.

# The End
# Where Do We Go From Here?

The superintendent was playing dirty, and he was so damn obvious about it. Take a little rumor and speculation, add a little disgruntled administrator or two, and the grand lie, and presto! You have a case to involuntarily transfer a teacher midyear and to then place him on a second-class certificate, ready to terminate at the slightest or even no provocation. Did it matter that I had done nothing wrong and that I had many more excellent observations and evaluations than critical ones? No. Did it matter that despite the superintendent's claims that I couldn't get along with anybody and that I was aggressive, arrogant, and obnoxious, I had never, not *once*, been written up for it? No. He made it up as he went along. But what was the saddest part was my union representatives went right along with it.

Right here in the spring of the year when I should be counting down the days to summer, I am plunged into the depths of depression. And so under these sunny circumstances I head off to my spring break in Florida and my parents' fiftieth wedding anniversary. Here I am wondering how I'm going to clear out my office and what to do with twenty years' accumulation of school psychologist "stuff." It would be a first, moving from an office into a classroom. Not to mention a classroom I would share with another teacher and a band of unruly kids. Lesson plans and daily objectives and other nightmares flowed through my brain, but we were determined to head to Florida and enjoy ourselves. And the best way? Not to mention a word to anyone about my "reassignment." I had called my teacher's association attorney hoping she could intercede, but alas, all she had to offer was go in and do your job, let me handle the rest. That would be okay if she did, but here I was two months after my formal conference with her and my local rep, and despite my warnings that they were out to get me, here the trap was sprung and I was just left sitting by myself, my leg firmly chained to the ground.

When I got back from Florida I met with the teacher association attorney for over an hour. During this hour she spent the better part of it brow-beating me for my "bad attitude," "chip on your shoulder," "behavior bordering on insubordination," "acting like a clown," "acting the buffoon," "challenging the superintendent to fire you," and much, much more. "Learn to keep your mouth closed. Even if they are unprofessional and insulting you, they hold all the cards. Keep your mouth shut!" She went on and on. I mean, whose side was she on? Sure, I had spoken up, but I was a whipped pup. All I asked for was some help. I promised to be good. But all she did was holler and humiliate me even more. I was never so glad to get out of there. She did agree to file a formal grievance on my behalf citing the reassignment as "arbitrary and capricious" and not in the best interest of the school system. In the mean time I would have to report to work on April 9 and take whatever they handed me, and like it. But if it was true that they held all the cards, how is it that they still don't have to play by the rules? And why do teachers spend all that time (and money) drawing up contracts if they can't be honored?

I was standing behind what I thought to be my rights as written in the negotiated agreement I signed as president of the teacher's association. It was our contract. Binding. It was clear that only principals could evaluate you, and they had to do it in a carefully prescribed fashion. A superintendent and his underlings could not override this procedure and gather information (dirt) from planted sycophants and use it against you. But they did. And when I reacted that he couldn't fire me, I'm the buffoon? Would it have been better to have been contrite and apologetic, and put my tail between my legs? "Sorry, Mr. Superintendent, I shouldn't have been talking while Miss Sheila, that wonderful spay-shell edu-ki-shun teacher from the high school was interrupting, and it was rude of me to tell her to stop. Furthermore, I should have given them the inaccurate information they wanted, I mean, who am I to interpret my own test data and interfere with their hidden agendas. And I really didn't mean to tell those parents the truth. I meant to lie, but the truth it just…just… slipped out. Those kids don't deserve services anyway! And I know…I should have not been chewing gum in the meeting. I'm sorry. Can you ever forgive me?"

I am a proud man and I make no apologies for that, or for standing up to tyrants and other little men who think they can abuse their power to intimidate others. I had a right to an advocate and yet no one stood up for me. I was on my own to defend myself and I did it, and I am proud that I stood up to the man. One thing I learned is that when someone is going to cut your head off, you don't put your head on the block. I went down fighting and I went down proud. He had to throw me out of his office (ask me to leave) because he was tired of my arrogant remarks. And then my final one, "It ain't over til the fat lady sings." He even quoted that one in his letter to me. So I got demoted, and I had little to no support from my attorney other than go into the class and do a good job and let her do the rest. After the brow-beating she gave me, I really trusted *her* to protect my rights. I went out and hired another attorney to make sure my interests were protected, someone I could trust. But I did follow the association attorney's advice. I took my medicine like a good boy and I went to work, and I made the best of it.

# CHAPTER SEVENTEEN

# THE CLASSROOM FROM HELL— APRIL 1996, MY DIARY

## April 9, 1996

First day. This must be how hell is designed. Tedium, tension, and a queasy stomach all wrapped into one. ODD (oppositional and defiant kids), even if there are only two of them, they can make life very unpleasant for those around them. If this were the only thing on my mind it would be difficult, but with all of the other "stuff" it's almost unbearable. But what choice do I have? To get paid and finish the year I have to undergo this and all the rest of it. What a mess! Glad this is not December but April. Now that I've seen the personnel director's plan to dredge up all of the minor incidents from years past, two, six, and even seven years ago, and then place all of this stuff into my personnel file as though it was there all along, shows how they intend to fight: dirty. I was never given the chance to respond or defend myself from all of this stuff, primarily because it was never PUT in my file or used in any disciplinary manner. Now it is here as fuel for the fire they hope to set around me. It is beyond description. Who would want to stay and work with these people anyway? But I can't quit now, that's what they want. To quit now would throw everything away. I need to GET TOUGH! Find out what I am made of. Stay in there and FIGHT!

## April 12, 1996

Like flying, this job is best described as long periods of utter boredom interrupted by moments of sheer terror. I sit and just watch for the most part, noting minor infractions such as sleeping, not working, rocking in seats, playing with the blinds, instigating others. My mind is still reeling, seeking psychological comfort in *routine,* a standard one can get used to, a rhythm; security, comfort, familiar; versus insecure, uncomfortable, unfamiliar. Relaxed instead of tense. I worry about the due process special education hearing for Sarah coming up in ten days. My loss of status hurts, my identity as a school psychologist ripped away. Feeling the success of accomplishment, of helping kids and teachers...all gone. And what did I do to deserve this other than stand firmly behind my convictions? Yesterday I stood outside the school, waiting for the bus to carry the wild creatures back to their caves. Two parents I had helped earlier in the year walked up to me. The mom looked at me with these sad eyes. "We're going in to our IEP meeting now; I wish you could be there with us." I looked at her and said, "You don't know how much I'd like to be," and then I broke with emotion. It was humiliating, and it was cruel, not only to me but to the parents and the kids I serve. *Humiliation, embarrassment, loss, grief, sadness, anxiety, fear, depression* all wrapped into one with anger as a distant cousin. There's almost no room for it. Caroline calls once I get home to check on me, I tell her the story and I break down again, I hang up and I pound the kitchen counter "THEY CAN'T DO THIS TO ME, IT'S NOT RIGHT, IT'S NOT FAIR. IT'S NOT

HONEST. IT'S ALL A LIE!" Where is the cavalry when you need them?

## April 15, 1996, My Reassignment Hearing

Am readying myself for the hearing in a week. Got all of my documents together, need five copies, each an inch thick. Zip over to Parcel Plus to copy, collate, and mail. Watched *Braveheart* over the weekend. On a much smaller scale, I compare his independent thought and dedication to his own conscience rather than the voices of others, the true meaning of freedom. Freedom to think, to express one's thoughts, and for me, academic freedom to advocate for children. Countering the administration's argument that I have "assumed duties that were never assigned to me," that I have "created my own job description." Some duties don't need to be assigned; they exist by virtue of the education, training, and background of the professional in charge of the caseload. That is why you ARE a professional; you don't have to live to take specific orders, and you KNOW what to do. Those who have the responsibility, the accountability, should also have the authority to make decisions on behalf of students and the board of education. The central task: "to protect the student and school system from harm." The student from violations of his or her rights, and the system from legal actions arising from these same violations.

I knew in my heart of hearts that I had not invented my own job description, and that what I was doing was precisely what my professional organization supported. I sent away for the *National Association of School Psychologist's Professional Standards Booklet,* and was heartened by what I read. What was most interesting about all of this was that I had known it, followed it, and preached it for years before seeing it in print, and reading through it in the midst of this confusion was overwhelmed with a feeling of validation. I called aloud "YES!" "YES!" as I read the book. According to this book, my loyalties were of my own choosing, not my employers; and if there was ever a conflict between my loyalties to my students or my employer, my only obligation was "to inform all concerned persons of relevant issues in advance." More importantly, my dedication to the kids I served was clear: "school psychologists consider the students or clients to be their primary responsibility, acting as advocates of their rights and welfare…and is a top priority in determining services." In the darkest hours I read and re-read my professional standards book.

## Strategy Session

I sat down in the teacher's association office with my representatives. One was the current teacher's association president, and the other the UniServe director, the same gentleman who was so helpful during the Jackie incident when I could have been fired for attending a funeral. They reviewed the actions the superintendent took against me and decided that although he could reassign anyone, anytime, for the best interest of the school system (reallocating resources); he had made a number of technical errors. This was not simply the case of moving a third-grade teacher into a fourth-grade classroom. This was taking a fully certified, experienced psychologist and placing him into a position where he was uncertified and inexperienced. The timing of my daughter's cases and proximity to the "complaints" from the high school suggested that the move was not an innocent one, but one in response to actions on my part. In this case my "trouble with teachers and staff" and my response to the personnel director and the superintendent boiled down to "I can't fix what isn't broken." My position was that my problems were related not to my job actions, but my role as parent. They weren't punishing me for not doing my job, they were punishing me for taking them through hearings and court, and since they couldn't "get me" on those counts, they'd get me where they could: on the job. And since I had no problems on the job, they would have to create them, imagine them, or even set them up. The UniServe director was troubled not only about the disciplinary nature of the reassignment, but that fact that they warned me on the twenty-seventh to "straighten up or else!" and then scheduled a meeting less than forty-eight hours later, at which time I was reassigned. This did not give me much of a chance for improvement. Of even more interest to me was the fact that if all of this was "disciplinary" in nature, especially the Northern High complaints, then why did they not follow the requirements spelled out in the negotiated agreement: they had to be timely and they had to come out of a conference between the employee and principal. This never happened.

So in addition to 1) Sarah's expulsion case and 2) Sarah's due process special education case, I could now add my own personal/professional case: 3) reassignment.

## State Level Due Process

Having "lost" the case with the local mediator at the local level, the due process rights of my daughter, Sarah, were still in limbo. I had the right to appeal to the state, and after reading the mediator's decision, with its spelling and typographical errors, not to mention procedural errors, I was confident that at least I could expect a higher level of professionalism at a state level hearing. What do you think? We are prepared to present our case through several witnesses and then make arguments from the record subject to the board attorney's cross. Closing remarks can either close the record or you may leave it open as you wish to allow the opportunity for written memoranda from both sides.

## Office of Administrative Hearings

Dear Ms. Smith,                          April 12, 1996

In response to the school board's offer for mediation, let me quickly say that as far as my family is concerned, mediation is completely out of the question. As we are confident that we will have a fair and truly impartial hearing at the state level, we are anxious to proceed. Not only has the board's attorney rehashed his claim that "a Section 504 program could address (Sarah's) needs," when she is clearly eligible for special education and/or related services under IDEA, but he has indicated his intention to redetermine her eligibility yet again, referring to Sarah's "alleged disability in mathematics" in his recent *Mediation Information Sheet,* a fact he previously stipulated to at the local hearing! We never anticipated the level of "gamesmanship" some people are willing to engage in. For example, I find it odd that the board's attorney was " unavailable for the hearing during the week of April 15 through 19," yet is suddenly free to meet for the purpose of *mediation* on April 17, 18, and 19.

Throughout this sometimes grueling process over the last eighteen months, we have been more than willing to mediate this dispute, or to meet and reach compromise. Time and time again we have been rebuffed, and my daughter continues to receive none of the services she is entitled to. They have either ignored us or issued "take it or leave it" ultimatums. Although we are reasonable people and willing to compromise on any number of issues, our daughter's education is not one of them.

Thank you for notifying the attorney on our behalf that "the proper appeal forms" have been on file with OAH since April 5, and that he is free to request them at his leisure. Thank you for your assistance, you've been most helpful. I never fully appreciated the extreme disadvantage parents are faced with when they are up against the "deep pockets" of a board of education, even one of the smallest ones over here on the Shore.

Sincerely yours,<br>
Frank Matthews

## My Opening Remarks — April 22 Due Process Hearing

And so I proceeded to address the panel in much the same fashion as I had addressed the board of education many months earlier. I explained why I was bringing her case to them; because I truly believed that her expulsion from school for drugs was due in large part to her untreated attention deficit hyperactivity disorder and the impulsive nature of her personality, and how I was also convinced that her frustrations in high school were related to learning disabilities diagnosed in elementary school that reemerged when she moved up to the high school. I explained how her mother and I did everything we could as responsible parents to address her needs through drug counseling, individual counseling and family therapy. All we were asking was for them to recognize the findings of two school psychologists that identified her as a child with learning disabilities, and to do what the school system failed to do by providing her the special education and related services to which she was entitled.

## Monday, April 22/Tuesday, April 23 State Level Due Process Hearing

The day after. Took off Friday afternoon to see my personal physician. The week before I was pretty depressed. Eating, sleeping, bowels and brain all in an uproar. Not knowing whether I could handle the hearing, not being a psychologist, employment future in question, and being in a classroom of a dozen unruly kids with lectures, lesson plans, observations, grading papers, disciplining, and just being there for seven and a half hours, a challenge like none I'd ever faced.

As recorded, I began to fill in with constructive things to do, and the time in my new assignment passed more quickly. I structured the day with a student schedule with breaks built in at appropriate times (nine thirty when they were on task for ninety minutes and they were restless). Group counseling was moved to the afternoon and I began to actually look forward to coming to school/work. Stayed Friday past the time I could leave, at eleven thirty, for my half day personal day allowing my co-teacher to go to lunch. I left around noon. Met with my doctor and was straight with him. He was shocked and concerned and wrote me a script for cramps and Metamucil for stomach/bowels to work better.

I worked Friday and Saturday and Sunday, collating and organizing and coordinating my presentation. Witness order. Questions for my expert witnesses. Outline for my presentation. What book I was working out of, in what order, how to move smoothly through my transitions, cross referencing the quotes in the transcripts from previous hearings. Blue book, February 20 hearing, transition January 30 hearing, transcripts, blue book, witness.

I had six hundred pages catalogued from transcripts of the first two hearings. Summary statements and page/line references: page 122, line 6. I grouped them, sequenced them, and the flow was exquisite! I would feed their own witnesses' statements back to them to demonstrate how they contradicted themselves. I would effectively undermine their credibility and show them for the liars they were/are. I was ready. I did final run-throughs Sunday and again Monday and was relaxing on the back porch with Caroline and Diane at eight with an hour of breathing time. Diane, a respected college professor and friend with a Ph.D. in special education, would be my star witness. I was ready!

# The Hearing

The hearing itself was nothing like I expected. The administrative law judge (ALJ) arrived twenty minutes late, and then took additional time to settle in and meet with the two hearing officers. The ALJ allowed the personnel

## The Classroom From Hell—April 1996, My Diary

director to enter the hearing room. The same personnel director who was my contemptible supervisor, member of the expulsion committee for Sarah, head of the special education department, and my chief persecutor. The ALJ was going to allow him to attend the hearing as a "recorder." I complained. This was intimidation. It fell on deaf ears. How I detest that man. We didn't get started until ten forty. The board's high-priced attorney was there and, in what had to be a delay tactic on his part, failed to number his documents. This took another forty minutes. Then prelims. We wanted to be honest, so we explained to them that Sarah had classes and would only be staying for the morning. That was a mistake. So, without consent, they switched the order of proceedings and put her on first! The two hearing officers questioned her about why she wanted an IEP, didn't she know this would not follow her to college? Even they had her in tears. Then they allowed the board's attorney to question her, something we had hoped to avoid. She was a mess after he got finished. "Didn't you realize that just being learning disabled doesn't mean you were automatically ELIGIBLE for services? Needs have to be determined." By the time this first phase has gone down, I had this distinct impression that the hearing officers had already made up their minds. I said as much: "This feels more like the end of the hearing rather than the beginning!" I was not happy. I had not even presented, and yet they seemed to know what I was going to say, to do, and to present. It was like a done deal—their minds were already made up. Was this truly a hearing or an "already heard"?

The next surprise was the administrative law judge's ruling that I was precluded from discussing TIMELINES, since I had failed to bring it up as an issue at the "lower level hearing." I indicated that I had tried and was *prevented* from doing it. I also told them that despite their preconceptions of things, there was no *form* I had to fill out to state my issues on, or memoranda. I'd had no opportunity to lay out my case in writing at the lower levels. I had called and asked the mediator what I needed, and he said witness lists and documents, both of which I provided. This was starting to feel like a miscarriage of justice. A done deal. Timelines were our "fallback" position; with other issues in question, we had to hope we could at least prevail in timeline violations, the long delays they forced on us. Justice delayed, justice denied. But it looked like we would be prevented from including these.

So with Sarah upset, the personnel director allowed to stay, precious time wasted with late starts, the board attorney's numbering game, and now no timelines, what next? The ALJ wanted to make sure we did not bring up "things already on the record." Only new facts and contradictions (the thrust of my case). But how to convince her that these were in fact contradictions and not only a rehashing of the previous hearing? I would do my best. I launch into my opening. The board attorney only interrupted me once ("He's testifying, he needs to be sworn!") and then indicated that he would be briefer than me, and proceeded to go on for twenty-five minutes, fifteen longer than my ten-minute intro. He even lied about the time. By now it was time for lunch. But first I wanted to clarify one mistake in the transcript. Page 99, line 2. That's when the disaster truly began to take shape. "I don't have that on my copy," the board attorney complained. "Me neither," said the hearing officer. "Are you sure you have the correct page? Do you have the right transcript?" Something was very rotten in Denmark!

Turns out that out of the five copies — mine, the board attorney's, two for the hearing officers, and the administrative law judge's — four were identical to each other, and one was different. Guess whose? Mine. I was dumbstruck. Someone, either the board or their attorney, sent me an altered copy. All of my hours of cross-referencing were rendered useless. And since I had the lone copy, it looked like I was the problem. We broke for lunch and I got on the phone.

The company who typed out the transcripts from the tapes of the previous two hearings pulled up the original, and it matched mine! Come to find out that they had sent out five copies, one to me and four to the board of education. They

## The Classroom From Hell — April 1996, My Diary

also sent the board of education the ASCII disc! It doesn't take a rocket scientist to figure out what they did. They put their four copies on the shelf and pulled up the transcript off the disc. They justified the margins on theirs and made four copies, which they sent three of to the ALJ and hearing officers. Though they didn't change a single word, by justifying the margins it made their new copies completely different by line number and page.

I was so drained by now that when they started talking mediation and settlement, I was ready. They worked up a 504 plan that included everything we wanted except an IEP. They recognized her learning disability, they offered her tutors, consultation with special education, accommodations and modifications, weekly parent contacts. We took the deal. I was beginning to get exhausted. I was willing to run the race, but not with the weights strapped to my ankles. In the end I wrote a letter expressing my concerns:

"Office of Administrative Hearings            June 20, 1996

For the past twenty-two years I have been a practicing school psychologist and have followed with great interest the development and implementation of the federal laws that affect the children I work with, first 93-180, then 94-142, IDEA, ADA, and the older but newly revived Section 504. Never before have I been as concerned as I am now about the process by which parents pursue their rights to a free appropriate public education FAPE for their disabled children. This process turns out to be seriously flawed, in part because the deck seems to be stacked against parents and their children in favor of boards of education and their attorneys. Rather than a search for the "truth" and what is in the best interest of the child, it turns out to be more of an exercise in "blame and attack." The irony is that I only discovered this recently, not as a professional practitioner, but as a parent of a child with a disability, my daughter, Sarah. My concerns extend beyond the simple question of fairness to something more serious. From a layman's point of view many of these hearing officers behaved in a manner that belied the common wisdom that they "defer" to parents who lack the background, experience, and resources of a school board attorney. The three that we dealt with violated the spirit if not the letter of the law, that the parent and the disabled child should receive the benefit of the doubt. The following outlines our case and the difficulties we dealt with.

For starters, "free or low-cost attorneys" are supposed to be available to parents, and yet I had to go through twenty-five before I found a "specialist" who billed by the hour (and minute) at the rate of $175 per hour. Since I am fighting a battle on three fronts; my daughter's illegal expulsion from school for alleged drug use, the county's refusal to provide special education services to my learning disabled daughter, and most recently my reassignment from a position as school psychologist to a classroom teacher for disruptive youth, I was forced to take on the special education case by myself since I was unable to afford another attorney. I happen to be in the untenable position of being employed by this same school system.

How else is the deck stacked against parents? The LEA has access and control over all the records. They are free to add to or delete information at will. Our daughter's files were "lost" for over ten months, suddenly reappearing after the "five-day disclosure" period had passed for Sarah's local due process hearing. My home county prevented me from accessing my files after they announced they were moving me, and have taken entire file drawers from other special education teachers in an attempt to "clean house" in the event federal or state monitors show up. They have even threatened to "terminate" one colleague for "forging signatures," then denied her access to the files she is accused of altering. This same colleague made the tragic mistake of refusing to sign a letter condemning me for violating confidentiality rules (and informing me that someone was entering my confidential computer files). This cost her her job.

The LEA has extensive control over their employees, free access, and unquestioned loyalty. In our county people know

## The Classroom From Hell — April 1996, My Diary

their jobs are on the line if they take the "wrong" side of the issue. I was told as an employee that *my* job would be in jeopardy if I used my office phone to recruit character witnesses for my daughter's hearing, or was caught at the copying machine or using my computer for "personal business." Imagine their reaction when I ask fellow employees to come forward, for me or my daughter.

Still, the most surprising aspect of these proceedings was the conduct of the individuals who were charged with seeing that fair hearings were given. No matter how knowledgeable a parent might be (and I consider myself well-versed in special education law), we are no match for attorneys who can distort the simplest facts, put negative spin on every good intention, and confuse what should be simple issues. Even if you survive unscathed through the local administrative channels, you're then faced with a tight network of local boards, state boards, and circuit courts more oriented to the status quo than giving the parent a fair and truly impartial hearing. With attorneys who are more intent on winning the case than advocating for the child's best interest, boards, hearing panels, and courts are treated to an exercise in distortion where the truth is lost in a conundrum of legal arguments. I was almost excluded from offering expert testimony as a result of a clerical error in my professional directory listing me as having an Ed.D. instead of and Ed.S. I was prevented from bringing in the numerous timeline violations because I hadn't highlighted timelines as a major issue. This after the hearing officer assured me all I needed was the documents I would present for the record, and a witness list turned in five days before the hearing date. He then based his decision—which contained over thirty spelling and typographical errors—on the other side's closing arguments, rather than the evidence we presented. Cases cited by both the hearing officer and the attorney for the school system later turned out to be totally unrelated to this case.

The bottom line is that parents, even those with significant knowledge and background in special education such as myself, can all too easily be discredited and intimidated by questionable legal tactics that effectively destroy the true spirit, if not the letter, of the law for disabled students.

The ALJ (administrative law judge) from the state hearing also refused to allow us to introduce timeline violations, ignored the fact that they were given altered transcripts by the LEA, and forced my daughter to testify before we had presented our case, thereby prejudicing the panel. She was asked technical questions she was unable to answer and broke down in tears. I was frequently interrupted (objection/sustained) during my opening remarks, and almost forced into a settlement agreement by sheer exhaustion and frustration. My requests to present our case were ignored as the panel left for a recess that resulted in our waiving all of our rights for special education services in return for a 504 plan that has yet to be implemented in the classroom.

This entire case has been frustrating for us. A little girl identified in second grade as learning disabled and served with an IEP cannot receive a timely reevaluation, and when she does, still cannot receive services even after local and state due process hearings. The ALJ noted that we "looked happy" after the settlement. It was more like relief that it was over, and we at least came away with something. But two months later with the school year over, and nothing in place at the school, has left us feeling like we've been had. We've waived all of our rights for special education services for a 504 plan that has yet to be enforced, and a prevailing attitude at the high school that they can do whatever they want since the Matthews "lost" the case. I'm concerned about the Matthewses, all right—Frank and Caroline, who dragged their way through this, spending thousands of dollars in the process, but I'm most concerned about Sarah Matthews, who was supposed to be the object of all this, and for all of the other kids whose parents give up long before they get to this stage. Can you blame them?

        Sincerely yours,
        Frank and Caroline Matthews"

The Classroom From Hell — April 1996, My Diary

# Back To The Class Again

After a day off at the hearing (with appropriate loss of pay) it's back to the routine again. Even the routine was tough. As you got adjusted to one group of kids, they would add a few more. And in a room full of disturbed kids, even one can make a big difference. I tried to work out a compromise with the other teacher, who was far less structured than I was, but it was still her class. I was forced to participate in the charade. Even if she wanted to accept a few of my suggestions, they still had to go through the principal. And once she found out whose ideas they were, they were squelched. Can't have changes leading to success. They wanted me to fail, and they did everything in their power to guarantee it. They added kids, they switched schedules, they didn't provide a substitute when the aide was out, and they were leaving me alone with the kids on an increasing basis. I'm trying to teach kids in grades –seven through twelve from four schools (two middle, two high), different grade levels, different subjects. My association attorney, the one who browbeat me, is still putting together my complaint against the board, but will only be asking for a school psychologist job back, not my "old job" at the elementary level. I'm frustrated. Am I willing to work at the secondary level again? It's better than this, but what about the job I was happy in at the elementary level? Should I start looking for work elsewhere, or look for a career change?

**May 2, 1996**

The kids are restless. One new kid from the inner city. Derek questions everything. "How come I get points just for sitting in Mr. D's chair? Ms. Bates (the lead teacher in the Alternative School) lets me sit there." Meanwhile Daman (Demon?) is rolling around the room in the other desk chair. He slides over to the computer, where he is forbidden after messing up the password on the others. Kids are talking out, out of their seats, wrestling, talking across the room to each other and the other teacher, they're rocking furniture, sliding across the room, you name it. And the teacher is too busy on the phone making personal calls to respond to any of it. So am I to be the "bad guy with no support"? I just count the days and pray that relief is on the way. Summer, come on! Then what? A state job, aide to a congressman, mediator, psychologist, or financial ruin, degradation? What do I deserve for the stress and strain and humiliation, etc.? Isn't it my time?

**May 7, 1996**

We'd been waiting for some time, fighting the good fight, waiting for the cavalry to come. When they didn't show, I sent out scouts to find them and bring them to our rescue. I wrote letters to everyone I could think of. The governor, the lieutenant governor, advocacy groups, the ACLU, my professional organization, the National Association of School Psychologists, and, yes, even my congressman. I got a call from his office and spoke to his assistant, and she was very encouraging. It seemed that he was getting a lot of calls here lately from parents about Shore school systems that were less than responsive to parents of disabled kids. She had heard from more than one person that decisions were made before the meetings even began. Since I was both a parent and a professional educator, my perspective would be important. Would I be able to meet with the congressman on May 7? Without a moment's hesitation I said yes. Previously I rarely missed a day; in fact I had over eighty days saved up. Lately, though, my mental health was so low, not to mention by dedication, that I took off at the slightest sniffle. I could feel a headache coming on for the seventh.

After languishing for almost five hours, I finally built a sufficient case for the headache, and I left after Ms. Bates came back from lunch. We were still doing good, sixteen days without a referral, but Bates wasn't happy. She had a session on "respect, consequences, and all of that good stuff we do for you isn't payin' off, so it was back to the old ways. Mess up, get referred." Seems Bates thinks her words have an effect on these kids. I doubt it. Action. Setting firm limits,

## The Classroom From Hell — April 1996, My Diary

tying consequences to inappropriate behaviors, and providing incentives and rewards for good behavior. Bates is too wishy washy and breaks more rules than she keeps. She likes having the power and control, though she wields it inconsistently. She allows them to talk, to get out of their seats, to shout across the room, to do no work. She shouts across the room and disturbs them when they are quiet. This lackadaisical attitude will come back to haunt her. For me, I'm going to meet with the congressman.

Warren T. Hillcrest is a populist congressman. He still drives the same beat-up car and wears the same Sears shirts with frayed collars, and he looks you in the eye. He is a very down-to-earth kinda guy. He is one of only two Republicans I have ever voted for, and one of them went to federal prison for embezzlement (the former governor of West Virginia). There was supposed to be a group of parents there; only two showed, but since it was their meeting, I was willing to sit back and let things happen. They wanted me to go first, and when I did they sat back in stunned silence. I kept apologizing for monopolizing the conversation, but they were clearly interested. The conventional wisdom is that it is the parents against the bureaucracy (the school board), but when one of the insiders, a school psychologist, has the same problems with his own child, it suggests that something really is rotten in Denmark.

The other parents had their say. One didn't seem to have much of a case, the other did, but both were more willing to "cut and run" than stay and fight. Both were poised to enroll their kids in private school. Warren offered to help them with a few well-placed phone calls and took down some directory information. He turned to us and offered the same, but who to call? We told him about our case before the court of special appeals, the 504 for Sarah, and my complaint through OCR. He offered to call the superintendent, but we passed. He knew the superintendent personally and agreed a call might hurt more than help. He would do several things on our behalf. Follow up on the OAH to see about the status of our plan.

Work behind the scenes at OCR to move it along, and...he would be willing to attend a meeting at our home to discuss concerns of parents and teachers about special education and the school system in general. He said he felt that some of the wrong kinds of people were in education, that he was concerned about what he had heard today. I told him I had considered resigning, but was reluctant, he told me emphatically not to, that this was "not going to be swept under the rug." We left and he acknowledged with a look that he was very glad to have met us. I followed up with a letter to his assistant and a packet of material for Warren. It felt good to have someone in our corner!

## May 8 — The First Referral

Although my influence on the rules of the class were small, I did make some inroads. My dilemma was trying to perform the role I was assigned: teacher. To fail at this would be more grist for the superintendent's mill. To succeed would also present problems, for it could demonstrate that I was appropriately placed. Could I successfully "play" psychologist and "fix" all of the problems with their behavior management system? Certainly. Would this guarantee me a promotion back to my "old job" or a permanent place in the alternative setting? Rock and Hard Place 101. For my own sanity, as well as for the benefit and growth of this group of kids I was responsible for, I challenged them to go until May 5 without a referral for behavior, and I would talk to Mrs. Terry about returning their privilege of going to the high school for gym. This not only appealed to their own need for self-control, but to the need to be part of a team. I had been using the life boat analogy with them, that like a group of people cast adrift from the main vessel (the high school), they are dependent on each other for survival. They need to share and cooperate or they all will suffer. They have to support each other. This seems to have made sense, for they made the seventeen days and their

## The Classroom From Hell — April 1996, My Diary

gym privileges were restored. To keep things going, I change the count on the board each day to see how long they can go beyond the goal. We reached twenty today.

Yesterday 285-pound-plus Gary refused to stand during the pledge. By the time I had intensified the polite request to a demand, the pledge was over. He didn't have to recite the pledge, but it was disrespectful to sit while others stood. There are certain conventions that society expects, and these kids need to know them or understand the social consequences of violating them. Like sitting during "The Star Spangled Banner" or sitting down when the judge enters a courtroom, or sitting when everyone else stands up to sing a hymn in church.

Since the pledge was over I asked him to stand for thirty seconds. He sat. I then told him this was the "last time I will ask you to stand." He sat. I then threatened the "first referral." The kids went nuts. They started yelling at him and pressuring him to stand. Still he sat. So I separated him from the group; they didn't deserve a loss of privilege because of him, so I told him, "Fine...sit. Here are a few things you can expect today: 1) You remain behind while the others go to gym." The kids responded to this right away. There would not be a loss of a "class privilege" if only one student screwed up. This was fair in their eyes. But "who would watch him since you went to lunch and the teacher and aide went to gym?" they asked. I would eat lunch in the classroom to watch him. 2) At the nine thirty break he would sit. 3) At lunch he would sit, at his desk, and food would be brought to him rather than joining the group, and 4) He would only be allowed two bathroom breaks, one in the morning one in the afternoon. If he enjoyed sitting so much, that is exactly what he would get to do all day. Logical Consequences 102.

The remarkable thing is that he didn't complain and he complied. He tested the bathroom rule in the afternoon by trying to go for an extra visit, but when I caught him, he returned. He then slid his chair around the room, "I'm *in* my seat!" but we clarified his seat meant his chair under his desk.

At lunch I talked with him about respect for others, let him vent a bit, and let him be. Halfway through the afternoon he asked, "If I stand for the pledge now, can I use the computer?" I explained that he'd already made his choice for the day, and that tomorrow would be another chance. By the end of the day I asked him if tomorrow would be better. He didn't respond. The next day the pledge was announced, and Gary stood. Without saying anything, I patted him on the back. I also gave him the fantasy book I promised to bring in. Tough love worked. I really felt this was a breakthrough. Who was to know what was lurking beneath the surface.

## The Snack Machine

I went to lunch and all the kids went to gym. I don't know whether they were primed after a good day, or whether they were playing one teacher against the other, or whether Bates had some kind of subconscious desire to undermine what I had built with "her" kids. Whatever it was, she made a series of errors that lead to a crisis that could have, should have been avoided. Bates left the group unsupervised while she went to pay for the lunches. This was something that never should have happened. Left to their own devices, two kids, Gary and Daman, snuck off to get something out of the snack machine. The popcorn got stuck, so Gary proceeded to kick the machine. Hard. Harder. Just about that time the principal comes around the corner. Busted! Now Bates had to save face and regain her "authority" and control, so she proceeds to write them up, without discussion or consulting me. Problem was, I came back for lunch ready for group (counseling), and she has everything at fever pitch. Then Bates makes her next mistake. She leaves for planning, leaving me with seven angry kids. I had no idea of what had gone on other than she was writing Gary and Daman up for inappropriate behavior.

# The Classroom From Hell — April 1996, My Diary

I started out with the *Touchstones* program. To control the speaker, I used my paperweight, the rule being only the person with the paperweight could speak. I demonstrated by talking and holding the weight and then passing it on to the next person and "zipping" my lip. Daman took it first and made out like he was in charge, "Now you shoodoop." Next Gary grabbed it from Daman and went on about the unfair "policy" of no food in the room. I pulled out the handbook and read it for their benefit. Derek grabbed the weight and jumped on the wording of the policy which stated that "Food may not be brought into the classroom from home." "See, he didn't bring it from home, he got it from the school!" I provided a clarification that the intent of the policy was to prevent any food from being brought into the classroom, "You can't stop off at the 7-11 on your way to school and load up on candy and soda pop to bring into class." Derek, enjoying his control with the weight, "Shows how dumb you are, we don't got no 7-11 roun' here!" The way this kid twists things is amazing! He is a choice candidate for a prison cell if there ever was one. He takes words and twists them to gain psychological control, to contort the logic if it doesn't work in his favor. He also capitalizes on weaknesses rather than seek common ground and fairness. He is a "con man" more interested in the "con," the control, than a person-to-person interaction, especially where one has the authority and deserves the respect. Truth be known, he probably is a kid that has had no control over his life and has never received any respect. He hasn't learned how to trust. Try to treat him with fairness, and he turns it against you. It's perceived as weakness. He only understands strength, force, and someone who word plays like he does. Derek jumped on the rules I've established. "Hey, man, you ain't got the microphone (the paperweight), so you can't talk." When I explain, or try to, that I'm the group leader, so this doesn't apply to me, he jumps on this. "Oh, so you think you special, rules don't apply to you." I can feel my blood pressure boiling, but I am still calm and in control. I tell him to please hand me the paperweight. He refuses to relinquish the paperweight; he wants control. He then lapses into personal attack: "Why you eyes get all big and your voice get high? Me, I'm calm. You all excited?! If you was in court you be like that and I be all calm, you be the one going to jail." I lower my voice and squint. I counter with, "I guess that's because you've had more experience in court than I have." Derek moves to talking about my daughter. "I think I know your daughter, what's her name, Sarah?"

I ignore this game and move on to talk about why they are in this classroom, because they don't respect adults or other authority figures and the rules they've established. That they will do better by trying to learn about rules like them or not. Show respect and you will earn it back. What did they see for themselves when they got out of high school? Derek says he don't need to worry about that " 'cos I make more money in a week than you could ever think about." "Doing what?" I inquire. "None of your business," he responds. "Doing something legal?" This strikes a chord with the group, especially the black kids. "You accusin' him of being a drug dealer?! You wouldn't ask Drew (the white kid who's the champion archer) that." They tried to draw the line in color and I refused to bite. I closed down group after Derek launched his final challenge: "Tomorrow I'm bringin' in two cheesesteak sandwiches, snacks, and a drink, and I'm gonna eat it right in your face!"

I was never so glad for a day to end. What had happened between yesterday and today? What had Bates said to them or done to turn them on me like this. Was I paranoid or did something happen? Had I screwed up that badly, or did I try to deal with them at the wrong time, when they were angry at Bates and Mel? Was I receiving the spinoff from that? I tried to be fair and in control, and it seemed like neither fairness or control was executed. I felt powerless myself. I would have to rethink my approach, I would have to regain control, and respect the next day.

I needed to be ready for them.

# The Worst Day Of The Term

I figured that the kids perceived my "nice guy" demeanor as weakness, so I was resolved to be tough. Firm, and not so nice. They came in a few minutes late in a group as though they had been outside talking amongst themselves. Usually they straggle in one at a time. They "entered laughing," wired with a total groove of "we've got his number." I wished them good morning and asked them to take their seats. Everyone sat except Derek. He stood by his desk. I then asked the group to stop talking; it was five after eight and they needed to settle into work. Derek complained that he wasn't talking and sat down at his desk. I wasn't going to argue with him. I thanked him for sitting. He stood up. I told him firmly, "Sit down." He approached my desk where I was seated, standing over me with a threatening look on his face. I had to make a decision: sit there and ignore him, ask him to return to his seat, and get into an argument with him, or confront him. The one thing I could not afford was to show that I was scared of him. Derek had moved the game into a different arena. Now he was not just insubordinate and disrespectful, he was physically challenging me, trying to intimidate me physically. I stood up and faced him. I said, "If you want a piece of me...take it." And I stood with my hands to my sides in a nonthreatening manner. Two of his friends came over and grabbed him by each arm and led him back to his seat. I think they did this for my benefit as well as Derek's. It would have been fine if it had stopped there, but it didn't. From his seat he started running his mouth about how he "scared the teacher. He nothin' but a chicken. We got his number," etc. Once again I had to establish my position, my authority in the room. With a group of adolescent males, especially ones like these who believe fighting and physical solutions are viable options, the only way you hold them at bay is to earn their respect. They have to have something to lose, to fear. Maybe it was being on the losing end. To get humiliated by a good beating or a superior force, handcuffs and custody by police, being removed from the area, suspension, etc. Right now it seemed

I had to show these boys I could take a good punch, that I would be a man about it and show him I wasn't afraid of him. I stood up and slowly walked back to his desk. Both hands were on my hips in a nonthreatening posture. He stood and faced me. "Come on, here's your last chance to do something. You want a piece of me, take it now." He had a pen in his fist which he was clutching and unclutching. I looked down at it. "I think you can put the pen down." He stood for another few seconds, and I finally said, "That's what I thought," and walked away. I had stood up to him and he didn't rise to my challenge. I made my point. I called his bluff. As I walked back to my desk he called me a "bitch" and then he pulled out a Rice Krispy Treat and shoved it in his mouth, chomping on it loudly as he approached my desk. He came to within a foot of my face, fulfilling his promise to "eat it right in yo' face." I went over to the file cabinet and made a point of pulling out a referral and said, "Consider yourself written up." He walked out of the classroom.

Clifford pulled me aside and said I should consider myself lucky. "Hey, man, I pulled him away the first time. He's crazy. Last night he got arrested at the ball field for hitting the coach with a baseball bat. He was out there flirting with my sister, who plays third base, and the coach kept telling him to get away, and when he didn't he sailed a fastball over his head. Derek got mad and came at him with a baseball bat." I wish I had known that before I challenged him. Who was to know?

Meanwhile, Gina, the lone girl in the classroom, has been reacting to all the excitement. She is mouthy and carrying on with Roland. Right after this incident over eating in the room, he starts giving Gina some candy out of his box. I ask him to give the box to me and he protests, but complies, after counting them to make sure I don't eat any. I give him his space around that. I explain to them that it wouldn't be fair to write Derek up for eating in the classroom and then let them eat candy. I put his candy in my desk and turn around and here Gina is drinking a Coke. Testing, testing. I walk over and tell her to give it to me. She drinks. I tell her once more that

## The Classroom From Hell—April 1996, My Diary

students are not permitted to bring food or drinks into the room and that she had best turn over the soda can. She drinks. I warn her, "You take one more drink...." She drinks, trying to finish the whole can in one gulp, and I go to take the can. She pulls away and I'm not going to play tug-o'-war so I let go to return to my desk to write her up. Now she comes up and makes a production of pouring the soda can into my trash can, saying, "I hope you get to dump this trash!" I tear up the referral. (Boy, I'm nice). She then returns to her desk, packs up her stuff, and starts to walk out of the room. I call out to her, "Gina! " "WHAT! I'm sick of you!" and starts running off at the mouth as she leaves the room. Now I have both Gina and Derek not only out of the classroom, but over in Terry's office telling her all so many nice stories about what happened. It's not hard to imagine whose side she'll take. There is also the question of racial loyalty. Now Derek is mixed race, Gina is a white but most of her friends are black, and the principal is African American. I'm at a definite disadvantage already because I am white, and then I am on the superintendent's shit list.

Derek tells her I wanted him to hit me, and I called him out. Gina tells her I put my hands on her. Terry is lapping this up. Talking to students first before talking with the teacher, empowering them and quite effectively undermining me. I get my chance to explain, but it's clear I have lost control of this situation, in no small part due to my lack of training and experience with these kinds of kids, as well as being dropped in midyear with no authority to call any of the shots, no support from administration, and a teacher and aide (both black) that feel I am not doing my job right with the young black males. I leave her office totally disillusioned. It's only ten o'clock and we've five hours to go. All of this a direct spin-off from Bates's indiscretion yesterday, leaving these kids alone and turning them over to me angry and frustrated. As big a setup for me as them.

I return to class depressed and anxious. Daman starts messing with Gary while I'm taking the lunch orders. I don't know what is going on because my back is to them while I write down, "Two Sunny Delights, no gravy, one Hawaiian Punch, chips, but no potatoes." Daman, a ninety-pound black kid, has just slapped Gary, a 285-pound white kid, in the back of the head for the last time. I turn just in time to see Gary with a chair over his head, and before I get to utter a sound the chair flies across the room. Luckily he missed. Now I'm really angry. No more time for polite intrusions of "please" and "do this now or else"..."SIT DOWN!" I yell, even scaring myself. Silence. I turn to finish the order; I want the whole meal and two snacks and one chocolate milk and one green (2 percent) milk. Daman has slipped into the bathroom. At least there he's out of trouble. He exits, Damien goes in. Hey! Who's been burning stuff in here? Seems old Daman set fire to the paper towels. Both he and Gary get written up. After twenty days, I've just written four referrals sending students out of class to the office for discipline in less than twenty minutes, and it's not even eleven o'clock.

# CHAPTER EIGHTEEN

## THE NEXT DAY

Gina is back. She's telling a student who missed all the fun the day before what happened. "He even suspended me for having a Coke can!" I correct her; she got herself suspended. Though she told the principal I had put my hands on her, the only physical contact that was made was my fingers touching her fingers that were wrapped around that Coke can that she refused to relinquish as she tried to suck down the last few drops. She got a day out of school and was back the next. She mumbles under her breath, but quietly. She then proceeds to tell the class about the flying chair and the fire in the bathroom and the standoff between Derek and me. I detect more than a little pride and respect in her voice as she describes the interchange: "And then Mr. Matthews stands up to Derek and says, 'You wanna piece of me?'" Maybe I was learning to speak their language and earning their respect. Maybe I was making a connection and reaching them in a way.

As I sit and reflect on this, I still feel that I am powerless in this position; I am not cut out for this job, emotionally or intellectually. Twenty-two years' experience, eight in this school district—I have earned the right to move up, not down! It should be getting easier, not harder, yet here I am in a grunt-level, first-rung position everyone else has moved out of. I should be a consultant to this program, not a glorified aide. It's not fair, it's not just, it's not right, it's just…not…right.

A week later Derek is back. Sits at the back of the room and says he "ain't doin' no work, gonna earn zeroes, and gonna make trouble all day. Make it worth your while. Gonna box Mr. Matthews, gonna hit him like this (shadow boxes)." I ignore him. Then he calls across the room to two of his African American friends, "Hey Roland, dja' call Sarah last night? Oh…she called you. Is she good?" By talking about my daughter he is obviously trying to get me going, but I don't bite. It's amazing what these kids do and what they can get away with under these circumstances. I mean, can you imagine a male student going into any classroom in this nation and talking about the teacher's daughter like this? And getting away with it? But I was powerless to do anything about it. I was a toothless lion. And they sensed it.

These kids act like hyperactive two-year-olds. They show off for each other, they laugh, they walk around the room, they instigate. They tell me to "shut up" or call me "fool," insult my daughter, threaten me physically, challenge my authority, overrule me in class, don't pay attention, laugh, play mind games, and get the rest of them going. The thirteen-year-old, in here for gross insubordination (as well as breaking and entering and trying to sell the guns he stole), is like a shrew; small but mean as a snake. He enjoys insulting the bigger kids, knowing full well I have to protect him, or, if not me, then one of his other big friends who doesn't like the kids he's teasing and calling "You big fat asshole!" "Runt." "F*#k You!" Bates actually does something! She takes him to the office! Teaching this class is like one of those hand-held little games with the steel balls you try to get into little holes. You might get one or two balls set, then lose *them* trying to get the other ones in line. You almost never, or rarely ever, get them all in place, and when you do, someone comes along and bumps into you.

Since I started here April 9, eight new kids have been placed in here—kids who have been suspended or expelled from their home schools for fighting, weapons, or assault against teachers. One kid's in here for B&E, another for assault with a deadly weapon (shot this kid's eye out with a pellet gun—"Well, he shouldn't have got in my way!"), and a few have also sold drugs. Not one for even simple possession. These kids are ADHD (attention deficit hyperactivity disorder), ODD (oppositional and defiant disorder), LD (learning disabled), and ED (emotionally disturbed). More kids are coming, and they tell us now that the aide is leaving and they aren't replacing him. Can it get any worse?

Before the year ends, I break up a fight and get punched in the mouth, Gina threatens to "really get me in trouble if I'm not careful" (false accusation of sexual contact, I suppose), and the fun, if there ever was any, has simply gone out of it. Caroline is seeing me get torn apart and thinks I should take a medical leave of absence. Use up my sick days and stay home on doctor's excuse. But how will this look? A psychologist taking leave for mental reasons? Exhaustion, stress, acute anxiety, all of the above. I agree to see my doctor. I meet with my doctor and he convinces me to hang in there. He gives me some anti-anxiety medication. Caroline is mad at me because I continue to go back. She doesn't fully understand the consequences of taking medical leave for psychological reasons. Beyond that, I have to prove to them—and myself—that I can't be beaten.

## Thursday, May 30, Evaluation

The principal of the vocational school where this program is housed evaluated me yesterday and wrote me up for failing to have a lesson plan. I was doing "group" and no one told me I had to. It was the worst evaluation I have ever received.

## No Good Deed

Thirteen *Needs Improvements (NIs)* compared with her previous observation with only two NIs. It appears that someone must have informed the superintendent that he couldn't fire me unless he had bad evaluations and failed improvement plans on file. Since he had none, he would have to get them. They would now attempt to *evaluate me* out of my job. How clever and creative these folks can be.

On Tuesday, May 28, the principal came into the room and sat down at the table, notebook in hand. I was sitting at my desk, doing what I usually do. Nothing. Sitting there keeping the peace. It sure looked like she was there to observe me, so when Gina asked if we were going to do group, I reckoned we would. I pulled out the *Touchstones* book to lend some structure to the session. I went through one story about greed and sharing that went well, and the principal left after about forty minutes. She indicated that she would do the conference the next day. On Wednesday she called me in to go over it, and it was not good. She found little good and more bad, a highly critical assessment that ended in many "Needs Improvements."

Friday was my "year-end evaluation," and my fear was that this last and most recent evaluation would set the tone for the conference. The personnel director, my arch foe and second in command to the superintendent, would be sitting in and the principal would be leading it. The handwriting was on the wall and it seemed pretty obvious it was going to be an execution. I asked the principal if my primary supervisor, Jack, could be included, and she said she would check. After all, I spent the first seven months of the school year under his direct supervision, and only two under hers. And I trusted him. Why shouldn't he be included? On Friday the principal told me she had called my house at three forty-five Wednesday and "talked with my daughter," though I got no message, and neither Sarah nor Andrew remembered taking the call. The principal indicated that they would be holding a meeting at the board office that morning, with the principal from my high school, the principal involved in my hearing for

## The Next Day

the personal day, and my lone ally, the principal of the middle school and building level supervisor, Jack. They would all provide additional input to my annual evaluation. It would not be based solely on the principal from the vocational school's observations. The personnel director would still be sitting in, although this is rarely, if ever, done unless there is another agenda. Evaluating someone out of the system would be my first pick. I responded that we were told at the beginning of the year that three people would be involved in our evaluations: the lead school psychologist, the special education supervisor, and our building supervisor, in my case, Jack. Why was the personnel director sitting in on a routine year-end evaluation? Why were two other principals involved, and where was the lead psychologist and the special education supervisor? It was simply amazing how they changed the rules to suit themselves and the current situation.

Later in the day the vocational school principal indicated that this had changed (I must have made my point) and that the personnel director would not be sitting in after all, but the special education supervisor and my friend and primary supervisor, Jack. The vocational principal, Terry, introduced the special education supervisor as the supervisor of school psychologists, which she clearly was not. I explained that she was not my supervisor. Then Terry rattled off something like, "The personnel director said several individuals served in this role." I'd already been around the barn with the spec ed supervisor over Sarah's case, so I could reasonably predict her take on things; I just wanted a fair chance. I am sure they sought legal counsel for every step.

The meeting was scheduled for one o'clock. At one fifteen I was ready for the meeting. The special education supervisor was already in the room while I waited outside, and Jack arrived at one twenty. They met behind closed doors for fifteen or twenty minutes and then Terry called me in. The special education supervisor led off about the purpose of the meeting and then turned to Terry. She pointed out the two sections on the evaluation form for "Interpersonal" and "Professional" with a "1" in the first and "2" in the second. She indicated her concerns were in the professional area, although she did not elaborate. The special education supervisor then turned to Jack. Jack was clearly uncomfortable with the proceedings and, staring down at the table, said, "I'll pass." The supervisor homed in on one section, "Interpersonal," citing "violation of rules" and documentation provided on April 9. When I tried to tie her down as to the documentation for "rules violations" or specifically what were the specific problems or behaviors I engaged in that resulted in a "2" (needs improvement), she mumbled something about the "documentation had already been provided."

I told her that the improvement plan form she presented to me was a form I had never seen and was not familiar with, much less the categories, and since they were all blank with only a summary number on top, it was difficult for me to know what behaviors I was having difficulty with and therefore which to change. I also explained that I had had no explanation of the April 9 material, much less an opportunity to respond to any of it. She replied that she "believed the issues have already been discussed in detail." She also indicated that this was based on Terry's recent observation, her own observations over the year, and the input from the other principals. The form was a "summary" of their deliberations. I then asked if I could see a copy of their input. If there were complaints about me from other principals, I needed to know what they were. To date I'd heard or seen nothing. She repeated her statement that these had already been discussed with me at the April 9 meeting with the personnel director and Terry. We both knew this simply never occurred.

At the bottom of the form was a statement referring to my status. It read "second class." In six years I'd never seen this used. When I asked about the "second class" designation and what it meant, she was unable to explain, so Jack did. Essentially it meant I would be more closely supervised next year, with additional observations and evaluations. My improvement plan would remain in effect, and I would

## The Next Day

receive no step increase in salary. Even more significantly, my tenure, in effect for six years, no longer applied. In other words I could be dismissed at any time...without cause.

I again asked her if I could get a copy of the principals' deliberations and comments about my job performance, since their input was included in this action. I also asked if I would be given the opportunity to know what the material the personnel director gave me on April 9 was all about. I then indicated that I felt uncomfortable signing a form I had never seen, with the wrong title, "coordinator," at the bottom instead of "psychologist." I also pointed out that there were no details on the form, only summaries, and that I had never seen the supporting documentation. I asked if I could share this with counsel, since I rarely signed anything without having my attorney check it first. No one could answer. So I was allowed to leave the meeting and went back to the room. Our teacher's contract allowed all personnel to have a representative present when job actions were taken, and here I stood alone against three administrators, two who were essentially setting me up for dismissal. The three of them remained behind to talk. I didn't just fall off the cabbage truck, and my senses were keenly tuned. I was not going to give them any ammunition. Terry came back to my classroom and asked me to return to her office. The supervisor had left and it was only her and Jack. They indicated that it would be in my best interest to sign, as I might be considered insubordinate if I did not, and I asked if I could call my attorney, and they agreed. I had until the end of the workday at four thirty to sign, according to Jack.

I returned to my room to get my teacher association's lawyer's number and then to a phone. She was out and no other attorneys were present, so I called Pat, my association rep. She basically said, "Sign, you're not admitting to anything and you just need to cross out coordinator at the bottom." Terry came in my room while I was talking to Pat and told me quite clearly that I would have to sign or be considered insubordinate. I made it clear this was not my intention, so I returned to her office to sign the documents. She said the supervisor and Jack would be back at three ten. Later she came by the room and said I would have to go to the supervisor's office at the board of education to sign, and Jack would be there, too. I went back to the room and the union lawyer's secretary got her on the car phone and she told me the same thing, "Sign it and we'll take it from there." She was always full of such great advice.

I drove over to the school board office and signed and made idle chitchat waiting for Jack to get there. The supervisor had indicated that he had called and wanted me to wait until he got there. When he got there he looked at the supervisor, and he looked at me with a serious but supportive look and said that he was signing this evaluation, however, his signature on the form did *not* reflect his experience working with me over the years, and that he was signing only based on the personnel director's indication that he had gathered "extensive documentation" on me. Jack signed on faith. I made it clear to the supervisor that I wanted copies of any notes or documentation from the morning meeting they had held with my other supervising principals. She wrote it down and indicated she would see about this. I would never receive any of this documentation, of course, because there never was any meeting with my other supervising principals, but that shouldn't come as a surprise.

Here was my response to this "evaluation."

1) There is no credible evidence that would support any of these actions, much less a reduction to second-class status. Even in the Alternative School I did the best I could. Most people who are lowered to second class are less than competent and have been given a year or more to straighten out their act with a great deal of support from administration. They also remain in their same position while trying to make corrections and improvements. I was given less than a year, and it was after first being yanked out of the elementary setting I had enjoyed for

## The Next Day

six years and placed in a secondary setting, and then removed midyear from my role as school psychologist and placed in a classroom as a teacher, a position I was uncertified, unqualified, and inexperienced for. To then judge me for "corrective action and improvement" under these circumstances was simply not fair. I was a school psychologist, not a classroom teacher.

2) Though a lot of documents were shared with me on April 9, the "complaints" were flimsy and weren't specific enough to support a case for unprofessional conduct. Holding one's hand up to stop someone who was constantly interrupting him, reporting test results honestly and accurately, and chewing gum were hardly grounds for reprimand. The rest of the April 9 packet that the personnel director dumped in the file were an amalgam of letters I wrote or others wrote over the eight years I'd been in the district, some that should have been taken out of my file after I filed grievances (4-205 [c] actions). Others were dealt with years ago through mediation. Many were five and six years old. Ninety percent of them were never a part of my personnel file (I made sure of that), and yet they were pulled from a secret file and literally dumped in my personnel file to bolster the current actions.

    Note: I had begged/pleaded with Geraldine to purge my personnel file months ago, but nothing was done. It was like someone stopped by your house and left a dead body in your basement. You call your lawyer to ask her what you should do, and she tells you not to worry. Then the police come over and you get charged with murder. Hello?

3) None of my immediate supervisors from the high school or middle school or Jack were involved with observations or conferences with me this year. The principal from my high school and I got along fine. He insisted he "had no trouble with me." The middle school principal and I had limited contact, especially after the incident in

the fall involving the funeral and my lost personal day. Jack and I got along fine and he did one positive observation, which is part of the record. My inappropriate language with his teacher never made the light of day, so I didn't have to worry about that coming up.
4) When they moved from the evaluation system to the improvement plan, no one reviewed it with me. No one reviewed the observations; they just lockstepped through the process to lower my status with no discussion or opportunity for improvement, much less due process.

This clearly demonstrates that rules can be bent to the breaking point, and that—board policy and procedures and union/association contracts aside—if someone in administration is determined to get rid of you, tenure or not, you are toast and they are the blow torch designed for maximum burn.

# Caught Between Sarah's Bad Attitude, Geraldine's Charms, And My Future

Between fighting for my professional life (not to mention my sanity) and Sarah, who had been embroiled in a "250 lines or I won't grade it" controversy with her history teacher, plus her expulsion case and 504 plan, not to mention her weekend mind games she lays on Caroline and me, I didn't know how much more I could take. I really didn't. I wanted out of this school so badly I could taste it. June couldn't come soon enough. My daily baby-sitting with these kids I can't reach was wearing me down.

I called my union attorney to ask about my reassignment appeal and my current evaluation, and she told me that they made an offer to return me to my old job with "no access to parent meetings, since that's where the problems are." I would just test kids and not meet with parents or teachers. How come she sounded like she was agreeing with them that

## The Next Day

I "had problems in parent meetings"? I mean, what am I supposed to do in these meetings, roll over and play dead? I told her I was not going to operate as a psychometrist and they could go "stick it." She chastised me again for my attitude and how it would get me nowhere. I told her she didn't have to quote me exactly, but give them a sense that I wasn't just taking whatever they offered. It's like she hadn't read all of my observations and evaluations prior to this situation, or hadn't talked with any of the people I referred her to; she simply talked to the superintendent and the board's attorney and bought their line that I'm *trouble*. I thought that your advocate was supposed to *advocate* or speak up on your behalf, not just take the other side's version as gospel and offer the client a crappy deal. I've attended over a thousand special education meetings of all types over eight years, not only with no problems, but with a record for establishing excellent rapport and facilitation. How can she make a statement that it's okay for them to restrict my duties "because that where the problems are"? She would pursue my second-class appeal, but she would not pursue my reassignment. There was no chance of winning, according to her, my record wasn't spotless, and superintendents can move people at will "in the best interests of the school system." So after begin yanked out of my job, humiliated and all, all she's going after is my lost of status from first to second class. They say you get what you pay for, and this was my free attorney.

I would have my paid attorney, Morris, pursue it, as I was not going to accept this without the board being involved at least. To take me from my job of twenty-two years where I am fully certified and move me to one for which I am uncertified and inexperienced doesn't make sense. How can this possibly be "in the best interest of the school system"? It was disciplinary, following on the heels of this stupid meeting with the superintendent held on March 28. In response to the gum-chewing complaints? I mean, really. My record may not be spotless, but no one's is. I have a reputation of being too direct and not considering the impact of my explanations or the political ramifications. My focus is and has always been what is in the best interest of the child, and I often suffer from kill-the-messenger syndrome. But I have never been rude or unprofessional. I tend to be a little intense at time (passionate) and I may take a little getting used to, but once people know who I am and where I am coming from, they are fine, even supportive of my positions. Most of my "problems" were due to lack of support from the personnel director. I was not moved due to problems with people, I was moved due to problems with the superintendent, period. His actions were retaliatory and they were railroading me, and my attorney was helping them. Where was my advocate? What was I to do? I wasn't just looking at the loss of my job, but quite possibly my career.

## CHAPTER NINETEEN

# JULY 16, 1996, ANDREW TAKES HIS TURN AT CHALLENGING HIS PARENTS

I managed to survive until June, but the joy most educators experience at the end of a long year was not mine. How can you enjoy your summer when it's filled with hearings and trials and no idea of where you will be come fall? But one has to suck it in sometimes and just make the best of it. It's another one of those days. You know the kind. Starts out with the sun shining and that *great to be alive* feeling and then the stuff starts flying all over the place and you have to duck because it's coming from so many directions you can't help but get hit.

I decided to take my sister for a ride in my '62 Buick Electra 225 convertible. The scenic tour included the Cambridge to St. Matthews Ferry followed by a trek to Tallman Island, lunch, and a quiet drive home. The sun was shining and the top was down and Caroline told us to go on without her, so just the two of us, baby sister and I, headed southeast. We stopped at the ferry landing and stood in the warm sun and cool breeze off the bay. The group traveling in the car behind us lined up for the ferry and stood admiring La Bomba, the affectionate name I gave my big red car. We struck up a conversation with one family. We took pictures for each other going across on the ferry. He told us about his house on the water and his boat, and his other house in New Jersey. Offered to trade his $40,000 Lincoln Town Car for my red beauty. My "deuce and a quarter." It's true there's a thousand of his for one of mine, but monetarily I would have gotten the better part of that deal. He was only kidding, of course. As we drove off the ferry I told Julie I should have offered to let him trade cars for the ride out to Tallman. His family and friends (from Brazil) would have gotten a kick out of driving in the big convertible from the 1960s, I'm sure, and I probably wouldn't have minded getting behind the wheel of a $40,000 car. We turned up the road leading away from the ferry and I told Julie she could crank her vent window for more air. Back in the day they had vent *windows*, little triangular shaped pieces of glass that swiveled vertically allowing as much or as little air into the car as you chose. Little did I know the side mirror was pushed in and very loose. A short crank and the side mirror was history. I caught a glimpse of it as it smashed on the road and flew into the bushes. Our friends in back honked their horn and we both pulled over to the side. He was very nice, recovered the mirror, and consoled me, "It's only the glass. Tell you what. You get a mirror, I'll cut you a new piece for that." And he was serious, too. I asked him if he was a glazier and he pointed to his shirt, resplendent with tools, "I'm into all sorts of things. Woodworking, for one. We come down every weekend. Got a piece of paper? I'll give you my name and number and you can come over and I'll fix it for you."

 The idea of visiting a house on the water, complete with boat, to get to know someone who is into woodworking (as well as all sorts of things) and is of generous spirit sufficient to offer to fix a stranger's broken mirror was intriguing at best, exciting at most. I knew Caroline would enjoy meeting

## July 16, 1996, Andrew Takes His Turn At Challenging His Parents

them as well, and I knew this might be a nice thing to do. They followed us to Tallman, but we sort of got separated at St. Matthews, and although they ended up at the same restaurant, we were outside and they must have been inside, so we missed them until we left and noticed their car in the lot.

I tried to talk Julie into trying a soft-shelled crab, but she opted for the next best thing, a crab cake. Something about a sandwich with six legs sticking out of a hamburger bun was not something on her list of Things to Eat. We sat on the porch watching the boats come and go, drinking strawberry daiquiris and eating french fries and genuine blue crabs. It was great. We drove back through St. Matthews and home. I pulled in the parking lot with thoughts of asking Julie to open the garage door so I could pull Bomba in, when my eye caught hold of an unbelievable sight. My "Z," my tender little Z-car, was sitting in the driveway with the front end caved in! The entire front fender of my vintage 280-Z was crushed — headlight gone, fender buckled, rim shattered. Pretty obvious what happened. The Z is usually in the front of the driveway out of harm's way. Both kids know not to park there or in front, blocking me in. There are plenty of places on the circular driveway. Earlier that day they both came home and the Z was out, so they just pulled the truck in and filled in my space. I had no place to park when I came back. Where was I to park now without blocking them in? So I pulled over close to the side of the driveway to give them plenty of room to pull out. One of my two lovely children had backed my truck out without thinking, without looking, and BAM! Slammed right into the Z sitting there on the side of the driveway. Now, at this point I had no idea which child did it, Sarah or Andrew, but I needed to know. So I head in and asked in my gentlest fatherly tone, "Which idiot ran into my Z!?"

You might figure it was Andrew, and you might figure Mom was quick to jump in to Andrew's defense. Andrew's bicycle had been hanging in the garage, in the way, for well over a year, unused. Ever since he took to the highway, the two-wheeler was history. When he came back from college, I asked him if he was going to use it, and he responded in a noncommittal sort of way. I told him I was sick of having to move it every time I wanted to get to the ladders, and I would give him one month to take it with him or dispose of it; sell it, give it away, take it to the dump, I didn't care, just get it out of my garage. If it was still there in thirty days, I would dispose of it. Predictably it was still there that Saturday morning, and so he had his last warning. "If I get back and the bike's still here, it's history. So he threw it in the back of my truck and he flew out of the driveway in a fit and plowed into my 1975 280-Z. My pride, my joy, my first brand new car that still was in showroom condition. He drove *my* truck into *my* car. And whose fault was it? You guessed right if you said Dad's. Caroline: "If you hadn't asked him to get rid of the bicycle, this never would have happened!" My car, my first new car, my Z, is sitting with its front end smashed in, and it's my fault? I asked her nicely to stay out of this and let Andrew and me deal with it. I was angry yes, but in full control. She wouldn't stay out and, worse, he hid behind her skirts. Why? "Because you might get physical," he whined. I asked him to step outside to discuss this man to man, not in a threatening way. I mean, I didn't say, "Hey, want to settle this outside?" But I did want to get Mommy out of the picture. He refused. He made a lot of excuses like he "didn't see it in my rear view mirror" as though he actually looked in it. I think my comment was something along the lines, "Did you ever think about sticking your fucking head out of the window?" I mean I wasn't one to hurl profanities at my children, but this was my prized possession, my sports car, my Z. Andrew told me he would pay for it, so that was a start, but it was like burning up someone's house and personal possessions and saying, "No sweat, man, you got insurance." The money was the least of it at this point. But I was trying to be accommodating and fatherly and understanding. The Z needed a little work body and a complete paint job. It was not on the top of the list, however, and now it had to be done. Very unhappy. Then, without asking me, Mom

## July 16, 1996, Andrew Takes His Turn At Challenging His Parents

lets him get in my truck and drive off. I felt this was quite inappropriate; but I had other things on my mind, as follows:

Sarah's case was scheduled to come before the court of special appeals in November. We had a very good chance of prevailing. The brief had to be filed by Wednesday, July 17, the very next day, and our attorney wanted us to look over the draft before submitting it. He faxed it that day, and I had to read over it for any major changes. It arrived about twelve thirty, and I needed to give the corrections or all clear by three so he could get it to the printer.

Not as though my mind was not clouded enough by the front-end damage to my favorite sports car, the busted mirror from La Bomba, not to mention the rear end damage to the truck. Enter Caroline, the bearer of glad tidings, who hit me with another zinger. Can you spell t-i-m-i-n-g? This bit of news she shared with me was from our pal the superintendent. Seems he didn't like the idea I took out a formal complaint against his attorney for changing dates or springing them on us last minute, and for screwing not only with timelines, but the transcripts as well. The attorney grievance committee, who usually ignores complaints unless they are taken by clients against their own attorneys, did investigate, which boiled down to asking the board's attorney for his version of the controversy, and of course he lied as usual and they believed him, and shut down the investigation without giving us a chance to respond. Hey, I did my best. I mean he did play games with the dates, and he did violate timelines and then fight to have them excluded, and did his client receive not only the transcript but a computer disc as well, and was it a coincidence that I had the only original copy where everybody else at the hearing had a different one? I never accused anyone of altering the transcripts, but put it together yourself. Why would four copies have justified margins and mine didn't? Why would the board's attorney accuse me of ordering my own copy when he knew I didn't? Why would he send the wrong letter to the transcript company as "evidence" to give the false impression that I had ordered my own copy? And why would he call me a liar when he knew I was the only one telling the truth? That's because that is how he plays the game. What did I have to lose? I filed a complaint with the attorney grievance committee and he had to spend his own time, unbillable hours, defending himself. Too...darn...bad.

Now the superintendent was even more upset with me, as though that were possible. He decided he would jump on the bandwagon and write us a letter complaining about our continued string of false allegations, now these directed at his attorney and his dear sweet special education director, and how if I continued, he would have to pursue legal action within the limits of the law. What was the expression, *The best defense is a good offense*? Right. I can't exercise my rights as a parent to file due process actions on behalf of my daughter? I can't appeal his wayward decisions to the school board, state board, circuit court, and any and all other courts I have a right to appeal to? I can't turn his attorney in for what I consider to be unethical practices? I have no rights as a teacher, or as a professional educator to file grievances when I am prevented from doing my job or accused of unprofessional acts? Now I'm to tremble in my boots because he's threatening me with legal action if I continue to exercise my rights? I'm sorry if I feel that playing games with procedures is wrong. If meetings are to be set up at the convenience of parents, then they are to be involved in these decisions, not let in on them at the last minute. And if timelines are sacred and can cost the board the case, then they should be considered, not cast aside with legal maneuvers. And if transcripts are to be shared, then they should be the same copy, not altered by unseen hands. They sure didn't get that way by themselves and when they were caught, why didn't they just admit it rather than lie and blame it on me or the reporting company? I make no apologies and I make no concessions to liars (if you say those two words real quickly they sound pretty much the same: *lawyers/liars*). I refuse to back down to tactics that can only be described as intimidating. This man simply didn't know when to quit. Trouble is... neither did I.

July 16, 1996, Andrew Takes His Turn At Challenging His Parents

# July 19, 1996, Falsifying County Documents

Had a rather interesting day today. Got another note from the superintendent. PROOF I was deceiving him all along! HA HA HA HA HA! I sent him two letters in one day, maybe that was too much for him to process. One was an apology about confusing the issue of my job assignment; am I a psychologist or a teacher? This was a direct result of my assignment notice listing me as a "teacher" for the 1996-'97 school year. Previously I would never have given a thought to being listed as a "teacher." That's just for salary and benefits, workday and school calendar, even for bargaining purposes. I am considered a "teacher" along with other noninstructional staff: media specialists, guidance counselors, teacher specialists, etc. Somehow this year was different, though, after being pulled out of my *psychologist* position and placed in a classroom as a "real" teacher, I was a little reluctant to sign the bottom of the sheet listing me as TEACHER. So I had a friend type "/ PSYCHOLOGIST" next to TEACHER, since that is what my primary role and job description was. By pure coincidence, her typewriter had exactly the same font as the board of education's, and so it was a perfect match. I thought it made for a more professional job; the superintendent thought I was trying to pull a fast one on him, trying to "lock myself into my psychologist position." I was trying to clarify my role. At any rate, I get this irate phone call from the superintendent, who insists I come into his office and sign a fresh copy, otherwise he will consider my contract null and void. I contacted my attorneys and on their advice did just that. I followed up with a letter apologizing for "altering a county form," as he termed it. The irony is that when I first got hired on here, back in July of 1988, they sent me this very same form with several schools listed on the assignment sheet. Midsummer they changed their minds and decided to give me a different set of schools and called to tell me to "cross out Lake View Middle School and write in Blueville, Statesburg, and Presley." I did exactly as they instructed me to, crossed out the schools listed, wrote the new schools in, signed and dated the bottom, and, keeping a copy for my records, sent the altered white original back to them. So the first duty I had for the county system was to "alter a county form," a heinous crime that would be ignored for eight years only to catch up with me later in the midst of the current brouhaha. I still had the copy of my "altered form" from 1988. I wrote the superintendent to let him know I had no intention to deceive, only to clarify my role for the 1996-'97 school year. I was tempted to enclose a copy of the altered form from '88, but figured they would turn that around on me as well and left this document in my file drawer.

The other letter was a more cleverly disguised letter; an appeal of my reassignment to a teaching position last spring. AHA! Proof the first letter didn't mean a thing. All the while I was trying to sound contrite and apologetic, I was poised for the kill! Appealing one of his holy orders. Not trying to deceive him? "Then why were both letters DATED THE SAME DAY!?" They were dated the same day because I wrote them the same day, and though I fully acknowledged that "altering forms" was not the politically correct thing to do in this heated climate, I felt just as strongly that I was trained as a school psychologist, functioned as a school psychologist for over twenty years, and, most importantly, I was *hired* as a school psychologist by this system, and it was highly inappropriate for them to place me in a position I was untrained, uncertified, inexperienced, and completely uninterested in. I had a right to appeal this decision, which, in my opinion had more to do with my pending litigations than my success or lack thereof as a school psychologist.

I've dealt with paranoids a little, and some have a tendency to make connections where there are none; they're called Clang Associations. But even this was a stretch. In my own mind, my desire to cling to my position as school psychologist, one for which I have been trained and educated and am rather attached to after twenty-two years, is right up front. My putting it next to "Teacher" on the assignment notice makes it rather clear that I expected to be a school psychologist, and I also expected the superintendent to keep to his word that

## July 16, 1996, Andrew Takes His Turn At Challenging His Parents

I truly "had my old job back" and that he was not going to re-reassign me to Title I Reading since I have an interest in kid's reading skills. And my appeal of his decision to take me *out* of my school psychology position and then give me only half of my "old job" back is entirely consistent with my wants and desires and with my honest attempt to clarify my position as teacher/psychologist. Now about the only thing that gets in the way of this logic would be my "attempt" to pin the superintendent down to keeping his word. If he planned to reassign me again next year, then he would be a little nervous about me trying to lock him in or keep him to his word, and be upset about me putting the term down on paper. But then who would be deceiving whom? At any rate, he wrote another one of his letters rambling on about how I'd proven I wasn't sincere about my apology, and maybe he misunderstood my true motives. He wouldn't know a sincere apology if it reared up and bit him in the ass, and forget about him ever offering one. Perfect people never make mistakes, and he had a nickname, one quite descriptive of him. His nickname? "God."

By the seventeenth, I was looking at one more day until the board office closed and my union attorney would be out of time to deliver my appeal due in on Sunday the twenty-first of July. Since I had faxed her several letters and material, and called her several times as well, I sort of figured she would have something out this week. When nothing materialized on Wednesday, I called her secretary. She assured me that she would (1) see *if* it went out or (2) make sure it *went* out. By Thursday I still had nothing and secretaries were away from their desks and the attorney was out of her office. I asked Maxine to please find out and call me. Maxine said that Daniel, the head attorney at the state teacher's office, and my attorney, whom I'll refer to as "Geraldine," had discussed it and were intent on filing the appeal on the second class, and that she believed that it already went out, but she would check. When I got home from Baltimore at four thirty-five Thursday, the last day the board office was open, with no call from Maxine, I called the state office. "Offices closed at four thirty." I was in a spot. Were they trying to screw me? Miss the deadline on purpose? Even I was a little paranoid. I finally got Geraldine on her car phone at five ten. The woman sounded annoyed, and told me we had until next week. Here I am telling her thirty days is thirty days and they are up Sunday. She assures me when the day is on a Sunday they give you to the next day, and anyway she will have it out by Friday since she is going on vacation. Next morning I called Mr. Bourbon (one of my private attorneys) for advice, and Maxine, and got her first. She didn't call me Thursday because Geraldine told her 1) she had already talked to me and 2) the deadline was Wednesday the twenty-fourth. This made me real nervous. I knew it was the twenty-first. And with this twenty-fourth stuff, I was starting to get real paranoid. Was she trying to screw me up? I couldn't take a chance.

When Mr. Bourbon called back at noon, I laid it on him. First off he told me what I suspected. They rarely give you more time. Thirty days is just that, and to wait for Sunday was not recommended. If I missed the thirty-day deadline to file an appeal of my second-class status I could pretty much kiss it goodbye. And as far as faxing, what if the board FAX is off or out of paper? Best thing to do, write my own letter and get it to the board president and the superintendent's office that day, the nineteenth. So I whipped up a letter, stuffed two envelopes, and got into my fast-forward mode. Caroline and I rode out to *Fisk Brothers* and asked Mr. Spinner's secretary if he was in. He was president of the school board. He came out, invited Caroline and me back to his office, and, after a cordial vacation chat, asked us how he could help. I apologized for bothering him at his office, but explained that since the board office was closed on Fridays I had to hand deliver this appeal to him that day, timelines being what they are. He understood perfectly. He said he knew about my second class appeal and wanted to put things in "perspective." He said he knew we wouldn't be in education if we didn't care about kids, and that we'd both spent a lot of money on this business so far. I truly believe he was expressing his desire to be done with this thing, and, as he said, "Let's get back to the business of kids. Too much time and energy is being misdirected." I just told him I wanted to get back to my job. It was a gracious and professional meeting and he walked out with us, shaking hands and feeling good about the contact. It was much more than I expected, but it made us both feel great. We headed over to the board and found the hallway open, so I stuck the superintendent's letter under the door to his suite. It was noted "hand delivered July 19," and, with the official one in the board president's hand, we felt we were in good shape. I was appealing their placing me on second class, and I might even have an ally in the board president, who was as tired of all this stuff as we were. We were anxious to put all of this behind us and I was eager to get back to doing my job.

Maxine finally called at six fifteen and assured me (again) that Geraldine had the appeal filed and it would go out certified mail that day. She was unable to get a copy to fax to me, however. The way I look at it, better two than wait for her certified letter (probably snail mail) to roll in one day next week, two days past the deadline. Mine is in hand and if she did send one out, hers will expand on my request to set things right. If she didn't send anything out, or the superintendent is laughing at a bar somewhere in Ocean City with her right now that they really put one over on old Frankie, then the two of them can choke on the letter sitting on the superintendent's carpet, even as we speak...

## July 28, 1996, Mom And Pop's Vacation

It's summer and still it's this torrent of nonstop rain with the sun popping out for only a brief moment or two. Here is the rundown for this last week. Saturday, Sarah dropped us off at the airport for our trip to Florida. Just Mom and me, a chance to be together as a couple, like our April "honeymoon." There was a little bit of difference this trip, thanks to Andrew. The last trip Caroline and I took by ourselves was to Connecticut, and we came back to find our house invaded. By the kids' friends. Seems like they had one helluva party while Mom and Dad were out of town. We took action and set consequences; sad thing is that in trying to accommodate Sarah, who has been grounded for the last five years, we took a different tact with her, just a few simple rules, and she could have her freedom to make her own choices. It brought peace to the house. She was ready to leave and that would not have been good. Trouble is that in returning her privileges, no consequences were set for the "party." Caroline felt that Andrew shouldn't be punished if Sarah wasn't, so he got to go to his rave after all. This was *not* my idea, I felt it was a mistake to let them abuse our trust and our house, and then to let them get away with it by suffering no consequences, but I said nothing until we attended our four-man counseling session with Dr. Mom. I expressed my concerns that Sarah needed a different approach than Andrew, and that he was beginning to get away with too much just by virtue of being nineteen.

It peaked when I insisted he get rid of the bicycle he hasn't ridden in two years, and he backed into the Z, causing between $500 and $1,000 in damages. He offered to pay for it, but what got me the most upset was the scene. I was angry, but in control, and Mom got right in the middle. Andrew played "Momma's boy," refusing to step out of the house to talk with me, complaining that I, "…might get physical." He then left in the truck to do his thing with his friend Eric, so he essentially got away with it all. When I expressed these feelings at the session, Caroline said something that put everything in perspective, and burned more than a few bridges between us. "I'm afraid of losing Andrew because of Frank." Not, "I'm afraid of losing my husband because of my son's behavior," but losing her son over her husband. Now I'll admit I never had the close relationship with Andrew that I would have liked, but this was largely due to his tendency to identify with Mom instead of me. He was getting too old to hide behind Mom's apron strings, and I resented his coming between

## July 16, 1996, Andrew Takes His Turn At Challenging His Parents

Caroline and me. Dr. Mom tried to put it in perspective for Caroline—"You'll never lose your son..."—but the damage was done. We left for Florida with a hole in my heart that even a week on the beach couldn't cure.

We had a good time, mind you, flying in, air-boating, swimming in the pool and ocean, visiting with my aunt Virginia and my great-uncle Fred and his wife, Mary, both in their nineties. We also got to spend some relaxing time with my little sister Julie and her boyfriend, Gator, Mom and Dad, Cousin Jean, Aunt Muriel, and Caroline's great-uncle Dewey. Ate plenty of good food and came home tanned and healthy. To one hell of a mess.

Andrew picked us up at the airport with his trusty green backpack full of who-knows what. The thrust of his conversation was the rave and how great it was; *jungle music, house music,* and other terms which I was both unfamiliar with and uninterested in. He went on about the scene and how cool it was to have stuff like *Winnie the Pooh* backpacks and stuffed animals at the raves. Talk about retro! This scene looks like a move back to childhood, and with his fascination with action toys, computer games, comic books, Japanese animation (cartoons), and stuffed animals. I'm worried about the level of this scene for a nineteen-year-old college sophomore. When we got back to the house to find more *toys*, including a *Winnie the Pooh pacifier* he walked around sucking on, I was nearing the end of my patience. But that turned out to be child's play compared to the scene that greeted us at home.

## Welcome Home To A Full House And Royal Flush

For starters all of the toilets were plugged. They hadn't flushed for a day or so and everything was backing up in the sinks and bathtubs, I mean foul-smelling yellow and brown excrement. After a week on the clean beaches of Fort

Lauderdale, to return to a toilet plunger was a bit much. Come to find out that despite the last fiasco, they (he) had another party! "Just a few friends" and no beer, but people at the house. What triggered it was a baggie that reeked of stale cigarettes, and when I opened it I found at least twenty butts and a broken glass. Confronted, Andrew admitted to having people over despite our request not to. "What part of NOBODY IN THE HOUSE WHEN WE ARE AWAY do you not understand?" His defense, laced with more profanity in three minutes than I uttered in three years, was "This is fucking stupid, we're part owners of this house anyway, since our father's Social Security helped pay for it, and we're tired of all these shitty rules...yadda yadda yadda." Andrew then went on about how he was screwed up like a lot of kids who had "psychologists for parents." Sure, blame it on the shrinks. His mother isn't a psychologist but a guidance counselor. Another freaker of children's minds! We weren't really sure what consequence was suitable for this one, but not leaving them alone again (who does this punish?) and losing out on raves were starters. Sarah came home and got the same business for the party, though she insists they were all *his* friends this time, and she did cop to putting her tampons into the commode, which started the blockage. She also admitted to still smoking cigarettes. When will they learn?

Mom and I were completely stressed out. Sarah went to work and Mom and I went to work in the yard. That is when I noticed that the Buick didn't look like it was parked the way I left it. The back end was way over to the center and it was pulled up too far. I mentioned this to Caroline (who never drives it) and she insisted I put it away in a hurry after I realized Andrew had wrecked my Z. But no, I remember leaving the Buick in the driveway, not wanting to chance banging it up with my adrenaline flowing from the Z disaster. I looked it over carefully, and the tail was at least eight inches over, and the front was six to eight inches too far forward. Now keep in mind, this is a 1960s-era car, all nineteen feet of it, and it is residing in a 1990s garage designed for vehicles of a more compact design.

## July 16, 1996, Andrew Takes His Turn At Challenging His Parents

In order to get the car in the garage, get the garage door closed, and get in and out of the vehicle, one must be extremely precise in positioning it in the garage. For someone like me who parks in a precise position every time, it didn't feel right, but I wasn't ready to start accusing. Especially with Caroline defending. One more thing to check. The engine shuts off in the "Off" position, but I always turn it one more to "Lock" for obvious reasons. Anyone else less than forty years old who would drive it wouldn't know this. I leaned over to check and noted that not only was the key not in the "Lock," position, but it was one past...the "ACC," accessories, or *Battery On* position. A quick lean on the horn button and pull on the light switch was all that was needed to know I had a dead battery and a solid case for someone using my car without permission.

Armed with this evidence, Caroline and I (she was finally convinced) went back into Andrew's room. Although he had been asked to clean up ten ketchup packets left in the driveway by one of his burger-eating friends, he still laid in bed. He admitted that he and Sarah had just taken the car for "a little spin." As it later turned out, it was twenty minutes, and Sarah did not go along for the ride, his pal Mike did. And they went into town, to McDonald's. I was livid. I explained the repercussions of his taking my car, for which he was uninsured, and having an accident. I couldn't believe that he would take my classic '62 convertible, an irreplaceable car, and drive it two weeks after smashing up my Z! He was still in bed under the blanket, and I could feel my temperature rising. It was even pissing Caroline off, and he was not responding, so with a wink to Caroline I figured I would wake him up a little. I told him I was calling the police and turning him in for unauthorized use of my car. This got his attention. He yelled and screamed about how INSANE this was, and threw in a few *Fucking crazies* and *You're fucking nuts* and a few accusations to boot. I told him as far as I was concerned, his mother and I would discuss it, but he would lose all his car privileges for a time. He escalated to a point that I suggested, and his mother followed up on, his need to find somewhere else to live for a while. He was told to pack it up and go. Mom was right behind it, too, bless her heart. Take a week to think about what he wanted to do with his life and then get back to us. Caroline made him pay his debts before he left, and he called a friend and was gone. She didn't stop crying all day and blamed herself emotionally, if not rationally, for failing her kids. After all she has done for them, why have they turned on her? Has she (have we) done too much for them? Have we spoiled them? Has she put them first so many times that they know she'll love them no matter what they do? Are they (or at least now he) testing her limits? I'm proud of her, she stuck to her guns and was tough on him, something she is able to do for Sarah and has never done before for Andrew. And now he'll really have to think about what he is going to do. He had $800 in the bank a while back and was earning a good paycheck working forty, fifty, sixty hours a week, but his hours have fallen off and two thirds into summer he has only $400 in the bank. What happened to the rest? Came to find out later in the summer that he spent $900 in the month of July alone. Raves? Drugs? Parties? Friends? Who knows?

## Andrew Returns

Andrew tried to convince his mother that the reason he did all these things was because I hate him and he now hates me. Caroline talked with him, and then she came out to fill me in. I stopped her and said I was not going to let him put her in the middle. If he had anything to say to or about me, he needed to say it to me directly. I was not going to let him get between us again. He was playing the big "M," the manipulation game. He was trying to separate us. Andrew and I have not had a great relationship, but he was, and is, a hard kid to like at times, and a lot of it has to do with the games he plays. Getting between his mother and me is one I resent more than any. And when she takes up his banner, it not only hurts our relationship as father/son, but my marital relationship as well. Dr. Mom once said it, "The greatest gift you can give your children is to be together." Parents need to stick together, and though it's acknowledged that there is a special bond between different-sexed parents and children, mother/son, father/daughter, one that is of a more forgiving nature, there should also be a special (and protected) relationship between same-sexed parents and children, father/son, mother/daughter, one that is based on role modeling, high expectations, and a desire to prepare that child for the world he or she is destined to exist in, a man's world for the boys and a woman's world for the girls. And only someone living there can show you the way.

## It Takes A Man To Make A Man

A man has got to do what a man does, and that means forming a relationship with your father. Love your mother, but relate to your father. As a man, I had to come to grips with that in my own relationship with my dad. You have to meet him on HIS terms. A father will not change for his son; the son must adapt to the father's ways in order to learn the way of men. That's just the way it is. I have told Andrew that to get along with me, he has to relate to me as a man, which means face to face, and that getting to me by going through Caroline will backfire every time. He might get what he wants in the short run, but at the expense of his relationship with me. I readily admit that I am hard on my son, and though part of it is conscious, a large part of it is instinctual, or flows from lessons I've had at the feet of other men, my father, and my friends' fathers, from my cousin Bill and my uncle Fred, and from neighbors and friends. Men learn from each other not through talk as much as through action; you learn from competing with men or working with them. Andrew hasn't learned these lessons yet, and he still gravitates to his mother for support and protection. I felt badly when Caroline made him leave, but he had some valuable lessons in life to learn, and a week or so away was worth his the rest of his life.

# CHAPTER TWENTY

# JOB SEARCH 1996

I managed to survive the '95-'96 school year with my new school assignment in the middle and high schools, and even when I was exiled to the Alternative School I made the best of it. I stayed the high ground and made sure I kept the hearings and court cases out of the classroom. I worked hard and did my best. Of course, it did me little good. With the principal of the Alternative School's help, the superintendent built his case against me. Contrived as it was, he maintained that I demonstrated the "same problems" in my fourth assignment that I had demonstrated elsewhere. Now I couldn't even get along with kids in the classroom. Forget the fact that these "kids" were street smart and were violent and aggressive kids with substance abuse problems. I would have to show "significant improvement" or I would not be renewed. The handwriting was on the wall. They were going to "evaluate me out of the system," as my private attorney predicted. My best bet was to get out while the getting was good, and I started a serious attempt to find another job.

Trouble is that when you're forty-six years old, you're looking at the downhill side of your career. You've got more years behind you than in front. Forgetting about the first thirteen years in public education for a moment, I had six more to get my degrees in English education (B.S.), psychology (B.S., M.S.), and school psychology (Ed.S). Add to that twenty-two years of practical experience in the field, three states, in four school districts, and you can imagine how what some might see as advantages (diversified experience in a variety of settings, maturity) can also be perceived as disadvantages (unsettled, old, high end of the salary scale ). I'm not at the bottom of the scale exactly, and some rural (i.e., poor) districts would rather hire someone who is young (i.e., entry-level salary). Forty-six may not feel old, but it certainly sounds old. I would need to expand my horizons: my home state first, then neighboring states, and then distant states if I had to. More importantly, I had to establish a positive frame of mind. Difficult to "sell yourself" if you're depressed and sound desperate. Why are you out looking for your fifth job at forty-six? For me it was moving toward better opportunities rather than running from bad ones. In the end I realized I loved what I did, and I was good at it. I had experience over a twenty-three-year career, I was active, involved, creative, energetic, and I cared about the kids, their teachers, and their parents. I could write well and communicate well, and I was well-organized. I got the job done. I was honest and I was direct—too direct, according to some—and I didn't mince words. I spoke the truth though it was difficult for others to accept at times. This was who I was and what I had to offer. Now to find the right place.

I contacted my old professor at Redford and got a few names from him. I also contacted Ron, my previous superintendent, to let him know I might be looking. I also contacted friends from the State Department of Education. I got a few leads and followed up on them. I went through the now-familiar routine of upgrading my resume, sending for applications, filling them out, contacting references, arranging for transcripts to be sent, paying fees, addressing envelopes, and

## Job Search 1996

making the personal contacts, calling people on the phone so they'd have more to go on than just a name on a pile of papers. Transcripts are always fun, for in addition to my main two institutions of higher learning, where I took 90 percent of my courses, Virginia and Redford University, I have a course here and there at College of Graduate Studies in West Virginia, James Madison University, West Virginia University, Salisbury State, and Loyola. Although each was a pain at the time, six hours for my second certificate and six more for third one, then three more to work on my administrative certificate (the course alone was enough to convince me I did not want to be an administrator), I now sit with a master's plus forty-five hours, and this is sufficient to earn me a few more dollars once I find a system that recognizes it. Most only recognize master's plus thirty, which I have had for the past twenty-two years. School psychologists have the highest entry level in education, plus a full year (usually unpaid) internship.

I applied to Washington County and Jefferson County and Lincoln County. I then put in for Duke County and Duchess County, and even a private catholic center, a private school run by nuns for kids with serious issues. Here are the results: not hiring, looking for an intern, recommended (with reservations), too late, too old, and sorry, don't call us, we'll call you. This last one (the private school) was a surprise. I figured they'd be glad to get someone with my qualifications, and I knew they could afford it; they had a $7 million building program last year for residential supported living. I put in my application and references and they called to set up an interview. On the day of the interview they called to cancel. The educational consultant conducting the interviews was "sick." Since it was the school psychologist who called me, I asked if I could at least come over and talk to her, to find out about the job and see the school. She reluctantly agreed. I went over and had a nice chat with her, and a tour. It was when we were walking out that I knew I was dead in the water. She wished me luck. That was a bad sign. She said someone would call, and when no one did, I called the school...twice. Even talked with the receptionist, who was real nice, and told her quite honestly that I was afraid that my current employer might have disparaged me. She told me that to her knowledge no one had called from the board office. That wouldn't have prevented the educational consultant from picking up her phone. I guess she was still sick. She may even have died, because to this day she has never returned my calls. It just didn't feel right. I had worked with her a number of times, and I felt she owed me the professional courtesy of a call at least. That goes on her tally of sins, though, not mine.

By July I was looking at an ever-worsening situation. No prospects anywhere. Even having to move to have a job looked good. And when nothing happened I was forced... forced...to look back at the job I had. Try to be positive about it. I wouldn't have to move. I would have the same salary. I would be a school psychologist. Even if I couldn't sit in on parent meetings, I'd be with more normal kids. It would be closer to my original situation. So I softened my position. I had told my union attorney in the early summer that they could take their "school psychometrist" job and "stick it." Maybe they could "unstick" it. Trouble is, when you tell someone to "stick it" and then you go back, you usually find out that's exactly what they did. And when they pull it out.... Well, let's just say the return to my "old job" wasn't exactly what I had in mind.

## Meeting Monday, August 26, 1996

Initial Purpose: To discuss my role and job responsibilities
Actual Purpose: To provide me an updated performance improvement plan
Present: The personnel director, the special education supervisor, the principal

"I've got some good news, and I've got some bad news."

## Job Search 1996

As the 1996-'97 school year got started, I knew things would be different. I would be returned to my home base at the middle school; however, my mentor and chief supervisor would no longer be there. He'd had about all he could swallow after twenty years in the system, and he took a better job as principal of another county high school further north. In his place was...the same principal who did the superintendent's bidding against me at the Alternative School! It's truly amazing how many career advancements I can take credit for. Coach moves into an assistant principalship, and now this young woman gets principal of the middle school...where she can keep tabs on me.

The principal called me on Friday, August 23, to notify me of the purpose, date, time, and location of the meeting as well as who would be in attendance. The personnel director arrived early and was in the principal's office when I arrived. She was in the hall and observed me and my private attorney walking down the hall at 10:55. That's right. I wasn't relying on the teacher's association attorneys to tell me I had no right to representation, and then lambaste me when I spoke up to defend myself in these meetings where I was verbally attacked. I contacted my private attorney, who was more than happy to attend this meeting as an observer or adviser, as it were. My job reassignment was being appealed, as was my demotion to second-class status. This was a meeting about my job assignment and responsibilities as well as the manner in which I was to be evaluated. I had a right to representation. The special education supervisor arrived fashionably late as usual, and after a brief meeting the principal came out and called me into the meeting. I brought Liz with me and introduced her, indicating that I had asked her to accompany me to the meeting as my representative. The personnel director sprang to his feet and authoritatively insisted that this was not going to happen. I argued that since this matter was in litigation, I had a right to counsel. He reiterated once again that this was not to be. My attorney graciously indicated that she would be willing to sit in as

## No Good Deed

an observer and not participate, but the personnel director barked "No," so my attorney pulled me into the hallway. She posed two options: 1) walk out and reschedule, or 2) attend without her. Option 1) would prevent us from finding out what they had in mind, so we decided on 2), and I attended. It was just so sad that the board, the school district, had the deck stacked in their favor. They could double or triple team me and have other staff members make up information about me and affect my job, my income, my career, and yet I could not have an advocate along to witness if not defend me. It was sad indeed.

The personnel director also refused to allow me to tape record the meeting. I expressed my formal dismay that I was not being allowed representation or to tape a meeting in which there were three of them and only one of me. He countered that it was a "non-adversarial" meeting to only discuss my *performance improvement plan* (PIP) as required by procedures consistent with my second-class status, and that there would be another meeting Tuesday at 9:30 at the board office with all four psychologists to discuss "evaluations, observations, forms, assignments, and related matters."

He then handed out the *PIP* and I noted that there were additions from the previous one handed me in April 1996. I asked him and he indicated that additional "bullets" had been added. I asked him when he would be reviewing my previous *PIP*: I think I asked, "What was the result of my efforts in meeting the criteria established in my previous plan?"

He indicated that this was already accomplished during my May evaluation conference. I indicated that I still was confused about which specific areas I was marked down for. A "1" over an area listing five separate criteria made it difficult to tell where my strengths and weaknesses lie; was it one, two, or all five criteria? If they were going to use this PIP as a means to fire me, then I wanted to make sure they included every detail of my performance, good or bad.

He responded, "You should be familiar with this form, as it is in your personnel file," and, "One low rating in a single category is enough for a low rating in the main area. The lines weren't there for separate notations; they were not for the purpose of averaging. In fact we plan to change the form." If the true purpose of the form is to indicate areas of need and the employee is motivated, as I was, to make those changes, then he or she deserved a clear outline of these changes. This was not the intent, and the more confusing and arbitrary it was, the better it was for them. It all looked clean on the outside, but it was rotten to the core. I signed the form, which was not dated, after they corrected my name, which was misspelled. The least they can do is get the name right. The meeting lasted no more than fifteen minutes.

# Phone Conversation With My Mentor, September 2, 1996

I needed to know what my rights were and I didn't know anyone knowledgeable enough and yet trustworthy at the same time. So I called my former principal and mentor. He addressed the following issues:

Seniority — A principal has the right to move a teacher from one grade to another based on her experience and need to cover the class load...but it is typically *the same job description*.

Moving a teacher into a *different* area — math to history, or English to art, or *psychologist to teacher*, or psychologist to psychometrist — is a different job description.

Second Class — RULE OF THUMB, when a teacher has been placed on second class as a result of poor performance in a job, leave them in that same assignment to allow for corrective action.

In the interest of FAIRNESS, it would be inappropriate to put a math teacher on second class and then throw him or her a curve and set him or her up by moving him or her to history.

This is clearly what they failed to do in my instance. I was taken from a position I was successful in and placed midyear in one in which I was untrained with little to no support. I was then evaluated in this setting and marked down for "failures" that were overblown and not unexpected under the circumstances. It was patently unfair to evaluate me in this setting.

PRECEDENCE—The superintendent does not always support the principal's recommendation for putting a teacher on second class. He told of a case in which a classroom teacher was recommended by the building principal for demotion to second class, but because the principal failed to follow the procedures, the superintendent overruled him. The teacher retained his first-class status.

In my case, the superintendent reminded my principal/mentor that he had supported him on another occasion. My mentor had recommended one of his teachers for a demotion to second-class status. He had followed all the proper procedures and the teacher was still doing a poor job, so he deserved the demotion. Here the superintendent wanted my mentor to support him where the demotion was not warranted. The superintendent told him, "I supported you on (the one teacher); why won't you now support me on the Matthews case?!"

Problem is that my mentor was the supervising principal in both cases, and the recommendation should have been from the bottom up, rather than the top down. Why would a building principal be supporting the superintendent on an employee the principal was responsible for supervising and evaluating? Especially when the building principal had no adverse information on me, in fact only positive observations?

The superintendent insisted that he "read the Matthews file" so he could be a witness against me on the second class. When he declined to do this, he was reprimanded by the superintendent for it. My mentor refused to read the file because 1) he was not part of gathering the documentation as required since he was my primary supervisor, and 2) he suspected that the information gathered was worthless. He was not going to be party to this process. Good for him!

PERSONNEL FILE— Anything that goes in your file must be subject to review and response. Any letters/memos about a teacher that do not pass this test cannot be placed in the personnel file or any file at school, etc. They also cannot be used in any disciplinary action against the teacher. They have to be pulled and placed in a "correspondence" file for a principal to use to refresh recollections only. The superintendent's use of old letters was blatantly illegal.

The only "evidence" the superintendent had against me were these memos that were solicited from people at the high school. They were never discussed with me or made part of my improvement plan until they served the superintendent's political agenda.

During my evaluation conference on May 30, 1996, the special education supervisor took notes, which she shared with the superintendent, including my mentor's refusal to sign the second-class recommendation. He knew I was getting railroaded. He had a solid reputation in the system. He was respected, but he was feared, too. He had sealed the fate of more teachers who weren't doing their jobs than all the principals put together, and his cases held up. He did it by the book. He believed in being fair and giving teachers a chance to improve and to change. And he understood how administration was required to help the teachers, to work with them. He knew how it was done, and this...wasn't...it. He was my primary supervisor. Without concrete evidence, how could he sign "on faith" that the personnel director and his cronies had gathered evidence against me supporting the second class status? He would sign, but he would also make it clear it wasn't based on his experience with me. The superintendent wanted me and he wanted me bad, and he didn't care how he did it. He had his supervisors and teachers all out there gathering dirt on me. It was like the Nixon White House where they were trying to build in levels of administrators to assure "plausible deniability" for the superintendent while building a case out of thin air. They were being asked to misrepresent a teacher's record to support the superintendent's case. And they all did it, gladly, everyone with the exception of my mentor, my middle school principal. He was the only one who stood up to the superintendent other than me, and for this I will eternally be in his debt. Here was a man with integrity.

## October 18, 1996 — Happy Anniversary

Happy anniversary! Two years ago to this very day I walked Sarah into North to turn her in. There's a bright idea for you now. Do the right thing and the Lord will smile on you. Well, he's been showing his teeth all right, but more on the order of an angry dog snapping at my rear end, the target of his hostilities. And once again I feel like I've had to drop and turn to catch the action.

Yesterday started off fairly normal, yet I woke with this sense of anxiety, of impending doom. Sarah and I haven't been on the best of terms, and Mom has been rising to her defense as of late. Forget the fact that she "snips" at me when I ask her what she'd like for dinner, or that she refuses to return calls to friends when I take the message, leaving them wondering if I even gave her the message. Sarah stays depressed much of the time, locked up in her room, then when she is happy, Mom is ecstatic. Me, I'm wondering what she wants, as that's about the only time she engages us in a positive frame of mind anymore. Mom says it's just that she's "bonding" with her, and that I might do a little of the same. Caroline was out for a parenting class she's teaching and left Sarah and me alone.

I'd spent thirty minutes on hold trying to get with Sarah's doctor to discuss Sarah's medication, and finally worked out a compromise: she would write a prescription for a week's worth. As it stands, we are working very closely with Dr. Mom, who we trust and has been through it with us as a family as well as with us as individuals, me, Caroline, Sarah, and even Andrew. But she cannot prescribe medication; that is Dr. Stromberg's privilege. But Dr. Stromberg is reluctant to place Sarah on the medication we (Caroline, Dr. Mom, and I) feel she needs, Ritalin or its equivalent to deal with Sarah's impulsivity. Dr. Stromberg is recommending antidepressives like Prozac, which clearly have not been effective. We are not your typical parents, since we all deal with kids on meds in our jobs all the time. So Dr. Stromberg is apparently a little upset that we are going over her head with the medication—on Dr. Mom's advice—and I'm feeling more than a little caught in the middle.

On this evening when Caroline is out teaching her parenting classes (how ironic), Dr. Mom calls to speak with Caroline. Sarah picks up the phone and, rather than put me on, she ends up talking with Dr. Mom, neglecting to tell her I am home and available to talk. I was a little upset that Sarah didn't put me on the phone. Of course, Sarah didn't know what was going on entirely—we handle everything for her—but it gives Sarah this feeling of being in charge when we're doing all the work. Anyway, I complain to her that I would have liked to have spoken to Dr. Mom, and Sarah shouts back that she didn't ask to speak with me. I try to explain my frustration of being on the phone for thirty minutes trying to work out her medication (on Mom's instructions) only to get stuck in the middle again while Sarah chats with Dr. Mom. I also try to explain this to Caroline when she gets home. Once again it is "my fault." "I can't leave you two alone for three hours...." That makes me feel like she is talking to me as one of two children she left unsupervised. It makes me feel like a child rather than the adult I am. What she says next is even more telling.

She describes her group of parents and the complaints mates had in biological situations, and how similar they are to our situation with me as the adoptive parent. Fine, I'm with you so far...then she rattles out a dissertation of how, "when the mothers are gone, all hell breaks out with the kids and Dad, and yet when Dad is gone, how smoothly everything goes." What they neglect to mention is that these are both short-term settings and may say more about who is really "in charge" than who lacks control of the kids. My guess is that if moms were out of the picture long enough to let dads regain control of their families, the same harmony would reign with dads as it does when moms are home. At the risk of sounding sexist, I will speak up on behalf of men, fathers, who are not allowed to parent their own children. Part of the reason this generation of children have the problems kids have today may be due to the rising power of women in the family leading to the demasculinization of men, and the removal of their position in the family. Women run families, the kids and their husbands, and the results are not always good. Anyone that doubts this, think of how many women laugh at:

*When momma's unhappy, everybody's unhappy...When poppa's unhappy, who cares?"*

I sleep on the couch with the feeling that if she thinks she can do so well without me, then fine, I'll absent myself from her life and theirs. But don't ask me to help with your homework, or to fill out this form, or to make phone calls to doctors because I "understand medication so well." I look back to all the times I stood out there alone, unsupported, and how it always backfired for me...and the kids. I also think back two years ago when I got so tired of fighting both Caroline and the kids that I gave up at one point. I told Caroline I was literally tired of fighting both of them, and that I was stepping down, I was stepping out of the ring. If Sarah had a problem or question, ask your mother. Don't ask me anymore, I was finished. Sarah, want to go out tonight? Don't ask Dad; ask your mom. Sarah and Caroline began to get into more squabbles (what happened to the mother/daughter bonding?), including the remark that Caroline wished it was Sarah going off to school instead of her older brother, Andrew. It wasn't long after this discussion that Sarah pulled her October surprise at school. If this sounds like I'm blaming Caroline for Sarah's problems and her actions at school, to be honest it can't be put down to any one thing in particular. But my stepping back as the primary disciplinarian surely didn't help. Kids respond best when both parents are involved in the discipline, when they support each other. In effect I have to bear my share of the blame because when the going got tough, I bowed out, leaving Caroline to do it all by herself. Once Sarah had us separated, her downfall was inevitable.

*The greatest gift you can give your children is to be together and be supportive of each other.*

## And Seldom Is Heard A Discouraging Word...

Thursday was okay until I called my private attorney. She essentially informed me that my case, strong as it might be, wasn't going to bring me the results I expected. I would not have an option for civil action, nor would I even get any of my money back. If I was really committed in continuing my career, it would have to be somewhere else. In other words, give this all up, settle, and do it in a way that I left here without the pressures and with a good recommendation, but leave with no money, and a pyrrhic victory. She further indicated that since I was paying her to discover all of this wonderful advice, I'd be smart to follow it. She also alluded to my union attorney's remark about what kind of client I was — difficult — and that I embarrassed my union rep at the last hearing by things I said to the superintendent. I have no idea what I said at this hearing to embarrass her (that would take a lot). It was like my private attorney, rather than be a positive influence on my union attorney, was being influenced by her negativity. *I* was the problem. A problem client, rather than one with a strong case. I hung up very discouraged, thinking that this whole process over the two years has lead to nothing more than a mass of headaches and sleepless nights, leaving me $25,000 poorer, with a ruined career. Is it fair, or honest? No, but it is real. I was at the high school that day, the site of my classroom of alternative kids. I had nothing to do, so I left to go over to the alternative school, just to change channels.

## No Good Deed

It actually felt good leaving the high school and heading out into the warm sunshine toward the alternative building. It didn't seem so long since I'd left the place for the last time in June, but it was four months ago. I walked up the ramp, and first person I see is the teacher in her usual place—on the phone, gossiping I'm sure. Ol' Mr. D, the aide, was back again and he came over. I thought he was moving on to bigger and better things, but here he was back. I sometimes wonder if his leaving three weeks before the end of the school year had more to do with squeezing me than furthering his career goals. At any rate, we all chatted and then one of the female students sauntered over and dropped a bombshell. "How'd you ever let Sarah pierce her tongue?" One of the students asked what she'd done, and Gina went on, "Oooh, she's got these brass balls, one on top and one on the bottom." I think she realized by the look on my face that I didn't know until that moment. She blanched and looked down, "Oops. You didn't know, did you? Oh my God!" She was genuinely embarrassed and shocked, and she felt bad for me hearing it from her the first time as much as she was sorry she let the cat out of the bag for Sarah. I was cool, but they all knew. The teacher went on about how she knew, they'd been talking about it for some time. You can't imagine the feeling a father (or husband) has as he finds out he's the last one to know. Here this flaky teacher of the alternative school knows more about my personal life, more about my own family, than I do. After fighting the good fight, fighting for my little girl, risking my job, my career, and spending twenty-five grand to do it, too, how does she show her appreciation? By piercing her tongue? I could feel things building up inside me. Betrayal was the best descriptor. After school I was in the library when Sarah came in and sat down next to me. She began to make some light conversation when I told her to stick out her tongue. She did about an inch. "More," and I saw the glint of brass. The most I could say to her at the time was that I was not happy about it. On the way home she told me when, "two months ago"; where, "Fells Point Chat Street"; who, "Liz"; and how much, "$40." Part of the money was what I had given her for her birthday when I allowed her and her friend Liz to go into the city as a special treat. Once again, how does she show thanks for this favor? By violating my trust and my respect. I couldn't wait for Mom to get home. Though she was shocked and disappointed, I think it paled next to my emotions. They were heading to Dr. Mom's for a medication update, so I said that under the circumstances, I thought I should go.

## Dr. Mom's—The Break Is Made

Not a whole lot was discussed in the car on the way over. Dr. Mom took Sarah in first and then called us in. I got to talk first and expressed my feelings of betrayal and disappointment: how I looked at this as 1) a violation of the team contract not to alter hair color, etc., without team permission; 2) a direct violation of the "no piercing rule," something we'd been quite clear about; and 3) an outright deception. Caroline had her say, but it was mild, and then Sarah spoke and justified her actions, of course. We did a little back and forth with Caroline and Dr. Mom trying to settle me down—they thought I was being hard on Sarah, who was "very fragile." About as fragile as a black widow spider. Sure, you can crush it with a quick jab of the thumb, but let it crawl inside your shirt...I guess I felt Sarah had sort of crawled into my head a bit and now was crying to get out. I mean, she didn't have to pierce her tongue. It's not like having to go out with your friends, or having to see your boyfriend, or even having to take that drink or toke that Mom and Dad say "No" to, but you do it anyway. This was a needless, senseless act, something she could have done without. She did it not because she wanted to and needed it, as much as she wanted to defy us. It was more against us than for her in other words. The mark of the oppositional and defiant personality, and I guess I had been as far down that road as I wanted to go. I wanted off, I wanted out.

The scene is best described as Sarah crying, playing on Dr. Mom and Caroline. "See, I can't do anything right, he's always on my case, he never talks about anything but his job and the case, the case. I *hate* it around there. That's why I want to go out every weekend." Meanwhile I'm soaking all this in...she usually spends her time ensconced in her bedroom with MTV and the telephone, and we don't bother her. I certainly don't go into her bedroom to ask her to review a file for me. I try not to talk about negative stuff about my job, but good stuff. And in the midst of it all, I am totally frustrated that she can't see, or is trying to hide the connection between, HER BEHAVIOR and MY REACTIONS. Hasn't she figured out by now that I only get angry when she outwardly defies me or lies to me? That her freedom and privileges are directly tied to her honesty and cooperation? Be honest and try to respect the rules, and have more freedom. Lie and openly defy and violate the rules, and consequences kick in, including less freedom.

I took Dr. Mom and Caroline's cues to ease off, and let Sarah spout. Dr. Mom sometimes goes off on what I think are irrelevant tangents, using "counseling techniques" that may sound great in the textbooks, but not in the real world. This was one of those tangents. Rather than focus in on what "wasn't working" between Sarah and Dad, Dr. Mom was focused in on Gina and Dad. Like Gina really matters in the scheme of things. Dr. Mom's point? That I needed to let Gina know that she should have let Sarah tell me about the piercing. Like that was either important or relevant at this junction in the road. Like if Gina hadn't said anything, when would we have found out?

After a while she refocused on the tongue piercing from a clinical standpoint. She talked about how these wounds don't always heal and how they are ripe for anaerobic bacteria for infections that can linger for months. Now I'm clicking on how Sarah has been sick for the past several weeks, sore throat, fever, ear infections, and now I'm wondering, is she doing this to herself? Where is the common sense? This isn't helping my headache, it just makes me more upset. It's like watching someone you love self-destruct in front of you. Sitting there with a razor blade, slicing off pieces of flesh, while you sit back and wax poetic philosophies. After a few more back-and-forths, I hit the brim and begin to unload—if she is so tired of living at our house, then fine, pack your bags and get the hell out, move in with Nikki, her ex-junkie pal, see how you enjoy that lifestyle. My feeling is that she would 1) never do it or 2) if she did, she'd be back in a minute—too much to lose. So fine, GO! Just stop trying to blackmail us with this "If you're mean to me I'll leave!" Call her bluff and tell her to go. But Mom and Dr. Mom intercede. "No, now that's not what you really want...." I am at a point that I really don't know if I don't want her out. I love her and I want to help her, but I can't. Maybe she would be better off on her own. But will I then blame myself if I am the one "responsible" for her leaving? Should I change my behavior, my expectations, to accommodate Sarah, so she can stay and be happy? Should I just back off and let Caroline handle it as before? Or should I be me and tell the world what I think? It is really a moot point, for the fuse has been set and is ready to light. I cry out that I am feeling that Mom and Sarah have bonded at *my* expense (first Andrew, now Sarah), and that I feel very left out. I mean, I am totally frustrated with the turn of events over the last two years, and all we've asked of Sarah is to work with us, don't fight us all the time. I am so stressed out with things, I don't know how much more I can take. Dr. Mom interjects that that is a subject not for here but a private session, and it's back to Sarah and the tongue.

Now that she knows the trouble it's caused, if not for anything other than health reasons, why doesn't she take it out? "I can't." I offer to take her right to the emergency room, where I know they'll take care of it. Mom and Dr. Mom concur, and then me, and it's on to Sarah, who insists that she's NOT TAKING THIS OUT! I'M 18 AND I CAN DO WHAT I WANT WITH MY BODY! I give her an ultimatum: lose the thing or find another place to live. Sweet Dr. Mom, always trying to find common ground, says, "Now, now, that's not

## No Good Deed

what we want," Oh no? At this point I am feeling so totally betrayed by this kid, I don't *want* to live with her anymore. I'm sick and tired. I've put my reputation, my livelihood, my finances, my friendships on the line for her, and all we've gotten is grief and more grief. I had to leave. I would allow them to work something else out and I would accept it. I got up and walked out the door to wait in the car.

Caroline eventually told me that we were going to have a twenty-four-hour cooling off period and were due back Friday, same time. I knew then, as I know now, twenty-one hours later, that I want no part of that. Let them work it out. For me to be involved, the hardware comes out first. It is not a subject for negotiation. Hardware first, then we talk. Dr. Mom seems to think I need counseling. I have a temper and I am under stress, but come on, I've been doing great controlling it. But everybody has his or her breaking point, and I'll be damned if Sarah's going to sit there and tell me what she is going or not going to do. Where I came from, your parents rule, right or wrong, and you might not like it, but you did it. Or you left. And this little gal who has cost us so much already is not going to dictate to me. If she hasn't the sense to keep cool until she is out of the house, than she's not as smart as I thought she was. For the second time in as many years, I hear my mother's words when I first told her about my new girlfriend and her new wonderful little kids: "Oh…don't get involved." If only I knew then what I know now. The heartache, after so many years of dedication just doesn't seem fair. But despite it all, there is so much love there for Sarah, and even more for Caroline. I have to stick with it for her sake. For the marriage. Sometimes you just get tired of fighting them all. You have to surrender. For your own sanity and peace of mind.

## CHAPTER TWENTY-ONE

# OCTOBER 30, 1996, MARRIAGE QUAKES

It's only one more week before my hearing on Monday, November 4, and I don't know if my association lawyer has called any of my witnesses or if she is fully prepared to defend me on the grounds I expect (substance not technicalities—"He can be difficult to work with at times; what did you do to help him improve?" vs. "He does his job, he fights hard for kids, and you have no legitimate proof he has done anything unprofessional or incompetent that would rise to the level of dismissal or demotion"). I also don't know if she has demanded that the board remove documents from my personnel file that should not be in there. My private attorney Liz wrote her last week and called several times, and still we wait to hear on this essential point. I don't know how things work in the real world of legal documents, but it seems these attorneys don't take things very seriously. I mean, if the board is using your personnel file against you in a hearing, and it's loaded with illegal documents (letters and such that have never been discussed and signed off as required), then they are clearly inadmissible as evidence in any legal proceedings, especially one that may lead to dismissal from a job, yet my association attorney doesn't seem all that concerned. I am not an attorney, but it's like going into a gun battle when you've had a chance to take all their bullets and you just sit there while they load up. Isn't that what evidentiary hearings are all about?

Last week Sarah and Caroline visited Dr. Mom on Friday, and the piercing came out. She was allowed to drive up to her friend Alexis's, in Pennsylvania, not a choice I would have made…but who was I to interfere? Caroline basically spent Thursday and Friday on Sarah. I went shopping with Caroline Saturday (Boston's, T. J. Maxx, and Value City—site of the infamous shoplifting incident), and then Sunday she went off to Wilmington for the Regional Counselors Conference and an opportunity to present her program on "Kareer Day for Kids." She spent much of Saturday night working on her presentation. She left Sunday and was gone Monday and Tuesday. She was back for a few minutes Tuesday before going to teach her parenting class Tuesday night. Wednesday was uneventful, and then Thursday it was zip in from work, and zip out to a junior college for a tour with Sarah. They met Andrew across the bridge and toured together, just the three of them. I was still "okay" with all this until I asked when they expected to be back Friday night, and I got the "We'll be back when we'll be back," response from Caroline. I was beginning to feel isolated and even abandoned. Caroline took time for herself and her career, she took time for her children—where did I fit in? Once again I was made to feel like the "bad guy" as Mother takes her two little chicks under her wing. Forget that it's they who have transgressed. I didn't get drunk or wreck the car, or lose the family money gambling, or go out with some bimbo. All I did was defend my family and try to keep it together, not separate it. Caroline didn't have to play the "We'll be back when we get back" routine. That was insult on injury and was uncalled for.

## October 30, 1996, Marriage Quakes

They were actually back before me, at four. I stopped off for dinner at the pizza place in Cambridge, and got home around six. It was the next day that pushed me over the edge. Caroline had time for Sarah Thursday, the seventeenth, and Friday, the eighteenth. Herself and Guidance on the twentieth, twenty-first. Herself and parent group on the twenty-second. Sarah again on the twenty-fourth and twenty-fifth, and then she comes home and hits the couch. Nothing left for me. She gets mad because I grimace when she says she started her period (another month without the intimacy that holds a marriage together in rough times). She is upset because I "don't understand her pain." Oh I do, I do. But why am I the only one who has to "understand"? Where is *my* understanding? Why do I only get leftovers?

On Saturday Caroline says if I want she'll take a hot shower and see how she feels and maybe she'll go to a movie with me. I appreciate the gesture but it feels like this grand favor she is doing. Rather than doing it willingly because she a) likes movies and b) enjoys my company, it's this "favor" coming off her deathbed to keep hubby happy. Knowing full well I will hear from her about it later—"I went to the movies with you"—this little light went on, and I thought, boy, it would be nice if I had a wife who enjoyed some of the same things I do. And it would be nice to have a wife who appreciates a husband who takes his wife to dinner and a movie instead of going out with the boys. Her next comment was the turning of the knife when she said, "I'm sorry if you don't have any friends to go and do things with. That's not my problem." Within seconds I knew what I was going to do. Go and treat myself to dinner and a movie. Though part of me, the good husband, wanted to stay and wait on her and keep her company in her pain, a larger part of me was saying, "She has beat herself ragged running for her kids, and her job, and her school parents, and her counseling association, and I deserve more." So after expressing this feeling as quietly as I could, I dressed and left for Annapolis, where I had dinner and a movie by myself.

I joined this family because I wanted to be part of it. And one day, when they were eighteen and gone, I could enjoy my wife alone. And here we are, one nineteen and one eighteen, and the problems are worse, not better, and the couple is struggling to stay together. She is so afraid of losing her kids because of me, and yet she doesn't realize that if something doesn't change…she may push me so far out of this marriage that I won't find my way back. Somehow, there is a core of feeling, of love, for each other that keeps us coming back to center. Though we often tiptoe right up to the brink, we never fall over the edge; we always step back and find each others' arms. These behaviors, the focus on *her* children and career and self to the exclusion of the marriage, its joys and pleasures, and its obligations, will continue for years, well past the day the two children leave the home, as you will come to see.

## Bumper Cars At The State Fair

This week the days are melting away as my hearing approaches and I don't know where I stand. I've paid $1,700 and more for my private attorney's services to make sure I get a fair hearing, and I still don't know if I will. Monday at work was another snoozer, with only one kid of two present, so I had time on my hands. I am a work-oriented person; I need to stay busy and have things to do, and downtime on the job is like watching paint dry. This is the first time in over twenty years that I have not been in charge of my own schedule. My activities are so restricted that I just sit and wait for something to happen. Tuesday and Wednesday were my counseling rotation at the elementary school, which was okay, except I am still not hearing from my attorneys and I don't get home until four fifteen now. I check on my '61 Buick, which was running poorly, and the mechanics can find nothing wrong with it. I head home, and for some odd reason the truck is still in the driveway and the taillights are on. The front fender sure doesn't look right either. And by the time I get out of my car and around the front of the truck, my truck, I notice why the fender is crumpled. The entire front end—grill, front bumper, turn signals, air conditioner—are all four to six inches back from their original position. Now I want to be calm. I really do. But with Andrew having just caved in the front of my Z in July, and then caving in the front fender of the Volvo in August, not to mention taking my '62 Buick for a joyride, I'm a little testy when it comes to my cars. Add to that Sarah's speeding ticket, and then rear-ending that kid in the school parking lot, who then called my insurance company with a $400 bill. The Volvo has had over fifty thousand miles poured into it since we got it less than eighteen months ago. The back bumper has been pushed in, trim ripped off, fog lights smashed, and the front fender modified by a pole. Take all that body damage plus $250 for a fuel sensor and another $250 for the fuel pump plus $250 plus for rear seal and transmission fittings! They drive the poor car to death, tear it up, and then Dad lets them drive his truck, only to find the front end all caved in. Do I have a reason to be upset? Is any of this my fault?

I walk into my home to me confronted by the team. Are they apologetic and contrite? "Sorry, Dad, I didn't mean to wreck your truck. It was just an accident. I'll pay for it"? Oh no. They have their head of security assigned to deal with me. Caroline, who feels the best defense is a good offense, starts on me about how many cars I wrecked when I was young, and how about that time last week when I almost hit that guy, and how this is not "my" truck, but the family truck (convenient except that it is my chief transportation and I pay ALL the bills on it).

Caroline's strategy appears to have Dad, who has every right to be mad, to empathize with poor Sarah (Hey, man, you drove crazy when you were young, so why get mad at her for doing it?), and it isn't working. It's making me angrier. I calmly...calmly...explain this to Caroline. "Look, this is not what I need to hear. I am calm, but this shifting of the blame

## No Good Deed

is not making me feel better. I have a right to be upset. I have a right to be angry. Allow me that right, and I will exercise it with restraint." I'm sort of asking for a chance to be good. But nooooo. Caroline knows how I "am" and Sarah is afraid how I'm going to react, etc. I am not going to be given a chance. It's called being set up for failure. And Caroline continues with her attack. At this point I haven't done a thing except look at the front of my truck smashed in. I haven't raised my voice or kicked a tire, I have just calmly surveyed the damage and waited for an explanation from the driver (Sarah) as to what happened. But Caroline won't allow this to happen. Instead of calming the situation, she adds fuel to the fire. As she walks into the house she exclaims, "I'm tired of twelve years of verbal abuse." (This is a new one.) Now she is bringing in all of this other baggage that has *nothing* at all to do with the fact that Sarah just wrecked my truck. I haven't raised my voice or really said anything. But I ask again, "Please let Sarah and me deal with this." This is not my fault, I did not cause this accident, and I am not about to excuse Sarah from accepting the responsibility just because I might get mad. And, most importantly, I'm the dad, she is not. If I get a speeding ticket or wreck a car, I take care of it. No one else is responsible. And I am the adult, meaning I can do a lot of things that an eighteen-year-old can't. Why? Because with over thirty years of driving and a million miles with only two minor accidents to my credit, I don't have to answer to anyone. Except the police and my insurance company. Pay the fines and the premiums, and I don't bother anyone. This is a kid, driving Dad's car, on Dad's insurance, living under Dad's roof and financial support. And this is a kid who only last month smashed the front end of another car, and it's our job to teach responsibility…not make excuses. "Sarah had a bad day, and Dad should calm down" doesn't cut it. I *am* calm at this point. "She's a good driver" also doesn't cut it at this point. The evidence doesn't support that right now. She has made the same irresponsible, careless mistake, not watching where she is going, twice in a row. The first she got away with little damage to her car, just a $400 pain for Dad. This time my truck has sustained hundreds of dollars of damage. Thirteen hundred, to be exact.

I walk into the house. As if this weren't enough, Caroline shoves this letter in my face. "Here is the superintendent's response to our request for Sarah's transfer." Now I am beginning to understand where all this anger is coming from. Why Caroline is mad at me when I haven't done a thing. He turned us down. Seems as though he was going to require Sarah to stay at North Caroline, the same high school she had trouble in, next year. We had requested that she be able to transfer to another school in the district for a fresh start. We would provide transportation, of course. "We have to call Dr. Mom!" she shouts as I attempt to absorb all of this.

Talk about bad timing. At this particular moment in time, I am not into exerting any extra energy into helping Sarah. I mean, do some women do these things on purpose or do they simply not know any better? For one thing, I'm on stimulus overload and don't need to worry about this letter. And I say as much. Caroline's response: "Well, fine, I'll just call Dr. Mom and *tell* her you're not going to worry about it." (Bad dad, bad dad.) Women…you can't live with 'em…. I'm told that maybe I should have understood that members of the fairer sex get overwhelmed, too, and that I should have understood that, but to me there is a basic difference between men and women on how they present and solve problems. Women can solve numerous problems on their own, they take pride in their independence and not needing a man to do things for them, but some of them, when they run into a tough one, when they get in over their heads, they look for their man to fix it. "Here, you deal with it!" Men, would never dump one of their own problems on their woman to fix; that would be a sign of weakness. We don't say, "Here, you solve it." We solve it or we ignore it; we rarely lay it on our wives or girlfriends to fix. We also know when to leave them alone. We are all fully conditioned to the PMS, time-of-the-month, don't mess with 'em blues, and believe me, we steer clear. We ain't stupid. We like having our eyes full and round and inside our heads rather than bleeding and scratched, lying on the side of the road like two squashed grapes.

Many women, on the other hand, seem to have no sense of danger when they get on a roll. They don't care if we've had a bad day or are completely stressed out; we are there to fix it, and do it now. I was always taught from the time I was a very young child that it's prudent to let sleeping dogs lie. This suggests that it's advisable not to haul off and kick a pit bull in the testicles as he lies sleeping and then stand around, hands on your hips, waiting for a reaction. Some women do this all the time. And not only do they kick you in the balls, they grab and squeeze them for you. As a man, it's difficult to excuse men who hit women. I have hit (slapped) one woman one time in my life, and that was after she hit me. It was more of a reflex than a preconceived idea. She whacked me and wham! I whacked her back. That was almost twenty-five years ago and I still feel bad about it. This young woman was my friend and lover and we had been living together in what could be described as a volatile relationship. On several occasions she pulled my hair, kicked me, and one time grabbed my privates and wouldn't let go until I cried uncle, which I gladly agreed to do. The four-year relationship ended when I caught her sleeping with one of my friends. Emotions were high, so I think I can understand how some women may unknowingly invite abuse.

If you watch these made-for-TV movies about spousal abuse, though, there's usually a scene where the quiet little lady cooks the guy's dinner, and gets his slippers and beer, and says, "Anything else you need, dear?" and he sips the beer and spits it across the room. "This shit's too warm, get me a cold one!" he says as he hurls the can at her. Then he takes a bite of his steak and peas and tells her to "Get over here!" and when she does, he grabs her by the back of the neck and shoves her face in the plate, shouting, "I told you I don't like salt on my peas, it makes my blood pressure too high!" In reality, I would honestly guess that there are many occasions where women bait their men until they explode.

Why they do this, I can't begin to tell you, I just know that I don't get mad easily, and I put up with a whole helluva lot until I can't take it anymore, and then yes…I do get angry. I explode. But I do not hit, or throw things, or strangle, choke, or pinch. I just react. My nervous system explodes in release. Today I mostly yell, but in my younger days I would end up hurting *myself*. I'd punch a wall or kick something, you know how that goes. So here we are, Sarah has wrecked another car, and Mom is shoving things in my face demanding that I do something about it. At this point, though, I am still containing myself.

Enter Sarah, fully empowered by Mom's defense, coming on like it's no big thing. "Oh," I reply, "It's no big thing that a few weeks ago you run into someone's rear end, and now here you go and do the same thing again?" Sarah's response? "It wasn't the same thing, it was a *different* guy! It was an accident. I didn't do it on purpose." Somehow the logic of that argument escapes me. While I am trying to develop an intelligent reply, the phone rings. It's the Volvo man "Well, I got the rear seal in, but you're right, there is a lot of play in that shaft. It will need a new bearing. Do you want me to replace that while I got the drive shaft out?" "Yes, fix it up so my son and daughter will have their own car to smash up instead of mine." I hang up and turn to Sarah. "Look, you and I need to talk about this without your mother getting in the middle. I was fine with this until she started making this my problem, talking about my driving history and my problems with communication." Mom doesn't take the hint and inserts herself square in the middle. It escalates predictably. Sarah is leaving, if she has to walk. Mom says, "No, honey, I'll take you." If there is one thing I can't tolerate, it's being directly challenged. "If bad old dad won't let you go to your concert, then I'll take you." Team up against me, fine…challenge me and I'll parry with the best of 'em. No cars are leaving this house, and I storm out of the house to remove spark plugs from each vehicle. Then I stop…this is stupid. I replace the wires and return to the house. Caroline is on the phone to Dr. Mom. No way is this triad going to set up—I don't need three against me—so I pick up the phone, get on, and we do battle over the phone.

To me, the closeness and intimacy Caroline and I enjoyed this summer was because it was couple vs. kids. I mean to tell you, they were opening our house to strangers when we were not at home, they were allowing underage drinking and drugs in our home. We had reason to be upset and a responsibility to clamp down on them. With Andrew gone and Sarah settled down, we remained intact, that is, until the tongue piercing. Now Caroline and Sarah have "bonded" and Sarah can do no wrong in her mother's eyes. She needs her freedom and her space, and Dad needs to forget everything that has gone before. "If Sarah is happy, leave her alone." That is something I can't accept. But it puts me in the uncomfortable position of being the bad guy. Mom gives consent, I am pulled in to say yea, for if I say nay, I've got two against me. Give her money and a car and freedom and sit back…and she (Caroline) doesn't seem to care that she is once again driving me away and playing into Sarah's game of manipulation and separation of Mom and Dad. Sarah tells me she feels caught in the middle, that Mom is always telling her this stuff about me. Is this the basis of their bonding…women against men? Don't be the victim of verbal abuse. Don't let your man be a man. Sorry, once again, I can't buy into this. I am even tempered, but I'll make no apologies for a woman who lines up against her husband with the kids, especially in a situation like we're in, when her kids have lied, concealed, destroyed, manipulated, and exploited us…not me, us. I'll never sell the kids short, but they don't deserve the protection she affords them. Where are the consequences? This is clearly enabling. Where do I fit in? By all intents and purposes, Sarah should have lost her right to go to the concert. She wrecked the truck, she was careless, bang! Consequence. Instead, she gets to go, will not be driving to school for a while, and will have to get a job to pay for the damage. I'm lost in this mess somehow. Am I being too tough or am I simply trying to follow the rules that call for immediate consequences, and logical consequences?

Emotionally I'm driven away from Caroline. I don't want to sleep in the same bed. I'm beginning to prefer my own privacy. I don't want to ask to go to a movie. I see myself withdrawing from her physically and emotionally. I have fantasies of landing myself a job and a new girlfriend in Virginia, one who likes to go to movies, and dinner, and doesn't have the health problems she has. Someone who likes to take hikes and go snow skiing, or jogging or riding a ten-speed bike. I am longing for someone else to fulfill what is missing in my marriage. A companion and friend as well as a lover. My fear continues that we (I) will never be rid of these kids, they'll be stones around my neck for years, separating me from my wife as they grow into their twenties and even thirties, and we move into our fifties and sixties. Are her model brother George and her parents enabling her? She does not, cannot, see what her role is in this. She talks a great show, teaches a great parenting class, but when it comes to seeing herself, and seeing me, she is blind. How much longer do I remain on this course? As I approach fifty and look to the day I am no longer sexually marketable, I look for an out. I still love Caroline deeply, and when she started being nice to me this morning I felt bad, but I also felt manipulated. I am a man, with my caring, and my deep emotions, and my anger. It is all part of me. Do I want to get rid of the anger? In some ways, yes. In some ways I need it. It empowers me. For so long I never could exercise it, but now it is my armor, my protection. Don't mess with Frank, man. He'll listen to reason, but try to force him to swallow something and he'll spit it back at you. It's my pride, it's my defense, it's my protection. It's who I am. Frank!

## It's November, And What Do We Have To Be Thankful For?

When we left off, Sarah was still moping about after tearing up Dad's truck. Friday I came home and she was here with a few of her "friends," Travis and Mike, her little tenth-grade buddies who have this mad crush on her. Her girlfriend Kyle was there, too. I was sociable and fed them a bowl of chili, and asked Kyle to do me a favor and take Sarah over to pick up the Volvo. It had been in the shop for over a week now and it was time it came home. Last month we spent $250 to fix the stalling problem. New plug wires, new plugs, and a fuel pump resistor. It still stalled and was getting ever harder to start in the mornings. So we took it back. He ended up putting new brakes, a new fuel pump, and oil seals in the old girl, and replaced a brass bushing that was ready to blow. I gave Sarah a blank check, and she came back with another bill for $650. So that made the total $900. After putting that kind of money in her car, and looking at my poor truck, I managed to convince Caroline that one very logical consequence was to let Sarah drive the wreck while I drove the Volvo. Sarah wasn't too happy about that. She went out Friday to a movie (it was sold out, according to her), and then had the SAT Saturday. It was scheduled for eight thirty to twelve thirty with an extra ninety minutes for her based on her diagnosis of ADHD. We figured she'd be home around two. Oh yeah? She made it home at ten after twelve, before the other kids had even finished! It was the hardest test she ever took, and she was never going through that again. We debriefed her a bit, but you know you can't study the night before for an SAT. That's a lifetime of reading and using a dictionary. Sarah used to read a lot, but stopped when she hit her teens when MTV and music took its place in her life. I made some grumbling sounds about "if you think this test was hard, what do you think college is going to be like?" She wanted to stay over at her friend Liz's, but Mom wasn't in favor of that and used an excuse of being in such pain that Dad might have to take her to the hospital. Stress was taking its toll on Mom. She wanted Sarah to stay close. Go to Liz's but come home. Sarah griped but complied. She rolled in at twelve fifteen.

# The Chickens Come Home To Roost

Sunday Sarah was to go over to Dr. Mom's for a tutoring session. I don't know, I had this feeling she was going to do something, sabotage. With her wrecking the car, and no real consequence (like get a job and pay for it), and with my hearing coming up Monday and hers Thursday, the air was rife with tension. I told Caroline I thought Sarah would pull something, but she doubted it. I had an appointment with my attorney Sunday at one and Caroline had to pick up a little fellow in Ridgely for a mentoring day, so we left out around twelve to hit the bank up for some cash, Ridgely to get the little kid, and get me to my one o'clock. Sarah was still in Easton at her tutor. Caroline mentioned that Sarah wanted to go to mass Sunday night, and even though I was glad she was getting back to church, I thought that it was suspicious. She never goes to church. Turns out *mass* was not a religious ceremony, but a drug-infested all-night dance marathon, a Sunday night rave. Definitely not, I say. Hey, it's a school night, she went out Friday and Saturday, give it a rest. We agreed. Sarah hadn't really asked, just dropped hints (mass is tonight, mass is tonight, Liz is going to mass tonight). I felt this was going to be her blow up, but Caroline didn't feel it was any big thing. Imagine our surprise when we got home and Sarah wasn't there. Oh, she left this full page note about "needing to get out" and how we never had anything for her to do until she wanted to do something, and then we had an excuse (staying close to Mom). She talked about having no friends and how these tenth graders were not on her level. She also left a trip ticket for mass, back at ten! You'll recall that the trip tickets were her contract between herself and us that documented where she went, who she went with, how she was getting there, and most importantly what time she was getting home. There had been way too many curfew violations where she would insist we had agreed she could come home at one in the morning when we had said eleven. The problem with this unscheduled outing was that we never agreed to her going. We never signed the trip ticket.

We called Dr. Mom and agreed to make Sarah drop a level, and take a urine specimen. Sarah called at ten fifteen, fifteen minutes past curfew, to say Liz got them "lost in Annapolis" and they were still there. Mom told her quite calmly that she needed to be heading home, now.

## Whose That Knocking On My Door?

After we realized that Sarah had gone to the rave without permission, we just sat back trying to figure out how to calm our jangled nerves a bit, and, more importantly, how to handle Sarah's homecoming. Her best defense was often a formidable offense, and one had to prepare for a challenging engagement. At the same time we are dealing with this new wrinkle in the long-running Sarah saga, I'm trying to relax before my second-class hearing, which was scheduled for the very next day. If my union attorney has done her job, then maybe I keep mine. If not... We decide that Caroline will handle Sarah when she comes home, and it will just be a drop in level and no more discussion. That way I can remain calm and focused for the events of the next day, a day that held my job and my career in its grip.

Suddenly there's a knock on the door. Strange, trick or treat was last week. And when I go to answer the door, it was not a small child dressed up as a policeman, but a real policeman, a grown man with a mustache and all. First question he asks is am I Frank Matthews. What is going on in my mind at the time? *Has Sarah been in an accident? Has Sarah been arrested?* He asks to come in. Sure. Next question does allay fears one and two. He asks, "Is Sarah at home?" At least she's not hurt or dead. And if he didn't know where she was, then she wasn't under arrest. But was an arrest imminent? With Sarah one never knew. Turns out, these two tenth graders she's been hanging around with, and their friend Curt, were trouble from the word go. According to the police officer, they had racked up tidy criminal records and were known by both the State

Police and the County Sheriff's office. The current incident involved Curt's running away from home. It appeared that the last person he was seen with was Sarah.

The officers were also asking questions about an apparent feud with this youngster named Brian, who had been calling her names and harassing her and who, according to Sarah, brought a knife to school on Thursday. Seems Curt or Mike or Travis, Sarah's loyal acquaintances, had made threats including the use of a gun to resolve the dispute. These later proved to be unfounded, according to Officer Powell, but just the same, it spoke to the caliber of Sarah's latest group of acquaintance. She says they aren't close friends, but in a sense it's amazing how she continually seeks out the worst characters, or rather the worst characters seek her. And the trouble she gets into comes directly from it. Who is the good/bad influence? Who is the leader? Who is the problem solver? Why does she dwell in this muck? We've tried medication to help her impulse control, special help at school, counseling, drug education, family talks, behavior management, and tutors, and yet the problems are relentless. What will happen when she is out of here and is living on her own? How long will it be before we get the call from the jail? And what will we do then?

Though it only takes forty-five minutes for Sarah to make the drive back from Annapolis, it was over an hour, 11:25, before she rolled in. "I'm home." We called her in and had a conversation. I had told Caroline I couldn't handle it, she could, but I jumped in anyway. We discussed a number of items, including the visitors we entertained earlier that evening.

======= CHAPTER TWENTY-TWO =======

# THE CASE BEFORE THE COURT OF SPECIAL APPEALS

## November 7, 1996, Hearing Day

After all that we've been through, starting from October 18, 1995, on, this day of all was one of the most crucial. After going up the proverbial chain of command from the bottom of the ladder, Coach, to the building principal, and then the expulsion panel (the personnel director, assistant superintendent, the principal [again] )and then the superintendent and the local board of education, and the state board of education, and the circuit court judge, we finally made our way up to the state court of special appeals. It took us a year from our circuit court date, but here we were, poised and ready for a hearing at the state's second highest court, a forum consisting of three judges steeped in the law and free from the shackles of political expediency. Finally, the deliberative body that could look at the evidence and give us a fair and unbiased ruling.

Over the summer months we had provided the court with copies of various briefs and memoranda from all the lower levels. Their clerks and the court officers, the three judges, had ample time to review them and think about or research them further. It seemed so clear cut to me, I wasn't surprised when our attorney told me they sometimes made up their minds before you even argued before them. They had to "go through the motions" to give the appellants a sense of justice, that real people were involved (and here we were sitting in front of them), and that real arguments were to be made. We were paying our attorney $10,000 for this, our *day in court*. You couldn't believe everything you read, for people lied in briefs, but you had a better chance of discerning the truth with the miscreants right there in front of you having to answer questions. And our attorney told us the judges would fire questions at lawyers, holding no quarter for either side. So we went in prepared as much as anyone could be. Here were our arguments:

Sarah's due process rights were violated as a result of the manner in which the information she provided was gathered. A football coach who was mixing roles as neighbor and friend/teacher and investigator pumped a little girl for information, using inside information, exploiting her and his relationship with her family. This was not in the best interest of the law or a student's rights. It was a violation of the constitutional protections against self-incrimination and the rules of gathering evidence.

Couple the way in which this information was obtained (coercion followed by voluntary cooperation) with the fact that that is *all* they had—no blood samples or urine specimens, no powdery substances, no witnesses, no corroborating testimony—the chain of evidence wasn't just flimsy, it simply didn't exist. Sarah's word, her admission, was the word of a scared little girl who really couldn't discern fact from fiction, lie from the truth.

And last, though certainly not least, the fact that kids with drug problems deserve some kind of special consideration, help not hurt, treatment not torment, and Sarah clearly had a problem with drug use as demonstrated by previous use and treatment. Our brief focused on the erroneous impression that

## The Case Before The Court Of Special Appeals

the circuit court judge expressed: "if she had been involved in counseling then (it would be different)...." We provided the documentation that she had been involved in counseling. As well, Sarah deserved protection, like it or not, as a child with a disability. Having previously been diagnosed as learning disabled in second grade, having served in special education in second, third, and fourth grades, she qualified for protection, spelled: manifestation hearing.

These arguments were spelled out clearly and in detail in the brief that our attorney wrote. He charged us $10,000.00 for this research, this brief, and his representation. Altogether we had three short meetings, one in his office after the circuit court fiasco, one this summer to pull things together for the appeals court, and one final meeting after the board's attorney filed his brief. The remaining time was spent driving to and from Annapolis for the hearing, and the twenty minutes he would spend behind the podium. That's right, all we (he) had was twenty minutes, fifteen to present and five to rebut. I figured it out. That's $500.00 a minute, or $8.33 a second. Hell, I would have just spent over $40.00 dollars just writing that last sentence.

We arrived and the courthouse was impressive. Wide steps a la Lincoln Memorial, leading up to this main entrance replete with marble and a huge atrium that went up four floors. Lots of glass and expensive woods. And you wonder where your state tax dollars go? When we looked around we found our attorney already there, and he indicated he had some good news. They had seven cases on the docket, and would be running to five o'clock; however, we were slated for the second slot: nine forty-five. We would literally be in and out before ten thirty. There was a case before us, so we went in to feel it out. The courtroom was small in the sense that there was only seating for maybe twenty people, no jury box or gallery to speak of, just leather chairs along the side and rear of the chamber. The dais was separated from the rest of us, the observers, and attorneys, by a walnut rail that curved around from their bench on either side. Unlike the circuit court, we would have no access to our attorney. Any attempt to speak to him or even pass him a note would be met with ejection from the arena. At either end of this rail were two attached tables of walnut or mahogany, with red and white lights at the corner. Reserved for the occasional witness, I imagine. In between this rail and the bench were two tables on either side of a podium. Each table had two chairs pulled up which were also highly polished wood. The podium had a similar sheen and red and white lights attached. This is to signal the attorney when his/her time is up. This more sophisticated procedure replaces the hook. The ceiling of the place was also quite elaborate and seemed to go up to the sky. I was impressed. The bench, and that hardly seems fair to use to describe it, was this huge, curved wooden structure, rising above all below, attorneys and clients alike. All you could see of the judges were their upper bodies and heads. If it was meant to be intimidating, it clearly met the task.

When we arrived court was in session. Two attorneys, one for a homeowner and one for the bank that foreclosed on his loan, took his house away, bought it back at auction for far less than it was worth, turned around and sold it for a profit, and then went after the poor sap because he didn't make good on the original loan. His lawyer argued quite logically that since the bank didn't lose any money on the deal, in fact they profited handsomely ($45,000), they shouldn't have to go after this poor guy who lost his house, and all of his previous payments, not to mention the chance of making any money on the deal. The bank, of course, claimed a right to the house and profit since they took the chance of playing Realtor and spent money cleaning up the place. I had visions of a cleaning lady running a vacuum, dusting, and squirting some Ty-D-Bol in the privy.

Their red lights having come on, they weren't even out of the holding pen when the judge called out, "Next case." This was us. Morris and the local school board's team included the local board attorney and their hired gun from Baltimore. They both stepped forward. I wanted badly to take the seat beside our attorney, but, lacking the necessary credentials,

## The Case Before The Court Of Special Appeals

had to stay in the observer's gallery. Our attorney did an admirable job of presenting despite constant mean-spirited and somewhat arrogant interruptions from the head judge. Though all three made comments and asked questions during the previous case, the other two remained strangely silent on this one. Judge Murray quickly shut down our arguments that evidence was not properly obtained. She confessed; that was good enough for him. Unless they "beat it out of her," the confession stood. He gave the school credit for "being kind enough to not involve law enforcement as required by the policy." Sure. She walks in on her own accord and gives a complete confession and they arrest her and slap her in handcuffs. For what? Possession? No...admission. When she came in on that Tuesday morning with her dad, she did not possess anything and was not under the influence. All that was supposed to have happened four days before the confession. Our attorney countered quite well that it would have been kinder if in fact they had called the police, for no police officer would have taken her into custody on her word alone that she had taken "something." Police needed hard evidence. He also raised the point that if procedures were unwritten or open ended, then a variety of approaches were acceptable; however, with a policy clearly written and established in case law from previous events, without the substance itself, the drug, without any evidence other than her confession, the investigation and the case itself should have gone away.

Apparently Judge Murray was an "expert" in the gathering of evidence and cannot be argued (reasoned with) on this matter. It's too bad criminals are treated better than high school students. He did comment on the shortcomings of the zero tolerance rule, that the only kids who remained in school are those who "ratted" on the others, a clear reference to my testimony that the kids who were honest and came forward were expelled while those who lied remained in school.

Our attorney moved on to the issue of Sarah's disability, and held his ground well here. He described her previous history of substance abuse and her involvement in counseling, and how the school knew or should have known about both. Knowing her history, they should not have used her confession against her, as it was given in the spirit of seeking help with support from appropriate state laws. At the very least, they should have held a manifestation hearing to rule out any causal link between her learning disability and her admission of drug use. This one seemed to interest the head judge a bit more, but he suggested that we were trying to "use this" after the fact as an excuse, though Morris stood his ground that this was established well before her act and was brought up well before she was expelled by the board. In fact the building principal, the expulsion panel, and the local board members were well aware that she was disabled and ignored the impact of this and the requirements of federal law. The lead judge felt that we expected too much to expect the "investigation" and wheels of justice to come "screeching to a halt" just because we raised the specter of a disability. (In fact that is exactly what federal law requires.) His focus was so intense on the disability aspect that he quickly tossed off the other aspects. "The judge in the circuit wasn't impressed with your plea that there was sufficient evidence, so why should I be?" Maurice countered that it would only have halted the process for a mere thirty days, a mere pittance in contrast to the loss she experienced over the interim. Murray's analogy included an attorney who brings up some minor technicality to stop the wheels of justice. Something along the lines of a brutal murderer getting off because they didn't have the right date on the search warrant. But this wasn't about murder, it was about a disabled kid with a drug problem. This wasn't a ruthless criminal, this was a five-foot little girl with a learning problem and emotional problems who was very likely self-medicating. And the federal statute protecting students with disabilities and drug problems was clear that suspension or expulsion could not take place until hearings, manifestation hearings, were held at the local level.

The lead judge seemed concerned about the kind of disability Sarah had. Testimony by Dr. Mom referred to co-morbidity

## The Case Before The Court Of Special Appeals

of drug use and ADHD, which is what she felt was the primary problem. I believe and continue to believe that her learning disability is primary, her receptive language and math skills being only two of many manifestations. Our attorney brought this to the forefront, mentioning her specific learning disability. He did his best with more interruptions from the bench than opposing counsel, then concluded after fifteen minutes with a right to rebut the other side's presentation.

It's interesting to note that when the federal law for the disabled (IDEA) was renewed in October 1997, it clearly came down on the side of the child. If the student was disabled, the manifestation hearing had to be held before the suspension/expulsion. And in the case of a student who was not identified, but who might be disabled, if the parents had even called the school concerned about their child's grades or progress, then (sorry, Judge Murray) the administration's process ground to a halt while the child was tested to make a determination about the disability. As you know, we had been concerned about Sarah's education for years. Not only had she been identified with a recognized disability, a learning disability, but she had received special education services under an IEP for three years.

When the other side presented, the Baltimore attorney stepped forward and overdramatized how serious this event was, and how there was a need for law and order in the school. He conjured up this image of drug-crazed students running amok in the buildings. No one seemed concerned about the guns and knives and bomb threats or the sexual predators that were not held to a similar standard of zero tolerance. It was clearly aimed at the kids with substance abuse problems, the so-called druggies. Morris made his rebuttal and they cried out for the next case. Before we even realized, it was done. That was the quickest ten grand I ever spent!

## Overview

This case dated back to the December 6, 1994, a hearing before the local board of education. We presented expert witnesses and documentation to demonstrate that Sarah was coerced into coming forward by a coach on an unofficial basis, and that nothing was done officially until I brought her forward four days later. The only "evidence" they had was her confession. As well, she had protections, first from Maryland state law, which encouraged students with drug problems to come forward seeking help. If they did, information they revealed would not be used against them. Secondly, as a student with a disability (learning disability), other steps had to be put into place before they suspended her, much less expelled her, specifically the holding of a manifestation hearing to determine if there were a causal link between her act and her disability. The board had no witnesses or physical evidence. The *chairman* of the expulsion panel admitted in sworn testimony that they would never have known were it not for the fact that I brought her forward, and finally it was thoroughly demonstrated through documentation as well as sworn testimony (unrefuted) by expert witnesses that Sarah was identified and enrolled in special education classes both in West Virginia and here in the district. Simple case. Open and shut, right? From local board of education to state board of education, it took four months. From state board to judicial review at the circuit court, seven months. And now, at the door of the court of special appeals, twelve more months, for a total of twenty-three months, just short of two years.

Questions presented:

1. Did the reviewing court err in affirming the decision of the state board to affirm the local board's decision to uphold an expulsion where credible evidence was offered that the expulsion was undertaken without consideration for the child's handicap?

2. Did the reviewing court err in affirming the decision of the state board to affirm the local board's decision to uphold an expulsion where the record indicated that the only evidence offered in support of expulsion centered on the student's own coerced admission?
3. Did the reviewing court err in affirming the decision of the state board to affirm the local board's decision to uphold an expulsion where proceedings revealed noncompliance with statutory authority concerning the investigation and disability assessment of students identified for expulsion?

It was with a sinking feeling we left the hearing. I was not optimistic. I was neither surprised nor disappointed, therefore, when the decision came in. They give you a –thirty-to-sixty-day timeline, and I figured with Thanksgiving and Christmas, we'd hear after the first of the year. We didn't have to wait that long, and the sad thing is that I had to find out from my teacher association attorney, who was contacted by the board's attorney. The word was that the board had yet another favorable decision and that the wording was good as well. I called Caroline and she had heard nothing, and even our attorney was also in the dark. We were in Florida before my attorney contacted me with the official results.

## Murray's Law

Once again we were handed a ruling that was insulting to the judicial system as I understood it. Rather than a clear examination of the facts, it demonstrated that justice was not only blind but deaf and dumb. And although we had decided that we would go along with this decision, win or lose, it lacked the logic, the valid explanation, I had sought for over two years. It also ignored the established facts of the case, facts that were well documented and on the record. So once again I found myself refusing to accept this and wanting to go to the next level, to whatever level it took, until someone provided me with a logical explanation instead of a ruling that ignored the simple facts. Don't tell me, "No." Tell me, "Why."

Here is what the judge offered in way of explanation.

He outlined the parameters the court is required to stay within, that he is "limited to determining if there is substantial evidence in the record as a whole to support the agency's (the state board's) findings and conclusions." He also indicated that "because the state board of education is an administrative body specifically created by statute to comprehensively administer the public education system, its decisions are afforded great deference." The only problem with this logic is that the state board did not render a decision. They responded in a one-page form letter. They gave no reason for their judgment, only that they affirmed the local board's decision. And the local board made the original error. To support the state board's decision-making process is to support a house of cards. Murray did allow that his court could "substitute its judgment for that of the (administrative agency) on questions of law" and that our inquiries involve mixed questions of law and fact. Why then appeal any lower decision?

Murray's first error was in his lack of understanding of the local board's decision. He wrote: "Appellants first challenge the local board's determination that Sarah was *not handicapped* and therefore not entitled to the special statutory protections afforded to students with disabilities".

The local board never said she was "not handicapped"; they said she "…was not a special education student." That's a big difference. The issue here is not whether or not she had an IEP, or was currently enrolled in special education classes; but whether or not she was disabled, which she clearly was.

Murray went on at length about Maryland law protecting the "handicapped" or disabled and then stated, "Despite evidence indicating that Sarah suffered from attention deficit hyperactivity disorder ('ADHD'), *she had not been previously*

## The Case Before The Court Of Special Appeals

*classified as handicapped*, and should not benefit from the procedural protections of Maryland law ".

I was dumbfounded. What do you mean she wasn't previously classified as handicapped!? *This was an established fact.* She WAS! Didn't he read the record? Were they making a ruling on the so-called facts the local board's attorney gave them? I was extremely disappointed to say the least. This grand body failed to do their homework, and chose to believe the liars! Again!

Murray's second error related to the "evidence." He wrote, "When initially approached by school officials (Coach was not operating in an official capacity) Sarah admitted to possessing and using a controlled dangerous substance while on school grounds".

It still has not been made clear that there was no "official" knowledge until we brought her forward (the assistant superintendent's statement was clearly in the record) and that the only "evidence" they had was her confession. Even more ludicrous was Murray's suggestion that Sarah failed to exercise her option for "retracting or mitigating or rebutting her statements." What this justice was suggesting, was that she could have lied or stonewalled. She is now faulted for sticking by her original story, the truth. Yet another confirmation that the justice system does not always seek the truth.

His third response is related to the lack of due process, that we were not notified while they were "investigating" her, and that since she was "under investigation" it precluded protection for coming forward seeking drug counseling. There was no "formal investigation" until she came forward, as there was no official contact until four days after the incident when I brought her in. They make it sound like they "caught her." The truth of the matter was Coach only knew because she confided in him as friend and neighbor, not teacher, not an official from the school system, and he also provided a cover story for her. The story, the lie, would have held, too, were it not for honest Dad convincing his daughter to come forward with the truth. They didn't catch her; she turned herself in. So much for their investigation, and so much for Murray's argument that she didn't deserve the protections afforded kids with drug problems who turn themselves in.

Murray also erroneously wrote, "Furthermore, appellants have not provided any support for their assertion that parents must be notified before an investigation can begin." If their investigation began on Thursday, October 13, and continued on Friday the fourteenth, and they had reason to suspect she had ingested a controlled dangerous substance, one for which a student already had been hospitalized for an adverse reaction, then how could they in good conscience send her home for the weekend and allow another three days to pass, the fifteenth, sixteenth, and seventeenth, until *my* phone call on the night of Monday, October 17? County policy was clear that parents were to be notified. "If there is an immediate and dangerous threat to the student (loss of consciousness, inability to communicate coherently, or threat of suicide), the staff shall inform the principal, who shall contact the parents, nurse, or medical doctor," none of which was done. On the Thursday in question, Sarah was crying uncontrollably in the restroom, and no one had the presence of mind to call and tell us, her parents.

So we lost the case for the same reasons we lost earlier: no one with any sense was looking at the facts and making a fair and just decision based on them. I still did not have what I considered to be a reasonable response. Justice had not been served. I wasn't giving up. Not yet.

## November 11, 1996 — My New Job Duties

Another day, another exercise in boredom on the job. At least when I'm bored at home I can go out in the yard or watch TV or listen to music or sleep or go downtown or find a project to work on. Here, once I've finished all my "work" for the day, there isn't anything else to do. Today was report writing day, so once my two twenty-minute reports are done (by nine thirty), the rest of the day is mine. I read the newspaper and reviewed my schedule for November, sending the personnel director an e-mail about having eight kids to test and two weeks before I get to write a report. And with a Thanksgiving holiday in between, that makes it even worse. Too many kids, not enough fresh memory. I asked to switch a day to get the reports written and be on schedule. For those of you who might say, change it yourself, let me introduce you to my job responsibilities: Though I am a professional, I cannot arrange my own schedule. I am told where to go, who to test, and what to give the student in the way of evaluation instruments. I am told when to write reports and when to get back to the testing regimen again. If I dare to alter anything—the report format, the day I test, or the kids I test—I am in big trouble for "not following directions." Of the three-hundred-plus employees here in the district, only my job hangs in the balance over some of the most trivial nonsense you could ever imagine. You changed "Behavioral Observations Observed During Testing" to "Behavioral Observations" without approval! You added a "Summary Section" without approval, etc. You think I'm kidding, but I was written up for just these infractions! Reprimand number six.

Although the flow is a little better between reports and evaluations, it is still a trickle, and the boredom is making me kinda crazy. Frustration is that there is so much to do, and I can't do it. An object lesson on dedication. Work too hard, dedicate yourself too much to your work, and you will find yourself with no work. Meanwhile life goes on, and nobody gives a damn, not the teachers, not the parents, and certainly not the kids themselves. Kinda speaks for doing what you have to and no more; nobody appreciates it, and even if they do, how soon they forget. But I guess this is better than the classroom from hell. Do I sound bitter? Well, I guess I am.

## The Second-Class Hearing

We were scheduled to have my hearing on my "second-class" status on Monday. My union lawyer was there, as were my personal attorney and, of course, the rest of the superintendent's staff. I had several people of character who were going to appear on my behalf. A parent I helped out with a case involving his stepdaughter was one. Several teachers were there at risk of their own jobs, one who was eight months pregnant. Apparently some discussion had occurred prior to this gathering and my attorney wanted to know if I would consider a settlement offer. Maybe we could all come out ahead. With this in mind we met without the witnesses, went on the record, and talked. The two attorneys talked, then my attorney talked with me. Then their attorney talked with them. In the end they laid out a settlement agreement that sounded like it would allow me to regain my first-class status, have a shot at returning to my old job, and get them off my back. In return I would have to withdraw any and all complaints and actions against them, promise not to engage in any future actions, and honor the confidentiality of the agreement. It sounded good, so they drew it up and promised to have something in writing for us to sign. I proudly went out into the hall and thanked my witnesses for their courage and caring, and told them that their presence may have swayed the board to deal more fairly with me. We would not go to hearing; we had settled the case to my satisfaction. They could go home. We all walked out into the cool night air. Maybe we had finally cleared the air inside that building as well. A cease-fire had been declared between the two warring factions. I felt great.

# The Forecast: Partly Cloudy With Afternoon Thundershowers

Last week we "settled" my appeals, and yet here we are a week later, and what's changed? I am still in this awful rotation, stuffed back in this office, with no change in my duties much less the role I play or the way people treat me. A

## The Case Before The Court Of Special Appeals

teacher approached me the other day and asked if I could sit in on a meeting for one of his kids. He was concerned about possible drug use, and when he mentioned a meeting to the parents, they asked specifically for me to attend. I referred him back to the building principal. He did, and wow, did he get a response. "Under no circumstances is Mr. Matthews to attend any meetings with parents! He is a tester and that is all. In fact he is not really even considered a member of this school faculty." Nice. And if I'm housed here and this is my "home school" and I'm not considered part of this faculty, where do I belong? You can imagine what the feeling is like in outlying schools. Half this staff is afraid to talk with me, and the other half doesn't want to.

It made me realize how dirty the water is and how it will never get clean. Any thoughts of staying here are not only pipe dreams, but senseless. Why would I want to stay? Because of my house and our lifestyle is why, not because of this job. That is why we came here eight years ago, but it has been eight years of hell with the last two hotter and lower. A few short years of peace and quiet and then all of this stuff. I wish I could take my house and go...but life doesn't work that way. It's a package deal, with options tied in. We built our house and put ourselves into it with our time and blood and sweat and money and all of the things that are unique to it: the church window (which comes with us), the mantle from the railroad bridge, the floor from the trees we cut off the land, the spiral staircase I ordered, designed, and assembled, the oak wainscoting, the cherry wood paneling in my study. We will never get our money out of this. It's worth $200,000, and yet we'll be lucky to get $180,000. How many $200,000 houses are there in this county? How many people are there to live in them? Same answer to both questions: few. Still, our house is unique and beautiful, and there are many folks in town who've seen and admired it. So maybe we will luck out. Just so they know we aren't desperate to sell and will rent it for $1,000 per month before we'll give it away. No dogs. No smokers, please.

## The File Room Incident

Last Friday we had a minor controversy spring up. For any one of the other three-hundred-plus employees in Caroline County, it would be nothing. But for Frank Matthews, double agent, it was a major catastrophe. You may remember it all started innocently enough, a "talk while we walk" conversation with my friend and the guidance counselor, Tony. He asked how my hearing before the court of special appeals went, and I gave him my brief summary of our fifteen minutes of fame for ten grand. I asked him why he was limping. He admitted to twisting it tripping over a piece of furniture or something. He turned off the hallway into the conference room across from the guidance office and, indicating he had to copy something, stepped into the file room. I stood in the doorway and held the spring-loaded door open. He copied something and walked out past me, and I quickly asked him, as an afterthought more than anything, "Is my old file cabinet in here?" On the principal's instructions I had wheeled it down to the assistant principal's office when I left that spring. The same AP (assistant principal) now at the middle school was the AP at the high school at the time my daughter was a student there. And, yes, he was the same AP that called her in to interview her on Coach's recommendation. After working with Lou for a couple of years, I felt I could trust him. He later told me he had relinquished the file cabinet. Wanting no part whatsoever of my hot files, he had called the assistant superintendent to report that he had them. My files of students over an eight-year period were placed in the file room with all of the other confidential records. They then changed the locks to the file room, with only two keys issued. This was reportedly to make sure I didn't get into the files. Like I was going to use confidential files as evidence against them or something.

Although I was never instructed to stay out of the file room, much less the files themselves, I exercised a great deal of judgment in those days and kept my nose out of where it had no purpose being. I did not need to see confidential files on my own cases, much less anyone else's. My new job description was very limited and that was fine, I followed it though I didn't agree with it or think it was necessary. Oh, it might help the hundreds of kids I've seen, but since I wasn't allowed to use "background information" in my reports, and no one was allowed to consult with me anymore, isolating the files served no real purpose other than to ease the mind and paranoid tendencies of the superintendent. He was afraid I was going to use something in my files against him. To tell the truth, I had everything I needed for my cases and complaints already, having copied and removed critical documents when they were under my control. I saw the storm clouds coming, believe me.

So...fifteen seconds in and out of the conference room ended up into a major blowup. Seems Miss Manners, the three-hundred-pound watchdog put in charge of the file room along with everybody else's business in the school, saw Tony and me go into the conference room. Her adrenaline pumping, she leapt into action, surging from behind her desk, knocking kids out of her way in her futile attempt to "catch us" in the file room. But alas, she was too late. By the time she squeezed her rather generous derriere out the door and waddled across the hall, Tony and I had finished our dirty deed of conversing and were coming out of the room back into the bright lights of the hallway.

I never knew anything was amiss until a few hours later when Tony, quite upset, stopped me in the hall. I don't think I'd ever seen him this agitated. Seems Miss Manners gave Tony the standard lecture on access to the file room and how he was not authorized to enter, much less allow *Most Wanted Candidate of the Year* access as well. Her job was on the line! Tony tried to put her fears and suspicions to rest, but it was no good, she was taking this to the top. The building principal (remember, this is the same individual who was principal of the vocational school where I was placed in the classroom from hell). She was now in my new building and would hear about this serious transgression. Tony, wanting to head this off at the pass and put it back in the tiny bottle it belonged in, asked me to meet with him, the principal, and Miss Manners in the office. We sat down and I was cool as a cucumber. After all, I hadn't done anything wrong. The principal gave Miss Manners a chance to talk, and she deferred, then when he got started she left the room in tears. Tony and I were on the same wavelength…it was perfectly innocent, a conversation that took place while we were in and out of the area of the files for ten to fifteen seconds at most. Miss Manners, having regained her composure, returned and took her seat. Tony and I attempted to get her to clarify the amount of time she saw us in the file room. Was it ten minutes or ten seconds? "I'm not on trial here!" she wailed. "I can't afford to lose my job!" she blubbered. I quietly and calmly told her that there was only one person in that room whose job was on the line, and that was me, and that I certainly didn't need anyone accusing me of doing something wrong—something that I did not do. "Nobody is accusing you of anything," she snarled.

We made it quite clear to the building principal that I had not looked at any files, nor had I asked to look at any files, and my question about the location of my file cabinet was due to the fact that we were presently in settlement negotiations with the superintendent, and that was one of the requests I made, that I would get my files back. I was only trying to ascertain their current location. I admitted to not having seen them since the previous April. The building principal made it abundantly clear…I had no business in the file room because there were files there. I asked her if that meant I wasn't allowed in any room where files were, because they were in *every* special teacher's classroom. Am I to be accused of looking through files every time I go to pick up a kid for testing? "No, but then you'd have a reason to be there; you have no reason to be in the file room." We further explained that I was not "in the file room," only in the doorway, and even Miss Manners agreed with this. I asked that this conversation stay in the room, only because it really amounted to nothing, and I could ill afford any problems while my settlement agreement

## The Case Before The Court Of Special Appeals

was taking place. She agreed and came down to observe me later in the day. Everything seemed back to normal.

Five days later, on Wednesday, November 13, the building principal left a note in my mailbox to meet with her at two forty-five to go over my observation. I was ready. She asked her assistant principal to sit in as an observer (where was mine?). Her AP, by the way, was the ex-wife of my first principal, who left town six years ago. She didn't like me before he ran out on her, and now that he was gone and he and I were still friends, she wasn't really fond of me, you could say. And now she's sitting in as observer for my observation/evaluation. Wonderful! The first half went great, though I kept waiting for the other shoe to fall. Positive comments, excellent this, great that. At the end, before she gave it to me to sign, she mentioned that I was also continuing to be monitored for my performance improvement plan. "With that in mind," she said, "I wrote up the little incident from Friday." After agreeing not to mention the file room incident outside the discussion we had in her office, here she was formalizing it in my observation as part of my performance improvement plan. More hearsay and innuendo, now adding walking by the file room to chewing gum and holding up my hand. My ship was sinking again.

"**Office of the Principal**                    To Mr. Frank Matthews

Dear Mr. Matthews,

I am writing this letter so that I may clearly communicate to you my expectations regarding your access to student records and the records room. During our conference, on Friday, November 8, 1996, you admitted to being in the student records room having a conversation with Mr. Geronimo. In your present position as testing psychologist, there is no need for you to have access to student records, nor do you have authorization to enter the student records room. All student information you require to administer tests is included on the student referral form, as completed by the referring school psychologists. The student records room is locked at all times and only authorized personnel have permission to enter the room.

Also during our conference, you admitted to asking Mr. Geronimo about the location of your filing cabinet. This is a clear violation of a directive which was issued to you at the beginning of the school year that you address any questions or concerns related to your job duties and responsibilities directly to me. In summary, you are to abide by the following guidelines:

1) You have no access to student records.
2) You are not authorized to enter the student records room.
3) You address any concerns or questions directly to me.

The school district will not tolerate the actions of employees who violate established rules and guidelines. Not following the guidelines as directed by your building level administrator represents poor judgment on your part and seriously violates our standards. Future violations may influence your job status in our district schools.

Sincerely, The Principal"

This signature indicates that the employee did have the opportunity to discuss the letter, received a copy, and is aware of its existence. It does not mean that the employee necessarily agrees with the contents.

This reprimand (number seven), handed to me four days after our settlement conference, demonstrated most clearly the lengths the administrators would go to stifle dissent. Although it was clear that I was never told to stay away from student records or records rooms, I had a clear sense that I was not to cross this line. I exercised keen judgment in this respect. All I wanted to know was the location of the hundreds of file folders I had produced over eight years in the district employ...my records. Test booklets I had filled out, tests I had

## The Case Before The Court Of Special Appeals

administered and scored, reports I had written, and notes I had taken. Everything in my handwriting as part of my job. And I didn't want to see them, I just wanted to know they were safe. And so a simple conversation, and an even simpler question, is turned into a major incident that "represents poor judgment on your part and seriously violates our standards." Give me a break! The irony is that this district has no written standards, and those they do have are ignored and/or violated at a whim. And I had a reputation for being knowledgeable and consistent about respecting federal, state, and local procedures. It just wasn't fair. But it was clear what their bottom line was: "future violations may influence your job status in our district schools." One thing for sure, I don't make the same mistake twice. That's why so many double binds are built into their evaluation procedure. It was time to walk like Jesus again, 'cause I was about ready to get nailed again.

More significantly, coming on the heels of the cease-fire, it suggested that rather than ceasing hostilities, the war was still on. So I was forced to gear up again. I had the same feeling I had after my meeting with the board president: first, relief that we could work things out amicably, and then disappointment when I realized that he didn't want peace, he didn't want to settle anything, he wanted me gone, and he wanted me ruined. As someone said, "The superintendent will never let anyone leave this county alive."

Well, you can imagine my reaction to the letter. I said that I was under closer scrutiny than anyone else in the district. I was forced to watch every little thing I said, did, or thought about doing. I looked her in the eye and said, "You know none of this was intentional; don't you think this wording is a little strong?" Her reaction was most interesting. She said that she wrote it up to protect herself (as though she needed any protection), that I had made some inaccurate statements about her failing to provide any technical assistance at the Alternative School in the spring, and that this was not the case, she had given me a great deal of materials and support. I explained that I never said that. Maybe my attorney said that as a defensive position. She stood by her letter. I signed it and left.

And that's when it hit me. How in the hell did she know what my lawyer wrote or said about her in a closed hearing? Unless…the superintendent himself leaked a bit of information. She'd had two days to write me a letter, and did not… that is, until she went over to the board office on Wednesday and got an earful from the superintendent himself about how I had "made some inaccurate statements about her at the hearing, and how this is typical of me making up facts, and that she better protect herself and put this incident into writing." I'm sure he threw in some good stuff like, "Under the circumstances, if he were to reenter the file room and provide more incriminating evidence to the state or federal government, then you would be responsible for not putting him on notice, and *your* job might be in jeopardy." It fit the pattern all too well. This man is so mean spirited, so conniving, he won't order someone to "get someone," he merely puts the pressure on him or her, puts the gun to the person's head and gives him or her a choice he or she is forced to make. He did the same thing to another principal, as you'll remember, when he had him lie to "get me" on the funeral case. But that's how the man works. Put the pressure on his principals to "do the right thing" or, more accurately, the "wrong thing." I once had a conversation with an attorney who used to work with this same district. He resigned because he could no longer be associated with what he termed the unethical tactics he witnessed on a regular basis.

This is precisely what the superintendent had the personnel director and the assistant superintendent do to my mentor when he refused to be a party to my loss of tenure back in the spring. This time it was his dog soldiers doing the dirty work. They came at the poor guy. The only administrator with the integrity to say no. They came after him like dogs to a kill. "Don't you trust your colleagues' judgment? Where is your loyalty to fellow administrators? What about your friends? Trust us. We have the goods on Frank, he's history. You don't want to go down with him, do you?" In other words, "Aren't you willing to lie and ruin this man's career to keep your job?" Apparently we all know what his response was. He no longer works in the district. He had integrity, and he left rather than sell out. That says a hell of a lot about the ones who remain, and to what lengths they'll go to save their own hides and jobs.

So I can now add to my list of serious offenses not reporting a full scale IQ, holding my hand up in somebody's face, telling a parent to go to the school board, chewing gum, writing my current job title on my assignment form, adding a summary section to my report, holding a door open, and holding an unauthorized conversation with a colleague. It's enough to make you scream.

## CHAPTER TWENTY-THREE

# NOVEMBER 25, 1996—
# PSYCHOLOGICAL WARFARE

And what a week it was, folks. I mean, I got the phone call from the EEOC (Equal Employment Opportunity Commission) last week, and then I finally got their complaint form in the mail. I set it aside with the other stuff. Funny thing about those complaint forms, I mean, here is a formal branch of the United States Government, and the forms they send out are barely legible. They look like badly smeared copies of copies of copies. No space to fit anything, and don't they know nobody writes in pen and ink anymore? The quill went out with the computer. Anyway, I set the form aside, having other things on my mind. My complaint to them about the way I was being treated at work would have to wait.

Friday was a professional development day, and the personnel director had me scheduled for testing two kids. Trouble is, kids don't come to school on professional development days. I e-mailed him to find out if I was still to report to the two schools in question. Thursday I got word to test those kids December 3, though still nothing about where I was supposed to go or whether I was allowed to attend the personnel director's staff meeting. With someone else trying to set a complete schedule for me, a professional schedule with a thousand things to do is like someone writing a script for driving your car from your house to town with all the turns and stops and possibilities with changing dynamics coming at you from all directions. I figured I would play it safe and assume it was another "report-writing day." A day I could just stay in my office and…write reports. Turns out I got to sit in on seven hours of conflict resolution training. Somewhat irrelevant, but still it was nice feeling part of the middle school staff. Made the mistake of checking my e-mail and found this question from the personnel director, my boss and master, about some kid I was supposed to test. Trouble is I never heard of him, and ran around in a panic trying to figure out if I'd "screwed up again" and would be reprimanded for the eighth time in less than a year. This was beginning to constitute psychological warfare, with pressure as intense as it gets. Under it you better not make mistakes, but you do simply because of the pressure. Add to that the crazy schedule someone else sets for you with mistakes built in, last-minute corrections, and last-minute notice, and complete lack of flexibility, "Don't do anything without checking with us first." It's cruel, even sadistic. How do these people sleep at night? Between the personnel director shouting commands and the special education supervisor calling the plays from the sideline along with the principal from the vocational school, not to mention the man behind the curtain, the superintendent redrawing the play book on a daily basis, it's a wonder I haven't run away screaming. I begin to understand how some men under similar circumstances resort to violence. Go postal. The pressure is intense, beyond intense.

In addition to this test-on-demand stuff, I have a counseling rotation at the elementary school. You'd think I'd be happy getting back to my old home base and getting to work with kids again. But wait till you hear who I got to counsel: several kids from the SED (seriously emotionally disturbed)

## November 25, 1996 — Psychological Warfare

class. That was fine, I got along great with my boys, read them stories, drew pictures, worked on getting along with each other. It was other two groups that challenged the imagination. I was required to counsel several kids in the autistic class. You know...kids who are nonverbal and don't even make eye contact. These were "counseling" subjects. I ended up pushing cars back and forth and bouncing them up and down on this big rubber ball. They like the movement and the physical contact, though like small children they sort of throw themselves into it with no thought to safety; they trust you to "save" them, and I had to be ever vigilant. That's all I'd need, to have some kid bounce off the ball and break an arm. They'd have me up on child abuse charges. But the kids liked the play and the teacher felt it was good exercise for them (and me). It was kind of fun making contact with kids who usually treat adults as objects. Once again they threw me in the proverbial briar patch and I made the most out of it.

It was the last group that was by far the most challenging to counsel. The severe and profoundly mentally disabled class. Kids with IQs 25 and below. Nonambulatory, nonverbal, and nonresponsive. I would talk to some, play music or car sounds for others, and played catch with another. This one young man was sixteen, in diapers, and loved to throw things. Hand him a toy...he'd throw it. A book...he'd throw it. A ball...he'd throw it, and with deadly accuracy. Aha! Trained to be flexible, I used this to my advantage. We'd go in his room and I'd throw things to him, and he'd throw them back. He'd laugh and drool and off we'd go for thirty minutes. I'd throw, he'd throw, and he was a pretty good catcher. I figured, heck, if they wanted to pay me $30 an hour to play catch with a sixteen-year-old disabled student, that'd be fine with me. I'd keep him entertained and help his teachers out at the same time. I made the best of yet another difficult situation. Sometimes I felt like a leper, at other times like the phoenix. No matter how badly the superintendent burned me, I'd rise from the ashes again. Like a burr in his saddle or a booger stuck between his tiny little fingers, I was tough to get rid of.

## Dirty Tricks Continue

I checked in with my personal attorney on Thursday. Seems the board's hired gun (attorney) wrote the state board of education a letter withdrawing my appeal of the reassignment. He indicated that the matter had been "fully settled and resolved." Trouble is that wasn't his place to do that, especially since I had instructed my attorney to hold it open until we had something in writing. We were going on three weeks since the "settlement" with no word from my union attorney, and all I heard from my teacher association representative was that they had received a copy of the written agreement and that the union lawyer sent it back to the board's attorney. The wording in the settlement agreement was "too offensive," according to my rep. By law their attorney had to send a copy to my personal attorney. When she saw this letter, she called him. We were *not* withdrawing the appeal until we had a settlement in hand, she said. "Sorry, I'll retract it. Didn't you get a copy (of the agreement) yet? I sent it to the union lawyer two weeks ago." "No." So he sends her a copy of the agreement and the "laudatory letter." I could see why the union attorney didn't send it to me. The laudatory letter was so robotic as to be laughable. Here was what was supposed to be a complimentary letter about my strengths and my positive contributions to the county over the eight years I was employed there. It was a letter that would enable me to move on to another position elsewhere without all the recriminations of the last two years. It was part of the settlement agreement, and they sent a form letter instead of the genuine, complimentary, laudatory letter we had agreed they would write on my behalf. Here is what they came up with:

## "To Whom It May Concern,

"This is a letter of recommendation for Mr. Frank Matthews. Mr. Matthews has served as a certified school psychologist in the county's Public schools since the 1988-'89 school year.

November 25, 1996 — Psychological Warfare

"During this time Mr. Matthews has shown a strong understanding of the psychological testing process. In testing situations he has consistently been able to form productive rapport with individual students. His testing results are useful in determining the proper educational programs for students.

"Mr. Matthews has effective communication skills. He is articulate and has demonstrated excellent skills as a writer and as a speaker. He has also demonstrated a work ethic that includes good attendance and a willingness to put in the time necessary to complete his assigned duties.

"Mr. Matthews has been an active member of the community. He has served as the president of the local County Council of PTAs. In that capacity he was active in helping local PTAs work with schools for the benefit of students. He also served as president of the local County Teachers Association. In that role he was instrumental in helping reach a mutually beneficial negotiated agreement.

"For the above stated reasons, I feel that Mr. Matthews could be an effective addition to any school system as a school psychologist."

Very bland and so generic that it would apply to almost any school psychologist with a pulse. Commendation? Hardly. It would raise more questions than it answered.

Even more upsetting was the settlement agreement. The document we wrote up to avoid the hearing with all my witnesses was fine except for one thing. Every clause ended with "at the sole discretion of the superintendent." The man who wants me not only out of a job but my career would only sign the settlement agreement if he had the final say on my: 1) first-class status, 2) job responsibilities, 3) recommendations, and 4) termination. And oh, by the way, I was to drop any and all rights to appeal, sue, complain, or even talk with parents, agencies, politicians, or the press about the events over the last two years. I was to go away, quietly, while they or he could reduce my pay and job status, my job description, the recommendations that would follow me to my next job, and, yes, he even reserved the right to fire me rather than allow me the option to resign. I was to trust this man who had made my life, my daughter's life, my family's life, a living hell for the last two years. I don't think so.

## The Best Defense...

After agreeing to a cease-fire, I get a harshly worded reprimand for holding a door open. The personnel director is still handing out crazy schedules and questioning me on who I tested when. Then who do I bump into last Thursday but the superintendent himself. He tried to pass me by without acknowledging me, then stopped in his inimitable way to let me know, "Gee, I'd really like to grant your daughter the leave for second semester, but I don't know if I can. I don't know if it's legal." I mean, here is this son of a bitch who breaks every damn law he can and wields so much power he can just say, "Sue me, I'm part of the good ol' boy network," and then says he can't give my daughter permission to graduate early to leave to go to junior college. I asked him about dual enrollment; didn't this cover her at both locations? Oh no. "That's just for credit purpose, not attendance. But if there were any way I could do it I would. I just don't want to establish a dangerous precedent." And so Sarah is stuck in the rear again.

## Sarah's Next Surprise

This started things crashing for Sarah. There was nothing she wanted more than to be done with school. Just thinking about having to stay at that high school seven more months was too much. Then Sarah's SAT scores came in: 570. "Verbal or math?" Both. Yup. That's right folks, *combined*. She answered so many questions *wrong* on one section that she actually had a negative score. I tried to be calm, but it was obvious she didn't apply herself or follow the basic rule to only answer questions you are sure of, not to guess. I pointed this out. She

## November 25, 1996 — Psychological Warfare

argued (so what else is new?) that she *didn't* answer every question. I pulled out the test response sheet and pointed out the "*5 Right, 30 Wrong, 1 Passed*," and suggested that this demonstrated my point. I did this in a positive way — that she wasn't dumb as an ox, she just didn't know how to take the test. Next time she would do better (How could you do worse?) Oh, that high school really prepared her for college.

Sarah wanted to go see her brother Andrew in College Park, but we felt she didn't need to be involved with the college scene as of yet, so we said no. To give her some other treat, she was allowed to attend a slumber party at her friend Danielle's on Saturday. To be honest, I thought they were coming here, but it turned out she wanted to go there, and I felt I was being coerced, but went along with it. "Have Danielle's dad call," I told her, which he did. She came back Friday and bopped around with another acquaintance, this little fifteen-year-old gal pal, Judy, and then asked if she could stay over at her house Friday night. I said no. One night is enough. Mom and Sarah both felt that I had agreed to *something special*, and Sarah stood four feet away from me saying, "You said I couldn't go see Andrew, so I could do something special. Why can't I stay over?" She knew she had Mom in her corner, and she was well-practiced in separating us. So I gave in (as usual) with the usual requirement of *parent to parent*. This was to make sure she had adult supervision. Well, she complained, and I quickly pointed out that this was what compromise was all about. I didn't want her to go, she didn't want to have Judy's dad call, so...you get to go, and I get my call. She agreed and walked out the door. That was the last time I would see Sarah for a very long time. When she failed to call in, Mom called Judy's for the now-not-so-unexpected, "I thought Judy was staying at your house tonight.?" Judy's dad is a police officer, so you can imagine how pleased he was with his fifteen-year-old out who knows where with our eighteen-year-old.

If there is a reason, a justification, for my strict and consistent positions, my discipline, it was because I did not trust Sarah, and knew she could not trust her own judgment in many cases. Teenage substance abusers need structure they cannot provide themselves with. At any rate, all the while Sarah stood there whining about not getting to see Andrew at the university, and she was asking, "Why can't I stay at Judy's?" Sarah was planning on seeing Andrew at College Park. And not just to talk to her brother, but to attend a party at a mutual friend, Cosmo's. That girl can lie, and despite Dad's radar, she got to go anyway. Who feels like a fool now? Mom figured she would be back in time to go to her SAT prep class Saturday and then home by twelve thirty Saturday afternoon. Well, she didn't make it. She didn't make it to class, or make it home by twelve thirty. So here we are waiting and wondering, knowing she got us again. Knowing she was pulling all of this stuff behind the wheel of my truck, we resorted to more forceful action. We called Andrew's machine, threatening to have the police pick her up for taking my truck without permission. My patience was done. For your information, *it's unauthorized use of a motor vehicle if someone takes it without permission or doesn't have it back in time. Police can seize the vehicle and tow it back to the owner. Juvenile referral or criminal charges, depending on age.* Sarah finally responded by calling to tell us the truck never left town. She stashed it at the local supermarket and rode across the bridge with friends. This is the same truck, my truck, that she smashed up when she had her second rear-end collision. She didn't want to drive the wreck, so she left it in town. We told her she was well past curfew and needed to find a ride and get home ASAP. We'd discuss the situation when she got home.

## Consequences

We figured after consultation with Dr. Mom that losing a level for this was not enough. It was all the way down to Level 1, no privileges, and working her way back up. When she called at five forty Saturday night in response to our threats to have her arrested if she did not return my truck, she of course said

## November 25, 1996 — Psychological Warfare

she didn't have the truck. Well, we said she still needed to get home. Caroline had given her a seven thirty deadline, but Sarah informed her that she wasn't coming home Saturday night. "You don't understand! I need a break!" She didn't want to talk to her stepfather either (that's me). First time in fifteen years I'd ever heard that one from her. Put aside the money ($25,000) that's been spent dragging her hind end out of this mess. And forget the hell I've been put through at work over this. And forget all of the friends we've lost, and the fact that we will probably have to sell our house and relocate and find jobs elsewhere. Forget all that. This gal has been the apple of my eye since she was three years old, my reason for doing it all. My sunshine. And now she's here throwing it all right back at me. "Thanks, man, but you're not my real dad." (As though he would have done better.) He never even bought them a freaking loaf of bread.

I got on the phone and calmly, quietly gave her a choice. In a soft voice I said this: "Your mom said seven thirty was your deadline. It's now five forty. That gives you twenty minutes to think about what you're going to do, and another ninety minutes to get across the bridge to our home. It's your choice. If you come home we won't yell; in fact, you can have a twenty-four-hour cooling-off period before we even talk about it. Then we'll involve Dr. Mom and the team to decide how we're to handle this." "I'm not coming home tonight," she said. "I need a break" I repeated, "Listen, you need to come home. You lied about where you were going last night, you went where you weren't supposed to go, and you are way past curfew. You need to get home and deal with your consequences." She repeated, "I'm not coming home tonight." "If that is your decision, then I need to explain our position," I told her. "If you choose not to come home tonight, you won't be allowed to come home. The doors will be locked and you will be on your own. Do you understand that? Do you have any questions?" All I heard was silence, and a repeat of "I'm not coming home tonight." At seven forty-five (fifteen minutes grace) the house was locked and the lights were turned off. Her clothes and personal belongings still in her room. She had no money, no clothes, no car, and now, no home. Mom was hopeful she would be back within a week. I wasn't holding my breath. So I continued to field the 504 calls from school about the wonderful things they are doing for her. And I was asked to help her with her English paper due December 2. And I hung my head in embarrassment, for the only team member that counts, Sarah, had left the team. Neither Caroline nor I would see or hear from Sarah, though we did find out she was staying with friends in the next town.

## November 26, 1996, The Settlement Agreement Fades

I am still reacting to the change in wording in our settlement agreement with the board. Everything was fine with the exception of the final disclaimer, "at the sole discretion of the superintendent." As Dick, my union rep, said yesterday, he usually puts a few "tweakers" in when he writes a settlement, but takes most of them out before he mails it to the party. "This is four pages of tweakers!" he says. I want to withdraw my offer to settle, but Dick says we can't. We settled already with the conference, and the drafting of the paperwork is just a formality. Does this mean they can shove anything they want down my throat? "No. The superintendent won't get everything his way." But this remains a concern to me.

The superintendent's attorney originally agreed to withdraw his letter and put the state board appeal on hold, then called back and said he was letting it stand; after all, we made the agreement in conference to "drop all appeals," so what's changed? Ignore the fact that he wrote the letter to the state board of education as the local board's attorney when he is not (he is the administrators' attorney). He can't represent the plaintiff (the superintendent and his fellow administrators) and the judge (the local school board who heard the superintendent's case). This could be considered an inherent conflict of interest. So what else is new for this guy? My attorney was upset and would call him on this and the fact that until we have a document in writing we all can agree on, all bets are off and the state board can keep us on the agenda.

My fear is that since the superintendent's attorney contacted the state board to withdraw the complaint, he might also do this with OCR as well. The state investigatory agencies have already done their thing, and even if I withdraw my complaint, they are still bound by federal law to make sure the disabled kids in the county schools are receiving appropriate services. My other fear is that this deal has effectively silenced me, cut me off from federal agencies, state agencies, the press, parents, the courts, and anyone else who might listen. I have given up my rights across a broad spectrum of agencies, and what have I received in return? I still don't have my first-class status or my old responsibilities back, and all I really get is a mediocre recommendation after they kick my behind out of here. I have to sell my house, pack up and move, find a job elsewhere, and they're gonna be real gentlemen and say nice things about me? As though I deserve less? And after looking at the agreement, the personnel director's robotic letter that was supposed to be "laudatory" and the agreement to stick to the content of the letter if asked for information about me, it sure doesn't sound like I want them speaking on my behalf at all. Sounds like they are not only out to get rid of me, but to ruin my career as well.

After talking with my attorney on Thursday and then reading the superintendent's attorney's brief Saturday, I was not in a settling mood. Especially after Sarah pulled her latest and most significant act of sabotage—running away from home. I blame the superintendent in part for this latest hassle. It's Sarah's fault, but it's kinda like she may have been the one who brought the wolf to the door, but you have to blame the wolf, too. And maybe, just maybe, if they had worked with us two years ago Sarah would be further along than she is now. They made it hard on us, we made it hard on Sarah. The superintendent's latest shot—his refusal to allow Sarah to finish her high school requirements at the junior college—was what drove her over the edge last weekend.

I pulled myself out of another depression by completing my referral to the EEOC (Equal Employment Opportunity Commission). At least it makes me feel like I'm doing something. I don't feel so powerless. And the section on harassment for reprisals really got my attention. I probably would have waited under ordinary circumstances, but my union attorney hasn't contacted me since the hearing twenty days ago, and after dealing with the games the board's attorney was playing, I called my personal attorney, who promised to call me back in thirty minutes. It took three hours and I was already out of the house. She then promised to call me back before noon, and I'd still be waiting for that call. It never came. So, feeling lonely and isolated once again, with the distinct feeling that I was NOT getting good representation, I took matters into my own hands and sent the EEOC complaint off myself.

Call it rationalization if you will, but I sincerely was pleased and relaxed after the settlement conference November 4. Then, when I received reprimand number seven, four days later, I felt sick to my stomach. That was dirty pool. It was a sucker punch. And then to read the agreement itself, with no hint of bargaining, or compromise, much less good faith, it was too much. I was hearing nothing from either one of my attorneys. I considered the EEOC complaint to be my last attempt for justice. If the settlement falls apart I may need this as backup. If it holds together, then I can always withdraw it. If my attorneys find out and complain, I can say it was a follow-up on the original referral back during the summer. At that time I was more concerned about OCR and the complaint based on harassment based on a disability, and let the EEOC thing slide. Come to find out OCR has to wait until all the other "pendencies" had run their course. We were a half step from this with the hearing then got "sidetracked" by the attorneys. I just hope it turns out like they portray it. I hope they haven't sold my civil rights to the highest bidder in return for a few crumbs. It might give them peace of mind, but it sure doesn't make my life any easier if they're taken away all of my best defenses—agencies and politicians I have curried for months now in return for a swift kick in the seat of the pants. My attorneys assure me that's not the case, but I guess I'm still a bit leery.

## Sarah Blows It Again

Sabotage. Defined in *The American College Dictionary* as "any malicious attack on or undermining of a cause." It's a term Dr. Mom used when a person intentionally disrupted a process, often one that might favor him or her in the long run. Sarah does it every time she breaks a rule, not caring about the consequences until she has to pay up on them. Staying out past curfew, going somewhere she isn't supposed to go, smoking cigarettes, piercing her tongue, lying about where she's going, crashing our vehicles. I thought back to her first and most significant act, taking the alleged drugs at school. Was this the ultimate act of sabotage, and did I feed into it by waging this fight all these years? Should I have ignored it and just waited to see if they discovered her and made her face the consequences? What if they didn't come after her? Would I be enabling if I let her slip away? Was I enabling her by turning her in only to turn around and trying to get her out? By making excuses for her—"she's learning disabled"? To be honest, I stood up for her not because she allegedly took drugs at school, but because she was willing to stand up and admit it and seek help. The school system was taking information she brought forward and using it against her, to punish her, instead of helping her, and that was just wrong. And she is a kid with problems. She is learning disabled and more than a little ADHD with ODD (oppositional and defiant) thrown in. My ultimate goal was to clear her record because she tried to right her wrong, and to encourage others to come forward who were stuck in the quagmire of drugs.

## December 3, 1996

Another glorious day. We figured that after a week "on the road," Sarah would run out of money, clean underwear, food, and friends. Ten days later and she is still out, though she is changing plans faster than anyone can keep up with. Her brother was in a panic yesterday when she didn't show up for two days, having left a party with some guy named Dave. He was intent on finding her. Mom was ready to turn her in to missing persons, but I envisioned the cops finding her shacked up with some guy and her telling them in no uncertain terms that she was "eighteen and had no intention of going home to those assholes," a.k.a. her parents. When Andrew did find her, he still wasn't convinced that home was the best place for her, so he was still playing the game of them (Andrew and Sarah) versus us. "She doesn't want to come home. She's afraid." Andrew was convinced that we were physically assaulting her. "I've heard her cries of agony," he exclaimed. Welcome to the torture chamber. But then he is a loyal brother who has reason to be angry with us, too, since we interfered with his lifestyle. Since he hasn't been home for months, I take it she cried over the phone to him or he has some pretty spectacular hearing acuity, hearing cries of agony seventy miles away. He did call and let us know that her friend Lexi found Sarah, and that Sarah's plans were to stop by Cosmo's and then Andrew's dorm to get her stuff, then she was heading back to town, not to come home, but to stay with her friend Liz and get back in school. This was good news for us. Mom was hoping she would call or stop by, but I wasn't as optimistic. At least she was "found" and not on a morgue slab. This wouldn't be the last time we (Caroline) filed missing person's reports on Sarah. The fact that she a) left the party with this guy Dave she just met whose phone was disconnected and b) that she didn't have the courtesy to let her "friends" or brother know where she was for two days gives you an idea of how she exercises good judgment and why she can't keep friends. I think she wore her welcome out over in College Park, and that's why she is returning to the shore.

November 25, 1996 — Psychological Warfare

## Any Port In A Storm

This morning I saw Sarah's friend Liz and asked her about Sarah. She confirmed that Sarah was supposed to be coming back to town, and staying with her. She had spoken with her on the phone Monday night. Trouble is, she never showed. Several hours later I was filling in the guidance counselor at Sarah's high school when guess who shows up? Sarah. I walked out of the office right past her, treating her like a piece of furniture. Later the counselor came up and informed me that since Sarah was eighteen, he had no control, and she was transferring out of Northern High, over to the Western Shore. No school was mentioned, much less residency requirements. So, since last night, she has changed plans and is *not* staying over here, but on the Western Shore, though she had no place to live as far as I knew. How credits will transfer or how they will treat her expulsion and all is beyond me, but if she can get a diploma from a Western Shore school, I will be pleasantly surprised. I hope she brings her 504 plan with her. It stretches the imagination....

## December 5, 1996, Reaching Out

Whoooooooo ah! Another day gone by, and boy was it easier to swallow. I took a "sick day" and crammed it full of appointments with doctors and therapists. I needed it. Later in the day I met with an administrator in a neighboring county. I called him two years ago when all this mess started to check and see about getting Sarah into school over there. He explained why he couldn't, but put me on to their night school program for her. This earned Sarah six credits and kept her busy during her expulsion. He also expressed interest in her legal case and asked that I keep him informed, which I have from time to time. The most recent call I made was a few weeks ago to find out about protections for me. I told him about my current job status and how I was in the squeeze. He asked me if I was looking, and I said yes. I never would have figured a neighboring county; figured it was too close to this one. The local superintendent's reach was far. Apparently not that far, or maybe not that effective. He told me to come over and meet with him, that from time to time things came up and maybe he could help me out. We chatted for fifty minutes and seemed to hit it off pretty well. A real likable guy. By the end of the conversation I felt he had a good sense of who I was as a person. We both lived up to our "phone personas," and my sense of it was if there was a job open in my area of certification, he'd recommend me for it. He'd even put in a good word to the superintendent (who happened to come from West Virginia). Apparently our local superintendent's reputation was well known, so it provided a measure of credibility for what I told him about my situation. He knew that what was being done to me had more to do with the "political situation" than my lack of competence or professionalism. Thank God! I grabbed an application on my way out and felt good for the first time in a long time. From there I called Caroline, who was home sick, and she confirmed my eleven o'clock appointment at Dr. Mom's. After Sarah pulled this last trick, I hit bottom and needed to bounce it off somebody, and Dr. Mom was top on the list.

I still had thirty minutes, so I popped over to see my attorney, whose office was down the block from Dr. Mom's. My intention was to stick my head in the door to set a time for an afternoon meeting, but she was free, so I went in. We talked about my case. I expressed frustration that a strong case was going nowhere, and this drew a strong reaction from Liz. "You *don't* have a strong case. You have *no case*. The cards are stacked against you, there is no case law there to protect you, and the case is not unique enough to establish new law. If you were a member of a protected class (black, female, disabled), maybe. But you're not. You're white, male, and in pretty good health. And your record is not spotless." (No, I guess chewing gum and talking with your hands are serious infractions, not to mention changing the name of a report section. The

## November 25, 1996 — Psychological Warfare

fact is, over a twenty-plus-year career I never had any legitimate infractions, just petty nonsense trumped up by a series of sycophants who were challenged by my leadership.) She continued, "I'll show you the cases that are similar, and when an employee has a blemished record, the board can point to it and rule out your charges of retaliation. And when your union attorney showed me the state law where *personality* is a factor in employment cases, I knew we were dead in the water. It's wrong. Personality should not be in the law, but it is."

So I guess being a forceful (strong) advocate for students largely goes unrewarded; in fact, it is soundly discouraged. Do your job and keep your mouth shut like everybody else seems to be the way to go. Trouble is, I'm one of the few school psychologists who not only reads my code of ethics, but take it to heart, especially that one line that reads: "School psychologists are expected to speak up even when it is difficult to do so." She went on about all the time she has spent on this case over the last two months, and how my bill was approaching $3,000. I almost fell off my chair. Now granted, November 4 was the hearing, so she had a lot of preparation and conference time, and I was glad she was part of it. But I ended up paying $5,000 for two things: research into my rights to pursue civil action against these folks, and an advocate, someone I could trust, involved in my second-class hearing. Count one came up empty, I have no case, and her review of my record wasn't as positive as I thought it would be. She still hasn't talked with another attorney I referred her to, but I can tell from her attitude that she will not give him an argument convincing enough to warrant a positive response from him either. So unless I seek a second (third?) opinion (where do I get the money?), I'm stuck with her and no case. Even though every fiber of my being says that what they did to me, and are doing, has nothing whatsoever to do with my professional competence, or my personality and everything to do with my actions as a parent and advocate for my child. None of this came up before I took them to task over my daughter.

Writing me off as having a personality problem...that isn't fair either. I am tough, firm, and admittedly I have little tolerance for people who don't do their jobs, but I have a lot of friends and, more important, the respect of the people who count: the teachers and guidance counselors and parents. I am from New York, where folks are assertive to the max and go by the credo "Don't take any shit off anyone." To write me off because I sometimes piss people off without looking at the particulars for each case is simply not fair. I really thought my own attorney would give me a fair shake, and now it seems she is being swayed somehow by the union attorney and getting discouraged, rather than the other way around, with my personal attorney acting as my advocate and encouraging the union rep. And I'm paying good money for this service. To listen to my $5,000 attorney tell me my bad record and lousy personality are losing this case for me is insult on injury. You'd think that five grand would at least gain me some affirmation from my own attorney. And even if I was a total jerk, which I am not, there were ways of getting rid of people who don't do their jobs, and yet here I am eight years later doing a fine job, earning people's respect and causing no problems for the longest time until Sarah...then bam! And even more importantly, they tried to get me without following their own procedures, a cardinal sin in the law. Even ax murderers get off if procedures aren't followed. I have documents (they don't) and witnesses, and I still feel if I could get it to a jury, we'd prevail... but she won't take it. "I have to be careful they don't apply sanctions against me!" Everybody is afraid it seems, except me. And maybe that's because I'm stupid or something. In my mind I am convinced my case is strong and worth pursuing, but I can't do it alone. If I have nothing left, I have this, the strength of my convictions. Knowing I am right is my only claim to sanity.

I pointed out to her that the board attorney's eagerness to settle was a classic sign they knew they would lose eventually. I suggested that conventional wisdom supported this. I pointed out that all of the "exclusions" he included in the

## November 25, 1996 — Psychological Warfare

"settlement" addressed his fears, especially no contact with the press, parents, or members of the general public, and an admission of "no harm" preventing me from ever suing any of the board employees! I mean, hello! Does this sound like he's convinced we don't have any legal challenges? My attorney's take: "they just want you to stop harassing them." Excuse me? Me to stop harassing *them*? It sure felt like it was the other way around. "No, all of the actions you have taken have come up empty. They just see you as a pain in the ass and want you off their backs, period." Who is on whose back? I just wanted to go back to doing my job. I was only defending my daughter and now my career. And I was tired of fighting. I wanted peace so bad I could taste it, but on terms I could live with. Who started this fight in the first place?

So I guess that all of these complaints (fighting my demotion to second class and my reassignment, and contacting OCR, EEOC, MSDE, and OSERS), all of whom were filed AFTER they started putting the pressure on me, are considered groundless, and *harassment* on my part? What about the findings from the state? What about whistleblower protection? I've worked with these folks for too many years and been party to some outrageous acts that violate both the spirit and letter of the public laws protecting the disabled. I had names and dates and real events, and if the investigations came up empty, it wasn't because there was nothing to find. And most of their investigations were cursory. They would simply ask the accused if they did it and to send them explanations. They never sent representatives down to check on the charges I leveled, and when they did the state department representatives only talked with the supervisors, not the teachers or special education staff or parents. And if they did talk with anyone in a position to know, it was with their supervisors present and subject to intimidation. No one was given "immunity" or even the privacy to tell what they knew without fear of repercussions similar to my own. I mean, they made a grand example of me, and who in their right mind would say anything? People who knew me and my knowledge and experience of the law and saw what happened to me knew it could happen to anyone.

Note: In a back-to-the-future moment, in the year 2008, federal law provided protections to individuals who brought complaints similar to mine under three provisions: 1) whistleblower protection—retaliating against an employee who raises legitimate complaints; 2) age discrimination—protection from action directed against someone fifty-five or older who also happens to be at the high end of the salary range; and 3) the Americans with Disabilities Act (ADA), which protects not only individuals with disabilities, but those who act on their behalf. But this was 1996.

I have done more soul searching than any man I know. I am one who is greatly affected by what others think of me. As my former superintendent in West Virginia once said, there are two types of employees: shit givers and shit takers. Shit takers take the shit and let it roll right off their backs; very little affects them, and it's tough to change their behaviors. Shit givers give a shit and get nervous and anxious when the boss calls them in, they take to heart anything that is said, and they are always willing to make adjustments to change their behavior to make the boss happy. He readily acknowledged that I was a shit giver. I worried myself to death when my boss wasn't happy. I made every effort to do what was expected me. This is why I was up on the rules and regulations. This is why I went back to the principal at Blueville to apologize and try to work things out. This is why I went back to the other principal time after time to figure out just what went wrong (what I did wrong). I cared, I tried to do the right thing, but in this county where the right thing is wrong, I was odd man out. The only trouble with me wasn't that I was the lone honest man, it was that I was so outspoken about it. I couldn't leave well enough alone. When I was told to lie and sit quietly because others did so, I just couldn't. And for this I was an outcast? Is this what is wrong with education today? Everybody looks the other way? Does being a "team player" mean you have to cheat, or shut up about it when they do? I was trying so hard to walk that line and listen to others about what I should do and think, including my own attorney — after all I paid good money for her advice, why not follow it? But when I knew in my head and in my heart of hearts that I was right and they (even she) was wrong, I simply could not accept it. I couldn't. Not stubborn, just committed.

I wanted a number of things on the record, the documents they dumped on me April 9, for one. Not only were all of them completely without substance, but they were gathered illegally and not in conformance with the negotiated agreement. But we passed by this for settlement. My sense of it: negotiated agreements aren't worth the paper they are printed on without binding arbitration. Only state law. And so it really doesn't matter that they failed to follow procedure. And it really doesn't matter that they have no "legal documentation" about my "personality problems." The superintendent can drag up any letter, supported or not, and use it against you. Even though it was never in my personnel file and couldn't legally be placed there. As well, the superintendent could make false statements about me with no supporting documentation and these would stand as well. Their case, built on a house of cards, would stand, and I would be history. And my own attorneys would support me only if I settled and took this deal now, while I still had the chance…then they would probably terminate me and there would be nothing… they…could…do. So I decided to settle. What choice did I have? They'd beaten me in the due process hearing for Sarah, they'd beaten me on the civil case I brought against them on Sarah's behalf, and they beat me on all the complaints registered with state and federal agencies. Guess I should have expected they would beat me on their last mission to destroy me personally and professionally. My choices were limited. I had to settle, my fight was over. The only thing I was clear about was the terms of the settlement had to change. A month had passed with no written agreement, and the board's attorney was out trying to cancel the few lifelines I had left (my appeals to the state and federal agencies). And what do I get out of this great deal!? I get to leave my job and they'll give me a good recommendation. Period. But they reserve the right to fire me if I don't improve, and they base this on this performance improvement plan that is diabolical in its inception. *Follow the rules*, which they change at every turn, and *treat administrators with respect* when they harass and insult me, and contact your *principal for directions* and then write me up for asking a question about the location of a piece of office furniture: "Is my old file cabinet in there?" It simply wasn't fair or just. It was a formula for disaster with too many traps ready to be sprung.

My attorney wrote a letter to the state board asking them to hold my appeal, but she omitted any language about the board's attorney. You see, he really wasn't their attorney. Another local barrister was. This hired gun from Baltimore, who they brought in later on, represented the administrators (at taxpayers' expense). But he also took on the role of board attorney though it could be considered a conflict of interest. She left out the section about his needing to remove himself from the case due to inherent conflicts. I mean, this guy was there for Sarah's hearing before the board, and then at all the due process hearings, and then again at my own hearings. The letter she wrote was good, but it wasn't strong enough. More importantly, she still hadn't grasped the big picture, that the superintendent was behind it all. And she can't begin to see things from my perspective. To be sure, I am too close to the case (emotional/too subjective), but I know it inside and out. If I am one thing beyond obsessive, it's compulsive, and I thought things were cut and dried. I had laid the conspiracy out, and if she couldn't see it.... She is still convinced that the three principals wrote me up on their own without any guidance or pressure from the superintendent. She couldn't be more wrong. My own private attorney still figures the Baltimore attorney is doing all this on his own, and then wonders why he included all this garbage in the settlement agreement. And wonders why he was at first willing to withdraw his letter to the state board and then later in the day changed

## November 25, 1996 — Psychological Warfare

his mind. Sounds to me like the superintendent overruled him. And after a month with no response from my union attorney, my attorney contacted the Baltimore attorney to give him a ten-day clock, and he calls her in a panic: "We've got a board meeting tomorrow. If we need to reschedule a hearing, then I need to know what's going on." But he doesn't want a hearing, he still wants to settle. I personally don't think either the superintendent or his attorney want a hearing, they just want to try to shove this settlement down my throat. And my union rep sits in silence.

At least we are on the record that I will not accept any agreement unless it has my blessing, with my signature on it. After my union lawyer's move last summer, allowing an agreement to go through I never accepted, I don't trust her completely. I will allow her to bargain in my behalf, but not agree or accept on my behalf. So right now, as it stands, my attorney will contact my union attorney to determine the status of the settlement. She will review with her my latest concerns as well as what I expect to get out of this settlement. And we go from there. In the meantime, I'm not afraid to let people know I am not happy with their new tactics, that the cease-fire was broken by them, and though we tentatively reached an agreement to settle the dispute, the document they wrote up afterwards was not worth the paper it was written on. And in my inimitable way I let folks know in no uncertain terms what I thought of it. When the superintendent got wind of it, he wanted my head. He wanted to fire me. Oh God, what did Frank say now?

I finally get a call from my union attorney. "I understand you rejected their settlement offer. Is that true?" I admit to that being the case. "I also understand that you made a rather unprofessional, even obscene remark about it." "Oh yeah? What did they tell you?" "They said that you wouldn't use the settlement agreement for toilet paper! Did you say that?" "No." " Then what did you tell them?" "I told them I wouldn't wipe my ass with it."

Of course my union attorney exploded and explained the pitfalls of my approach and how they were ready to fire me and how I should conduct myself in a more professional manner in the future. Yada yada yada. Desperate men take desperate measures, and I was not one to mince words. They didn't name me Frank for no good reason. I speak my mind and always will.

## Sarah's Future

Meanwhile, back at Ranchero 504 (remember Sarah has that 504 plan on file), my request to allow Sarah to slide OUT of North and IN to Chesapeake College in February, which had been sitting on the superintendent's desk since September, finally worked its way through the system for approval. Did Sarah's last act of desperation have anything to do with it? Or maybe Caroline's attack on the personnel director? Seems he made the mistake of poking his head in her office door right after Sarah moved out, and Caroline gave him an earful. She made it clear that if anything happened to her, she was holding the board responsible. Did they get scared that if something happened to Sarah they'd be liable? I mean, his last words to me on November 21 were, "Gee, I wish I could grant this, but it would be illegal and set a dangerous precedent." This word back to Sarah (staying in high school until June) followed by her abysmal SAT score, 570, and, well…I think this, coupled with the rest of life's stressors (how to pay for the $1,000 damage to dad's truck, and how to get into college and out of here, and will I even make it in college? And why am I even doing this for? And I'm sick of this stupid case and my part in it) were too much and she lit the fuse on yet another one of her bombs. This one blew up in all our faces…thanks, boys. Sarah moved out and her whereabouts were unknown.

November 25, 1996 — Psychological Warfare

# Dr. Mom And Me

Dr. Mom and I had a very productive conversation. She basically told me to get it out of my head that Caroline's lack of support for me, siding *against* me and *with* the kids, undermining me in the process, was the cause of our current problems. Keeping it in the brain meant it could escape during an argument. Things said in anger...actually I don't say things in anger I wouldn't say in frankness. I rarely lose control of my lips; it's usually my body that storms around slamming doors and tearing spark plug wires from cars I do not want leaving me behind. Last time this occurred it was almost funny. I went out, trouble is I couldn't find the damn spark plugs in this maze of wires and sensors. I cooled down pretty quick. I usually do. I actually felt stupid. I don't stay mad for long, as long as folks leave me alone anyway, I'm more like a rocket that shoots up into the sky, fizzles out, and falls harmlessly back to earth under the billowing folds of a parachute. Dr. Mom has given me some insights into what makes me angry: Caroline not only failing to support me when the kids screw up (like wrecking my cars), but taking their side against me. "Leave Sarah alone, she had a bad day, she didn't mean to run into the car in front of her, and she hasn't rear-ended anyone for over a month now, and the insurance company paid for that. They'll probably pay for this one, too, and she'll come up with the $1,500 to fix your truck, don't worry." Now, granted, this preceding segment was not only paraphrased, but exaggerated somewhat. Point is, when they are acting crazy, I have to be the sane one. Getting upset not only makes the situation worse, but it plays into their hands: "See, he *is* a maniac, just like I said." Cooler heads prevail.

The rule was this: two people cannot be angry at the same time, so if I recognize Caroline getting angry, then I cannot be. I have to remain cool. In fact, staying calm while someone else is acting in an irrational manner can be quite empowering. You watch as his or her face gets red and his or her eyes bulge and he or she flails about, getting even angrier because you are cool. Try it sometime.

## December 11, 1996, Damned If You Do… Anything

Today was an interesting day. Yesterday I had reports to write. However, the fact that three kids were sick last week, and I had all morning to write those I had on Friday, left only two lonely little reports to write Tuesday. So, I looked at the schedule and said to myself, *Self…you got lots of report writing days and room to squeeze a kid in for testing*. Why would I want to do extra work, you ask? Simple. Though this week is an easy breather, I am required to spend three days at Reston Elementary School, including six more kids to test and no days to write reports in my crowded schedule until after we get back from Christmas break two weeks later. Not a good idea. So…if I can test the Friday afternoon kid now, that will give me the whole afternoon to write reports before the Christmas break. Good planning. That's what competent professionals do. They schedule assessments leaving time to gather data and notes and enough tme to write a report or two while the facts and faces are still fresh in your mind. Too many kids, too many unwritten reports and they overlap and run together. Under this new schedule imposed from on high, I have no flexibility, I have to be creative to continue to do the professional job I am accumstomed to doing. I am required to provide a list of all the students by name who I plan to test, the day I plan to test them, and the date I complete the report on them.

    So I come into work Tuesday and guess what? I leave my briefcase with the last two evaluations inside at home. Great, now I can't write reports and I can't remember who I'm supposed to test next. Tyron was on my schedule, the one I had turned in to the boss, so I went to get the little guy. Trouble is he wasn't there! Now what? Easy, pick another to do today

November 25, 1996 — Psychological Warfare

and do Tyron tomorrow in that kid's place. No problem. What was that name...Siegler! So I snuck down the hall and got her, and snuck back up the hall and tested her. Whew. Now all I gots to do is sneak her back into her room and it'll be cool. No one will see me TESTING on a REPORT WRITING day. So I slip down to sixth grade with the little gal and face...an angry teacher. Bonnie Smyth. "I didn't know you had her. We had the adolescent state survey to complete." "Sorry, I had no idea," I apologized. "When I took her out of music no one told me anything about a survey. Is there anything I can do to help?" "No, I'll just have to see if she can do it second period." That's the thing about some people. Have to make a federal case out of nothing. And in my situation I don't need it. All Bonnie has to do is complain in front of the wrong persons (the building principal e.g. ) and it'll be, "What do you mean you were testing someone on Tuesday? That's not your testing day." And it will be *reprimand time* again. Also, I am now at ten o'clock in the morning with nothing to do, and if I ask to go get my briefcase, it will be a major case (no pun intended). Major infraction and demerits for failing to bring in required materials. Forget the fact that my schedule is so screwy I can't tell if I'm coming or going. Hmmm. I decide to take a risk. In the Volvo, I'm less conspicuous than my other vehicles, so I'll slide out at lunch, ten minutes home, grab the briefcase, and ten minutes back. They'll never miss me. And I do. Zip, zoom, zip, and with the exception of a near-miss head-on collision with the art teacher (going home to tend to a sick kid), I make it back to school undetected. Whew! I mean, really. I spend the rest of that afternoon writing reports.

## The Next Day

The building principal wants to observe me testing someone, so it would be better to pick the kid scheduled today rather than the one I'm trying to slip in. I had this nightmare of the kid I'm supposed to test being sick and I have to go get the one

I did yesterday and give her the whole test again (shhhhhh) in front of the principal. I ask her when she plans to observe me, first thing or ten o'clock, when I start the second one? "Oh, first thing." Great, and I head down to get Seneca. I try a couple of locations and then get the bad news. *He's been suspended.* Oh shit! With Siegler done and the only other kid on the list gone, what am I to do? The jig is up. I explain to the principal that the kid I planned to do was suspended, can I pull in another? *"What's wrong with Siegler? You have two on the list, don't you?"* Well…I did her yesterday. *"You'd better wait."* So I get to stand and then sit for twenty-five minutes waiting for her to do her rounds and then figure out how it is that I tested a kid the day before? My brain is reeling, but I have a solid explanation. With all the kids sick on my schedule I needed to move some kids around. I mean, this is so petty, so ridiculous. I mention Tyron. The principal pulls out her sheet, unrevised, and I breathe a sigh of relief. "You don't have him on yours. *He's at the high school,*" she says. "Not really," I respond, "that's John's error. He is one of yours and I can slip him in today and stay current with the schedule." *"Fine,"* she says, and I breathe another even bigger sigh of relief.

It's really crazy what I have to go through to sort through this stuff. Just to do my job, even things as simple as testing Kid A on Day B. Especially when they're sick and I have to have a requisition from on high to modify or alter my plans. It's as though they don't trust me to do my job. I've always done that, on time, completely, at 110 percent. Never a problem. This is their way of humiliating me. Demeaning me. Keep me on a tight leash as though I can't be trusted, be here on this day, test this kid, go here, write reports, back here, test, etc. It's their way to set me up for failure. It's nuts and a totally ineffective use of my time. I waste more of it doing this (writing in my diary for the big book) than anything else. They so badly want me to quit. They don't know me very well.

Funny thing is that the other psychologists don't seem much happier. They have to do my work since I can't— explaining test results to parents, setting up and attending

## November 25, 1996 — Psychological Warfare

placement meetings, filling out behavior checklists on my kids (I can't talk to teachers, after all). I also understand that despite all the grand press about all this time for the referring psychologists to expand their roles to attend SIT (school improvement teams) and SAT (student assistance teams — prereferral interventions), the power brokers (the guidance counselors) are now calling the shots as to who gets tested and who doesn't. Eighteen months ago I was trying to get on Blueville's team and five years ago Statesville's. The lead psychologist keeps maintaining it's a communication thing, but to me it's simple. It's a power and control issue. Who has it, who wants it? Small people with big egos making life-and-death decisions about small children, without the least bit of knowledge and understanding. Do they look at the child's medical folder? See if there were any problems like seizures? Nooooo. Do they review his grades and test scores and retentions and moves? Nooo. What *do* they consult other than the current teacher's frustrations and the guidance counselor's whims? Good question.

So the lead psychologist suggested they get the personnel director to the meeting. Yeah, right. This dog don't hunt. Like he's ever solved any of the other fifteen "longstanding unresolved issues" in the district. It seems that schools are still not making effective use of the psychologists, just relegating them to the role of psychometrist. They aren't happy (except maybe Bernie, 'cause that's all he knows how to do, test), and they want to tell someone about it and have something done. It's funny (ironic) that after I left, the power shifted, and the schools (principals, counselors, teachers) are deciding how screening should be done (who gets seen) and, even more, who gets tested and what tests to do. So, if a psychologist wants to try to put an intervention in place, they look at you as though you've grown two heads. "Whadyamean you're not gonna test? We already have done everything. Put the kid a) on medication, b) in special education, and c) refer him to somebody else to handle." Why, they are even trying to tell the most senior psychologist in my absence how to conduct her ever-precious behavioral programs. And whether I agree or disagree with her approach to ADHD, I'll defend her right to case manage students any way she feels is appropriate for her. She is worried about being rushed into "quick and dirty evaluations" that will miss something about the kid. She is worried that her name is on the bottom of the report. She is also worried that our pupil personnel handbook says that any suspected ADHD kids are to be referred to the 504 committee. This is not being done. The newest psychologist is concerned that they wanted him to rush through an evaluation on a kid, and when he reviewed the records he found out that there was a family history of seizures and the kid himself had them—wonderful. Because they are trying to keep me on a tight leash, I am totally unable to advocate for the other psychologists, and psychological services suffers as a direct result. Kids suffer.

The handwriting is on the wall. The superintendent couldn't care less about special education and the psychologists. The personnel director couldn't care less about anything he has to do something about. Even when I was on top, I was extremely frustrated, not only at the lack of competence of those below me, but at their unwillingness to become competent, to hear out someone who knew how to do the job. They continually put it into *Frank always has to have his way.* It became a struggle of egos when it only had to be common sense of doing something the *right* way, the way the federal government, state law, and local policy and procedures expect. But when you have no support or no enforcement from the top, and those on the bottom don't know a sack of shit from a pinup girl, than this can only be an exercise in frustration. When I was in my old job I built a rapport with colleagues by being consistent and doing it one way—the same way. If the powers that be wouldn't inform people, I would fill the vacuum. They respected me and it worked. Except for a few places where they wanted to hold on to the old ways. What would it be like going back? Can you ever go home again? With so much micromanagement going on, they won't let anybody make a decision without them and make the only rule *their* rule rather than the written understanding. It's time to leave, my friend, and go somewhere, anywhere but here.

Later that evening, Caroline says that Sarah called in. Apparently she wanted to come by and get her stuff. First thing Caroline told her was that she couldn't allow her to come by unless I was home. "So Dad gets to make all the decisions, huh?" Sarah asked, still trying to separate. Caroline straightened that out, saying that we both need to make the decisions. Good for Caroline (and Dr. Mom's sage advice). She also told Sarah that, as promised, we cleaned out her room and redid it. In fact, all of her stuff, all eight bags of it, was sent to Goodwill. What didn't was on its way to the landfill, having been dropped off in truckloads at the dump.

## Sarah Stops By

So Sarah arrived at the house. We set some ground rules about taking only clothes and leaving TVs and VCRs. Since we were allowing her back to get this stuff instead of dumping it, she would have to take it all. Caroline told her this as we sat around the table, and I repeated it while they were in the room. "Take what you want now, because we aren't storing anything for you. What's left is going out." This prompted her to ask about her couch, her wooden art project with my classic magazine glued all over it. "What do you expect me to do with this, cram it in the backseat of the car? Why can't you take it into West Virginia?" I mean, this kid is not thinking. Here we are talking about severing our familial ties, she's leaving home on bad terms, and she's asking us to move her furniture into West Virginia? Hate to say it, but I really enjoyed throwing that couch into the trash bin. Too bad she wasn't sitting on it at the time.

## So This Is Christmas?

The weeks between Thanksgiving and Christmas were charged with electricity. What was the status of my job? Would Andrew pass the term? Would he go to Florida with us? What was Sarah planning for Christmas? I was ready for a break, but as much as I wanted to go, just us, Caroline and I, I wanted to bring the family down as well. We talked about extending a Christmas amnesty. A last opportunity to go to Florida as a group. Sarah contacted us and we agreed to meet with her. We took her to dinner. She arrived with presents, a movie for Dad (*Stand By Me*) and a watch for mom. We'd already returned her gifts and really didn't feel badly that she was giving us something and we had nothing for her. Over the dinner table at the Greensboro Restaurant, we had pleasant conversation. We offered to take her to Florida; she declined. We would be taking Andrew. We dropped her off and went our separate ways.

## How About Some Good Drugs?

Throughout this discussion of drugs was Sarah's introduction to the illicit ones and the relative ease with which she got hooked on them. The term was used early on about her tendency to "self-medicate" or take illicit (illegal) drugs to help her to fill in what was missing in her own little brain. Drugs to make her feel better. Drugs are sometimes viewed as an escape, like a vacation, where everything changes around you to give you a break from the routine. In the case of drugs (the illicit ones), the view is that it changes everything around you by first changing some things inside you, like your hearing and vision and body image and so on. Drugs do that, and much more, but the essential bottom line is that they make you feel better for the most part. If they didn't why else would hundreds of thousands of people do them? "Let's go do some drugs and feel bad, whatdya say?" Trouble is, with most of the illicit drugs, they are unregulated, which means the dosages are not controlled very well, and there's no one to be there for the side effects, like addiction, for example. Most illegal drugs are quite powerful as well, by factors of ten, a hundred, or even a thousand in the case of LSD.

These days psychologists, physicians, and psychiatrists have finally come to an agreement that many of our mental health problems today are due to chemical imbalances in the brain. Too much of one brain chemical or too little of another will generally make people feel happy, sad, confused, agitated, distracted, angry, suicidal, homicidal, etc. The two brain chemicals we hear the most about these days are dopamine and serotonin. They are the two chemicals known as neurotransmitters. In case you don't know, your brain is not hot-wired. Your eyes and ears and fingers and your thoughts all travel from the outside to the inside of your brain on nerves which are like wires that have been cut into thousands of little pieces. So instead of the signal running easily from one end to the other, it gets stopped at the break like a car that realizes the bridge is out. The neurotransmitters are the little ferry boats that take the car across the river to the other side. Too many boats and there's a log jam on the other side, too few boats and there's a lotta honking car horns. SSRIs are selective serotonin reuptake inhibitors. Without confusing you even more, let me just say that in the brain circuitry, ferry boats are constantly being built and sunk. A car needs a ride over, a boat is there, takes it across, and disappears, its mission accomplished. Some folks' boats disappear too fast, leaving their cargo to sink or swim. SSRIs make sure the boats (serotonin) don't disappear (get taken up—*reuptake*) too fast. Prozac and Zoloft are two of the most commonly prescribed.

There are many other medications that serve very specific purposes to enhance or maintain imbalanced brain chemistry. Ritalin is one such medication, used for individuals whose brains can't shut off the flow of information and are so bombarded with it they can't concentrate on what they need to. They have the attention deficit hyperactivity disorders we spoke about earlier. Although no one really knows, it's thought that Ritalin and other drugs like it allow the brain to work better at controlling and organizing information (nerve signals). In Sarah's case, we would really have liked to have her on this, but we never quite got that far. Though we worked with a family doctor and family therapist who was a former nurse (Dr. Mom), these two could never get together and so Sarah was on Prozac and Zoloft and other medications that really did not deal with her primary problems: impulsivity and risk-taking behavior. By the time we were ready to get her on Ritalin, she was gone, working out her own regimen of pharmacological substances. To this day we are unsure of what drives her and what she relies on to get her through the day. But as we did in any number of other circumstances, we tried our best.

# CHAPTER TWENTY-FOUR

# MY LUCK HAS GOT TO CHANGE

Some say that people make their own luck, and though it's probably true that you have to exert some effort to make good things happen, not going on to college and sitting in the house all day munching potato chips waiting for Publisher's Clearing House to stop by being a rather hollow exercise. You might want to find a good job or apply to an accredited institution of higher learning to secure an even better one. Genuine good faith efforts go a long way to enhancing your luck. The bad news is that just as many bad things happen to people who make the good effort. Like the time I was clearing fallen branches out of the roadway after the ice storm as a neighborly gesture, and tore my favorite shirt. That's when I figured out that a) there was no God, or b) if there was one, he had a sick sense of humor. On the upside of this was the time shortly after we moved here and were facing financial ruin. We were unable to sell our house in our previous state, having dropped the price on our three-bedroom, twenty-five-hundred-square-foot home from $70,000 to $65,000 and then $60,000 and getting ready to

## No Good Deed

descend into the $50,000s. We were paying $500 a month rent for a two-bedroom shoe box with no garage (a lot of money in those days) and assuming an ever-expanding construction loan on the house we were building. We'd tapped out on our relatives and were wondering what to do. I'd be less than honest if I told you we never thought about torching the place, but there were a lot of factors that held us back, arson being a major felony on the top of the list. Just as we were hovering on the brink, wondering what to do, I heard a voice. It wasn't this "Sermon on the Mount/Charlton Heston/burning bush" voice. It can best be described as an inner voice, and not the one who talks to you every day. It was different, more…confident. I don't always believe my inner voices; some tell me to do all sorts of crazy things that would get me in big trouble, like grabbing some beautiful woman on the beach and planting a lip lock on her. Others are just boring, guilt-laden voices. This one was different. It was credible, and when I heard it, I didn't argue or debate, I just said "I hear you." And I sat back and waited. What the little voice said was this: "Don't worry, I'll take care of it."

Two months later, at seven thirty in the morning, we were awakened by a telephone call from Caroline's dad back home. Our house, some three hundred miles away, had burned to the ground. It was a total loss. I can't begin to describe our feelings. We were set to go in since it was Easter weekend anyway, so we packed up the kids and headed in a day early. Sure enough, what was our house was a still-smoldering pile of blackened rubble. My 1962 Buick convertible that was parked in the garage was parked out in the driveway. It had one small burn hole in the car cover. Seems the firemen knew it was in there and chopped a hole in the garage door and pushed it, all 4,000 pounds, out onto the drive. Though the concrete garage didn't burn, the heat was so intense, it set anything leaning on the back of the garage wall on fire; several wooden doors, ductwork for the heating system, plastic piping. The car was parked with the rear (gas tank) a foot off this same wall, and it would have turned into a bomb and major car-b-que.

## My Luck Has Got To Change

The house was a complete loss, along with approximately $12,000 worth of stuff still in the house. Though we'd moved most of our possessions (good luck) to our new location, where it was in storage waiting for our new house to be finished, we had beds, dressers, lamps, kerosene heaters, hall trees, clothes, carpets, appliances, etc., still inside waiting for our final move to the new house. When we went back home to visit Caroline's family, we'd always stop by the house, turn on the heat and lights, go visit with the family for a few hours, and then come back up the hill to our warm little house to sleep and have milk and cereal. That would never be again. It was gone for good.

The neighbor up the street said she woke up when the cat was doing a dance on her bed. She figured it had to go to the bathroom or something, but when she opened her eyes the entire ceiling of her bedroom was glowing red. Rushing to the window, she saw our house fully engulfed, the sky of the entire valley lit up. This was two o'clock in the morning, but cars were still driving by, no fire engine in sight. She called and asked if anyone had reported a fire on 119 north of town. "No," the dispatcher mumbled tiredly. "Well, you got one, and you'd better hurry," she exclaimed. It took fifteen minutes before the first engines arrived on the scene, and by then the fire had burned through the roof. Her husband said he saw the second story sliding glass doors blow out shooting flames across the yard. Apparently once it got going, the built-in kerosene heater in the bottom floor burned as well. The copper line feeding it melted along with it. This allowed some two hundred gallons of kerosene to gravity-feed into the basement, adding plenty of fuel to the fire, literally. It musta been hot; glass and aluminum melted and there wasn't a shred of my solid cherry paneling, just a few remnants of the decks, the T-111 siding, and the front porch we just built over the front door to keep the ice from freezing the front door knob.

We had the fire marshal and the arson squad on scene, of course, but our consciences were clear. They interviewed Caroline and me separately and asked a lot of questions about our finances and debts, our marital relationship, and other normal stuff, interspersed with questions like, "Did you burn down your house, Mr. Matthews?" just to check your reaction. "How much money did you make last year, Mr. Matthews? How old are your kids? Do you have any idea who *did* burn down your house?" In the end they were convinced that somebody did, though there had been a storm that night and the power had gone off and then on again. We had appliances running (refrigerator) and rats were known to frequent the place when we were not in residence. To be honest I have no idea how the fire got started, but I do remember that little voice. He said "Don't worry, I'll take care of it," and, well, who was I to argue? And to tell the fire marshal "God did it"? Well, I didn't think that was prudent. Who was I to argue with God, much less rat on him? No, I figured we'd keep that little secret between him and me until things cooled down (no pun intended). The insurance company eventually settled with us for an amount well in excess of the original asking price, and we paid off the mortgage on the house and one-third acre, cleaned up the site, and applied the rest to our construction loan. This gave us a fair amount of equity in our new house. And so, I tell people that the Matthews have an equal share of both good and bad luck. Just wait around long enough and one or the other will come a-knockin'. That was over twenty years ago, and here we were in another two-year run of terrible stuff and hoping and maybe even praying for a miracle, and, well…what do you know?

## Christmas Shopping For A Surprise Gift

Caroline invited me to go along Christmas shopping in a neighboring state with her and Nancy, who teaches at her school. She also taught at my home school when I was there. We hit the mall around ten and shopped and shopped. Around lunchtime we got hungry, but the food court was crazy. "Why don't we check out the restaurant behind Bosco's?"

Nancy suggested. We'd never eaten there before or since, but why not? We sat along the wall on padded seats with tables and chairs lined up in front. While we waited on our food, Nancy asked how things were going. Ha! I filled her in on the settlement gone badly and the reprimand for holding the door. I waxed poetic about a need to be truthful to parents. I could not sit in silence while others in the school system lied to parents, and if they wanted to fire me for that, then, well, so be it. I had to focus on what was in the child's best interest and make sure that his or her folks were willing partners. The woman at the next table eating with her daughter couldn't help but overhear. She was only three feet away. "Excuse me for eavesdropping, but are you a school psychologist?" she asked. "Right now I am," I cracked. "Well," she said, "I'm an elementary principal from a school district just down the road, and our school psychologist just left. Do you think you might be interested?"

Well, you could have knocked me right over. I told her I was very interested, and she wrote down some names and numbers. I also asked her to write her own name and number for reference. As we all walked out of the restaurant she remarked that the thing that caught her attention was my discussion about advocating for children and the importance of being honest with parents. "That's the kind of employee we want in our district," she said. That was who I was and the kind of position I was seeking. The principal told me that her district wanted people who cared about kids. That's me, and after working in a district that was about power and control and the rest be damned...well, this sounded like a perfect fit.

I made the phone calls that Monday and sent all my information in. The personnel director informed me that their psychologist had in fact resigned to take a job in the next district in October, and that they had advertised more recently up and down the East Coast. They were currently in receipt of a number of applicants and would be setting up interviews after the Christmas break. January 2 they would be back in the office to schedule the dates and times. I felt good about this. Real good. What was the chance of being there in Bosco's at that time? Talking about advocating for kids. Maybe my luck was on an upswing.

## Three Months Later

You can't really tell by this huge gap that a whole lot happened between pre-Christmas and this eighth day of March, 1997. We went to Florida, "we" being Andrew, Caroline, and yours truly, and had a good time for the most part. Sarah chose to stay back. The weather was perfect, the best I've seen in twenty years of going down during the Florida "winter" in December. Sun out and bright every day, good swimming weather, and plenty of time to visit the folks. Andrew had his moments when I regretted bringing him, but when Mary, Fred's ninety-eight-year-old wife, fell and I needed him, he was there. He spent more time in the apartment than at the beach, but that's Andrew. We spent a lot of time with Fred and Mary, in part because we needed to. Mary was not doing well, and Fred was resisting taking her in to the doctor. Her physical condition was poor, especially with her leaking bladder and weak legs. They wanted to stay put for Christmas but told us not to worry, go on to cousin Bill's Christmas gathering in Miami, and just bring some turkey and ham back for them. So we bid them good-bye, Fred at ninety-nine and Mary at ninety-eight. You might know that Mary would fall while we were away. Fred didn't know we had come back from Bill's late Christmas night (we were worried about them), so poor Mary spent her Christmas on the floor for twelve hours. We checked in with them the next morning to find Mary sitting up in the kitchen leaning up against the stove. I insisted the paramedics be called, and I made the call with Fred's approval. They came and my Aunt Virginia insisted they take Mary to the hospital. Virginia was tired of being the only one on call for two geriatrics approaching the century mark—I mean, Virginia was eighty-five at the time.

## My Luck Has Got To Change

By the time the paramedics got there, Mary was in good spirits, shaking her fists at them in mock challenge, "Do I feel all right? You wanna go a few rounds?" Her heart was strong and her lungs were clear (I was worried about pneumonia, lying on the floor all night, and her voice was a hoarse whisper). Her blood pressure was better than mine: 106/70. They asked her if she wanted to go to the hospital and she said no, so they gave her a pat on the back and left. We did convince Fred to let us bring in a lady to bathe Mary and help her out a bit, and I left with the girl coming in three days a week. I figured that they could help out with Mary, but my ulterior motive was to have someone outside the family coming in to supervise and evaluate the situation. Mary was fading and Fred was suffering in his valiant attempt to take care of her. She needed to be in a rest home, and the inevitable was close at hand. I spent the month of January on the phone with doctors, health care providers, lawyers, caretakers, relatives, and managers from the apartment to make sure things happened. Fred never knew the groundwork I had set in place when he went to the doctors to talk about Mary's condition. It was just as well. He didn't get mad at me for interfering, and he felt proud that he got Mary into the hospital with just one visit to the doctor. "Good job, Fred."

Mary held on until the week before Christmas 1997, a full year later, and then, after another surgery, finally gave up the good fight. Fred spent every day, eight hours a day, at her side well past his one hundredth birthday in April of that year. He continued to drive (yes, drive) his car to the nursing home and then back to his apartment. Amazing man. He made it to 101 before he finally joined his Mary in the afterlife.

Another highlight of the Florida trip was Christmas at Bill's. My little cousins—Miriam and her husband, Dan, and kids, and Miriam's sister Haley and her husband, and Tom and Less and kids—were all there along with Aunt Meam and Virginia, my mom's two older siblings. Mom and Dad made it, too, which was nice, as well as my younger sister, Julie. We ate and yakked and had a good time. Near the end, the little cousins and their families had left, so it was just us old poops sitting around. I received a great deal of support from the little cousins and husbands. They heard our story and were there to support us. It felt good. Bill was silent. He would walk away if I was into a conversation with someone. Around nine o'clock we sat out on the porch and chatted. I felt the same vibe from Bill that I had from my old friend Murphy. He finally put it into words. "If you work for someone and they pay your wage, you either support them or...leave." Bill always was direct and honest with me, dating back to the days when he flew fighter jets in Vietnam and I strolled the Mall in DC protesting that same war.

I tried my best to explain that this was not a situation of a disgruntled employee finding fault with his employer, as much as an employer who had declared war on an employee. First on my daughter, and then me. Whether it was the many little discussions we'd had over the years or my role as president of Teachers and Parents, the superintendent had an opportunity to get back at me when Sarah opened the door, and he took it. From that point on it was purely defense, defending Sarah and then myself and my career. All of my complaints and counterattacks and appeals (not suits) were to place me in a stronger bargaining position. One thing I learned was you don't negotiate from a position of weakness, especially with someone much more powerful than you. I had to stake out my ground. I explained this and I think Bill was truly surprised when he heard the details. He said as much. Mom and Dad were tiring, so we left.

The other highlight of the visit was the phone calls between Florida and home and my two attorneys. My union attorney was trying to put together the deal, and Liz, my personal attorney, was staying right with her. And me. When I would get excited about the strong language and fast deadlines they set, she would point out that they weren't for me so much as for my union attorney, who let the other agreement languish for six weeks. By the time I was ready to leave for home, we had faxed a number of documents back and forth and the agreement looked like it was coming together. I would voluntarily resign on January 2, the day after I arrived back home, and all other matters would be dropped. I would write my own letter of resignation, and I could get on with the rest of my life. Sure enough, in time I walked into the superintendent's office, handed him my letter of resignation, read over the agreement, signed it, and walked out. I think I might even have shaken his hand. If nothing else, he had to have some respect for me. I proved to be a worthy adversary. I left feeling like the weight of the world was off my shoulders. The agreement was sealed, as were my lips.

## Time Off For "Bad" Behavior

I now had some time to sit back and evaluate my situation. And find a job. I had several irons in the fire, a neighboring county for the fall, one over the bridge for a possible half-time position with "per diem" at $250 per kid, and was starting to look in other districts. I really didn't want to move. We had $190,000 in our house and we'd be lucky to get $160,000 in the depressed market. The whole idea of moving was downright depressing. I'd jumped through all the hoops for jobs and still hadn't heard from any of them. I really wasn't excited about a two-hour commute each way or moving to the other side of the bridge in high-priced real estate land, with no money to put down and a twelve-month position with only a slight increase in pay. They base your salary not on what other people are making in the same system, or even your year's experience, but what your salary is in your current job with a 20 percent increase for the extra two months. A $9,000 raise might sound real sexy, but when you figure out what it costs to live there, it fades quickly. I did not get a good feeling about it. I hoped something would open closer to my house, or in a rural county close by. If not, carry me back to Ol' Virginny. That's where I got my start. Maybe I was destined to finish my career there as well. Southwest Virginia, look out. But maybe, just maybe, I'd get real lucky and that job in the district in the next state, the one I learned about in the restaurant, maybe that one would come through! With the district being just over the border and only a twenty-five- to thirty-minute commute down country lanes, it seemed ideal. Out of the corrupt system that let me down, from the teachers and superintendent all the way through the courts, state department of education, and governor's office. A fresh start with no baggage and only five schools in the whole district with another psychologist already on board. I would have to wait two long weeks for the call. But I finally got the invitation for an interview. The principal who put me onto the job was on the team, along with another principal, the school psychologist, and two special education coordinators. It went well. I left out of there feeling good and went home with fingers and toes crossed. A little over a week later I got the call. "Could you start work Monday, February 3?" Could I start work? Are you kidding? Just tell me where to report!

## Forest Schools

I've been working here for five weeks now and couldn't be happier. The commute is easier than I thought. A straight shot to either an elementary school or middle school. The people are great and the kids are...well, kids. Everywhere I go, I get the same thing: "we are glad to have a school psychologist again." And now that they have gotten to know me, it's "we're glad you're here," which means they like me. They like me, they like me, they really like me. And to tell the truth I am a different person. I am a better person. More appreciative, more flexible, more anxious to please, more willing to accommodate. It's nice being liked and doing my usual good job. In the back of my mind are the things people I respected said (how they didn't like me at first). Did I snub people? Not anymore. Did I come on like a know-it-all? Not anymore. I am here to do a job and get along, and there will be little left of the "abrasive, arrogant" man that people who don't know me can suppose. My union attorney brought me down a few notches, and even Liz, my private attorney, set me up for a reality check. She was good at mitigating that angry side. I am so happy to be back at work with teachers and kids again, and my anger has drained away. I am truly happy, positive, and completely energized. It's funny, but people I haven't seen for a while can see it. I'm wearing it on the outside, too, I guess.

## The Kids

As for the kids. Well, Andrew got back to College Park with the Volvo and a plan to get job. Two months later he still had no job and the Volvo sat in a parking lot broken down. Three thousand miles in thirty days may have had something to do with that. We visited him on his birthday, February 6, and took him to *Star Wars*. I took a new distributor cap (his mechanic friend said the old one was cracked) and we got a new battery since his was dead. We still couldn't start it. The deal was, pay us for the Volvo and Z damage in thirteen payments of $200 plus his $60 insurance. You'll remember he backed my truck into my Z and we held him responsible for that little glitch. He had to pay for the damage he caused. Miss one payment and you're okay, next month pay two-and-a-half times the amount; last month's, this month's, and half of next month's in advance for good faith. Miss two payments and we repossess the car and sell it. We gave him one month's grace and yet got nothing February 15 or 28, and we are less than a week from March 16, the day we come to get the car. Who knows? Where we have seemed to fail Sarah, we are trying to keep Andrew straight, provide him the support without enabling him, making it too easy to stray. Part of you says, oh, give him the money, let him get his car fixed, but then the "tough love" voice comes along and says, "Ah ah ahhh. They have to learn to fend for themselves and to keep their part of the bargain.

Giving in now will only teach him to be a welcher." So you hang tough and hope they get the hard lessons on life.

## Sarah Takes A Step Forward

Sarah stayed at her friend Liz's house in Blueville, not far from home, during the week, and spent every weekend at her "boyfriend's" across the bridge. We got a call from her mid-January. She complained how she wanted to just finish high school and not have to go on to Chestnut College, and why didn't we support her? We explained how we'd spent $25,000 in legal fees to settle with the school board to let her finish high school in January and then go to a community college. We were not comfortable or able to afford a four-year university right now. We weren't able or willing to renegotiate this deal. She then told me that she had decided to sign up for classes at Chestnut, so could I take her over? I agreed. It was a cold ride over. First off she comes out of the school with toboggan (wool hat) in hand, then gets in and shoves it over her head, knowing I dislike the hat routine. Skaters and druggies and antiauthority types all wore wool caps pulled down to their eyes, even on a hot July day. Though I was a certified member of my own counterculture, after dealing with all of Sarah's rebellious moves, I was expecting, even demanding, a little more cooperation. I was running out of patience. We did the college thing. A counselor I knew professionally from having taught there extended us (me) the courtesy of helping her directly. She wanted to take a full load but was unable to because she failed the entrance exam. When he pointed this out, she came up with some story (lie) that the printer didn't work at the high school, and she'd send them the results. He wasn't buying (good). She signed up for two classes, and then I wrote the check since she said her Social Security check hadn't come in yet (another lie). When the counselor asked if I wanted to sign her schedule, she quickly indicated that she was eighteen, she would sign it. She didn't jump when

I signed the check for her tuition. She would subsequently retake the exam, pass it, and come back on her own to sign up for two more classes and buy her books. She came by the house to pick up her mail and show us her books. She had her nose pierced now and was sporting a dime-sized gold ring in it. The hole was red and infected. Real class job. Tongue and nose. Sarah always was good about the in-your-face stuff.

## The Mad Bomber Strikes Again

Less than twelve hours later, Sarah transferred out of Northern High School, dropped all of her classes at the college, the ones we had just paid for, returned her books, and moved out of her friend's house, heading for her new home on the Western Shore. Though we've spoken with her, we haven't seen her since this fiasco. As far as we know she still has not enrolled in a high school, and will not graduate. She called a few times, usually asking for money (Why can't I have my college money?) though one time she left a message on our machine, "Mumble mumble…call me, I want to come home." Trouble is she left this message at four o'clock (the second day of my new job) and then she left the house we were to call her at. Hard to return calls when you're not there. She then called Nunny and Pap Pap, Caroline's parents, and cried the blues about how we wouldn't return her calls. I called back, but she still wasn't in. Later discovered she stayed out partying until one in the morning, got up, and made herself breakfast at her boyfriend's parents' house, and when asked about returning my call said, "Oh, I got in late last night, so I didn't want to wake them." She finally got back to us the next afternoon. I hung up on her when I heard her response to my statement, "Sarah, I can't really say I agree with some of the decisions you've made lately, but I've given up giving you advice." What she said just pissed me off: "You gave up on me from day one!" Right…

## The Greatest Fear—Call From The Police

It was eleven thirty at night when we received the call from the police. "Frank Matthews? Is your daughter Sarah Matthews?" I thought this was the "worst fear" call, but instead of asking me to come down to identify her body, he merely wanted to know if I knew where she could be reached. Whew! A fifteen-year-old runaway was last seen in her company. I gave the police officer her phone number. Boy, was she surprised when the police came knocking on her door looking for the fifteen-year-old kid she was hanging with. She now has an apartment and a job: hostess in a restaurant where she can wear anything she wants. Baggy jeans, three shirts, rings in her nose and tongue, toboggan hat pulled over her pasty face. I can't wait to bring some of my colleagues to have dinner over there. Grass burgers and soy tofu! Wow, man, cool! But at least she's alive and I was spared having to identify her body on a slab in the morgue.

Andrew, who seems like he is joined at the hip with his sister, flunked out of college and has no job or money. Though he has a car, it sits in the parking lot outside his apartment in College Park, out of commission. If he doesn't come up with $650 by Saturday, he won't have a car or insurance. He too will be quite effectively cut off.

Mom is strong now. She understands that she does not want these two kids hanging around her neck when they are in their thirties. She looks at her own brother George, and even our counselor's kids who are still taking advantage, and she says "NO." Dr. Mom told us only the other day how she bought one son a car and he turned around and sold it, bought an old VW bus, and headed to California the long way, through Florida. Like all of us, Dr. Mom is learning, too. Professionals are sometimes better at giving advice than implementing it, but then we all learn, don't we, and it ain't an exact science. And by definition, professionals in the education and mental health fields care about kids. Maybe too much at times. How far do you go to help kids with problems without feeding into the problems? Can cutting them off help them or hurt them, even kill them? I worry about this every day. If you maintain even a small link, you might have just a little influence that will sink in and keep them alive another day. To turn your kids out on the street, quite literally, and have them run afoul of the law or, worse, a killer, can force you to share in their deaths as well as their lives. You can tell your kids your worst fears, and I mean to tell you, we have. But short of locking them up and making them hate you for it, what else can you do as parent but sit back and let them make their own mistakes? Just like we did.

## CHAPTER TWENTY-FIVE

## NOTHING LEFT TO GIVE

Not exactly Chapter 11, but it does feel like I am bankrupt. Emotionally speaking, that is. I am so far in debt emotionally when it comes to my daughter, Sarah, that I haven't got the emotional resources to break even. So the only way I can handle matters these days is to "cheat," to sell short and just not allow myself to feel anymore. Last Wednesday I looked at my daughter for the first time in a long time, and I told her that as far as I was concerned she was already dead to me. Pretty harsh words for someone who used to be the light of my life. How'd we get to this cold and barren place? Read on.

Sarah has been out of the house five months since her decision to not come home that night just before Thanksgiving. Her friends and her boyfriend Rob's parents have kept her afloat, so though she has moved from house to house, bed to bed, she has stayed off bottom. We talked with her a few weeks ago and she said she was "thinking about coming home." She asked me if we wanted her to come home to live. I didn't answer. Why didn't I answer? Because the house has been peaceful since she left. No battles about her hair color (red/pink), clothes (baggy and layered), whether she is going to get a tattoo or another part of her body pierced (ear and tongue are already done), or where she is going or where she's been. We got tired of fighting with her moods, and with her lies, and with her tendency to do precisely the opposite of what we asked her to do. There was no compromise; it was her way or the lie-way with no middle ground. And she didn't have the sense to just *do it*. She always had to get caught...had to put it in our face where we were forced to deal with it. And we weren't convinced her medication would work as long as she was still into the illicit drugs. I told her we wanted her home, but that she would have to consider our conditions. She said she just couldn't handle our rules, which is why she left in the first place. Being drug free and coming and going as she pleases were the most difficult, it seemed.

As June graduations grew close, Caroline became more obsessed with the *diploma* than I did with the *case*. She wanted her kids to graduate from high school, at the very least. After that, Sarah could do what she would with it. We'd spent too much in time and money to get that diploma and Caroline wasn't about to let it get away this close. I mean, Sarah had all the credit hours (twenty-five when she only needed twenty-one). She had all the state-required courses and passed all four functional tests. All she lacked was the four-year residency (attendance) requirement. Her expulsion wiped out one year even though she was working at the rest home and then child care and taking six credits at night. The superintendent finally waived this after Sarah moved out, but she still needed her senior year. Sarah has attacked us with the concept that she shouldn't have been retained (in second grade), and she should have graduated last year, but the kids graduating this year *were* her class, the one she has been with since 1988 when we moved here when she was in fourth grade. She might be somewhat older than they, but maturitywise, many have it all over her. She wanted out of the high school. She got out. The 504 agreement allowed her to attend Chestnut College this spring, taking four credits, art, and child care, and graduate on time with her friends. She stayed in class more or less even after she left home from November through January. Come January she signed up for her classes and even bought her books. I wrote out a check for $200. For tuition. A week later she dropped her classes, returned her books, and dropped out of high school. We never got the $200 back we loaned her for tuition. Turns out she had her SSI check after all. Suckered us again, all right. She paid us a short visit after Andrew came home in March (see the next chapter), but she was just there to "nib." She asked about her college money again, and if she could take a few more things out of the house. She surely didn't come to see us. She and her boyfriend, Rob, spent most of the time in Andrew's room. Mom agreed to let her have a few more things. Sarah asked Rob to give her a hand. "Carry them out yourself!" he intoned. She did. Nice guy. She got what she wanted, and she departed. She left, leaving us feeling used again.

## Andrew Moves Back To The Nest Again

Andrew, our last hope, flunked out of school and screwed up his car from road trips to raves in North Carolina, and now he is burning out. We were all set to go and get the car he hadn't paid us for, as promised. Andrew had failed to meet his obligations to pay us back and get the car running. Mom called to clear the way and he started on her. "I've got to get out of here. I'm depressed, I'm going crazy. I wanna come home." I'm sure there were a lot of tears on the phone, mostly his. We talk with Dr. Mom, and she suggests a thirty-day stay at rehab to dry him out, clean him up, or whatever. She feels he's gotten into the drugs, too, and I agree. I suggest we share this with him, but Caroline says no, we'll talk with him when we get over there. Now there are two problems: one which involves his stuff, which will fit in his car and ours; the other is his car, which is still sitting in the parking lot outside his apartment. I will either have to fix it and drive it back or have it towed to someplace over there to have it worked on. The frustration is that I have seven cars. We sold this one to him so we would have one less to fool with, and here we are fooling with it…again. I begged on the indulgences of a true friend, i.e., someone you can count on. Dave, my chief mechanic, drives over with us, and the two of us try everything he knows to get it running. It won't. So we have it towed to a local garage. Dave heads back to the other side of the bridge in my truck. The three idiots, Mom, Andrew, and I, get in Mom's car and start out. While we are waiting for them to tow the car to the garage, we talk. If he is coming home, does he understand that it's because he failed out here at the university? He failed his classes last spring, he abused our trust living at home last summer, and then he flunked out of school. He went off to live on his own, and with car and apartment taken care of all he had to do was find a job. And two months later the car was a mess and he was running away from his experiment in communal living. If he came home, it was it was on our terms. Our way. He muttered and mumbled, but agreed. We threatened a few times to haul his ass right back to the apartment, but he agreed. I knew, and Mom, knew that part of "our way" meant thirty days in rehab. He didn't. I wanted to tell him, let him know it was part of the plan before we took him over the bridge. Mom was of the mind that he'd refuse to go if we told him now. She preferred to spring it on him. Bad idea…

    The tow truck arrives and hooks up his car and we follow it over to the garage. We sign the necessary papers to have the work authorized and pack into our car with all Andrew's stuff and head east over the bay. We cross the bridge and head east. When we get to the intersection where we usually turn toward home, Andrew realizes something is up. "Where are you going?" he asks in a rather agitated tone. Caroline then proceeds to explain that we wanted to have him seen by a professional drug counselor and have him evaluated for drugs. We'd follow whatever recommendations they made.

Mom felt, and I partially agreed (what choice did I have?), that if the counselor recommended a stay, then it would be the counselor, not us, putting him there. I was still of the mind to let him know upfront that a residential stay might be in the cards. So we arrive at the facility, and he sees these adults and older adolescents lounging around, and when he is called for the interview, he closes up. He is not forthcoming about his drug use; according to Andrew, "I have no problem," and we are called in. "He's twenty years old and he is denying any drug problem. We can't keep him against his will." Well, after thirty minutes and lots of phone calls and confusion, we are faced with a choice: 1) take him back to College Park, 2) drop him off in the nearest town, 3) leave him there at the center, or 4) take him home. He doesn't want any part of going back to College Park. Mom will not leave him off on a sidewalk somewhere (my suggestion). The treatment center does not want him there and can't take him against his will, and 4) Dr. Mom says, and I agree, under no circumstances should he come home. He agreed to our terms; here they were. He was in tears. "You tricked me," or rather *I* tricked him. He hated me, I wasn't even his real dad (first time for him on this one, too), and we went round and round with him and Dr. Mom (on the phone) and the center. He was too old to keep and we could not leave him there. So guess what? We loaded him up and took him...home. Talk about feeling trapped. All the plans we had, and all the commitments from him and Caroline, and Dr. Mom's strong word to refuse to give in by taking him home, and here we were bringing him home without the rehab we had all agreed to.

I was never so close to leaving Caroline at that point. Here he was coming home after failing at school, at work, at maintaining his car and his financial affairs, not to mention family affairs. I told the two of them I had had all I could stand with Sarah and her bullshit, and here we were having to play the same games with him. I was beyond my breaking point. If something didn't change, I was leaving this marriage, this family. Caroline countered that wouldn't be necessary...

they'd leave. That's right, she was siding with her son against me. She was choosing him over her husband. What a fuckuvamess! What was I to do?

We drove home and let things cool down for a while. We agreed that we would allow him to stay under certain conditions. His stay at home would be a trial period. There were some ups and downs, as you'll see later, but for the most part it went better than I thought it would. I just felt so strongly that you couldn't continue to bail out these kids who continually failed and came running home. He was twenty and had to grow up sometime. His little sister had taken a position and she stuck with it. She survived. Now it's his turn. You do everything you can, but when they take positions that are so alien to yours, you can't help them. And when they're nineteen and twenty and have a drug habit/problem, any help you give them falls into the category of enabling. But Mom felt she'd lost one child, and here was one who had a chance. She wasn't going to let him fail. So Andrew came home. And once again…what choice did I have? Dr. Mom insisted that we keep him busy and get him two jobs, eighty hours a week, to keep his mind on something other than drugs and social life. What choice did I have but to give him another chance? I was not ready to walk away from my marriage or my home. The kids? Well, they walked away from me.

## Jacque To The Rescue Again

To go back a little bit, as April rolled into May and graduation drew near, Caroline wanted to try anew to work out something to get Sarah's diploma. She made inquiries and found out that Jacque Cook, who helped us out two years ago when Sarah was expelled, was willing to help her again. We transferred her records and he began to work out a program for her. Fine…we reached out to Sarah to go to Florida with us (Christmas amnesty) and she said no. We invited her home to have dinner and spend the night so she could see her counselor and get her Prozac prescription refilled, but her ultra world party was more important. Fine...now here we were with another offer. Come home and get your diploma. We'll come get you, you can stay here and eat and sleep, and we'll transport you back and forth to class. We'll pick you up Saturday. She agreed. Was I optimistic about the outcome? No. Did I want any part of it? No. Did Mom? Yes. So I stood back, offered no ultimatums, but offered no support either. This was their game. I would let them play it for a while. Maybe Caroline had to find out for herself what these kids were capable of and what they weren't. Instead of listening to the old doomsayer Dad predicting more bullshit. Let them wear her out and let her get as angry at them as I was. I would support my wife in my silence.

Rob, Sarah's stellar "boyfriend," went to court for his DUI on the military base. This is a federal installation, so it's under federal jurisdiction, so they get tough and give him a choice: dry out in rehab for three weeks or go to jail. He chooses rehab. That meant Sarah wouldn't have a place to stay. Rob's father calls us up Thursday to say she's gotta go and that her choice of places to stay in Baltimore is unsavory. He wouldn't recommend she stay there. He was trying to shame or scare us into taking her home and off his hands, I think. But so be it. We wanted her home for school *Monday*, so if he could wait a day or two we'd come by Saturday and get her. He agreed. Sarah wanted to come Friday, but Caroline and I were having dinner with friends and didn't want to have to deal with her then, and told her we had plans. Sarah was to call Saturday to tell us where she was and we'd come get her.

Friday she calls, surprised to find us home, "I thought you had plans." She is questioning *our* activities?! Well, anyway, I'll save you and Mom some trouble, I have a ride over...see you Sunday. Turns out the rave is Saturday (can't miss that) and so we wait all day Sunday, and Monday. No Sarah. No call. I am heading for Virginia next weekend and I begin closing doors to her. I leave that following Friday, still no word from

Miss M. She finally calls Caroline. Had to take care of a friend, sorry, but can I still come home? If I were there, it would have been NO. I wasn't home, so despite the fact she is coming into our home on her terms, a week late, she is there when I get home Sunday. I decide that she is using us again, and I want no part of her. I refuse to take her to school or pick her up. I want nothing to do with her. Her window of opportunity had closed when she failed to show up as promised and made no attempt to call Sunday, or even Monday, Tuesday, etc. She has not changed—it's the world according to her, and I want no part of that world. It's the only way I can protect myself—by insulating myself. I am a bit upset with Caroline for allowing her in on these terms, but it is her (Caroline's) choice. So, she (Caroline) can live with the consequences. I will not enable Caroline to enable Sarah. I steer clear of the two of them.

## Dad Unloads

We coexist while Caroline picks Sarah up and drops Sarah off. Tuesday her buddy Rob calls and I don't let him talk to her. She calls him and I tell her that won't do. "It's my calling card!" "But it's my house and my phone." I'm ready to kick her ass back across the bay. I tell her in no uncertain terms that I was not impressed with her new beau, that I know she doesn't want to be here or finish her diploma but just needs a place to land for a few days, and I couldn't care less about either. But if she persisted on doing the opposite of my requests, in my home, she could just get the hell out, and I'd be glad to have her removed if she didn't leave. That was Tuesday night. Oh, what a joy it is to have children about the house.

I did feel I owed Sarah an explanation. From her perspective she was doing everything we wanted—she was home and working toward her high school diploma. So why is Dad giving me the cold shoulder? She doesn't process things auditorily and perceives "tones of voice" that aren't there, and I write as well as I speak, maybe better. So I wrote her a letter.

I read it to her at the last counseling session with Dr. Mom last Wednesday. We told Sarah we knew she was still into the drugs and produced a letter she wrote Rob on the subject. We told her we knew she was probably dealing to support her habit, and that she was headed for the same fate her father "enjoyed": jail and death. She reacted only one time while I read my letter to her in the session, about her being foolish for having unprotected sex. "You don't know what I do! And I haven't even had sex for the last month! You just think all I do is have sex and do drugs all the time." My comeback was that if she hadn't had sex with her boyfriend Rob for the past month, then there was something wrong with her relationship, and that drug use and dealing wasn't anything we supported. The three of us, Caroline, Dr. Mom, and I, all read her the worst-case scenarios: death, disease, assault, imprisonment. She sat stoically. Caroline got up and left first, and then I did. I didn't want to be in the same room with the little creature, and I sure didn't want her in my car. Caroline brought her back on these terms; let her deal with it. I was out of there for a two-day conference anyway.

Here is the letter, unedited:

# A FATHER'S LETTER TO HIS DAUGHTER

Sarah,

What changed between the phone conversation we had ten days ago and this weekend? I did. You didn't. When you called a day early on Friday to tell us you didn't want to inconvenience us, that you had your own ride over, and that it would be Sunday instead of Saturday, I was suspicious. When I later found out *Base Rush* (Rave) was Saturday, and that you had no intention of helping us out, you were just taking care of Sarah again, I was disappointed. Then you made us wait around all day Sunday and never showed up, and no courtesy of a phone call? Your mom was ready to write you off right there. But not Dad. No. I gave you until Monday night. Time to make it to class. When Monday came and went, so did the last remnants of my faith in you. I changed, my hopes for you dashed once again. *You* hadn't changed a bit. Still taking care of Sarah and still leaving out the truth, and still toying with our emotions. Right now I don't care what you do. I do care very much about what you do to *me*, and to my wife. That is why I do not want you in my home.

You can't imagine how nice it is since you left. It's quiet and peaceful. We don't have to worry about what kind of mood you're going to come into the house with, or what situation you've contributed to at school or on the highway. We don't have to dread the weekend battles about where you go and who you go with or what you do. And then to realize the whole scene is a charade because you invariably lied about where you went anyway. Our house is a home now, and we deserve the peace and quiet that is there for us. It's pretty obvious you have no respect for us. If you care for someone, it's more than feelings and talking about it. It's acting on it. Caring means giving up for someone else. It means sacrifice. I don't think you understand what that means yet. It's all for Sarah. Rules, only Sarah's, not those we deserve to have in our home. Drugs, they are the most important thing to you as they are to any addict. And sex? If it's true you haven't had sex with Rob for a month, then there is something wrong with your relationship. Unprotected sex is stupid. And if you are living on the streets, your chance of getting raped are increased significantly, so get ready to get pregnant with some stranger's baby. I hope Rob will still want you then. And his parents, too, because they have allowed this to go on, way beyond where we would. They can bring it up. You can imagine how healthy it will be too with all the drugs and booze you've consumed. It might be disabled or worse.

You are not ready to "come home." All you want is a place to stay until something else comes up, Rob's in rehab and you've worn out your welcome everywhere else, it seems, and if night school and getting the diploma your mother wants is part of the price, then even you can swallow your pride and play the game for a few weeks. But all I've heard from your mother is how your attitude is still the same. You don't want to work to earn your keep; no, you want to finish your class and get back on the streets again. What are your goals? Fun, raves, parties, drugs. We know you're dealing and that you've already overdosed once. You have no direction and no future, you don't want our advice, but you have none of your own! Back when I was still experimenting we had a term for people who did drugs and nothing else: lost souls. We had "hangers on" who lived in town who didn't go to college, or who did and flunked out. No direction, no balance between work and play, no goals for the future. Most of them are dead now, like your father. You seem to have this "thing" about him. You were four when he died. What do you even know about him? If anyone knows who he was, it's your mother. She knows how violent and aggressive and self-centered and immature he was. He stole from you and your mother. He never stopped for a minute to think about you kids before or after your mother left him. That is *why* she left him. She did not want you to be around him. She put together a very different life for you, and yet you have cast it aside for this dream of what it might be to have him around. If you truly believe you are like him and want to be, then get ready for what's next. He went to jail. He is dead. Some future.

\*\*\*\*\*\*\*\*\*\*\*\*\*\*\*\*\*\*\*\*\*\*\*\*\*\*\*\*\*\*\*\*\*\*\*\*\*\*\*\*\*\*\*\*\*\*\*\*\*\*\*\*\*\*\*\*\*\*\*\*\*\*\*\*

Sarah announced that she would be finished with class Thursday anyway and was heading back to her house. Come to find out she has a living arrangement with some guys who live in a townhouse. Dealers, I imagine. Caroline supervises the last day and lets her know 1) she is not to take anything from the house or she will be arrested for theft; 2) she may take her clothes; 3) she is to take her last look at the house because she is no longer welcome there; 4) she is not to call; 5) any serious problems, she is to call Dr. Mom. And that was it. Sarah did not want to stay until Saturday to meet with Dr. Mom's psychiatrist partner because she didn't want to have to fool with three-month updates. So she is now off her Prozac. She is back across the bridge, and the last links to her mother and the only real father she's known are gone. Tough, love. But at least she has her diploma…

# CHAPTER TWENTY-SIX

# GRADUATION PICTURES

It was a bit hard seeing Sarah's face smiling out of the Class of 1997 photo spread in the local newspaper, especially when we know it's a lie, but even harder is seeing the faces of all the other kids, the same ones we encouraged her to stay away from because they were "bad influences." Seems as though they managed to graduate. And those "rotten kids," those "bad influences," they are all heading on to colleges or junior colleges or jobs. They are all heading off to their futures, while Sarah is still stuck in a thirteen-year-old dream world of "party till you drop." That hurts. Not only has she robbed us of the pride we should hold in seeing her graduate after fifteen years of schooling, but she's robbed us of the joy of the prom, and seeing her friends stop by to say good-bye. Friends who were here as much as their own parents' homes, overnight, at slumber parties. Dad pushing them on the swing or the zip line I had run along the back yard. Making pancakes for eight, or cramming three into the back of the red convertible for a ride to Annapolis or the beach. It's over, and I guess I would have liked to have had some closure, a hug or a sad good-bye, instead of the silence that greets us every weekend.

Amber and Ariel did come by, and I can't begin to tell you how nice that was. These were the two kids who accompanied Sarah and me to Woodstock '94. Amber has finished her first year at college, and Ariel is finishing up high school. She has the look of a professional model, thin, brilliant red hair, and a face that makes Kate Moss look like Roseanne. Two kids, two friends that will go on with their lives, leaving Sarah behind. They called on their way to the beach last weekend and I encouraged them to stop by. Told them I'd cook them dinner before they headed to the beach. By the time they got here from Pennsylvania it was seven thirty and they were tired of fighting the beach traffic. I offered them a place to crash for the night and they ended up going into Acropolis to see a movie, *The Fifth Element*, with Andrew and me. They headed to the beach the next morning.

I looked around the house the other day at the photographs of Sarah. The family portrait from two years ago, and last year. That was before she cut her hair and she began her descent into drugs. It was like looking into a completely difference face. And I remembered my photos, before I got into drugs and after, and imagine my parents felt the same way. Their clean-cut son with long hair and a mustache. But throughout it all, they never saw death in my eyes like I see in Sarah's. I always kept one foot on the planet even though I drifted off into space more than a few times. I always knew that line. I maintained that balance. Kept that tether strong. I stayed in school and I continued to pursue my career. Even when I was out of the university and in between college and graduate school, I did not bother my parents. I lived on my own and I moved forward and I kept my eyes on doing something else with my life other than digging ditches or running a fork truck. And when the opportunity came along for graduate school, I was ready with money in hand to go. And I didn't burn any bridges with friends, or professors, and, most important, I never burned the bridges between my family and me. Sarah has burned bridges with friends and family.

## Andrew's Turn To Hassle

Andrew returned to the nest on our terms, but, his long-term memory being what it is, he quickly forgot his promises to us. He is working and paying off his car and insurance, (room and board are gratis) and we pretty much let him come and go as he pleases. It's just that when he asks to go somewhere or to bend the rules, it brings back memories of Sarah on the weekends. He knows he cannot stay overnight anywhere. This was one of our preconditions. This was a way of keeping him straight and away from Raves. Dr. Mom suggested it, and I felt very comfortable with it. He comes to me Wednesday when Mom is at a meeting and says, "I need to talk about weekend plans, but I guess I'll wait until Mom is home since I'm supposed to ask both of you at the same time." I agreed, suggesting that, "Since Mom has been at work for eight hours, plus her second job at Dr. Mom's teaching social skills to kids, and the CHADD meeting till nine o'clock, she might be a little tired, so don't hit her with it the second she walks in the door.

I am in my lounge chair when Mom arrives home. First words out of her mouth: "I guess Andrew and Jackie are going to the movies tomorrow night." Seems like Andrew was waiting out in the parking lot for her to drive in. Or maybe the front door. At any rate, he hits Mom up and asks her BEFORE we (Mom and I) have a chance to discuss it. What happened to asking both of us at the same time? I bring up my earlier suggestion to Andrew that he wait until Mom came home and settled in before talking to her, and Mom rises to his defense (and truth be known I wasn't there, so maybe she did ask him first): "I asked him what he was doing!" This is a rough start to a discussion that goes downhill from there. He wants to go to a movie Friday (*Jurassic Park*, the movie he and I had planned to see together for months—now he is going without Dad, but I can deal with that), and then work; the pool ten to six Saturday and head to the beach after work, coming home at three in the morning only to get up and work the pool again from ten to six Sunday and Monday and then regular work Tuesday. When I respond that I think three in the morning is a bit late, he starts with the "pout and shout" routine…"I'm an adult, I'm paying for my car, I'm saving my money for school," etc., etc. "I used to be able to stay out overnight—what's changed?" I point out to him that *everything* changed when he got involved in drugs and flunked out of school and had to come home to live after failing to do so on his own. More importantly, when he had a nine o'clock curfew several weeks ago and chose to call at twenty-five after nine to say he would be late, he'd arrived at eleven, two hours *past* curfew. I felt it was time to set some ground rules and consequences. Dr. Mom had suggested no overnights, and no fifteen-minute grace—curfew time was firm (I had added a fifteen-minute grade period so he wouldn't get killed rushing home to get there before the clock struck curfew time). I also explained that violations would mean he would not go out the next week. He had violated curfew and here was the consequence. Of course he moaned and groaned, and when I pointed out that his mother and I would discuss it and let him know, he moaned louder. Mom got up and left. I then told him I felt he was trying to manipulate me. He accused me of playing my stupid psychology games on him. I left the room as well. It's so hard, even impossible, to do this by yourself.

## Separation Anxiety

Thursday night before he came home, Caroline and I talked. We agreed that Dr. Mom's ground rules were sound and that we were to ask him to set his curfew, adjust it accordingly, and then explain the consequence for violation. He arrives. Caroline is lying on the couch. He says that Jackie wants to go to the late movie and that since she doesn't have a car, he will have to pick her up and drop her off. This means a two thirty to three in the morning arrival back home. Mom reminds him that he went to a late movie a few weeks ago, and made it back by one fifteen, and she thinks one thirty is fine on Saturday. I express my concern that with it being the first Saturday of Memorial Day weekend, cops will be out aplenty, and he is at risk being out at three in the morning. As well, there will be other nuts and assorted drunks out at this same time. And even more importantly, since he worked five days this week including until nine o'clock Thursday, and would be working Saturday, Sunday, and Monday at the pool, and then back to his full time job on Tuesday, maybe he could consider the effects of burning his candle at both ends, including sinus infections he gets, not to mention having mononucleosis *twice*. This launches a pout fest of how healthy he is, and how he won't get sick because the more times you've had mono, the more immunity builds up: "THAT'S A PROVEN FACT!" he shouts. When I ask him to modulate his tone, Mom gets up and leaves. Now I could have used a little support about now, but Mom simply walked away. Now I don't see this as an argument, but a discussion in which only one adult is playing…me. Is her silence consent that he can go, or that we are sticking to our original one thirty and two o'clock curfews? She leaves before I get a clarification. More importantly, when I set the consequence—"If you violate curfew Friday, don't expect to go to the beach Saturday"— not only does he protest, but Caroline speaks up: "That's not what we agreed. It was for the *next* weekend." Well, maybe that's the way she heard it (next weekend), but anyone in behavioral management knows that immediacy is crucial. Violate curfew one night and then you don't get to go out the next. The consequence has to be immediate (the next night) and the duration is the week. I know Dr. Mom had talked about violating curfew one weekend would lead to grounding the next weekend, but that was more the spirit of the idea. Violating curfew Friday should lead to a more immediate consequence on Saturday. That was the point that Caroline seemed to miss. But even more importantly, she has disagreed with me in front of him, then she leaves. He stays and keeps on with his argument, but his kicker line is when I tell him the decision has been made: that one thirty/two o'clock and violation means grounding, and that Mom and I have discussed it. "Doesn't sound like it," he says and leaves. The urge to kills is strong.

Andrew then knocks on Mom's door, and though she shoos him away, she gets out of bed to go into his room for a discussion of who knows what. I stay in my seat half watching TV and half listening. He walks into the living room with her close behind and I politely inquire as to the status of this situation. "Did you go in to your mother's room?" I ask. "STAY OUT OF IT!" he tells me. Mom jumps to his defense once again: "I went into his room to discuss something on a completely different subject!" And though that may well be, she will never win any prizes for her sense of timing. I can feel my anger boiling. Caroline is in bed feigning sleep. I go into the bedroom to tell her that this feels exactly like it did when Sarah lived here. Everything is calm until the weekends, and then all hell breaks loose. I don't remember exactly what she said at this point, it was lost in the explosion, but it had to be something along the lines about how tired she is of me "mistreating" her kids. That triggered my detonator. I exploded. I lost it. I leapt up on the bed, straddling her like a horse (she was on her side) grabbed her face in both my hands and, with my nose a quarter inch from hers, screamed: "*YOUR* KIDS ARE DRIVING ME FUCKING CRAZY!" I then hit her with my pillow and attempted to jump off the bed. Adrenaline pumping, I missed. My leg got caught in the sheet and my momentum twisted my body backward. My head and shoulder were heading toward the floor at the same time my feet were heading toward the ceiling. Our bed is an antique and is every bit of three feet from ground level. I flew across the room, landing with the full force of my 190-plus pounds on my right shoulder. As soon as I hit I knew I was hurt. I could barely breathe, much less move. Andrew heard the noise and came in to find me lying on the floor. I told him I'd fallen out of bed and that I was all right, please close the door. I told Caroline I was hurt, and, mad as she might have been at me at that moment, she figured I got what I deserved, but she wasn't going to leave me there to suffer. She helped me into the bathroom, where I got sick from the pain. She helped me into bed with assorted icepacks. My rage cost me an injured shoulder. Better me than her. I took Friday afternoon off to see my doctor, who gave me a sling and muscle relaxants. I also went to see Dr. Mom. I told the whole truth. Here's what she told me:

## Dr. Mom's Advice

"The bond between a mother and son is like no other in the world. In many ways it is stronger than husband and wife. We carry our children for nine months and know them that much longer and in a different way than any father can. When we have a child who is needy (and Andrew certainly appeared to be that), we develop an even stronger protective bond. We want to protect him from the world. Andrew has always been a challenge, a whiner, a pouter. If he doesn't get his way, he fusses. I know, I've seen it here in my office. He blames others for his own failings; he criticizes and complains and never accepts responsibility for his own shortcomings. His failure at college, it was the professors' fault or the assistants', not his. And then it was his roommates', and the employers who failed to give him a job. If he gets fired it will be the boss's fault. And now it's Dad's criticism and ridicule and lack of faith that are to blame. How do you combat this?

"Criticize him or argue with him and you bring yourself down to his level and allow his mother to align with him. Remain silent, don't get drawn in to his games, and you won't be reactive, and it won't give her the chance to line up with him against 'bad Dad.' Be proactive. If he suggests a time, don't disagree; ask Mom what she thinks about it. Negotiate, don't make edicts or say no, and keep the discussion open (like a meeting at school). If he begins to argue, fall back on the agreement to discuss it with Caroline at a later date. If you already have and agreed on a time, then say so. 'Caroline, didn't you say one thirty was fine for Friday and two for

Saturday?' If she says yes...discussion over. If she says nothing...silence is consent, discussion still over. If he argues, leave. If she leaves, leave. Don't let him pull you into his trap. Remove yourself first."

## June 2, 1997, Motherhood/Fatherhood

Kids. You'd think anyone who liked/loved kids as much as I do would have had a better shot at parenting. To this day I don't know if the problem I have with my kids is with them or with their mother or with me. Caroline and I are almost constantly at odds over them, and though they are young adults on their own at nineteen and twenty, when things should get better, it has actually gotten tougher. Whoever said *eighteen and over* doesn't know much about life sentences.

Andrew continues to manipulate. I talked with Dr. Mom last week and her strategy is for me to let Caroline deal with Andrew first; then she can get mad at him, not me. She still defends him. I spent the day with him at WHFS-Tival on Saturday. Sixty thousand people gathered in RFK Stadium to listen to twenty bands play Alternative music. A real rock festival sponsored by WHFS radio station. It gave me insight into the age and current fashion trends—the blue hair and dreads (dreadlocks akin to the Rastafarians in Jamaica), the clothes, the baggies, the layers, the music, loud, boisterous, more to mosh to than listen to, the rave scene, dancing and moshing for eight to ten hours under the influence of a range of pharmacological substances. It's not that much different than the sixties, really, rebellion and all. I told Caroline Sunday that I didn't see any problem with Andrew going to one "party" this summer and that I might even be invited to go along. I thought this was positive. Her reaction? "Well, I trust him completely. I don't see why you don't." I said I thought he was still too close to the problems with raves and drugs and anger from last July ('96) to completely trust him. I mean he went from there to flunking out of school in the fall, and then

## Graduation Pictures

his rather unsuccessful venture on his own January through March, and his homecoming hasn't been 100 percent successful. No, I am not ready to open the trust gates completely. A little at a time.

This discussion quickly went downhill, with the usual attack and blame—he could do better if I wouldn't "CONDEMN HIM ALL THE TIME," and my response, "WELL, IF YOU WOULDN"T TAKE HIS SIDE AND BABY HIM," etc. I told Caroline I didn't always agree with the way she always took up for him. She said she did for him like she does for all of us, me included. I made it abundantly clear that I did not feel she did for me half what she did for Andrew. Taking a day off from work for me? Never happen. For Andrew, to go visit Bradford Academy, in a New York minute. I told her I would do my best to let her relate to him as she needed to, mother to son, but that she needed to allow me to relate to him as I needed to, father/son, without always characterizing it as CONDEMNATION! She reacted defensively, "Don't lecture me...," and we ended it by just ending it. Nothing resolved. She did toss in how forgiving she was, citing as an example how she forgave me for the Sunday night incident and how that was the closest she's come to leaving me. If that's forgiveness, you can have it. The term is *forgive and FORGET*, meaning don't bring it up later. "Well, I forgave you! I should have left you!" Thanks for nothing. Though I didn't mention how many times I have wanted to leave her because of her manic obsession with these kids, I did remind her that I was the one hurt in the Sunday night incident, and that if Andrew hadn't behaved in the way he did, and if she hadn't as well, I would certainly not have reacted in the fashion I did. I mean, I was a little bit stressed out. It was after Sarah had been here, and after I found out I didn't have a guaranteed job for the coming school year, and all she could think of was, "How am I going to afford the bills if you lose your job?" Gee, thanks for thinking about me. Oh yeah, I almost forgot. That wonderful job I got in a neighboring state was still great, but it was one that I started midyear, in February, as you will recall, and as such I did not have a continuing contract. In fact, I would have to re-interview for it and I would not be the only one in line. Apparently the nationwide search had turned up a few more candidates after I was hired on, and the personnel director, who wasn't too keen on me anyway, thought he might open the job again. There was no guarantee I would get it, so come summer I would be back on the job search again. And all Caroline can think about is how we are going to pay the bills. A man can only take so much. Thanks for the support. I just wish she gave me half the support and trust and encouragement she gives Andrew, but, then again, he needs it more than I do.

## Uncle Dewey's Gift

In the midst of all this, Dewey, bless his heart, left Andrew and Sarah each $1,000 in his will. Andrew got his to put in the bank for expenses, Sarah's, well...we agreed we did not want to give it to her if she was still into the drugs. We would encourage her to invest it in her college fund. On the other hand, I reminded Caroline of the deal we'd discussed if she graduated. Give her the Florida plane ticket and $50 to fly anywhere in the Continental Airlines routes. I even would kick in another $50 for spending money. Caroline kidded about her going out to California. Boy, was that a glimpse of the future! We also talked about her parent's upcoming fiftieth anniversary party. After coming back from WHFS and seeing two thousand Sarahs there, red hair, pierced faces, smoking weed, I couldn't help but think maybe she wasn't that much different than we were back in the sixties. I mean, there were kids with tattoos and shaved heads and that really "lost" look. I thought about my expectation to see her dead if she didn't change her lifestyle. Was that what I wanted...or expected? What if I closed the door permanently and she did end up dead? I came home and talked with Caroline. Maybe we would call and open the door a crack and see if Sarah

## Graduation Pictures

wanted to go into West Virginia with us to enjoy the family get-together celebrating Caroline's parent's fiftieth wedding anniversary. Caroline put me up to talking to Sarah about the $1,000, and having her call Caroline for arranging the transfer. I added the plane ticket, and what about West Virginia? "You call," Caroline said. I did. Sarah returned the call tonight.

I told her about the $1,000, that it was hers, though Dewey had strings attached; it would have to be invested. She didn't complain. I also told her we would do something for her finally earning her high school diploma, although I didn't say what. And I told her about West Virginia, how Caroline's mom, Nunny, wanted to see her. She said she was planning on going in anyway. At this point I handed the phone to Caroline with a brief summary. Caroline's tone and demeanor were negative and accusatory from the get-go. "What's this about you going into West Virginia? How are you getting there? Who invited you? What, were you just going to drop in? You don't even know what we're doing and they don't want you there anyway." This was not the truth. I decided to get on the downstairs phone. If Mom ran interference for Andrew, then maybe it was my role to do the same for Sarah. Caroline was every bit as tough on Sarah as I was on Andrew as of late, and Sarah needed some slack. I told Sarah Pap Pap (Caroline's dad) had been there for us throughout my job problems and Sarah's problems and court case. He felt that some of the decisions Sarah made, leaving home and dropping out of school, betrayed him as well as us. Nunny was Nunny; she would accept her anyway. She is the classic enabler. I also told Sarah that we had two reasons for wanting her to attend the party: one, because it was a time for the family to get together to celebrate their fifty-year marriage and the family that resulted from it, and two, so that Nunny could understand better what kind of lifestyle Sarah was living, with the baggy clothes, crayon-red hair, and body piercings. I wanted Katie to get a taste of what we had to deal with with Sarah. Sarah said she didn't care, Nunny would still be there for her.

When the discussion got around to the money, I tried to set up a time and place for them (Caroline and Sarah) and a notary to make the transaction. Sarah made it known she was in Easton and would be there the next day. How about our attorney George's office? Caroline: "Not until we talk with him first!" "How about somewhere in Weston, a nearby town?" I ask. Caroline: "I'm not taking time off from work for that." I reminded her that she took a day off for Andrew, and she could make similar arrangements for Sarah. That's when she got on her power trip of "I HAVE THE CHECK, I'LL DECIDE WHAT TO DO WITH IT. IT'S AT MY CONVENIENCE, NOT SARAH'S. AND I'M NOT TRYING TO HUNT HER DOWN TO CALL, EITHER." That's when I suggested that I would just give Sarah $1,000 if Caroline just wanted to play her power/money games. What a turnaround this was—here I was defending Sarah from her mother, much like Caroline defends Andrew from me, and as right as it felt, inside I knew it wasn't. How could I criticize Caroline and then do the same thing? Side with a child against my partner?

Sarah called because we told her to. All Caroline had to say was negative. We both get angry with Sarah, but when she calls because we ask her to, we don't have the right to attack and blame. We should have worked out West Virginia and her inheritance. According to Sarah, she was not in too deep with drugs, no more than the rest of her friends (how deep are they?), no more than I was in the sixties (how does she know what I did or didn't do ten years before she was born?), and she does no more drugs than dear sweet Andrew, who hung with the same circle of friends and did the same stuff she did. Her clothes were the style, her hair and piercings the same, and nothing was permanent. No tattoos (not yet), just pins and rings she would take out one day. She wanted to go to a community college for art, and she had a job at a piercing parlor—not exactly Rhodes Scholar material, but better than dealing drugs. She was planning on living in Ocean City and had a temporary place to live. She needed money and was insistent that if Dewey left it to her, it was hers to do with as she pleased. I stuck with the story that it had to be invested and counseled her that any hard-line approach with her mother would backfire. Caroline had the papers and lawyer's name and the check. Without Mom, there'd be no cash. I suggested she adopt a tack of forgetting about the thousand, and ask if she could have something for graduation. We had agreed to this. I further suggested that she call Dr. Mom, for practical reasons as well as to serve as a liaison between her and her mother. She agreed. She said I could call her friends anytime or come over and see her, and that she'd get me a phone number or her beeper number once she got it activated. She never called Dr. Mom, and she would continue to ask for the thousand.

## CHAPTER TWENTY-SEVEN

# BLOOD—IS IT THICKER THAN WATER OR JUST THICK?

Not too many men would have pursued this fight for their own flesh-and-blood kids, much less someone else's. But I made the commitment when I adopted them and loved them as my own. And though Caroline and I have grown closer over this at times, since Andrew has moved back it has been a wedge between us. We leave last summer for a break and they turn the house over to friends. They wreck my cars. They jack up my insurance. Sarah almost ruins my professional reputation and my livelihood. She steals from me and betrays me and embarrasses me. Still I am there for her, and I am condemned for it by their mother? And when my new job is in question for a time, do I get support? Instead I get, "You turn people off. You're too abrupt. What am I going to do if you don't get rehired?" Any words of encouragement ("Just hang in there, it'll work out") or just a sympathetic ear? No. And when I snap, when I break, and I hurt myself in the process? Though I don't expect or even deserve sympathy, I don't deserve condemnation. "I should have left you." No. I should have left *you* a long time ago. I was in this for eighteen years, and I'm looking at ages nineteen and twenty and still no end in sight. And for all the talk of "I'm not my parents and don't want a George (her brother) hanging around in his thirties," I want to know when it will end, and when will we have a life? When does the couple work together? Do I get any credit for my efforts, or only the blame for things that didn't turn out the way they should, through no fault of our own?

## June 7, 1997

Maggie's birthday. It's easy to remember, as Caroline points out, because our English bull, Maguerita Maybelline, Maggie May, or just Maggie, was born on 6-7-89. Maggie is the only member of my family I can count on. She is loyal, she is faithful, and she does not judge me. She simply loves me without question. She's a great dog. It's been an interesting week. Busy, productive, depressing. Had the notorious Child Find Event Monday Tuesday, and Wednesday.Child Find was a Federal Requirement for school systems to do outreach to identify children entering the school in the fall who might be suffering from a disability. We screened all four and five-year-olds with a battery of tests that included bean bag toss, jumping on one foot, skipping, counting, identifying colors and letters and drawing pictures and cutting, lot of fun stuff but very intense. It was busy with forty-minute evaluations with the little guys and gals and follow-up meetings with their parents, but I felt comfortable with the work I did, and the right kids got the service they deserved. I also had enough free time to do the real work of a psychologist, touching bases with the teachers. Sat in on a few extra meetings and solved a few more problems. My new job is starting to feel like home, like I belong there. Though I haven't heard about the interviews, I'm not really concerned that I won't have the job next year. Mary has been nice, and Elaine and Meredith are cool (special education people), and I got to spend the week with Mallory. She is quite a remarkable person, four kids and program chair of early childhood and teacher, and always has time for you. I pray she is on the interview team. I also got another support letter for the interview team, and WOW, it was one of the best I have ever gotten. From Betty, one of the special education coordinators I work with, and it was right nice. Nice to know somebody appreciates what you do. There are four others interviewing for "my" job, and I have no way of knowing if I will be the candidate selected. In case you're wondering why I am interviewing for my new job, the one I already had, well...since I was hired midyear, in February, I had to reapply for my position, and district policy required that they advertise and open the position for applicants. Six months ago there were none, now there are several. I had competition. As well, I had a few bruised egos who preferred no psychologist to one who actually wielded a little influence. My job was not a sure thing. Anxiety set back in again.

## Sarah Eases Back In

Still reverberating from last week's crisis with Andrew and Mom, the inseparable duo, I have learned to stay out of the arguments (though I thought fathers had a right to make statements and any retorts from the kids were considered "fresh" or "back talk"). I have learned to let *her* criticize him, not me, and to just hold on until he moves on and we can get back into a groove, if that is possible, again.

When I think of Sarah and the other kids whose smiling faces have appeared in the newspaper this week, winning scholarships and going on to sports teams and winning awards for academic excellence, and I look around the neighborhood and see all the "good kids," I shudder. But then again, how will they fare when they follow the straight and narrow course, and marry their college (or high school) sweetheart, and have two lovely kids and nice jobs, and wake up some morning and realize they haven't lived a life? Midlife crisis. That's one thing I never had because I lived my life full! As did Sarah. I guess it's a balance between "What have *I* done (all this time with my life)?" and "What have I *done* (with my life?)!?"

I met with Dr. Mom Thursday, and though Sarah called, she got the answering machine and never called back. We have not heard from her since, so I did what I could...I filled in Dr. Mom the best I could, but it's tough. I explain how Caroline defends Andrew and allows him to do whatever he wants now. He has essentially moved back in all the way. He's back using my office as his playroom, which includes computer time. When he first moved back he was restricted to his own possessions, not ours. He sleeps all afternoon and is up all night, falling asleep with lights and TV on. He is working and putting his money aside, but all his deals and understandings about lifestyle (his living ours, for example) are gone. I told Dr. Mom I was ready to just back off and let Caroline handle him, and she discouraged this. She reminded me about what happened when I backed out of Sarah's discipline. Apparently without me there will *be* no limits, no structure or consistency. Then again, if Caroline is the one setting the limits and he breaks them, then she gets to deal with the consequences.

I tried to explain to Dr. Mom about my frustration when Caroline and I weren't together on discipline and how it hurt me when she would take Andrew's side, defending him, speaking for him, how it turned me against both Andrew and Caroline. Of course, Dr. Mom suggested that it was my fault. She didn't use these terms, but that was the gist. I had to assume some responsibility for the events in my family. Now I have to use EMPATHY. I had to take Caroline's words, her feelings, and reflect them back, not judge her for them, but let her hear them repeated back so she could judge them for herself! *So you trust him more. That's different from last summer. That's good; why is it that you feel you trust him more, etc. etc.* I know this will give me more information and avoid an argument, but it puts me in the role of playing the therapist instead of the husband and the role I know best: being a man. Dr. Mom has ways of working that are unclear to me at times. What it looks like is that she is taking sides when she is really trying to help me avoid the pitfalls. Although it is true that I often feel like the husband committed to the marriage but frustrated by kids who break in between himself and his wife, wreck his cars, and abuse his house, not to mention him, Dr. Mom knows that she has to work through the strongest member of the duo, and the one that has the best opportunity for change. Caroline was too close, she was not able to change; I was. I was more motivated and I was more flexible. I would have to suck it up. Caroline was so committed to her children and so blind to what it was doing to her husband that Dr. Mom reasonably concluded that I was the stronger and more malleable mate. So the plan was, get Frank to give a little, to let Caroline be Mom, and ask me to step back.

Dr. Mom consequently asked Caroline to work with her, to tutor some of her clients, to help Caroline shift her focus away from her own problems to those of Dr. Mom's clients. Even that has backfired somewhat. Dr. Mom brags on Caroline in my presence like she's the greatest thing since pasteurized milk, and though I too am proud of her professional accomplishments, how does that help us with our conflicts over our own kids? By working with Caroline professionally (employer/employee) and me clinically (patient/therapist), the line between therapist and colleague are blurred. I get lost in this new strategy and feel threatened by it. When is someone going to build me up, take my side? I feel very alone and isolated and can't see the big picture. But then again, maybe it's Dr. Mom's strategy to boost Caroline's ego a bit so she doesn't feel so downtrodden and defensive. Make her strong and confident again. I'm okay as long as it works, and I have to trust Dr. Mom to do her thing.

# The Nose Knows

I have been so stressed out this week from the pace at work and the depression at home that I have my first sinus infection in two years. I stopped by my doctor's office Wednesday to get an antibiotic. He wasn't there and the other doctor only wrote a prescription for a decongestant. Great! By Friday I had a full-blown sinus infection with my throat on fire. I stopped in on my way home and my doc wrote a script for Ceclor, thank you, thank you. I am sitting in my downtown pharmacy, sitting in the waiting areas, chatting with a woman I worked with in my old school district. A number of other folks were also waiting for prescriptions, and the girl at the counter was a girlfriend of a guy I knew who was killed over Christmas. The pharmacist, seeing the prescription for Matthews, calls over to me some twenty-five feet away. "Frank, did you have someone call in a prescription for you today?" Well, I never gave a thought to Dr. Mom or her partner psychiatrist, Dr. Castro, so I hesitated; I wasn't sure. "It's for an ANTI-DEPRESSANT. You haven't used anything like that before. That's why I was wondering." Well, thank you very much. Now the whole world knows Frank Matthews, the school psychologist, is depressed. When I walked up to the counter to make this conversation a little more intimate, I was so shell-shocked I could not think of his name. Finally Castro came to mind. Forget his first name, it starts with a "V" and has twelve or more letters. He's Filipino, I think. The last time I was this embarrassed was in the 1960s when I went into a drug store to buy some prophylactics and the druggist yells out, "RUBBERS, you mean?" at the top of his lungs. Oh, these pharmacy guys are great comedians. So much for the privacy act.

I faxed Dr. Mom a note last night about my thoughts. Dr. Mom was suggesting that Caroline was modeling my behavior in cussing out the superintendent ("She's taken on your demeanor"). After I had a chance to think about that for a while, I realized that she has always been angrier at him than me, and it's more like I've taken on her demeanor. Take the article published in the local newspaper about Sarah's case. Finally, after three months, the *Daily Planet* made good on its promise to give our side an opportunity to be heard. Friday, the week of graduation. Did it have anything to do with the letter I wrote the paper's editor last week asking her to honor her commitment to publish Sarah's story, or was there more to this odd timing? Caroline is convinced it's because the superintendent asked the editor to hold it off until after graduation. Time for the first article to cool down. I'm sorry, but I don't think he has this much pull in the county and don't see what advantage it would be to wait until June when everybody is reading about graduates and wondering about some who might not have made it, like Sarah. Caroline's take is, "He got the last word." I don't see it that way. The story was balanced and is clearly a father/employee who reached out to his employer and got screwed. Anyone who knows me and who knows the superintendent can read between the lines. His "I wish Sarah well" was as empty as his heart. I feel vindicated. My side has been heard, and even though the phone hasn't been ringing off the hook for interviews, I have more closure than I did when that first article appeared.

## Marital Troubles Peak Again

So Caroline is mad at Sarah and me, and money crops up every time. This time Caroline expresses her anger that I "wasted $10,000 of (her) money on this court battle (for Sarah)." It was my money, too. And it was our family's money, too. Her parents kicked in $10,000, my mother $2,000, my aunt $3,000, and her uncle $2,000. The rest came from our paychecks, Sarah's account ($2,500), and the equity loan. It was a joint venture. And though Caroline was with me all the way, even pushing to continue when I wanted to settle a long time ago, when we lost, Caroline blamed me. Why? Because I lost it? No, because I thought we'd win and get our money back. According to Caroline, we should have just hired the DC attorney for $175 an hour for the special education case and won it, instead of me trying to take on the high-priced attorney from Baltimore the board hired. What she forgets is that we didn't have the $10,000 to $50,000 to fight the case with the DC lawyer, not with two cases going on simultaneously: Sarah's special education due process hearings and the expulsion case, not to mention my own case later on with the board, all continued drags on cash resources. What Caroline also forgets is that it was I who put it all together, researching the cases, reading and critiquing the briefs, preparing the special education case, and presenting it at two local hearings and a state-level hearing. I was the one who wrote literally hundreds of documents and made scores of phone calls and wrote scores of letters to keep this case alive for over two years. Hours upon hours of my time. She forgets I suffered the humiliation and loss of my job of eight years due to dirty tactics by shifty lawyers and less-than-competent judges. And it was my career that suffered. I was a school psychologist for six years before I met Caroline, and was a successful one for fourteen before we moved here to Maryland. After twenty years in a tenured position, I almost lost it all in a fight over her biological daughter, the same one I adopted when her own father abandoned her. And I get blamed for losing? For spending her money? Come on now. Don't I deserve a little credit?

# CHAPTER TWENTY-EIGHT

# JUNE 17, 1997, CLOSURE

When we last left you, Sarah was still not "present and accounted for," and with her history we were a little suspect. The adage we'd all like to live by, "Forgive and forget," or "Let's forget the past and take it forward from here," only works until someone repeats a past mistake, and then the whole rotten thing reemerges from the grave to haunt you again. It's the way of human nature. We want to forgive and forget and pretend that people will change and that we won't/can't/shouldn't hold their pasts against them, but in the end people are people. They can grow and maybe even change after a serious trauma, such as a near-death experience or religious conversion, but for the most part, they play the same roles, repeat the same mistakes, and continue on as they always have. Katie and George, Caroline's parents, were "celebrating" their fiftieth wedding anniversary in June. I qualify this because Caroline's mother, Katie, has said very little, and "Pap Pap," George, has made it clear that while he thought it was nice what we did for my parents' fiftieth last year, according to Caroline's father, he wanted "nothing."

"Why would I want to celebrate the unhappiest day of my life?" So much for his view of married life. Did this have anything to do with Caroline's view of ours? Despite George's edict, we couldn't let either of them down, so we arranged a family gathering at a local restaurant. That way they couldn't argue. George probably wouldn't get her anything, as he is also famous for saying he won't buy Katie another thing, since she never used the last present he bought her…a cemetery plot. Katie, champion of the underdog, and a child advocate in her own right, asked so many times about Sarah that we talked about extending special amnesty and inviting her to West Virginia with us. She agreed to go and would arrange to get to the house the day before we left. So…when Sarah told us she would catch a ride and be at the house Thursday, and didn't show, we figured she was sabotaging the family again. She called and said she would be there Friday, that *Dave let her down*, but we were not going to get our hopes up.

Friday morning she called Caroline crying about Dave letting her down again. She needed a ride, so Caroline drove an hour and a half over and an hour and a half back from Ocean City. Just in time to head into West Virginia for the fiftieth anniversary party for Katie and George. Caroline was ready to take it as it was, to be positive, and to allow no negative energy to interfere with the weekend's activities. I had already made my conversion that Sarah was probably no better, no worse, than thousands of other kids her age, and no better, no worse than I was at her age (though I graduated from high school with 1200 on my SATs and managed to finish college as well). Under terms of the amnesty, and accepting them as they were, I would have to do the same for Andrew—forgive/forget/accept. She wasn't as bad as she seemed, he wasn't as bad. Caroline reminded me of this whenever I said something to Andrew on the way in, in her firm lecture tone: "No negative." I bit my tongue more than a few times, but here we were, all four of us, in a car heading into West Virginia, just like old times. One big fucking happy family. We stopped for dinner, and all in all it was pretty good.

## June 17, 1997, Closure

Sarah's hair was pretty red, lipstick red, and in addition to her half dozen or more ear holes, she had nose, tongue, eyebrow, and now a chin piercing. Real nice, but we'd promised ourselves to take things as they were. We even let her smoke outside the car. It was like we had all moved several years down the road in six months and were trying our best to be more accepting of who they were. I even had this proud poppa feeling as people stared at Sarah as we went into restaurants, thinking, "Hey, whatta you lookin' at? They're just kids." This made for a more pleasant trip. Saturday we went down to Katie and George's, and of course Katie was happiest to see Sarah. It actually took a few days before she started asking us why we couldn't do something about all those piercings. Hey, now Katie knew what we were talking about. Sarah is nineteen and on her own; she can do what she wants.

During the visit I had an opportunity to go for a ride with Sarah and Andrew and Atlee (their cousin), without Caroline. I actually got to talk to them, father to children, without the defensive maneuvers Caroline constantly interjects when I say anything negative about *her* kids, especially Andrew. It felt good, and they accepted it a lot better. As well, it was a more honest conversation, because they knew that while I was more judgmental and critical of them, I had more than a little experience, not only than they did, but than Caroline did. I was also a father, a male figure who was programmed to accept or reject his children based on their *behavior*, not merely the fact of their birth, as mothers do. And though I rarely talk about my own experiences in front of Caroline and the kids, I could in this forum, and being honest allowed them to be honest with me. It was a wonderful conversation amongst the four of us. It would stop when Caroline was there. We all knew.

In a way my respect for Sarah has increased. I don't like the piercings or her lifestyle, but I understand it better now. In a way I admire her for staying out on her own. Andrew couldn't handle it; he came running back to shelter. She stayed out. It will take her longer to tire of her lifestyle because she likes the excitement so much more than he, but then too, being poor and without a car will weigh on her, too. I just hope she doesn't get in too deep with the drug thing. Easy money can be addicting and as dangerous as the drugs themselves. Andrew has it easy; I just hope he uses his second opportunity to pull himself up so when he leaves for Tech School in October, he will stay on his own.

The weekend, hatched in auspicious beginnings, developed into something beneficial and healing in nature. We all drove home together a family again, bonded by blood and circumstance. Sarah not only fit in, but there was a glaring contrast between her and Caroline's brother, George Jr. Everyone "dressed up" (Sarah even polished her piercings) for the fiftieth anniversary dinner. George Jr. showed up late, straight from the lake, in shorts and T-shirt with the sleeves ripped off, *TOPPS Rolling Papers* emblazoned across the front, long hair streaming down his back, leather HARLEY-DAVIDSON hat perched on his head. He brought only one of his four boys; one made it there on his own power, and the other two were "stayin' at the lake" with no further explanation. I mean, we reached out to our daughter after a monumental battle so that she could come in to West Virginia for this family celebration, and George can't drag his son away from the lake ten minutes away for a family celebration of the fifty-year relationship that gave birth to them all? The missing son, his oldest, is the same thirteen-year-old son he bought a Harley-Davidson Sportster for. No, not for when he grows up, NOW. He wanted to bond with his son and have someone to ride with, so he and this kid tear around the countryside on two motorcycles. Today George brought his youngest son with him, his seven-year-old. I wonder how old he'll be before his dad buys him a bike? Talk about different lifestyles! And parenting styles!

So George sat down at one end of the table with "his boys" and interacted very little with the rest of us. Sarah was front and center and fit in well, laughing and carrying on. Despite her protests about "family stuff," she valued being a part of a

## June 17, 1997, Closure

family and enjoyed being there. As well, family enjoyed having her there. To be honest, a large part of getting along was acceptance—an attitude on all our parts (mine included) of not condemning, not judging, just taking her as she was, red hair, body piercings, baggy clothing, drug use (marijuana, tobacco), and lifestyle. We even let her smoke in front of us, though not inside the restaurant or in the car. She respected this. With no "rules" she seemed relaxed and more willing to trust us again. Everything was fine as long as we "didn't get in her business." As far as accepting George, well, that was a bit much to ask.

We all came back to Maryland refreshed after the anniversary celebration. On the way back Sarah hinted about wanting to come back to live. Little things like offering to stay with Aunt Liz, who broke down in tears when everybody left. Consider Sarah telling her mother how much she would love a job with a five-year-old autistic child or serving a Down syndrome child as a nanny. When Caroline complained about being in pain Monday, she said, "I guess I'll have to stay and take care of mom now." Part of her wants to come home, but part of her wants to go back to Ocean City and the fast life. It's not too dissimilar from the *Call of the Wild*. Not having to account to anyone, coming and going as you please, staying up all night, not having to report in, not having anybody worrying (caring) about you. Running with the wolf pack, free and unfettered. It's got its upside, and maybe just a little she is starting to see the downside. Too, she wants to have the best of both worlds, and this isn't always possible. As parents, we have our limits.

By Monday night, the honeymoon began to fade a bit. Nothing major, just little things. Sarah announced that she was going out instead of asking, and that was cool, and she didn't get mad when I asked about what time she'd be back (twelve thirty to one). Cool. She headed off and I went to bed early. She came in around twelve thirty with Kyle and the two boys, Brian and John, Sarah's old boyfriend. Mom woke me up at one thirty to tell me they were heading out again.

After Caroline got my heart pounding in the middle of the night, she indicated that she wasn't making excuses for her, but she did say Sarah told her she might head up to the club for a midnight swim in the pool. They woke me up when they came back, all four of them. Thumping around, opening and closing doors. This was around two thirty. Then they headed to the hot tub. I asked Caroline to check on them because I felt it might lead to a confrontation if I went out. Bottom line? When they aren't living with you, you don't know and really can't begin to care about the hours or friends they keep. That's their lifestyle. When they are in your house…all of a sudden there is a clash of lifestyles, and they disturb your rest. I had to work the next day. She came in well past her old curfew, and she came in with friends, and she came in loud. She wasn't considerate or cool, she was inconsiderate and objectionable. The honeymoon was over. She was back to her old tricks of in-your-face politics.

## Clash Of Lifestyles

What came to mind was Andrew's moving back in. True, he kept to himself, but when he wanted to stay out till five in the morning, I let him know it didn't really matter to me, just that I didn't want him coming in and waking me (us) up at that hour. As well, there is the intangible worrying about them while they're out. Responsibility for them and all. Andrew seems to understand this better than Sarah, and he also seems to need some limits, some restrictions. Unlike Sarah, who is out there (remember *Call of the Wild*?), Andrew is just as happy staying at home in his room watching TV or playing on the computer. Last weekend he spent over four hours playing one video game. His lifestyle fits ours better, though he pushes the limits at times and complains about how he doesn't do anything (by whose choice?) and then when he asks to do something (like staying out all night, which is off limits) we say no. Caroline says that the reason he lies and

## June 17, 1997, Closure

doesn't always ask is we always tell him no. Dr. Mom and I felt he was too close to the situation last summer, and with fall failure and winter/spring crunch, going out to all-night parties was not in his best interest. At this point, I'm ready to let him fly a bit, as much to let him try his wings while he is here with us as for convenience. Arguing with him is so tiresome. Having him back continues to reinforce my theory that God's great plan is to ease the transition your children make to leave you by making them so darn obnoxious you can't wait to send them packing. I mean, if your kids stayed small and lovable and cute and compliant, you'd never want them to leave, and you'd be heartbroken when they did. This way you're glad, relieved that they have left. Peace and harmony reign once again.

With Sarah coming and going at all hours and bringing guys to spend the night, and the clothes and sleeping bags and cereal boxes emptied, I think it's time for her to head back to the beach. She is quick to condemn our lifestyle ("I'd rather be happy than rich"), but she sure enjoys the amenities: the hot tubs and cars, stocked cupboards and pleasant accommodations. I guess that's what it all boils down to. By the time they're in their late teens and venturing out on their own, you have to let 'em go. The line is crossed only when they disrupt your lifestyle. Then you set limits, and if they don't like (respect) them, then it's an incentive to move on. If you make home too comfortable, then they won't go after all. Bit by bit we are letting out the rope, including cutting off the car insurance. Andrew was given six months after he flunked out of college this winter, and in June I canceled his insurance. He was good about getting a job and has gotten his own insurance. He is also paying for his car and phone bills. We let him ride on the room and board. Mom's started charging $200 per month now to be put aside for him later after he spent all of his savings and dipped into Dewey's money to the tune of $700. He's been home five months, and if it weren't for Dewey he'd be $700 in debt. Sure, he pays his bills. He has paid his own insurance and car payment to me and phone bills ($50 to

$75 per month), not to mention the $650 it cost him to repair his Volvo when he skidded off the road and bent the front end. At least it was his car this time, not one of mine.

He still goes out at night late and is still into the rave music, though we've cut back on the scene itself. He is signed up to go to Bradford Academy in October, where he can spend eighteen months learning about computer animation/graphics, etc. It blends his love of computers with his talent in art, and we're trying to build in success. We have the money for it (his college fund) but are afraid if it's just handed to him like the $10,000 for college, he might not take it seriously. I'm lobbying for him borrowing it; Mom is into paying for it and hoping this will be it for him. With $20,000 in tuition in eighteen months, plus apartment and living expenses, it is going to be tough if we don't help him, but he still is spending hand over fist, mostly on car insurance and phone calls. I'm optimistic he'll make it this time, whether he comes up with his own money or we pay the freight. I'll tell you what, though. If he doesn't make it and tries to come home in two years, I'm outta here. It will be the straw that breaks this camel's back.

I gave Sarah thirty days after she moved out and then canceled her insurance. Shortly thereafter I got a notice that they were increasing my rates due to her two rear-end collisions. I called them to say I had already kicked her off, and they made the necessary adjustments. With Sarah off and credit for the time I paid when she wasn't on the policy, plus Andrew being off, they keep discounting my rates so I don't have to pay anything until August. Now that's nice. A bright light at the end of the car insurance tunnel.

Sarah called in July before we left for Florida, wanting to see us before we left. We'd even offered to give her her plane ticket so she could accompany Atlee down while we were there, but she declined. "I'm going to California!" she exclaimed. Looked like Mom saw this coming months ago. California dreamin'. So far she has no diploma or ticket. She never called us back to see us before we left for Florida. Over the past eight months, Sarah has lived in Daton, Blueville,

June 17, 1997, Closure

Acropolis, Baltimore, Crofton, Tolson, College Grove, and Lake City. She also held a brief job or two at Subway, a restaurant, and a piercing parlor. She is currently unemployed but enjoying the good life. She called last week wanting to come see us, and we basically told her, get a job and a stable residence and we'll talk. Short of that...have a nice life. We cannot support or condone your lifestyle and really don't want you coming around. "But I'm your daughter!" she cried aloud. But both Caroline and I aren't interested in her pleas that we owe her. We've paid our debts to her and then some. Now she'll have to earn her way back into our family...or not.

Dr. Mom asked us what we would do if she never changed. Do you engage in what is so casually referred to as an "estranged" relationship, which really means that you don't talk or call or see each other? Do you see her on her terms on occasion, leaving the door open a crack? What about birthdays and holidays? Do you ignore/condone continued drug use and her illicit lifestyle? Is that enabling or is that no longer a factor once they're out on their own and making their own way? If you aren't giving them any money, are you still supporting/enabling them if you continue to see them on their terms? These are questions to be considered. Once again, the greatest fear, death, is ever present with her out-of-control drug use, so there's the need to keep a finger held out, if not a whole hand, just in case she needs the lifeline...and just in case she falls off the edge. Maybe it will make it a little bit easier on our collective consciences that we did the best we could...we did all we could.

## I Find My Place In The Sun

I was interviewed for my job, and on a Friday, the thirteenth of June, I was informed that I would be recommended to the board. Blessed relief! As well, I would receive my pay raise for my master's plus forty-five...and it would be retroactive to February 3! That meant two checks on June 30! And just in time for vacation. I would be making $6,000 more in the new job at Ocean Pines compared with staying in the old job. Another dose of good luck. The family is back on speaking terms and the cases are all closed. EEOC, OCR, OSERS-OSEP, MSDE-DSE are all just government agencies with bureaucrats going through the enforcement motions with no serious intent. If they did care about the federal law, they wouldn't have written my complaints off as a disgruntled employee and pursued them even after I withdrew my formal complaints. I have to put this behind me. Time to get on with the rest of our lives! And who said Friday the thirteenth was an unlucky day?

I guess if you have to end somewhere, this is as good a place as any. It's been three years of unmitigated hell with one bad thing after the other. Sarah is living on her own and seems to be surviving. She is who she is and has a spirit that will keep her above water. I worry about the drugs and the lifestyle, but even more I worry about her thin grasp on reality. Telling lies was just too easy for her. You just take her on the surface and go with it. Not living with her, you don't have to get tangled up in the webs she weaves. She will have her diploma and maybe after a few months or even years of hand-to-mouth blue-collar jobs, she'll be ready to try another route to living. She'd rather be happy than "rich," but there ain't nothing worse than being miserable and poor. She had all the advantages and threw them away, and though that might be easier to live with than being on the bottom without the choices, it too gets old. One day she will pull herself up by the bootstraps. She may be a Stewart by blood, but she's got her mother's Cassell blood and spirit, and hanging around me has rubbed off on her some, too. I am the only father she ever knew and I was there for her from age three to twenty, seventeen years of her life. I am not too worried she'll make it. I just hope that her addictions to drugs and easy money don't get the best of her. She wants to do well, she wants to work with children, but knows that she is certainly no role model for them now. Our position as this point is, call us when you have

1) a job worthy of respect and 2) a place to live. We really don't want to see her or hear from her until she's at least made this commitment. Maybe that will be enough to keep her moving forward.

Andrew will probably make it too, for different reasons. He is more cautious than Sarah and lacks her spirit of adventure; that should keep him safer. He has more book smarts compared with her street smarts. He also has a lot of talent in the art area, drawing, painting, and he is more focused, more dedicated to his interests. He is also big on computers. His new job at the graphics store has him drawing/creating on the computer, and he has produced T-shirts with his own original designs. He followed through and has a bunch made up. His weakness is leaning too much on home. He likes being here and so does Mom. He now talks about coming back here to live after school — if he hasn't found a job yet. "Brian might hire me back until I find something." Though I know that can get too comfortable and he might not "find" something and be here for long, I also know that stuff happens and he might very well meet with success outside and find it preferable to living here. I'll hope for that.

Caroline, well, we were getting so close and then the kids popped back up and wham! we drifted apart again. The dynamics of Andrew living here just keep it that way, even when everyone is getting along. She lives for him, and my position and status as husband and soul mate decline. Her lack of respect for me and her outright display of same are sad. The competition between Caroline and me is so intense, she even brags about beating me out in the life span game. She brags about outliving me. She also makes quite the thing about being able to get along just fine without me, without any man, as she counsels her sister and friend Jill, who are currently in bad relationships. She has this role of "Look at me. I'm strong I don't need a man!" played to these women who are currently being dumped on by their men. Easy for her to say this with a good man standing right behind her. It's almost like a well-fed person surrounded by food, counseling others who are starving on how they don't need food, "Be like me and stand strong without food. You don't need it, look at me." And though I don't doubt Caroline would do just fine on her own, and that if I left or died she would not seek comfort in another's arms, it's still sad to hear her go on like this when I'm standing right there. You can say all you want about the "fragile male ego," but I know mine has taken quite a lot of blows. I look to my inner strength that allows her to carry on like this. I know deep inside it has little to do with me, and I love her enough to allow her to be a little crazy. I know we are successful because we are a team. Kinda like the "She's not heavy, she's my wife" version of Boys Town, "He's not heavy, he's my brother."

We're very different people sometimes, and though I know that marriage is for "your pruning" as well as your growth, it would be nice to have a glee club, a wife who was proud of me. And I haven't found her pride in me for a long time. In her son, yes; in me, no. And should she be? I survived the fight with the school district. I put up one hell of a fight for our daughter, and lost, and am working my way out of the bitterness. I did it by doing something about it—giving the interview to the newspaper to get the *rest of the story* out. I was proud when it appeared. Caroline insisted they would never publish it, and when I insisted they would, she told me I was naive. When they did, not only did I not receive any praise or admission that I was right; she got angry because it appeared in June, was the superintendent's last word, and because "she would now have to answer a thousand questions at work." I can never win. Now it was MY FAULT the paper ran the article. She was mad because it appeared so late after the first article, and after graduation. She was convinced that Little Man had orchestrated even this final word. When do I get just a little credit for the hundreds of hours I devoted to this case and suffering the humiliations and loss of a job and almost my reputation for our daughter? Could a lesser man have done what I did? Would any other father? How about stepfather? I'm proud of what I did, and Sarah is, too.

June 17, 1997, Closure

Is that part of it? I could do for her daughter something she was unable to do? Though we were in it together for so long, I really feel like I am out there alone sometimes. It's why I reached out to Sarah again, maybe not so much for her as for myself. I needed my ally back. Caroline has hers (Andrew), but mine has been gone since that day in November when we lost the case. And though I am not pleased with who she is and what she does, there is that link, that bond, that love that only a father can have for a daughter. And I miss it. Deeply.

# Hindsight

Do I regret taking on this fight? Did I really have a choice? I had to do it. When did I waiver? When I saw what it was doing to my family and my career. I wanted to back out. I got savaged by Caroline for being a coward. I stayed in till the end. I lost. I lost my job, almost my career, some of my family's money, the case, some friends. I lost part of me. And I am condemned by my wife because I thought I would win and I was wrong? I committed the unpardonable sin; I lost. Condemned for being positive and having hope, seeing to the truth in the case? That's what kept me going, and though we "lost," the truth got out. Even though the board and the courts turned their heads, they know I was right and that what they did was wrong. That doesn't change anything, but I was true to my mission, and I stuck it out till the end. And I have my self-respect back. And I'm sorry if my wife is upset or angry, but her target should not be pinned onto my back. I was true to her and her children. It's tough to think about, but our marriage could end not with a bang but a whimper. Or it could pull back together. If you look at men, those who walk away from their own children, and those who are devoted to theirs, I deserve some credit for being there. And as much as I love Sarah, I've been tough on her. I meted out discipline when it was called for. Andrew, it was easier to dole out. Why? Because he was coming between my wife and me. If

Caroline could only see that. We sat over dinner not too long ago and I told her how happy I was. The cases were closed, we had some extra money, I had a new job with a bigger salary, our house and garden were in great shape, we didn't have to move, and look at our lifestyle, flying off to Florida three times a year, and Connecticut to enjoy friends, and dinner and a movie in Annapolis. And she looked so sad. "You're not happy, though, are you?" I asked her. She said she just didn't feel like her house was a home. A home like her mother's, with kids coming around and all. I said that this was a time when they were leaving the nest and that she shouldn't blame herself for the problems Sarah and Andrew had. She said she didn't blame herself. She blamed me.

Here is a woman so hopelessly devoted to her kids, that she is ready to let her marriage fail to have just a little piece of them as they go out the door. Yet I have hope for the future. I have to. That's who I am. I have friends both male and female, and options outside of this marriage if I am forced to leave it. But just because *you're* happy in a marriage doesn't mean it's a happy marriage. Both of you have to be happy, and Caroline hasn't been for a long time. Her kids have not turned out the way she wanted, and she can't always blame herself, so I'm the target. And I'm tough. I looked to my primary role model, my aunt Meam, and hoped that things would work out for the best. I had to. Little did I know what surprises were in store in the coming years. There would be a calm before the storm, but yet another major battle lay ahead of us, another one that would challenge our marriage, and ourselves.

## CHAPTER TWENTY-NINE

# NOVEMBER 1999

Been a while, hasn't it, and yes, a lot of water has flowed down this stream. Caroline and I were finally settling into a much-deserved rest, empty-nest syndrome extraordinaire. For the first time in our sixteen-year marriage, we were able to enjoy each other without the kids. Just little Maggie Mae and us. We heard from them both on a regular basis, Andrew more than Sarah, but usually by phone. According to schedule, we got our six-week update from Sarah. Caroline had the pattern down. Sarah would call about every six weeks just to check in, to let us know she was still amongst the living. Sarah left Maryland to join forces with a dude she'd met in Baltimore. He was also involved with drugs, but had been shipped off to Texas to live with his uncle to get clean. Sarah flew out to join him and get herself clean, according to her. Shortly after her arrival in Texas, the two headed further west to…California. She had phoned us from there surprised that we didn't know, assuming we had followed her travel adventures across the continent. To be honest, once she left "for good," out of sight/out of mind was safer for everyone. Though we hadn't completely written her off, our patience had worn pretty thin, and all we needed to know was whether she was still alive; anything more was more drama than we were willing to entertain on her behalf. This call, however, was a little more eye opening than usual. "I'm pregnant," she said. "I'm pregnant." Now, with her history of drug use, especially the IV stuff, not to mention her consorting with who's-to-know undesirables, my first thought was all of the high-risk factors this pregnancy was subjected to. We suggested that she be tested. Though we never suggested it (knowing how oppositional she was), her decision to take the pregnancy full term, to have the child, should be based on its health, her health. She needed to rule out STDs, AIDS, hepatitis C, etc. She also needed to make sure she was both clean and sober. We raised these concerns calmly and rationally, focusing on the health of her baby, though terminating the pregnancy also crossed our minds when we considered all the high-risk behaviors and the effect they would have on her growing fetus and the child she would be bringing into the world. To be honest, Caroline and I both agreed that having a child in her condition was the last thing anyone would recommend. We shared our concerns, wished her well, and then waited to see what she discovered. She put us off for a number of phone calls and finally said she was going to do it, "Quit buggin' me, I'm scheduled to get tested, so get off it," was her general attitude. To be quite honest, I was almost hoping something would be found to provide her with an excuse to terminate this pregnancy. I was worried, and not only for Sarah. For someone like Sarah, with untreated co-morbid (co-occurring) conditions such as ADHD, ODD, LD, depression, panic disorder, etc., just taking care of herself was a major undertaking. The strain of having to take care of a baby with no post-high-school education, no career, no savings, no husband, was even more daunting. Most people wait until they have all those things mastered before thinking about starting a family, but then again, Sarah always did do everything backwards. I was worried for this child and the

November 1999

bouts of depression and drugs its mother was subjected to. And, yes, I was worried about this baby's effect on our lives, Caroline's and mine. If Sarah fell off the wagon and this baby was neglected, would we be in the same position as many of our clients/parents who are grandmothers, bringing up their children's children? At fifty and looking forward to retiring in ten years, I was not wanting to be dealing with a child and then a teenager in my sixties. In my mind I was getting ready for my fallback position if that happened. I was considering leaving the marriage. I had reached that place in my life and my marriage where the "straw" of a squirming, screaming baby was more than sufficient to send me packing. I had run out of patience.

To compound the fears and the issues were two phone calls Sarah made after her tests. The first, she tells us that the doctor told her the baby might have Down syndrome. Oh, boy, a lifetime of child rearing, and the added stresses a mentally challenged child provides: mental, financial, marital. Next phone call it was, "No, not Down, a neural tube defect." Oh, wonderful, everything from mental retardation to paralysis and even death right after birth with the baby's brain outside of the skull. Sometimes my education and training opens the doors to too many bad scenarios. We were on this roller coaster with Sarah receiving questionable medical advice, without the benefit of someone in the know (Caroline or myself) able to talk directly to her treating physician. And with her three thousand miles away on the opposite coast in California, with her new half-Iranian boyfriend "Mohammed" Aminimackmahood, it was crazy. Then the word came back that everything was okay; her doctor said so. Took a sonogram and saw the fetus and the heart was beating and everything was going to be just fine. Like I trust this doctor who couldn't give a straight reading of the lab report. Or was it Sarah's inability to understand what the doctor was saying? Or, even more likely, Sarah playing the big *M*, manipulating us, playing with us as always? Toying with our emotions, pulling us along on her roller coaster ride? I didn't know but I was becoming increasingly uncomfortable with the whole scene. It was easy to throw Sarah to the curb; heck, she reveled in lying in the gutter, but with a little baby at her side? We didn't want to push the abortion issue, or Sarah would go the opposite way; at the same time, we hoped that our concerns would put the fear into her and maybe she would decide having this baby was more than she could handle. Sarah seemed to be willing to see it through, and like a child who just has to have the toy, only to leave it aside, Sarah was not capable of seeing the consequences down the road. Whether she got pregnant by accident, to mend her relationship with Mohammed, to provide someone for her to love (and be loved by), or whether she did it to weasel her way back into the family, we might never know, but with no thought or plans for termination of the pregnancy, and the nine-month clock ticking away, we began to consider the long-term effects ourselves. Caroline was moving in the direction of "since it looks like this pregnancy is going full term, maybe we should be planning on going out there to California." I took a wait-and-see attitude.

For me, it was more like…what's changed? Sarah still has not paid back any of the money she took from us, or paid us for the car we gave her. You'll recall that she cashed in tuition money and money for books and school supplies we gave her, not once but twice. She also owed us for the car we bought for her to get back and forth to classes at the community college. When she screwed us the second time, Caroline and I were adamant: until she paid back the money she owed us, she was not welcome in our home. Did she get pregnant as a way of getting back into the family fold? Were we being prudent to make any major changes in our plans based on her "mistake"? I was still holding the ground for her doing the right thing, but now here was this new factor that literally had a life of its own. And Caroline, being blood, was being drawn into this thing a lot faster and sooner than I. Once again I was starting to feel left out again. I made it clear where I stood. I

November 1999

was *not* raising my daughter's child. I would not send money to her, and I wasn't sure about supporting this new entity. I resented being forced to accept choices someone else made (to not take proper precautions, to get pregnant, to bring the pregnancy to term, to raise the baby, etc.). But Caroline was starting to make grandmotherly sounds and the phone calls to California were increasing, now almost weekly. I was starting to get anxious. I loved Caroline, and loving means being willing to make sacrifices for your loved one to make them happy, but when is this love reciprocated? When does Frank get to be happy and to have someone make a sacrifice, a difficult choice, for him?

I got on the phone a time or two and learned that Sarah's baby was a girl, and she was putting on weight, and the due date was at the end of June. Caroline wanted to be called *Nunny*, in the Italian tradition. "What do you want to be called?" Caroline and Sarah (long distance) asked. I only had to think for a minute. *Grandfather* was too formal and I hated the Southern tradition of double names, *Mom-mom*, *Ma-maw*, *Pa-Paw*, *Pap-Pap*, etc. How about *Uncle Frank*? That seemed to work for my many nieces and nephews, and little cousins? "DAD!" Sarah didn't like that too much. "I'm just not ready to be a grandfather yet," I told her. I'd have to think about it. So here I was, never saying never, considering how I would deal with being a grandfather.

Well, fall 1999 turned to winter 2000, and then spring, as it usually does around that time of the year, and we got pictures of the sonogram. It looked more like static on an old black and white TV. I got on the phone a few more times, but had yet to speak with Sarah's significant other. I hadn't met him or talked with him, and here he was not only going out with my daughter, dating her, boffing her, but impregnating her. Whatever happened to asking permission for this stuff? Heck, in his country they would have chopped his winkie off for the out-of-wedlock sex, and I would get to wield the axe for his defiling my precious daughter. I'm glad we live in the grand ol' USA, though, cause I would have been dewinkified years ago if I lived in Iran. He was sticking with her, and he seemed to want the baby as much as she did, so maybe this could work out.

## Spring Break 2000

April always brings the great Easter break into play. This year snow has shortened Caroline's vacation, but mine was still intact: Good Friday and the entire week after. I planned on going to Florida, and Caroline was allowing me to bring a buddy of mine. We were going to have fun in probably my last visit to my aunt's apartment. Meam died a year ago January, and I missed her terribly. It looked like the apartment was going to be sold to my sister so I would get to have one last visit. Caroline would be going into West Virginia and then back to work. Then Sarah announced she was coming in. Now I hadn't seen her since February 1999 when she flew off to Texas, and then California, and my feelings were still mixed. I would be in Florida when she arrived, but she would still be in town when I got back. Did I want to see her? Sure. How about meeting her significant other, Mohammed? "I guess." "Great! We'll all meet you at the airport when you get back from Florida!"

Now here's the rub. A week in paradise; swimming pools, bars, bikinis, beaches, dinners on cool canals, views of the city in lights at night from the twelfth story, etc. Coming back home to reality is tough enough, and as nice as it is to see my wife, it's going to be tough seeing my prodigal daughter after a year or more, and to also have to meet her boyfriend, lover, father of her child-to-be for the first time. Well, let's just say I know my nervous system pretty well, having lived with it for fifty years, and I know what stimulus overload is all about. I agreed to meet Sarah at the airport, but Mohammed could wait until I was ready.

I arrived at the airport, and no one was at the gate. So I started walking toward the baggage. Here came Caroline. Hugs and kisses were exchanged; I did miss her. But where was Sarah? Seems she had taken offense at my refusal to meet Mohammed, so she wasn't coming either. Caroline was to call from her cell phone when I landed, and then she would decide. We got our luggage and our car and headed down the road to the shore, and I said sure, call her, we can meet in Annapolis, halfway home. So she called and it rang and rang and rang. We were past Annapolis and over the bridge before she picked up, had to go out to get milk or something. Did we want to meet for dinner in Baltimore at eight? According to Sarah, the whole family (his family) was gathering: Mohammed, his mother, stepfather, half brother, full brother, and who knows. Having just returned from Florida, and driven ninety minutes home, having to unpack and unwind, did I want to turn back around drive another ninety minutes across the bridge to meet and break bread with Sarah, whom I hadn't seen in a year, plus the rest of this crew of strangers? The nervous system again was saying, *I don't think so, Frank. We might make something very nasty shoot out of your lips on this one.* So I declined. We'd call her in the morning and we could get together for breakfast in the morning, just the four of us. Mom, Dad, Sarah, Mohammed.

Well, Sunday morning came, and I was actually looking forward to seeing Sarah and meeting her mate. This wasn't to be, however. After a litany of excuses, they ended up staying home all day, and then left for California later that evening. Caroline had gotten to spend some time with her and even met Mohammed, but I was deprived (spared?) the opportunity. From what Caroline had to say, maybe "spared" was more like it. Sarah did not make a pretty pregnant woman. In fact, with her baggy pants and ethnic cornrows (red), not to mention her new tattoo, she looked more like some refugee from the trailer park Laundromat than a daughter we could be proud of. Our mother-to-be now sported a six-inch-high graffiti-style tattoo of her street name, "GURL," emblazoned across the small of her back. Oh well. Caroline was glad she didn't get to see me. "You would not have approved," she said. "I told her if she was going to the airport dressed like trailer trash, then she could just stay home." So the rest of that story came out, but then again, I would have been embarrassed by a bloated, braided, tattooed lady in sweat pants claiming to be my long-lost daughter in the crowded airport. If we didn't go to California in July when the baby was born, then maybe we could work something else out. Sarah still seemed lost to me. What had changed? Soon there will be a fresh set of arms and legs to tattoo, and a fresh pucker of mouth to shove a cigarette into. I could hardly wait to see my new grandbaby.

Somewhere along the line I brought up the subject of establishing some connection with our new in-laws. I mean, if our daughter was going to have a baby with this man, and we were one of two sets of grandparents, well, then, shouldn't we get to know his mother, his family, a bit? Caroline called Mohammed's mother, who only lived about forty-five minutes away, and suggested we meet over dinner. She agreed to meet us at a local restaurant near where she lived, and we would drive across the bridge for the rendezvous. I told Caroline to ask her to bring a picture of Mohammed so I could see what he looked like. Caroline described herself — five-four, shoulder-length hair — and yours truly, six foot, 190, blond hair and mustache. His mother described herself as five six, brown hair and eyes, and maybe fifty pounds overweight.

We got to the restaurant before her and sat down waiting for her arrival. When she stomped in, I said to myself, fifty pounds? She was more like one hundred pounds over the top. She plopped herself down, nervous to the max, and yammered along a mile a minute as though she only had five minutes to tell us everything about herself and her son. She apparently had met his father, a citizen of Iran, in the States and then returned to his native country, Iran, where she gave birth to her first son, Mohammed's older brother. When she was pregnant with Mohammed, Iran was experiencing some minor political upheaval involving an ayatollah and some American hostages. Dad felt it would be in her best interest to leave Iran and return to her native country. He would join her later. So she came back to the United States of America and gave birth to Mohammed. Later that year when Daddio finally returned to the United States, he received a rather cool reception at the airport, and then when he went to grab for his new son, Mohammed broke into a loud cry. Rather than accept the fact that the little tyke never set eyes on this swarthy stranger from a strange land and might be a little scared, he reportedly grew incensed that his wife had turned his son against him. He apparently made such a scene that he was not permitted to remain in the country and took the next flight back to Iran — and don't let the cargo door hit you in the ass on your way back. A divorce followed and Mohammed's mother remarried. Stepdad had little to nothing to do with her boys, as he had a son of his own, so the boys essentially grew up without a father, just Mommy. At the restaurant she brought not one, but a whole album of photos of little Mohammed; the chubby baby pictures, the fat-faced little school pictures, and the fat kid in the band uniform pictures. I was starting to get a sick feeling in my stomach. Of all the co-morbid conditions my daughter had, we had failed to address her most significant one: her vision.

At any rate, we talked a little about Sarah's upbringing and her troubles with drugs and how we were concerned that this might have an impact on the baby. We also made it clear that the message we sent to Sarah and Mohammed was that this was their choice and their responsibility. If they decided to have this baby, they would be raising it, not us. His mother, whom I will not so affectionately refer to as Big P, short for Penelope, quickly responded, "Oh, I'll raise her!" This woman apparently had issues beyond the weight problem and the ex-husband problem, and the problems she had raising both her boys, who admittedly had a few of the *D*s themselves: ADHD, ODD, and the big *D* for drug problems. Older brother had even spent some time in jail for his indiscretions. What were we getting ourselves into, or what were we being drawn into? Caroline and I came out of there shaking our heads, resigned to letting things happen as they may, but resigned to not stepping forward to take this responsibility off these kids' hands. If they decided to have this baby, they would have to straighten their acts out, grow the heck up, and get ready to be parents to this new life they had created. Maybe, just maybe, it would help them. Beyond this, the message you must send to your children is, "This is your child, you raise it," NOT "This may be your child, but if you get in a pinch, Momma will step up and help you raise it." WRONG MESSAGE.

# CHAPTER THIRTY

# SUMMER 2000

Despite the lightening speed with which life passes us by, sometimes it slows down. Like a river eddy or a current moving within the larger faster-moving stream, it takes a life of its own and it slows down, giving us a chance to savor its essence. When you look back on it, it seems like too much has gone by, and yet the time was so short. So have the past six months been.

June 2000 was welcomed in with a new colleague at work. She came to replace the previous one, who only landed for less than eight months, realized her certification didn't go through, and resigned mid-April, the busiest time of the year. Just when I was in the process of readjusting to this, another candidate popped up, one with a Dr. in front of her name, a few years of experience, and a certificate. So rather than feel guilty like I did last summer about leaving for six weeks without someone to fill in for me, we had a full-time employee hired on, and I was determined to make sure she stayed on. I treated her royally. June would be a winding down, and then the summer plans kicked in; Lake in the Berkshires for the

## No Good Deed

Fourth of July, three days in New York City, Florida for ten days, and camping at the beach. I was excited. Caroline, well, she was excited as well, but for different reasons; she was going to be a grandmother. Sad to say, I didn't quite share her enthusiasm. I was still a bit gun shy; I still felt that Sarah might was using this pregnancy to weasel herself back into the family. She failed to meet any of the other conditions we'd set, so how else could she work her way back into our good graces other than being with child? And not just any child, but a grandchild. The first grandchild, and for Caroline her natural grandchild, with her DNA, her connection to the future. I couldn't be more disconnected. As much as I loved Sarah, it was less the unconditional love of a father and more of, "I will let myself feel something again when I know it's safe. " So I was wary. As the date approached, I kept strangely silent. We were all at the lake with friends, real friends, from way back. Caroline and the kids both knew these folks, from fourteen summers up there. Me, I've known them for forty years, from the days I spent at their houses when I was ten. So we all sat on the deck overlooking the lake on the Fourth of July 2000, and waited, counting the CCs of dilation. And when she finally popped out, Sarah's little baby girl already had a whole series of names: Betsy Ross, or Sparkle Starr. Of course she (Sarah) wasn't so keen on that idea, and I don't know what the little tyke herself might have thought. Sarah's man was coming into an age where his heritage, his Persian heritage, was beginning to rise in its significance for him, so he suggested a Persian name. They arrived at "Lily," with an even more flowery/street name of Jazmyn for a middle name, and his surname, which is appropriate under the circumstances. Though his father was and still is from Iran, a ten-letter name that no one can spell is tough to swallow, but it does render some level of commitment on his part. He is acknowledging the child and will have some responsibility to care for her. I still had mixed emotions; I mean, I had yet to meet the fellow, and Sarah had long ago used up any "chips" — you know, as in "bargaining chips." I wanted to be stress free for a while on her account; she'd put me/us through enough stress. And all the worst-case scenarios were still swirling about my brain; what if she gets back into drugs again and the baby is left on its own? Sarah swore that she stopped using drugs, even tobacco, when she found out she was pregnant. She was still clean. We had to believe her; what were our choices? The thought of her back on hard drugs and a poor little baby being left on its own was frightening. But how could Caroline leave flesh and blood to be farmed out to foster homes? I was filled with more fear and caution than joy. Caroline, of course, was edging towards joy. I explained it away in this fashion: Sarah is her child. Of her blood. This baby is her direct descendent, her blood also. She carried Sarah, and now her baby, her little Sarah, was carrying a child of her own. This was a bonding, a sharing experience between mother and child, one I could not share. If Caroline had her way, she would have been in California with Sarah, not sitting here at a lake in the Berkshires, but it seems Mohammed's mother, all three hundred pounds of her, beat Caroline to the punch and was right there for the birth of her grandbaby. It was Caroline's place to be with her daughter at this time, but Big P barged in. Wasn't room, quite literally, for two grandmothers. I was glad that Caroline was with me, but I feared the worst. I had reason to. What if this relationship didn't turn out? For all the talk of "We're not bringing up your baby," once the little human being is on the planet and takes on increasing value, things can change. This was not a pregnancy, or an embryo, or a fetus, it was, for real, a CHILD, a BABY.

I was being a little selfish. Summer was all planned out, a couple of days at the beach in June, the lake in July, New York City, and then Florida. When we got back, Sarah would be on her way to the East Coast. One more trip to see the ponies run at Chincoteague with Caroline's sister and niece, and we would come home to greet Sarah and child. Caroline was calling on an increasing frequency, and the days and the trips all converged to the last week in July. When we pulled into the driveway after our four-day camp out at Chincoteague (it rained all four days), they were there. Was I nervous? Darn right. It had been over a year since I last saw Sarah, and a lot of dirty water had been under that bridge. But when I saw Sarah and she ran over to hug me, it was as though it was all gone. And then we got to see the little squirt, all fuzzy eyed but beautiful.

I had a few days to observe, and watched Sarah with her little girl. It didn't take long to figure out whether the two had bonded, and whether love and affection or resentment ruled the relationship. It was obvious that Sarah was completely devoted to this little girl, and it was as though all of it was gone—all the pain and frustration and anger and rules were gone. Washed away. I can remember a moment when she was lying on the couch with Lily, and I was sitting in the command center (my recliner). I looked over and I said, "Sarah, it's been a long time since I could say I felt this way, but I am really proud of you." She beamed and said, "Thanks, Dad."

The next few days we took our granddaughter out to show off, at the beach and to town, hoping to bump into people whom we might have ducked earlier. I had little Lily in a harness over my neck that held her close to my chest, and her little nose was usually pressed into it. I was worried and asked Sarah if this was the way it was supposed to work. "Yeah, Dad, she likes to hear your heart beat." And it was beating a beautiful rhythm of love and affection and pride for my little granddaughter. I spent a lot of time holding the little creature, talking to her, and even marveling at how I could calm her down when she cried. Yes, folks, rather than hand the screaming, squirming little devil over to her mother, I would talk to her and make funny noises and lift her up, up, up, and down, down, down, and she would calm and begin to gurgle and coo. This was the beginning of bonding with my little gal. She was just three weeks old and already I was in love with her. It was a wonderful time for all of us, reconciliation.

We saw Sarah a month later, in September, when Caroline's dad passed away. Sarah and Lily flew in for the funeral. We took her shopping and she bought a nice suit with a long coat that covered her belly that was only recently was with child. Caroline's niece, the princess of the family, working on her law degree, was stealing the show as usual, setting up the memorial service with many opportunities for her to lead the congregation in song. I don't think much of church services anyway, and the singing sticks in my throat at times, but having to listen to this barrister howl at the moon was too much. So I decided to talk with Sarah about speaking on behalf of her grandfather. I didn't even get the chance to ask; she asked me if I would help her write something, and I quickly agreed. We worked on it for about an hour, her ideas with a few suggestions and literary embellishments from me. She practiced it and was ready for the service. Caroline wanted to read it (edit it) beforehand, but Sarah and I were adamant, she'd have to wait like the rest of them for the reading at the service. Caroline loved us both, but she didn't always trust us. Sarah, for obvious reasons, and me, well, let's just say I have a mind of my own, speak it at will, and sometimes even Caroline doesn't know what will come out of my mouth. There has been more than one occasion when she is kicking me under the table or making faces at me to shut it up, but I am a grown man, and believe it or not, when it comes to funeral services, especially for an in-law, I wasn't about to launch into anything controversial. I may have a big mouth, but I like to think I have some degree of discretion and good taste. Here is what Sarah said:

We are gathered here today for two purposes. To mourn the passing of my Pap Pap, and, more importantly, to celebrate his life. He was George to his many friends and coworkers at the railroad. He was George to his wife of fifty-three years, my Nunny, Katherine. He was dad to his three children, Liz (the first girl born into the Cassell family in fifty-two years), Caroline, his middle child and my mother, and George Joseph, his youngest son. But he was Pap Pap to his eight grandchildren, my brother, Andrew, Haley, Atlas, Jeremy, Johnny, Mike, Tim, and me, Sarah. Above all, he was a true friend to everyone he met.

He was special to me for a lot of reasons, but most of all because he loved us all without question, and he was always there for us when we needed him. He was not only a good storyteller, but he was a great listener. If you had a worry or trouble you knew you could sit down with Pap Pap and he would listen to and give you the advice and the encouragement to work through your troubles.

Pap Pap always had good advice, about working hard in school and saving money. He also told me about drugs and how they might look good at first, but that they were a dead-end road to nowhere. When I was in my darkest days, I remembered his words and it helped me to find my way back out. He'd always tell me, "Sarah, you keep your head up, don't ever let anything get you down."

Pap Pap taught me about the importance of family and how they are the only people you can truly trust. When I was a teenager and had some troubles of my own, I didn't always feel I could talk to my parents, but Pap Pap was there and he helped me to learn about who you could really count on. He told me that as mad as I might get at my mom and dad, they were the only people I could really depend on, and that they would always love me no matter what I did.

One of my best memories occurred during Nunny and Pap Pap's fiftieth wedding anniversary. He sat at the head of his family and he looked so proud of his family and his place in it. Then he gazed around the room at all of his kids and grandkids, and then at my Nunny, and a look came over his face that I will always remember. Without saying a word his eyes told everyone that he was glad he married her, glad that he had chosen her to be his life mate. He seemed so proud of my Nunny at that moment, and the love they shared filled the room that day.

Over the past year his battle with emphysema grew. His eyesight failed him and he could no longer do a lot of the things he loved to do, hunt and fish or even drive himself around. I didn't realize how sick he was until I came in to see him from California this July after my baby was born. It was the first time he got to meet his great-granddaughter, Lily. Pap Pap looked at her with the same look he gave Nunny, filled with love and admiration. He bent down close as he held her in his arms so he could see her tiny little face, and as she fell asleep in his arms, all limp, he looked up at me and my mom and said, "She's just like a little pup."

Lily will never get the chance to know her great-grandfather, but she will learn about him from me and the rest of the family who loved and respected him, and she will learn the value and importance of family...the lessons that he taught all of us.

It was a sad occasion, but one that strengthened some family bonds just as it loosened others. Our family bonds grew stronger that day. Sarah and Lily flew back to California that weekend and we stayed in touch. Christmas was the next scheduled visit, and despite a couple of false starts, tickets were purchased and Sarah, Lily, and Mohammed, Lily's father, arrived on the East Coast. We got together at his mother's house in Annapolis and the next event was the Christmas holiday. We'd decorated the house and cleaned and were anxious and excited about their arrival. For the first time in a long time, the warmth of family was filling our home to overflowing. Mohammed seemed to be a decent guy, even likable, intelligent, and a willing conversationalist. Sarah had lost all of her post baby bloats and looked beautiful (despite the new tattoo *"Lily"* emblazoned across the back of her neck; what can you do?). At this point, we are a family again, and with Andrew and Sarah at home and now two new arrivals, Lily and Mohammed, the family grows to even larger dimensions. It has been a long journey, and it still has some distance to go. But for now, there is much joy and happiness to behold, and we all have learned a great deal from it. I look at my own family in total disarray from my Aunt Meam's death and my sister Sue's nervous breakdown, and I thank the spirits for giving me my own family, one that is based on love and mutual respect. We are a long way from perfect, but the balance has been restored.

# CHAPTER THIRTY-ONE

# CHRISTMAS BLUES

We were all looking forward to Christmas. Lily would be six months old, and we paid Sarah's way back east and ending up paying for a nonrefundable roundtrip airline ticket, LA-BWI (Baltimore Washington International). Our original plans (hopes?) had been for us to pick them up at the airport and bring them to our home, but that's not exactly the way it worked out. Mohammed's mother, Penelope, stepped in and offered to pick them up at the airport. Her explanation was that since she lived closer to the airport on the other side of the Bay Bridge she would just go and get them. She would get to see them first, but we just stepped back, disappointed but resolved to let things work out. After all, we had planned to spend time with them at a ski resort in western Maryland, so let her enjoy the first few days. I had booked two rooms at a ski lodge in the mountains where we could ski, swim in the pool, bask in the hot tub, eat good food, and generally enjoy each other's company. Caroline and I suggested that we all ride together in our car, but they didn't want to drive out with us to the lodge, which was about three hours away. They would follow right behind us. They had already spent Christmas Day with his family, so we were disappointed that we wouldn't even get to exchange gifts until we met at the lodge. We drove the four hours to the lodge and checked in. By late afternoon we were getting a bit worried so we called and had a difficult time tracking them down. When we finally did make a connection, Sarah was full of all sorts of crazy stories and excuses: they had to visit with his brother and his cousins and they were all sick with the flu, etc., etc. Bottom line was that they would not be joining us at the lodge. You can imagine our disappointment. We didn't get to greet them at the airport, we didn't get to spend Christmas Eve or Christmas Day with them, and now they were backing out of the three-day vacation I had already paid for at the ski lodge.

We returned to our home and made arrangements for them to join us for a few days there. Disappointment turned to frustration and anger when Sarah and Mohammed continued to make excuses for not coming to see us at all. I pointed out to her that I had paid for her trip in, had not seen them since they arrived, and that they stuck me on the ski lodge vacation, and I expected to spend some time with them. They eventually relented and came over and spent the afternoon and evening with us and left the next day. Less than twenty-four hours. Out of ten days. Little did we know at the time that there were extenuating circumstances that drove their need to be in Annapolis. Other than family.

They returned to California with very little face time with us, but what could we do? Sarah had a significant other, she had a child with him, and had in-laws who wanted to see their grandbaby, as well as great-grandparents and assorted nieces, nephews, and cousins. We wanted to stay on good terms with them, so we continued to make nice and make regular phone calls to California. By January and February of 2001 we begin to notice a return of Sarah's depression. It began with her breaking down in tears, crying on the phone, complaining about Mohammed's frequent trips on the road, leaving her alone with Lily, coming in at all hours when he *is* home, etc. When Mohammed did return in the wee hours of the morning, he expected Sarah to get up and see to his needs. Mohammed also had the habit of bringing in roommates or friends who needed a place to stay, forcing Sarah to have to clean up after them as well. One of these individuals, Teddy C., was a known drug user and was the subject of a federal warrant. On one occasion federal marshals burst into the apartment next door (Sarah's neighbor and friend Ruth B.) looking for Mr. C. because he had used Ruth's phone to conduct business. They subsequently went to Sarah and Mohammed's apartment and took Mr. C. into custody. They burst in guns drawn. Lily slept in the next room. This was all straight from Sarah.

Sarah indicated she has no time at all for herself. When Mohammed was home he refused to help out with Lily, even insisting Sarah take Lily into the shower with her. This was confirmed by their neighbor Ruth. She also reported that when Sarah would leave Lily with Mohammed for a few minutes to visit Ruth for girl talk, Mohammed would bring Lily over and drop her off. When Sarah asked to go out for the evening with a female friend, Mohammed would demean her and call the friend a "whore." He had control of the family vehicle, leaving Sarah to fend for herself. There were occasions when Sarah had medical appointments for either herself or Lily, only to cancel them because Mohammed left her without transportation last minute. There were occasions when he left her without money or without purchasing enough food or diapers for Lily, forcing Sarah to rely on neighbors for both. Ruth turned out to be a wonderful neighbor. We got to know her because she had the phone Sarah would use to call us and for us to call her. Ruth would always run next door and get her. When we had Ruth on the line we would ask her how things were going. She did not think a lot of Mohammed, and told us Lily spent a lot of time playing with her kids in their apartment just across the outdoor walkway from Sarah's.

## Spring 2001

Through regular phone contacts with Sarah, we became concerned that she was beginning to sound more and more depressed. With her history, we began to worry that she might start self-medicating, and began to notice slurred speech and conversations during which she was unable to maintain a train of thought. We asked to talk with Mohammed and attempted to impress on him the need to take Sarah to a doctor to have her evaluated and treated for depression. When I spoke with him, I told Mohammed that she might need to be back on her Prozac to stabilize her mood swings. His response was, "We don't believe in medication — we do things the natural way." How was I to know what he meant by that? As it turned out, his natural way was through the use of opium poppies' primary derivative, heroin. Sadly, they both were back to using heroin.

By May I was convinced she was back using drugs but had no proof, and Sarah was denying it. Caroline was also very defensive about it and got angry at me when I suggested it. In a series of e-mails between Sarah and me, she began to talk about marriage to Mohammed, prompting a long e-mail from me encouraging Sarah to think long and hard about the decision. I posed questions about her need for an education and career to assure her independence in light of her overdependence on Mohammed. Sarah's response was that she didn't need a lecture, she needed support. After an exchange of e-mails, some of which asked for our help in setting up the wedding (finding a location, arranging for food, sending invitations, etc.), I attempted to explain that a wedding, even a simple wedding, requires lead time (residency, blood work, licenses, guest lists, return time for RSVPs, meal counts, etc.), and that it was difficult to impossible to plan it in a little over a month, three thousand miles away. Sarah's next e-mail described her wanting to come home so badly, but Mohammed "is making a big deal of it. I don't know what is going on with him, he never wants to talk to me, and he is so negative." She sounded so desperate and so lonely, and she was so, so far from home.

## June 2001

Sarah indicated that they "are getting married July 2, then will celebrate Lily's (first) birthday, and then my vacation starts. I want to see all my friends and my niece and Mohammed's brother and his wife (girlfriend), and we will make no plans until we get there." When I inquired in an e-mail about the location of Lily's July Fourth birthday party, her *first* birthday party, Sarah insisted we should already know. It was at Mohammed's mother's home in Annapolis. Sarah complained about having more problems with Mohammed. "I'm having doubts about this marriage. We're having problems…I never see him unless he's sleeping and it seems like all we do is argue about petty stuff." Once again we were on the wild roller-coaster ride with blind curves and no assurance of safety.

Five days later, the marriage was back on again. We were expected to plan for a wedding that we did not support, that we were unsure would ever take place, and now it was clear they were having personal problems that extended well beyond cold feet. I e-mailed back that she could do what she wanted, but we would not be involved in any way, planning or attending the wedding. Nothing more was heard about it for a while. I just had to get off that wild ride, I couldn't keep up.

By the end of June Sarah's calls were more incoherent and her speech more slurred. Caroline was still trying to cling to a mother's hopes that I was wrong, but in my heart and my head I sadly knew I was right. My earlier suspicions about her being back on drugs were so strong that I called Mohammed's mother to find out what she knew about the relationship, the wedding, etc. She admitted that she too was worrying about drug use, and regretted sending them money for the baby. Penelope indicated that over the last few months she had sent them between $500 and $600. We were incredulous. We told her not to send Sarah or Mohammed money under *any* circumstances. If they were on drugs, the money was going in their arms, not to the baby in their arms.

Sarah and Mohammed had no phone in their California apartment, so they continued to rely on their neighbor Ruth's phone. On occasions when Sarah wasn't home, the women started talking. Ruth would tell Caroline about her concerns, especially her suspicions that drugs were being used. Remember, it was her apartment the police barged into looking for Teddy C. On one occasion Caroline called Ruth to inquire about Sarah's physical condition and state of mind, and she said things appeared normal to her. It turned out Sarah was there in the room when we called. Ruth shared our concerns with Sarah, prompting a phone call to us the next day (June 22) in which Sarah cried, shouted, and screamed at us over the phone that she was not using drugs and that Mohammed's mother and everyone else were liars, etc. Furthermore, she was not coming into Maryland for Lily's birthday; in her words, "I don't need this shit."

We knew that Mohammed was on the road. Apparently he was an accomplished videographer and was under contract with a hip-hop group and on the road. His mother had given us his pager number. We called and left three urgent messages with his message service (live voice) on several occasions, telling Mohammed that Sarah was having a breakdown and we desperately needed to talk with him. He never returned any of the pages. We couldn't figure out why he was so bent on avoiding us and not helping his girlfriend and child. All this strange behavior would soon begin to make sense.

Two days later, on the twenty-fourth of June, Sarah called us back to tell us she would come back east for a visit with us but only under the strict understanding that we not discuss 1) drug use, 2) marriage, or 3) Mohammed. After consulting with our family therapist, Dr. Mom, she counseled us to hold Sarah to her word and *not* discuss any of the above. We agreed to meet Sarah and Lily at the airport. Mohammed would follow in a few days when he returned from New York.

June 24, Mohammed's stepbrother Richie, who lived in California, gave Sarah over $100 for her trip to Maryland, according to Mohammed's mother. Despite our vehement urging not to give Sarah or Mohammed any money, just arrange for their flight, Penelope convinced her stepson Richie to give Sarah cash to travel on. As you might expect, the money went to buy her the drugs she injected into her arm in the bathroom at the airport prior to the flight home.

June 25, Sarah arrives at BWI. She steps off the plane with baby in arms and a summer dress with short sleeves. Needle marks are clearly visible up and down both her thin arms. She was emaciated. From a postbaby 130, she dropped to a healthy 120, and now she weighed less than a hundred pounds. Sarah had lost a significant amount of weight since December and was pale and sickly. Lily was an emotional wreck, refusing to let Sarah out of sight or contact for even thirty seconds; she screamed when Caroline attempted to hold her. Children who are abused or neglected often exhibit what is known as an extreme attachment disorder. They are afraid to leave the parent, they need to take care of the parent, and they refuse to let anyone hold them or take them out of their mother's sight. This was what we observed with our little gal.

We'd promised not to discuss her drug use, so Caroline and I bit our tongues and waited anxiously for their luggage and our ninety-minute ride home. Our Uncle Paul was visiting from Ohio, and he had offered to let us use his Cadillac, a larger car with more room for luggage and passengers than our small cars. His only caution, in jest, referred to something about baby puke on his leather seats. Of course, that is exactly what happened. We had barely pulled out of the airport terminal when Sarah started yelling, "Pull over, pull over, Lily is getting sick!" And sick she was. The poor little thing was so stressed out from it all that she lost whatever she had in her little belly, all over the back seat of this luxury sedan. We pulled over and did our best to clean her and the car on the side of the highway.

The next morning we told Paul about the accident in his back seat. He laughed, reminding me of his earlier caution when he offered the car, "What can happen other than the baby throwing up in the back seat?" He was okay with it, especially when I assured him it was cleaned up and smelled fine the next morning. We spent a pleasant day with Paul, Caroline, and Lily, though Lily was very subdued for a toddler. Almost depressed. Paul left the next morning and we headed to the beach for our three days of camping. We got the pop-up set up and went out for a bite to eat. Sarah looked over the menu at the Long Horn and ordered a filet. At twenty-five bucks I pointed out to her that even I didn't order filet mignon out, that she could order anything but the filet. She settled on a salad and a $16.95 sirloin. I point this out only to place into context what happened next. The salads arrived and Sarah took one bite, then excused herself to use the restroom. When Lily saw her mother leave, and leave her with strangers (Caroline and me), who had only been with the little gal two days, she began to scream. Not cry, not whimper, but scream. There was no consoling her, and after being with her for the past forty-eight hours and observing her behavior of scream/withdraw/scream/withdraw, we knew there was nothing we could do to intervene. Of course everyone in the restaurant felt they had the key to this little girl's heart; they looked at the uncaring grandparents sitting there coldly while their little granddaughter screamed, unaware of the history that was coming home to roost at that table.

When Sarah returned to the table we made it clear she was not to leave again without taking Lily with her. "I was sick!" she said. "I threw up everything." About that time her $16.95 steak arrived, but she had already established that she was not going to take even a bite of it. When I reacted in kind (I'm glad I didn't pay for the $25.00 filet) all she could offer was, "I do this to Mohammed all the time" — order a big meal someone else is paying for, and then leave it to spoil. Always faithful to consequences, I told her she could take it back to the campsite. It stayed there in the fridge for a while, followed us home into the big fridge, and then, as you might have predicted, made its way to the landfill by way of the trusty trash can. Sarah managed another "Got ya!" to the small tune of $16.95.

We traveled around the beach as little as possible, only because Lily screamed every time we tried to get her into the car for the ten-minute drive. By day two at the beach, Sarah was still sick and pale and pasty, and wasn't able to relate to what we had planned to be a quiet family time at the beach. Though we all agreed to not discuss her problems, she was rapidly bringing them to the table. She insisted that we leave the sunshine of the beach and take her back to the camper. Sympathetic? Knowing full well that her vomiting and cramps had little to do with a virus, and everything to do with her withdrawal pangs from drug use, we had little sympathy. The sicker she got, the more we experienced the ultimate consequence, self-imposed: her sickness. The only sympathy we had was for the innocent in all this, little Lily. When the stress finally got to Caroline and she threw up on the beach, it was the first time I had ever seen Caroline sick in twenty years. I knew it was time to head back to the camper. Caroline and I lay down on one side of the pop-up and Sarah and Lily on the other. Sarah was out cold with little Lily sitting on her stomach wanting to play, wanting to make Mom feel better, a classic role reversal with a one-year-old child patting Mommy's face and stroking Mommy's hair. We cooked out on the grill, Sarah ate little, and then we left her at the camper and took little Lily to the boardwalk for an evening stroll in her stroller. She screamed all the way to the beach, and then clammed up at the beach, depressed, withdrawn, unsmiling. The crowds, the sea gulls, the kiddy rides weren't enough to shake Lily out of her sullen mood. An anger began to build up inside of Caroline and me, but mostly inside of me. Anger at my daughter for doing this, not to us, but to herself and her daughter. This was a complete abandonment of the parental role. That night was one of the worst I have ever spent. After seventy-two hours Sarah was in full withdrawal, and she was sick with fever and chills and cramps and nausea and she could not remain still. At three in the morning Caroline and I were on one side of the see-saw camper, Sarah and Lily on the other, with every shudder, every movement, every toss of her tortured body translated in full dynamics to Caroline and my side. Shake, boom, toss, turn. I finally had enough to speak up. "Sarah, can you keep Lily still?" "It's not her, it's me…I can't get comfortable." After several more hours of this, I was strongly suggesting that she go sleep in the car, but where would Lily go?

Somehow we made it through the night and into the next day. By day three at the beach we had had our fill of Sarah and took Lily to the beach, leaving Sarah alone in the camper. Things were better but we were still concerned that Lily was in a daze, unresponsive, and not even beginning to warm up to us. By day three we were all ready to go home.

June 29, we drive home from the beach. Mohammed calls the house and gets into an argument with Sarah on the phone. We put the baby to bed and confront Sarah on her drug use. We'd agreed to not talk about it, but when she so blatantly thrust it into our faces, we had to respond. If not for Sarah, then for little Lily. Sarah still denies using, and I challenge her to prove it with a drug screen. "Let's go!" she says, and we (Caroline, Sarah, and Lily) drive to Annapolis to the ER at the hospital. Unbeknownst to us, Sarah had called Penelope, arranging to have her to meet us there. When we get to the hospital, Sarah grabs Lily and runs ahead of us, attempting to hook up with Penelope in hopes of escaping out the back door. For once, Penelope doesn't play along and insists that Sarah wait for us. After some discussion, Penelope agrees to take Lily home with her, and we sit with Sarah waiting for the drug screen. With Lily out of the way we can focus on our daughter. Still insisting she did not use drugs anymore and that the black marks (tracks) up and down her arms were old ones, Sarah starts to waffle on the test. "I don't have to

## Christmas Blues

do this, you know, and even if I do, I don't have to share the results with you. It's private and confidential." I explain that that's not the deal. To convince me she is clean, she 1) has to take the test and 2) has to share the results with us. She reluctantly agrees and goes off with the nurse while we (Caroline and I) wait in the waiting room. We are exhausted physically and emotionally after the past three days and are feeling ever more helpless. Caroline stops for a moment to realize that today is her birthday. Happy freaking birthday!

Within a few minutes the duty nurse and the attending physician came out to speak with us. The doctor acknowledged that they knew she was of age and that they didn't have to share their findings with us, but that they were concerned enough to bring us into the loop. Sarah had admitted to them that she was heavily addicted to heroin, and though she'd been clean throughout her pregnancy and for months afterward, when they were in Maryland for Christmas, they had both used, hence their flulike symptoms and reluctance to meet up with us. Though Sarah resisted after they returned to California, she finally caved in and starting using on a regular basis. Mohammed had started using again and having parties at their apartment and encouraged her to as well. The physician and nurse at the hospital asked us if we would talk to her and try to get her to admit her drug use to us. We agreed and followed the doctor and nurse back to the bed and pulled the screen back. She was hooked to an IV to rehydrate after three days of vomiting and diarrhea. After a few moments Sarah finally admitted her use and Mohammed's involvement with her relapsing. We both hugged her and told her we loved her. We talked quietly for a while and then told her how important it was for her to get well. We would take care of her little girl, and she needed to focus on herself. We were doing this for her and secondarily Lily. We just knew we had to do something for the both of them.

We had hopes that this would be the bottom we had long expected, but Sarah quickly reverted to her earlier defensive strategies; "I can do it myself, I don't need rehab." After ten to fifteen minutes of attempting to apply logic to an irrational situation, we hit an impasse. I issued an ultimatum. Part of my voice was from exhaustion over the last three days, but it was also from the roller-coaster ride over the last seven years. "Sarah, you are out of choices. You either get your ass into rehab or we are done with you. We will cut you off completely as before. You'll be dead to us." It brought back to mind a previous intervention with our family therapist when we told her what her funeral plans would be if she didn't stop using and get some help. In addition, I also told her that we would do everything, everything, in our power to take Lily away from her. We then turned and walked out of her room. We left Sarah in the ER at the hospital. Maybe with no place to turn she would make the right decision to go into rehab. We walked down the hall, pausing only to talk with the doctor, nurse, and social worker, got information on a rehab facility, and left the hospital. We left to go home knowing Lily was safe and Sarah was…well, out of our hair after three of the worst days of my life. We went home to relax and recoup.

We called Penelope later in the day to check on Lily and told her we had left Sarah at the emergency room and the circumstances. We told her that Sarah had few friends and would face being homeless, or going into rehab. Under no circumstances should she pick her up at the hospital; Sarah needed to hit bottom. I wasn't even sure Sarah would call Penelope, but if she did I strongly discouraged her from allowing Sarah to stay there, especially with Lily being there. These two, addicted mother and child, needed some time away from each other. Penelope failed to hear a word we said. Sarah called and Penelope went to the hospital and took her home. Sarah ended up in her finished basement apartment. Unlike like the four of us trapped in a pop-up camper, unable to separate mother and daughter, Penelope could stash Sarah in the basement and leave Lily free to roam the main floor without seeing or hearing Mommy. This went on for three more days, Saturday, Sunday, and Monday, with Sarah throwing up and losing even more fluids and any remnants of her self-respect.

Caroline and I felt completely helpless. Penelope taking her in was akin to a parent down the street taking your daughter in when she ran away from home. But Sarah was of age, twenty-three, and all we could do was hope that this woman, Penelope, would respect our family enough to follow our wishes with respect to our daughter. She was not married to her son, she was still our daughter, and we expected more cooperation from her. But Penelope had a different view of things, one that involved playing into the manipulation, giving in to the demands of her sons and their girlfriends, and running around trying to fix things. She was the classic enabler. If her oldest son's girlfriend drove her car into the ground and failed to get needed repairs and it subsequently broke down, Penelope would not only pile in her car late at night to rescue them, but drive all over creation trying to find them a cheap starter and then wait along the side of the road while her son tried to put it in. Too much drama, too much craziness in that family dynamic for me. So when it came to our daughter, who was a de facto member of that family by virtue of her boyfriend/father of her child, then our rules no longer applied. Instead of Penelope joining with us parents, adults in support of the child, united in our stand against the substance abusers, Penelope sided with Sarah against us. In this way she would gain access to Lily, playing the good guy to our bad guys. Any hopes for Big P were lost.

Her plan to fix everything backfired, and by Tuesday Sarah ended up in the emergency room again. We got the call from Penelope. Sarah had to be taken back to the emergency room; would we go and get her? We certainly did not want to, but were almost forced into it, and we figured we put in our three days, Penelope put her three days in, maybe we could exercise some influence over Sarah this time. Now keep in mind, this was the day before the Fourth of July, and you can imagine what the traffic looked like going both to the beaches for the holiday and away from the beaches for the holiday (to the mountains). Off the shore to vacation points to the west and on the shore to the beaches. There was a huge bay between those two points and a bridge which funneled traffic down to two or three lanes in each direction. It typically backed up for miles each way, and we would have the exciting opportunity to enjoy the traffic jams both going and coming back. But we got in the car and crept along with traffic from the light at the end of our road all the way through the second light a mile down the road and then the bypass, clogged with cars. By the time we got to the next light I was ready to try a different route and headed north off the main road. Had a little red car in front who was making good time, 58–65 mph, and no one ahead of us. We cooked along for about five to ten minutes and then came upon two slowpokes, a blue car in the lead and a white car cruising along behind him at 45-–50. How patriotic, blue car, white car, red car. The red car pulled in behind the white one and I in turn. We cruised along like that for miles and miles with no one passing anyone, not the white car, who seemed satisfied with the pace, or the red car, who was earlier on a roll with me. After five miles stretched into ten I saw a straightaway and made my move, shifted into third, and punched it, moving along to 50, 55, 60, 65, which is what I was doing when I passed the white car…the State Police cruiser…and realized, Oh shit! What do I do now? Hit my brakes and unpass two cars or maintain my speed and a safe maneuver and pass the third car? I maintained my speed, signaled my lane change, pulled in front, and slowed down from the 70 I was doing in a 50 zone. He hit me with the lights as soon as I pulled over. No explanation about beach traffic and unfamiliarity with the road or the fact that I was on the way over to retrieve my daughter from the emergency room was well received. I waited the interminable minutes watching the other idiots continue on while I sat and sat and then continued on to my destination…the four-lane highway less than a mile ahead of us. No further comment is indicated.

We finally arrive at the hospital and Sarah is waiting for us out front. To say she looked horrible doesn't begin to describe this ghostly apparition who was enduring her I-don't-know-I-lost-count-of-how-many-times-I've-done-this  withdrawal.

She slinks into the back seat of the car and asks if we'll take her by the house to pick up clothes. What part of "No way" do you not understand? We head back into traffic for the ride home and tell her she will not be attending Lily's first birthday party the next day. She didn't deserve to see her baby, she hadn't earned the privilege, and if she was counting on us to come and pick her up at the hospital after our last conversation, she should consider herself fortunate and not press her luck. We were in no mood for compromise. The traffic and speeding ticket alone were enough to have me in a less-than-generous mood, and when I considered how little I liked being drawn into other people's problems, I was in an even less giving frame of mind. We would enjoy Lily's birthday. She would miss it.

## July 4, Tuesday

Mohammed arrived from his tour with the hip-hop band in the wee hours of the morning and took charge. He started shouting orders to his mother and other members of his family. He got into an argument with his mother when Penelope told her son Chris, Mohammed's eleven-year-old half-brother, that he could not go to the movies. Mohammed insisted he should be allowed to go if he wanted to. Picking up on his big brother's attitude, Chris talked back to his mother and she slapped him in the face, precipitating a major family argument. Not as though there isn't enough stuff going on. All of this was in Lily's presence. Mohammed indicated that he was heading back to California with Lily. Sarah was on her own, there was to be no birthday celebration. The extreme unhealthiness of this family dynamic was shocking to us. Since when does the son, the drug-abusing son, come in and start calling the shots? His place is with his woman, Sarah, not to leave her alone and take her daughter and run off. After all, he was the one who got her back into drugs; now he was walking out on her with the child? We are mystified that Penelope would allow this to happen. Is she afraid of her own son? Who's in charge? Sure sounded like the lunatics were running the asylum.

I called to talk with Mohammed, telling him he lacked the authority to take the baby back to California without her mother, and Mohammed responded angrily, threatening legal action. He subsequently called the police department, asking them to come to his mother's home to prevent us from "taking his child away from him." We had no intention of doing this, only wishing to celebrate Lily's first birthday. Caroline and I had purchased gifts for Lily and had baked two cakes, one for Lily to enjoy by herself and another for the adults to share. We simply wanted a quiet day to celebrate Lily's first birthday. This family, these people, were not working with us or for a peaceful resolution to the mess.

I also did not believe it was right to take Lily out of state until things were settled with her mother. She was heavily addicted to heroin and needed rehab. It all appeared to fall on deaf ears. Mohammed agreed to come and pick Sarah up at our house so that she could say good-bye to Lily before he left again for New York and then California. So we sat back to wait for the arrival of Mohammed, whom I now referred to as the Prince of Persia for the airs he affected. After he failed to show up at our home, we began to get worried. He subsequently had his mother call to tell us not to come to the house for the planned birthday party, and that he was sending a cab for Sarah. We talked with Penelope and made it quite clear that this was not going to happen. Maybe she was inclined to take orders from her son; we were not. We would be driving Sarah over in time for the long-scheduled birthday party. Although we had planned on a straight-line consequence for Sarah—do drugs, lose access to your child, and no birthday party—with Mohammed threatening to take the child away we had to choose between our consequences and Sarah losing her child and becoming even more depressed. We didn't know what this family had in their heads, but I was not about to let this crew start calling the shots. She was still my daughter and she needed help, and I wanted to be able to have one positive outcome, a child's first birthday, my granddaughter's birthday.

For someone with a heroin problem and a girlfriend in dire straits, this guy sure had delusions of grandeur. He thought he was still in charge of all the adults around him. Mohammed called and left a message on our machine (we were outside when he called) telling us that there would be no party and not to come because no one would be there at the house. In the background of the call, Mohammed's mother asked to him to at least let Sarah come to see her baby, Mohammed cut her off, saying (on our answering machine), "No! It's all Sarah's fucking fault! There *is* no fucking party. I'm taking the baby and getting out of here." I was beginning to really dislike this guy.

We subsequently drove over the bridge, arrived at Penelope's house, and knocked on the door. Despite Mohammed's declaration that there would be no party, the house was full of relatives. Mohammed's mother, stepfather, two elderly aunts, his grandmother and stepgrandfather, younger brother, older brother, sister-in-law, and niece all were there. Sarah was reunited with her Lily, and they disappeared into the basement with Mohammed. We mixed with the relatives, ate cake and ice cream, and tried to make the best of an extremely awkward situation.

The house was full of people and all, but beyond that, one would assume that Penelope would have cleaned up or straightened up a little before the family arrived. The place was downright filthy. There were paint cans in the bathroom and clothes and newspapers and boxes on every piece of furniture that was unoccupied. The floor was unswept and the kitchen stove and fridge were resplendent with food from days gone by. Dogs and cats roamed wild amongst the partygoers. Caroline and I had recalled the conversation with Penelope when we first met her. We originally made it clear that we were not raising this child—remember, "If Sarah and Mohammed choose to allow the pregnancy to go full term, then they are responsible for the baby." Penelope, on the other hand, quickly agreed to take the baby. "Oh, I'll take her, I'll raise her." We tried to communicate to her that this was the wrong message to send to the kids; they had to know it was their responsibility to raise this child, not the grandparents', and to give them this out—"Oh, go and have the baby; if you don't want it I'll take it"—might lead them to continue the pregnancy and bail out if it didn't work out. In the same way one can enable an addict by bailing him or her out or calling him or her in sick for work, allowing the addict to avoid the consequences for his or her bad choices, his or her bad behavior, Penelope was effectively enabling their failed parenting. And here we were, Caroline and I, Sarah, and, most important of all, the little innocent in all this, Lily.

After Lily was born we thought, "Well, if Penelope wants to raise her so badly, then let her. We can just sit back and have her over on weekends or vacations and let Penelope have the work of raising her." But here we were in this filthy dirty house with all these crazy people running around, a prime example of a dysfunctional family, and Caroline and I had the same thought. "No way would we ever allow Lily to live with this woman." I said to Caroline on the way home, "Can you imagine little Lily crawling around on the floor in this mess? Can you imagine her living with all this craziness?" And do you think for a moment this woman would work with us on visitation? I don't think so. Forget everything I said about not raising this little gal or leaving Caroline if she chose to. I had BONDED with this little human being, and I would protect her at all costs. Little did we know that this was the start of an even more harrowing adventure.

We agree to allow Sarah to remain at Penelope's in Annapolis that night to spend time with Lily and to mend fences with Mohammed. Remember, he was threatening to take Lily back to California without her mother. Mohammed agreed to bring Sarah to our home the following day (Thursday). They arrive late in the afternoon with Lily and stay for an hour, but leave on the pretext of attending a Narcotics Anonymous meeting in Annapolis (they attended no such meeting). Before they leave our house, Sarah wants to take her clothes, but we only allow her to take a change of clothes. She was staying with us under our supervision, and we took that responsibility seriously. Although we could not keep her from Mohammed, or Lily from them, we knew a long-term plan had to be put into place under our direction and supervision. It was clear Penelope was not equipped to deal with these two. The following day (Friday) we meet in Annapolis and drive into Baltimore's Inner Harbor to walk around and have dinner with Mohammed, Sarah, and Lily. Mohammed spends most of his time on the cell phone. Big shot. Remember, this was ten years ago, before everyone had cell phones glued to their ears; only businessmen had cell phones.

We leave Sarah and Lily with Mohammed because they plan to visit Mohammed's paternal grandparents on Saturday, the Iranians who live in DC. We arrange to pick Sarah and Lily up on Sunday at his mother's between six and seven in the evening. We arrive at six thirty and wait until after eight, when they show up over an hour and a half late. We were a little upset but decided to not make an issue of it. We were not going to leave until they arrived. We would persist. They follow us home to Denton and spend the evening. After some discussion Sarah agrees to look into rehab at a local clinic, Hope Center.

On Monday morning Mohammed leaves for New York at six o'clock, leaving Lily and Sarah with us. He promises to return for dinner. He fails to show for dinner or for the rest of that night or the next day, staying over one and then two nights with no word. When he does return to Maryland, it's to his mother's. Sarah calls over twenty times trying to locate Mohammed and admits to us that "he does this all the time." On Monday, in keeping with our agreement Caroline takes Sarah to the Hope Center and is not allowed to sit in on Sarah's interview. Sarah reports that they won't admit her to their program because she is a California resident. It is later revealed that Sarah had no intention of signing into rehab, and that if she couldn't convince her mother to take her home,

Mohammed had arranged to meet her and take her to his mother's. Sarah is trying to avoid the inevitable. She returns to our home. We are trying to do everything in our power to do the right thing, which is to 1) get our daughter the help she needs and 2) to protect our granddaughter. We are overcome by the efforts by Sarah, her boyfriend, and his mother to work against every plan that seems workable.

## Wednesday, July 10

Sarah is eager to return to Annapolis and is extremely restless. Lily is starting to get upset again. She cries and is inconsolable. Tension builds as Sarah paces the house, calling various numbers on the phone, trying to locate Mohammed (a total of thirty-three calls were logged on the bill). Caroline and I aren't used to that tension and agitation and just want peace and quiet to be restored to our home. Having a junkie in your house, even if it is your own daughter, is like having a wild animal pacing back and forth in your living room. You don't know what they are going to do next. She was making us all crazy, and just for peace of mind we agree to let her return to Mohammed's mother's house. We call and agree to meet Penelope half way and drop Sarah, Lily, and their clothes off at the meeting point. We make the dropoff, buckle little Lily into her car seat, and head back across the bridge.

The next day Sarah calls us to indicate they are extending their stay a week to July 18 (original plans were to leave July 12). Remember, we bought her a round-trip ticket and it was nonrefundable. With neither my knowledge nor consent, she lies to the Priceline.com agent about a death in the family and charges $105 to my credit card for the extension. I subsequently file a complaint with Priceline and refuse to pay the charge. I figured I paid good money for a visit with my daughter and granddaughter and it was anything but enjoyable, and I would be damned if I had to pay extra for her to remain longer, especially when I wouldn't even get to see

## Christmas Blues

them (Sarah and Lily). As it turned out, the next seven days were anything but enjoyable for anybody that came in contact with this couple.

During the time period between July 10, when Sarah and Lily left our home, and July 17, when Mohammed and Lily left Maryland, a number of incidents occurred. It all started when Penelope smelled something burning and, upon investigation, discovered Mohammed and Sarah cooking up something in the bathroom. Heroin. When she confronted them, a scene developed in which Mohammed grabbed his belongings and Lily and left the house screaming that Penelope would never see her granddaughter again. His exact words, as quoted by Penelope, were, "Take a good look at Lily's ass, because it's the last thing you'll see of her as I walk out this door." Sarah didn't even have time to grab her clothes, following Mohammed and her daughter out of the house and into the waiting car. Penelope followed and tried to stop them from leaving and engaged in a tug of war with Sarah's car door, resulting in Sarah's leg getting squeezed. When Penelope tried to stop Mohammed from getting in the car, he struck her and shoved her onto the ground. Penelope called us in a panic, laying out the whole sordid incident. All this occurred in Lily's presence. Now Penelope was trying to do the right thing, prevent these two morons from getting into a motor vehicle and driving just after shooting a load of heroin into their arms. But she had allowed this whole scene to get out of hand, and now that she lost control, she needed to seek our help. The cows were already out of the barn and tearing down the road when she called. We told her what to do. Call the police.

We encouraged Penelope to contact the police and report the assault on her, file charges, and let the police know that they were under the influence and likely possession of drugs. Penelope insists that she did, but no police report was ever filed and neither felon was ever taken into custody. Instead, Penelope drove all around town looking for Mohammed and Sarah on the pretext of returning the baby's toys and clothes.

All of these incidents of domestic violence were initiated by Mohammed's actions and carried out in the full view of our granddaughter. Once again Penelope failed to do the right thing and hold them accountable. Instead she enabled them.

After we were drawn into this sordid soap opera involving drugs and violence and family dysfunction, all in the presence of our little one, we had to do something. The threat (promise) to cut Sarah off and make every effort to protect little Lily would carry no teeth unless we acted on it. It was now clear Penelope would never hold them accountable. And once Sarah got back with Mohammed and his doormat mother, she was lost to us. Little did we know the power and control he had on Sarah, the pimp with his drug-addicted-girl mentality coupled with his lack of respect for women. How much did this have to do with his Persian (Iranian) background, a culture that did not exactly revere women? What could we do to stop them from getting on a plane and flying back to California, where we would have little to no control? What could we do to help our precious little gal? I contacted security at BWI airport and reported that two known heroin users were about to board a plane to California. One of them, Mohammed A., recently returned from a trip to New York and might be in possession of drugs. There would be with a minor child and they might want to check them out. Neither Sarah nor Mohammed was stopped at the airport. Now keep in mind that this was July 18, 2001. Had this report of mine been made two months later, on September 18, 2001, the swarthy guy with the Iranian surname might very well have been stopped. But these were different times.

We subsequently followed up on our promise to have Lily removed as long as Sarah was using drugs by contacting the Department of Children and Family Services (DCFS) in California on July 18. We told them we were concerned about the minor child and reported the facts as we knew them, including Sarah's two hospitalizations for heroin withdrawal. One of the classic ironies in all this is the fact that Mohammed, who never stopped using, continued to get by with it, while

Sarah, who desperately tried on numerous occasions to kick the stuff, went through withdrawal and brought more attention to her addiction.

Because Caroline and I are both educators, we are mandated reporters, which means that we are required by law and the tenets of our profession to report any known abuse of children. Our jobs, our careers, are on the line if we fail to do this. Funny thing is, so is Mohammed's mother, Penelope. That's right, she was an elementary school teacher! Guess she doesn't take any of her responsibilities seriously. Quite obviously the choice was easy for us. Many ask us whether it was difficult to turn in our own daughter, or commend us on how brave we were to take this step. There was no question in our minds; the choice between our adult daughter, age twenty-three, able to come and go as she pleases and make her own choices good or bad, and the little innocent year-old child... was no choice, it was automatic. We made the call and followed up to see what DCFS did in response.

We are told that Sarah tested positive for drug use, although results were inconclusive in regards to Mohammed. It was later revealed that he was not screened (urine, blood, or hair samples) at this time, and not for six to eight weeks. Since he was still using and always had a ready supply for himself, he never got sick, and he put it all on Sarah. As well, Sarah covered for him, telling authorities she was the junkie, he was trying to get her clean. What a joke, but it guaranteed that her supplier would stay out of jail.

What the child welfare department did was ask Sarah to leave the home, leaving Lily in her father's care An even bigger joke! For starters he never cared for her in the first place, and in a city the size of LA, it was all too easy to sneak Sarah back in to see to Lily's needs. So even after all this is brought to a head, nothing has changed. We stay in touch with Ruth and she tells us Lily is now old enough to crawl out their apartment, push the screen door open to the balcony, crawl down the outside hallway to Ruth's apartment next door, and call for the kids, Ruth's daughter and sons, who adore Lily.

Talk about independent! And not even walking, just a year-old baby.

We maintain steady contact with DCFS and the caseworker, Almira, who drug tests Sarah three times. She fails, and Almira begins to initiate the detaining of Lily, meaning taking her away from her parents. We had hoped that they would have taken Lily right away, but there are steps that have to be followed, and Almira has other cases. After several weeks of inaction they eventually respond to our pleas (many, many phone calls to Almira and her supervisor) to get this child into a safe place, including setting up live scans (electronic fingerprinting for background checks) for Caroline's second cousin, a minister in a large congregation in LA, whose wife is a family therapist. They expressed a willingness to take Lily in or find a family in their church who could. Perfect, or so we hoped. We were three thousand miles away, but we had Ruth's eyes and ears and we were persistent, calling, calling, and keeping DCFS caseworkers and their supervisors aware that we were not going to let this case slip away.

In what was to become standard operating procedure for us, we contact Almira's supervisor Nestor on September 10, insisting that they investigate Mohammed's background. Several phone calls back and forth and DCFS agrees to contact the neighbor Ruth to verify our concerns about Mohammed's failure to care for Lily when Sarah was there, as well as to confirm the living arrangements with people coming and going, federal marshals breaking in, etc. They agree to talk to Ruth about the marshals only, but rule her out as a suitable witness due to Ruth's prior history of drug use. We call back insisting they talk with Ruth, the only reliable witness to Mohammed's physical and psychological abuse of Sarah and his acute neglect of his daughter, Lily. More importantly, Ruth has been clean for years, has three great kids, and is more tuned in to the situation with Mohammed and Sarah precisely because she was in a similar relationship with her children's father.

She knows; she's been there and come back. She works in an attorney's office and is as credible as they come.

Sarah returns to the house, apparently against the ruling, to care for Lily and keep the house clean. DCFS claims they were unaware at the time and gave Mohammed credit for the clean house and Lily's healthy condition. During the last weekend in September, Almira told us that Sarah was allowed into the home during the day, but could not stay overnight. Sarah was later accused of violating her restraint order. Throughout this affair, mixed messages have been routine, lack of supervision and follow-up the order of the day, and a plethora of excuses given for Almira's frequent lapses.

We always started with calls to Almira and, failing there, call her supervisor. We rarely take "We're too busy" as an excuse and keep the pressure on. This little girl will not fall through the cracks. Why won't they let Caroline's cousin Bob and his wife, Judy, or their adult children step in to care for Lily?

## October 3

Ruth calls to inform us that Sarah has been assaulted by Mohammed and has marks on her throat and a black eye. We contact DCFS yet again to insist they remove the child from this now dangerous environment. On October 5, ten weeks after our first referral, they come in and remove Lily. Thank God! And Ruth!

We fully expect that DCFS will turn Lily over to Bob and Judy. Instead they turn her over to...ready for this? Mohammed's stepbrother, a twenty-two-year-old bachelor with no blood relationship to Lily, much less any knowledge or experience of how to care for a year-old little girl. Although Almira indicated that as a result of the domestic assault against Sarah in front of the baby, neither was allowed unsupervised visits, later we are told Mohammed has rights to unsupervised visits while Sarah does not. Go figure. Seems that even though Lily has been detained, i.e., removed from the parental home, the goal is still reunification with her parents.

When we indicate our desire to make the trip out to the West Coast to visit Lily, we are told *we* have to have supervised visits. When we react in disbelief, Almira explains that we were not cleared and had to have the live scan evaluation first in her office. We arrange to have this conducted by our local Department of Social Services in Maryland, who refers us to the Sheriff's Department. We are also told by the caseworker in California that we will be required to answer certain questions about ourselves. The twelve questions Almira sends amount to a proof of identity: height, weight, eye color, hair color, place of birth, alias, etc. No fingerprint cards or directions are provided. We return the identity sheets (live scans) and two sets of fingerprints for each of us to DCFS California.

Almira informs us that a hearing will be held on November 8, 2001, at which time the court will decide to return the child to Mohammed or to keep her for up to six months. Almira didn't tell us if we could attend the hearing, but hey, this is our case, we made the original complaint and the follow-ups, and this is our daughter and granddaughter, so if there is a hearing, we want to be heard. When I ask who Lily's court-appointed advocate is, Almira is unable to provide it: "I don't know her name, I'll have to get back to you on that." We indicate that we will be out to California for the hearing. Who can we trust if the DCFS caseworker and her department supervisor aren't there to protect our granddaughter's safety? We prepare for what turns out to be our first of many trips to California to stand up for Lily's rights

## CHAPTER THIRTY-TWO

# DEPARTMENT 410, LOS ANGELES COUNTY FAMILY COURT

We have spent so much time in this waiting room, I was afraid they were going to start charging us rent, but we really didn't get to do much with it ... other than wait. That's right, we're in California, in a waiting room *outside* the courtroom while all the action is going on *inside* the courtroom. Oh, to be the veritable fly on the wall. Eighteen months ago we got to observe firsthand the effects serious addiction has on a small child. As always, we stepped forward and demanded action. Either our daughter would get herself professional help in a rehabilitation center, or we would cut her loose from the family circle, again. But this time would be a little different. We could ill afford the luxury of allowing her to completely enjoy her current lifestyle with no interference from us. Now there was a child involved, and, mandated reporters or not, we could not, we would not stand idly by while they dragged this child into their maelstrom of addiction. The proverbial ball got rolling when we made that call to the proper authorities in California, DCFS (Department of Children and Family Services). We'd tried to stop Sarah and her significant other, Mohammed, at the airport in Baltimore, but they snuck out ahead of us. To be honest, I don't think any of the security team was that worried about a man and woman and small child traveling out of state with possible drugs in their possession. A man with Middle Eastern ties at that. But this was July 2001, two months shy of September 2001 and the wake-up call to airport security. No, he was not a threat to the United States, just to a small citizen of the country, our granddaughter.

We were impressed with the response we got from DCFS in California. Within twenty-four hours of their arrival in LA, a social worker made a home visit. This eventually led to our daughter being tested for substance abuse. Why our daughter and not Mohammed? Because we had no firsthand knowledge of his use, only Sarah's, and his mother, Penelope, was not of the same bent as us. Her MO was to enable, to hide, to lie, to make excuses for her son. Her first priority was her son; everything beyond that didn't matter. And so it was that the first person to get caught up in the snare was Sarah, and it was Sarah that was forced to leave the family home, considered a threat to her own child. Was it fair that she had to leave when the father, the man who reintroduced her to drugs, remained at home with their child? No. But Sarah made bad choices: to take drugs, to remain with a man who took drugs, and to lie, to take the rap for him when the social workers came to call. So she was the one to pay the full consequences for acts they were both fully involved in.

The irony is that he was left home to serve as the primary caretaker when in fact he was no caretaker at all. Even forced into this role, he still had to sneak Sarah home to do the twenty-four/seven routine of feeding, changing, and protecting their child. Fortunately for us, their lack of funds and lack of phone opened a channel of communication that would otherwise be closed: the next door neighbor with a phone. Ruth became our eyes and ears, as the situation we so desperately tried to change remained status quo. When the already dysfunctional domestic situation reached an even greater level of dysfunction, and father assaulted mother, only then did little Lily escape. But where did they send her? To a relative of ours, empty nesters with excellent credentials and the hearts to match? No. Lily was sent to the father's family; a single, male member, his stepbrother, Ritchie. No blood ties even; a stepbrother. And because he was also ill equipped to serve as caretaker to a fifteen-month-old girl child, he too gave in to the demands of the father, his stepbrother, to allow Sarah to care for the child, to allow them to continue to control Lily's life. When this charade was finally unmasked, only then did Lily move to a neutral corner away from harm. She entered the foster care system.

This came about, once again, through our efforts, our eyes, and our ears, and our phone calls and letters bemoaning the fact that this child needed to be in safe place. When we made our first trip to California for the first hearing in November 2001, we were not allowed unsupervised visits with our own granddaughter. Despite our efforts to provide background information on ourselves, including live scans (electronic fingerprinting) and several sets of inked fingerprints, we were only allowed to visit our granddaughter with the stepbrother sitting in. We spent more time in the airplane than we did with Lily, but we had the opportunity to observe the blatant disregard Mohammed and his family had for the law and restrictions they were obligated to respect. We only got to spend a court-allowed three hours with Lily on our first visit, and when Ritchie, the stepbrother, offered a longer opportunity, we rejected it. The court specified three hours of supervised visits; we would stick to three hours. We would enjoy the time with her and give her back to her caregiver.

This was difficult for many reasons, most significantly that the caregiver, Richie, was providing domicile for the other grandmother, Mohammed's mother, Penelope, who enjoyed many more hours with Lily by virtue of her relationship with her son and stepson. She didn't need a background check, no fingerprints live or inked; all she had to do was go visit her stepson, who just coincidently had Lily under his care. The unfairness of her access, for the one who contributed to the dysfunction to have access when we did not, well, it was extremely frustrating. When we pointed out this inequity to the department, we were told it was our fault because we lacked a similar close relationship with our own daughter. Ah, hello! There was a very good reason we did not have a "close relationship" with our daughter: she was neglecting our granddaughter! She was taking drugs! We turned her in. We did what we had to do. And we were punished for the difficult steps we took, while Penelope, the paternal grandmother, was in essence rewarded for her bad choices: her support and friendship with two seriously addicted parents, our daughter and her son.

On day two we were to enjoy our second three-hour visit with Lily. We were dumbstruck that Richie, the primary caregiver, failed to appear with Lily at the dropoff location, the IHOP in Glendale, and instead sent his stepmother, Penelope, to make the dropoff, spinning her tales of seemingly more important priorities, Richie's having to fly out of town to work, and having to step in to take care of Lily, and her willingness to allow us as much time with Lily as we chose. Even this tempting situation failed to deter us from our agreement with DCFS. We would respect the three-hour visit and return her to...Penelope, since Richie was no longer available. And when Penelope ranted and rambled on the inequities of the system and the "communist dictators" at DCFS, who so unfairly removed the child from her son and were now setting even more ridiculous limits...we walked off. We had to. We couldn't stomach the wide difference in perceptions—equitable and reasonable limits to us, designed to protect the minor child, but "dictator's rules" to her. Caroline's cousin Bob remained in the parking lot outside the IHOP to hear Penelope out, and to gather intelligence. Caroline and I went inside to enjoy the few precious hours we had with our baby girl. When we went to return her several hours later (three), who do you guess accompanied Penelope to pick up Lily? Sarah and Mohammed! Not only were they prohibited from visiting the child unsupervised by the stepbrother, but they were prohibited from seeing her together as a couple! And here they are: three adults, none legally allowed to be with the child alone, all sharing in the conspiracy while the caretaker traveled out of state. Sarah literally grabbed Lily out of my arms as she sat on my lap, laying her down on the carpeted floor to change a diaper that had just been changed. Going through the motions of being a good mom. The motions...

Their refusal to respect the guidelines, the restrictions established by DCFS, would eventually lead to the loss of the little gal as DCFS increased their scrutiny based on our reports and caught them in further violations. We would call Richie every Sunday to talk to Lily, at least to let her hear Caroline's voice. Invariably Lily would be "sleeping" or "not feeling good," according to Ritchie. We would then place a call to Sarah, and what do you know, there was a little voice in the background. "What is Lily doing with you?" we would ask. "Oh, Richie had a date and let us have her for a while, please don't tell." But tell we did, documenting the date and time of the phone calls and precisely what we heard. Their blatant disregard of the rules eventually caught up to them all.

But back to the IHOP parking lot. As the fates would have it, our relatives, our family in California, turned out to be a perfect sounding board for Penelope's rants. They entertained her in the parking lot for almost thirty minutes as she rambled on about the system and then moved on to the unfair treatment of her son and our daughter, and then into a new realm. Her reaction to our requests to step in to care for our granddaughter was filled with tales of misery and woe, not about her son or our daughter, but about me. Stories my own daughter concocted to portray us as evil monsters bent on taking her child, and justifying her fight to prevent it at all costs. They ranged from "forcing Sarah into therapy three times a week when she was growing up" to "physical, emotional, and even sexual abuse." Our daughter, who portrayed her childhood as violent and restrictive, strict beyond reason, recounted tales of a stepfather who controlled her and her mother, not allowing them to attend church, one who insisted on listening in on phone conversations and subjecting his family to a reign of terror. All complete fabrications. In all the years with my daughter, from the first time she called me "Daddy" at age four, through the adoption at age seven, up to the present time at age twenty-three, she never once, not even once, referred to me as her "stepfather" or assaulted me with that hurtful accusation, "You're not my real father." Having seen photographs of him she did take some pride in looking like him, but she knew the difference between her father, and her dad, which was me, She was steady until this family got involved to poison her mind along with her body. Penelope's loose lips revealed Sarah's lying lips.

Though my first reaction was hurt and anger, in the long run the context in which it was offered began to take on a general pattern of diversion: the best defense is a good offense. When we first appeared in court that November, we were treated as pariahs, and we were left to ourselves with support from only one quarter, and that was our family out there, Caroline's second cousins Bob and his wife, Judy. They alone stood beside us, encouraging us to take it all in perspective, to let it slide off our backs, to know that we were doing the right thing. Just as Mohammed's actions eventually lead to his losing Lily, Ritchie's also resulted in the same. We were to stay the high ground and let things just sort themselves out. It was hard listening to the unfounded accusations, being stared at by caseworkers who believed the worst about us, and feeling isolated. We were out in the cold. In the California sunshine. Bob and Judy took us in, they gave us a place to stay, a car to use, and, most importantly, the emotional support we so desperately needed in a place so far away from home.

When we next returned to California two months later, in January 2002, it was no better in the court battle. The mud was still being slung and we, or rather I, was now accused of homophobia, calling my son a "faggot," and even encouraging my daughter to take drugs. I was somehow responsible for her addiction. I was the "cool dad" who took his sixteen-year-old daughter out for her birthday to get high on marijuana. Yeah, right! For the record, my son is quite heterosexual as far as his wife and two sons go, and I would never use that term, period. I also would never encourage my daughter or anyone to use drugs, much less take her out for her sixteenth birthday to get high. On her sixteenth birthday I took her and one of her friends to Baltimore for lunch. No drugs, just sandwiches.

Although we had high hopes, we did not get to take Lily home with us that trip either, and our hopes for a visit with her took a sharp turn. When we left the courthouse Department 410 after the hearing (which we could not attend, but we took our seats in the waiting room) we asked the social worker if we could arrange a visit with Lily who was now in foster care. "Oh, didn't you know? She's in the hospital." No, we did not know and were very concerned. Turns out she was hospitalized with a staph infection, a rather serious one. It appears that most children have the bacteria in and on their skin but are able to fight it with normal immune systems. This poor little gal's system was compromised with all the stress she was subjected to, most recently in her new foster home with Mrs. Watson. The infection caused all of her skin from her chest over both shoulders and down her back to become significantly inflamed, and it peeled like a third-degree burn. This affliction is also known as "scalded child syndrome" because it literally looks like someone has poured boiling water over the child's tender flesh. By Thursday of that week, Lily had been in the hospital for four days on intravenous antibiotics and was responding to the treatment. A sick little girl in the hospital needs her parents, and they were nowhere to be seen, so we stepped in for the first time to support and nurture this little gal. It was an occasion we seized to be near her for an extended period of time and resulted in Caroline's significant bonding with her. Though we (Caroline and I) were quite attached to this little gal, Lily was dealing with the primary features of an attachment disorder. Not being in

## No Good Deed

a stable setting, with Mom addicted, Dad abusive, and both neglectful, not to mention moving from one home to another (theirs, a Chinese family's, Ritchie's, Mrs. Watson's), this little girl didn't know who to latch onto.

When we arrived at the hospital she was in a crib with high, shiny steel sides (bars) and she looked like she was in jail. When we walked into her room, she was lying in the bed, and when she heard our voices she quickly stood up and smiled. The nurses said we could take her out, but we had to be mindful of her IV tube taped to her left wrist. Apparently she had pulled one out, so she was taped up pretty good, almost like a cast. The tube reached up to a drip bag that the nurse attached to a portable stand with rubber wheels. As soon as we lowered the sides of her crib and set her on Caroline's lap, she squirmed to hit the floor running, and run she did, with Caroline and me trying to keep up with those little pudgy legs charging up the hallways. She wanted to explore and knew we were right there with her. At one point she ventured into another little boy's room and, spotting his Mylar "bwoon," pointed and made her intentions clear. I asked the folks where they got it and they directed me to the gift shop downstairs. Caroline took over the drip stand and I took the elevator down. As I walked across the courtyard to the gift shop, Lily was looking out the window in Caroline's arms.

When I made my way back across the courtyard, balloon in hand, Lily spotted me instantly, calling out, "Bwoon! Bwoon!" I proudly relinquished the red Get Well trinket and Lily grabbed it and let Caroline know she wanted down! I grabbed the drip stand and almost had to run after her as she made it out the door, turned left, and ran down the hall, turning right at the intersection and right again at the next and down to the last room on the right, the same room with the little boy, and, entering, held her hand out to him, showing him her bwoon, bwoon! Her focus, her intent, her desire to show this little fellow that now she had a balloon just like his at sixteen months of age, impressed us to no end. This was a bright and engaging little girl. Over the course of the

## Department 410, Los Angeles County Family Court

next few days we spent as much time as the liberal visiting hours would allow, and the nurses were glad for some respite that family was finally there so they would not have to spend all their time entertaining the little gal. Where were her real parents?

When they finally did make a show of concern, it was late, around eight thirty at night, when the lights were down and they were getting Lily ready for bed. First Sarah walked in, and shortly after Mohammed, who marched in like the Prince of Persia, failing to show ID or signing in as we had. He made everybody very uncomfortable, and because there were reportedly restraining orders against both parents visiting at the same time, we stepped out to inform hospital staff and then left to avoid any further stress. When we got a chance to speak with our daughter, she denied having any contact with Mohammed; he "just showed up." When we asked why she had failed to be there all day for her little girl, her only explanation was that she just got a new job and couldn't take off. My anger quickly rose to the surface as I attempted to digest this. Come on! What boss would fail to let a mother off to be with her sixteen-month-old baby in the hospital!? What mother with a sick child would allow a boss, a job, to come between her and her baby? But Sarah was not functioning like a mother. We asked how she was getting home and she made like we could give her a lift, but bowed out to catch a bus, though by this time it was pretty obvious she was waiting on Mohammed. They were still together, together on everything with the exception of this child. Lily would be released to Mrs. Watson, her foster mother, on Saturday, the day we were leaving to return to Maryland, so we had seen the last of our little gal for a while.

It would be shades of things to come. When we went to court, we may not have gotten her, but neither did they, for the detainment order remained in effect, in part due to their lack of cooperation and in part due to more evidence, more documents we provided about their family. I had gone to great lengths to secure the police report recounting the violent scene at the grandmother's home the previous summer. Another insight into the dysfunction they all enjoyed, mother, son, and now, our daughter and granddaughter. I'd made inquiries and got a copy of this police report, a public record of the birthday visit when he'd knocked his mother to the ground when she tried to stop them from driving off after getting high on heroin. Their continued neglect of her when Lily was in the hospital and their insistence on both meeting with the child despite court orders to the contrary would also work against them in the long run, with our documentation carrying the day.

Two visits to California, and six months of efforts on the part of DCFS to affect some kind of change in this family dynamic, were appearing to be futile. Our daughter was to get involved in parenting courses and drug counseling. Mohammed needed domestic violence and anger management counseling. He was still clean as far as drugs were concerned; Sarah was still covering for him there. And so January moved into February and March, and the foster mother, Mrs. Watson, provided the direct caretaking and allowed parental visits, attempting to reunify the parents and child. But their visits with Lily were few and far between, their cooperation with rehab and anger management and domestic violence sporadic. And as April turned to May and another hearing, they were told either get your acts together, or risk the first step in losing your child…forever…the end of reunification and move toward termination of parental rights. One of the court officers, Lily's advocate, commented that the judge had said he never saw two parents less motivated to get their child back.

When the hearing was held in June, Mohammed had failed to meet even half his requirement of courses in anger management, and tried to pull a fast one on the court, showing up with a bogus counselor and the phony document he'd purchased for two thousand dollars. Sarah had bottomed out, thanks for Penelope's gift of $1,500 that fueled a two-week drug binge that landed her in detox and rehab. Clean for the first time in months, she started feeling good about herself and bad about her treatment at his hands, and she broke, and she came clean; he was using drugs, too, and he was her main supplier, and she was tired of getting abused and blamed for everything that went wrong in their lives. But was she willing to testify to this in court? Yes. So Caroline made trip number three out to LA and to support her. Caroline was to wait at the courthouse, and the social worker would drive out to Acton Rehabilitation Center and have Sarah released to her custody to testify against Mohammed. With her testimony about her attempts to get clean and Mohammed's efforts to work to keep her addicted, they finally decided to take action. Sarah indicated her willingness to allow Lily to go to live with her parents, Caroline and me, on the East Coast.

The court had little choice but to follow the recommendations of the department and terminate reunification efforts. The course was set: either the parents made the effort required to change the paths they were on, or their child would be lost forever. In front of Caroline, the caseworker told Sarah, "Take a good look at that little girl over there. It is your choice. She will either be your daughter or your sister. You know what you have to do." And while they were thinking about their choices, the baby, little Lily, would be placed with the folks who were best equipped to love and protect her: the maternal grandparents, the Matthews!

When we both made our trips to California, five hours in the air each way with stopovers in Denver or Las Vegas or Minneapolis, all for a few hours with our gal and a few more hours in the waiting room outside Department 410, we did what we had to. Caroline had been to a conference headlined by a nationally recognized author, David Peltzer, who was seriously abused as a child. He survived intact and is an outspoken advocate for children who are abused. Caroline gave him a business card with a note on the back: "I have a granddaughter in foster care in California. What do you recommend I do?" Several weeks later she was sitting at home when the phone rang. It was David Peltzer. His advice: "Even if you have to sit in the waiting room, do it, just to let her know you are there and that you care. Make your presence known." It was advice we took to heart, and when we went to the courthouse we always signed in as potential witnesses and we sat quietly, respectfully, while the two parents walked in to do their thing, casting dirty looks at us. After the hearing we would respectfully approach the attorney representing Lily, and the one representing Sarah, and offer our support. After Sarah made all her false accusations against me, I confronted her and insisted she sign a statement I had written out retracting all the false allegations. I had her sign and asked Lily's attorney to witness the statement, which she did.

I don't know what turned the page on this, Mohammed and Sarah's failure to make even the slightest effort to meet the court requirements, Sarah's testimony against Mohammed, or Mohammed's threats to send Lily out of the country to Iran to live with his family over there. The court deliberated and told Caroline to return to Maryland and prepare for Lily's arrival within the next few days. We were jubilant, to say the least. For so long I contemplated the impact of the lack of consistency for this child at so important a developmental stage, I wanted so desperately to have this child with us, protected by our circle of love we held for her. The unwanted pregnancy had so quickly turned into this beautiful little gal whom I held closely to me at three weeks of age, three months, six months, one year, sixteen months, eighteen months, and now at two years she would be there to have and to hold in the safety and sanctuary of our home. As a school psychologist and one who fully appreciated the need for safety and security at this young age, I so desperately wanted her with us, to have and to hold, to love and protect. How wonderfully this had turned out.

This was the one trip I had missed, so I was back in Maryland waiting to hear the outcome. It's probably just as well, for as happy as I would have been at the outcome, I don't know if I could have controlled myself for what was to happen next. Mohammed and his mother did not accept the

# Department 410, Los Angeles County Family Court

court's decision, as you might expect. They were so enraged, so mad that Sarah had turned against Mohammed, that he and his mother turned on Sarah with a vengeance. As Sarah left the courtroom after testifying, they yelled and screamed at her, You lying cu*t, you fu**cking whore, blah blah blah. The baby's attorney, Sarah's lawyer, and the social worker, not to mention Caroline, had to spirit Sarah out of the building ASAP. They had already decided to schedule a visit with Lily after the court proceedings, and Almira phoned ahead to see if Mrs. Watson was home. She was, and had just woken Lily from her afternoon nap. They would be awaiting Sarah, Lily's caseworker, Almira, and Caroline. They drove out of the parking garage at the courthouse and headed to Monrovia, just a few miles down the road. Little did they know that Mohammed and his mother had taken the freeway and, at breakneck speed, beat them to the house. Unannounced and uninvited, they barged in to Mrs. Watson's and grabbed Lily up. When Sarah and Almira pulled into the driveway, they noticed a BMW parked out front. "Didn't you say they were driving Uncle Mark's BMW?" Caroline asked Sarah. "Yeah, but I don't know if that's it." Almira cautioned them to stay in the car while she investigated.

Almira, Lily's social worker, walked up to the front door and, noting it was uncharacteristically closed, knocked. Hearing no response, she returned to the car and told Caroline to hand her her cell phone. "Mrs. Watson, so you are there, we were knocking on the door...." "Well, I'm in the back room with the other children. Penelope and Mohammed are here and they have Lily." "Hmmm. Well, could you please come and open the door for me?" As Almira began to exit the car, the front door opened and out walked Penelope and Mohammed with Lily in his arms. Sarah panicked, but Almira counseled calm. "Just stay in the car and let me handle this." As she approached Mohammed, he let loose a string of expletives: "Why are you in my fu**king business? Maybe if you were into their fuc*king business instead of my shi*, we wouldn't be in all this shi*," etc. etc. Almira calmly informed Mohammed that they had a scheduled visit with Lily, and that she was still a ward of the state of California and as such he needed to hand her over…now. As she reached for Lily, Lily reciprocated and reached for Almira as if to say, "Get me away from this lunatic!" As they walked to the car, Penelope flashed Sarah and Caroline the universal sign of utter disdain, her middle finger. Penelope would later deny it, and then, when her action was confirmed by Almira as well as Caroline and Sarah, would change her story to indicate that, well, she might have given them the middle finger, but they were sitting in the car sticking their tongues out at her. You be the judge.

Sarah, Lily, Almira, and Caroline headed to a distant McDonald's, where they enjoyed the birthday cake they'd brought for an early birthday party, and time was spent between parent and child. This would turn out to be the last time Sarah would see her child until over six months later when they (meaning Mohammed, Penelope, and Sarah) would be allowed their final visit in California on January 13, 2003. Funny how Sarah would slither back to these people who had so demeaned her only months before. Oh well…a testament to the powers of addiction. But whereas she could not put Lily ahead of her own addiction, her own needs, she was no longer in charge of the little gal; we were. Since Mohammed made the threat to take Lily out of the country, he was restricted from seeing Lily without security close by. His mother was also required to have supervised visits as well. Just to be on the safe side, little Lily packed her bags from Mrs. Watson's home and headed to the airport. On July 1, 2002, three days before her second birthday, little Lily and her social worker, Almira, made the flight to Maryland and to our home and loving arms. All Mohammed and Penelope could come up with was more unfounded accusations and ill-timed excuses, little in the way of action. As summer turned into fall and the next hearing approached, the recommendation was made: terminate parental rights for both parents.

October 18h, 2002, was the first sign that we might be keeping the little gal for good, and despite Mohammed's last-minute appeals and contested hearings, no changes were made in their lives, which were only spiraling deeper and faster into oblivion. Evicted from their apartment, cars wrecked, cars impounded, licenses lost, drugs still the main priority and the crime that it spawned, four arrests for theft, and grand theft, and transportation of narcotics, and distribution of narcotics, dirty drug tests, all at the direction of Mohammed A. By the time the December 2002 hearing arrived the court, the department, the caseworker, even our daughter's attorney were ready to take the only step left, termination of parental rights.

So for the fourth time, Caroline and I, this time with little Lily in tow, made another plane trip to California. Lily was still a ward of the State of California, though we enjoyed guardianship and physical custody of Lily. We were now invited to attend a hearing in regard to permanently ending Mohammed and Sarah's parental rights, a termination hearing. We were poised to get a definitive ruling on this were it not for one final surprise which postponed the decision for one more hearing. That's right, we flew all the way out to LA (our fourth trip), drove over to the courthouse, waited patiently for our case to be called, and WHAM! the lights went out. They literally went out. The outage apparently affected the entire neighborhood, for traffic lights were inoperable as well. We were willing to attend the hearing by candlelight or flashlight, but apparently there was a prison lockup in the basement, and without electricity, security was breached. So the entire building had to be evacuated. But before we left, could we reschedule for next week? they wondered. Uh…we aren't from around here, in fact our neighborhood is over three thousand miles away. They did agree to work with us and rescheduled the hearing for January 2003. My fifth, my wife's sixth visit to Edleman's children's court now scheduled, we headed back home.

## January 13, 2003, Department 410

What would they come up with next? What card would they could they play? The hearing about their fitness as parents could focus on only one thing, their complete lack of fitness. We arrived at ten after eight, early as always for the eight thirty check-in. They arrived at ten after nine—Penelope and Mohammed and Sarah. Oh yeah, she dropped out of rehab; Mohammed made sure of that. Then she disappeared for two months, popping up in Maryland at the end of August to "be closer to my baby." Funny thing, even after four months and only forty-five minutes from her baby, she never made any attempt to contact her. Sarah would finally see her for the first time on January 13, over six months since the last visit in California. Even Mohammed succumbed to his mother's nagging and showed up for three visits at the visiting center in Maryland, back from California himself. We figure his rapid dismissing of charges, including three felonies, might somehow be connected to his rapid departure from LA and the associates he ratted out.

We were somewhat surprised to see them together, all three, and what was even more surprising was the fourth person to accompany them, to be called by the father as a witness *for* them and *against* us: Mrs. Watson, the kindly old lady who supervised Lily as a foster parent. What was she doing here? She arrived first alone and took a seat in the waiting room just down from where we were sitting. I got up and walked across the room and said hello. When I asked her who invited her, who called her to testify, she hedged, then said, "The family." The family? Which one, Penelope, Mohammed, Sarah, or all three, the holy trinity? She told me she did not want to get in the middle, she just wanted to see this thing settled for once and for all. And she wanted to see Lily. She later changed her story…twice, saying that 1) she was not called by anybody, that she just wanted to see Lily and was told that she would be at the court, and 2) then changed it again, saying that Mohammed had called her. By then it was obvious what her role in this was.

## Department 410, Los Angeles County Family Court

Although it might not be fair to characterize them as con artists, Sarah and Mohammed (and many addicted individuals) share many of the same personality traits as con artists. They will lie quite convincingly at the drop of a hat, especially to protect themselves when caught, and they will construct the big lie to garner what they covet: drugs, stolen goods, or, in this case, the little gal. They convince others to believe what they believe as well, and with the three of them, Sarah, Mohammed, and Penelope, all working together, a poor God-fearing woman like Mrs. Watson didn't stand a chance. I imagine they told her many of the same lies about me that they foisted on the court: that I was an abusive father and husband, a control freak who never allowed my wife to go to church and listened in on her phone conversations, That I abused my daughter physically and even sexually (though no details ever came out about how, when, where, etc.). That I forced my daughter into therapy three times a week and wouldn't let her go anywhere or have any friends. Furthermore, that I took drugs with her when she was sixteen, and was a homophobe and a racist, having called my son a faggot and Mohammed and others of his ethnic persuasion "sand niggers." That was the first time I had even heard that term, and thankfully the last.

I was the last person on earth who should raise this two-year-old child! Sad thing is, they not only convinced Mrs. Watson I was all of these horrible persons rolled into one, but they convinced her that even she heard me use the racial epithet. This despite the fact that I only had a single conversation with her and that was in the hospital room when Lily was sick with the staph infection. No, I do not like Mohammed, but it has little to do with his ethnicity and everything to do with his behavior. Granted I have my prejudices, and the idea of this huge man (250 pounds) having sex with my trim little hundred-pound daughter turns my protective-father stomach, but I hold no ill will about his father's birthplace. The fact that his father hates Americans, and that the threat was made to spirit Lily out of the country to his waiting arms, adds a factor that would otherwise be absent had Mohammed and his father been from Hoboken, New Jersey, but I judge people by their behaviors. But I digress…

So, Mrs. Watson goes in to the courtroom and repeats the racial epithet I reportedly issued and revises her earlier testimony about the parents failing to visit their child during the six months she was in Mrs. Watson's care. "I hate to lie, but Sarah has not seen her child in months and Mohammed has only been by a time or two." This was updated to be, "Oh, they visited on a regular basis!" When she was questioned by Lily's court-appointed advocate about her documentation, however, it all fell apart. I can remember Caroline reminding Mrs. Watson to jot it down on her calendar when they came to visit as a way of easily documenting their visits. She brought no such item to accompany her perjured testimony. Oh well…

And so we sat, me waiting for an opportunity to clear my good name, and Caroline and I for the chance to hear the final words: *termination of parental rights*, which would open the door for adoption and a permanent home for our little gal. As one thirty moved to two thirty and three, Caroline commented that she figured it would be all over by three. Within thirty seconds of that remark, the door opened and the bailiff called out, "Mif Maf-use." We both sat there; did he say Mr. Mathews or Mrs. Mathews? Caroline asked for a clarification—"*Mrs.* Mathews." And so up she went and was gone for maybe thirty minutes. When she returned she seemed okay. They'd asked her about me, and whether she heard me make any derogatory remarks about Mohammed. "No," she quickly responded, and they asked her what her intentions were relative to Lily, would she be willing to adopt her. "Yes." How would she respond if her daughter asked to see her? "Well, that would depend on whether she had lived up to our family standards." And what might they be? "Clean and sober, gainfully employed, and (how best to describe being free from the bonds of slavery Mohammed seemed to have her in?) self-sufficient." Spoken like a former single mom who knew what having a job and an income provides a woman and her

## Department 410, Los Angeles County Family Court

children. The advocate remarked later that it must have been difficult for a mother to say that about a daughter, but they recognized her values and her placing Lily first above all else, and they did the right thing: they terminated parental rights and recommended permanent placement, adoption, with the de facto parents (us) having first option. After a home study to see if we had a fit place for her to live, the wheels of justice would turn to a six-month hearing where little Lily Jazmyn A. would become Lily Alexandra Matthews. My new little daughter. After eighteen months, and two years from when we made our first report, we would fulfill our promise to Sarah and to Lily, that we would do everything in our power to take that child from her. And so we can get on with the rest of our lives, raising the little gal to become all that she can be. We deserved another shot, and so did she.

# CHAPTER THIRTY-THREE

# BREAKING UP IS HARD TO DO—FIGHTING FOR OUR GAL

We fought so hard for Lily, even against the attorneys who represented her, and the department (DCYF), and Sarah, and Mohammed, and we finally convinced the court, the judge, that we not only had Lily's best interests in mind, but we were the best individuals to bring them to pass. On July 1, 2002, three days before she turned two, Almira brought our little gal to us. After appearing to line up with the biological parents against us, believing all the lies and half-truths, and being overwhelmed with an overpowering caseload, Almira finally knew who was telling the truth. Caroline and I were glad it was she that was bringing little Lily home to us. Lily had two phrases—"hot dog" and "french fry," no doubt a result of her frequent visits to McDonald's. She weighed thirty pounds and was a little pudgy bundle of love. One year later, when she was three, she still weighed 30 pounds, though she had grown into her weight with some muscle and long bone development. Green vegetables and corn and squash and fish took the place of the cakes and cookies and hot dogs and french fries. Never could break her of that chicken nugget habit, though. Even today at age twelve, she still loves those chicken nuggets, though she has branched out to chicken tenders and barbecue wings.

Looking back, it was odd to consider the simple fact that had Sarah and Mohammed fought their addictions as hard as they fought DCYF and us, they could have beaten their drug problems hands down, and they would have still had this wonderful child. But individuals who are ODD—oppositional and defiant—don't do what is expected of them or what is asked of them; no, they do exactly the opposite. Their attention deficit disorders also prevent them from considering or even understanding the consequences of their actions, and they act impulsively. Sarah was given a choice, though she insists to this day that drugs are not a choice; "they grab hold of you and you do what they tell you—free choice is gone!" according to her. But in the world of the rest of us straights—straight-thinking people—given the choice to stay in rehab and quit drugs, or lose your child, most would do whatever it took to quit the drugs. Given the choice to have Lily as a daughter or a sister, she left rehab less than a week into the program when Mohammed came to spring her, and she quickly returned to the world in the clouds. Lily flew into the clouds on her way to a better life.

I don't know how much his Iranian ancestry drove his actions, but Mohammed, who never considered Lily his responsibility, suddenly was focused on getting her back. I think it was more a property right than a child, but he filed appeals and pursued them through his pro-bono attorney, as Sarah did through hers. Penelope was right there with them as always, urging them on so she could have "Day Day" to raise herself. Since we now had custody of Lily, Penelope insisted on visitation rights at least. So within the first few weeks of having Lily, we were forced to bring her to the visitation center every other Sunday, drop her off for two hours, and allow Penelope to lavish gifts on the little tyke. This was not allowed, according to the center's rules. They did not want adult visitors, usually ex-spouses, trying to buy a child's love and affection. But Penelope somehow convinced them that she never got to enjoy Lily's second birthday, so why couldn't she bring a few birthday presents? We were glad we had our pickup truck with us to haul all the stuff she brought that day. The same gift extravaganza reoccurred for Halloween and Thanksgiving and Christmas, of course the only traditional gift-giving holiday.

In the fall we found out that Mohammed had returned to the East Coast and wanted to enjoy his visitation privileges. Though his parental rights were terminated in October 2002, their appeal allowed them to maintain rights to visit in Maryland. And though the rules only allowed one visitor at a time—the center was designed for parents primarily—once again Penelope convinced them that Lily would do better with both of them (Penelope and Mohammed) present. Unbeknownst to us Sarah had also returned back east, though she did not join the visits for reasons still unclear to us. Mohammed was back three months before he joined his mother for a visit, and Sarah would wait until six months after her return before she would visit, and ironically it would take place not in Maryland, but California, when we were all out there for a status review hearing in January 2003.

We had hoped to spend some time with Caroline's family in LA, her cousin Bob, his wife, Judy, and their married children Rob and his wife, Maggie, and David and his wife, Nonnie, and Bob and Judy's single daughter Becky. They were always there for us, from the day we let them know Sarah lived around the corner from them, through the court battles and termination hearings. They adored Lily and provided a safe place to bring her for our short visits before she was brought to us. Instead of letting them enjoy Lily unencumbered, we were forced to allow the parents, Mohammed and Sarah, and his mother a visit in California. They actually allowed all three to visit her at the DCFS department office. It would be Sarah's first visit with her daughter in six months.

It would also mark an even longer time since we saw our daughter. Our cousins were familiar with the neighborhood, having ministered in the church across the street from the department. All of our trips were to the courthouse, Department 410; we had never been to the main office of the Department of Children and Family Services (DCFS). The office on Colorado Street was right across the street from the main entrance of the church, so we decided to do a little spying of our own. The visits were set up to avoid parties meeting, so when we dropped Lily off, they were already there waiting. We would then disappear for two hours and then return to pick her up. They would have to leave the property before we arrived. So we snuck back a bit early to watch them leave while we hid across the street in the church. The three marched out, Mohammed in the lead with Penelope and Sarah walking together in the back. She looked wasted away under the influence of Mohammed and the drugs he provided. She was a shadow of her former self. It was difficult to watch, but increased our resolve for having stepped in to protect Lily.

One of the outcomes of this visit to California was to continue her placement with us, and to allow the parents (Sarah and Mohammed) to visit together. We were not pleased with this, but one crumb they tossed our way was the ruling that curtailed Penelope's visits. She no longer had any legal standing. When we returned to Maryland we now played the every other Sunday game with Sarah and Mohammed. It was tough dropping her off with the parents who had broken their parental bond with Lily in favor of drugs, and yet here they could continue to play the role of the loving parents every other Sunday. We would drop her off and hear Sarah call out to her in the hallway, "Come to Mommy." Lily would reek of perfume on the way home. It was a sad charade.

These visits would continue for several months, with Lily's behavior deteriorating as visits approached and falling apart altogether after they took place. Consider the perception of a two-and-a-half-year-old child whose parents weren't there for her, who allowed strangers to step in and take her from them and place her with a stepbrother, with them showing up when it was convenient, then moving her to live with a complete stranger and then traveling across the country to live with two more individuals she hardly knew. Then, just when that starts to feel good, a stable home with two loving parents, you're back with the old ones for visits. Does that mean they might be back for good? Does this mean a trip back to California and the chaos it represented? Will I be taken from the two people who have provided a stable and happy home?

Possession is nine tenths of the law, they say, and after fighting so hard for this, and now having her, we would fight even harder to protect this security. The visits were working against us, against Lily's development, but how could we stop them? We pleaded with her attorney and with the social worker and with anyone with influence. We were advised to gather any documentary evidence of her biological parents' negative influence. We decided to document her behavior after the visits, but were told no one would believe us since we had a powerful vested interest. We would have to find a neutral party to support our contentions. So we engaged a clinical psychologist to observe Lily and get to know her and us, and then provide her with the opportunity to see her after the visits. The clinician was okay, but we were not impressed and sought another who was willing to work with us even to setting up Sunday appointments immediately after the visits. So we took Lily every week and then arranged for a session after a visit with the "parents."

The day of the big visit was rather strange, for rather than waiting in the waiting room at the DSS visiting center for the visit to be over, Lily was waiting for us in the arms of the social worker. They herded us out and on our way. We headed over to the psychologist's office and Lily went immediately into the toy room. She was somehow avoiding us, and when we went to check on her, we realized why. This little gal, who had been toilet trained since the first weeks after her arrival ten months earlier, had wet herself. She just stood there playing with a toy and let the warm pee just run down her legs. The psychologist agreed that that was significant and felt that any more of these behaviors and he would be able to recommend that the visits be reconsidered in light of the negative impact on the minor child. It would turn out to be a moot point.

Wednesday of that following week, I got a call from the supervisor of the visitation center informing me that Sarah's privileges at the visitation center were revoked. Why? Because she had violated the rule regarding drug use on the premises. I would have to wait until later that week to read the visitation notes before I would realize the exact circumstances. Apparently Sarah excused herself a few minutes after arriving for the visit to use the restroom. When she did not return immediately, the state police officer on duty for security purposes knocked on the bathroom door and asked if she were all right. She indicated she was and presented herself a few minutes later. Her speech was noticeably slurred and she staggered slightly when she walked. This gave the officer reason to suspect that she was under the influence of something. He asked the social worker to have Sarah leave the visitation room and meet with him in an adjoining room. He asked her permission to search her purse and discovered two vials with the residue of a white powder. She was taken into custody and arrested for suspected possession of a controlled substance and being under the influence of the same in a state-run facility. Since the Family Service Center was dually funded by DSS and the local board of education, it fell under the provisions of the Drug-Free Schools Act as well.

Sarah's privileges at the visitation center were suspended, so once again she was prevented from seeing her daughter. Caroline and I had mixed feelings about this, for once again Sarah was the only one suffering the consequences of the couple's shared behaviors. The bigger question I had was the status of Mohammed's visitation privileges. When I called the center to inquire, they indicated that he did not appear to be under the influence and was not in possession of illegal drugs, only Sarah, so once again he seemed to be sailing along scot-free. I called Lily's attorney in California and lodged a protest. She agreed with me that with his history of supplying her with drugs, and his knowledge that she was still using drugs, he was equally complicit, and his rights would be stopped, if not by the visiting center, then by court order from California. This was wonderful news and was accomplished just prior to his next visit. We would no longer have to suffer through the indignities for parents who quite obviously were still living the lifestyle they were supposed to have left behind in California.

You will remember that when Lily was taken from their home in the first place when Lily was just a year old, it was because Sarah was a drug user and Mohammed was an abusive mate. The total irony of it was revealed when, two years later, their visitation, their last contact with their daughter, was revoked for precisely the same reasons: Sarah was using drugs and Mohammed was allowing it. And to fulfill the last piece, he got so angry that Sarah had lost him his visits that once again he assaulted her. And for once, this would turn out to work for all our benefits, Caroline's and mine, Lily's, and even Sarah's.

## Joe, Our Guardian Angel

It seems that Mohammed was a serial batterer. Several weeks prior to this most recent beating, he had punched Sarah and given her a black eye. She went to work with it and it garnered the attention of one of her customers at the restaurant/bar she worked at. He was a computer technician from Chicago in Baltimore for business. He seemed to be somehow taken by this fragile young woman and was sympathetic. "How'd you get the shiner?" he asked. "Oh, I have this guy I'm living with who's a little free with his fists." "Wow, nobody deserves that.

Look. Here's my business card. You ever need someone to talk to, give me a call. I'm not married and I live at home with my folks, so maybe I can be of some help to you." "Sure why not?" she replied, and took the card, placing it in the pocket of her uniform. Over the next few weeks, Sarah called Joe and they spoke. Next time he was in town he came to the restaurant and they met after work for a conversation. Joe seemed harmless enough and kinda nice even. He was very laid back and seemed genuinely interested in Sarah. A friendship developed over time, with phone calls, and Joe made it clear to Sarah, if she ever needed a place to go, he would be there for her. So here she was, several weeks later, at the receiving end of more brutality. She decided to give Joe a call. Was the offer still open? He asked her if she wanted a roundtrip ticket or one way. It didn't matter, she just wanted to get out. One way would be fine. "Can you get away safely?" was his main concern. "I can handle that part." So Joe arranged for a flight from Baltimore to Chicago that very evening. Sarah grabbed up all her clothes and personal belongings, threw then in a laundry basket, and told Mohammed she was going out to do laundry. He even dropped her off at the Laundromat. She never looked back. She somehow got hold of a suitcase or travel bag, threw all the stuff inside, caught a bus to the airport, and was in Chicago by the end of the evening. Joe was waiting for her there at the airport.

    It wasn't until four years later that I heard the rest of the story—at Joe and Sarah's wedding. Joe was living in his parents' finished basement and suddenly realized that he knew very little about this young woman who was coming to move in with him and his parents. He just had this strong feeling toward her (love at first sight?) and went by his gut. When she arrived, it was all hugs and kisses at first, then the heroin began to wear off. Here we go with withdrawal…again. Sarah was sick, with all the chills and fever and cramps and vomiting and nausea. She was honest with Joe and told him why she was sick. "What can I do for you? How can I help?" Her response? "Take me to the dirtiest ghetto in Chicago." Without a moment's hesitation, Joe told her, "I'm not gonna do that." Instead, he called one of his gal friends, who came over, and, between the two of them, they got her through the sickness, and then got her to a clinic and into a program. Sarah worked the program and got onto methadone, and between Joe and his friends, and, yes, even Joe's mother, they made sure Sarah stuck with the routine and took her methadone. Three years later she weaned and got off the methadone, and to date she has been clean and sober for almost ten years now.

After Sarah left Baltimore, Mohammed called us searching for her, but we had no idea where she was, and wouldn't have told him if we had. Five months later, in October 2003, the court in California rejected Mohammed and Sarah's appeal of the order of termination of parental rights, and Lily became a child without parents, without even relatives. She was a ward of the State of California in a preadoptive placement with us. It was at this point that Lily began to heal, to bond with us, and to begin to show herself in all her glory. Her bad dreams stopped and she developed the wonderful, if challenging personality she has today. Mohammed never called or tried to contact us again. Sarah called him a time or two from Chicago, but when Joe found out, that stopped. To date no one has heard from Mohammed, or his family. I am convinced that he only looked at Lily, and probably Sarah as well, as property, his possessions. And once he knew they were gone, he lost interest in any other emotional attachments. Say what you will, but there are certain cultures that have little to no respect for women, and with his Persian ancestry, his father being Iranian, it may have affected an attitude or belief system that hurt Sarah and Lily when they were with him, but gave them a clean getaway once they were clear of him.

Four years later, an article appeared in our local paper about a shoplifting scam at our local Walmart. Seems a man, Timothy J. A., was arrested with another man after secreting a number of CDs in an empty fan box. Timothy J. A., also known as TJ, turns out to be…Mohammed's brother. The same one who shared the drug problems and proclivity for crime with his brother, Sarah's ex-boyfriend and Lily's biological father. Seems like nothing changed in that family.

## Reunion

From the fall of 2003 to the spring of 2004, we would be held to the standard of Caroline's words in court. Under what circumstances would we allow Sarah to see her daughter? Since Sarah had met all of the conditions, i.e., she was clean and sober and on a maintenance dose of methadone, she had a job in a check-cashing business, and she was independent of Mohammed and, to a certain extent, anyone else. She lived with Joe in the basement of his parents' house. Joe, it turned out, was the youngest in the family, with siblings who were significantly older than he was at thirty years of age. His mother was in her seventies and his dad was pushing eighty. In addition to Joe and Sarah, Joe's sister Robin also made residence in Mommy's house with her two children, a twenty-year-old son, and an eleven-year-old daughter. One happy though somewhat eccentric family. Though Joe was the youngest in the family, he seemed to be the bedrock, the foundation of the family. It was a far cry from what Sarah was living in, and she was clean, sober, employed, and paying her way. And they were her support system, so we had to give them a lot of the credit for her recovery. After all, we weren't so good at it, were we?

## Reconnecting With Sarah

Somewhere along the way, Sarah called Caroline, and they began to open channels of communication. Caroline had noticed that Sarah's family contacts were cyclical. Every six weeks she would need to talk with her mom, so she would

## Breaking Up Is Hard To Do—Fighting For Our Gal

give her a call. Mom was always there for her. I remained skeptical and was the reluctant one. Never begrudged Caroline's contact with her daughter, our daughter, but in the background I remained. This went on for several months, and then Caroline told me she wanted to see Sarah. I was not enthused about it; I thought it was too soon. We were only a year past the visits and the recriminations, and she was only away from Mohammed a year. It just seemed like yesterday when she was accusing me of abusing her, and her mom and me of forcing her into therapy and keeping her locked up in her bedroom. We had been through a great deal over the last four years since Lily was born, and I wasn't ready to jump into anything. Six trips to California and fighting Sarah, Mohammed, and his mother for custody left a bad taste in my mouth that wasn't cleared with the visitations with them. But Caroline felt that Sarah had met the criteria and that we needed, she needed, to reciprocate. She wanted to see her daughter. I was still so focused on Lily that I could not justify taking time away from our summer with her for a visit to Chicago, especially with Connecticut and our house project on the summer docket, but Caroline was insistent. "Fine. I'll go myself, you can stay home with Lily." I was okay with that, then she added a critical element. "I've talked with Andrew and he wants to see her, too, so he is going to fly down from Canada and we're gonna meet in Chicago." Now wait just a minute, there was no way, NO WAY, I was going to allow this dynamic to take place, the "terrible triad" I had suffered for all those years. The thought of it reemerging from the primordial ooze was stomach churning. If Andrew was going, so was I. We booked flights to Chicago for a long weekend. We arranged for Lily to have a sleepover with her day-care mother, who had a ten-year-old daughter. She also knew Miss Karen's husband, Mr. Curtis. She would be safe and sound while Caroline and I made good on reconnecting with Sarah.

We decided that we would not stay with them (Sarah and Joe), as if they had room in a house with four adults and two kids. We would stay in town, in the Loop of Chicago, and rent a car so we would not be dependent on them for transportation. We wanted to be independent in case the dynamic went south. We booked a room at the Hard Rock Hotel, which had just opened. We checked in, Andrew was picked up at the airport by Sarah and Joe, and they arrived to meet us in the lobby of the Hard Rock. The reunion was a joyous one, with a lot of hugs and good feelings. We liked Joe, a quiet, easygoing guy who seemed to worship Sarah and had the patience of Job. To his great advantage, he had never fooled with drugs. We spent the next few days having dinner at Ed Debevics, a hamburger rock and roll joint, the Navy Pier, and other points of interest. We took the time to visit with Joe's parents, and got to meet Robin and her daughter, though Jeremy, the wild one, was elsewhere (good thing). We parted with the same hugs we started with, leaving Andrew to spend a few more hours with Sarah and Joe.

## Back To School And The Christmas Reveal

The next school year was uneventful, with school starting up and Lily attending preschool in Caroline's building. Her status as a foster child helped get her in the pre-K program, and we enjoyed the holidays without any intrusions of gifts from overbearing grandparents like Penelope. We spent Christmas in Florida and got to spend some quality time with my cousin Tim, Lisa, and their children, Rachel, ten, Ryan, eight, and Katrina, four. We also scheduled some time with my mom, who had moved over to the east coast of Florida after being displaced by Hurricane Charlie. The trip over Christmas was good, and Lily seemed to be relaxing and settling in.

Over the past year or so we had continued our contact with Sarah. I even got on the phone to chat with her on occasion. What we didn't do was let on to Lily who we were talking to or about. We used code. "M" called, or "M" is trying to get Joe to move out from his parents' house. Lily was receiving counseling from a mental health professional at school. Just someone she could talk to and iron out any wrinkles her early years and the effects separation might have wrought. We also wanted to keep a pulse on her developing curiosity about her past and how she fit into her new family. We, Caroline and I, agreed that we would never lie to her, yet would not volunteer information, just respond to questions she put to us. Along the way the therapist let it be known that Lily knows that Caroline is her grandmother and that she has another mother. "She knows that Frank is her grandfather. She also knows that Sarah is her mother, and that you talk with her." We knew that sooner rather than later we would have to have "the talk" with little Lily, a very bright and perceptive little girl who didn't miss a trick. Even at four years old, we knew we had what some refer to as an old soul. She was definitely wise beyond her years.

So here we are, Christmas 2004, Vero Beach, Florida, eating dinner with our cousins, Tim, Lisa, their kids, Rachel, Ryan, and Katrina, and Lily looks over at me and out of the blue asks me, "Do you know my mom?" I look over at Caroline. We both, we ALL, knew she was not referring to Caroline. Do I answer? Do I make light of it and say, "Caroline? Sure, I know your mom, Caroline." But this would not be honest, knowing the true import of her question. So with a knowing look of consent from Caroline, I responded honestly. "Yes. I know your mother." Pause... "What's her name?" Wow! Talk about being put on the spot. I am now being required to utter the name, for the first time in years. Again the eye contact with Caroline and the assurance it was okay to respond, and I uttered the word, "Sarah." Just as quickly Lily responded. "No it's not! It's Katie!" Whoa! She tiptoed to the edge, then just as quickly backed away from the cliff. Was she testing us? You bet. We never did figure out who Katie was. The closest Caroline could come was Sarah's great-grandmother, Lily's great-great grandmother, Kevin's grandmother. And if Lily is an old soul...who was she channeling? That was essentially it for the discussion of relationships. Lily continued to be focused on family groups; all her stuffed animals had a mother, father, and a baby. Baby animals had a mother and father as she started to conceptualize her place in the family, our family.

I got down to Florida for my Easter trip, and we started talking about returning to Florida for a ten-day summer trip. Maybe even sneak Disney World in for Lily, who would turn five July 4, 2005. We made our plane reservations and planned on visiting my mom in Lake Worth, along with my cousins in Vero and Parkland. As summer approached, discussions ensued about another reunion with Sarah. "Like when?" was my response, with three days at Rehoboth Beach, and a long weekend in Connecticut, and ten days in Florida. Well, Connecticut got cut, and then Sarah suggested we just meet in Florida. She missed the days we all congregated in Fort Lauderdale with my family; why not meet there? Maybe we could leave Lily with Heather and James in Lauderdale or with Tim and Lisa and the kids in Vero. Then Caroline suggested that maybe, just maybe, it was time to bring Sarah and Lily together. I was not ready for that one. I didn't think that Lily was ready either. Caroline and I went back and forth a number of times and we could not agree; her argument was that Sarah had met all the terms, mine that Lily was still fragile and only two years away from the torment of two mothers and two fathers. I suggested that we get some advice from Dr. Mom. I called and spoke to her and she seemed to agree that the time might not be right. Had Lily asked to see her mother? No. "I'll talk with Caroline and see what she thinks, and offer her my opinion," Dr. Mom offered. When Caroline debriefed me after her conversation with Dr. Mom, a new insight emerged. Lily might be able to handle it, but how about Sarah? She was only clean and sober two years, and only recently weaned off her methadone. It was Sarah that was the fragile one. Where we see Lily as a beautiful and vibrant child, Sarah sees her as the child she had with Mohammed, and the life she had with him, a life filled with drugs and deception and dysfunction. "Seeing Lily could set her back," Dr. Mom told Caroline, and we were back on the same wavelength. We can go see Sarah in Florida; Lily would not go along for the meet.

As it turned out we decided to leave Lily with Tim and Lisa. Lily was getting along fabulously with the kids, Rachel, Ryan, and Katrina, so we just told Lily we were going to see some friends in Lauderdale, and my mom. We would only be gone a night. And off we went to see my mom...and Sarah and Joe. Once again the reunion was great, with lots of hugs and heartfelt conversations. Drank a few beers in our favorite spots, and swam on the beach in front of the apartment that belonged to Aunt Meam before she died. Took some pictures and then headed back to Vero. Lily was never the wiser. I don't know if it was something we said, or somebody else, but five months later, December, and Lily informs us, out of the blue, that she is mad at us. Why are you mad at us? "Because you went to see Sarah in Florida and didn't take me!" How she knew this was beyond us, but this child was no dummy, in fact she could read people like a book. Follow-up questioning revealed that, yes, she wanted to see Sarah. Why couldn't she? We briefly explained that Sarah was still not able to take care of her, that she had been...sick, and was only now getting stronger. But one day, if she wanted to see Sarah, and she was ready, then we would work it out.

## Television Stars

Some months back, we had established contact with a national news program (ABC *Primetime*) to do a story on grandparents raising their grandchildren. For several months two producers from ABC News spent time in our home, in our schools, on the soccer field, at the doctor's office, filming everyday life with Frank, Caroline, and Lily. In the fall the producers asked us, would it be all right to contact Sarah? I responded this way, "If you had asked me that two years ago, I would have said no, but she has been clean and sober for two years, and she has a job and a new boyfriend, and, well, sure, go talk to her." We called Sarah to make sure she was okay with it and her answer was typical Sarah: "I don't care, send 'em out." We talked with her on basic etiquette such as not ordering the most expensive thing on the menu if they took her out to eat; she did anyway, and left half on her plate…typical Sarah. So the two producers flew out and spent a few days with Sarah, and got her views on film.

## What's In A Name?

And so we moved on to November 2005, and were getting ready for the big day, the finalization of our adoption of Lily. After having her over three years, and fighting Sarah, Mohammed, Penelope, and the bureaucracy for four years, we were going to have our little gal, our legal daughter, with all rights and privileges. I was tremendously excited. We had hired an attorney to file all the paperwork and to appear in court on our behalf and he sent us papers to sign. One important piece, of course, was her name. I told Caroline that having no natural/biological children of my own, I now stood ready to adopt my third child, and, having missed the opportunity to name any of them, wanted to name this one. I had no problem with "Lily," and "Matthews" was automatic if not temporary pending her marriage one day. As for her middle moniker, it was given to her by her birth mother, Sarah, who had piercings in her ears (five each), nose, eyebrow, tongue, and who knows where else. Sarah, who had a Chinese pagoda running from her right shoulder to her elbow, and her street name, GURL, emblazoned in four-inch-high graffiti letters across the small of her back, not to mention the letters L-I-L-Y' across the back of her neck (to show she really cares). Sarah decided to name her little daughter Lily' Jazmyn A. The nine-letter ethnic "A" name would be history along with the accent and the middle name with the street spelling, with a middle name worthy of this old soul: Alexandra, with the accent (spoken only) on the third syllable with the proper pronunciation "on," not "an" — Alex-ON-drah. *Lily Alexandra Matthews*. Initials LAM. That's what I wrote on her adoption papers.

## California For The Adoption

Somewhere along the way, one of the documents I signed noted that in order for the adoption to take place, "ALL PARTIES MUST BE PRESENT." Looked like we were going to California. Again. The sixth time for me, the seventh for Caroline. ABC News and the two producers who were following us around wanted to be there for this momentous occasion, and we planned on dual Disney for our little gal — having spent a day at Disney World in July, we would also spend a day at Disneyland in November. We would fly out to LA a few days early to settle in, take in the sights at the Magic Kingdom, and then appear in court. Now the original plan was for the two producers to fly out with us, but as the date approached one of the producers came up with another plan, one we were not excited about. While Vivian would fly out to LA with us, camera in hand, Anna would fly to…Chicago to be with Sarah in her time of need. Time of need?! Sarah was fine with our arrangement. She knew she was not in any shape to raise Lily when she was sick, and only fought us because Mohammed made her do it. He wanted Lily so he could give her to HIS mother. You remember the home with the hot and cold running dogs and cats, paint cans in the privy, and food and other indescribable detritus covering every horizontal surface? Sarah was glad we had her; in fact, she couldn't think of a better place for her to be than with us. And she was in no position to take her anyway, living in Chicago in a basement with her boyfriend, working for a few bucks to pay for her cigarettes (and tattoos). Why would she need support as her mother and father finalized what was inevitable, and what had been in place for forty months following Lily's arrival three years earlier? What was Anna up to? But we had more important things to consider, like getting to LA and getting the adoption worked through. We decided that since this was a celebration, and the family, our family, in California, who were there for us at every step, Bob and Judy and their grown children and their spouses, Rob and Maggie and David and Nonnie, and Bob and Judy's daughter Becky, would have to be there to celebrate with us, where else to celebrate but DISNEYLAND! So nine of us, Bob, Judy, Becky, Rob, Maggie, Frank, Caroline, and Vivian (David and Nonnie were eight months pregnant so they passed) and Lily went to the Magic Kingdom. A grand time was had by all as Lily chased all the princesses down.

Friday we arrived at the courthouse, and with cameras rolling headed into the parking lot. We parked our car and walked up the portico, dancing our way up the sidewalk, when… Caroline's cell phone rings. Who is it but Sarah. "Can't talk now, we are on the way into the courthouse. Call you when we get out. Bye." We took the elevator up to Department 410, a building and waiting room we were all too familiar with, but this time, this time, there was no anxiety, just joy. The service was great and they paused for photos with the judge and, well, it was a great time for all of us.

Caroline, mind you, is Sarah's mother, too, and whether it was her phone call as we headed into the courthouse or her motherly instincts, Caroline was having some pangs of conscience and sadness that she was having to adopt her daughter's daughter. So when we exited the courthouse, she felt obligated to ring Sarah back, I was a bit annoyed. This was OUR happy moment, our moment of triumph, and why was Sarah trying to spoil it? What was going on in Chicago? Try to imagine the scene: Here sits Caroline, on the LA courthouse steps, with cameras rolling. There's a guy with one of these big professional ABC Television news cameras, a sound man with a mike on a long boom, the producer with a clipboard, Lily, Bob, and Judy, and me. There sits Sarah in a Chicago hotel, cameras rolling, a mother/daughter confrontation brought to you by…Jerry Springer. In tears, "Why did you have to ADOPT her, why couldn't you just have been her guardian?!' Calmly, Caroline responds, "Sarah, you don't understand. Guardianship is for someone to step in for the parents, on a temporary basis. You lost your parental rights. They were ready to put Lily up for private adoption. She might have been lost to us all. You should be glad your dad and I stepped in to take her, to keep her in the family." Sarah: "That's not true!" "Yes, it is true, Sarah...and I love you, too." Caroline was in tears at this point. "No, you don't." Sarah was crying, too. "I don't want to talk about it now. Bye." Very sad, heartbreaking even.

Anna, the producer, picked up the phone from Sarah and went into lecture mode. All of us, including Vivian, our producer, were telling Caroline to say good-bye to Anna, hang up, gotta go. We finally convinced her to do so as we were getting into the car to leave the parking lot. Now Caroline was upset. Our celebration spoiled somewhat for that moment of drama that sells television time. The thing is, that moment was just that. A moment. We didn't need the gray cloud looming over our California sunny day. Sarah was sad, but this day was the one she was warned about so many months ago by the DCFS case worker when she told Sarah straight out, "Look at that little girl. It's your choice to straighten up and she will remain your daughter, if not, she becomes your little sister." Choices were made, and what we looked on with joy and happiness, she looked on as something we did to her...we took her child and made her our own. And we did, but not for any selfish reasons, but because this little girl deserved better.

Once we got back to Maryland and the phone calls resumed between Caroline and Sarah, all was well. By Christmas we decided maybe it was time to open a link, small as it might be, between Sarah and Lily. So on Christmas Eve when Sarah called and I was talking with her, I asked Lily if she wanted to talk to Sarah, and she did. The next day they spoke again on Christmas Day, and she told her all the things Santa brought her. It was the start of a reunification between biological mother and daughter, with small steps balanced by the routine of life in Maryland with Mommy and Daddy, Caroline and Frank. We sent Sarah photos, and Lily sent her a birthday card when Sarah turned twenty-eight in March of 2006. In keeping with the theme "Sarah couldn't take care of you because she was sick," Lily put together the fact that Sarah smoked cigarettes with being sick. So in her birthday card, with no suggestion from us, she wrote, "Happy Birthday, Stop Smoking, Love, Lily." All we did was tell her how to spell the words she asked us to. Boy, did Sarah get mad! "You put her up to it!" "No, we didn't," but who was to believe it? Not Sarah. What a smart little girl, though.

At the end of March we were told that a final interview would take place with the ABC News television anchor and the three families who were the focus of a *Primetime* special. Cynthia McFadden would sit down with each of the families for a face-to-face interview. We looked forward to it, and took the day off from work to meet with her in Wilmington, Delaware. We were used to our producers, Vivian and Anna, with their hand-held cameras shooting "home movies." We had also experienced some bigger stuff, with microphones on our lapels, and a sound man with a boom mike and cameraman with a big camera on the tripod or carried on his shoulder. This setup (with some of the same personnel) was much larger. In a conference room upstairs at the elegan*t Hotel DuPont,* we peeked in to see lights, reflectors, three large cameras on tripods, and miles of cables. Three chairs were in the middle with blue curtains, Cynthia's, and Caroline's and mine, side by side.

We sat for sound checks and powder for my shiny nose. Cynthia asked them to move her chair closer—she felt too far away—and then we began. The interview lasted over ninety minutes and never dragged. She asked some difficult questions, but Caroline and I agreed that it gave us the opportunity to respond with our well-considered thoughts on a wide range of subjects and experiences. One of the more direct questions was about how we somehow "failed our daughter," and here we were a school psychologist and a guidance counselor.

Yeah, well, we were human beings, too! And we realized we were too close to the situation to be objective, so we sought professional help for Sarah, for our marriage, for our family. I told Cynthia on camera that we were pretty much a normal American family, we didn't drink or take drugs, we ate dinner around the table every evening, we did everything we could for our kids, yet Sarah still decided to go in another direction.

Did I feel like I had erred along the way? Maybe being a child of the sixties and glorifying that period of my life may have lead Sarah down the wrong path, but once we realized the drugs were leading her, we stepped in. Hard. Drug rehab and counseling and house rules, close scrutiny, and a clear message: whatever Dad did or didn't do, you are not going to be abusing drugs under our watch, and we will make every effort to make sure that you don't, and that you pursue a more meaningful course in life.

The other "difficult" line of questioning revolved around our current relationship with Sarah. "When was the last time you spoke with your daughter?" "Tuesday," Caroline responded. Miss McFadden looked surprised. "Do you talk with her often?" "About once or twice a week," Caroline replied, and I supported. She looked even more surprised as a puzzled look came over her face, "Because she (your daughter) seems to be pretty angry with you." Now it was Caroline and I who were genuinely surprised. We couldn't believe it, didn't believe it. Our relationship with Sarah had been quite strained throughout her adolescence; it peaked when she left home at eighteen and moved to first Texas, then California, with Mohammed. It eased with contact relegated to phone calls every few weeks, then peaked when she was pregnant. We were very nervous about her bringing this pregnancy to full term with her history of intravenous drug use. She gave us a few scares. "Oh, I might have a baby with Down syndrome." "No, it might have a neural tube defect or something." And then, just as matter-of-factly, "The baby's fine." We may have been annoyed, but the anger was gone.

Caroline was always there for Sarah. Even when she had to be tough, she loved and kept the door open.

Fathers tend to be tougher, their love tends to be more conditional, and their kids have to earn their love and respect. I loved Sarah, but withheld affection until she had earned my respect by actions. The past few years were tough, but when she was with her little girl, straight, sober, and focused, it gave me the sense she was back on the right track, and I let her know that. I so wanted to be truly proud of her. We had our ups and we had our downs, but we thought that the anger and recriminations were behind us. That is why we were so surprised to hear Ms. McFadden ask about the current status of our relationship with Sarah as though it were strained when we thought everything was so good.

Sarah knew and respected her limits. She didn't ask to talk to Lily and knew better than to ask to see her; it was "Parents know best, and I'm glad you're taking care of my little girl." That is the way it was for almost three years until ABC descended on her in Chicago, apparently. The interview in the fall of 2005 with Vivian and Anna, and the confrontation during the adoption in November, stirred something. The kicker is that Sarah never shared any of it with us. Not with Caroline and certainly not with me. She said very little of her first interview and nothing about the second. And within days it was back to business as usual, calling us, talking nice. We thought we had a very good relationship with Sarah, working toward the reunification with Lily down the road. So you can imagine our surprise when Cynthia McFadden informed us that Sarah was angry with us. For taking her child. For dropping the dime on her when she returned to California that summer. For suggesting that her child was in any danger. "She was never in any danger." Sarah, like most addicts, had a difficult time with the truth, and with accepting the consequences of her actions. This was a prime example of that. Talk nice to Mom and Dad, from whom you want something, then bad-mouth them behind their backs. More importantly, she was minimizing her role in Lily's neglect, putting her in danger, and then refusing to acknowledge the actions that followed by the courts and by us. This made us worry about her trustworthiness in the future. Until you can face up to your acts and, if not apologize, appear remorseful, the healing can never begin. You can't get better. And if she wasn't going to get better, Caroline and I had to carefully consider how much contact Lily would have with her biological mother.

Caroline and I flashed back to the worst three days of our lives, back in July 2001. About the conversations with Sarah's neighbor Ruth in California about a toddler not yet walking making her way out of her apartment and down the open balcony to Ruth's. We saw that balcony when we returned to California with Lily, the open wrought iron railing with a six-inch space underneath, just enough for a child to crawl through and drop fifteen feet to the pavement. No, if Sarah wanted to be mad at us for taking Lily away from that, well, then she could just be mad. It wasn't about her, it was about Lily. Her safety and security.

The next time Sarah called after the McFadden interview, I made a point of getting on the phone. "Hey," I said, "what the heck did you tell Vivian and Anna when they interviewed you?" "I don't know, why?" "Sounds like you were pretty mad at us and said some pretty nasty things," I said. Defensively she replied, "Why do they (the media) always have to focus on the negative things? Why can't they focus on the good? I said a lot of good stuff about you, too." "Well," I said, "they can only focus on bad stuff if you say it, and you know drama sells. And besides, you're the one that's gonna look bad if you bad-mouthed your mom and me." "What d'ya mean?" "Well," I said, "twenty million people are gonna hear you try to justify your actions and how you were such a great mother while addicted to heroin." Her response, so typically Sarah, was: "I don't care...I don't know any of them anyway!" "Well, they are certainly going to know *you*!" I responded. And that was it. Our relationship, our phone calls from Sarah, returned to business as usual.

## Lily And Sarah Reunite

By April, between our conversations with Sarah, and Lily's conversations with her counselor, and Lily's conversations with us (she was mad that Vivian and Anna got to see Sarah and she couldn't...in her words, "That's not fair!") we decided that maybe Lily was ready to see Sarah. Sarah was three years sober and a year off her methadone, so maybe the time was right. We talked with Lily's counselor and prepared for the reunion, the first time in three years. Lily was now five years ten months of age. We stressed the temporary nature of the visit and compared it with visits with her big brother Andrew. He comes and sees us and leaves, and sometimes we go up and see him at his house and then we leave and come home.

We decided to meet Sarah at the lakehouse, a neutral location closer to Chicago and an opportunity for Sarah to visit with Caroline's mom, who was eighty-six and hadn't seen Sarah in years. We talked about the visit, and Lily was the one who voiced it: "We're gonna go see Sarah. She used to be my mother but now she's my big sister." Sarah seemed okay with everything and demonstrated an ironic sense of detachment, one I had difficulty coming to grips with but accepted under the circumstances. I love kids. Enjoy being around them, watching them, teaching them, playing with them, entertaining them. I have played cousin or uncle to generations of kids, including my cousin Bill's kids when they were young and now their kids (Rachel, Ryan, and Katrina). I enjoyed Andrew and Sarah when they were little and the neighbors' kids when my kids grew up and moved away. I've taken kids to the beach, to the lake, to the park, to amusement parks, and seaquariums, and monkey jungles, and science museums.

I like kids and they like me, and when I realized what was happening to Lily, neglected, set aside, then bounced from home to home away from family that could love and nurture and support her, I was willing to step in knowing that I would probably get attached. And having bonded with this little gal over the last six years, and especially the last four when she came to live with us, I enjoy watching, playing, entertaining, supporting her. And, as I watch her grow, she comes up with gems. On diets: "I don't know about you and Mom, you're always on diarrheas." Or, the time I remarked on all the sad little shacks on the side of the hills in West Virginia and she responded, "Yeah, Dad, but inside those little houses are beautiful little things." Or her take on religion and church: "I know they have food there…chips and dip." I sit back and I enjoy my time with her, and I wonder how Sarah could give this up, how she could have just let it go.

Sarah seems happy, almost relieved at times, that she doesn't have to deal with a child twenty-four/seven and glad we have her. I have commented that she (Sarah) should set some money aside, even $25 a week, and put it in a bank account, $100 a month, $1,200 a year, and when Lily is ready to go to college, she can say, "I may not have been there for you all those years, but here's a little something I set aside — here's some money for your personal expenses in college." "That would mean a lot to her," I said, "and show her you were thinking about her and willing to make a sacrifice, however small, for her all those years." But it never happens. Cigarettes, tattoos, fingernails, haircuts and dyes, and fun money always come first. Sarah still spends more on her own personal expenses, making even this small contribution to her daughter difficult; the child she brought into this world. Sarah makes promises with all the best intentions — "Oh yeah, let's buy her that expensive doll, I'll give you money toward it…." Yeah, and the check's in the mail. And beyond the money, beyond the box of clothes that was not yet mailed and never was, where is Sarah emotionally when it comes to her child? Does she care? Does she miss her? Does she regret losing her? Doesn't she know what she is missing in this wonderful little girl's everyday life? But maybe the detachment is protection from emotions that are too painful to deal with. Wishing you were on the cruise ship after it's sailed isn't very healthy either.

The other question running through Caroline's and my minds was something broader, more mature on the scale.

What if something happened to Caroline and me, thrusting Lily into the world without parents again? Would Sarah be the first choice to step back in? Is she ready (she's met the criteria—clean and sober, employed, independent)? Is she able? Most recently she moved out of the basement at Joe's parents. For a while she was living on friends' couches, even less stable than the basement room, homeless for all practical purposes. Even more recently Joe and Sarah set up housekeeping in a one-bedroom apartment. If she had to, could she afford to provide for this little gal the minimal provisions? We all know she would not be able to maintain her current standard of living, her ballet lessons and her swimming lessons and her soccer team play, and her own room filled with toys and games and books. And as for lifestyle, could she change how she has lived these past five years to become a parent, to make the daily sacrifices, putting her first? Sarah has lived for herself, by herself, for so long, it would be difficult to impossible for her to make the adjustment to be a mother to Lily. So maybe the detachment, ironically works in support of what is: Frank and Caroline are Lily's parents, and Sarah is a distant relative soon to be reintroduced to the family. We set the stage, but we had no idea how this reunion would play out. Did we want to do it in front of the ABC cameras? No. We needed this moment of privacy, of safety and security, for all our benefits, but Lily's most of all. Memorial Day weekend was the time we set aside to bring birth mother and daughter together for the first time in over three years.

We were already at the lake and were waiting for them (Joe and Sarah) to arrive. They planned to drive from Chicago to Caroline's home town, about ninety minutes away from our lake house, to visit with family. Sarah's grandmother and aunt and uncle, Caroline's sister and brother, and an assortment of cousins would all be there. Many of them had not seen Sarah for years. After spending the night there they would drive the final leg to the lake, where we waited. I looked for them early, but they slept in, had breakfast, and arrived around noon. I gave Sarah a big hug, as did Caroline, and Lily stood back holding onto Caroline's leg. Sarah had her dog with her, an all-black pug named Onyx. Like all small dogs, he introduced himself by barking his head off at everybody in a frenetic "hubba hubba hubba hubba…hubba hubba hubba hubba." By the time he had settled down, Sarah and Lily hugged. The weekend was very low key with a lot of laid-back family time, sitting around the dinner table, talking family stuff, swimming, riding the Jet Ski. No tears or smothering or any of the things we feared most about the reunion. Just like when we got together with Sarah and Joe, pleasant communion. We made it through Saturday and Sunday, and on Monday we parted, we heading back to Maryland and Sarah to Chicago. It went so well and Joe and Sarah had so much fun at the lake that they indicated they would be back for Lily's birthday in July. We hugged and went our separate ways.

Lily did not mourn her leaving, or ask a lot of questions. It was just like her big brother Andrew coming and going with the notable exception that she didn't really talk about Sarah like she did Andrew. He was a full-fledged member of the family, drawn in Lily's pictures of Mommy, Daddy, the cat, and Andrew. When he was in Canada she missed him and asked about him. Sarah was just now reentering, so it was no big thing. She had yet to earn the status of being a full-fledged big sister.

May turned into June and then July. We agreed to allow the ABC News Producer to attend the birthday party at the lake, where they could film whatever, and we even agreed to restage the reunion as though it was the first time Lily and Sarah got together. The weather was beautiful and the Jet Ski and sailboat and beach were put to full use. Even Caroline and I could go out by ourselves on the Jet Ski, leaving Lily on the beach with Sarah and Joe providing the entertainment and supervision. Andrew and his friend Dan were also on hand. ABC arrived late because poor Vivian got lost, arriving well after dark. We'd all been together most of the day already, so we talked about restaging the reunion in the morning after Lily got up. When the next morning arrived and Lily got up, she was tired and a bit groggy, but we went through the motions anyway. Sarah drove her car up the hill, drove back down the driveway, and greeted Lily, who was in Caroline's arms. She was tired and clingy and the staged reunion did not exactly replicate the original performance in May. But the show must go on. There were plenty of other opportunities over the weekend to show the relationship between Sarah and Lily. We fully expected a repeat of the previous weekend, with Sarah displaying her general detachment and sisterly attention to her little sister. In truth, Sarah was more focused on the darn dog, worrying over his running out of the yard or bothering the neighbor's dog. Good thing, Onyx was her new "baby" now.

There were several cringeworthy moments, of course, Sarah's choice of language is not always child appropriate, and the whole lifestyle of many members of generation X is a bit hard to take at times. We all smoked cigarettes during the sixties, but not in front of our parents; in fact many of our parents (like mine) never knew. We protected them from that. These kids light up right in front. They are more "in your face" than even our wild and crazy generation. Our motives may not have always been the purest; for me, I never told my parents about my wild life to protect them, yes, but to protect myself from an endless stream of hassling by them. What they didn't know wouldn't hurt me. Gen X doesn't seem to care, and if I try to offer parental advice, I am the one that gets hassled. Then again, maybe it's not a generational thing, this "in yo face!" behavior, so much as a Sarah thing.

Sarah was, you'll remember, an "in your face" kinda person, a personality honed by fierce independence and that raw mix of ADHD and ODD. The ADHD brought impulsivity and an inability to connect behaviors with consequences; the ODD (oppositional defiant disorder) brought the "I'm gonna do *whatever* I feel like *whenever* I feel like it, and you'll just to have to deal with it" to the mix. For example, I never minded the occasional rose tattoo, or the name of a child and a dove on a shoulder, but Sarah always went over the edge as described earlier with tattoos large and plentiful as her piercings. Not exactly what you have in mind when you think *mother*. Tattooed, pierced, smoking lady, someone you would see in a bar, or a circus even. The fresh mouth also accompanied the "look." Vivian (sans camera), Joe, Sarah and I were out front pushing Lily on the swing. Sarah thought it was cute that she taught Lily to say "cheese" when her shorts got caught in the crack of her behind. "Wedgie" would have been more appropriate, "cheese" having so many other connotations, and then Sarah had to explain herself to Vivian as she laughed at Lily's "I got cheese again." Vivian and I both looked a bit taken aback, so Sarah explained, "I shortened that so it doesn't sound so bad." I had to stop and think for a minute to consider what could be worse…Butt Cheese, Crotch Cheese? Yuck! I wasn't about to pursue that one.

Your mind goes to the kind of life Lily would be living had she stayed with Sarah and Mohammed. The clothes she would be wearing, the language she would be using, the behaviors she would be showing off to adults for their amusement. For the occasional moment, I think about how it "should have been" with our roles as grandparents with occasional visits from Sarah, her man, and Lily, and the long weekend with Grandma and Grandpa or the long vacations and then we send the child back to her parents with a return of so-called freedom for us. You know you've heard grandparents who brag that they spoil the grandkids, get 'em all sugared up, then send 'em back home to their parents. There's even that little bit of payback in their wildness for adult children who didn't listen to, "Wait until you have your own kids." I've thought about that long and hard, and the anxiety I would have experienced sending Lily back to the lifestyle she would be "enjoying" with Sarah and her man of the moment, and I consider myself very, very lucky to have Lily twenty-four/seven. We are not "typical" grandparents, if there is such a thing. Being educators keeps you in touch with youth, but more importantly we have the energy and the expertise and the patience and the heart to love this little gal like she deserves to be loved. I often kid that having a young child in our home at our age will keep us young and make us old at the same time. I wouldn't have it any...other...way.

Things appeared to be going well as other family members arrived for the party. Caroline's sister Liza and their mother, Katie, and our niece Holly and her husband, Darren (both successful attorneys), with their little girl Marnie, not quite two. Things appeared to be going well up to the opening of the presents. It was here that a certain tension descended. Lily is looking sad and asking where Sarah is. Lily has been attached to Sarah's side, waiting on her and doing everything to please her "big sister." Big sister apparently has been distant and is now among the missing.

Vivian, to her credit, was busy filming the rising storm and though her role as journalist was to remain detached and uninvolved, her relationship with us, her feelings for us as people, took precedence, which is why I respect and trust Vivian explicitly. I couldn't say the same about the second producer, Anna. Vivian pulled Caroline and me aside to share some footage. She also shared an observation that supported what we were about to see. Seems like Sarah called over to Lily, asking her to, "Come sit on *Mommy's* lap." Lily quickly complied and went to sit on...Caroline's lap. Maybe this was the start of it, maybe it was the family all around, maybe it was seeing her cousin Holly and her husband, Darren, both successful professionals, with their child living with them, traveling with them. Maybe it was a flash of what could have been for Sarah and Lily. Whatever it was, Sarah disappeared downstairs. We all figured it was for a smoke, but with Vivian's journalistic skills, she sensed something more serious, and followed Sarah downstairs. The footage was brief, a few seconds of a happy little girl opening presents with her family around her, and then Sarah leaves and Lily's expression changes to one I had not seen for five years. Eyes down, sad, depressed. No doubt picking up on Sarah's state of mind. The camera then follows Sarah downstairs, where she is obviously upset and in tears, crying about how phony this all is.

"You're all trying to make this look like a happy family when it's not, it's just not—this is so fake!" She walks away from the camera. That was reality TV for you.

And so it appears that despite our perception that all is well, and that this reunion is working out, there is another larger reality going on. Nothing out in the open or that anyone else would notice or remark about, just a few subtle hints that things are not going well. Later Sarah wanted to leave to go down the mountain for something, and was taking Lily with her. Our trust was gone, and we were not comfortable with Lily spending time with Sarah alone. Our fears from before the first reunion were now being realized. Sarah adopted her resistant, oppositional attitude, and we were nervous about the two of them going off for some impromptu mother/daughter talk. We were glad when the rest of the family started to leave so we could deal with the rising storm.

Sarah avoided us, rode the Jet Ski until she couldn't move, and started doing stupid things like taking the Jet Ski out with the gas running out and the switch on reserve instead of heading back to fill up, and running completely out of gas. Run on "reserve" and you not only have no gas, but often have to you drain the carburetor and get a mechanic to prime it again. We had to get a neighbor to run out to rescue her and tow her in. I was starting to lose my patience as well. I was returning to the mode, the dynamic, we experienced when she was the oppositional teen. Sarah was twenty-eight years old, but her ten years of drug use left her stuck in adolescence, still rebellious, oppositional, and often annoying. Sarah also had the uncanny knack of pushing the limits right to the very edge. Give her an inch and she took a mile. Invite her for a visit and she moved right in. Allow her to reconnect with Lily, and she wanted to have all the rights and privileges of being her *mother*. The only thing missing was the responsibility. That was assumed by Caroline and me.

Caroline pulled me aside later and suggested that maybe it was a time for a father/daughter talk. I waited for Sarah to take a smoke break and followed her downstairs. Joe (what a great guy) made a polite exit within a few minutes of my introductory remarks. I typically don't beat around the bush and got right to the point. I wasn't angry, more disappointed. I frankly told her what my expectations were about Lily's adjustment to their new relationship as sisters, and that she needed to make the shift as well. "This is so phony!" she cried. "Faking the reunion when she was all tired and didn't even come and hug me, that wasn't *real*. And all this running around with family and how *nice* everything is for everyone; it isn't nice for me! I don't want to be her sister—I'm her MOTHER, and she will always be my baby girl!" It was heartbreaking. I tried to focus on the choices she made years ago, the ultimatum her mother and I gave her, her lawyer gave her, Lily's attorney gave her, the judge gave her: "clean up or lose your daughter." She chose drugs and lost her daughter. She was shouting now: "I didn't CHOOSE drugs. You don't UNDERSTAND, I was under their control. It's NOT a choice, it's a sickness!"

She was right, I didn't understand, didn't want to, couldn't. Yeah, I did my share of drugs, and drank my share of alcohol, and ran through women like a kid in a candy store, but I grew up. And I gave it all up, for family, ironically, to raise her and her brother and be a good husband to her mother and to be a good father to them. Sarah was also upset because she could not have another child with Joe, not with Lily out there. "How can I have another baby when my first baby isn't even with me?!" I think it was a more self-centered notion, that she could not have a family with another child while her first child was not with her. It was all or none for Sarah— she wanted all of her kids with her, or none. I reinforced this notion from another perspective, one honed from real world experience. How could she have another child, a sister or brother, a "real" sibling for Lily, when they would never be together? Would that be fair to Lily that she had a little sister who lived with Sarah when she did not? How would that settle with Lily? Would Lily see this as more rejection by her birth mother? For different reasons Sarah and I agreed on that one. "And that's not fair to Joe. He wants kids!" My heart ached for Sarah, but I had to protect Lily. Lily didn't belong to her anymore; she belonged to me, to Caroline and me. The adoption made legal what we had already put into action. Sarah was just another sibling now, not her mother. She could not be her mother. She simply wasn't getting it, despite thousands of words and e-mails and handwritten letters from me about the "worst thing in the world" for Lily to begin to reattach to a mother who couldn't be there for her. She wasn't getting it, and I didn't have the luxury of waiting until she did. Lily came first. She would always come first.

I sat down with Joe later and laid it on the line. It was apparent that Sarah was having a hard time with this transition. She was also, in my opinion, behaving badly, and not willing or not able to accept her role as big sister. I told him about Vivian's and my observations. I told him about the footage. I told him that either Sarah got with the program and accepted her role as sister and put her history of being mother to Lily behind her, or the visit was over. She could pack her bags and hit the road. That was her choice. I was not going to subject Lily to any more confusion. And stop and think about it. What if Sarah had her way, and Lily bonded with her as a mother, as a primary caretaker? How would Lily react when Sarah left and went back to Chicago? Could she deal with another loss, another rejection? Did she have to? I wasn't going to allow it.

The next morning Caroline noted that Joe and Sarah had packed everything up and it looked like they were leaving. The plan was to stay for the rest of the week, but Sarah got the word from Joe. I tried to explain it to her so she would understand, and failing there made sure she knew where we stood. The four of us were all up early, Sarah, Joe, Caroline, and I. Lily was still sleeping. Sarah was ready to go. She was in a sour mood and just wanted to hit the road. The conversation was between the four of us and it was short, I told her I was sorry it had to end like it did. There were no hugs or good-byes, and she never stopped a minute to say good-bye to Lily. She just walked outside, threw her bags in the car, and got in the driver's seat. I can remember being a bit nervous of her navigating the twisting roads out of the lake with her mind in a bad place, but Joe knew better than to cross her. He lingered a few minutes after she went downstairs, packing up his things, and thanked us. He said he was sorry things ended like it did, but he appreciated our hospitality. He said good-bye and we shook hands and gave him a hug. I thanked him for being there for Sarah. Joe seemed to understand; he agreed with our take on things, especially that Sarah's lifestyle was not conducive for children, and he was not ready for children. He went downstairs, got in the car, and they pulled out of the driveway in a cloud of dust.

Lily got up and asked where Sarah was. We told her she had to leave. "She didn't say good-bye to me. Did she say good-bye to you?" "No. Joe did, but Sarah just left." Several weeks later Lily was in the back seat talking to two friends, Katie, six, and Tim, eight. They were talking about a movie they recently saw, *Cars*. Lily said this: "It was a good movie, but it was kind of sad, too. The one sad part was when he didn't say good-bye to Mater. That was kinda like real life for me."

Since then Lily has mentioned Sarah's next visit, and we told her we didn't know when that would be. We explained how we would be going back to school and how Sarah had to work and didn't have the time to take off like in the summer. Memorial Day and July Fourth were special times for special visits, and it might be a long time before she could come visit again. A week or so later, Lily mentioned again that she would like to see Sarah, and we told her that just because she wanted to see Sarah didn't mean that Sarah wanted to see us. In fact she was kind of mad at us, and we didn't know when she would be ready to visit again. We told her that sometimes Sarah just got mad easy, and it took a while for her to calm down. Lily moved on to other subjects.

According to Andrew, who has spoken to Sarah, she is mad, real mad, at us. It will be a while before she cools down enough to talk to us again. Her loss, I say. Once again we tried to do the right thing, for us, for Lily, and for her. Sarah played her game of sabotage and destroyed what could have been a smooth transition to reforming our family along different lines. I understand how this was difficult for her, and how she was unable or unwilling to accept the conditions, but they were all clearly spelled out. She can be mad at us; she's been mad at us before and comes back when she needs us, as she will this time, I'm sure. Maybe sometime later she will be ready to meet our terms and enjoy any relationship with her daughter, even as her sister. Better than nothing, but maybe in her eternal stubbornness that's where she'll leave it. Maybe that is better for her; no contact, like a drug addict or alcoholic—even a taste can be fatal. No impulse control. Thing is, where will Lily take all this? Will she understand why her mother, her "big sister," can't visit anymore? Will she mourn the loss without the proper good-bye? Only time will tell.

# CHAPTER THIRTY-FOUR

# THE AWAKENING

Sarah and I were estranged once again after the Fourth of July 2006 visit. It wasn't just that she was selfish and self-centered and bothersome to us. More importantly, it was because she had hurt Lily…again. Our job, Caroline's and mine, was to protect her as best we could, even from further insult by the parents who brought her to this world. We agreed it would be a long time before Sarah would get to see her little sister again. Sadly, Lily felt the same way. After some reflection we were struck by one of the many ironies in this situation. When Sarah was using, drugs came first. And second and third and on and on; nothing else mattered. Once she got clean and sober, and her head began to clear, she began to realize what she lost, she began to have regrets, she began to care. If a little too late. We could ill afford another bout of rejection. If not for a family tragedy, it's hard to tell how long we would have waited to bring these two together again.

January 18, 2007, the phone rings at the Matthewses'. Caroline's brother George is on the line ranting and raving about what turned out to be a secondary problem, his middle son's sharing information he should not have with Caroline's eight-six-year-old mother. The information, regardless of its delivery, was devastating. Caroline's sister's son Adam was dead, killed in a motor vehicle accident earlier that evening. He was twenty-five years old, living with his mother Liza, and struggling to find himself. After several years of mediocre jobs and failed attempts at putting his creativity and amazing intellect to good use, he found himself...at the bottom of a ravine. Some years back, when he was only fifteen, he had been involved in another car crash, and alcohol and drugs were suspected. I wrote him a long letter about where he was heading and expressed my worst fear at the time, that he would "find (himself) wrapped around one of those sturdy oaks." Sadly, he never took my warnings under advisement and ended up fulfilling my worst fear for him. His mother, Liz, also ignored the letter I sent her with the same message and what actions she needed to take to protect her son.

Calls went out to friends and family, including Sarah and her Joe, and Andrew and his new wife, Carla.. Against our wishes they eloped in the fall of 2006, and quickly became pregnant. They arrived late from DC, Andrew looking like he just woke up and had slept in his clothes. Carla ignored conventional wisdom and behaved as though this whole ritual was for her benefit. At the very moment the family lined up behind Adam's coffin in the church preparing to follow it up the aisle, she insisted that Andrew locate a bathroom for her. Addressing Caroline, he asked, "Mom...where is the bathroom?" Caroline was understandably annoyed by this request and told Andrew in a stern but quiet whisper, "Not now, just cross your legs! " After another moment, "But Mom...it's not for me, Carla needs to use it." "Andrew," Caroline intoned, "tell her to just toughen up, this is NOT the time for this." Once we followed the coffin up the aisle and took our seats, Carla, in her best dying swan routine, leaned on Andrew's shoulder with a sad face. Considering the fact that she hardly knew Adam, only meeting him on one brief

## The Awakening

occasion, her long face was for garnering sympathy for herself, not an expression of grief and empathy for those who had lost a friend, a nephew, a cousin, a brother, and...a son. They arrived late, left several times to attend to Carla's needs, and generally annoyed Caroline and me to no end.

Sarah, on the other hand, was great. She always seemed to rise to family occasions with the utmost sense of decorum. At the fiftieth wedding anniversary for Nunnie and Pap Pap, at his funeral four years earlier, and now here at her cousin's funeral. The previous day friends and family were allowed to visit the funeral home to pay respects. We had a private family time set at noon (Andrew and Carla were late) and the home was opened for guests at one. Liza stood by her son's coffin from one until nine that night, eight hours without leaving to eat, drink, or even visit the restroom. Who else could stand in her place to greet the eight-hundred-plus guests?

Caroline and I ran interference, greeted folks, and made sure the food that was brought by family members was properly displayed and served. Lily was a trooper, and when it was clear that other family members would not help out with Lily, Sarah stood ready. She knew her place and communicated an air of maturity, respect, and responsibility that was somehow missing in her older brother, Andrew. Sarah and Joe took Lily to get food (McDonald's) and entertain her while we provided support for Liza and Haley, Adam's older sister. It was a sad occasion, but brought the family together in the way it should. But as happens in all weddings and funerals, it brings out the best and the worst in family. It would be months before we would, err, Caroline would speak to Andrew again. We made it clear we were embarrassed by Carla's behavior and counseled him about setting the tone regarding family expectations for his wife. It was *his* place to keep her in *her* place. I keep thinking about that scene in *The Godfather, Part II* when Freddo's wife is drunk and hanging all over other men. Michael, through the family's consigliore, made it clear to Freddo, "Take care of your wife...or we will." It just had to do with family values and respect; wives were to honor them, not disregard them as Carla had and continues to do to this day, but that's another story.

Sarah done good and it opened the door for more contacts between families and we talked about getting together again...soon. As it turned out, it would be for Sarah's birthday on March 17.

## Coming Home

Sarah decided that she wanted to come home for her birthday, so we arranged to fly her and Joe in for St. Patty's Day. We drove over and picked them up at the airport and Sarah came home back to our house, for the first time in five years. It was pretty special. Lily was so excited. Seems that nobody believed that she had a big sister much less one who was twenty-eight years old, so Lily worked it out that Sarah would be brought to school for show and tell. It must have been a real hoot. Sarah helped Caroline out with things and got introduced to her staff. I demanded equal time, so the two of them, Sarah and Joe, headed over to Delaware, where I got to introduce my beautiful daughter number one to my friends and colleagues. It was very nice, and those who had heard so much about her were glad to put a face to the stories. We enjoyed the few days, went out to eat, and they drove into West Virginia to visit with Nunnie before heading back to Chicago.

Summer 2007 was good, with another family reunion at the lake with Bob and Judy and their son and daughter-in-law, Maggie, from California, along with twenty other Cassells from Ohio, DC, West Virginia, Virginia, Pennsylvania, and Maryland. Since Andrew's wife Carla was with child, the women put on a baby shower and made a big to-do of the newest member of our family. Despite our earlier reservations about Carla, her marriage to Andrew and pregnancy seemed to smooth down most of her rough edges. She especially enjoyed being the center of attention. Sarah was able to fit in just fine and enjoyed the family time again.

## The Awakening

Caroline's hope for a double wedding with Andrew and Sarah and their spouses standing at the shore of the lake with the sun setting and family standing on the shore wasn't to be. It was preempted by Andrew's rush to the courthouse in the fall of 2006 to marry Carla, and Sarah insisting on having her wedding in Chicago, where Joe's family lived. We couldn't fault her for that, so we arranged to fly out at the first of September to marry our daughter off. His family would arrange for the chapel and the reception in his sister's back yard, and we would take care of food. We ordered a roast pig and all the trimmings, and his mom jumped in with more food, like chicken and beef for people who don't like pork. We also kicked in for soda, wine, and beer. They had a tent and chairs and tables on order, and we had contacted a firm to roast a pig who offered to take care of the entire gig—tables chairs, beans, potato salad, plates, spoons, etc.—but Joe and Sarah had their own ideas, so we just went along. It was their wedding; we were just trying to do our piece as parents of the bride. It turned out to be a battle of the caterers, the one we hired and the one her family hired, vying for space in a small back yard. There was little room on the tables for all the food, but we worked it all out in the end. The wedding, the food, the DJ playing all our favorite tunes, the dancing, the friends, it all turned out to be just right. No stress, no arguments, just two families merging as one.

Caroline and I decided that if the wedding had been at our location, the logistics would have been much better and more of her family could have attended. As it were, it was just the three of us, Caroline, Lily, and Dad. Andrew was on a short leash, having fathered a little boy two weeks before the wedding, so he wasn't going anywhere. Once we got to meet Joe's family and, most significantly, their friends, and heard their stories about Sarah's arrival and how they kicked in for her…wow, we were so glad the wedding was there and that we had a chance not only to be a part of it, but to meet and get to know her circle of friends. Caroline and I were both disappointed that Sarah's brother, Andrew, couldn't attend his sister's wedding, but considering the erratic behavior of his new wife, Carla, it was probably better they weren't there. Carla would have managed to make it all about her and create a scene that would have directed the attention to her and her alone. This was really all about Joe, Sarah, and the Chicago family.

Just think about it. Joe lives at home with his family and has never really had a long-term girlfriend. He works and goes out with the guys and his female friends, and they go to Cubs and Bears games and live the good life. Then he meets this beautiful girl, wild, tattooed, pierced vision of loveliness, who complements his quiet personality and captures his heart. She needs a prince and he recognizes a damsel in distress. He makes a genuine offer to this maiden, so taken by her he is, and when she follows up and asks him if his offer still stands, he doesn't hesitate; he sends her a ticket. Now what is he to do? He has just committed to have this beautiful stranger come to live with him at his parents' home and he knows nothing about her. But it feels right. He picks her up at the airport and within a few days she is bad sick. What's going on? She is honest and tells him her whole story of being addicted and trying to get straight. But she is sick, vomiting and cramps and fevers and chills. What can I do? he asks. "Take me to the dirtiest ghetto you can find in Chicago, I'll do the rest," she says. "I'm not going do that," he insists, and he calls a female friend and she comes over and they get Sarah through the worst of it, then they get her to a clinic and into a program and they all work the program with her. She gets on her methadone, and she gets clean and she stays clean. She gets a job, and then a better one, and she weans off the methadone and she starts taking classes again, and they move into a place of her own, and they get married. A truly happy ending to a fairy-tale story. But it almost didn't happen. The wedding, that is. Here's what happened ten days before she walked down that aisle on her father's arm. When you're dealing with addiction, and Sarah's often unpredictable personality, you have to accept the roller-coaster ride. The month

## The Awakening

before this September wedding, events stepped in that could derail even the best-laid plans. Sometimes even when things are going well, the past is not far behind.

Summer vacation always a special time for me, from the days on the lake as a child, to spending time with my own family. Someone I know once said this: "I'm going to make sure I enjoy myself because I don't have that many more summers left." I started to think, hmmm. You always know another summer will roll around, so if you don't have anything grand planned you can always wait for another one to come along. But when I look back over my life (fifty-eighty summers down, _?_ to go), I realize at best I may have twenty-five to thirty left, and how many of them will I still be able to water ski and jump off boats? Makes you think. Can't waste even a single one. All those plans and trips out West and to the pyramids better get scheduled before the calendar just... runs...out. So this summer I got to the beach, got to canoe down the river, went into a cave and on top of the mountain, and got to just sit back by our lake house and watch the sun come up and go back down. One night Lily and a little friend wanted to sleep in the boathouse, so I slept downstairs, standing guard duty. Had to do my usual two-in-the-morning pee call and stepped out onto the dock, looked up, and saw one of the most brilliant night skies I have ever seen in my life. There were billions and billions of stars just shimmering against the black night sky. It was simply amazing. When the girls woke up and wanted to come downstairs to sleep, I walked them out to glory, the majesty of that night. They too were amazed, even at the ungodly hour, four o'clock in the morning.

July turned to August and we had to drag ourselves down from the mountain and head back to reality of the workaday world. I started back on the thirteenth and the rest of the folks came the following week. Two days of professional development were planned for the twenty-second and twenty-third, and our team was working on a program to be presented to the entire faculty on the twenty-third, kindergarten through sixth grade in the morning and seventh through twelfth in the afternoon. We were trying to communicate about the changes in special education law, and we had *Apollo 13* on the screen—FAILURE IS NOT AN OPTION—and how we had to solve our problems like they did, midflight, with what we had on hand, no more. I dressed up as the Statue of Liberty and gave the speech: "Give me...your poor...the wretched...tempest-tost," etc., changing it up later to "Give us your learning disabled and mentally challenged and visually impaired." It was fun and they got the message of change loud and clear.

Wednesday night as I sat preparing my speech and getting my green gown and crown together, the phone rang. It was Joe. Sarah's Joe. Sarah was in jail. And just so I wouldn't get mad and hang up, he explained that she didn't do anything other than lose her wallet in a bar. Seems some of her girlfriends were taking her out for a bachelorette party and she left her wallet in the bar. When she returned the next day to get it, they referred her to the local police department. The bar's policy was to turn in any lost possession to the police. Let them sort it out. The police, having nothing better to do in this podunk town, decided to play with some of their newfangled com-puter equipment and ran her name and numbers, and lo and behold if Sarah didn't have some outstanding warrants from four years ago. You'll remember that Sarah left in a hurry after being found under the influence of drugs at the visiting center. When they lost visitation privileges at the visiting center, Mohammed blamed Sarah, beat her up again, which is why she called Joe and left town to join her future husband in Chicago. Several months earlier, Sarah was staying with Mohammed's brother TJ and his girlfriend. Some merchandise came up missing and Sarah got the blame. Charges were filed and it would all have gone away once she went to court and TJ's girlfriend testified that it was really her *brother* that took the stuff, not Sarah. The court hearing was for the last week in May, one week after Sarah left for Chicago. As a matter of course, a fugitive warrant went out, and since she hadn't committed murder or assault or even grand theft, no one was in any hurry to go after her. But here

## The Awakening

Officer Barney Fife got him a real criminal, all 110 pounds of her, and he wasn't letting her go. He arrested her and booked her, and they would just wait and see whether Maryland wanted to extradite her on these charges. They could hold her for thirty to ninety days.

Joe called and was beside himself. They had only held her overnight at the local jail at Barney's place, then they sent her up to the big city lockup, the Chicago Women's House of Detention, Cook County, where Sarah was surrounded by junkies and prostitutes and killers of small animals. When Sarah tried to tell the guards this was only a case of mistaken identity (it was Lisa's brother that took the stuff, not her), they laughed and told her, "Yeah all you fucking bitches say the same shit. Shut up and go to sleep." Sarah called me one afternoon, and it was heart wrenching. "Dad, you gotta get me outta here, these women are disgusting, they're throwing up and shitting all over the place and it's horrible. Dad, you gotta get me out!" "I am, sweetie, you just stay strong and keep to yourself." It just about broke my heart. You can get pretty mad at your kids and want nothing to do with them, but when it comes right down to it, you can't turn your back on them when they need you, when they reach out. She had made great strides to get her life back on track, and she did not deserve this.

For the next sixty hours, all day Wednesday and Thursday and into Friday, I was on the phone to everyone I could think of in Chicago and here at home: lawyers and sheriffs and state police officers and secretaries and district attorneys and courthouse clerks, most of whom I was on a first-name basis with once things got going. It all boiled down to one thing: The police here would not extradite her on a misdemeanor theft charge by an individual. They could not justify sending an officer on his shift on a plane to Chicago to fly her back or drive her back to here for a petty charge. But I needed to get the district attorney's office here to talk to the sheriff's office here, and send word on to Chicago to cut her loose. Papers had to be filed and approved, and, well, things just didn't move that fast, they had thirty to ninety days. I told them who I was, and who she was, more importantly, and, even more importantly, who she is today, and the simple fact that in ten days she was supposed to be in a wedding with scores of guests and tuxedos and roasted pigs and flower girls and plane tickets and, well, SHE was the one who was walking down the aisle.

On Chicago's end they couldn't release her until they got word from here, and they had not heard a word. The folks on our end insisted they'd notified Chicago. Turned out the local person here who sent the papers, insisted she sent the papers to the sheriff in the town in which she was arrested, but the clerk in the sheriff's office insisted she never got 'em. Several calls back and forth over several days solved that mystery. The gal in the DA's office who insisted it was her job to send the notices, would have taken care of that...except for the fact that she was out of the office for two days. Wednesday and Thursday. Here it is Friday and would she move Sarah's to the head of the stack so she could spend her last weekend before her wedding making arrangements? She did, and Joe was soon on the phone saying they said they were gonna release her but didn't know where she was. He is standing at the front of the building at "Intake," while Sarah is standing on the street at the other side of the building under the sign that read "Discharge." And here I am a thousand miles away trying to get the two of them together. He soon called and they were together. Free she was, and my heart, and Joe's heart, and Sarah's heart, and Caroline's heart, all soared when we know she was OUT! "Oh, my God, Dad, I love you sooooooooooo much!" "I told you I'd get you out."

With me working this end and Joe on that end, we were so exhilarated at the end, I told Sarah she had Joe to thank as well. One of the few friends I shared with misadventure with, asked me, do you think her fiancée will stand by her? Her being arrested and all that? Without a moment's hesitation I answered, "He won't leave her there. He is in it for the long run." And I knew then and there that this marriage would

## The Awakening

take place and would be a strong one. And I was glad, too, that she married him so I wouldn't have to. I had told her months back, "Sarah, this guy is the real thing. If you don't marry him, I will!" Imagine the force of emotions when we got off that plane in Chicago and into our daughter's arms a week later. And what a wedding it was!

As I put the finishing touches to this long journey, Christmas is around the corner. Joe and Sarah are living back with his parents, trying to save money to buy a house. Andrew and his wife and son are seventy-five miles away, and we are trying to deal with the challenges the new wife presents. Our love for Sarah and Joe is strong, as it is for Andrew and his son, Ethan. Carla, his wife, is still a stranger to us in many ways. I don't know if I even *like her*, much less feel any warmth or affection toward her. She will take some getting used to. Ethan, our new and only official grandson, is cute as a button, but distance and emotions keep us apart for the time being.

Lily, well, she is the light of my life, and the love is deep. I have no blood children of my own, but I love my three children as my own. Caroline and I bonded and, moving forward, though much of the passion is gone from our marriage, we are friends and enjoy each other's company. We still have our occasional *discussions*, though we always communicate. She is devoted as always to her son and now his son, and to Sarah and her man, Joe. Lily is still central in her life, and once again I come down to the bottom of her list. Kids have to come first, but isn't that what parenting is all about? Making the sacrifices for them? And isn't that what love is all about, for a child, for an aging parent, for your life mate? Making sacrifices for them, to make them happy? As Dr. Phil always says, "It's not about you!"

# EPILOGUE

All good things must come to an end, but so must all the bad things, too. Life goes on and you make adjustments along the way, accepting things you swore you never would, giving up and moving away from things you swore you would never abandon. What was it that John Lennon said, "Life is what happens while you're busy making other plans." As I sit here on my birthday, November 28, 2012, I can reflect on the turn of events over the previous twenty years. Here's what I came up with:

My father passed away in 2003, but not before I had the opportunity to reconnect with him in a meaningful way. I got to tell him all the things he meant to me and how alike we were. I also came to the realization that he was who he was, he was not about to change on my account, so I had to remember that love meant sacrifice and adjustment, and I needed to change for him. It was the key to our reconnecting, the prize well worth having. Both of my sisters proved to be self-centered "all about me" type individuals, and I have no interest in reconnecting with them and have no contact as a result. Don't miss them a bit. Fifty-plus years of playing second fiddle to them also has a bearing on the joy I have in leaving them behind.

They say that there is nothing like a mother's love for her children, that it is both forgiving and unconditional. Trouble is, my mother never got the memo. When my dad got sick and fell into a coma, though my sisters were both a few hours' drive away, they never made it to his side in time. I flew in from four states away and was there by midafternoon. I was able to support my mother as she made the decision to suspend his life support. He had drawn up advanced directives, or a "living will," as they call it, and you could clearly understand his wishes. His neatly scribed initials, *GRM*, were to the right in the space provided next to each statement. We went home and they called us from the hospital telling us he was gone. My youngest sister, on a horseback ride somewhere, unable to figure out how cell phone messages are retrieved, never made it back before I left. My older sister rolled in with tales of car troubles and intestinal distress.

The following year, when Hurricane Charlie swept through her park, destroying her home along with over three hundred others, once again I was there within hours to help her sort through the mess and load up what we could on a trailer to put into storage. After she was forced to move six times, trying to find a home she was happy in, ending up in a moldy trailer, Caroline and I convinced Andrew to take the money he'd made on the townhouse he bought at preconstruction prices at our direction, then sold at the top of the market, clearing a cool $100,000 profit, and invest it in "rental property" in South Florida; a brand new double-wide home my mother moved into. She paid rent to cover the mortgage, and Caroline and I covered the rest of the expenses. That's what kids do for their aging parents.

Andrew had moved to Canada, where he met his future wife, Carla, and when they married she quickly insisted that he sell the place and get "their" money back! We did not think much of her at first impression, and our opinion of her continued to slide further into the depths as time went on. Getting married to someone whose first set of marching orders is to throw your grandmother out of her home and onto the street does not demonstrate good judgment, or compassion, for that matter. My mom was in her eighties and comfortable in her new home, so Caroline and I decided to buy the place from Andrew. When Mom expressed concern about the unfolding events, we assured her that she could stay put, she would just have a new set of landlords, us. Caroline and I took out a

# Epilogue

loan for over $100,000, paid Andrew off, and became property owners in South Florida.

Everything was fine until my youngest sister moved in with Mom. When I indicated that I would have to raise the $800 a month rent to $1,200, to cover Caroline's and my expenses (we were covering the mortgage, insurance, taxes, and maintenance fees), and since she was using the spare bedroom that was never used, and the bathroom that was never used, and cooking and doing laundry, it was only fair that she pay her share. I suggested splitting the $1,200 in half, so mom's rent would go down and she would be paying the same as she had charged housemates in her house before she sold it and moved in with Mom. She raised holy hell, moved out, and threatened to have Mom move out too. Six months later, she bought a house up north in Florida, and Mom calls me to let me know she will be moving out to help little sis with her mortgage. Uh...what are we supposed to do with your place? "That's your problem," my dear mother told me.

I maintained contact with her even after she moved out, but when Mom told me on one phone call that she could have bought the place herself and didn't because she knew it was a bad investment, that I was essentially foolish for buying it, that was too much for me to swallow. She also insisted that I did not buy the house for her, but to help Andrew out (with profit from his townhome that might be subject to taxes), apparently oblivious to the fact that that arrangement ended when we were forced to buy him out. Mom's last words to me were, "I don't need all this confusion, just leave me alone," then she hung up. That was three years ago. I'm still waiting for her to call back—well, not really.

Andrew's wife continued in her campaign to alienate us. Full-blooded Chinese, she ran down his friends, and all Americans, for that matter. She insisted on driving us to dinner on one occasion and stuffed us in the back seat of her small sedan, cranked up house music to eleven on a one-to-ten scale, and careened around corners at high speeds, almost hitting a motorcyclist when she almost ran a red light. When

Andrew shouted at her to watch out, she berated him, telling him he should not talk to her like that and he could just get out and walk. We were not offered a similar option, which I might have exercised. She bragged about spending $300 on two pair of sunglasses she'd lost, and reportedly spent $1,000 on a pair of pants. For that kind of money the pants would have to take me on long walks and wash themselves in the kitchen sink. On another memorable occasion at our lake house with Caroline's aunt, cousin, his wife and her son, and uncle present, she began to berate Andrew in our presence on a sunny Sunday morning. It got so ugly as they were packing to leave—"You not need toothbrush, you never brush teeth… your breath stink! I not know where your blanket is, you pack own clothes!"—that despite or maybe because he was so embarrassed, Andrew cried out, "Carla, that's enough!" When she continued in front of seven of his family members (Lily was asleep), I stepped in, "Carla, I have to remind you that this is a no-nagging zone." My attempt at humor unleashed a torrent of venom from her none of us will soon forget: "You not tell me how to act! You have daughter who take drugs and both of your children all fucked up because of you, and you try to tell me how to raise my child!?" I was never so happy to see them go. I felt bad for Andrew, but he married her against our wishes, so he had to deal with her issues.

Though we were estranged right after they married, when she became pregnant for Ethan, her hormones gave her a taste of normality. We were there for her pregnancy and the birth of Ethan, our first grandson. That lasted six months and she turned on us again for some perceived slight. When she was pregnant with her second child, she started acting normally again. We enjoyed their company for about a year, time for Ethan and Lily to bond and time for Frank to be born. Finally! Someone that carried my name. That lasted eight months, then, hormones depleted, she returned to her totally unreasonable behaviors and attitudes. We have not heard from them for three years.

# Epilogue

Caroline's parents both died, and her sister Liza tried to abscond with half the estate. Once again into the breach with attorneys, this time to the tune of $30,000 to have the proceeds of the estate evenly distributed between the three heirs. Caroline and both her siblings are estranged as a result: her sister, for obvious reasons, and her brother, for his betrayal at the end and refusal to pay his share of legal expenses that netted him over a hundred thousand dollars that he would have relinquished to Liza were it not for our efforts.

Sarah and Joe brought two new little guys into the world, Bryce, who is now four, and Braxton, who is eighteen months. We travel to Chicago to visit them and they meet us at the lake house for visits. We cherish the time with the two grandsons we can enjoy. The sad part is that not only do we miss out on Andrew's children, but Lily who has experienced so much loss in her life, has lost two precious nephews she cherished, and the boys will never enjoy the childhood memories of time with two loving grandparents.

I survived the establishment long enough to earn my pension. Thirty-eight years operating in four states, five school districts, including the one I retired from after fifteen years. As I look back, I experienced just as much trouble in my new job as I had in the previous one. Despite my joy at a fresh start and new opportunities, I got written up for many of the same nonsensical things I did when I was fighting the other school district over my daughter. Ahhhh, you say. If you had all the same problems in your fresh new job that you had in your previous one, how can you suggest it was THEM, not YOU, causing the problems? I just think it boils down to irreconcilable differences or major incompatibility. I was there to speak up on behalf of kids, and they were more interested in the status quo. People are bound by human nature and the roles they have in work as well as in life. There are those who serve the kids in education, and those who serve their need for power and control. Unfortunately, the administrators, the ones with the power and control, call all the shots, and because they have moved out of the classrooms and the lives of children, they quickly lose touch with them and the teachers who live with them six hours a day every day during the school year.

The biggest difference between the two districts and others I worked over the years is that this time, I learned how to work within the system, gaining the respect and admiration of building administrators. They knew what I was all about, and that I was not only there to firmly advocate on behalf of the children I was assigned to, but to work to protect the school district and the administrators as well. If I told them one of their actions was illegal, I always had another approach that would meet their needs and remain in the bounds of the law. I always had the respect of teachers; they knew I had their backs and that I was good at solving their problems with students. Kids, well, they recognize someone who is genuine and who cares about them. *Firm but fair* was my motto, and I still managed to relate to all ages, from preschoolers all the way up to high school age students. They knew they could trust me, that I would be there for them even when no one else was. I always got along with support staff. I not only appreciated what they contributed to the team, be they a custodian or secretary or specialist, but I was light, I was funny, I was flirtatious, and, most of all, I was genuine. The only ones I had difficulty with were ones with other agendas, I did not, could not, would not suffer fools. Even when they held positions of authority over me.

And though I respected the chain of command (if *respect* is the right word…fearing charges of insubordination and getting fired were more the underlying motivation) unlike any other public school employee who must defer to their immediate supervisor, in this case the building principal, I could not. Administrators are so used to having people defer, give in, kowtow to, relinquish, etc., to them that when one comes along and disagrees or points out another way of handling a situation *according to the law*, they take extreme offense from it. I always believed that my code of ethics was my first priority, that I had to consider the child as my client and had to speak up even when it was difficult to do so. The fine line between advocacy and insubordination is just that, fine, but I managed to straddle it for years, fifteen in my last position. In fact, I wrote a series of articles on just that topic. All were published in national publications like the National Association of School Psychologists' newspaper, *The Communique*. I was respected by many, including my peers and colleagues. They knew I would stand up for them and for their children, and that I wouldn't back down. I was not easily intimidated. And for all the allegations of my "aggressive nature," I maintain that I never wanted things that did not belong to me, only protected what was mine. What was "mine" was my knowledge of the law, and protection for the kids under my care. It was never about ME, and always about them. For all the complaints—"He always has to have his way!"—some never understood, it wasn't "my way," it was the carefully written laws, regulations, and guidelines I read, understood, and shared with anyone with the time to listen. I was *assertive* in protecting my role as protector of the weak, and my knowledge of the law as it applied to disabled students. I could not, would not, betray them, even at great expense to myself both personally and professionally. Asked one time, "Wouldn't it have been much easier to just sit back and not make waves?" I responded, no, it would have been impossible, because I could not have lived with myself. It would be like sitting quietly while someone struck a child. Easier to turn the other way? Not hardly.

But, yeah, I had eerie deja vu experiences in my new district over the fifteen years I was there, getting written up for improper language, overstepping the bounds of my authority, and for generally being an arrogant, assertive pain in the ass. I remained true to my profession throughout it all and focused on what was in the best interests of the student and his teachers. As such, I earned the respect of teachers and my building administrators. Never a complaint from them, just from the scattered sycophants who fought for the power of making decisions without the encumbrance of one surly school psychologist. The big administrators, those ensconced in the ivory towers of the administration building, try as they might, never quite understood me. And the petty stuff they hurled at me was from the same playbook from the previous district.

I am almost convinced that with tenured teachers, administrators take lessons on how to remove them by gathering "documentation," some genuine, some contrived, then throw it together with false accusations, hearsay, and innuendo. They learn how to "evaluate an employee out of his or her job" by building a case out of cards. All they need is a loyal (to them) employee to get the goods on the target, to observe, challenge, then complain about the response. No interest in the truth, or the target's version of events, just the story the loyal rat-employee spins. They "stack" charges, hoping you'll be so intimidated you'll back down. I once had six letters written and handed to me on a single day, the day before summer break. They were hoping I would just leave. Instead I held on until an outside mediator from a neighboring state sat down with both sides and it all went away.

Folks in my previous district where my kids went to school might be surprised that I STILL had issues in my new job; I mean, those out to get me weren't following behind me. Oh, there were phone calls between districts, I am sure, "off the record chats," but they still hired me because good people provided a perspective for my behavior. By the same token, folks who liked me in my new position and knew what pressures I endured there would be surprised that I had similar problems in my previous position. The only folks who wouldn't be surprised would be the board office level administrators in both settings, who KNEW I was a bad penny, a trouble maker, a rabble rouser. They never stopped for a minute to think about our shared responsibilities to the students, *all* the students, but most especially the difficult students, the "bad pennies, the trouble makers, the rabble rousers" the ones I most identified with, because...I was one of them. Antiauthority,

## Epilogue

independent, assertive, not-gonna-take-no-shit-off-anybody proud.

I survived in a conservative, regimented, hierarchial society, always looking over my shoulder, always one step away from a reprimand or warning of impending doom; "Further Disciplinary Action and Possible Termination" highlights a certain amount of resiliency or stubbornness. It's one thing to be beaten by a worthy adversary in a fair fight, but when someone tries to take you down with lies and unfounded allegations and hearsay and innuendo and oversteps the bounds of their authority and common decency, it's time for someone to say, "No!" And though I paid a heavy price for my resistance, as I said in my retirement speech at the end of thirty-eight years, "Whenever I came to that fork in the road, the easy path or the treacherous one, I really had no choice;, I had to take the one that beckoned me, where I was most needed."

At my retirement dinner I told my gathered friends and colleagues, "I started going to school when I was four. Boy, that was a mistake! For the next fifty-eight years it has been pretty much the same routine: get up…get dressed…eat your breakfast…go to school…do your work…try to stay out of trouble…and….keep your mouth shut. I've done pretty well with the first five on the list; it's those last two that have been more difficult for me. And while it's not that I go out and look for trouble, it has an uncanny knack of finding me, and as for that last bit about keeping my mouth shut, well, you might just as well tell a dog not to bark."

Having survived another coup d'etat in the spring, I entered the 2011-12 school year with assurances from the head of personnel that she would have my back. "No one should have to work in fear" were her words to me when I explained not wanting to spend what might be my last year looking over my shoulder all the time. In October, after saving the district thousands of dollars in retraining fees, I organized a program to allow eight trainers to each have eighteen hours of contact time training over thirty staff members across six schools who needed six hours retraining, and a half dozen new trainees who needed twelve hours (the group I trained in nonviolent crisis intervention). It was a logistical nightmare, but we pulled it off with my help, and I got all the manuals and tests mailed in before the November 5th deadline for recertification. The next day I get called into the supervisor's office (the supervisor from hell) and was told to bring my union rep with me. To thank me? Hell no! Turns out she had a list of allegations (all from the same individual, who had been complaining about me for years), most of which fell by the wayside, with several remaining: *interrupting the coordinator while she was running a meeting, using a racially charged expletive, and...an obscenity.* The reason I interrupted her, all three hundred pounds of her, was because she failed to follow procedures, in this case addressing the need for an aide on a bus for emotionally disturbed students.

There was nothing written into the IEP about special transportation, other than the fact that it was "special transportation." "Uh, isn't there supposed to be an aide on this bus?" "Of course there is," she answered. "Then why isn't it written in, 'Aide on the bus'?" "Well," she said almost indignantly — and this is in front of a dozen IEP Team members, including the grandmother raising the student in question — "That would lock the district in to pay for it." "That is precisely why you do it," I explained. The IEP Team recommends what is needed, what is in the best interests of the student, and the district provides funding to support it. She puffed herself up and exclaimed rather loudly, "Well, I don't have the authority to do that, we'll just have to adjourn the meeting and reconvene with a supervisor present." Now, mind you, this is a duly constituted IEP with a dozen members, including all the essential ones, parent, special education teacher, general education teacher, specialists, even two school psychologists, and a social worker. The school had sent out notice of the meeting, prior written notice, etc., and she wants to adjourn and call the same meeting again with a supervisor present? I responded quite calmly, firmly, but calmly, "Are you not the

## Epilogue

designee? I mean, you signed as the designee. That means you are here to represent the district administration for the purposes of funding. You *have* the authority." By law every IEP meeting is required to have an administrator or an administrative designee present at all meetings. "Well, I'm not going to do it," she responded. "Well," I said, "if you don't have the authority, then get someone here who does. Where is Mr. Black (the building principal)?" I inquired. "He's out of the building," she replied. "How about Mrs. Motel (the assistant principal)?" "She's doing observations and Mr. Dart is doing testing." That's when I blurted out the so-called "racial expletive" by calling the impasse "a Mexican standoff." According to my *Funk & Wagnall's*, it's in common usage and not considered offensive. Besides, there were no Mexicans present, so who was upset?

The coordinator's position was that they had an aide on the bus in the afternoon, that they didn't need one in the morning, and they didn't have to record that on his IEP. I maintained that since he and another ED student had decided to smoke a bowl of marijuana on the special ed bus in the morning that maybe, just maybe, there needed to be an aide on the bus for the morning trip to school as well. This also needed to be agreed on by the IEP Team and, if so, recorded in the IEP document. The team agreed, but she refused to acknowledge it. We moved on. Later, when discussion of his drug use at age fourteen came up, I weighed in. As a grandparent raising a grandchild myself due to the simple fact that my own daughter got addicted to drugs, I had sufficient standing to advise this grandmother to be vigilant and keep her grandson straight by asking him to pee in a bottle. "That way," I said, "when one of his peers tries to get him to have another taste, he could simply say, 'I'd like to, man, but I gotta pee in a bottle for my grandma.' "

Just to add fuel to my funeral pyre, I was also accused of "not following procedures" at *another* school building despite the fact that every member of the IEP Team there agreed with my recommendation. The supervisor was not consulted, and this was the *failure to follow district procedure*. The frustration is that supervisors and administrators all have notice of these meetings well in advance, and though they have the opportunity, some would say the responsibility to attend, typically they defer to their building coordinators. If they choose not to attend, they lack any standing to complain about the decision their IEP Teams arrive at. Though out-of-district placements (as in this case) require funding from the district office, all that is required is that they be notified; they don't have veto power. This supervisor insisted that she have final say, though we disagreed that "say" meant that she could countermand a decision rendered by a duly constituted IEP Team. This is precisely what she proceeded to do anyway.

Four months and several levels of grievance later, I finally got my sit-down with the superintendent. I presented for thirty minutes: "here's her memo, here's her e-mail, here's the regulation, here's what I did." Page after page after page. The law, the regulations, were clearly on my side and reinforced by her memos and her e-mails and state department clarifications, not to mention federal regulations and a number of legal clarifications in newsletters I presented. I did exactly as I was directed to by law and, quite ironically, by her. My "Perry Mason moment" came when I pulled out the two letters of reprimand, one citing me for *failing* to inform the team (including the building principal) that they weren't following procedures...and the second letter reprimanding me for doing precisely *that* in the other meeting, telling the three-hundred-pound coordinator that she *wasn't following procedures*. "You can't have it both ways," I told the superintendent, "and write someone up for doing what he is required to do: explain procedures, then let the IEP Team render its decision." He downgraded the "reprimand" to a "warning," which accomplished only one thing. It prevented me from moving to formal mediation by an outside arbitrator because it was "only a warning," a preliminary step prior to "further disciplinary action or possible termination," not a formal "reprimand" that warned that the next time you could be "further disciplined or terminated." Even my union was powerless to act. The letters stood, and though they removed the wording that my acts were "unprofessional," the superintendent still dragged up the unsubstantiated accusation that it appeared to him that I somehow "frightened and intimidated people into doing my bidding." Just goes to show how they try to marginalize anyone who goes against the grain. I so wanted an impartial mediator to examine the record, and the facts, and rule. I had done my job and would have been easily vindicated. But I was not to have my day in court. I simply had to start my countdown to retirement when I would no longer be under their control or any public school administrator's control. I would be free to speak out, "unshackled from a paycheck." And I could sleep well at night and, like a lot of idealists, keep fighting at every occasion, and I never betrayed myself. Not many people can say they have never betrayed themselves. I can.

My last official act as an employee was to write a letter to the board president documenting the hostile workplace my supervisor had created and how the board of education members were, "*...hereby put on notice...*" that they were duly informed regarding her bullying tactics and intimidation of me and numerous others. Should anything ever come up about her performance—harassment, hostile workplace, etc.—THEY could and would be held accountable. I attached the administrative survey I completed on her job performance. Asked about her leadership style, I wrote, "Are you familiar with the recent documentary entitled *Bullies*? In reference to her setting high standards, I said it was "Everest without the Sherpas." I understand they still renewed her contract for another three years. That only reinforced my decision to move on.

In October as contract renewals for administrators approached, including my favorite supervisor, I made some additional phone calls and sent another letter enclosing my earlier correspondence and the administrative survey to all five board members. This finally got their collective attention for they started to make some inquiries as I had suggested, calling employees who had also worked under her. They were surprised when they heard much the same as I had outlined in my letters. When it came to a vote, one asked that her contract not be renewed at all, but the superintendent convinced the remaining four board members to give her another chance. Rather than extend that "chance" for the traditional three years, they only granted a single year. In the field of education this is a message to start putting your resume' together. I received numerous calls, emails, and texts, with the news, many of my former colleagues thanking me for my efforts.

Several months later, it was revealed that the primary reason the superintendent had been supporting the supervisor in spite of all the arguments against her, was, simply put, they were having an affair. His wife filed for separation and divorce, he moved out, and the community was in an uproar. Funny how karma works.

Caroline's and my marriage survived as well and we moved on. We will be married for thirty years in 2013. She is still working in the district that shunned our daughter and me and is well respected as a guidance counselor. Every bit as feisty as I am, her longevity has a lot to do with her style, and the fact that I took the lead and drew most of the fire over my daughter. We were granted custody of Lily when she was two, and by age four she entered preschool in Caroline's elementary school. She moved through the grades quite easily and graduated to the middle school after seven years with her mom. Thirteen on July 4, 2013, Lily is an honor roll student who plays the piano beautifully, takes dance lessons, has lots of friends, and loves life. She worships Sarah's two boys Lily's two little brothers (insisting there is no half to it) and, though she enjoys spending time with Sarah and Joe and the boys, is glad to come back home, where she is surrounded by our love and attention. Life is good, and if you learn to make adjustments as you move through life, so long as you remain faithful to your values, you can look back with no regrets. Love doesn't mean not having to say you're sorry,

## Epilogue

from that seventies movie, it means always remembering that loving someone is to make *them* happy and hope the love comes back to you in spades. Sometimes it does, sometimes it doesn't. All you can hope for, is the best that they can do.
THE END

www.ingramcontent.com/pod-product-compliance
Lightning Source LLC
Chambersburg PA
CBHW031609160426
43196CB00006B/72